Four Square Leagues

FOUR SQUARE LEAGUES

Pueblo Indian Land in New Mexico

MALCOLM EBRIGHT, RICK HENDRICKS, AND
RICHARD W. HUGHES

UNIVERSITY OF NEW MEXICO PRESS
ALBUQUERQUE

© 2014 by Malcolm Ebright, Rick Hendricks, and Richard W. Hughes
All rights reserved. Published 2014

First paperbound printing, 2015
Paperbound ISBN: 978-0-8263-3972-0

Printed in the United States of America

LIBRARY OF CONGRESS CATALOGING-IN-PUBLICATION DATA

Ebright, Malcolm.
Four square leagues : Pueblo Indian land in New Mexico / Malcolm Ebright,
Rick Hendricks, and Richard W. Hughes.
pages cm
Includes bibliographical references and index.
ISBN 978-0-8263-5472-3 (cloth : alk. paper) — ISBN 978-0-8263-5473-0 (electronic)
1. Pueblo Indians—Land tenure. 2. Land grants—New Mexico. 3. Indians of North
America—Land tenure—New Mexico. I. Title.
F791.E37 2014
978.9004'974—dc23
2014001548

DESIGNED BY Lila Sanchez
COMPOSED IN Minion Pro 10/14, Caligraphic 421 BT

FOUR SQUARE LEAGUES

Pueblo Indian Land in New Mexico

MALCOLM EBRIGHT, RICK HENDRICKS, AND
RICHARD W. HUGHES

UNIVERSITY OF NEW MEXICO PRESS
ALBUQUERQUE

© 2014 by Malcolm Ebright, Rick Hendricks, and Richard W. Hughes
All rights reserved. Published 2014

First paperbound printing, 2015
Paperbound ISBN: 978-0-8263-3972-0

Printed in the United States of America

LIBRARY OF CONGRESS CATALOGING-IN-PUBLICATION DATA

Ebright, Malcolm.
Four square leagues : Pueblo Indian land in New Mexico / Malcolm Ebright,
Rick Hendricks, and Richard W. Hughes.
pages cm
Includes bibliographical references and index.
ISBN 978-0-8263-5472-3 (cloth : alk. paper) — ISBN 978-0-8263-5473-0 (electronic)
1. Pueblo Indians—Land tenure. 2. Land grants—New Mexico. 3. Indians of North
America—Land tenure—New Mexico. I. Title.
F791.E37 2014
978.9004'974—dc23
2014001548

DESIGNED BY Lila Sanchez
COMPOSED IN Minion Pro 10/14, Caligraphic 421 BT

CONTENTS

Preface		vii
Introduction		1
1	The Pueblo League in New Mexico, 1692–1846	11
2	Santa Ana Pueblo's Ranchiit'u Land Purchases	49
3	Picuris Pueblo: Spanish Encroachment and Pueblo Resurgence	89
4	Sandia Pueblo	123
5	Santa Clara Pueblo and Its Struggle to Protect Santa Clara Canyon	149
6	Cochiti Pueblo	169
7	Jemez Pueblo	189
8	The Surveyor General and the Cruzate Grants	205
9	The Pueblos Come Under U.S. Rule	237
10	The Pueblo Lands Board	267
11	Taos Pueblo and the Return of Blue Lake	293
Epilogue		321
Acknowledgments		327
Appendix 1	*Confirmed Pueblo Grants*	329
Appendix 2	*Documents Relating to the New Mexico Pueblo League*	331
Abbreviations		337
Notes		339
Glossary		421
Works Cited		423
Index		441

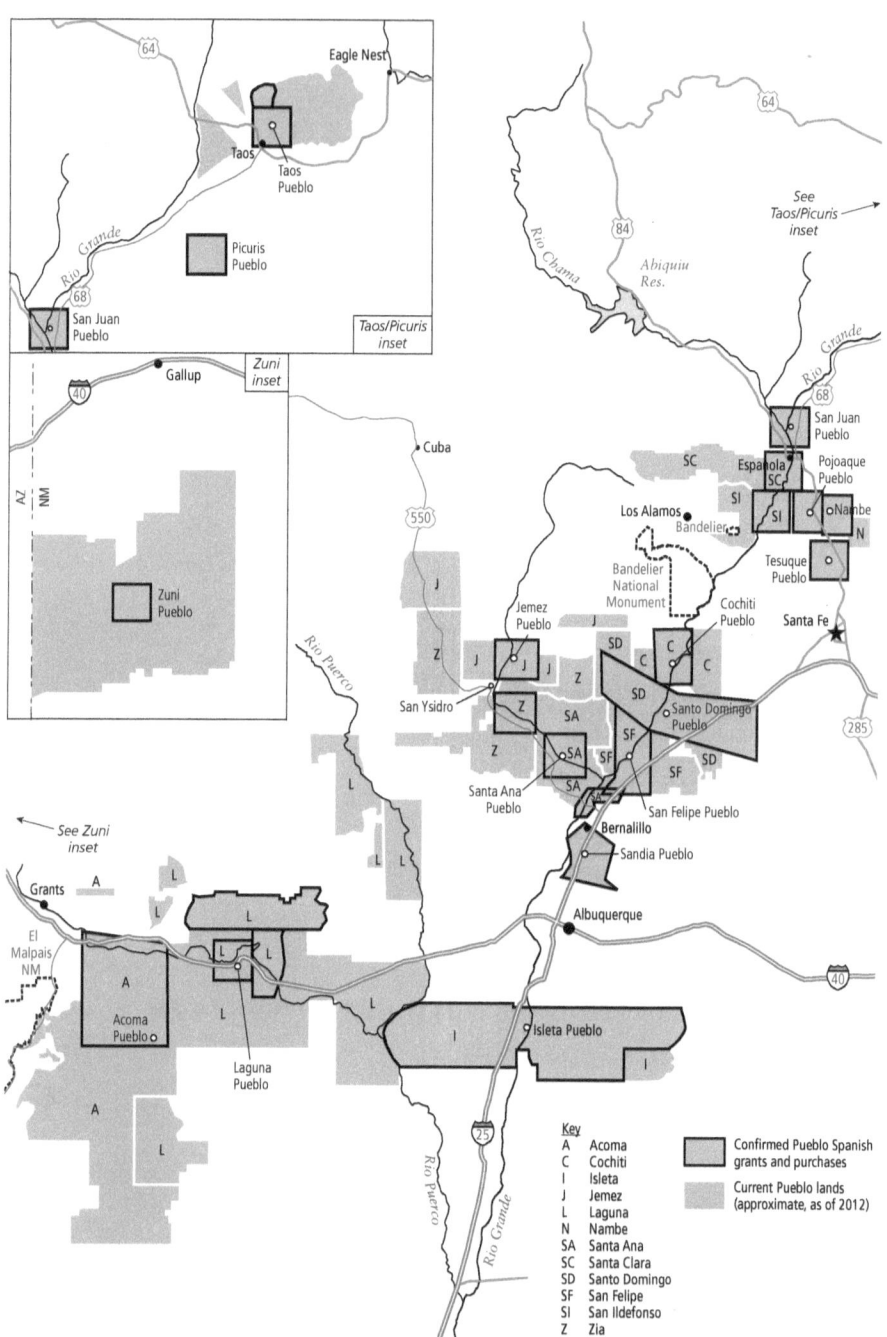

Lands of the Pueblo Indians of New Mexico. Map by Molly O'Halloran.

PREFACE

When legal historian G. Emlen Hall assessed the need for more scholarship about Pueblo legal history back in the late 1980s he delineated four major areas related to the subject of Pueblo Indian land in New Mexico that merited additional "detailed work," given how little was known about the topic. This book addresses all four points and goes beyond this ambitious agenda. First, according to Hall, "we need to trace document by document, law by law, the rise of the mysterious Pueblo league between 1700 and 1821 as the basis, measure, and limit of the Pueblos' claim to land under Spanish rule." We have tried to do that in the first part of chapter 1, although our research shows that Pueblo land was not necessarily limited to four square leagues, an area amounting to 17,350 acres that came to be known as the Pueblo league.[1] The second part of chapter 1 responds to Hall's second point: the need for "a detailed, exhaustive analysis of Pueblo lands between 1821 and 1848 to determine how in fact the Pueblos and their non-Indian neighbors reacted to the change from Spanish to Mexican sovereignty." While not comprehensive, our analysis shows that the Pueblo league continued to be used as the measure of the Pueblos' claim to land as pressure from non-Indian encroachment built up and confusion over the Pueblos' status as citizens and their right to sell their lands increased.[2]

Third, as Hall notes, "we need specific studies detailing the changes in Indian policy in the late nineteenth and early twentieth centuries that both foreboded and predicted the fundamental changes in Pueblo land status that the Sandoval decision and statehood brought," and fourth, "we need to know more . . . [about] the precise state of affairs in New Mexico that preceded passage of the 1924 Pueblo Lands Act." Chapters 8, 9, and 10 deal with these topics, as do the individual chapters about Santa Ana, Picuris, Sandia, Santa Clara, Cochiti, Jemez, and Taos. Although this book does not provide an in-depth treatment of every pueblo, we do respond to all of Hall's four points. We have, in Hall's words, "sliced the problem [horizontally] along the divisions that changes in sovereignty provide" and vertically across the chronological division brought about by the imposition of new legal regimes on the part of Spain, Mexico, and the United States.³

Other scholars who have written directly about Pueblo land besides Hall are Herbert O. Brayer, Joe Sando, and Ward Allen Minge. Numerous scholars have indirectly contributed to the subject, such as those who prepared reports in the *Aamodt* case regarding Pueblo Indian land and water, including Daniel Tyler, William B. Taylor, Michael Meyer, Susan Deeds, and John Baxter.⁴ The Vargas Project at the University of New Mexico has translated and annotated many Spanish colonial documents dealing with Pueblo Indian land. Land grant scholars such as Malcolm Ebright and Em Hall have studied Hispano land grants, their adjudication, and their relationship to their Pueblo Indian neighbors. PhD candidates at the University of New Mexico, such as Jacobo Baca and James Dory-Garduño, have begun to examine Pueblo land grants in tandem with Hispano land grants, as has Malcolm Ebright in his recent *Advocates for the Oppressed*. Frances Levine has written with the cultural sensitivity of an ethnohistorian of the "dominant cultures inventing categories of meaning to explain the subjugated place of indigenous peoples" at Pecos Pueblo.⁵ We observe this process at work throughout this story of Pueblo Indian land. We have built on the work of these scholars, but the core of this book is based on U.S. legal decisions, legislative documents such as U.S. statutes, and most particularly on original Spanish documents.

The story of Pueblo Indian land told here relies primarily on Spanish and Mexican documents up to 1846. Although we have made every effort to find indigenous voices and points of view in these documents, in the main they reflect the views of their non-Indian authors. We have discovered, however, some documents that Pueblo leaders wrote in which it is possible to discern distinct Pueblo voices, as well as a complete set of documents from the archives of Santa Ana Pueblo that record the pueblo's purchase of valuable irrigated land called the Ranchiit'u tract, which is still farmed today.⁶

This study began as a report on the history of land tenure of Ysleta del Sur Pueblo in El Paso, Texas. In the course of preparing this report, Ebright and Hendricks began to explore the origins of the concept of the Pueblo league. They subsequently wrote reports for Santa Ana and Picuris, for whom Richard Hughes provided legal representation. When Ebright and Hendricks conceived the idea of a book-length study of the history of Pueblo Indian land in New Mexico, they asked Hughes to collaborate with them. We eventually dropped

PREFACE ix

Ysleta del Sur from the book as it became more tightly focused on central and northern New Mexico.

Because this is a long, detailed book, there is a certain amount of duplication when it seemed necessary for the reader to understand the broader context of the pueblo under discussion. To aid the reader who is not satisfied with any translation, in the notes we have frequently supplied the original Spanish text in modernized orthography. We have also modernized Spanish names and place names. Spanish words and phrases retained in the English text appear in italics on the first instance and in Roman type on subsequent instances. According to *Webster's Third New International Dictionary of the English Language Unabridged*, which we have taken as our authority, certain words, accented in Spanish, such as "alferez," are now accepted as English words of Spanish origin, without accents. Titles of Spanish nobles we have retained in Spanish. We have left saints' names in English, unless they are part of the name of Spanish churches, organizations, or places.

In keeping with contemporary scholarly usage, we capitalize "Pueblo" when referring to the Pueblo people and when using the name of specific pueblos, as in Taos Pueblo, for example, but not when making a general reference to an Indian community ("the pueblos' boundaries," for example). We have opted to use the term "Hispano" to refer to non-Indians who peopled New Mexico during the historical periods covered in this book. This decision was made to ensure consistency and to avoid using different terms to refer to the same people with each major political change in the governance of the region. This includes people who might more accurately be called "Spaniards" or "mestizos" for the period 1598 to 1821, "Mexican" for the period 1821 to 1846 (or beyond), and "nuevomexicano," "Spanish-American," or "Mexican-American" after 1846. Our usual term for non-Indians who began to arrive in 1846 is "Anglo-American."

The authors wish to thank Carroll Riley, Cordelia Snow, Lolly Martin, and Robert D. Martínez for reading and commenting on early drafts of the manuscript. Of course, we take responsibility for errors that may remain in the book. Grants from the New Mexico Public Records Advisory Board provided partial funding for the research and writing of early versions of chapters 4, 5, and 7 on Santa Clara, Cochiti, and Jemez. Funding for Molly O'Halloran's maps and Glen Strock's drawings came from Tamaya Enterprises, Inc., Southern Sandoval Investments, Ltd., Santa Ana Hospitality Corp., and Santa Ana Golf Club, Inc., and we thank each of them for their assistance. The authors also wish to thank Sandra Jaramillo, former New Mexico state records administrator; John Hyrum Martinez, current state records administrator; and Bonnie Coleman, history projects coordinator of the Office of the State Historian, for their support. They also acknowledge Faith Yoman and Virginia Lopez, librarians, Southwest Room of the New Mexico State Library; Alison Colburne, librarian, Laboratory of Anthropology Library; Michael S. Poulson, New Mexico Supreme Court law librarian; and Mark Adams, Peggy Trujillo, and Bruce Mergele for their research and interlibrary loan assistance. Finally, the authors would like to thank Robin Collier for facilitating the circulation of electronic files as work progressed on the manuscript.

Reading the Acts of Vassalage and Obedience at Acoma. Drawing by Glen Strock.

Introduction

The chapters that follow focus on Pueblo Indian land in New Mexico, exploring its history from the late seventeenth century to the present. To provide some context for this long period of history, it is useful to examine briefly the nature of land tenure before the Pueblo Revolt of 1680. That story began when Governor Juan de Oñate (1598–1610) took possession of New Mexico and claimed for the king of Spain what had been Pueblo Indian land since time immemorial.[1] Oñate and his colonists were looking for mineral riches and did not realize that the true wealth of New Mexico was the land. Of course, Pueblo Indians knew this, and they developed a highly sophisticated religion based on intricate and secret ceremonialism to bring about fertility of the earth long before Europeans arrived in the Southwest.[2]

The Pueblos did not share the European concept of private property ownership, although they did have boundaries marked with shrines, petroglyphs, and other rock art, and they knew how to map their lands. Some Native American rock art reveals partial and complete maps. In the Galisteo Basin, there is a petroglyph on a boulder depicting an irrigation system centered on two reservoirs, with irrigation canals leading the water to cornfields.[3] Recent mapping projects demonstrate that Pueblo Indians had their own maps showing areas of land use, sacred shrines, and the boundaries or spheres of influence of each pueblo. One Pueblo leader noted that "indigenous people have always had maps. We've had songs, chants, prayers, migration stories, shell arrangements, drawings on hides, drawings on wood and stone. These maps aid our memories; they give reference to our places of origin, places we have visited, and places we hope to go. They also provide us with a reference of where we are within the universe and help to define our relationship to natural processes surrounding us."[4] For Europeans, maps delineated boundaries, but they were also instruments of conquest. Pueblo Indians today have said that "if we had had maps from times past, similar to what the Spanish, Mexican, and United States governments have today, we probably would not have lost all of the lands that we've lost."[5] The land and the sacred shrines were embedded in the stories and memories of indigenous peoples throughout the Americas. Landscapes were so crucial to the stories that if the land was lost or altered, the stories forming the basis of the religion could not be told.

Because Pueblo Indians did not have the same concept of land ownership as Spaniards, they were ill prepared for the arrival of Europeans who came to occupy the mountains, deserts, and river valleys the Pueblo people always had known to be theirs. European thinking about land was initially alien and incompatible with Pueblo ideas about land, but some Pueblos learned to use Spanish concepts of property ownership to their advantage.[6]

Under the Pueblo land-use system, the land used most intensively for farming was closest to the pueblo. More distant land was often where shrines were located, pilgrimages were made, and offerings were placed.[7] Resources such as clay deposits, salt, and hot springs were frequently used in common under the guardianship and with the permission of one pueblo. Thus, the Zuni Salt Lake was and is under the guardianship of Zuni Pueblo, but other pueblos and even nomadic tribes obtain salt there after getting permission from Zuni and making offerings.[8] Since the pueblos were in movement before they reached their present locations, "the idea was to have boundaries to create a place—to fix a place—temporarily within the larger idea of movement." Thus, unlike European boundaries, pueblo boundaries could be somewhat fluid. In fact, boundaries were often the most sacred places to the pueblos; instead of being places of contention, they were often places of healing. Other sacred places were well established in the sacred geography of a pueblo but often did not fit into the Spanish concept of the land an Indian pueblo owned.[9]

In the early years of the conquest of the Americas, an adelantado, or governor, officially took possession of land in the name of the king of Spain by means of a special act called the *requerimiento*.[10] The requerimiento preceded submission of the Indians to Spanish political and religious authority. According to Patricia Seed, the requerimiento was a military and political ritual with no parallel in any other European culture. Read aloud to Indians from a written text, the requerimiento was an ultimatum requiring Indians to acknowledge the superiority of Christianity or face punishment, often war.[11] This instrument was an attempt to provide legal cover and to legitimize and regulate the conquest. The requerimiento informed the Indians that the power of Jesus was transmitted to Saint Peter and from him to all the popes who came after him, one of whom granted to Spain the rights to America (and in part to Portugal).[12] If the Indians willingly accepted Spanish authority, they could not be enslaved, but they were subject to tribute, and resistance brought punishment. The requerimiento forced Indians to "choose only between two positions of inferiority."[13]

After the adoption of the Ordinances for New Discoveries of 1573, the ritual placing Indians under Spanish authority and the Catholic religion became known as "acts of obedience and vassalage." At Santo Domingo Pueblo on 7 July 1598, the first such acts of obedience and vassalage in New Mexico took place. This renamed ritual possession was essentially putting into practice the requerimiento; only the name of the act had changed.[14]

The 1573 ordinances also forbade crown expenditures for expeditions bent on expanding the Spanish empire. Entrepreneurs such as Oñate, who invested their own money and that of their financial backers, could grant encomiendas, and the Indian tribute earned by encomenderos helped to offset some of the expenses associated with conquest of new territory.[15] Initially, anyone who served the crown in New Mexico for five years at his own expense could become a hidalgo and was eligible to obtain an encomienda. The number of encomiendas granted in the early years of the colony is unknown.

No land documents formally granting land to Hispanos or Pueblo Indians are known to have survived the events of 1680. There are, however, references to grants of encomiendas and estancias in wills and other documents, such as the 1662 inventory of the possessions of Francisco Gómez Robledo. His encomiendas included all of Pecos Pueblo, less the twenty-four houses held in encomienda by Pedro Lucero de Godoy; two and a half parts of Taos Pueblo; half the Hopi pueblo of Shongopavi; half of Acoma Pueblo, less twenty houses; half of Abó Pueblo, which Gómez Robledo received in exchange for half of Sandia Pueblo; and all of Tesuque Pueblo, which for more than forty years neither Gómez Robledo nor his father, Francisco Gómez, collected payments from because Indians from the pueblo performed service instead of paying tribute. Gómez Robledo collected tribute payments twice a year in *piezas* (units), which corresponded to the number of Indian heads of household. In all, Gómez Robledo collected 610 units annually from his encomienda holdings: 340 from Pecos, 110 from Taos, 80 from Shongopavi, 50 from Acoma, and 30 from Abó. Payment came in the form of buckskins, mantas (pieces of cloth), buffalo hides, and elk skins. In addition to the grants of encomienda, there were estancia grants for San Nicolás de las Barrancas and a piece of land a league above San Juan Pueblo and another on the Arroyo de Tesuque.[16]

Around 1640 the viceroy of New Spain limited New Mexico governors' authority to grant encomiendas to no more than thirty-five colonists at any given time.[17] The encomenderos in New Mexico around the middle of the seventeenth century consisted of a group of some thirty-five heads of household. These men and women and their families, along with another fifteen or so families involved in ranching, comprised about 10 to 15 percent of the population.[18] According to Eleanor M. Barrett, most of these properties, more than fifty-five by 1666, were located in the Middle Rio Grande region where suitable agricultural land, water for irrigation, and a source of labor could be had. Some pueblos were practically awash in Hispano estancias.[19]

In the 1641 census, eight estancias are listed for Santa Clara Pueblo, fourteen for Isleta Pueblo, and an indeterminate number for Sandia Pueblo. The 1663–1666 census mentioned several estancias each at Santa Fe and Nambe Pueblo, six at San Ildefonso Pueblo, three at San Marcos Pueblo, thirty at Sandia Pueblo, fourteen at Isleta Pueblo, and two at Socorro Pueblo.[20]

Nevertheless, widely separated properties rather than clusters around Pueblo communities characterized Hispano landholding before 1680. It is worthy of note that the Franciscans also held extensive estancias associated with the missions located in Pueblo communities, and it is unclear whether they are included in the statistics these censuses provide.

New Mexico encomenderos received annual tribute from the Pueblo Indians of the kingdom, including those of the Zuni and Hopi districts. Payments were assessed on the number of households in a given pueblo. Encomenderos or their agents made collections in the spring and fall.[21] The term "dos cobras" (two collections) referred to one full year's tribute. Generally speaking, encomenderos received trade merchandise worth one peso per pueblo household.[22] Encomienda grants typically entitled the recipient to receive so many mantas per pueblo, although other trade goods could be substituted, and one fanega of maize per head of household. Tribute payments did not make New Mexico encomenderos wealthy. The encomienda system had its roots in the Reconquista of Muslim Spain. On the Iberian Peninsula, encomenderos were granted the right to collect tribute from Muslims and other people who worked the land that Christian Spaniards conquered and settled. In the New World, this institution did not imply land tenure on the part of encomenderos, and they were enjoined from living on the land where they held Indians in encomienda. In practice, however, some encomenderos resided on the very land where the Indians they held in encomienda lived. According to James Lockhart, "One can say with some assurance that during the Conquest period encomenderos in all the major regions of the Spanish Indies regularly owned land as private individuals and that many of their holdings were inside the limits of their own encomiendas."[23] The exact territorial limits of encomiendas in New Mexico are unclear because encomenderos were assigned a pueblo or part of a pueblo based on the number of inhabitants within a pueblo. In New Mexico there is evidence that some encomenderos lived in or near the pueblos they held in encomienda, a specific example being Ciénega and Cieneguilla Pueblos.[24] Authorities sought to justify this violation of the law by arguing that only by living among their tribute-paying Indians could encomenderos protect them from marauding Apaches.[25]

In theory, the New Mexico encomenderos were obligated to provide military protection for the pueblos of the Indians they held in encomienda as well as the Hispano colonists. In reality, an encomendero living in Santa Fe could do little to protect his tributaries at Zuni or Senecu, even if he had the inclination to do so. Colonists and missionaries complained bitterly that many encomenderos were reluctant to leave the relative comfort of Santa Fe to go on Indian campaigns. Military considerations were secondary to the economic importance of New Mexico encomiendas. France Scholes concluded that "the rivalry for encomiendas was probably keener than that for political office, inasmuch as the encomiendas were an important source of income and could be held for more than one generation."[26]

The size of New Mexico encomiendas varied enormously, from those comprising more than six hundred tributaries to those made up of fewer than thirty. Since encomienda income was based on population (the number of households), the best encomiendas were the largest. The larger pueblos, however, were usually divided into several encomiendas. Total annual encomienda revenue from all New Mexico pueblos, including Hopi, was probably four thousand pesos or less. In 1698 former governor Diego de Vargas (1691–1697, 1703–1704) received a four thousand–peso stipend from the crown, which was to be collected in New Mexico encomienda tribute.[27] This figure may have represented more than the combined annual value of the thirty-five-odd New Mexico encomiendas.

There is no consensus among scholars about whether encomienda tribute was onerous for Pueblo Indians in the pre-Revolt period. David Snow argued persuasively that, at least initially, the encomienda was not a hardship on Pueblo households.[28] By contrast, Elizabeth A. H. John asserted that tribute payment was the Pueblos' "greatest economic grievance and worst source of friction between Spanish and Pueblo populations."[29] In her recent book, Tracy L. Brown argued "that *any* labor or craft production Pueblos did for Spaniards was burdensome because it was required of them—it was not done voluntarily."[30] We find that it was always a burden, and it seems clear that in the famine years of the 1670s encomienda tribute became a major irritant and one more item on a growing list of complaints against the local Hispanos that eventually led to the conflagration of 1680.

Vargas requested an encomienda after successfully carrying out the reconquest of New Mexico. He also resurrected the term "requerimiento" when he met the inhabitants of Cuyamungue and Jacona in January 1694 during the campaign to reconquer New Mexico militarily. He continued to have the requerimiento read until the summer of 1696, including when he confronted Pueblos who were withdrawn on to mesa tops.[31] Ironically, one of the charges brought against Diego de Vargas in the lawsuit with Pedro Rodríguez Cubero was that he executed eighty Indians (who had surrendered) without first having notified them of a declaration of war through a reading of the requerimiento.[32]

The situation regarding Pueblo Indian land tenure before the Revolt of 1680 is even less clear given an almost complete lack of documentary evidence. The first indisputable documentary evidence for a definite area of land as a property right of each pueblo appears following Vargas's reconquest of New Mexico, although there are indications that Pueblos measured and monumented their land before the 1680 Revolt. The emergence of the four square league (approximately 17,350 acres), otherwise known as the Pueblo league, can be discerned in documents from this period held in both the Spanish Archives of New Mexico and New Mexico's pueblos. By 1704, it was taken for granted that the

INTRODUCTION 7

Pueblo league concept was based on a law or decree issued by the king. Thus in subsequent cases the Pueblo league was referred to as "the league that the king our lord grants to each pueblo," or "what was ordered from the time of the ancient kings," or simply, as based on "the laws of our sovereigns."[33] During the eighteenth and early nineteenth centuries, the Pueblo league was measured many times, and each time it was noted that granting four square leagues was based on royal law or a grant from the king to each pueblo, which reinforced the idea that this was an entitlement guaranteed to every pueblo.[34] Chapter 1 traces the development of the concept of the Pueblo league in New Mexico.

As described in chapter 2, by the eighteenth century, pueblos such as Santa Ana saw that Hispanos encroaching on their land were basing their claims on written documents. The people of Santa Ana realized that by purchasing land from their Hispano neighbors, the pueblo could recover some of the land Hispanos had usurped. Of the six case studies of specific pueblos included in this book, only the treatment of Picuris in chapter 3 covers the history of a pueblo from contact to the present day. This is because there is no complete published history of Picuris Pueblo.

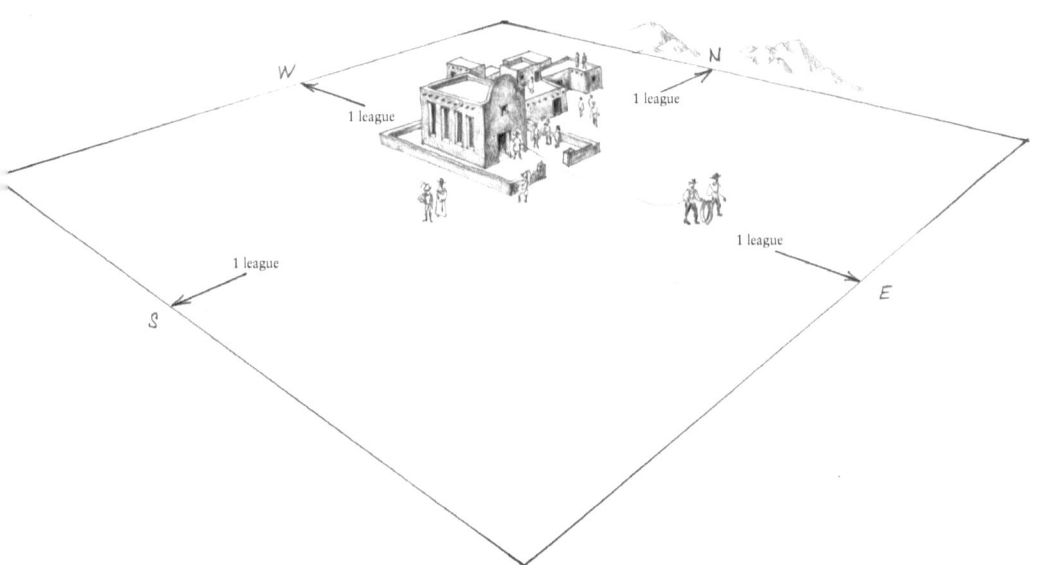

Schematic drawing of the Pueblo league. Map by Molly O'Halloran.

Some pueblos received land grants when old pueblos that were abandoned because of the 1680 Revolt were resettled, such as Sandia Pueblo, which is the subject of chapter 4. In 1748, through the intervention of fray Miguel Menchero, former residents of Sandia Pueblo, their offspring, and a group of Hopi speakers received a grant to resettle the site of the old pueblo. Chapter 5 deals with Santa Clara, another pueblo that received additional land beyond its four square leagues. Governor Tomás Vélez Cachupín (1749–1754, 1762–1767) awarded the Cañada de Santa Clara Grant to the pueblo to protect its water rights from Spaniards who were illegally irrigating upstream from the pueblo along the Santa Clara River. Chapter 6 investigates the case of Cochiti, which became one of the first pueblos to receive land beyond its four square leagues in 1722 when its Pueblo league and that of Santo Domingo were measured. On that occasion, both pueblos received land beyond their leagues. Jemez, the focus of chapter 7, also received a grant in addition to its Pueblo league, the Ojo del Espíritu Santo Grant. Made jointly to Jemez, Zia, and Santa Ana in 1766, this grant was soon overlapped by several grants to Hispanos, which called into question the pueblos' exclusive ownership of the grant and led to its rejection by the Court of Private Land Claims.

Spanish then Mexican officials continued to measure the Pueblo league until the U.S. invasion and occupation of New Mexico in 1846. In 1854 Surveyor General William Pelham was charged with investigating, adjudicating, and recommending Spanish and Mexican land grants for confirmation by Congress. Chapter 8 examines the curious and mysterious case of the Cruzate Grants, a group of documents purporting to be 1689 Spanish land grants to eight pueblos, which Congress confirmed in 1858 (a ninth, purporting to be a grant to Zuni Pueblo, was confirmed in 1931). In the 1890s, Will Tipton, a translator and document examiner for the Court of Private Land Claims, determined that the Cruzate Grants were not authentic. Although the documents were not genuine land grants, the measurement of the Pueblo league made it clear that New Mexico pueblos were entitled to at least four square leagues of land with or without documents. Many questions about the Cruzate Grants remain unanswered, but their central role in the establishment of a permanent land base for the Pueblo Indians is undeniable.[35]

Pueblo Indians greeted the imposition of U.S. sovereignty over New Mexico as a result of the Mexican War and the Treaty of Guadalupe Hidalgo with some trepidation. This change of national administrations and its impact on the Pueblos is studied in chapter 9. Chapter 10 takes up the story of the Pueblo Lands Act of 1924, which had the effect of costing the Pueblos tens of thousands of acres of the best farmlands within their grants, for which they received only minimal compensation. The book concludes on a hopeful note as chapter 11 turns to an account of the struggle of Taos Pueblo to achieve greater self-determination and the return of its most desired sacred site: the Taos Blue Lake.

Measuring the Pueblo league. Drawing by Glen Strock.

CHAPTER 1

The Pueblo League in New Mexico, 1692–1846

With the notable exception of the 1748 grant for the resettlement of Sandia Pueblo, no documentary evidence has surfaced to support the assertion that the primary landholdings of the Pueblo Indians in New Mexico during the more than two centuries of Spanish rule were based on written land grants. Instead, the Pueblo Indians' land base rested on a recognized minimum entitlement to land that was considered to be part of Spanish law applicable to the Pueblos. This was the "Pueblo league," a square oriented according to the cardinal directions, each of whose sides is one Spanish league distant from the center of the village. A league was 5,000 Spanish varas, and it is generally accepted that in New Mexico, a vara was 33 inches in length.[1] A league was thus 13,750 feet in length, or about 2.6 miles, and a Pueblo league was thus a square, measuring two leagues (or about 5.2 miles) on a side and containing four square leagues, approximately 17,350 acres.[2] Numerous documents from the Spanish archives of New Mexico affirm that this was routinely recognized as the minimum amount of land to which each pueblo was entitled. The documents also make it clear that the Pueblo league was at least nominally protected from encroachment by Spanish settlers and that the pueblos themselves were well aware of, and vigorously asserted their rights to, this entitlement.

In addition to this minimum land base, Spanish officials gave pueblos additional land in the form of grants in the interstices between two pueblos' leagues, for example, and in the form of large grazing grants.

Although, as we show, the principle of a square of land centered on the native village was established early on in New Spain as a standard entitlement of native communities there, the size of that entitlement was much smaller than in New Mexico—600 or 1,000 varas, for example, rather than 5,000. The Pueblo league as it was applied in New Mexico was unique in the Spanish empire; when and how the concept originally developed is unclear.[3] Less than ten years after Vargas restored Spanish rule in New Mexico, the Pueblo league was routinely cited as a rule of Spanish law that barred encroaching grants to Hispanos, suggesting that it was well established prior to the Revolt. But since virtually no records of the pre-Revolt Spanish administration survived the Pueblo Revolt, there is no way of reconstructing with certainty how or when the Pueblo league came to be.

The *Recopilación* (which was not published until 1680) contained numerous laws protecting Indian land and water rights, but none provided an unambiguous minimum property right for land. Law 4-12-18 directed that "the Indians shall be given all the land (and more, if possible) that belongs to them," and it specified that such lands were inalienable, but it said nothing as to quantity, seemingly leaving that to the Indians to determine.[4] Law 6-3-8 provided that newly established Indian towns (*reducciones*) should have ample water, lands, woodlands, access routes, farmlands, and "an ejido [commons] one league long." Presumably, some similar principles would have been applied to existing towns, such as the pueblos. Law 6-3-20 prohibited cattle ranches from being situated within a league and a half of any existing Indian community and prohibited sheep ranches within half a league. Otherwise, however, the *Recopilación* is silent on the extent of Indians' land rights in New Spain.

In central New Spain laws protecting Indians were enacted largely because of the influence of the reform-minded Bartolomé de las Casas and his writings.[5] The New Laws of 1542, which were enacted largely as a result of Las Casas's advocacy on behalf of Indians, who were placed under the protection of the crown, provided for the abolition of the encomienda, forced labor, and tribute payment.[6] The response of encomenderos was quick and entirely negative. In Peru the promulgation of the New Laws sparked an encomendero rebellion and civil war; in New Spain the laws were suspended.

The Ordinance of 26 May 1567, issued by the viceroy of New Spain, the Marqués de Falces, Conde de Sanestéban (1566–1567), provided a measure of protection for Indian land by granting pueblos 500 varas in each cardinal direction.[7] Subsequently, the distance was increased to 600 varas measured from the *casco* (the outermost houses from the center of the town). According to the ordinance, a Spanish hacienda could be no closer than 500 varas to Indian land, and a cattle ranch had to be at least 1,000 varas distant from Indian land. In 1687 the minimum distance from a Spanish hacienda to Indian land was increased to 600 varas measured from the casco of the town.[8]

These laws established a buffer zone between Indian towns and Spanish haciendas, which came to be called the *fundo legal*.[9] The fundo legal became a minimum endowment for each Indian town. Indian towns filed numerous suits in the General Indian Court in Mexico City to protect their fundo legal not only from Spanish haciendas but also from each other. In one case the Indian village of Xocotipac sought to have the boundaries of its fundo legal established over the objection of a neighboring Hispano whose ranch would be affected. The viceroy ordered the boundaries to be fixed for the fundo legal of Xocotipac.[10]

Two different leagues were in use in New Spain: the *legua común*, or common league, and the *legua legal*, or statute league. The legua común was four Castilian miles long and was never used for measurements of area in New Spain; rather, it was used to measure distances, such as those a traveler covered. The legua legal was three Castilian miles long and contained 5,000 varas of three Castilian feet. The legua legal was employed for land measurements in New Mexico.

The measurement of a league on the ground, which was routinely done when disputes arose, was a considerable undertaking. The parties to the dispute, the alcalde or other presiding official, those physically handling the measurement, a "counter," and witnesses had to gather at the site. While individual varas could be measured fairly accurately with a wooden stick with the correct length marked by two notches, the measurement of a league required the use of a cordel, or thick cord, preferably made of horsehair, 50 or 100 varas long.[11] The documents recording league measurements suggest that these cords frequently broke and that ropes and other materials were often tied onto the cord to make it the correct length. Authorities often ordered waxing the cord to keep it from stretching. Sometimes the cords shrunk and had to be soaked in water to get them back to their full length, but the wetting could also enable them to stretch quite easily beyond the prescribed length. Consequently, league measurements of the same land frequently came up with different distances, depending on who was doing the measuring, the condition of the cordel, the terrain, the weather, and related factors.

The measurement typically began at the door of the mission church in the pueblo, although other central locations were sometimes selected. One official held one end of the cord at the starting point, and another walked it in the desired cardinal direction, which was checked by compass, until the cord was tight. Then the first official walked from the starting point with the cord past the second, until the cord was again tight. Plainly, the vagaries of the terrain could make the process devilishly difficult.[12] With a 100-vara cord, 50 lengths had to be measured. It is not surprising that in three of the recorded measurements of the San Ildefonso league, the midpoint between San Ildefonso and Santa Clara was reached at 5,042 varas in 1736 and at 4,980 varas and 5,118 varas in two different measurements in 1786. Indeed, these measurements, showing a variation of less than 3 percent, suggest that the process was considerably more accurate than one might expect, given the conditions, and it had the advantage of involving the parties fully in the measuring process. The Pueblo Indians in particular were often present during the measurement of their leagues, giving them the chance to make sure the measurement was done properly.[13]

The orientation of measurements in the Americas was occasionally at variance with compass directions. In New Spain, for example, the predominant orientation of fields was eighteen degrees north of west, which corresponds to the position of the sun at the time of planting maize in the summer. This orientation was used even for lands that were described as empty, though the survey stated that the parcels were oriented in the cardinal directions. Another local variation of importance occurred in the El Paso area in southern New Mexico. There directional calls followed the axis of the Rio Grande Valley, which lies on a diagonal tending from northwest to southeast, such that what was referred to as the south to north boundary of the Ysleta del Sur grant on the west side actually bears from southwest to northeast.[14]

The fundo legal concept was first mentioned in New Mexico, so far as is known, by Diego de Vargas during the reconquest. Vargas was faced with trying to strike a difficult balance between attempting to secure the loyalty of the Pueblos during the reestablishment of Spanish rule by assuring them that their rights would be fully protected and restoring to Hispanos who helped with the reconquest the land they owned prior to the 1680 Revolt. Since there was a finite amount of high-quality irrigable land, and the pueblos originally held most of the best of it, Vargas had to make decisions on requests for land grants on a case-by-case basis, generally not granting all the land requested.[15]

As he approached Santa Fe in 1692, Governor Vargas found the pueblo of La Ciénega, 10 miles south of Santa Fe, abandoned. Writing to the viceroy from El Paso in January 1693 Vargas stated that "should some Keres Indians return to settle there [at La Ciénega], they will be limited to five hundred varas from the door of the church in the four directions, and no more."[16] Vargas was familiar with the practice in central New Spain of measuring 500 varas from the center of an Indian community, having served in Teutila in Oaxaca and in Tlalpujahua in highland Michoacán before becoming governor of New Mexico. He might have been unaware that the buffer zone had been increased by an additional 100 varas in 1687.[17] But the fact that Vargas told the viceroy he would "limit" the pueblo to 500 varas in each cardinal direction and not allot more could also indicate that he knew that were it not for his directive, the Indians would be entitled to more land. In any case, La Ciénega Pueblo was not resettled, and Governor Vargas did not have occasion to make any land grants to Indian pueblos. He did, however, make grants to Hispanos near Indian pueblos without specifying the exact boundaries of the Indian land. Typically the boundaries of Spanish grants were described as "the lands of the Indians," with no measurement or boundary marker on the ground to mark the extent of that Indian land; presumably, however, everyone understood what was intended.

The earliest known mention of a league of 5,000 varas for a New Mexico pueblo came in Lázaro de Mizquía's unsuccessful 1696–1697 proposal to reorganize New Mexico to facilitate the province's defense. Mizquía, who was the procurator general of the cabildo of Santa Fe, presented his proposal to the viceroy of New Spain, José Sarmiento de Valladares, the Conde de Moctezuma y de Tula (1696–1701), on 1 July 1697. Mizquía proposed establishing two presidios and relocating Spanish communities and Indian pueblos at intervals along the Rio Grande. The river bank would be settled in such a way that the two proposed presidios would have three leagues, one and a half each for grazing livestock and for fields, the relocated villas of Santa Fe and Santa Cruz would have two and a half leagues in each direction, and each pueblo would be given "one league in length."[18] That Mizquía failed to specify a league in each direction probably indicates his familiarity with *Recopilación* 6-3-8, which, as we have noted, called for reducciones, or new pueblos of resettled Indians, to receive "a commons one league long" without indicating how the league was to be measured.[19] He even repeated the key phrase from the statute: "una legua de largo." Regardless of what Mizquía might have proposed, his plan did not meet with the approval of authorities in Mexico City and was never implemented.

The earliest surviving record of a measurement of the Pueblo league in New Mexico—albeit an incomplete one—involved a measurement by *pasos* (paces) rather than varas. In early 1703 Juana Baca requested a land grant encompassing lands west of the Rio Grande, located between Santo Domingo and Cochiti. Governor Pedro Rodríguez Cubero (1697–1703) agreed to make the grant and directed Alcalde Diego Montoya to place Baca in possession of the land. But before doing so, Montoya had to determine the two pueblos' boundaries. On 22 February 1703 Montoya recorded that he "went to measure the league that according to royal ordinances and laws each pueblo possesses. Extending the cordeles, thirty [lengths] of a hundred paces [each] were measured, which makes three thousand, as well as another six hundred paces that the party gave to said Indians of Cochiti at their request."[20]

The next case in New Mexico to deal with the issue of Pueblo property boundaries involved land south of San Felipe. The San Felipe case began in early 1704, when Cristóbal and Juan Varela Jaramillo asked Governor Vargas to grant them land occupied by the Indians of San Felipe at Angostura, claiming that the Indians "have more [land] than the law allows, and it is not fair . . . [that] we should have nothing."[21] Governor Vargas ordered Alfonso Rael de Aguilar, the protector of Indians, and alcaldes Fernando Durán y Chaves and Diego Montoya to determine what land the pueblo owned. After the officials went to the land, Rael de Aguilar argued on behalf of the pueblo that the Indians had possessed land the Jaramillos sought "since [the pueblo was] founded," and that it was planted in grain and cotton.[22] He said that San Felipe did not want the Jaramillos to receive a grant adjacent to pueblo land because Hispanos would bring their cattle and sheep and damage Indian crops. To define the land the pueblo owned the protector of Indians cited the Pueblo league as "granted by royal law to the Pueblo Indians."[23]

The Jaramillos asked Governor Vargas to measure a league in only one direction, to the south of the pueblo in the direction of the grant they were requesting. Rael de Aguilar argued in response that "the league is understood to surround the pueblo. This cannot be given to the pueblo of San Felipe to the west because the mesa is next to the pueblo. Therefore, all the four leagues must be assigned wherever it is most advantageous to the Indians."[24] Rael de Aguilar thus urged that the measurement be made in such a way that would assure that the pueblo had the full benefit of the four square leagues and that the measurement be extended in one direction if the terrain blocked it in another.[25] Unfortunately, the San Felipe case ends here with no response from Governor Vargas, who died six weeks later.

A few weeks after the San Felipe decision, the socially prominent and powerful Hispano, Ignacio Roybal, requested a grant from Governor Vargas for land on the west side of the Rio Grande opposite San Ildefonso. Vargas made the grant on 4 March, but the local alcalde failed to make the customary investigation or notify adjoining landowners, including the pueblo, and give them an opportunity to object to the grant.[26] Had such an inquiry been made, the grazing grant would have been found to be encroaching on land planted in squash and watermelons and irrigated by an acequia the San Ildefonso Indians had dug.[27] Six months after Vargas made the grant, Rael de Aguilar filed a protest on behalf of San Ildefonso with Vargas's successor, Juan Páez Hurtado (1704–1705, 1716–1717; Páez Hurtado was lieutenant governor under Vargas and was interim governor following Vargas's death). Protector of Indians Rael de Aguilar gave several reasons why the grant to Roybal was invalid. First, he pointed out the failure to notify San Ildefonso "by the nine public proclamations for the period of nine days."[28] Not only was the protector familiar with the royal ordinance and custom requiring such notice, but he also had personal knowledge that the pueblo had not been notified, since he was serving as secretary of government to Vargas at the time the Roybal grant was made and the grant was in Rael de Aguilar's handwriting.[29] Second, Rael de Aguilar argued that San Ildefonso had owned the land "since ancient times," that the Indians planted crops on some of it, and that Spanish officials set monuments showing the boundary of San Ildefonso's land. Roybal's land overlapped the pueblo, and the *Recopilación* protected Indian land from Spanish encroachment, particularly land the Indians farmed and irrigated.[30] Third, Rael de Aguilar argued that San Ildefonso owned four square leagues of land (a league in each direction from the center of the pueblo) whether or not the Indians planted the land or received a previous grant. This land was "theirs by his majesty's will."[31]

Acting governor Páez Hurtado called for an investigation, in the course of which the officials found clear evidence that the pueblo had irrigated fields and cultivated crops on the west side of the river. In addition, the Indians pointed out a monument that they said was established as their boundary on the west by Spanish officials before the Pueblo Revolt, which suggested that at least some sort of land entitlement, possibly a league, was recognized prior to 1680.[32] Páez Hurtado then directed Alcalde Cristóbal Arellano to measure a league in each direction from the center of the pueblo and to establish monuments at each league's endpoint, noting that Roybal's grant would be understood to extend only from such monument westward.[33] On the ground, however, Arellano measured a league to the north but only half a league in the other three directions, claiming "there was insufficient farmland for the league in each cardinal direction, which is what the natives say they are asking for and not woods, hills, or land that cannot be sown and farmed."[34]

Since Alcalde Arellano's measurements did not encompass the full four square leagues, the pueblo filed one more petition hoping to change Páez Hurtado's mind. Although the governor of San Ildefonso, Matías Cuntzi, made the request for reconsideration, asking for "the customary measurements of land," Rael de Aguilar composed it in his handwriting and followed it with his distinctive signature and rubric. The protector claimed that the land in question was cultivated by and for several priests who ministered to the pueblo prior to the Revolt, beginning with fray Antonio de Sotomayor. Not only had the pueblo used the land, but also "the first Spaniards and [their] justices designated it for us as our own."[35] Acting governor Páez Hurtado curtly denied the request for reconsideration, stating that he already made his decision in the matter.[36]

Rael de Aguilar was careful, however, to underscore in his initial petition that what the pueblo was asking for was merely what it was entitled to: namely, "the four leagues in each cardinal direction that are theirs by his majesty's will, with the pueblo of San Ildefonso marking its boundaries, by which action disputes and lawsuits will cease."[37] For San Ildefonso litigation did not cease, however; the pueblo was involved in three more disputes over its league later in the eighteenth century.

This record shows not only that as early as 1704 the Pueblo league was considered a firm dictate of Spanish law but also that the pueblos themselves were aware of that right and had been for some time.[38] Whatever the origins of this important doctrine, which may have started out as a protective measure for Indian land in central New Spain, it was clearly a well-established property right in New Mexico.

Replacing Páez Hurtado was another interim governor, Francisco Cuervo y Valdés (1705–1707). Cuervo received only an interim appointment as governor from the viceroy, the tenth Duque de Alburquerque (1702–1710), so instead of hearing cases of encroachments on pueblo land, he spent much of his time lobbying for a permanent appointment as governor.[39] Cuervo did sign an important decree in 1705, however, that gave some protection to Indian pueblos. Noting that he had received complaints about Hispanos living inside the pueblos of Pecos, Taos, and Picuris, Cuervo ordered all Hispanos out of the pueblos under penalty of a two-hundred-peso fine and confiscation of their property. Judging from his later actions, however, Governor Cuervo was more interested in appearing to side with the Indians than in ejecting Hispanos living within the pueblos.[40]

Antonio Montoya, who had his eye on land between Santo Domingo and San Felipe, tested the Pueblo league concept in 1716. Montoya asked Governor Félix Martínez (1715–1717) to measure the land "that belongs to each one of the pueblos" and then to make him a grant of the *sobrantes*, or surplus land, between the two. Montoya left it up to Governor Martínez to determine what specific measurement should apply, assuming that there would be a surplus after the land was measured.[41] The governor did not tell Manuel Baca, alcalde of San Felipe, Santo Domingo, and Cochiti, how to determine the extent of the land Santo Domingo and San Felipe owned. The governor simply told Baca to examine the land Montoya requested, "leaving that which belongs to the pueblos of Santo Domingo and San Felipe."[42] When Baca arrived at the land, he met with the governors of the two pueblos who had received notification of Montoya's petition. The Pueblo Indians themselves, without the benefit of the protector of Indians or any other advocate, told Alcalde Baca that "their league should be measured for them so that they might know what was theirs." The document ends abruptly at this point, leaving the impression that Montoya did not pursue his petition when he learned that the Pueblos would insist on their league. Inasmuch as the two villages were only about

5½ miles—or just over two leagues—apart from north to south, it is likely that very little land would have been left for Montoya after both leagues were properly measured.[43]

In a 1722 case between Cochiti and Santo Domingo, former protector Rael de Aguilar was appointed *juez receptor* (temporary magistrate) to conduct a hearing in a lawsuit Santo Domingo filed over a sale of land to Cochiti by Juana Baca—the very land she was granted in 1703, in the earliest known mention of the measurement of a Pueblo league.[44] Santo Domingo was concerned that the land Baca sold was in a disputed area between the pueblos on the east side of the Rio Grande. Testimony from Juana Baca's son established the location of the land his mother sold as lying west of the Rio Grande. After examining the 1703 grant to Juana Baca, Rael determined that the Baca purchase was indeed west of the Rio Grande, on the opposite side of the river from the disputed boundary. The former protector of Indians was acting as a judge as well as an advocate for both pueblos when he told them that he "would measure the land, giving each of the pueblos the league granted to them by his majesty (may God keep him), and if there was any left over, would divide it between them in equal parts."[45] Rael de Aguilar then measured with a cordel 5,000 varas from the cemetery of the Santo Domingo church toward Cochiti and then did the same from Cochiti toward Santo Domingo. When this measurement left a gap of some 1,600 varas between the two Pueblo leagues, Rael de Aguilar split the difference and awarded each pueblo an additional 800 varas. He then set boundary markers on the ground and gave each pueblo a certified copy of the results, acting as judge rather than as an advocate. Nevertheless, as he did in the San Felipe and San Ildefonso cases, Rael de Aguilar recognized the Pueblo league as the norm for the amount of land Pueblo Indians could claim as their own and then granted them additional land.[46]

The Cochiti–Santo Domingo case is the earliest known instance in which local authorities recognized that a pueblo could be entitled to land beyond the Pueblo league. It was also the first post-Revolt case in which the Pueblo leagues of two pueblos were measured in the same proceeding. Since Governor Juan Domingo de Bustamante (1722–1731) commissioned Rael de Aguilar to hold a hearing and award the disputed land to the true owner, Rael de Aguilar's awarding 800 varas (in addition to their 5,000-vara leagues) to each pueblo had the same effect as a land grant. Although the Cochiti–Santo Domingo case arose out of a dispute between the two pueblos, both emerged from the case as winners.⁴⁷ Cochiti subsequently sold some of the land between the two pueblos to a settler named Alencaster (no relation to Governor Joaquín del Real Alencaster). According to the pueblo, some of the land sold belonged to Santo Domingo and was then transferred to Antonio José Ortiz. To determine the boundary between Santo Domingo and Ortiz, Santo Domingo asked that its league be measured.⁴⁸ Alcalde Juan José Gutiérrez measured the Santo Domingo league on 19 April 1815. When 5,000 varas were measured from the center of the pueblo toward the Rancho de Sile, the area was found to include most of Ortiz's land and all of his buildings. Only 219¾ varas beyond Santo Domingo's league belonged to Ortiz. Although he did not protest the measurement of the Santo Domingo league at the time, by September Ortiz had filed an appeal with Bernardo Bonavía, the commanding general in Durango.⁴⁹

In 1724 Governor Bustamante commissioned Páez Hurtado to hold a judicial inquiry regarding a grant Governor Rodríguez Cubero had made in 1700 to Mateo Trujillo of land between the pueblos of Santa Clara and San Ildefonso. The central issue to be decided was whether Trujillo had ever occupied the grant. Páez Hurtado examined the "principal Indians" of the two pueblos, who told him that they always planted the land in question, which Páez Hurtado said was "shown by an acequia on the site" and that Trujillo had never resided on the land.⁵⁰ Páez Hurtado started to measure the pueblo's land "to give them their league" but measured only 2,200 varas when he reached the boundary markers Trujillo had erected. Páez Hurtado told the governor that the witnesses all testified that Trujillo had never resided on his land grant, although he had erected boundary markers in the form of a cross and two forked props. The surviving documents do not reveal any final decision, but they do confirm the recognition of both pueblos' league entitlement.⁵¹

Twelve years later, however, José Riaño, one of the wealthiest men in New Mexico, who lived in the La Ciénega–Alamo area, purchased the Mateo Trujillo grant.⁵² Although Riaño must have been familiar with the 1724 case, in his petition to Governor Gervasio Cruzat y Góngora (1731–1736) he made no mention of measurement of his land or of the leagues of the two pueblos. Instead of asking that the Pueblo leagues of Santa Clara and San Ildefonso be measured, Riaño asked that the pueblos "present the documents they have for the recognition of what belongs to them"⁵³ Governor Cruzat y Góngora ignored this reference to Pueblo documents, describing Riaño's petition as "requesting that the two leagues belonging to the two pueblos of San Ildefonso and Santa Clara be measured, one league for each pueblo."[54]

Páez Hurtado again received the appointment to make the measurement. He proceeded to San Ildefonso with two witnesses and Alcalde Juan Esteban García de Noriega and started the measurement. When Páez Hurtado measured the San Ildefonso league, he found that the monument marking the lands Riaño purchased encroached on it by 400 varas, and when he measured Santa Clara's league, he discovered that Riaño's land was encroaching by 169 varas. There were only 84 varas between the two pueblos' full leagues. He informed the governor that this relatively small amount of land was what Riaño owned.[55] Governor Cruzat y Góngora, in a move that showed clear favoritism toward the wealthy Hispano, told Páez Hurtado that "nothing new should be done in the matter, and the boundary markers [shall] remain in the places and positions where they are found"—that is, encroaching on the two pueblos' leagues.[56]

Governor Cruzat y Góngora received at least one other request for measurement of the Pueblo league during his term. The case itself has not survived, but a reference to it is contained in the inventory of documents Governor Cruzat y Góngora turned over to his successor, Governor Enrique Olavide y Michelina (1736–1739). The outgoing governor apparently left unanswered a petition from the Indians of Isleta "requesting that the league belonging to them be measured."[57]

In 1748 the site of the abandoned pueblo of Sandia was the subject of a grant to a group of resettled Tiwa- and Hopi-speaking Indians. These individuals were Sandia people who fled to Hopi country (and their descendants) after Governor Antonio de Otermín (1677–1683) destroyed the pueblo in the course of his retreat to El Paso after being driven from Santa Fe in the Pueblo Revolt. The documents relating to this grant are the earliest extant for a Spanish grant to Pueblo Indians that is agreed to be authentic. It took the intervention of fray Juan Miguel Menchero to make the Sandia grant come to fruition.[58] The Sandia grant is an example of a pueblo grant whose boundaries combine measured distances and natural monuments, in this case the Rio Grande and Sandia Mountain. The grant also appears to reflect an application of the policy, suggested by Rael de Aguilar in the 1704 proceeding at San Felipe, that when a league could not be measured in one direction because of preexisting settlements, natural obstacles or other reasons, the difference could be made up by adding land in another direction. The Sandia grant and the modern controversy over the proper location of the eastern boundary are discussed in detail in chapter 4.

In 1754 Governor Vélez Cachupín made the Abiquiu Genízaro grant in compliance with Law 6-3-8 of the *Recopilacíon*, which set forth a property right for Indian settlements (reducciones). This law applied in cases in which Hispanos forced Indian communities to move or to settle in specific areas. Hispanos originally settled Abiquiu, but because it was on the frontier of the territory, it was constantly exposed to Comanche and Ute raiding. By 1747 Governor Joaquín Codallos y Rabal (1723–1749) ordered the remaining settlers to abandon their homes, because he could not assure their protection.[59] But his successor, Vélez Cachupín, made peace with the Utes, and the viceroy in Mexico City ordered the resettlement of Abiquiu. Inclusion of the Genízaros in the resettlement, however, was key to the plan, because they were expected to assist in protecting the community, and the viceroy ordered Vélez Cachupín to make a grant of lands to them, in accordance with Law 6-3-8, which he did on 10 May 1754.[60]

The grant boundaries were described by natural monuments, but the grant appeared to comply precisely with the requirements of the law in that it included ample frontage on the Rio Chama, along with lands that were irrigable from that river, woodlands, and, importantly, on the south, an ejido, or common lands, one league in length. Ultimately, the Abiquiu grant, though it was confirmed by the Court of Private Land Claims, was never treated as Indian lands by U.S. authorities. This grant is discussed in detail in chapter 5 of *The Witches of Abiquiu*.[61]

In the latter half of the eighteenth century, individual pueblos began to initiate lawsuits against Hispanos whom they believed were encroaching on the pueblos' lands. The first of these cases was brought in 1763 by San Ildefonso, represented by Felipe Tafoya, who identified himself as *procurador*, or attorney. Tafoya filed a lengthy petition citing encroachments on Pueblo land by Juana Luján, Pedro Sánchez, Antonio Mestas, and Marcos Lucero. Even though San Ildefonso's league had been measured in 1704, encroachments had occurred almost continuously since that time. In some cases the pueblo had protested, to no avail, when grants of adjoining land were made. Tafoya cataloged these problems, many of which went unresolved for more than half a century. Tafoya made his case in the name of the governor of San Ildefonso, Francisco Cata; the elders; and the other members of the pueblo.[62]

Upon receipt of the petition, Governor Vélez Cachupín lost no time in resolving one of the problems that had been festering for some time. He ordered Marcos Lucero expelled from land he was occupying "without the slightest recourse."[63] Apparently Lucero purchased land from an individual member of the pueblo, the pueblo protested, and Governor Francisco Antonio Marín del Valle (1754–1760) ordered that Lucero's money be returned to him and that he then vacate the land. Lucero took the money but refused to leave. Because of his familiarity with the earlier decision, Vélez Cachupín was able to act swiftly in response to Tafoya's request without requiring further proof.[64]

Tafoya's petition also achieved immediate results with regard to the claims against Antonio Mestas. Peremptorily and under penalty of a two hundred-peso fine, Vélez Cachupín ordered him not to settle at the Aguaje del Río Grande as he planned. The governor's order was effective in keeping Mestas and his father-in-law, Pedro Sánchez, from encroaching on San Ildefonso land, but Lucero was another story. In spite of Vélez Cachupín's eviction order, Lucero was still encroaching on San Ildefonso land in 1786 when Governor Juan Bautista de Anza (1778–1788) again ordered him to leave. Eventually, a new defender of San Ildefonso, Alcalde Carlos Fernández, obtained an order against Lucero from Governor Anza.[65]

Governor Vélez Cachupín ordered Fernández to examine the title papers of Matías Madrid and Juana Luján and to measure the San Ildefonso league. Fernández measured a 100-vara cordel in the presence of Felipe Tafoya, the pueblo's representative, and the pueblo's officers and leaders. The measurements, which were made in three directions, found all the Hispanos to be encroaching on San Ildefonso's Pueblo league.

When the measurements were concluded, the papers were delivered to Tafoya, who responded several times and in great detail to the various and diverse claims of the encroaching Hispanos. They argued that they were on the land pursuant to valid grants, that they had lived there a long time, and that it would be unjust to eject them. Juana Luján's son, Juan Gómez del Castillo, also argued that his ancestors helped conquer New Mexico and that he and his neighbors served in the militia at their own expense to protect the province from Plains Indian attacks. "It is a hard matter," Gómez stated, "that we should become as pilgrims in this kingdom, and not as natives." He also acknowledged, however, that the general right to "the league, which, according to law, the pueblos should have in each cardinal direction," was indisputable.[66] Tafoya rejected the notion that length of occupancy gave any rights to pueblo land, and he cited provisions of the *Recopilación* to show the royal mandate that Hispanos live apart from, not on, pueblo lands.

Now Governor Vélez Cachupín had the issue squarely in front of him, but his choice was an impossible one. Strictly upholding the Pueblo league would mean evicting Hispanos with valid grants, so the governor referred the question to Licenciado Fernando de Torija y Leri, a Chihuahua lawyer, for an opinion. About a year later, the lawyer replied with a compromise that took the pressure off Vélez Cachupín. First, Torija stated his opinion that the rights of the Indians and Hispanos were about the same. The royal laws protected the pueblos from encroachment, but the rights of Hispanos who had legitimate titles, such as Juana Luján, also had to be respected. As a practical matter, they were the ones most motivated to defend the province because they were also defending their own land.[67] The compromise Torija suggested was to recognize the basic right of the pueblo to four square leagues, allow Juana Luján to remain on the land, and measure additional land to the north and west to make up for the land the pueblo lost as a result of the encroachment.[68] Vélez Cachupín embraced the opinion wholeheartedly.[69] It was the kind of compromise he favored in other cases, allowing him to give something to both sides, while validating the mutually exclusive concepts each was endorsing. Tafoya, moreover, could claim a victory in the defeat of Pedro Sánchez's and Marcos Lucero's claims, or so it appeared.

Lucero was still there, however, when former Alcalde Carlos Fernández filed a petition on behalf of San Ildefonso and Santa Clara asking for a remeasurement of the leagues of both pueblos in 1786. Alcalde Fernández alluded to the long history of grievances that gave rise to the petition he was filing on behalf of the pueblos. According to Fernández, Santa Clara was not involved in as many lawsuits as San Ildefonso, so its need was greater. Santa Clara's Pueblo league, which by the 1780s was recognized as "the league that the king our lord . . . grants to each pueblo," was never measured, and Fernández wanted it measured properly.[70]

Governor Anza must have been aware that the method of measuring the league in each direction and of marking each pueblo's boundary was in question, for he specifically ordered that a "waxed cordel containing a hundred varas" be used and that boundaries be marked with lime and rocks.[71] If lime was unavailable, cedar stakes were to be driven firmly in the ground to form a circle or square measuring two varas around to be filled with four or five cartloads of stone. Anza's order indicates an awareness that the impermanence of boundary markers, such as a simple pile of stones, was a problem in the past. The measurement proceedings were turned over to Alcalde José Campo Redondo, who was even more specific about how the measurement of the Pueblo league should proceed. In the presence of Fernández and the still-encroaching Lucero and his family, the cordel was soaked in water because no one could find any wax to follow the governor's instructions. Then Alcalde Campo Redondo appointed officials to hold each end of the cordel and make the measurement and another official to count the fifty cordeles it would take to reach 5,000 varas.[72]

The first measurement started from the cross in the cemetery of the Santa Clara church. It headed in a direct southerly line and reached 5,000 varas, at which point a boundary marker was placed. Then the same procedure was followed from south to north: the officials started at the San Ildefonso church, and when they reached the Santa Clara boundary marker, they overshot it by 39¾ varas before reaching the full extent of the 5,000-vara San Ildefonso league. The measurement of the two Pueblo leagues being completed, Campo Redondo returned the proceedings to Governor Anza, who then referred them to Fernández.[73]

Fernández argued passionately how incredible it was for any New Mexico governor to make a grant of land between the pueblos when there was no excess land to be granted and when there was instead a shortage. As Fernández saw it, such a grant had to be based on misinformation or outright fraud, and in any case these grants to Hispanos were void, and no length of time of possession could change that.[74] Then Lucero took his turn. He made several technical arguments, but then he challenged Alcalde Campo Redondo's just-completed measurement. He said that the measurement was not begun at the proper location and was made with an old, unwaxed cordel spliced together with straps. He added that the Indians were trying so hard to stretch the cordel by pulling it that they broke it twice.[75]

Based on Lucero's statement, Governor Anza ordered the Santa Clara and San Ildefonso leagues remeasured in strict conformity with his previous order. A waxed cordel was to be used (apparently the parties found some wax), and the cordel was to be measured in full view of all the interested parties, a step omitted during the earlier measurement.[76] When the second measurement was made with a waxed cordel, instead of a 40-vara overlap there was a gap of 236 varas between the boundaries of the two pueblos. Campo Redondo measured the Santa Clara league twice with the same result. He then measured the cordel used in the first measurement against the one used in the second and found the first one to be longer "because the waxed cordel does not stretch, and the unwaxed stretches very much."[77]

Fernández and Lucero submitted further arguments in light of the second measurement, but by this time Governor Anza had all the information he needed to make a decision. He approved the proceedings leading to the second measurement, which showed a gap of 236 varas between the San Ildefonso and Santa Clara leagues, and he ordered that the pueblos were to each receive the land these measurements encompassed. Finally, he ordered Lucero to limit himself to the 236 varas between the pueblos. Should he decide to sell, he must first offer the land to San Ildefonso.[78] Anza was even more careful than Vélez Cachupín to set forth all the reasons for his decision. Vélez Cachupín's decree, which Anza cited, was based on the Chihuahua lawyer's opinion, whereas Anza took the *Recopilación* off his bookshelf and referred directly to royal laws.[79] He cited the law giving a league of commons to each pueblo and another providing protection to all the land the Indians farmed.[80] Fernández was unable to participate in the final step of this litigation because of illness. In his stead, Juan Ignacio Mestas appeared on behalf of the pueblos, overseeing the placement of permanent boundary markers. As Governor Anza ordered, a circle of cedar stakes was driven into the ground and three (not five) cartloads of stones were dumped into it. The Pueblo Indians saw too many so-called permanent boundary markers moved or disappear, so they took it upon themselves to build a wall of stone and mud one vara high as an additional boundary marker.[81]

Advocates Rael de Aguilar, Tafoya, and Fernández cited the laws in the *Recopilación* defining and protecting Indian property, but encroachers like Marcos Lucero ignored them. Lucero could do so because he was seldom penalized. Following Anza's ruling, however, Lucero was subject to a one hundred-peso fine if he failed to observe any part of the decree or attempted to move the established boundary markers. Another issue Fernández successfully laid to rest was whether the Pueblos needed to show grant documents to establish their property rights. Lucero argued, in May 1786, that the Pueblos should be required to provide documentation, but Fernández answered that "it is useless to ask that the Indians established in pueblos present the grants to the land they justly possess, because the same appear in the laws of our sovereigns."[82] The reasonableness of this response impressed the otherwise obstreperous Lucero, who agreed that the pueblos did not need grant documents. He even agreed to accept the pueblos' leagues as long as they were measured properly.[83]

A grant that Governor Pedro Fermín de Mendinueta (1767–1777) made to Santo Domingo and San Felipe in 1770 provides another example of a determination that the land between two pueblos' leagues should be divided between them as was done as in the resolution of the dispute between Santo Domingo and Cochiti in 1722. The two pueblos jointly petitioned the governor for a grant of land on the east side of the Rio Grande, saying they needed additional lands on which to pasture their livestock.[84] The lands described in the petition seem to have been east of the pueblos' lands, although the petition stated that the lands only measured about three-quarters of a league from north to south. The grant the governor made, however, consisted of the land between the two pueblos' leagues. Mendinueta said that it would be "extremely prejudicial" to the two pueblos if this land were granted to anyone else. He ordered that the two leagues be measured and that a monument be placed in the middle of the excess so each that pueblo would "recognize its appurtenance."[85] Bartolomé Fernández, chief alcalde, conducted the measurement. Then he took the two pueblo governors by the hand, and they "plucked up grass, cast stones to the four winds, [and] all shouted in a loud voice three times 'Long live our Lord the King,'" the standard ritual of the granting of possession.[86] Just over half a century later, these lands became a target of the Mexican policy of privatizing "excess" pueblo lands.

The next reference to the Pueblo league in the surviving records of the Spanish administration in New Mexico appears to be a letter dated in 1808, when fray Antonio Caballero, the priest at the mission of Cochiti, wrote Governor Alberto Máynez (1807–1808, 1814–1816) on behalf of Santo Domingo Pueblo. The Indians asked the priest to write because they were afraid they would be unable to explain themselves clearly were they to try to compose a letter. They explained through Caballero that "they were acquainted with the boundaries of their league," but they wanted the governor to know they purchased another piece of land west of the Rio Grande beyond their Pueblo league.[87] From all appearances, the pueblo had sent the letter solely to make sure that the governor had a record of its purchase of this land.

Beginning in 1811, the Spanish Cortes (parliament) passed a series of laws that reflected a significant change in the protective relationship between the Indians of New Spain and the Spanish government. These laws derived from the liberal philosophy coming out of the French Revolution and rested on the two pillars of equality between Spaniards and Indians and the preference for private over communal property. Equality vis-à-vis the Indians meant that Indian communal property would no longer be protected, according to the proponents of these laws. The preference for private property, as Mexican liberal José Luis Mora expressed it, was meant to allow Indians "to acquire individual parcels of land so that they might develop habits of hard work, raise agricultural production, and achieve 'a feeling of personal independence.'"[88] Not all of the members of the Cortes were as willing to privatize Indian land as was Mora. In 1812 a law reflecting a compromise regarding New Mexico's pueblos began making its way through the legislative process. Rather than privatizing all Indian land, the law that eventually passed on 9 November applied only to sobrante (surplus) land of Indian communities. When the law reached the overseas committee of the Cortes, it was modified on the grounds that "communal Indian land has always been viewed as a sacred place." The committee made an exception, however, noting that "if the communal land is very plentiful with respect to the towns to which it belongs, in this case it would be very fair to divide up to half the land into private property."[89] The law was adopted as article 5 of the law of 9 November 1812, and although it was revoked soon after it was promulgated, the Cortes reissued it on 29 April 1820. It was published in Mexico City on 2 September 1820 and eventually made its way to New Mexico, where Hispanos cited it again and again in their attempts to privatize parts of the Pecos Pueblo league. This new liberal philosophy first appeared in New Mexico as an argument against a pueblo's assertion of its rights to its league in 1815 during a serious contest over land rights that nearly turned violent and that the pueblo ultimately lost.

In April of that year, the governor of Taos Pueblo, José Francisco Luján, directed a petition to the chief alcalde, José Miguel Tafoya, in which he stated that although the king gave the pueblo "a league of land in the four directions," Hispanos who settled there usurped the land, preventing the Indians from making full use of it.[90] The alcalde, realizing that acting on this petition could stir up a hornets' nest, referred it to Governor Máynez.

Taos initiated this suit the day after Máynez made the Arroyo Hondo grant, northwest of the pueblo. In the petition for that grant, Nerio Sisneros, the lead petitioner, stated that the land requested was "distant from the league of the Indians," but Taos plainly felt threatened nonetheless.[91] The Arroyo Hondo petitioners were aware not only of the Pueblo league but also of the Cortes's decree of 4 January 1813. Sisneros based his petition on the decree's provision for "granting agricultural land to landless inhabitants of each town." Although Sisneros was not seeking land within the Taos league, the Arroyo Hondo grant still seems to have been the last straw for the governor of Taos Pueblo.[92] He asked fray José Benito Pereyro to advocate on the pueblo's behalf and to begin to deal with the settlers on Taos's league.[93]

The problem, as it turned out, went far beyond a few Hispanos chipping away at the edges of the Pueblo league. More than two hundred Hispanos were living inside the Taos league, mainly in the settlement of Don Fernando de Taos, surrounding the Taos Plaza. But Máynez, whose brief, second term as governor was marked by a number of actions intended to restrict Spanish intrusions onto Pueblo lands, seemed undaunted by the scale of the encroachment. Just a week after the petition was referred to him, on 18 April 1815, he issued a decree in which he stated that

> the five thousand–vara league, measured from the cross in the cemetery in each direction, which his majesty made as a grant to every Indian pueblo from the time of its founding, is to be maintained in order to support the natives of the pueblo, such that they [can] use it and cannot give or sell it without the king's permission because it is a patrimony or inherited estate. No judge or governor has the authority to sell all or part of the aforesaid league.[94]

He added that if Hispanos had in fact intruded on the pueblo's lands and planted crops or built homes, they ought to be forced to vacate and to forfeit what they built, but recognizing that this could cause "grave injuries," he recommended that the alcalde "temper equity with justice" and find a suitable compromise. He also directed Felipe Sandoval, protector of Indians, to assist in trying to come up with a solution.[95]

This was the strongest, most complete statement any governor ever made about the Pueblo league in New Mexico, describing a pueblo's four square leagues as its inalienable patrimony. Yet as Máynez seemed to realize, the ruling was almost impossible to enforce because so many Hispanos were already living inside the pueblo's league. And, as one of the advocates for those Hispanos later said, the pueblo itself sought Spanish presence within the pueblo in the 1770s and "congregated with the Hispanos in order to help defend the pueblo against Plains Indian [attacks]."[96] In other words, the settlers contended that Taos invited them to settle there. Now, it was trying to have them removed.

On 3 May 1815, the Taos alcalde, Pedro Martín, wrote the governor, saying that he measured the pueblo's league and that three communities of Hispanos, numbering about two hundred families, would be dispossessed if his order were carried out. Martín repeated the contention, which he claimed the settlers made to him, that Taos asked Hispanos to come and assist the pueblo when Comanches threatened it. He suggested a compromise to the pueblo whereby the Hispanos would be permitted to remain in return for a one-time payment to the pueblo of forty-five head of livestock, but the Taos Indians immediately rejected the offer. The frustrated alcalde was left with no compromise to propose to Governor Máynez other than the suggestion that Taos should give up the lands it purchased from the heirs of Sebastián Martín (which later became known as the Tenorio tract) and let Hispanos settle there, an idea he seemed to realize would have no traction with the pueblo.[97]

Martín clearly did not like being caught between the independent Spanish settlers of the town of Taos and the Indians of the pueblo. About this same time Taos residents revolted in protest against the imposition of a 5 percent land tax the governor announced in 1814. Alcalde Martín overreacted to citizen complaints about the tax, jailing 280 persons who refused to pay the new levy. He eventually lost his job in 1816, when he was forced to resign.[98]

Martín and Father Pereyro reported on 20 May 1815 that they were upping the offer to the pueblo to fifty head of horses and cattle, but the Indians again rejected it, saying they wanted their Pueblo league. It appeared that Father Pereyro was beginning to side with the settlers, as he and Martín then proposed that the pueblo should at least have to reimburse the settlers for their improvements, and they complained that the Indians had the best land in the province, that they did not cultivate most of it, and that they rented much of it to Hispanos. They reiterated Martín's suggestion that Taos return the land it purchased from Sebastián Martín's heirs, because "the Indians have more land than they need [and] . . . they are not capable of cultivating the land they possess."[99] They attached a statement by José Romero, who was speaking on behalf of the settlers, specifying that they purchased or inherited their land from legitimate grants, cultivated and improved it, and built homes and churches on it. In a thinly veiled threat of revolution, Romero stated that if the Hispanos were forced to leave, they might take desperate actions.[100] Father Pereyro and Alcalde Martín were even more direct, reporting that if the litigation remained unresolved, and the governor let his eviction order stand, "the result would be a sensational [battle] between the *vecinos* and the Indians."[101]

The dispute about the Taos league was never resolved, although Máynez remained firm to the end, stating that the pueblo's "rights to the league that his majesty granted them is incontestable."[102] The governor rebuked the settlers for threatening violence but seemed to soften his position, stating that he would not make a final ruling unless he was supported by a judgment from the Audiencia of Guadalajara. What the governor wanted was a compromise that would satisfy both sides, but both sides wanted the land (and Taos would accept nothing less), so there was no possibility of a compromise.

Although the decrees of the Spanish Cortes had been promulgated in the province in 1811, 1813, and again in 1820, by as late as the spring of 1821 the government of New Mexico still had not developed a consistent position on the question of privatization of Pueblo land. On 21 April 1821 Commanding General Alejo García Conde sent twenty-five copies of the Cortes's 4 January 1813 decree to Governor Facundo Melgares (1818–1822), telling him to put it into effect. The decree dealt with the privatization of public and common land, allowing grants of such land to landless citizens and military veterans. Its twenty articles set forth the procedures to be followed in the making of these grants, giving the newly formed ayuntamientos (town councils, for communities of more than four thousand persons) the power to allot such land, exempting from these provisions "the necessary commons of the towns."[103] In central and most of northern Mexico, "pueblo" usually implied a community of Hispanos, while in New Mexico it ordinarily referred to an Indian community. If there was any ambiguity about the use of the word "pueblo," New Mexican pueblos such as San Juan de los Caballeros had no doubt that the decree was directed at them. San Juan filed a petition directly with the commanding general seeking relief from the effects of the Cortes's decree. The pueblo's 11 October 1821 petition stated that "we have been read an edict stating that the land of the pueblos is to be reduced."[104] The San Juan people told Commandant García Conde that they had less land than other pueblos and could ill afford having it further reduced. The pueblo, speaking through six representatives, reported that it had "so little land that it does not extend to a league in any direction, for that is what was ordered from the time of the ancient kings."[105] According to San Juan, the other pueblos "have their full league."[106]

San Juan's representatives implied that, if anything, San Juan should receive better treatment than the other pueblos because it was the only one that submitted to the Hispanos under Oñate, "for the other pueblos were brought down by force of war."[107] Accordingly, the king "made us noblemen more than [the members] of the other pueblos," said the San Juan representatives.[108] The pueblo's argument impressed García Conde, who ordered the governor to act in such a manner that there was no change in the land belonging to the people of San Juan, "keeping them in possession, which they have enjoyed since the land was granted to them."[109]

San Juan chose to take its concerns to the commanding general in Chihuahua rather than the governor in Santa Fe and by so doing probably received a stronger ruling than if it had relied on New Mexico's governmental officials. It would be years, however, before a clear answer emerged from the Mexican government on the issue of privatization of Pueblo land. Pecos Pueblo, with a rapidly dwindling population, was the most popular target of requests for land by non-Indians in New Mexico. With only a few members, Pecos lacked the strength to defend itself. Moreover, it fit the model of a pueblo with large areas of unused land.

By 1823 San Lorenzo Pueblo near El Paso was reduced in population to a single Indian. This led its ayuntamiento to ask the New Mexico Territorial Deputation if the ayuntamiento could partition San Lorenzo's land between the lone remaining Indian and the many Hispanos in the area who needed land, citing the decree of the Cortes dated 9 November 1812 as the basis for the proposed action. They also asked whether it applied in New Mexico. The deputation did not provide an immediate answer but promised that a decision would be forthcoming.[110]

The Cortes's law of 9 November 1812 was ambiguous regarding what amount of Pueblo land would be considered "very plentiful," but it was to have a profound effect on some New Mexico pueblos. Throughout the second decade of the nineteenth century, the idea that Indian common land could be privatized was tested on several occasions. The first pueblo to be tested and the most drastically affected was also the most vulnerable—Pecos—whose population in 1815 had dwindled to about forty from a high of well over two thousand at the time of Spanish contact.[111]

Beginning with the 1794 San Miguel del Bado grant southeast of Pecos Pueblo, Hispano settlement around the pueblo began to grow, and as it grew, settlers and speculators alike began seeking new grants of land in the Pecos River valley. In 1813 three Santa Fe residents—Francisco Trujillo, Bartolomé Márquez, and Diego Padilla—asked Governor José Manrique (1808–1814) for land at Las Ruedas, a former satellite community of Pecos, south of the pueblo. They insisted the land did not infringe on the pueblo's land, although the description of the land requested was so vague it was impossible to verify the claim.[112] That petition was never acted on, but it was renewed in May of the next year, this time specifically identifying the place called Los Trigos as the locale being sought. Manrique referred the petition to the Santa Fe ayuntamiento, the first known instance in which this new body (another innovation of the Spanish Cortes) was asked to consider a petition for a land grant, and the ayuntamiento (whose membership included at least six land speculators) granted it.[113] A year later, on 22 June 1815, Governor Máynez approved the ayuntamiento's action but added the condition that the exclusive area of the grant would be limited to the lands that the grantees themselves cultivated and fenced.[114]

Three applicants, two of whom were members of the ayuntamiento, filed another request for a grant, this time north of the pueblo, in 1814. Again, there was no description of the land, although the petitioners claimed that the land was "beyond the limits of the pueblo" and that the protector of the Indians, Felipe Sandoval, knew it was. Governor Máynez asked Sandoval to report on the matter.[115] Sandoval measured the pueblo's league to the north and determined that the lands were in fact outside the league; he reported this to Máynez, who approved what became known as the Alejandro Valle grant.[116] He had Santa Fe alcalde Matías Ortiz place the petitioners in possession after again measuring the Pecos league to make sure there was no encroachment.[117]

The Spanish settler whom Pecos Pueblo considered to be the worst encroacher on its league was Juan de Aguilar. Sometime between 1815 and 1818, members of the pueblo asked Alcalde Vicente Villanueva to remeasure their league because they believed Aguilar was living on Pecos land. The measurement confirmed that Aguilar was within the Pecos league. This so angered him that he filed a complaint against Villanueva, arguing that the alcalde's measuring procedure failed to follow accepted practice. Aguilar argued that the measurement was not begun at the cross in the cemetery according to custom and that Villanueva used a 100-vara cordel instead of a 50-vara cordel. According to Aguilar, this distorted the measurement, wrongfully causing his land to appear to be within the Pecos league.[118]

Alcalde Villanueva responded with a detailed discussion of how and why he measured the league. His reason for not starting his measurement at the cross in the cemetery was simple and straightforward. "It has been the custom, which I have followed," said the alcalde, "to begin [the measurement] from the cross of the cemetery, and this had been a fixed rule because all pueblos (except this one) have the church more or less in the center."[119] But the church and cemetery at Pecos were situated at the south end of the pueblo complex. Since Aguilar was on the north side, a measurement from the church cemetery would not reach him, but a measurement from the center would. Plainly, Villanueva's approach correctly honored the spirit of the Pueblo league doctrine.[120]

Aguilar's other complaint was that Villanueva used a 100-vara cordel. Villanueva explained that the terrain was so broken that the use of a shorter cordel would prejudice the Indians.[121] This was because one hundred measurements with a 50-vara cordel would not reach as far as fifty measurements with a 100-vara cordel. The more measurements one made, the more walking up and down there was, and the greater chance there was that the measured distance would be used up in vertical rather than horizontal measurements. To demonstrate his fairness to both sides, Villanueva described how he wet the cordel before the measurement, fearing that it had shrunk while it was coiled up between measurements. The parties and the alcalde then stretched the cordel between two stakes and began pulling on it to stretch it to its maximum length before measuring it. It would be to the pueblo's advantage if the cordel stretched after it was measured but before the league was measured, since that would give them more land. The Hispanos pulled so hard they broke it. Presumably after tying the cordel together again the Hispanos were satisfied.[122]

Not since the 1786 lawsuit over the measurement of the Santa Clara and San Ildefonso leagues had the fine points of cordel stretching been discussed in such detail. The numerous measurements of the league and the jockeying for position through the stretching of the cordel show how each side sought whatever advantage it could get. At Pecos the prize was the rich land to the north of the pueblo known as El Rincón and the Ciénega of Pecos.

The battle between the dwindling Pecos Indians and the surrounding

Hispanos intensified in the 1820s. Even before Mexico achieved its independence from Spain in August 1821, the first effort to truly break up Pecos Pueblo's league had surfaced. On 10 February 1821, Esteban Baca asked Governor Facundo Melgares on behalf of a group of seventeen people from the Ciénega-Cieneguilla area for the portion of the Pecos league that the Indians were not using. According to the petition, the population of the pueblo had dwindled to eight to ten families, the church was in disarray without a priest, and less land was being cultivated because the church was not farming there anymore.

Not known as an activist governor, Melgares expressed no opinion about the ownership of the Pecos league; rather, he simply asked whether the petitioners already owned land, since if they did, they would be ineligible to receive a grant. The resulting report indicated all but seven of the applicants possessed land elsewhere, and no more was heard from either Melgares or the petitioners about this request for Pecos Pueblo land.[123]

The advent of the Mexican period in New Mexico brought significant changes in the administration of government that directly affected the Pueblo Indians and their land. At the request of New Mexico's representative, José Rafael Alarid, the Mexican Congress made New Mexico a territory on 6 July 1824.[124] As a territory, New Mexico came directly under the national congress's supervision. Remarkably, however, the 1824 Constitution did not provide for the internal administration of Mexican territories. Deputations, which were replaced with legislatures in Mexican states, continued to operate in the territories under regulations dating to 1812 and 1813, as did ayuntamientos. Lacking the authority to function effectively, these local bodies became merely advisory and had to seek recourse to national authorities to resolve local issues. Members of the deputation in Santa Fe appear to have been under the sway of the liberal philosophy of the Cortes of Cadiz, at least with regard to the principle of privatization of common lands. Officials in New Mexico began to redistribute the land of Pecos Pueblo in compliance with the law of 9 November 1812. When Pecos protested, the New Mexican officials had to seek clarification from the central government in Mexico City. Although Pecos was the focus of the assault on the communally held lands of the pueblos, the issue arose at other pueblos as well, and for a while it looked as though the Pueblo league would succumb. Ultimately, however, the Pueblo league survived, a fact that might have been due to the Pueblo Indians' stalwart insistence on respect for their rights.

The first assault on Pecos under the Mexican regime came in 1823, when

Domingo Fernández, an educated, manipulative member of the deputation, and thirty-two others asked Governor Bartolomé Baca (1823–1825) for the *sobras*, or surplus land, of the Pecos league.[125] According to Fernández, much of Pecos's land was unused, since there were very few Indians remaining at the pueblo. Fernández recognized that the pueblo still existed and owned at least part of the Pecos league. He wanted the other part, the surplus. He asked the governor to make a determination of the amount of land the pueblo needed and to allot the remaining land to him and the other petitioners. By so doing, he argued, the government would be allowing more land to be put into agricultural production, thus fulfilling a goal the Mexican government adopted, and the Spanish Cortes had previously enacted in the 1811 decree.[126]

When Governor Baca received the request in September 1823, he simply forwarded it to Alcalde Manuel Antonio Baca of the San Miguel del Bado ayuntamiento, asking for a report regarding the land requested.[127] The ayuntamiento issued a short report in a little more than two weeks, agreeing with Fernández's assessment that the land requested was the Pecos surplus but recommending that the petition be denied because "it would not be just to assign [the land] to other owners."[128] Fernández continued to argue in vain to salvage his petition, pressing the claim, which was apparently false, that he had spoken to the few remaining Pecos Indians and that they stated that they agreed to his petition.[129] The deputation denied the petition on the ground that "the Indians of Pecos Pueblo said that the land they farm scarcely provides them with their subsistence, and they were obliged to farm it all."[130] Pecos must have made its position known when the deputation's representatives inquired of them about the circumstances and quality of the land. In this way they contradicted Fernández's claim that the remaining members of the pueblo agreed to accept him and his group as co-owners.[131]

Pecos's victory over the Fernández petition was short lived. A year later, Miguel Ribera filed a petition with the deputation revealing that Hispanos were settling within the Pecos league and receiving grants there from unnamed Mexican officials. Moreover, the deputation granted to Diego Padilla the land at Pecos that the pueblo governor had previously assigned to Ribera. But in the deputation's view, the Pecos Indians had a right to sell land to Hispanos, and the deputation had the power to make grants to Hispanos of land within the Pueblo league. Now, in 1825, the deputation was getting ready to do just that.[132]

The few remaining members of the pueblo must have sensed that the final assault on their Pueblo league was about to begin, for on 3 March 1825, the deputation heard a complaint from the Pecos Indians claiming the right to their league.[133] The deputation dispatched representatives to advise the Indians that the Mexican government had altered the regimen followed under Spanish rule regarding the status of Indians, "so that as their ancient responsibilities have ended, [so too] their privileges have ended, and they are equal to all other citizens with whom they form the great Mexican family."[134]

The deputation prepared to put privatization into effect by appointing Matías and José Francisco Ortiz to distribute the land the Pecos Indians were farming to individual Indians and to then distribute the sobras to Hispanos who applied for them. On 19 March 1825 the Ortizes reported to the deputation that they had distributed agricultural land within the Pecos league to ten Pecos Indian and eleven Hispano families. They also had a list of seventeen more Hispanos who were to be given most of the remaining land after this initial distribution. In a gesture of approval of this first official privatization of the Pecos league, the Ortizes were sent back to Pecos "to mark the boundaries and put other claimants in possession of the former Pueblo land." As recompense for this work, the Ortizes were permitted to obtain plots of surplus land for themselves.[135]

The deputation also heard an application "from various individuals for surplus land from the league that belonged to the Indians of Nambe Pueblo." The deputation directed the ayuntamiento of Santa Cruz de la Cañada to investigate the status of the land and file a report with the deputation.[136] There is no record of further action in this case, but it is clear that the deputation under Governor Baca had no doubts about its power to make grants to Hispanos of land within Pueblo leagues. But that situation changed with the arrival of a new governor in Santa Fe on 13 September 1825.

At the same time that the Pecos league was under assault by Fernández and his associates, the tract of farmland located between Santo Domingo and San Felipe came before the deputation, in the session of 16 February 1824, at the request of eighteen individuals seeking a grant of the land. The deputation ordered Alcalde José Francisco Ortiz to go to the land, measure the amount of agricultural land available, and inform "those Indians that the excellent deputation can dispose of that land and seek the progress of the decadent agriculture of this vast territory."[137]

At its meeting on 12 March 1824, the deputation considered the request further. In the past, every time Santo Domingo and San Felipe received notification of a request from Hispanos for that land, they produced the grant that Governor Mendinueta made to them in 1770, and the new grant request was rejected. This time was different: Governor Baca was determined to support the movement toward privatization of Pueblo land. It is worth examining the fate of the land between Santo Domingo and San Felipe since it presaged the fate of the Pecos league.[138]

When the Santo Domingo–San Felipe issue came up, the deputation learned that Alcalde Ortiz measured three-fourths of a league of land considered "surplus land in San Felipe and Santo Domingo Pueblos."[139] By calling the land "surplus," the deputation was attempting to strengthen its case that it had the right to dispose of the land. To the deputation, surplus meant unused Pueblo land available for grants to Hispanos. No hearing was held allowing San Felipe and Santo Domingo to state their position. Even when the pueblos notified the deputation that they had a grant from Governor Mendinueta for the land, the deputation was unmoved. Instead of distributing the land to individuals who were not Indian, however, the deputation parceled out the land to individual Indians, who then had the power to sell it.[140]

Two days after his arrival in Santa Fe, Antonio Narbona (1825–1827) assumed the posts of governor and head of the deputation, replacing Bartolomé Baca. That same day, 15 September 1825, the deputation turned down the requests of Juan Diego Sena and others for surplus land of San Juan, stating that "it was resolved not to consider this and other requests of the same tenor until the supreme government of the federation is consulted seeking a general decision in so transcendent a matter."[141] Transcendent or not, the attitude of the Mexican government was changing with the arrival of a new governor, and the period of Pueblo league privatization was coming to an end. The Pecos Indians must have sensed this governmental change; a month later Governor Narbona received a petition from them, which left no doubt that pueblo members never consented to the privatization of their land and its transfer to Hispano hands. The governor reported that "the Indians of Pecos ask that the one league in each direction be declared their immemorial property, which has been considered as belonging to each pueblo in this territory."[142] Displaying more caution than it had during the Baca administration, the deputation under Narbona decided to seek clarification from Mexico City on the applicability of article 5 of the 9 November 1812 law to the privatization of Pueblo leagues. The deputation acknowledged the apparent conflict between the Pueblo league as established in New Mexico under the laws of Spain and the Cortes's subsequent legislative action. It recognized that only Pecos of all the pueblos had some of its league privatized, which it justified on the grounds that Pecos's population had dwindled to such a small number of persons. But now the pueblo was objecting, and the deputation was unsure how to proceed.[143]

The deputation's decision to seek clarification of the incongruity between the Pueblo league and the laws of the Cortes apparently discouraged any further requests from Hispanos for so-called surplus Pueblo land. Still, Hispanos who had already acquired land at Pecos were causing problems among themselves and with the remaining Indians. At this moment of doubt, when the deputation was unsure what to do, Pecos Pueblo seized the initiative and for the first time filed its own petition complaining about the grants of its land to Hispanos, about sales of that land, and about excessive planting by other Hispanos. Juan Bautista Vigil, the former secretary of the deputation, was singled out for authorizing these grants of Pecos land to Hispanos. For the first time, the Pecos Indians themselves were asserting their ownership of their league in their own words. How could the Mexican government expropriate only Pecos land "when we have acquired more merits than all the pueblos of this province and with much more distinction?" they asked rhetorically. If Vigil wanted to give away land, he should make grants to Hispanos in such places as Mora, Las Golondrinas, Las Vegas, Coyote, and Sapello.[144]

The tone of Pecos's March 1826 petition wavered between deference and outrage. The pueblo blamed Vigil for its plight and was not above the use of sarcasm in directing a barb at him: "Let don Juan [Bautista] Vigil donate to them [the encroaching Hispanos] and help them with his own money, if he wants to give them something." On the other hand, the pueblo addressed the deputation "with the greatest submission, respect, and veneration" and made cogent legal arguments about the shaky title of the Hispanos who were given deeds without the pueblo's consent and had not occupied the land for the five years required to obtain title.[145] The deputation was sufficiently impressed with the Indians' argument, and it halted further sales by Hispanos of Pecos land.[146]

A few weeks later, Governor Narbona sent another inquiry to Mexico City seeking guidance as to the proper procedure to be followed regarding unused Pueblo land. A response from First Secretary of State Sebastián Camacho in the Mexican capital sought more information about the extent of the land at Pecos that the deputation disposed of and the origin and nature of the pueblo's communal landholdings. The question reflected the central government's limited knowledge about conditions in New Mexico and was typical of a bureaucrat who had no idea how to respond to the question about the Pueblo league and so asked for a report instead. In fact, no clear answer was ever received from Mexico City to Narbona's questions about dispositions of land within Pueblo leagues.[147]

Governor Narbona's response to the request for more information, on 10 October 1826, was revealing in its details (as seen through Hispano eyes) about the landholding customs of the Pueblo Indians in general and of Pecos Pueblo in particular. The governor excused his delay in answering the secretary of state by saying that he was awaiting a report from the alcalde at San Miguel del Bado, which he finally had before him. Presumably, it was from this report that he extracted the following data about Hispano land ownership at Pecos. He stated that the total amount of Hispano land along both sides of the river was 8,459 varas, of which 200 were designated as *abrevaderos*, or watering places for livestock. This land was within half a league of the pueblo and was used by forty-one Hispanos, while the pueblo's population had declined to nine families consisting of forty individuals. The governor assured the authorities in Mexico City that although these Hispanos, who outnumbered the Pecos, were encroaching on one-half of the pueblo's league to the north, the pueblo had its full league in the other three directions. He failed to note that Hispanos possessed the best farmland within the league.[148]

Governor Narbona reiterated his recognition of the Pueblo league concept when he referred to the "ancient, immemorial possession that was given them, [which] ... occupies one league in each cardinal direction."[149] The entire pueblo owned the league in common "with equal rights in the pastures, watering places, and sown fields." But to Narbona and many of his elite colleagues in government, communal ownership of pueblo land was the reason for the pueblos' "backwardness." Narbona equated the Indians' lack of private property with their "uncivilized" state, and he claimed that the Pueblos lacked a spirit of cooperation because "they do not help each other to support or advance themselves."[150] Narbona's distorted view clearly applied only to Pecos, which was, admittedly, in a very bad state. The territorial deputation endorsed Narbona's report, stating that privatization of Pueblo land was "the remedy that is necessary so that the pueblos of this territory, in general, will flourish."[151] No record of a response from Mexico City has been found, although Emlen Hall and David Weber searched the minutes of the deputation from October 1826 to early 1829 looking for an answer from the government in Mexico City. They conclude that "if a reply did come, it must have told local officials to stop redistributing the surplus land of Indian communities for early in 1829 the deputation suddenly reversed itself."[152]

Pecos Pueblo filed another petition that year, through Rafael Aguilar and José Cota, in which they complained that they were being violently dispossessed of their land. The Pecos argued that, as citizens, their property should be protected by the laws of Mexico just as Hispano property was protected. They asked for a reversal of the 1825 grants of Pecos land to Hispanos.[153]

The deputation appointed a committee to study the 1825 documents and others related to the privatization of the Pecos league. The three-member commission composed of Pino, Arce, and Baca must have been struck by the ironies and incongruities of Narbona's report to Mexico City when juxtaposed with the Pecos petition. Narbona maintained that "no damage is caused them [the Indians of Pecos Pueblo] by the newly donated [land]," while Pecos Pueblo claimed in March 1829 that "nothing can be worse than to see ourselves despoiled of our land in which the oldest down to the youngest of our pueblo have shed the sweat of their brow."[154] In language quite similar to Pecos's petition, the committee recommended that "all their land be restored to the Indians of Pecos Pueblo, indeed, the most excellent deputation at that time [1825] of this violent taking without doubt did not consider the laws that speak of respecting the property of all individuals."[155] The committee concluded its report with a suggested order that was unequivocal in its repudiation of the deputation's 1825 decrees. First, it recommended that "all land that was taken from them be returned to the Indians of Pecos Pueblo."[156] Second, it suggested that "all [Hispano] citizens placed in possession of it be informed by the alcalde of that district that they have acquired no right to said possession because said grant was made of land that has owners."[157] The deputation approved the committee's report with one condition: that "the land that must be returned to the Indians of Pecos is that which has been granted [to Hispanos] and not that which they [individual Pecos Indians] sold."[158]

Pecos Pueblo's appeal for recognition of the integrity of its league was a triumph, but it was a hollow victory, containing the seeds of the pueblo's eventual defeat. The Pecos Indians sought protection of their property, as could any other Mexican citizen. By doing so, however, they forfeited any special status that Pueblo land might have enjoyed in the past, in particular its inalienability. At least as regarded Pecos, that protection was no longer available, and its land could be sold over the signature or authorization of a single pueblo member.[159]

Domingo Fernández headed a list of twenty-two Hispanos who were granted land at Pecos and wanted the 1829 deputation decision restoring Pecos land to the pueblo reversed. The petition of Fernández and company also spoke of being violently dispossessed when the alcalde notified them that they would have to leave.[160] A new deputation committee ruled against Fernández, so he and his group appealed to the supreme court in Mexico City.[161] As was their usual practice, the Mexico City authorities requested more information from the deputation. Surprisingly, the territorial deputation opted to take a stand on the ownership of the Pecos league and told the high court that "since time immemorial the land in question was the property of the Indians of Pecos."[162] This provided an easy way to avoid making a decision. The Mexican supreme court agreed that the case fell under New Mexico's jurisdiction and so ruled, sending the documents north to Santa Fe on 11 February 1830.[163]

Although this ruling left Pecos in possession of its league, it now had official authorization to sell its land. With only a handful of Pecos Indians left, José Cota, one of the signers of the Pueblo's protest of 9 March 1829, traveled to Santa Fe on 22 September 1830 to sign a deed that conveyed the most valuable part of the Pecos league to Juan Esteban Pino. Cota, who said he was acting for the entire pueblo, deeded the Ciénega del Pueblo de Pecos to Pino for eleven cows with calves and three bulls, which pueblo members were to select from Pino's herd.

Picuris Pueblo must have heard about the deputation's new, protective approach toward Indian land, for on 14 May 1829 a Picuris Indian named Mariano Rodríguez decided to put the deputation to the test by seeking to reverse a land grant within the Picuris league. Rodríguez told the deputation that a previous grant to Rafael Fernández and Miguel González was "within the right and property of the ejidos of the pueblo where I reside."[164] Governor Santiago Abréu (1832–1833) agreed with Rodríguez and wrote in the margin of the petition that any grant made to González and his associates was revoked.

The settlers were ordered to leave after harvesting their crops, but they did not depart. Instead, they petitioned the Taos ayuntamiento seeking validation of their grant. Although the ayuntamiento approved the grant at the Cañón de Picurís (present-day Vadito) to González and the others, a committee of the deputation made up of Sarracino and Baca overrode the decision to approve the grant, reiterating the 1829 order evicting the settlers. Two years later, in April 1831, the group headed by Fernández and González was apparently still in possession of the land upstream from Picuris at Vadito, for the deputation appointed another committee to sort the matter out. The Martínez, Salazar, and Quintana committee agreed with the 1829 decision upholding the Picuris league but went into greater detail about the location of the land. The committee reported that the Hispano settlers were fanning out "along the banks of the river of said pueblo in the area upriver, outside the league that by law belongs to the pueblo."[165] The committee not only recognized the Picuris league as belonging to the pueblo but also noted an area of commons, pastures, and watering places to be shared by the pueblo members and the Hispanos of the *alcaldía* (jurisdiction of an alcalde) of Taos. At this point it looked like a victory for the Picuris people in defense of their Pueblo league, but the settlers at Vadito were still not vacating their land, hoping instead for a more favorable ruling. It came in July 1832, when another committee appointed by the territorial deputation reversed the ruling of the 1831 commission. The deputation's new ruling upheld the Río de Picurís grant and earlier allotments of land at Vadito. In 1841 additional allotments were made at Vadito, which turned out to be within the Picuris league as surveyed by the surveyor general, just as Rodríguez claimed in his 1829 petition on behalf of Picuris.[166]

Two years after the Picuris case, in 1833, a similar question arose between Jemez and one of its Hispano neighbors, Rafael García. This time it was the Hispano who asked that the Jemez league be measured since he was not sure whether "the pueblo overlapped his land or whether his overlapped the land of the pueblo."[167] Alcalde Salvador Montoya measured the league in the direction of García's land. When he was finished, the alcalde sought guidance from the governor as to whether he performed the measurement properly.[168] Montoya began by measuring a horsehair cordel with the help of two men, one appointed by each party, using a rod that measured one official vara. When the length of the cordel was verified, the alcalde proceeded to measure 5,000 varas from the church toward García's land and found that the measurement overlapped his boundary by about 100 varas. Then the cordel was remeasured and found to have gained about one vara in length. Since the measurement was skewed in favor of Jemez, both sides agreed that the 100-vara overlap between García and the pueblo should be reduced to 50 varas. This would still put García 50 varas within the Jemez league.[169]

Alcalde Montoya began his measurement from the existing church, which was at a different location than the first church at Jemez, and the Indians protested that he should have measured from their first church, which was presumably closer to the center of the pueblo. The pueblo made other complaints about the measurement—initially, García and others wanted to use "light wooden rods tied together," but the pueblo, probably believing it would stretch more and give them more land, wanted the cordel to be made of fiber, which they claimed was the custom in past measurements of the Pueblo league.[170] The alcalde was unsure how to proceed and asked the governor "to tell me in detail how I should act, what vara should be used, what should the cordel be made of, and whether [the measurement] should be from the church that was established first, or from the one there at present, or from the middle of them."[171] But Governor Abréu was not interested. He told the alcalde to "ask an attorney."[172] This was a typical response of Mexican-period governors, who, unlike many of the Spanish governors, such as Vélez Cachupín and Anza, sought to distance themselves from Pueblo Indian boundary disputes. Nevertheless, the incident confirmed that the basic principle that pueblos owned at least a league in each direction continued to be recognized through the Mexican period in New Mexico.

That remained true as late as 1844, when Santo Domingo sought to have its league measured. The case began with a petition from the pueblo's representative, Miguel Antonio Lobato, asking the proper official to "make the necessary measurement of one league in the four cardinal directions that was adjudicated to them by the Spanish government."[173] Alcalde Juan José Gutiérrez made such a measurement in 1815 under the direction of Governor Máynez, but the boundary markers were lost or destroyed, and quarrels with the neighboring landowners resulted. In particular, José de Jesús Sánchez and Vicente Baca fought with Santo Domingo so vigorously that the pueblo was afraid the matter would be brought to court in a lawsuit. Santo Domingo believed its neighbors were encroaching on the pueblo's land and wanted the league measured to prove it.[174]

Governor Mariano Martínez de Lejanza (1844–1845) ordered the measurement made, and a former governor, Prefect Francisco Sarracino, carried out the measurement, after notifying the adjoining landowners and in the presence of an unnamed attorney representing Santo Domingo. Just as had been proposed during the Jemez case, Sarracino proposed using a wooden rod rather than a cordel to make the measurement, suggesting that with the passage of time, the Mexican authorities were becoming better equipped to deal with these situations. Fifty Castilian varas were measured "on a small wooden rod perfectly assembled, which had been made to that size for this purpose."[175] Then a hundred of these rods were measured to the north. Sarracino reported that "since each rod contains fifty varas, five thousand varas were measured, making one league, which is what has been designated as the ejido of the pueblo of Santo Domingo."[176] Surprisingly, no mention was made of how far the measurement reached in relation to the land of Baca and Sánchez, but it can be assumed that the Pueblo league did not overlap their land. Prefect Sarracino ordered Santo Domingo to "place a permanent boundary marker of stone at the point where the five thousand varas ended," a task that would take some time to accomplish.[177] In the meantime, Indians from the pueblo dug two ditches in the form of a cross and filled them with stone.[178] When the Santo Domingo Indians were digging, "they found certain and sure signs that boundary markers had existed in that very place, which must have been placed [there] at other times . . . just as some Indians of advanced age had stated, an indication that Prefect Sarracino's measurement was correct and in accord with the 1815 measurement of the Santo Domingo league during Governor Máynez's administration."[179]

The Pueblo league, whose origins remain obscure, as far as is known was never set forth in any written law or decree but was nevertheless a commonly understood principle of law, encompassing not only the definition of a pueblo's minimum entitlement to land but also the manner in which that entitlement should be located on the ground. Though sometimes honored more in principle than in practice, the doctrine retained its vigor through more than two centuries of Spanish and Mexican rule in New Mexico, providing the Pueblo Indians with far greater rights to land than were enjoyed by any other natives of New Spain. Though it was threatened by the egalitarian principles espoused by leaders of the new Republic of Mexico, the Pueblos' insistence on their longstanding rights ultimately prevailed, and the league entitlement withstood attack even at the declining Pecos Pueblo. Indeed, the Pecos league outlasted the pueblo itself. Today, the prominent squares that dot the map of northern New Mexico, marking the core landholdings of many of the pueblos, are based on the Pueblo league and constitute vitally important remnants of the Spanish colonial regime in New Mexico.

Santa Ana people delivering payment for the Ranchitt'u tract to Alcalde Miera y Pacheco. Drawing by Glen Strock.

CHAPTER 2

Santa Ana Pueblo's Ranchiit'u Land Purchases

After the reconquest in 1692–1693, some of the pueblos, particularly Santa Ana, reached an accommodation with local Hispanos that enabled them to participate actively in the Spanish system of real property titles and to make it work for them. Santa Ana, along with Zia and San Felipe, allied themselves with Vargas on his return to New Mexico and remained relatively loyal throughout the turmoil of the 1694–1696 period, during which time several other pueblos violently resisted the reimposition of Spanish authority.[1] That fact surely played a part in leading Hispano settlers to deal with Santa Ana as an equal player in the land title system.

Santa Ana began to purchase land from Hispano neighbors in the early 1700s to protect and extend its holdings under a legal system to which it was at first a stranger but that it eventually thoroughly mastered. Santa Ana became adept at using this system to its advantage even though its principles were at odds with the Pueblo world view.[2] Pueblos like Santa Ana used European conveyancing practices to attempt to reverse their loss of land. Like other successful pueblos, Santa Ana did not get caught up in that system. It bought land from Hispanos, but it did not sell land, realizing that land's value resided in its use and preservation rather than in the price it would bring. The pueblo paid whatever the Hispanos demanded, believing that no price could be put on land.

Other pueblos possessed the ability to understand and utilize the Spanish economic system to a degree, but Santa Ana developed that expertise to perhaps the greatest extent, as revealed in a remarkable collection of original documents dating from 1709 to the mid-1800s that the pueblo has preserved. This collection of deeds, land transactions, and lawsuits demonstrates the manner in which the Santa Ana people dealt with Hispanos, learning to hold their own and eventually prosper in those dealings. From 1709, when it made its first land purchase, to the U.S. era, Santa Ana acquired a sophisticated understanding of the Spanish and U.S. systems of land acquisition.[3]

When Santa Ana began making land purchases in the early 1700s, the theoretical concept of protection of Indian land was embedded in the Spanish legal system, but the government's specific recognition of Pueblo land was not a hallmark of Spanish legal culture in New Mexico. In spite of numerous royal decrees ordering Hispanos to respect the Pueblos' property, Hispanos routinely encroached on Pueblo land in the period before the Pueblo Revolt. When the Hispanos under the command of Governor Vargas returned to Santa Fe in 1693, a new accommodation between Hispanos and Pueblos gradually developed. The history of Santa Ana's land purchases from its Hispano neighbors provides a case study of how that accommodation took place on the ground.

Anthropologists believe that the Santa Ana people, Keresans who call themselves the "Tamayame," arrived at their present location from the San Juan region, breaking into two groups when they arrived in the Rio Grande valley. Eventually the two groups reunited and began living in a number of pueblos along the Rio Grande, between present-day Albuquerque and the area known as the Angostura.[4]

By the time of the arrival of the Spaniards, Santa Ana's main village of Tamaya was established on the north bank of the Jemez River (which was known in Spanish times as the Río de Santa Ana), about 6 miles upstream from its confluence with the Rio Grande. Water in the Jemez River was unreliable and of poor quality, however, and although Santa Ana did some farming in that area, its people established their main farms at an area along the east side of the Rio Grande, south of its confluence with the Jemez River, which they called Ranchiit'u. Hispanos apparently settled on those lands in the seventeenth century, competing with the pueblo, requiring some of Santa Ana's people to move. After the Pueblo Revolt, when the Hispanos returned, they resettled at Ranchiit'u, once again threatening Santa Ana's existence. To avoid the breakup of the pueblo, the elders decided that their best hope for remaining united was to reacquire the land they once farmed at Ranchiit'u.[5]

In 1700 Pueblo Indians were just beginning to learn from Hispanos that land could be bought and sold by means of a written document. Santa Ana began to enter the world of commerce that Europeans created and refined, where payment of a purchase price entitled the buyer to assert dominion over a tract of land—to own it. This is the remarkable story of how, beginning within just a few years of the reestablishment of Spanish rule in New Mexico, Santa Ana wholly engaged the Spanish system of land transactions to reacquire its Ranchiit'u lands and then made full use of the Spanish legal system to protect the titles to the land it obtained.

The pueblo's first purchase, a tract of land on the west side of the Rio Grande at the confluence of the Rio Grande and the Jemez River, well illustrates the problems that land transactions of the day presented: vague boundary descriptions, the uncertainties of title, and overlapping claims. Santa Ana bought this land from Manuel Baca, but it seems reasonably clear that the pueblo bought at least some of the same land again, thirty-three years later, from Baca's daughter, Josefa.

The 1709 deed from Manuel Baca to Santa Ana conveyed a tract described as farmland, although the pueblo later had considerable difficulty constructing an irrigation ditch to serve it, and it may have been partially watered by the flooding of the two rivers. The deed describes the tract as being at "the mouth of the Santa Ana River" (and, thus, on the west side of the Rio Grande) and bounded on the north by "the mesa," on the south by the Río de Santa Ana (Jemez River), and on the west by the lands of the pueblo (referring, presumably, to the lands appurtenant to the old village of Tamaya). The price was fifty pesos, a relatively low purchase price, probably reflecting the poor quality of the land and possibly uncertainties as to who held the title.[6]

The deed recites that Baca acquired the land by grant from Governor Vargas in 1695. That grant was listed in the archives of the cabildo of Santa Fe in 1713 as a grant of land "at the Angostura [narrows] de Bernalillo that belonged to his father, Cristóbal Baca."[7] The original document of the Manuel Baca grant has not survived, but the surveyor general's office made a transcription of the text and a translation when the grant was submitted for confirmation under U.S. jurisdiction.[8] The boundaries recited in the grant document were typically vague: "two leagues below San Felipe Pueblo from two cottonwoods on the bank of the Jemez River as far as [the place] they call Bernalillo and bounded by [land belonging to] Maestro de Campo Alonso García." The measurements of the requested grant were more specific but still did not locate the land with precision: "one league from north to south, a league on the west, and on the east the length of an harquebus shot." The distance that a ball could be shot from a smoothbore musket of that era (an harquebus) was a characteristically imprecise measurement but was generally considered to be about ninety meters, a little less than one hundred yards.[9]

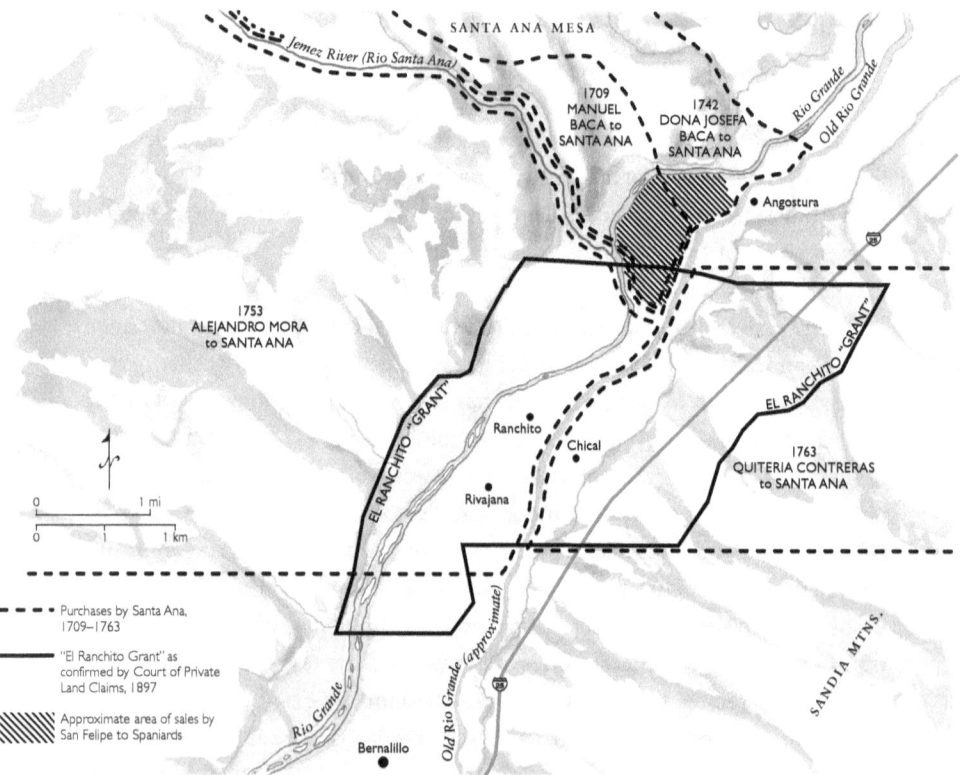

Santa Ana's "El Ranchito" lands, showing the approximate boundaries of the various purchases (dotted lines), the tract as confirmed by the Court of Private Land Claims (solid line), and the probable area within which San Felipe sold parcels to Spaniards (hatched). Map by Molly O'Halloran.

The Manuel Baca grant was more clearly defined in May 1700 when Baca was placed in possession of a tract bounded on the north by land belonging to Juan González Bernal and on the south by the property of an elite landowner in the Bernalillo area, Fernando Durán y Chaves. Baca soon ended up in a dispute with Durán y Chaves over the location of their common boundary, the history of which is part of Santa Ana's story.[10]

Boundaries given in eighteenth-century New Mexico deeds were frequently difficult to locate with any certainty, mainly because of the rudimentary land descriptions and forms of measurement. Measurements such as "the distance covered by an harquebus shot" or "the amount [of land] the throwing of a stone with one hand will cover," another measurement that was used in Durán y Chaves's dispute with Manuel Baca in 1704, today sound hopelessly imprecise, although they may have been somewhat standardized in colonial New Mexico. To see how the stone's throw and the harquebus shot came into play in this litigation one must go back three years to an earlier quarrel.

In 1701 Baca complained to the governor that Durán y Chaves had built his house on Baca's land, but Governor Rodríguez Cubero rejected his petition and directed Baca to deed to don Fernando the land north of Durán y Chaves's house up to "the distance that a stone thrown with one hand will cover."[11] That deed should have established the boundary between the two, but in 1704 Baca was again complaining that Durán y Chaves had moved his boundary further north and was encroaching on land that Baca planted.[12]

Eventually the dispute was resolved through Vargas's personal intervention. He provided the solution on 26 February 1704, when he rode out to the land on horseback and brokered a settlement between Baca and Durán y Chaves. Each identified a different tree that he claimed as the boundary. The tree Durán y Chaves pointed out was at the distance of an harquebus shot, while Baca's tree was at a stone's throw, which according to Vargas, was a distance one-third shorter than an harquebus shot. Vargas apparently prodded Durán y Chaves into making a concession. Vargas ordered Baca to place a cross at his tree, which would become the agreed-upon boundary. The governor hoped this settlement would resolve the longstanding dispute between the rival landowners.[13]

Their marriages to two daughters of Andrés Hurtado tied Baca and Durán y Chaves to Santa Ana. During the seventeenth century, Hurtado collected tribute from Santa Ana, for he held the encomiendas of Santa Ana and neighboring pueblos. This meant that he could collect a fanega of corn and a cotton blanket twice a year from each pueblo household. By 1680 Hurtado was dead, but his widow and her children escaped to El Paso during the Pueblo Revolt and returned upriver with Vargas in 1693. Among her children were Lucía Hurtado de Salas, who married Fernando Durán y Chaves, and an adopted daughter, María de Salazar Hurtado, whose husband was Manuel Baca.[14] Don Fernando and don Manuel thus thought that they should settle their 1704 lawsuit because they were related.[15]

After the settlement Vargas negotiated, Durán y Chaves decided to focus on his Atrisco landholdings and to leave the contested zone east of Santa Ana to Baca.[16] In 1706 Durán y Chaves sold his entire tract to Manuel and Juana Baca (Manuel's sister) for four hundred pesos, two hundred paid by each. Considering that at least some of the land was Captain Baca's to begin with, it must have grated on him that he had to buy it back, but at least that made an end to his problems with Durán y Chaves. Very likely, the land Baca sold to Santa Ana in 1709 included some of the tract Baca had recovered from Durán y Chaves.

In 1713 Manuel Baca transferred part of his remaining land to his sister. The complicated deed, which described the tract as San Antonio de la Angostura, did not include a good description of the land conveyed, and it seems possible that the deed covered at least some of the lands Baca sold to Santa Ana four years earlier. Baca stated that he did not intend to convey all the land irrigated by the Río de Santa Ana (Jemez River) to his sister but was instead keeping half of the irrigated land for himself.[17] Baca and Santa Ana did not mark the boundaries between them, leaving that for some future time. In 1733 Baca sold the remainder of his interest in the land, for which he had paid Durán y Chaves only two hundred pesos, to Cristóbal Martínez for seventeen hundred pesos.[18]

In 1713 Santa Ana purchased a tract of land from Juan González Bas, the second of Santa Ana's purchases. The deed by which González Bas conveyed the land to Santa Ana is fragmentary (and in fact contains no description of boundaries), but it is clear that the price was 120 pesos, that the land was acquired from Diego Montoya, and that González Bas claimed to have permission for the sale from his wife, María López del Castillo.[19]

Santa Ana's campaign to reacquire its traditional lands was temporarily sidetracked in 1734, when Governor Cruzat y Góngora annulled a potentially significant purchase. The pueblo negotiated a purchase of land just north of present-day Bernalillo and west of the Rio Grande from Baltasar Romero.

Before the sale was completed, the governor stepped in to nullify the purchase. He noted that he was advised of the sale but that the land could not be sold because it "was part of the *puesto* of Bernalillo, a very old settlement of Spaniards."[20] Cruzat y Góngora was definitely siding with Hispanos against the pueblo when he stated that the sale was contrary to Spanish law. The governor did not cite any law and simply noted that the law protected Hispanos from encroachment on land they received by grant, just as it protected Indians. Hispanos were prohibited from living in Indian pueblos, explained the governor, and Indians could not purchase land in the middle of Spanish settlements.[21]

The governor's motives for blocking the pueblo's attempt to purchase Romero's land remain unclear. As is obvious from Santa Ana's experience, no governor before or after Cruzat y Góngora took the position that pueblos could not acquire land from Spanish settlers. Whatever the underlying circumstances, the episode had no lasting effect. Twenty years later the pueblo was able to purchase this same land from a subsequent owner, although at a higher price.

In 1742 Santa Ana purchased a tract of land from Josefa Baca, the daughter of Manuel Baca, on the west side of the Rio Grande.[22] This was the pueblo's third major purchase. It seems clear from the description of the property that this purchase included much, if not all, of the land that the pueblo had bought from Josefa's father in 1709. Despite the overlap, however, the pueblo could be reasonably certain that it finally owned the land, and this turned out to be important, as this deed played a key role in the pueblo's subsequent boundary litigation with San Felipe.

The deed from Josefa Baca stated that she received the land "through inheritance from her father." It described the tract as being bounded on the north by "the place where the narrows widens at a stump of a tree that the Indians cut down," on the south by the confluence of the Rio Grande and the Jemez River, on the east by the Rio Grande, and on the west by the land of the pueblo.[23] The Angostura was an obvious and apparently well-known topographical feature where the low mesas on the east side of the river that enclosed the farmlands of Ranchiit'u came closest to the volcanic cliffs on the west side, constricting the otherwise broad river valley to a width of less than a mile. On a sketch map that was introduced into the Court of Private Land Claims El Ranchito proceedings in the late nineteenth century to depict the lands Santa Ana purchased, the place where the narrows widen was shown at the mouth of Arroyo del Cuervo, on the west side of the Rio Grande. For this parcel Santa

Ana paid nine hundred pesos, a relatively high price. By comparison, in 1709 the pueblo paid Manuel Baca fifty pesos for a tract described as bounded on the south by the Jemez River, on the west by the lands of the pueblo, and on the north by the mesa.[24]

A 1763 lawsuit that Governor Vélez Cachupín ruled on brought to light another land purchase Santa Ana had made three decades earlier, for which no deed has survived (if one ever existed). Were it not for this litigation, the purchase would probably have escaped the notice of historians. The land was located at a bend of the Rio Grande near Bernalillo on the west side of the river. Like most land in this area, members of the Baca family owned or claimed it. Exactly which Baca owned it and had the right to sell it to the pueblo was the crux of this litigation.[25]

Manuel Baca had four sons and four daughters: Antonio; Juan Antonio; Diego Manuel; Cristóbal; María Magdalena I; Juana; Josefa, who remained unmarried; and María Magdalena II, who married Diego Antonio Montoya and then Juan Márquez.[26] In this litigation, the two sons of María Magdalena II were fighting with their uncle, Antonio Baca, over land he sold to the pueblo. Santa Ana paid for the land sometime in the 1740s, but the claim in the 1763 lawsuit was that the pueblo paid the wrong person. Cristóbal and Nerio Montoya, sons of María Magdalena Baca II by her first husband, Diego Montoya, brought the lawsuit. The Montoyas claimed that their uncle, Antonio Baca, sold Santa Ana, land he did not own. Cristóbal and Nerio demanded the proceeds of the sale. Antonio implied that María Magdalena's second husband, Juan Márquez, sold the land to the pueblo.[27]

In New Mexico, a married woman's land was subject to joint control with her husband but could not be sold without her consent.[28] If Márquez sold the property in question to Santa Ana, Cristóbal and Nerio Montoya had no claim against Antonio. There was a sensational aspect to this case, because Márquez had been found guilty of having murdered his wife, María Magdalena Baca II, and sentenced to a period of exile from Santa Fe, and was thus unavailable to testify. Márquez was the perfect scapegoat for Antonio because it was plausible that Márquez sold his late wife's land to Santa Ana.[29]

Governor Vélez Cachupín ordered Alcalde Bernardo Miera y Pacheco to go to Santa Ana and ask the Indians who sold them the property.[30] Miera y Pacheco had completed a major Santa Ana purchase from another Hispano, Quiteria Contreras, just a month earlier, and the governor held the alcalde in high esteem.³¹ Miera y Pacheco went to Santa Ana, and when the pueblo's governor, cacique, war captain, elders, and others gathered to answer his questions, all said that Antonio Baca sold them the land and received the purchase price. None of the pueblo leaders had ever dealt with Juan Márquez.³²

Baca's case did not look good, and his own testimony did not help very much. In his statement he did not try to set the record straight but instead equivocated by saying that the members of the pueblo said different things to different people. Baca then presented the statement of Isidro Sánchez in his defense, indicating that the pueblo purchased the land from Márquez for a cinnamon-colored stallion and other property totaling 150 pesos. Sánchez had questioned four Santa Ana members, but they did not change their position as to the identity of the seller. They simply elaborated on what had been paid: three stallions (including the cinnamon-colored one), two oxen, and two bed sheets. In addition, Santa Ana paid Alcalde Luis García, who oversaw the transaction, ten wethers (castrated male sheep).³³

The proceedings were at a stalemate. Santa Ana had paid the person who claimed to own the land, Antonio Baca, and asked for a deed but was told that there was no paper available and that the deed would be prepared later. The Montoya brothers challenged Sánchez and Baca to produce the deed the pueblo requested and never received. Governor Vélez Cachupín ordered Miera y Pacheco to return to the pueblo to verify the statements of the men of the pueblo and obtain the deed to which Sánchez referred.³⁴ Miera y Pacheco and Vélez Cachupín must have maneuvered behind the scenes, however, for on 22 August 1763, the alcalde announced to the governor that Baca and the Montoya brothers had reached a compromise. In an implied recognition that he was at fault, Baca promised to pay the Montoyas 440 pesos in cows, oxen, sheep, wethers, and stallions. Santa Ana was allowed to keep the land, and Baca was permitted to collect 75 pesos from the other heirs to make up the total of 440 pesos to be paid to the Montoyas. It is not known what motivated Baca to seek this settlement, but it seems clear that Governor Vélez Cachupín believed the people of Santa Ana when they said they paid Antonio Baca for the land, and the governor and alcalde probably pressured Baca to settle. This vindication allowed Santa Ana to keep this tract of land at a bend in the Rio Grande on the west bank of the river near Bernalillo.

In 1753 Santa Ana made its fifth major land purchase, this time from Alejandro Mora. This purchase completed the acquisition of a large area west of the Rio Grande, stretching from where the Angostura widens on the north to the house of Felipe Gutiérrez on the south, and to the west, at least to the pueblo's old village of Tamaya. Reacquiring this land must have been a long-time goal of Santa Ana, since it encompassed all of the land between the old pueblo and the Ranchiit'u lands across the Rio Grande. As was explained in the Mora deed, by which the pueblo acquired the largest piece of this area, Santa Ana needed irrigable farmland because there was not enough land or water to support its members, and "many were scattered in various pueblos, searching for somewhere to plant."[35]

The "Rancho Viejo" tract that Alejandro Mora sold to Santa Ana in 1753 was described in the deed as stretching from the Rio Grande on the east to the Rio Puerco on the west and from the house of Felipe Gutiérrez on the south to "an arroyo where the road from Santa Ana ends" on the north.[36] When Mora decided to sell the tract to Santa Ana, he first went to Alcalde Antonio Baca to prepare for the transaction. Rather than simply executing a deed from Mora to Santa Ana as had been done in the past, Baca requested an order from Governor Vélez Cachupín and authorization from Mora's wife, Feliciana Miranda, for the sale, since she owned the property. Miranda had obtained the land as dowry from her father, Javier Miranda, at the time of her marriage to Mora in about 1742. Under Spanish property law, her dowry was her separate property, which Mora could manage and control but could not sell without her permission.[37] Instead of relinquishing her rights in front of the governor, Miranda appeared before him raising questions about the sale of her property. Vélez Cachupín listened but granted permission for the sale anyway, despite the fact that there was no indication that Miranda consented to the transaction. In fact, it appears from her testimony in a lawsuit she brought against her husband two years earlier that if she gave consent it may have been coerced.[38]

In 1751 Miranda brought suit, claiming that Mora had mistreated her and their Apache servant (*criada*) throughout their marriage. According to the testimony she gave, Miranda was "continuously lashed, beaten with sticks . . . and locked up."[39] Sometimes, she stated, Mora would "hang her totally nude and lash her with a whip."[40] Miranda told the judge that her torment was such that "neither now nor ever does she want to get back with her husband, Alejandro Mora, because of the bad life he has given her."[41] Mora admitted he punished his wife, although not as severely as she claimed. This seemed like a weak defense, especially when her burns and bruises provided their own grim testimony. Mora said he beat his wife because she did not attend to her Christian duty of praying daily. As for his Apache servant, Mora charged that "she had lost all his herds, and that she would go to the pueblos."[42] The real reasons for his anger became clear in the rest of his statement. Mora named several men with whom he suspected his wife had sexual relations, in particular an Indian from Santa Ana named Joaquín. There was no small irony in the fact that two years later, Mora sold Miranda's land to Joaquín's pueblo.[43]

Governor Vélez Cachupín must have believed Miranda and the servant because he moved the Apache from the house and ordered Mora imprisoned at Sandia Pueblo's jail. Yet when it came time to decide Miranda's complaint, the governor said that she and Mora had reconciled, "agreeing to live together as a married couple, embracing and making other verbal demonstrations of affection."[44] This apparent reconciliation often happened in other similar cases, but after Miranda's description of the abuse she suffered at the hands of her husband, it is difficult to believe that Mora suddenly changed his ways.[45]

In spite of Miranda's reluctance, the Mora land sale was consummated with the delivery of the purchase price of 739 pesos on 13 May 1753. The Mora proceedings demonstrate, for the first time in the records of Santa Ana's purchases, the lengths to which the pueblo had to go in order to complete these transactions. The people of Santa Ana did not have 739 pesos to pay for the land, so members lined up and proffered livestock and other personal property, each item of which was assigned a value, until the full purchase price was collected. The documents identify each pueblo member, his or her contribution to the purchase price, and its value. They further show that each pueblo member who contributed to the purchase price was to receive a specified portion of the land, and those persons and the amount of land allotted to each (in varas) is set forth. Because the tract was so large, however, there was plenty of land left over for those poor members of the pueblo who were unable to contribute any property. Vélez Cachupín finally approved the entire transaction on 28 May 1753, having previously ordered the land appraised by "disinterested and intelligent persons."[46] Alcalde Antonio Baca picked José Baca, a relative, and Salvador Martínez, but there is no indication that they ever performed a real appraisal. Alcalde Baca simply stated that the two appraisers "assessed and appraised [the land] as Christendom commands them."[47]

This was in sharp contrast to the appraisal procedures followed in a San Felipe land purchase that had occurred a few months earlier in 1753.[48] In that case, in which San Felipe was purchasing land on the east side of the river from the heirs of Cristóbal Baca (the fourth son of Manuel Baca), Governor Vélez Cachupín, apparently for the first time, fashioned a procedure to protect Indian pueblos in their land dealings with Hispanos. Concerned that San Felipe might be negotiating the purchase without fully understanding what the land was really worth, Vélez Cachupín appointed two appraisers to determine the land's value. He justified this procedure as necessary because "the Indians of San Felipe Pueblo . . . cannot and ought not make purchases or sales of real property [without government approval]," although they could sell personal property without approval according to local custom.[49]

Alcalde Miguel Lucero questioned the two appraisers separately, and each filed his own appraisal stating his valuation and the reasons for it. Although Baca's heirs asked for nine hundred pesos for the land when they approached the pueblo, each appraiser stated that the property was worth only six hundred pesos because there was no woodland, and water for irrigation was scarce. Governor Vélez Cachupín confirmed the appraisal at six hundred pesos, ordering Baca's heirs to deed the land to San Felipe at that price, which San Felipe paid with cattle, sheep, and other items of barter. The lands San Felipe bought from the Baca heirs were bounded on the north by San Felipe's lands and on the south by "the ranch and lands of Cristóbal Martin, deceased."[50] Sixty years later, this deed played a prominent role in the Santa Ana–San Felipe boundary dispute.

The San Felipe purchase appears to be the first time in New Mexico that land an Indian pueblo was purchasing was appraised in order to protect the purchaser. Vélez Cachupín further ordered that the procedure followed in the case should serve as a model for similar cases in the future. Later cases followed the San Felipe-Baca appraisal procedure, but Santa Ana's purchase of Mora's property did not. It seems apparent that the price the pueblo paid was Mora's initial asking price, but the size of the property suggests that Santa Ana was not overpaying for the land.

Attached to the extensive documentation of the proceedings of the Mora sale is a document that explains what happened after Governor Cruzat y Góngora thwarted Baltasar Romero's attempted sale to Santa Ana in 1734. The document is a declaration of a sale of land on 20 November 1739, from Pedro Romero, the son of the late Baltasar Romero, to Javier Miranda (the father of Feliciana, Mora's wife), for three hundred pesos, although he did not give

Miranda a deed. Thus, Santa Ana was buying from Mora the land it tried to purchase from Baltasar Romero nearly twenty years earlier, paying almost two and one-half times what Miranda paid for it.[51] Romero's declaration described the boundaries as being an arroyo where the road coming from Santa Ana ends on the north, Felipe Gutiérrez's house on the south, the Rio Grande on the east, and the Rio Puerco on the west. Mora took pains to point out that he was also selling to the pueblo a portion of the bosque situated on the east side of the river.

As Santa Ana slowly and painstakingly acquired land between its old village and the Rio Grande, the difficulties the pueblo encountered in irrigating the land led it to look across the Rio Grande to Ranchiit'u, the area it had farmed before the arrival of the Hispanos. Santa Ana needed those more easily irrigated lands east of the river to provide adequate food for its people. That land was almost entirely in the hands of the widow and heirs of Cristóbal Martín, also known as Cristóbal Martínez or Cristóbal Martínez Gallego, nicknamed "El Cojo" ("the Cripple"). Through a series of purchases, Martín had assembled a relatively large rancho of prime irrigable land east of the river.[52] Martín apparently died before 1753, as indicated by the Baca deed to San Felipe. His wife, Quiteria Contreras, remarried, and then apparently decided to sell the rancho that Martín had acquired. Santa Ana seized the opportunity, purchasing the entire tract in 1763. This was Santa Ana's largest land purchase during the Spanish colonial era. The originals of the extensive documentation of the transaction are part of the Spanish Archives of New Mexico.[53] Santa Ana received an exact copy of the proceedings, fourteen pages in all, bearing the original signatures of the all principals. That document, which Santa Ana used to establish its case in the boundary litigation with San Felipe in 1813, remains in Santa Ana's archive.[54]

The Contreras purchase was completed under the guidance of Miera y Pacheco, who was serving as alcalde of Zia and Jemez when he was called on to use his considerable talents to assist Santa Ana in its largest land purchase. It is striking how efficiently Miera y Pacheco handled Santa Ana's large purchase from Contreras. Between 5 and 8 July 1763, Miera y Pacheco completed most of the proceedings on his own. He summarized the background of the purchase from the pueblo's point of view, prepared a deed the parties signed, recorded a detailed itemization of the property delivered by individual Santa Anas, and administered a highly sophisticated appraisal of the property.[55]

On 9 July, Governor Vélez Cachupín confirmed Miera y Pacheco's actions up to that point and ordered the alcalde to "place substantial boundary markers that will serve as a sign of the boundaries called for in the deed of sale."[56]

Santa Ana explained to Miera y Pacheco that it needed this property because the pueblo still lacked sufficient irrigable land to support its members, despite its many acquisitions. The need for irrigable land was even more critical, since some families were planning to leave the pueblo unless additional farmland was found.[57] Contreras's land became available at just the right time.

Miera y Pacheco and Vélez Cachupín apparently understood that, especially in a transaction of this size and importance, it was critical to make sure Santa Ana did not pay more than the land was worth. Miera y Pacheco therefore ordered the pueblo to choose "a knowledgeable man of good conscience" to appraise the property on their behalf and ordered Contreras's representatives (her son, Mariano Martínez Gallegos, and her husband, José de Jesús Montaño), to select an appraiser as well.[58] This may have been an improvement over the procedure used in the San Felipe sale, for which Governor Vélez Cachupín appointed the appraisers, although the San Felipe appraisal was more favorable to the pueblo.

Santa Ana appointed Francisco Pablo Salazar as its appraiser, and the sellers chose Juan Bautista Montaño as theirs. It seems likely that they chose Montaño because he was related to Quiteria Contreras's husband. The two appraisers took an oath "to act faithfully and legally according to their true knowledge and understanding" and proceeded to appraise the land.[59] The appraisal was conducted in the presence of the sellers and the governor, cacique, principal captain, and other elders of Santa Ana. When the appraisers measured the irrigable land from north to south it came to a total distance of 4,340 varas (more than 2¼ miles). This was a substantial amount of irrigable land; the appraisers thus arrived at the relatively high valuation of 3,000 pesos, payable in local products.[60]

Once the pueblo representatives agreed to the appraisal, it was necessary to record the animals and other property that individual pueblo members brought to make up the purchase price. On 7 July 1763, eighty-one Santa Ana people appeared with their livestock and other property, which Miera y Pacheco tallied while the sellers looked on. One can picture the scene, as Miera y Pacheco, the appraisers, alcaldes and other Spanish officials, Contreras' family members, and Pueblo officials, gathered on a hot midsummer day. The pueblo members lined up to bring forward their animals to satisfy the purchase price for this important property. Most of the contributions were livestock, both large and small: sheep and goats at two pesos, bulls and cows without calves at twenty pesos, cows with calves and oxen at twenty-five pesos, mules from thirty to forty-five pesos, and horses from fifteen to fifty pesos. The most valuable horses were listed by name and color, for example, "Magua, the dapple-gray stallion, at fifty pesos."[61] The average amount contributed was thirty-seven pesos in property, a substantial sacrifice for these individual Indians and families.[62]

When it was over, Santa Ana had delivered quite a herd of animals as payment for the land. Apparently the Santa Ana people were particularly successful stock raisers, which was all the more remarkable given that the tradition of raising livestock for meat was unknown to the Pueblos until the arrival of Oñate in 1598 and that the opportunity to engage in large-scale stock raising only first presented itself to Santa Ana after the reconquest. In addition to the animals, a few items of personal property were contributed: several pieces of woven cotton cloth (mantas) and a basket (jícara). In contrast to the payments tallied in the Mora purchase, which were listed roughly in order of rank, the order of Indians delivering their property to Miera y Pacheco was somewhat haphazard. More important than observing strict protocol was assuring that the value of the property delivered equaled three thousand pesos. The scene at the time of the delivery of the property must have been hectic, with the small herds of animals and people milling about waiting their turn for Miera y Pacheco to tally them. The animals delivered that day in early July 1763 included eight horses, three mules, eight bulls, twenty-nine oxen, fifty sheep, and sixty-seven cows.[63]

This was by far the highest price that Santa Ana had ever paid for a single piece of property. Nevertheless, it was worth it to the pueblo to acquire a sizable tract of land east of the Rio Grande, land that it knew was fertile and irrigable. The boundaries listed in the deed that Miera y Pacheco prepared were on the north "the halfway point [la mitad] of the Angostura where a cross is placed to mark what belongs to San Felipe Pueblo, on the south three cottonwoods below the house where Cristóbal Martínez used to live, on the east the foot of the Sandia Mountains, and on the west the Rio Grande."[64] Miera y Pacheco included all the formalities in the deed, including Contreras's authorization of the sale and the acknowledgment by her son and her husband that they received the full purchase price of three thousand pesos.[65] Although Contreras did not sign the deed, she did sign a separate authorization, a step that neither Mora nor any of the other land owners followed when they sold their wives' property to Santa Ana.[66]

Governor Vélez Cachupín ordered the alcalde to place "permanent and substantial boundary markers," so Miera y Pacheco went to the pueblo on 3 August 1763 to set the monuments and deliver possession of the land. The people of Santa Ana were present, as were some people from San Felipe, when Santa Ana took possession of this prized tract of land. Individual pueblo members also received tracts of land in accordance with what they paid.

The Contreras tract continues to serve as Santa Ana's primary residential and farming area, and it is the location of its tribal governmental offices. Although the old village of Tamaya on the Jemez River is maintained and regularly utilized for tribal ceremonial and traditional purposes, the day-to-day life of the pueblo today is focused on the Ranchiit'u.

In addition to purchasing the Contreras tract, Santa Ana continued to acquire smaller tracts adjacent to that land. In October 1777 Santa Ana governor Melchor Chavarría, the war captain, and other pueblo leaders appeared before Alcalde Nerio Antonio Montoya to consummate one of those smaller purchases. Santa Ana was buying a tract of farmland 91 varas by 203 varas from Pedro García, which included a flat-roofed, two-room house at a purchase price of two hundred pesos. Attached to this deed was another whereby García purchased the tract to the east from Bernardo Sánchez. The boundaries of this Santa Ana purchase were, on the north, lands of Santa Ana, on the south, the property of the late Prudencia Gómez, on the east, the land of Bernardo Sánchez (at that time belonging to García), and, on the west, Santa Ana. It seems clear that by this time Santa Ana was interested in acquiring all the farmland it could.[67]

Through this seventy-year-long campaign of land purchases, Santa Ana finally reacquired its critically important Ranchiit'u farmlands along the east side of the Rio Grande, as well as the land west of the river all the way to the old village of Tamaya and beyond. It owned all of the land west of the foothills of the Sandia Mountains, from the town of Bernalillo on the south to the lands of San Felipe. As would soon become apparent, however, although the boundaries of the lands Santa Ana acquired were marked, there was some uncertainty as to where the boundary between the two pueblos lay, at least on San Felipe's part.

The first page of the fourteen-page documentation of the sale by Quiteria Contreras of her late husband's rancho to Santa Ana (José de Jésus Montaño and Mariano Martínez Gallegos acting on behalf of Quitera Contreras to Santa Ana Pueblo, sale of land, Santa Ana, 5 July 1763, SA 14).

The twelfth page of the Contreras transaction documentation, showing the signatures and rubrics of Alcalde Bernardo Miera y Pacheco and witnesses Alejandro González and Manuel de Miera. The text explains that this is an attested copy of the original, to be retained by the pueblo (SA 14). The original was sent to the archives at Santa Fe (SANM I:1349).

San Felipe made two purchases of its own: the Angostura grant, from Juan Jose Gallegos in 1752, and a tract from the heirs of Cristóbal Baca in 1753. The Baca deed described its south boundary as the land of Cristóbal Martín, the lands that Santa Ana purchased in 1763, and the Angostura grant was described as being bounded on the south by "land of the Indians of Santa Ana." Neither deed to San Felipe contained physical boundary descriptions, such as tree stumps, rivers, or arroyos. That lack of clarity, and the fact that sometime before 1779 the Rio Grande made a major avulsive shift in its channel, eventually led to a full-blown, nineteenth-century lawsuit between the two pueblos, which was adjudicated on the ground twice, both times in Santa Ana's favor and affirmed on appeal by the Audiencia of Guadalajara. There followed a five-year process of enforcing the decision through the eviction and removal of Spanish settlers who purchased from San Felipe land that was found to belong to Santa Ana. These events reveal a virtually unprecedented and largely successful effort by a pueblo to assert title to and control of its lands using the Spanish legal system, even though Hispanos occupied those lands and another pueblo claimed them.[68]

It is important to understand where Santa Ana's north boundaries lay, as established in its documents, on the eve of this dispute. West of the Rio Grande, the boundary was where the Angostura widens. East of the river, Santa Ana's north boundary was at the middle of the narrows, plainly somewhat south of where the narrows widen. The course of the Rio Grande linked the two lines. A full understanding of the resolution of the boundary requires an explanation of San Felipe's purchase of the Angostura grant, on the west side of the Rio Grande, a year before the Baca purchase.

In 1745 Governor Codallos y Rabal made the Angostura grant to a presidial soldier named Juan José Gallegos, a resident of Cieneguilla. Gallegos requested a tract of land at the place called Angostura, bounded on the north by San Felipe, on the south by land of the Indians of Santa Ana, on the east by the Rio Grande, and on the west by the Arroyo del Cuervo. The governor made the grant after very little investigation, leaving it up to Alcalde Andrés Montoya to notify the adjoining landowners.[69] Conceivably, the lands Gallegos claimed as part of the Angostura grant overlapped the land Santa Ana purchased from Manuel Baca in 1709 and from Josefa Baca in 1742. It appears, however, that Santa Ana never received notification of the grant and was therefore unable to object. Since the pueblo made no objection, Montoya, acting as alcalde and receiving judge, placed Gallegos in possession of the land and claimed to have erected boundary markers.

Gallegos held on to the Angostura grant for only seven years and then sold it to San Felipe in 1752 for three hundred pesos.[70] Thus, the southern boundary of the Angostura grant, which was described as the lands of Santa Ana, became San Felipe's southern boundary and its common boundary with Santa Ana on the west side of the Rio Grande.[71]

◆ ◆ ◆ ◆

In 1866 San Felipe sold at least a portion of the grant to José Leandro Perea.[72] That led the surveyor general of New Mexico to recommend to Congress in 1874 that the grant be confirmed jointly to Perea and San Felipe, but Congress never acted on that proposal. In 1897 Perea and others filed a claim for the grant in the Court of Private Land Claims, reciting the same boundaries set forth in the original grant document. The United States opposed the claim, arguing that San Felipe had purchased the grant in 1752, that the 1866 sale to Perea was invalid inasmuch as it lacked federal approval, and that the grant as claimed overlapped the confirmed San Felipe grant. The court was unpersuaded, and in 1898 it confirmed the grant to the plaintiffs.[73] As surveyed, however, the confirmed grant straddled the Rio Grande and overlapped with the surveyed San Felipe grant by about 880 acres, which included the area the community of Angostura occupied. That conflict was not resolved until 1930, when the New Mexico federal court, in the quiet-title suit filed for San Felipe under the Pueblo Lands Act, largely upheld the claims of the non-Indian residents of Angostura to virtually the entire area of overlap between the Angostura and San Felipe grants.[74]

Before the two pueblos became embroiled in litigation over their boundary, they had reached a settlement of the issue raised by a substantial shift in the Rio Grande's channel. Sometime prior to 1779 the Rio Grande moved in the Angostura area from the east side of the flood plain to the west, as a result of flooding. This left a substantial portion of the land covered by Santa Ana's 1742 deed from Josefa Baca on the east side of the river. Whereas the river previously served as a clear boundary between the two pueblos' lands on the east and west sides of the river, after the shift in the channel the location of that line became unclear. San Felipe was evidently on sufficiently good terms with Santa Ana at this time to negotiate an agreement regarding the boundary, and the two pueblos presented the terms of their settlement to Alcalde Nerio Antonio Montoya. Montoya wrote up the compromise agreement on 14 July 1779, under which the boundary was established in the middle of the former river channel, where it had been before.[75] Montoya ordered the two pueblos to "bury stones from the place where the river moved to where it came back."[76] This 1779 settlement agreement between Santa Ana and San Felipe was of critical importance in the adjudication of the boundary dispute between the two pueblos thirty-four years later.[77]

It is likely that Santa Ana people were also farming in the area, since the Angostura was one of the pueblo's traditional agricultural sites before and after the Pueblo Revolt.[78] After the Santa Ana purchases, the pueblo continued to farm the Angostura area and coexisted with San Felipe until San Felipe began selling land in the vicinity to Hispanos. The first such deed from San Felipe came just three years after resolution of the 1779 San Felipe–Santa Ana boundary dispute. Five surviving deeds from the period 1782 to 1816 record sales whereby San Felipe sold tracts of land for more than twenty-seven hundred pesos in sheep, cattle, horses, and money to Hispanos such as Pablo Montoya and Juan Esteban Pino.[79] As San Felipe sold more land that Santa Ana claimed through its own land purchases, Santa Ana began complaining to the Spanish authorities, first to the governor and then to the protector of Indians.

Felipe Sandoval was appointed protector of Indians on 20 August 1810 after Cochiti Indian José Quintana requested in Chihuahua that the post be refilled after a vacancy of almost a century.[80] One of Sandoval's first cases dealt with the dispute between Santa Ana and San Felipe. The litigation began with a petition from Santa Ana governor Eusebio Mairo to Sandoval, dated 5 May 1813, in which the governor explained that San Felipe took "our legitimate land, which we acquired by purchase," and sold it to Hispanos, who were now causing great damage to the land.[81] Santa Ana sought the opportunity to present its deeds so that "it can be determined who is the legitimate owner according to the documents we have."[82] Governor Mairo added another point to emphasize the need for prompt action. He reported that Hispanos who had purchased land from San Felipe were destroying the bosque (the riparian cottonwood groves) by cutting down the trees and taking wood from the land. He urged the protector to stop this until it could be determined who owned the land. Mairo stated that in order to decide that question the authorities would have to examine the boundaries, but "if there is any more delay, when the time comes to decide [the case] there will be no cottonwood remaining at the site, and we shall be incapable of demonstrating our right."[83]

On 10 May Sandoval transmitted Santa Ana's petition to Governor Manrique, who directed the alcalde of Albuquerque, José Pino, to meet with the leaders of the two pueblos at the Angostura. He was to examine their documents and attempt to resolve their dispute, with the assistance of the alcaldes of Alameda and Jemez and the protector of Indians.[84] The parties met on 13 May (although it appears that Sandoval failed to appear). Alcalde Pino took charge of the proceedings and examined the deeds of both pueblos in an effort to locate the boundaries, beginning on the west side of the Rio Grande. Santa Ana presented its 1742 deed from Josefa Baca, which referenced the tree stump where the Angostura widens as its northern boundary, and San Felipe seems to have presented the Angostura grant document, whose southern boundary is described as "the land of the Indians of Santa Ana." Pino and the leaders tried to find "the stump cited in their document."[85] But the alcalde reported that it "does not exist, nor is there anyone among the interested parties who could tell me about it."[86] The northern end of the narrows was clearly identifiable, however, and the parties proceeded to that location and placed a stone boundary marker there. Both pueblos seemed satisfied with that determination, but they indicated that the boundary east of the river also needed to be established.[87]

They attended to this on the following day, 14 May. The parties reassembled on the east side of the Rio Grande, at the place where the river shifted to the west. This was the area where sales of land to individual Hispanos had taken place, and Pino noted that the Santa Ana representatives told him that "the principal and most interesting object of their complaint was the land on this side of the river." After having determined that both pueblos were in agreement as to the location of the boundary in this area, apparently referring to the 1779 accord, Pino fixed this portion of the boundary between the two pueblos along the Santa Ana acequia, which established that Santa Ana owned the land on the west side and San Felipe the land on the east. He then determined that several Hispanos had purchased land belonging to Santa Ana from Indians of San Felipe, although he concluded that San Felipe as a whole was not to blame. According to Pino, the sales had not been made in good faith and should be annulled. He called for the individual San Felipe Indians to return the purchase prices to the Hispanos and for the land to be restored to Santa Ana, although he told Santa Ana it should not recover lands that were planted until the Hispanos harvested their crops.[88]

Alcalde Pino reported to Governor Manrique that both pueblos were satisfied with the boundaries he established, but just one week later, on 21 May, the governor and lieutenant governor of San Felipe asked Protector Sandoval to notify Manrique that San Felipe was *not* happy with the boundary. San Felipe believed it was losing land on the east side of the river, which the pueblo purchased from Cristóbal Baca's heirs. When Governor Manrique received San Felipe's petition, he appointed José María de Arce, the first alferez of the Santa Fe presidio, to review Pino's actions, ascertain whether they were fair and just, and report to the governor.[89]

Arce came from a military family, and Manrique presumably chose him because he was above reproach and not governed by self-interest or partisanship. He was the son of Antonio de Arce who served as alferez at the presidio of San Buenaventura in Nueva Vizcaya.[90] José María was a trusted military commander for the Spanish government of New Mexico who undertook important military as well as civil assignments.[91] Working out a settlement of the Santa Ana–San Felipe boundary dispute was very likely one of his most challenging assignments.[92]

Arce called the leaders of the two pueblos together on 5 June 1813 to review their boundary dispute. The alcaldes of Alameda and Jemez and the protector were also present, along with two witnesses whom Arce summoned.[93] He began by reviewing Pino's decision and the documents on which each pueblo relied. Importantly, neither pueblo disputed Pino's establishment of the boundary west of the Rio Grande where the Angostura widened. In reviewing the documents regarding the boundary on the east side of the river, which Pino had not considered, Arce correctly pointed out that none of San Felipe's documents was helpful because "none named the boundaries completely."[94] The principal document on which San Felipe relied, which must have been the deed from the heirs of Cristóbal Baca, stated that the lands San Felipe bought were bounded on the south "by the rancho and land of Cristóbal Martín."[95] The documentation Santa Ana produced showing that it had purchased the Martín rancho, however, convinced Arce that the 1763 purchase from Quiteria Contreras and Cristóbal Martín's heirs established the true boundary between the pueblos at the midpoint of the Angostura. The cross indicating the beginning of San Felipe land was no longer present, so Arce went to the Angostura to reestablish the line, placing additional boundary markers at the midpoint of the Angostura.[96]

Then Arce turned to the north–south line in the old riverbed, connecting the east and west segments of the boundary. Arce did not accept Pino's line along the Santa Ana acequia. He paid special attention to the 1779 Montoya agreement "regarding the land the river took from [Santa Ana]."[97] Arce went to the location where Alcalde Montoya ordered the two pueblos to bury stones as boundary markers, and he found only one stone. Rather than trying to reestablish the old Montoya line, Arce went to the place "where the river used to run a long time ago, next to the hills to the east . . . establishing for them a line [that] curved as the river bends, beginning where the center of the river seemed to be."[98] According to Arce, both pueblos indicated agreement with this new line. The alferez went to great pains to tell the pueblos how to preserve the boundary markers he was setting "near and in line with each other and with others that were buried in the ground and visible ones of stone and mud, so that they will not be lost again or be easily removed, ordering the Indians to examine them frequently and see that even the youngest members of their respective pueblos know them."[99] Arce reported that the Indians were satisfied with his determinations and concluded, as had Pino, that the Hispanos ought to return the land they purchased from San Felipe to Santa Ana but only after they harvested their crops. On 18 June 1813, Governor Manrique approved Arce's decision.[100]

Santa Ana had shown that it could keep track of its documents, watch over its boundary markers, and be its own advocate. These skills, prized in the world of Spanish property law and procedure, stood the pueblo in good stead when the Arce-Manrique boundary decision was appealed to the Audiencia of Guadalajara. It would be more than a decade before Santa Ana would rid itself of Hispanos occupying its land, but the pueblo found that, ultimately, the Spanish and then the Mexican legal systems honored the deeds recording the pueblo's land purchases.

The problem of Hispanos living on Santa Ana's land could not be immediately resolved because San Felipe claimed it could not return the purchase prices paid by the Hispanos and that it did not have other land to give them. Santa Ana prevailed in the litigation, but its effort to obtain full relief stalemated. Eventually, the matter came before the highest level of the Spanish legal system in the Americas, the Audiencia of Guadalajara.[101]

Beginning around 1815 several New Mexico pueblos began to take their grievances over land to higher courts in Durango, Guadalajara, and Mexico City. Cochiti was the first pueblo to take a case to the Audiencia of Guadalajara, with Protector Felipe Sandoval representing Cochiti and Santo Domingo in their dispute with Luis María Cabeza de Baca.[102] Sandoval died suddenly in early December 1816, and by June 1817 Ignacio María Sánchez Vergara had been appointed the new protector of Indians. Sánchez Vergara was highly recommended by Dr. Mariano Mendiola Velarde, judge of the Audiencia of Guadalajara, who appointed him because of the "circumstances of his honor and good conduct." Many of his earlier and later actions, however, suggest that this was probably more praise than Sánchez Vergara deserved.[103]

According to Santa Ana, Sánchez Vergara, who subsequently filed several petitions to acquire pueblo land on his own behalf, economically exploited the pueblo. In 1808 Santa Ana filed a claim against him for the value of crops it was forced to raise for his benefit. Sánchez Vergara was serving as alcalde of Santa Ana and considered it his right to receive the produce from a plot of their land, which the Indians cultivated in consideration of his services. He said the Indians provided their labor voluntarily until he destroyed an altar where the pueblo leaders were performing what he claimed were heathen religious ceremonies.[104] Governor Máynez did not believe him, however, and ordered Sánchez Vergara to reimburse the Santa Ana people for the value of their labor and to give them half of the current crop.[105]

As a protector of Indians, Sánchez Vergara was required to report to the audiencia regarding "the state of the Indians, the treatment they receive, if they lack [the teachings of Christian] doctrine . . . or are without the lands that belong to the pueblos in accordance with the ample royal provisions found in laws 12 and 14 of the *Recopilación*."[106] In January 1818 Vergara filed the report the audiencia required of him, becoming the first protector in New Mexico to do so. For someone charged with defending and advocating on their behalf, Sánchez Vergara had a rather low opinion of Pueblo Indians, describing them as "submerged in ignorance [and] preserving those heathen principles of idolatry and the forbidden life."[107] The protector's solution for improving the Pueblos' lot was somewhat ironic for a man known to desire Indian land. Sánchez Vergara told the audiencia that they should be made "to cultivate all the land they need without leaving any they do not work . . . [and leaving] free and unencumbered all the surplus land."[108] The implication was that if a pueblo did not farm all its land, the surplus should be available for land grants to Hispanos.

In the next part of his report, however, Sánchez Vergara reversed himself and began to advocate for the interests of Santa Ana. He pointed out that much of Santa Ana's land (especially around its old village) was relatively useless for agriculture because it contained large sandy areas and that the land the Indians purchased west of the Rio Grande was four leagues from the pueblo and "so limited that they can scarcely support themselves."[109] Sánchez Vergara then directed the audiencia's attention to the Santa Ana–San Felipe land dispute and the "land that the Indians of San Felipe usurped from them [Santa Ana], causing great harm, and sold to three or four [Spanish] citizens."[110] By bringing up the Santa Ana–San Felipe land dispute, the protector of Indians was in effect filing an appeal to the audiencia on Santa Ana's behalf. Sánchez Vergara proposed a resolution in his report: the Spanish citizens "should be relocated on unoccupied royal land or be returned what they have paid."[111] Either way the Hispanos would go, leaving the land to Santa Ana, which owned it, because "the sales [by San Felipe to the Hispanos] were in bad faith."[112]

The audiencia acted swiftly on the protector's recommendations—Sánchez Vergara sent his report from Jemez in January 1818, and in March, Mendiola presented a petition to the full audiencia that distilled Sánchez Vergara's report down to two main points: the need for more effective instruction of the Indians in Christian doctrine and the need to give final resolution to the Santa Ana–San Felipe land dispute. The key point was that San Felipe's land sales to various Hispanos were null and void. The remaining question was how to compensate Hispanos who paid San Felipe for the Angostura land in question. Mendiola suggested that these Hispanos be reimbursed from royal land in accordance with the provisions of *Recopilación* 2-31-13, so that the purchased land could be immediately restored to Santa Ana.[113]

Mendiola's petition reflected the mixed character of the audiencia as both a judicial and legislative body. The matter of religious instruction of the Indians was legislative and religious in nature and was handled with the recommendation that the bishop of Durango and the governor of New Mexico address the problem by reestablishing the *doctrineros*, priests who provided religious instruction to the Pueblo Indians. While the Santa Ana–San Felipe land dispute was legal in nature, it was not adjudicated by means of the procedure followed in other cases whereby all the parties appeared before the audiencia with their advocates and the protector of Indians.[114] In this case that was probably deemed unnecessary because the issues between Santa Ana and San Felipe were already fully litigated. The issues between Hispanos who purchased land from San Felipe were not yet litigated, and that, according to Mendiola, still needed to be done.[115] Instead of issuing a formal opinion, the four judges of the audiencia simply approved Mendiola's request that the land in question be restored to Santa Ana. Governor Melgares learned of the audiencia's decision on 20 May 1818 but took no action. Accordingly, the secretary of the audiencia, Rafael Cuentas, prepared another copy of the proceedings on 14 January 1819 and forwarded it to Melgares. The audiencia's action was a vindication of Santa Ana's position, but more time passed before the encroaching Hispanos moved.[116]

In April 1819, Sánchez Vergara wrote to Melgares, reporting on the audiencia's action and proposing that Hispanos who purchased lands from San Felipe should move and recover their purchase price and that the land should be restored to Santa Ana. Melgares finally responded, replying that the audiencia's decision should be promptly obeyed. He directed Sánchez Vergara to go to Angostura and in the company of the alcalde of Albuquerque restore the lands to Santa Ana. He suggested that San Felipe be given the opportunity to propose how to make restitution to the dispossessed Hispanos by repayment of the purchase price or provision of alternate land.[117]

When Sánchez Vergara and Alcalde José Mariano de la Peña appeared at Angostura with representatives of both pueblos, however, San Felipe complained that the proposed arrangement was unsatisfactory. Several Hispanos who purchased land from San Felipe were also displeased with the proposal. Up to this point, the Hispanos had not participated in the proceedings to any extent, undoubtedly believing they would never be forced to move. Hispanos in New Mexico were accustomed to taking Indian land as they saw fit. What made this situation different was that most of the Hispanos summoned to appear at Rancho Anaya on 9 May 1819 had paid San Felipe for the land they were occupying, and many had deeds to prove it.[118]

Only one of the ten Hispanos listed as having purchased land from San Felipe showed up at Angostura that day; two others sent representatives with powers of attorney. José Francisco Silva appeared for Juan Esteban Pino, who owned land throughout Santa Fe, Pecos, and beyond. Miguel López appeared for Pablo Montoya, who lived at Las Golondrinas and owned land in the

Ciénega-Cieneguilla area and elsewhere. Pino and Montoya notified the alcalde through their representatives that they would abide by the audiencia's decision. Peña told the governor that although some Hispanos did not come because of illness, all received notification that they would be granted new land in Socorro to make up for what they were losing at Angostura. The absent Hispanos were José García, Alonso García, Juan Domingo Archibeque, Pablo Archibeque, Diego Chaves, Francisco Gutiérrez, and fray Jerónimo Riega. The only Hispano who appeared on his own behalf was the largest purchaser, Juan Bautista González, who had bought several tracts of land from San Felipe between 1782 and 1816. González agreed to accept the audiencia's decision but wanted the twenty-seven hundred pesos in cattle, sheep, and horses he had paid for the land to be returned or else to be granted another tract of land between San Felipe and Santo Domingo, which González mistakenly referred to as "realenga," or "vacant royal land."[119]

Hispanos had eyed the land between San Felipe and Santo Domingo ever since Governor Mendinueta had granted it to the two pueblos in 1770 as farmland and pasturage for their livestock. Mendinueta ordered the league of each pueblo measured and then granted the land between the two leagues to them. The farmland was divided between them, and the remaining land was designated for use in common by both pueblos.[120] In July 1815 a group of Hispanos led by Domingo Fernández persuaded Governor Máynez to grant them some of the land between the pueblos, telling Máynez they were descendants of grantees who were granted the land in the early 1760s when neither pueblo objected. Whether the pueblos protested then, they were doing so now. Yet when they presented their 1770 grant, Alcalde José Gutiérrez dismissed it as being "without date or name."[121] Máynez did not investigate further as he should have and proceeded to make the grant.[122] Now, four years later, in 1819, González was trying to get some of this prime land between San Felipe and Santo Domingo in exchange for his Angostura land.

The land Máynez granted was at a place on the Rio Grande, about midway between Santo Domingo and San Felipe, called Santa Rosa de Cubero, and in August 1819 González tried to get land at or near the same location. He went to Cubero with Alcalde De la Peña and measured 2,875 varas of land to serve as compensation for the Santa Ana–San Felipe land for which González had paid twenty-seven hundred pesos. Before the land could be delivered to González, however, San Felipe and Santo Domingo Pueblos presented De la Peña with the

1770 Mendinueta grant giving the land jointly to the two pueblos. Unlike Alcalde Gutiérrez, who ignored the pueblos' papers four years earlier, De la Peña suspended the proceedings when he realized the land had already been granted to the Indians. Thus, the exchange González desired fell apart, and De la Peña had to seek another solution.[123]

Two days after the aborted land exchange with González, De la Peña called the parties together, ostensibly for the last time. San Felipe had given up hope that the audiencia's decision would be changed. The pueblo was unhappy with Sánchez Vergara (probably because he took Santa Ana's side initially), so it filed suit against him in May, but it appears that the suit was dismissed.[124] By early August San Felipe was resigned to giving the Hispanos other land it had purchased at Algodones as compensation for the Angostura land. At the August land distribution proceeding, Sánchez Vergara was listed as representing San Felipe, probably in an attempt to make up for his failure to represent the pueblo adequately in the past.[125]

The distribution proceedings went smoothly until it came time for González to accept a trade of Algodones land for Angostura land. Alcalde De la Peña measured with a cordel the amount of land each of the Hispanos had purchased from San Felipe, but instead of offering them the full amount, he assigned them one-fourth that amount of land "because all purchased uncultivated land, and now they were delivered cultivated land."[126] None of the Hispanos contested De la Peña's decision that the Algodones land was four times better than the Angostura land, and they all accepted the former in full settlement for the land they had purchased, except González, who held out for better land or a return of his full purchase price. The matter was deadlocked on 5 August 1819, so the alcalde told the pueblo and González to think it over. De la Peña returned the next day, which was taken up with measuring the land at Algodones and giving deeds to the six Hispanos, a long process that began in the morning and was not completed until six o'clock in the evening. It seemed that the only remaining step was to satisfy the very particular and contentious Juan Bautista González.[127]

By 12 August San Felipe agreed to trade González the land he wanted. The pueblo preferred to return the purchase price to González rather than give him other land, but during the 5 August negotiations Sánchez Vergara advised San Felipe more than once that it would suffer damages if it did not give González land. In the end San Felipe was persuaded it should trade González a tract of land the pueblo had purchased at Las Lemitas for the Angostura land. The land at Las Lemitas was part of the tract San Felipe had purchased in 1753 from Cristóbal Baca's heirs just north of Santa Ana's 1763 Contreras purchase. González would thus be acquiring a tract of land north of the one he was leaving but that was still in the Angostura area and closer to his old tract than any of the other pieces of land offered him.[128]

Still, this did not finalize the deal between San Felipe and González, and there were several more missteps before it was completed. On 12 August the Las Lemitas land was measured, and the governor of San Felipe told González that this tract would replace the property González had purchased from San Felipe. Alcalde De la Peña measured ten 100-vara cordeles equaling 1,000 varas as the land proposed to be delivered to González.[129] After some hesitation González accepted, but when San Felipe's governor told him that the exchange was only temporary because San Felipe was filing an appeal, González "refused and decided that this did not suit him." This left De la Peña without the compromise he had worked for so diligently. He wearily closed the day's proceedings, stating that the parties "retired to their homes at 6:30 in the evening, at which hour I had to recross the river, with those who were assisting me."[130]

The next day De la Peña was determined to close the proceedings, with or without the full agreement of San Felipe and González. He returned to Angostura, but this time he looked at the 1753 San Felipe purchase documents and asked representatives of Santa Ana about the boundaries. After listening to the explanations from Santa Ana's representatives, the alcalde decided that his earlier decision in May was correct: the disputed land belonged to Santa Ana and not San Felipe. The conscientious alcalde then sent the proceedings to Governor Melgares for a decision. He successfully relocated six of the Hispanos who were trespassing on Santa Ana land and came very close to engineering a settlement between San Felipe and González. De la Peña reported that he had concluded his mission of placing Santa Ana back in possession of its land. On 1 October 1819, Sánchez Vergara issued a report stating that the land in dispute had been returned to Santa Ana through the proceedings De la Peña had carried out.[131]

Santa Ana's success was almost complete when González signed a receipt to the pueblo on 16 October 1821, indicating his satisfaction with his new land at San Juan de las Lemitas. It also appears that the Indians of Santa Ana built

González a new house on the Las Lemitas land to replace the one he lost, which sat on Santa Ana's Angostura land. The receipt Santa Ana prepared recited that González was handing over the Angostura land "to Santa Ana, the preferred owners [who were] keeping and possessing the land."[132] The González receipt nicely caps Santa Ana's nearly forty-year quest to recover its land. Except for one other Hispano who did not leave the disputed land, Santa Ana was free of Hispano encroachment and was finally able to farm and irrigate its Ranchiit'u land without interference.[133]

The Hispano who refused to leave the disputed area was Pablo Montoya. He remained a thorn in Santa Ana's side throughout the 1820s and 1830s. Despite the audiencia's decision, Montoya believed his was a special case. To help him press that argument, Montoya induced Sánchez Vergara to prepare an unusual document in February 1821 that purported to interpret the audiencia's decision. Sánchez Vergara stated that the decision was not intended to apply to land that Santa Ana sold to Hispanos, only land sold by San Felipe. Presumably on the basis of an assumption that Santa Ana sold land to Montoya, Sánchez Vergara concluded that Montoya should retain ownership of his Angostura land.[134] There are, however, no known documents supporting the claim that Montoya purchased the land he was occupying from Santa Ana. Asked about Montoya's claim, Santa Ana's answer was unequivocal: "The Santa Anas state that they have not sold the land mentioned in these documents to don Pablo Montoya."[135]

Montoya remained at Angostura, where he farmed land Santa Ana owned. To make matters worse for Santa Ana, he and a few other Angostura residents claimed the right to irrigate from the pueblo's acequia. In 1824 Governor Bartolomé Baca issued an interim order giving those Angostura residents the amount of water they had used the previous year so that their crops would not be lost.[136] There is no evidence that Governor Baca issued a permanent order, but irrigation rights from the Santa Ana acequia were still an issue in 1829 when a dispute between Santa Ana and Montoya came before Alcalde Pedro José Perea. As a result of that hearing, the alcalde for water matters (*alcalde de agua*) of the Santa Ana acequia was ordered to allow Montoya to work on the acequia and to give him whatever additional water (*auxilio*) he needed. He claimed that Santa Ana was not permitting him to help clean the acequia and was then denying him water because of his failure to do so, but Santa Ana did not recognize Montoya's claim to irrigate from the Santa Ana acequia because he had no valid title to land on the acequia.[137]

Five years later in 1834, Pablo Montoya was still trying to get Santa Ana to recognize him as a landowner with water rights (*parciante*) to the pueblo's acequia. This time Antonio Montoya and Juan Pablo Archibeque joined him in a request to Governor Francisco Sarracino (1833–1835) that they be added as co-owners on the Santa Ana acequia. The matter was referred to the local alcalde, but there is no record of his action.[138] Then, in 1836, Alcalde José Andrés Sandoval ordered that Montoya and the others be allowed to work on the acequia and that the water be apportioned according to the greatest need.[139] Santa Ana continued to resist such orders because it did not believe Montoya had any rights to the land he wanted to irrigate, much less to the water. Finally in 1838, Montoya obtained a strongly worded water allocation decree when Alcalde Salvador Montoya (apparently a relative) ordered that "the water be given to the said Montoya because you know that even if he did not have any rights, necessity is the highest of all laws."[140] Pablo Montoya claimed to have lost some crops because of a lack of irrigation water and promised to prove his right to the land "when the time comes, by competent documents he has in his possession." There is no evidence, however, that he ever produced such documents, and Alcalde Montoya's statement that Pablo was entitled to some water based on his need "even if he did not have any rights," suggests that those rights did not indeed exist.[141]

Another elite property owner at Angostura who had extensive and complicated land dealings was Juan Esteban Pino, whom Francisco Silva represented at the 9 May 1819 hearing. Silva notified Alcalde De la Peña that Pino had papers that documented his purchase but said that he would obey the order to give up the Angostura land and move elsewhere. Pino, however, was not the only one with a claim on the land. He had acquired the Angostura land through a controversial foreclosure of a mortgage María Victoria Gutiérrez and her husband had given him, but several others also claimed an interest in the property. Santa Ana was caught in the middle. José García had purchased the land from two San Felipe Indians and then mortgaged the property to Pino as security for the eight hundred sheep Pino delivered to García's wife. The mortgage came to light in a complicated lawsuit between Gutiérrez and her brother, Pedro Miguel Gutiérrez, which also involved Pino.[142]

At one point in the proceeding, Pino's father, don Pedro Bautista Pino, provided telling testimony regarding Santa Ana's outlook on the world of land transactions. The elder Pino learned of the Santa Ana–San Felipe land dispute and went to Angostura in place of Juan Esteban to deliver the title papers for Pino's Angostura ranch. Since Juan Esteban's interest in Gutiérrez's Angostura ranch was only partial, it was being divided so that the portion the Pinos did not claim could be delivered to Santa Ana. On arriving at Angostura, Pedro Bautista suggested a deal to Santa Ana's representatives whereby the ranch would be consolidated. Either Santa Ana would buy the remaining part of the ranch from Pino or else he would buy Santa Ana's portion, so that the entire ranch would have a single owner. To this proposal the Santa Ana Indians replied "that they would not sell, but they would purchase." Santa Ana stood up to the Pinos by informing the elite family that as a matter of principle the pueblo did not sell its land.[143] Santa Ana held its own against the Pinos, Montoya, and González, adhering to a strict policy of refusing to sell its land and acquiring all it could.

San Felipe also purchased land from Hispanos and used it to raise crops, but unlike Santa Ana, San Felipe also sold land to Hispanos. In 1822 "the principal men of San Felipe appeared before Protector of Indians Sánchez Vergara, testifying that they had voluntarily given land in [the Angostura] area to Pablo Montoya."[144] Again, in 1823, San Felipe sold Montoya six additional tracts of land, one adjacent to Santa Ana land, one on the arroyo that ran from the Río de las Huertas, and others south and east of the main Santa Ana acequia. Not only did San Felipe manifest a different philosophy than Santa Ana with respect to land, but it was selling land to the one Hispano Santa Ana was trying to get rid of. The documents Montoya kept referring to as justifying his right to be on Santa Ana land probably included these deeds from San Felipe. Curiously, San Felipe still appeared to be selling land in the Angostura area to Hispanos such as Montoya in the 1820s even though Santa Ana had recovered it. A document in the Santa Ana archives may help explain the situation, although the story it tells seems as incredible now as it must have appeared to the pueblo then.[145]

In February 1822 the Indians of Santa Ana were summoned to Angostura, where they were met by the alcalde of Alameda, the alcalde of Jemez, and Sánchez Vergara, who was still referring to himself as the protector of Indians.[146] Without any explanation, Sánchez Vergara ordered Santa Ana to turn over to San Felipe the land Alcalde De la Peña and the audiencia had returned to the pueblo. He then asked the pueblo's representatives whether they agreed with his demand. They told him unequivocally that they did not.

Following the meeting they directed a strongly worded petition to Governor Melgares, explaining the bizarre circumstances of this meeting and asking him to intervene and, in the words of Santa Ana's governor, Andrés Maygua, "take care of us with justice."[147]

This new claim was unfamiliar to Melgares, so he asked the alcalde of Alameda to report to him "what has been done regarding this business," asking that all related documents be attached to the file.[148] Alcalde Baltasar Perea told Melgares that Sánchez Vergara asked him to be present at the delivery of Santa Ana's land to San Felipe because he was alcalde of San Felipe. Sánchez Vergara clearly wanted Perea to lend his authority to the proceedings. Perea stated that "he was informed that Sánchez Vergara had a summons that he was carrying in his hand, decreed as a result of the royal decision [and that] the protector proceeded to deliver the land to the body politic of San Felipe, dispossessing the body politic of Santa Ana of their land."[149] Perea included copious documents with his report to Melgares, most of them (twenty-four pages) from Santa Ana, explaining the history of the dispute with San Felipe and its resolution by Spanish authorities.[150]

Sánchez Vergara told the Santa Ana officials that he had in his possession a document from the commanding general ordering Santa Ana to turn over to San Felipe the land at Angostura that had been returned to Santa Ana. On seeing this report, Governor Melgares ordered Sánchez Vergara to appear before him, "with all that he has done and with [the] decree of the most excellent lord commanding general for the dispossession of the land of the Indians of Santa Ana [who] will accompany him."[151] No such decree was ever produced, and it seems likely that no such document existed.[152]

An important characteristic of Santa Ana in its legal dealings with the Spanish and Mexican governments was the elegant composition of the many petitions it filed. It is probable that Pueblo governors filing these petitions received help in drafting them, but it appears that the governor was the intellectual author of the document. That is, the governor told the scribe what points he wanted to make, a clear indication of how thoroughly the Pueblos participated in and understood the Spanish system of land tenure.

An 1846 petition that Santa Ana governor Miguel Lucero filed sheds some light on the inner workings of Santa Ana's governmental machinery. The way in which the pueblo reached decisions about filing complaints against the Hispanos is revealed in these 1846 documents dealing with another trespasser on Santa Ana's Angostura land, Ramón Gurulé. Governor Lucero brought the case against Gurulé in at least one other court before the dispute reached the alcalde of Jemez, José Albino Chacón, who made a thorough investigation after requiring Lucero to file a power of attorney proving his authority to act on behalf of the pueblo.[153] Following this procedural maneuvering, Alcalde Chacón finally made his decision. After pointing out that Algodones was the proper jurisdiction for the case, reviewing all the documents (including those Santa Ana had submitted), and going over the testimony of fifteen witnesses, Chacón made a visual inspection of the land. He ruled that Santa Ana, not Gurulé, owned the land in question at Ranchiit'u on the east bank of the Rio Grande.[154]

This was a fitting conclusion to Santa Ana's long struggle to acquire land for farming by relying on the Spanish and Mexican legal systems. Santa Ana consistently followed the rules of these legal systems and never succumbed to the temptation to sell land, always buying instead. In the process Santa Ana became adept at using Spanish and Mexican laws, customs, and practices to advance its own interests. A close look at the Santa Ana land disputes reveals an increasing sophistication on the part of the pueblo in the petitions it filed and the documents on which it relied. Beginning with the 1813 boundary dispute with San Felipe and continuing through Sánchez Vergara's attempt in 1822 to reverse the audiencia decision and on through the 1846 dispute with Ramón Gurulé, Santa Ana was successful because the pueblo stated its case clearly and concisely and had the documents to back up its contentions. Even when former allies, such as Sánchez Vergara, turned against it, Santa Ana stood its ground and was able to protect its rights. The acquisition of the Ranchiit'u land and Santa Ana's defense of its ownership of that property is of pivotal importance to the pueblo's history. This was the beginning of a long tradition in Santa Ana of resourcefulness and flexibility in protecting its land, water, and culture.

In 1850, just two years after the United States formally assumed sovereignty over New Mexico, Santa Ana officials went to Santa Fe and presented many of the Santa Ana title documents to Donaciano Vigil, who was then secretary of the territory and registrar.[155] Two years later, Santa Ana returned to Santa Fe and presented many of its title documents to John Greiner, the new Indian agent. Greiner prepared a transcription of all the documents, twenty-nine pages in all, dated 6 December 1852, certifying them in his capacity as secretary of the territory.[156] The pueblo probably believed that by presenting its documents twice to the new U.S. officials, the new government would confirm its titles.

It appears, however, that neither Vigil's records nor Greiner's transcriptions were ever turned over to William Pelham, the new surveyor general of New Mexico, after he arrived in Santa Fe in late 1854. Although the surveyor general in 1866, John Clark, recommended that Congress confirm a standard league grant for Santa Ana, centered on the old mission at the village of Tamaya, which Congress did in 1869, the pueblo's hard-won ownership of the lands along the Rio Grande, and from there west to Tamaya, was ignored.[157] Finally, Santa Ana filed an action in the Court of Private Land Claims on 2 March 1893, seeking confirmation of the Ranchiit'u deeds. The court agreed that the deeds were authentic and should be confirmed, but the pueblo's attorney (whether with its consent or not is unclear) apparently acceded to the insistence of the attorney for the United States that the area claimed was "excessive" and agreed to limit the claim (which, based on the deeds, would have comprised some 95,000 thousand acres) to a small area of less than 5,000 acres. Although this area included the best farmland along the Rio Grande, it excluded huge areas of good grazing land and left the pueblo's village of Tamaya once again cut off from the farms of the Ranchiit'u.[158]

Oblivious to the pueblo's long, continuous, and exclusive occupation of the lands between Ranchiit'u and the confirmed grant surrounding Tamaya, the United States assumed dominion over those lands beginning in the early twentieth century. When the land was brought under the federal grazing regime created by the Taylor Grazing Act of 1934, much of it was permitted to non-Indians, excluding Santa Ana from these lands it had striven for so long to protect.[159] In 1961 Congress finally began to recognize the injustice that Santa Ana suffered and restored to the pueblo in trust 22,976 acres of former Bureau of Land Management–controlled land, most of it north of Tamaya.[160] In 1978 Congress restored to Santa Ana in trust most of the lands remaining in federal ownership west of the Rio Grande, between Ranchiit'u and the Santa Ana grant surrounding Tamaya, comprising more than 16,000 acres.[161] In doing so, Congress acknowledged that these lands were "occupied, controlled and used for economic and religious purposes" by the pueblo from before the arrival of the Spaniards until 1937 when they were permitted to non-Indians under the Taylor Grazing Act.[162] Congress enacted further legislation in 1986 to correct errors in the 1978 act and to enable the pueblo to acquire additional lands adjacent to the lands transferred in 1978.[163] Santa Ana has never been able to reacquire the lands east of the El Ranchito tract, to the foothills of the Sandias,

The last page of the document concerning Ignacio Sánchez Vergara's attempt to reverse the decision of the Audiencia at Guadalajara. Pictured at the top of the page is the end of Alcalde Baltazar Perea's report on the matter, dated 4 May 1822. On 9 May 1822, Governor Facundo Melgares ordered the alcalde to have Sánchez Vergara appear before Melgares "with the decree of the most excellent lord commandant general for the dispossession of the lands of the Indians of Santa Ana." At the bottom of the page is Donaciano Vigil's certification that Santa Ana brought the document to him to be registered on 25 September 1850 (SA 23).

which were part of its 1763 deed from Quiteria Contreras, although it did finally secure control of its core landholdings, including the lands in the Jemez River Basin surrounding its traditional homeland of Tamaya and the agricultural lands of Ranchiit'u. In recent years, in a campaign harkening back to the single-minded determination of the land-buying program of the 1700s, Santa Ana has been actively acquiring valuable, privately owned land just west of El Ranchito, along U.S. 550.

Anthropologists agree that the ability of an Indian pueblo to maintain its culture and its religious life is closely linked to the pueblo's preservation of its land base. Anthropologist Leslie White, who authored the principal monograph on Santa Ana, expressed concern that the increasing movement of the pueblo from Tamaya to Ranchiit'u had the potential to weaken the solidarity of the Santa Ana community, socially and spiritually. As the distance from its sacred space increased, White felt that the pueblo's traditional beliefs and customs would be lost.[164] That prediction has not come true. The Santa Ana Indians who moved to their Ranchiit'u land did change, however, as a result of the move. They built houses of more modern construction and incorporated modern appliances into their homes. Instead of building their homes in clusters, as at the old village, the Ranchiit'u dwellers were more likely to build independently of one another. The individuality expressed in the house groupings was reflected in a decrease in friction and factionalism as the social distance expanded, and this did not lead to a loss of community solidarity. In fact, the opposite has proved true. Santa Ana still holds its ceremonies at its old village of Tamaya, has recently restored its church, and keeps its traditions alive, even as it continues to acquire land and support its people. If anything, the pueblo's traditional activities have strengthened as its land base has been restored. Santa Ana has mastered the complexities of the modern world and given economic independence to its members. By adhering to traditional beliefs as its people use land granted to them by the Pueblo league, obtained by purchase, and lost and reacquired from their Hispano neighbors, Santa Ana has indeed enjoyed the best of both worlds.

Picuris Pueblo celebrating San Lorenzo feast day. Drawing by Glen Strock.

CHAPTER 3

Picuris Pueblo

Spanish Encroachment and Pueblo Resurgence

Picuris, located on the western slopes of the Sangre de Cristo Mountains in southern Taos County, was the largest northern pueblo at the time of Spanish contact, with a population of about two thousand Indians. Juan de Oñate visited what he called "the great pueblo" of Picuris on 13 July 1598, soon after arriving in New Mexico. The thirteenth of July was the feast day of San Buenaventura, so Oñate chose that saint as patron for the pueblo, but the name did not stick. When a mission was established at Picuris in 1620, it was under the patronage of San Lorenzo, whose feast day the Picuris people still celebrate every year on 10 August.[1]

Oñate was not the first Spaniard to see the large pueblo of Picuris, although he was the first to mention the existence of minerals near the pueblo. Oñate reported that he found "a large quantity of ore which had accumulated in the riffles [small valleys between little ridges formed by flood water, where minerals might collect] of an arroyo."[2] The mineral referred to is unknown, but Picuris continued to be associated with mines or the possibility of mines for the next four centuries down to the present day.

Although the 1540 expedition of Francisco Vázquez de Coronado apparently reached Taos, Picuris remained untouched by Coronado because of its isolated location. It was not until Castaño de Sosa's unauthorized expedition fifty years later that the first known Spanish contact with Picuris took place, but the reception "was one of the coldest in southwestern history, both in climate and in human relations."[3] Castaño de Sosa arrived at Picuris an hour before sunset to find house blocks seven to eight stories high, making the pueblo the tallest recorded by any Spaniard. No one came out to meet him, not even the Indian he sent ahead from the pueblos he had previously visited. Eventually, Castaño de Sosa spoke to a few of the Picuris Indians, but the reception they provided was decidedly unfriendly. He opted to spend the night at the houses of nearby Plains Indians and asked the Picuris people to bring them corn, tortillas, and firewood, but "they brought [only] a little, almost nothing."[4]

The next morning Castaño de Sosa and his men saw the Picuris warriors preparing to do battle. The lieutenant in charge ordered his men to make ready two small bronze cannons but thought better of it after discussing the matter with his troops. Snow to the depth of three feet and the fierce reputation of the Picuris warriors decided the matter. "The men said . . . they should not go to the pueblo because the Indians were a bad sort," so the expedition departed from Picuris without trying to enter the pueblo. Castaño de Sosa's men got close enough, however, to take note of the large amount of jewelry set with turquoise and other "rich stones" that pueblo members wore. This piqued the interest of one of the leaders of the expedition, who sent word to the wearer of an armband of precious and semiprecious stones that he liked the jewelry and would like to look at it. The wearer declined, even after the Spaniard made clear that he only wanted to examine it. The Picuris people clearly mistrusted and were hostile toward the Spaniards from the moment of first contact.[5]

The Picuris Indians refer to themselves and their ancestors as the "p' inwél ené" (the mountain people; the mountain warrior people). Picuris is called "the mountain pass place" in Tiwa, referring to its location on the west end of the mountain pass leading to the Great Plains. Like Pecos, its proximity to the Great Plains meant that Picuris had a close relationship with Plains Indians such as Apaches and Comanches. Initially Picuris was one of the most traditional pueblos in its resistance to Christianization, and in 1609 it allied with Taos, Pecos, and some Apache bands against the Tewa pueblos near San Gabriel that had "shown so much friendship for the Spaniards."[6]

Fray Francisco de Zamora was the first priest assigned to Picuris. Zamora was also posted to Taos and the neighboring Apache tribes on 9 September 1598 when Picuris, along with the other pueblos, rendered their obedience to

Oñate at San Juan.[7] Zamora did not stay long, however, for by 1601 only a lay brother was living at Picuris. Picuris's strong resistance to Christianization turned violent after 1621 when the pueblo was assigned its second priest, fray Martín de Arvide. When Arvide tried to convert the son of a traditional Picuris medicine man, the healer became so angry that he picked up a club and struck the priest on the head. According to fray Alonso de Benavides's report, the Picuris Indians dragged Father Arvide around the plaza of the pueblo, and he barely escaped with his life.[8] In 1639 another Franciscan serving at Picuris escaped death when Taos Indians killed their priest, Father Pedro de Miranda, and then headed toward Picuris. The unnamed priest in Picuris escaped to San Ildefonso upon learning that the Taos Indians planned to kill him too.[9]

Taos continued to be so rebellious that Governor Luis de Rosas (1637–1641) sent a punitive expedition against the pueblo in 1639. Some of the Taos people fled to the plains rather than submit to the Spaniards, taking refuge among the Cuartelejo Apaches in present-day Scott County, Kansas, where they remained for a few years until Juan de Archuleta brought them back to New Mexico in 1642 or 1643.

Friars such as Benavides saw the spiritual battle between the Franciscans and the caciques at Picuris and other pueblos over differing belief systems as a contest for power. Benavides reported on a confrontation between the resident priest and some Picuris Indians who tried to grab the friar, who, according to him, by the intervention of "Our Lord" "became invisible and they were greatly confounded."[10] Although given to exaggeration, Benavides's account demonstrates the active resistance of the Picuris people to Christianization in general and to specific priests in particular. While the battle between Christianity and Pueblo religion was raging, Franciscans and the Spanish government officials also waged a contest over the use of Indian labor. Indians often worked without pay and were subject to physical abuse. Governor Bernardo López de Mendizábal (1659–1661) was one of the worst offenders in this regard. He often engaged in the slave trade, his troops raiding Apache country to take captives to sell in Parral in Nueva Vizcaya. López also forced Pueblo laborers to gather products that he sold in markets to the south, outside of New Mexico. In 1659 López forced Taos and Picuris Indians to build carts and wagons to ship these products to Parral. The Indians were not only ordered to build the carts but were also required to drive them. Yet when they arrived in Parral, the Taos and Picuris Indians found themselves stranded, since no arrangements had been made for their return to New Mexico.[11]

This kind of abuse and their active resistance to conversion to Christianity were important factors in the decision on the part of Picuris and other New Mexico pueblos to revolt in 1680, which culminated in their driving the Hispanos from New Mexico to the area around present-day Ciudad Juárez, Mexico. Pedro Nanboa from Alameda Pueblo was questioned about the reasons for the Pueblo Revolt less than a month after it happened. He stated that the Tewa pueblos and Taos, Picuris, Pecos, and Jemez had been planning to revolt and kill the priests and other Hispanos for some time because the Hispanos were killing the native spiritual leaders. The Hispanos' lack of empathy for Pueblo religion is apparent from the interpreter's use of the words "sorcerers and idolaters" to describe Pueblo spiritual leaders.[12]

Initial planning for the Pueblo Revolt took place at Taos and Picuris, under the leadership of Popé and Luis Tupatú, although a network of leaders from other pueblos participated, including a Taos man whom Hispanos called El Jaca; Cristóbal Yope of San Lázaro; Antonio Bolsas, the Tanos's spokesman; Felipe de Ye of Pecos; Juan of Galisteo; Alonso Catiti of Santo Domingo; Luis Coniju of Jemez; and Antonio Malacate, the interpreter of the Keresans.[13] Taos and Picuris were among the largest pueblos in New Mexico and were considered hotbeds of discontent.[14] Popé's anger against Hispanos was fanned into flame in 1675, when he and forty-six other religious leaders from the Rio Grande pueblos were arrested and charged with plotting to overthrow the Hispanos. Three were hanged, and the rest were punished severely. Popé, a San Juan native, moved to Taos and subsequently dispatched runners carrying a knotted cord of maguey fiber to all the pueblos. The number of knots in the cord signified the number of days before the revolt was to begin. There were two knots in the cord when Governor Otermín learned of the plot on 9 August, at which point the date was moved forward to 10 August.

Early on the morning of 10 August, Taos and Picuris, together with their Apache allies, rose up and killed their priests and most of the Hispanos living at or near the pueblos. Two Hispanos escaped from Taos: Fernando Durán y Chaves and Sebastián de Herrera. Father Matías Rendón, the priest at Picuris, was killed on 10 August along with Francisco Blanco de la Vega, his son Francisco Javier de la Vega, and many others.[15]

The Tewa pueblos also revolted, killing all Hispanos nearby and forcing the others to flee to Santa Fe. The plan seemed to be to kill as many Hispanos as possible upriver from Santa Fe to convince Otermín that the Indians were determined to regain control of their land. Picuris and Taos warriors went to San Juan, possibly joining Popé there. Two days after the outbreak of the revolt, reports reached Santa Fe, where the Hispanos were gathered, that the northern pueblos had revolted. Tano, Pecos, and San Marcos Indians attacked Santa Fe from the south through the barrio of Analco, which was populated, at least in part, by Indians from New Spain. Governor Otermín summoned the leader of the attacking Indians, a Spanish-speaking Tano headman, to meet with him in the plaza. Otermín offered a pardon to the attackers if they would lay down their arms and pledge allegiance to the king. The cacique replied that he was elected captain of all the Pueblo forces and that they carried two banners, a white one signifying peace and a red one indicating war. If the Hispanos wanted peace they must leave the province, otherwise there would be all-out war and the remaining Hispanos would be killed. Otermín tried to persuade the Indians to surrender and be pardoned. They responded that the Hispanos must give up all the Pueblo and Apache Indians in the service of the Indians of the barrio of Analco and in the service of Hispanos if there were to be any further negotiations. Governor Otermín was unwilling to accept this offer.[16]

The Hispanos skirmished with the Indian forces for two days and by the evening of the fifteenth were on the verge of victory when Tewa, Taos, and Picuris reinforcements arrived. The next day some twenty-five hundred warriors from these pueblos, as well as Jemez Pueblo and the Keres pueblos, attacked the villa, forcing the Hispanos to retreat to the government headquarters compound. The besiegers occupied the houses of the villa, cut off the water from a small acequia that supplied the government headquarters, and laid siege against the beleaguered Hispanos.[17]

The siege of Santa Fe lasted six days. The fighting was so intense and the Hispanos' hunger and thirst so great that Otermín finally opted to lead the surviving Hispanos south, hoping to meet the supply train heading north with food, weapons, and ammunition. If they could escape the Indians who were surrounding them, the Hispanos hoped to contact the people thought to remain in the southern settlements under the leadership of Lieutenant General Alonso García. The Pueblos merely watched as the Hispanos filed down the Camino Real toward El Paso, with four hundred animals "and for food, a few sheep, goats, and cows." The casualties of the Pueblo Revolt on the Spanish side were 21 Franciscan missionaries and 380 colonists. Although the number of Indian losses is unknown, the pitched battles fought in Santa Fe produced heavy casualties among the Indians.[18]

The Pueblo Indians burned and destroyed the abandoned houses of the departed Hispanos, appropriating household goods and cattle, desecrating and destroying churches. The Spanish archives were piled in the middle of the Santa Fe plaza and burned. Then Popé and the other revolt leaders toured the province. Accompanying Popé was El Jaca, the Taos cacique; Alonso Catiti, the Keres leader; Lorenzo Tupatú, the former governor of Picuris; and Tupatú's brother Luis, known to Hispanos as "El Picurí." They told the other pueblos that they should not speak Spanish, should cast aside all aspects of Christian doctrine, and should give up everything that came from Hispanos, including Spanish seeds. They should return to the old ways, abandon Christian marriages, and take whatever wives they pleased. During the twelve years that the Pueblo Indians lived in freedom in New Mexico, the Picuris leader, Luis Tupatú, was twice chosen leader of all the confederated pueblos. He also played a major role in the defeat of some of the aborted Spanish attempts to reconquer New Mexico in November and December 1681.[19]

In 1692 don Diego de Vargas carried out a ceremonial reconquest of New Mexico. After reestablishing a Spanish presence in Santa Fe, Vargas sought the surrender of the leader of the Tewas and Tanos, Luis Tupatú of Picuris. In early September Vargas sent a rosary and a cross as tokens of his peaceful intent to Tupatú, who was living in San Juan.[20] Luis Tupatú appeared in Santa Fe with his armed guards, Indians who were on horseback and on foot. Vargas received the Picuris leader at his tent where they drank chocolate with the Franciscans. Vargas gave Tupatú one of his saddle horses, and the Picuris leader gave Vargas some tanned deer or elk hides. Vargas noted that Luis Tupatú was very powerful, a fact the Hispanos needed to recognize.[21] The next day Tupatú conferred further with Vargas, and they agreed to an arrangement of mutual benefit: Tupatú would help subdue the rest of the Pueblo Indians, and the Hispanos would help Tupatú deal with his enemies. Vargas proposed that all the Pueblo people submit to Spanish rule and return to Christian ways; if they refused, he would destroy them "once and for all." Tupatú agreed to assist the Spanish forces with Indian allies under his command. Having reached this agreement with Vargas, Tupatú received permission to bring his people with their trade goods to the *plaza de armas* where they stayed all day "speaking and being friendly with everyone."[22]

The Picuris governor, Lorenzo Tupatú (Luis's brother), arrived at the plaza de armas asking for Vargas's support against the enemies of Picuris: Pecos, the Faraón Apaches, Taos, Jemez, and the Keres pueblos of San Felipe and Santo Domingo. In need of assistance in his campaign against Pecos and its Apache allies, Vargas accepted Picuris's offer "to provide men to aid in the war." Setting out in early October 1692 from San Juan for Picuris, Vargas arrived within sight of the pueblo after a day's travel and was met by Lorenzo Tupatú, his brothers Luis and Antonio, their children, and other principal Indians. Vargas commanded Lorenzo Tapatú to gather the people of the pueblo and then announced that he had come to reclaim possession of Picuris for the king of Spain and ordered the Indians to wear crosses and pray, telling the Franciscans to absolve and baptize them and their children. Fray Francisco Corvera and two other Franciscans baptized eighty-six adults and children. Vargas acted as godfather to Lorenzo Tupatú's daughter and many others.[23]

Vargas left Picuris for Taos but found the pueblo deserted. He dispatched Luis and Lorenzo Tupatú with their warriors to find the Taos Indians. During a parley Vargas informed the Taos Indians that he came to pardon them and return them to Christianity. Vargas made the Taos leaders embrace Luis and Lorenzo Tupatú, and the rest of the Picuris, Tewas, and Tanos; in his view, he had made them settle their differences.[24] Vargas was able to manipulate Pueblo factionalism and thereby further splinter the Pueblo coalition that had formed after the Revolt. Like earlier conquistadors, he relied on a strategy of divide and conquer, which was an important factor in facilitating the reconquest. Vargas obtained promises of submission to Spanish rule from twenty-three pueblos, including Picuris, before returning to El Paso in December 1692. The Pueblos may have accepted Spanish rule, but none were willing to give up their traditional religious practices.[25]

In October 1693 Vargas headed north from El Paso with a colonizing expedition. By November he was in the area of present-day Albuquerque, where he met Luis and Lorenzo Tupatú, as well as Cristóbal Yope of San Cristóbal and Domingo Romero of Tesuque.[26] Both Picuris leaders were visibly saddened to learn that Vargas's return was permanent: many settlers and soldiers had brought their wives and children, and many Franciscan priests were here to stay as well. Vargas learned that Pueblo alliances had shifted dramatically since 1692. All the pueblos were again in rebellion except Zia, Santa Ana, San Felipe, and Pecos. In December the expedition arrived outside of Indian-held and fortified Santa Fe. As the Hispanos huddled in the freezing cold and snow, Juan de Ye of Pecos arrived and warned Vargas, noting that the Tewas, Tanos, and Picuris Indians planned to attack and destroy the Hispanos. On the morning of 29 December, Vargas's force of some 100 soldiers and 140 Pecos Indian allies attacked Santa Fe, carrying the day in a house-to-house battle. Vargas ordered seventy of the rebellious occupants executed, including some Indians from Picuris.[27]

By June 1694, Vargas decided that the successful conclusion of his campaign of reconquest hinged on his subduing the most rebellious pueblos: Jemez, Taos, and Picuris.[28] In December 1694 Vargas received the governors and captains of the Tewa and Tano Pueblos and those of Picuris. The Pueblo leaders brought with them forty-five Indians whom the Hispanos had taken captive following the battle of Santa Fe in 1693 and who had subsequently escaped. Vargas returned them to their leaders and noted his intention to settle them at the abandoned pueblo of Cieneguilla, south of Santa Fe.[29] By the end of 1695, Vargas had consolidated Spanish control over most of New Mexico. Father Blas Navarro, who was said to understand the language of Picuris, was stationed there as missionary in August 1695, but in March 1696 Governor Vargas learned of a plot to murder Father Navarro, and other priests were reporting rumors of a general uprising.[30]

News of widespread acts of rebellion reached Santa Fe in early June. Six priests were slain, and many Indians deserted their pueblos for the nearby mesas and mountains. Eleven pueblos revolted, including Picuris. Allied with the Hispanos were Zia, Santa Ana, San Felipe, Pecos, and Tesuque. In the immediate aftermath of the outbreak of the rebellion it became clear that Picuris was in the forefront of the revolt.[31] By late July, Vargas turned the tide of rebellion, pacifying the Jemez and defeating the rebels under Lucas Naranjo of Cochiti. Naranjo's forces were defeated and his severed head was given to the Pecos as a trophy of victory, at which point the only pueblos remaining in revolt were Acoma, Picuris, and Taos. In late August when Vargas's forces launched a probe against the Picuris Indians living near Embudo, a crack appeared in the unified resistance Picuris had exhibited up to that point. Several Picuris Indians came into Vargas's camp and provided intelligence about Lorenzo Tupatú, their governor, and Antonio, his brother. The Picuris people were debating whether to accept the Hispanos' offer of friendship: some wanted peace and others wanted to go live among the Apaches.

During the first week of October, Roque Madrid arrived in Santa Cruz de la Cañada with three prisoners from Picuris: the wife, the daughter, and the elderly mother of Antonio Tupatú, who was the cacique and brother of the governor, Lorenzo Tupatú. Governor Vargas intended to return Antonio Tupatú's wife, daughter, and mother but only after the members of the pueblo returned to occupy Picuris. Madrid also brought Antonio Tupatú's nephew, the son of the late Luis Tupatú, Antonio's older brother, to Vargas. The governor told Antonio that the people of Picuris should gather the church furnishings and everything that belonged to the priest by the time he (Vargas) arrived.[32]

When Vargas returned to Picuris in early October he found a large cross set up at the entrance to the pueblo and smaller ones erected before the door of the church. A Picuris war captain and the fiscal greeted the governor, but not Lorenzo Tupatú, who was said to have been severely injured in a fall from a horse, twisting his leg. His injury and heavy snowfall made it impossible for him to come down out of the mountains. The rest of the pueblo was in the mountains, where they had their clothing and provisions. The Picuris Indians brought Vargas a chest containing some church vestments, although several of them were missing. Vargas told them to assemble the missing items and send them with Antonio Tupatú, who was to come at once.[33] Vargas returned to Santa Fe where he received a visit from Antonio Tupatú, the cacique of Picuris. Tupatú informed the governor that his brother Lorenzo was still ill and that the people were returning to the pueblo. When Lorenzo was well again he would travel to Santa Fe to see Vargas. On the strength of the news that the people were returning to the pueblo, Vargas gave Antonio Tupatú a letter for the alcalde mayor of Santa Cruz ordering the alcalde to hand over to Antonio Tupatú his wife, daughter, and mother, who were being held captive. Vargas asked Antonio to gather together and return the missing church furnishings and the santo (carved image of a saint) that was once in their church.[34]

Soon after the parley with Antonio Tupatú, Vargas realized that everything Tupatú had said at their meeting was part of a ruse to provide cover for the impending exodus of many Picuris. Most of the Picuris people did not trust the Spaniards to keep their promises to "treat them kindly" if they swore allegiance to the Spanish king and the Christian God, so they were preparing to journey to the Buffalo Plains and live with the Cuartelejo Apaches. The story about Lorenzo Tupatú's injury due to a fall from a horse was part of the clever stratagem designed to lure the Spanish into complacency. Lorenzo Tupatú was apparently making arrangements for the journey to the plains while his brother Antonio was securing the release of his wife, daughter, and mother. Antonio got the better of Vargas, but it would be the last time. Vargas received word that a group of Picuris Indians had gathered all their household belongings and departed to the east in the company of a group from Santa Clara, some Indians from Taos, and some Apaches from the plains.[35]

Vargas hastily prepared to depart Santa Fe in pursuit of the Picuris Indians, leaving to join the company in Santa Cruz. Vargas continued on to Picuris, which he found abandoned. A Tano captive said he heard the Picuris Indians say that they were going where the buffalo were running. Spanish troops left Picuris, following the tracks of the Indians and their animals for five days until they spotted one of the Picuris leaders, Antonio Tupatú. One of the soldiers struck Antonio a glancing blow in the chest with his lance and another wounded him from the other side with a gunshot. Together with Antonio, they brought in several women and children, who were then taken captive, including Antonio's wife. She and the other women stated that Antonio came to their pueblo to persuade the people to rebel. Given this testimony and the fact that Antonio was captured in open war, Vargas ordered him shot. Thus Vargas and the Hispanos wreaked vengeance on the man whose trickery made the exodus to Cuartelejo possible.[36]

A heavy snowstorm forced Vargas to order his company to withdraw from the field. Only with difficulty did they return to Santa Fe. Overall, Vargas captured eighty-four Picuris men, women, and children and five warriors and distributed them to the Hispanos who accompanied him on the campaign. Vargas explained to the Picuris people that he was doing this "in order to safeguard their lives in their [the Hispanos'] care" and that they were not to be taken outside of the villa of Santa Fe. From these captives the Hispanos learned that the rest of the Picuris people, led by Governor Luis Tupatú, had gone to live with the Cuartelejo Apaches in western Kansas.[37]

When Vargas reported to the viceroy about his campaign against the Picuris Indians, he noted that eight Picuris families had come down from the sierra to reoccupy the pueblo. These people visited Vargas in Santa Fe and told him that the absent pueblo members would return "toward the end of the next new moon." They asked the governor to return their relatives who were among the captured Picuris in Santa Fe and Vargas agreed to do so as soon as the absent Picuris returned. He said that he was "holding them as hostages until they [the Picuris Indians] informed [him] that those they had spoken of returned."[38]

Ten years passed before the Picuris people living with the Cuartelejo Apaches returned to their pueblo. By 1706 it seems apparent that many of the refugees had drifted back to their ancestral pueblo. In that year fray Juan Álvarez stated that there were about three hundred Christian Indians in Picuris and that "others keep coming in who have been among the Apaches."[39] Little is known about this Picuris group during the decade they lived with the Cuartelejo Apaches. There were at least sixty-four Picuris living on the Buffalo Plains, as Hispanos called the area, including Lorenzo Tupatú, the brother of the Pueblo Revolt leader, and his nephew Juan Tupatú. Also living with the Cuartelejos during this period were some Tanos, Tewas, and some Santa Clarans. What happened to the rest of the Picuris population, said to number up to three thousand in 1680, is unclear, although many were killed at the time of the Pueblo Revolt and during the reconquest, while others must have died during the sojourn at Cuartelejo.[40]

In July and August 1706, Juan de Ulibarrí led an expedition from Santa Fe to the Buffalo Plains to bring the Picuris people back to the pueblo. Governor Cuervo y Valdés ordered the expedition, having received news through a Picuris messenger that the Picuris people then living on the plains wanted to return to their pueblo. According to Cuervo y Valdés, the urging of the tribal members still living at the pueblo persuaded the Picuris Indians who followed Tupatú to return to New Mexico, but they lacked horses and supplies to make the journey. They almost certainly heard that conditions at the pueblo had improved after the revolt and wanted to receive the Hispanos' pardon and their sanction to return.[41] There was also the issue of the eighty-four Picuris captives Vargas took, whose return was promised when the Picuris people from Cuartelejo came back to the pueblo.[42]

Juan de Ulibarrí led the expedition out of Santa Fe on 13 July 1706 to bring back the Picuris people. When he stopped at Picuris the next day, he reported that the governor had collected a number of cotton and woolen blankets and as many horses as possible for the expedition to take with them to the Picuris people in Cuartelejo. The expedition left Picuris on 15 July and stopped at Taos for four days before setting out for the plains.[43]

The Apaches—accompanied by three Picuris—came to meet the Hispanos, bringing them buffalo meat and roasted maize. When the expedition reached the main settlements they encountered the Picuris people led by Lorenzo Tupatú, who were scattered among separate *rancherías*. "From their ranches and little houses came don Lorenzo and the rest of the Picuris Indians, men and women who were with him." These may have been the houses the Taos Indians built when they first arrived at Cuartelejo.[44] The next day Lorenzo Tupatú came to Ulibarrí's camp and told Ulibarrí that he would have to arrange to collect the remaining Picuris, "as they had no horses and were completely destitute." Ulibarrí provided Tupatú and his party with horses and assigned groups of Hispanos to go with them, "so that by their visit and the awe they inspired, there might not be any embarrassment." They split into three groups, each going to a different ranchería. Captain José Naranjo led the group that went to the largest ranchería, where the Apaches were "very friendly and agreeable." There "they handed over to them without objection or argument, Juan Tupatú, an Indian chief, a very young man who was the son of Luis [Lorenzo] Tupatú."[45]

After spending almost another week with the Apaches, Ulibarrí notified them that he was ready to go back to Santa Fe and that the remaining Picuris Indians must be delivered to him that day. After some negotiation the Apaches said they would deliver all the people they had by five o'clock in the afternoon. More Picuris were produced to join the returning group of Pueblo Indians, but five more were being held in the chief's house. Eventually the Apache chief delivered the five remaining Indians, albeit reluctantly. In return Ulibarrí gave the Apaches thirteen horses from those that Picuris had donated and those that Captain Naranjo purchased. All told, Ulibarrí brought back sixty-two Picuris, including Lorenzo Tupatú and his nephew Juan Tupatú, "the most noteworthy Indians of the entire kingdom and provinces."[46]

Governor Cuervo y Valdés reported the return of the Picuris Indians to the viceroy, the Duque de Alburquerque, in glowing, if somewhat exaggerated, terms: "He [Ulibarrí] entered the unknown land of different nations of Indians until he reached the new and widespread province of San Luis and the great settlement of Santo Domingo of El Cuartelejo inhabited by Apaches." The governor expressed the "hopes of extending into all those lands obedience to the dominion of his majesty and the Catholic religion, for the disposition of these nations seem to favor both."[47] Cuervo either misjudged or actively misled the viceroy about the Cuartelejos' disposition with respect to becoming loyal peaceful subjects of the king.[48]

Just how much the governor misrepresented the Apaches as peace loving with regard to the Pueblos and the Hispanos was demonstrated in the summer of 1715 when a band of Apaches attacked Picuris and made off with their entire horse herd. The Apache bands involved included the Lemitas and Trementinas (or Nementinas), who were enemies of the Jicarillas, Taos, and Picuris. Usually, Spanish authorities (and later Mexican and U.S. authorities) did not distinguish between different Apache groups or different bands of the Jicarilla Apaches. It was easier to consider them collectively for purposes of waging war, which often caused problems when one Apache group was attacked and punished for a raid carried out by another group. In this case, Spanish authorities, with the help of Lorenzo Tupatú of Picuris, got it right and selected the responsible Apache band to attack. The current governor, Juan Ignacio Flores Mogollón (1712–1715), called a council of war after taking the testimony of Lorenzo Tupatú, governor of Picuris. The Indians had left some of their arrows in the *ciénega* of Santa Fe, which Tupatú identified as Apache arrows, but not Cuartelejo Apaches. Before the council could get underway it was reported that the Picuris people themselves had recovered their horse herd and returned it to their pueblo. Governor Flores Mogollón ordered that a campaign against the Lemitas or Chippayne Apaches be sent out anyway under the command of Juan Páez Hurtado. The expedition included 151 Indian auxiliaries, including 12 Picuris.[49]

The Picuris Indians played an important role in this expedition, serving as reliable guides; they were familiar with the land, since they traversed it when they traveled to Cuartelejo and back between 1696 and 1706. The members of the expedition started from Picuris, but they never found the Apache rancherías they were looking for. In the end the campaign was a failure, for no Apaches were sighted. The expedition turned back to Santa Fe along the route it had come. Páez Hurtado assumed that word of the campaign had been leaked to some of the Apaches who came to Pecos to trade Indian captives.[50] In addition to the formal expedition comprised of 36 soldiers, 52 settlers, and 149 Indian auxiliaries, Páez Hurtado incorporated a group of 30 Jicarilla Apaches and 1 Cuartelejo Apache who was apparently living near Picuris into the expedition. Since the Cuartelejo Apaches had the greatest familiarity with the terrain where the enemy Apaches were to be found, the Cuartelejo Apache was appointed as head guide.[51]

It appears that the Apaches were warned of the campaign. After eighteen days, the Cuartelejo guide admitted he was lost. Páez Hurtado reported that "he was already confused and he did not know where he was or where he ought to go. Seeing that . . . he was guilty of such negligence, I condemned him to be given fifty lashes with a whip."[52] Páez Hurtado placed the blame for the failure of the expedition on a security leak by the Cuartelejo Apaches rather than by the Picuris Indians. While Páez Hurtado may have initially been wary of the Picuris scouts, he soon came to trust them.

Even before this 1715 campaign against the Apaches, Picuris warriors had fought alongside Spanish military forces and citizen militia in campaigns against various Ute, Apache, and Comanche groups. One such campaign against the Navajos took place in 1705, a year before the return of many Picuris Indians from Cuartelejo.[53] As Picuris Indians and Hispanos cooperated militarily against their common enemies, a gradual accommodation occurred whereby former enemies found it in their interest to work together. But Spanish protection of Picuris lands—part of the quid pro quo for pueblo military assistance—was largely ineffective.

The first Spanish land grant to mention Picuris was the 1703 Sebastián Martín grant.[54] The land was initially granted to three individuals who failed to settle on the land, so in 1703 Sebastián Martín and his brother Antonio asked Governor Vargas to forfeit the initial grant and regrant the lands to them. Vargas made the grant, but it was not until 1705 that the Martín brothers were placed in possession of the land. The grant was a huge tract whose boundaries were as follows: north, a cross erected in the canyon that runs to El Embudo; south, the north line of the Pueblo of San Juan grant; east, the river running between Chimayo and the Pueblo of Picuris (Río de Las Trampas); and west, the table lands on the west side of the Rio Grande. The two Martín brothers, together with three other brothers, settled on the land, built a large four-room house with two torreones, dug an acequia, and planted several fields. The Martín clan also ran a substantial herd of cattle on their land and beyond, causing Taos Pueblo to complain about encroachments on its land in the 1720s. Meanwhile Sebastián bought out his brother's interest in the land, and in 1712 he had his title confirmed by Governor José Chacón Medina Salazar y Villaseñor, the Marqués de la Peñuela (1707–1712), claiming to have lost his deeds and title papers. This was a tactic Hispanos sometimes used in the early 1700s to acquire more land than the government was willing to grant.[55]

By 1751 Sebastián Martín was the undisputed owner of this huge tract of land. Thus, when Governor Vélez Cachupín made the Las Trampas grant in 1751, Martín was able to deed the Las Trampas settlers 1,640 varas of land on the west side of the Río de las Trampas, which allowed them to plant fields on both sides of the river.[56] Congress confirmed the Sebastián Martín grant on the surveyor general's recommendation in 1860. Deputy surveyors Daniel Sawyer and William McBroom surveyed the grant in 1876. The grant, which was found to contain over 51,000 acres, was patented to Martín's heirs in 1893.[57]

Spanish encroachment on Picuris land began with the Embudo grant in 1725 at a place called the Embudo de Picurís. On 17 July 1725, Juan Márquez, Francisco Martín, and Lázaro de Córdoba, residents of Puesto del Río Arriba, asked Governor Bustamante for a grant of a triangular tract of land bounded on the north by the Rio Grande, on the south by the Sebastián Martín grant, and on the east by a dry creek bed running south to north. The petitioners told Governor Bustamante that the land was unoccupied and was three leagues (approximately nine miles) from the boundaries of Picuris Pueblo and therefore public domain. By 1725 the right of each pueblo to a Pueblo league was well established. In addition, Spanish law recognized the right of each pueblo to land it used before the arrival of Oñate in 1598, such as land members of the pueblo farmed.[58]

Although later surveys showed that the Embudo grant was indeed outside of the Picuris league, it did encompass fields that the Picuris people claimed their ancestors farmed when Oñate arrived in New Mexico. Petitioners Márquez, Martín, and Córdoba recognized that Picuris had some maize fields beyond their league, but they insisted that the proposed Embudo grant was "far ... from some fields cultivated by the [Picuris] Indians outside of their lands."[59] In fact the petitioners claimed that the maize fields were on the other side of the arroyo that formed the pueblo's western boundary.[60]

When Governor Bustamante received the petition in July 1725, he appointed the alcalde of Santa Fe, José de la Vega y Coca, to go to Embudo to examine the land requested by the petitioners. If there was no objection, he was to make the grant. Bustamante did not say anything about giving notice to potential claimants such as Picuris, however, or what kind of procedure should be followed. The pueblo was mentioned, but the method of determining the rights of the pueblo was not made clear.[61]

Governor Bustamante must have anticipated a protest by Picuris, yet he sidestepped appointing the local alcalde to make the investigation. Alcalde

Miguel Enríquez of the Picuris jurisdiction learned of the proceeding when Alcalde De la Vega y Coca appeared at the Embudo de Picurís one day in mid-July and showed him Bustamante's decree. Enríquez placed the governor's decree above his head, signifying his obedience to the will of Governor Bustamante and his intention to comply with the decree. Although Enríquez was present at the proceeding at which Picuris issued a strong protest, he was not asked his opinion, even though he clearly knew more about Picuris's land use than did the Santa Fe alcalde.[62]

On 19 July 1725, the two alcaldes proceeded to examine the land and to determine whether there were any objections to the grant requested by Juan Márquez, Francisco Martín, and Lázaro de Córdoba. The Picuris Indians were on hand and presented several objections to the proposed grant through Juan, their interpreter. The Picuris people claimed to have title papers showing their ownership of land within the grant and asserted that they farmed portions of the proposed grant, which would have given them rights to the land farmed under *Recopilación* 4-12-18.[63]

When the Picuris Indians presented the two documents they claimed gave them title to the land, it turned out that neither dealt with land ownership. One was an order from Governor Flores Mogollón to Alcalde Juan Ruiz Cordero to gather all the firearms in the hands of the Indians, and the other document related to "proceedings by the alcalde mayor relative to the removal of the Indians of the Tiwa tribes . . . of Taos and Picuris and their settlement at the Pueblo of San Agustín de la Isleta."[64] De la Vega y Coca summarily dismissed the Picuris Indians' attempt to base their objection to the Embudo grant on these written documents. The Picuris people then informed him that they used the Embudo grant "to graze their horse herd when they came to plant [their fields]."[65] Again he rejected their claim, on the assumption that grazing alone was not a sufficient land use, even though the Picuris Indians also implied that they planted some fields on the Embudo tract. The alcalde asked the Indians whether they had any fields on the proposed grant and, if so, to point them out. The Picuris Indians pointed to what De la Vega y Coca called "the two best pieces of land."[66] Once again the alcalde dismissed the Picuris Indians' claim, saying that the fields were "uncultivated and uncleared [so that] it is apparent that they never had been fields."[67] To this the Picuris people responded "that their ancestors planted there at the time of the conquest, when the first Spaniards came into this kingdom at the time of don Juan de Oñate."[68]

De la Vega y Coca knew that Spanish law required him to recognize land the Indians farmed as Picuris property, whether or not he was familiar with the details of *Recopilación* 4-12-18. Yet the alcalde did not specifically address this claim, the strongest advanced by the Picuris people. It is quite likely that Picuris was correct about farming in 1598, since the population of the pueblo was greater then and was spread out over a wider area.[69] Nevertheless, De la Vega y Coca quashed this final attempt by the pueblo, after offering to reduce the size of the Embudo grant somewhat, saying that the Picuris Indians were arrogant "and clearly manifested the desire to prevent the settlement of the Hispanos."[70]

Even though the Embudo grant was indeed outside the league, this was the beginning of a century of encroachment on Picuris land, so much so that by 1829 the pueblo was hemmed in on two sides. Had the pueblo been represented by an advocate, like the earlier protectors of Indians or later advocates such as Felipe Tafoya or Carlos Fernández, it probably would have had greater success, at least regarding its claim to land planted and farmed at the time of the conquest. Measurement of the Picuris league at this time might have slowed some of the later encroachment on Picuris lands.

Alcalde De la Vega y Coca stated in his report of the Picuris investigation that it was "well known since the time of the conquest of this kingdom they [the Picuris Indians] were not known to have any fields on this tract [the Embudo grant]."[71] This bald assertion without any supporting evidence effectively put an end to the Picuris people's protest against the Embudo grant. Alcalde De la Vega y Coca ruled that the Picuris people had "ample pasture for their horse herd in the wooded hills [behind the pueblo]" and that if Spanish-owned cattle damaged Picuris fields, the Indians would be compensated. De la Vega y Coca also ruled that the Picuris Indians had "ample cultivated lands," including those "at the embudo distant more than three leagues from the pueblo" and those surrounding the pueblo.[72] Here the alcalde was admitting that the Picuris Indians *did* own some farmland within the Embudo grant outside of the Picuris league.

The act of possession for the Embudo grant was completed by Alcalde De la Vega y Coca through the customary ceremony of pulling up grass and throwing stones to indicate the Hispanos' dominion over the granted land. This was the last time the Picuris Indians mounted such a strong protest against a neighboring grant, although they protested the making of the Río de Picurís grant in

1829 to the east of their league after suffering encroachment from the Las Trampas grant to the south and the Santa Bárbara grant to the southeast.[73]

The autocratic treatment of the Picuris Indians' protest to the Embudo grant by Alcalde De la Vega y Coca occurred during a period when relations with Hispanos alternated between hostility and friendliness. As Hispano settlers moved closer and closer to the heart of the pueblo, the Picuris people frequently allied with them as auxiliaries on their campaigns against the Comanches, Apaches, and other Plains Indian tribes.[74] During the first half of the eighteenth century, Picuris was exposed to Apaches who were being pushed out of their traditional hunting areas by the Comanches. Worse than that, by the time the Apaches were ejected from their historic land, the Comanches alone were beneficiaries of the French trade in guns. The Comanches then began a series of devastating raids in the 1740s that led to the depopulation of much of the frontier from Albuquerque north to Taos.[75]

Some individual Picuris Indians attempted to provide security for themselves and their families by acquiring land near the pueblo and selling it to Hispanos. In a 1732 sale, Governor Cruzat y Góngora was sensitive enough to Picuris concerns about land surrounding the Picuris league that he ordered that the pueblo be notified of a proposed sale by a Picuris tribal member of land at Embudo. Luis Romero asked Cruzat y Góngora for permission to sell the land he owned at Embudo adjacent to land of Francisco Martín. It is not clear how Luis Romero acquired the property, but it was probably in his capacity as *teniente alcalde* of the jurisdiction of San Lorenzo de Picurís. As teniente he had contact with elite Hispanos at Embudo, such as Sebastián Martín, and could have traded cattle for the land.

When consulted about the proposed sale, Picuris and the heirs of Luis Romero consented to it because the land was considered *tierras de riesgo* (dangerous land). Apparently the land lay in the path often taken by Apache and later Comanche raiders and was not land the pueblo was using, so the pueblo and the Romero heirs consented to the sale. Accordingly, the sale from Luis Romero to Pedro Montes Vigil was approved by Governor Cruzat y Góngora. The fact that Picuris was consulted about the sale suggests that the Spanish government recognized Picuris interests in land outside its league.[76]

In the 1730s, controversy continued to rage regarding priests accused of neglecting their duties. The charges included failure of the priests to properly administer the sacraments and to learn the native languages and failure of the

Indians to confess through an interpreter for fear of revealing secret information.[77] Fray Juan Antonio de Ezeiza was stationed at Picuris from 1730 to 1732, followed by fray Juan José Pérez de Mirabal and fray Juan Sánchez de la Cruz. In 1743 the church land was described as being between two arroyos and to the north of the Rio Pueblo.[78] During the two years that Father Sánchez was at Picuris he recorded thirteen marriages in the Picuris book of marriages, all apparently Indians from Picuris. Then over the next decade a series of priests recorded thirty-one more marriages, also between Picuris people. On 7 May 1741, fray Juan José Mirabal recorded the first marriage between two Jicarilla Apaches, Diego Pituse and María Antonia, and less than two months later he registered a marriage between a Picuris man named Antonio and a Jicarilla Apache woman named Rosa.[79]

In the two decades between 1720 and 1740, the Spanish government of New Mexico engaged in a policy regarding the Jicarilla Apaches that eventually resulted in their settling in the Picuris area. During the early 1720s, the Jicarilla Apache bands considered moving to Navajo country because they were not receiving enough protection from Hispanos against Comanche attacks. To provide more protection, the Spanish government proposed settling the Jicarillas close to Pueblos. This may have included areas surrounding Picuris.[80] Increased contact between the Jicarillas and Picuris are reflected in the marriage and other church records.[81]

During the three decades before 1750, the Jicarillas ranged between Taos and Pecos, more or less at peace with the Hispanos. By the 1750s, however, they had joined the Utes and began raiding settlements throughout northern New Mexico, forming an alliance that turned them into enemies of Picuris and Hispanos. One of the reasons for this shift in alliances was the severing of the Ute-Comanche alliance around midcentury after the Apaches were driven out of New Mexico. After coming to Taos in 1752, however, Utes sued for peace with the Hispanos. This began a period during which the Ute and Jicarilla Apache people engaged in relatively peaceful trade with both Hispanos and Pueblo Indians such as the Picuris people. The long period of interaction between Picuris and Apache bands, such as the Jicarillas and Cuartelejos, resulted in some intermarriage between the two, as well as a substantial amount of cultural exchange between the two groups.[82]

By 1744 the Picuris population had dwindled to eighty families comprising about four hundred people, according to a census taken by fray Juan Miguel

Menchero during his visitation in that year. Menchero noted that "[Picuris] is situated between two crystalline rivers which rise in a rough mountain; in them are found the best trout in the kingdom, which can compete with the most savory ones to be found in Spain." Assessing the reputation of the Picuris Indians as warriors up to the time of the Pueblo Revolt, Menchero stated that "[the pueblo] from the time of its first founding and before the uprising of the year 1680, had a large number of very brave and warlike Indians."[83]

The declining population of Picuris was related to reduced land and water resources resulting from Spanish encroachment. Encroachment on the Picuris league can be tracked in Picuris church records, such as the marriage records. The first entry of a marriage between Spaniards in the Picuris Book of Marriages is dated 1743. It is apparent that the settlement of Santa Bárbara was established by 1749 because on 18 September of that year the record of the marriage of Marcial Torres and María Martínez noted that both were from that community.[84] In the following years, more Hispanos appear in the Picuris sacramental records from Santa Bárbara and Las Trampas.[85]

In the two decades prior to the Comanche Peace, raids by marauding Comanches posed a serious threat to Picuris. Governor Vélez Cachupín tried to reinforce the ordinance available to the pueblos by distributing a small campaign cannon to Picuris in 1762, as well as quantities of powder and musket balls. Taos, Pecos, and Galisteo also received similar equipment, but in each case the weaponry was distributed to the local alcalde.[86] This armament did not prevent a Comanche assault in 1768, when fifteen raiders attacked Picuris, killing one Indian, nor a raid the following year, when the church was attacked and the supplies of the convent destroyed.[87] Father Andrés Claramonte, the priest at the time of the 1769 attack, considered himself lucky to have survived the raid unharmed. Governor Mendinueta ordered the church torn down because the raid demonstrated its vulnerability. By the time of Father Domínguez's 1776 visitation, the Picuris church was being rebuilt closer to the pueblo house blocks.[88] Comanche raids on Picuris continued: there were five raids in 1772, another in 1774 that resulted in two Picuris deaths and the loss of the horse herd, and several in 1777 that claimed the lives of four Picuris.[89] Governor Mendinueta, during whose term in office these attacks took place, proposed in 1778 that fifteen trained cavalrymen be stationed at Picuris during the summer months to help ward them off.[90] In 1773, when two hundred Comanches attacked Picuris and wounded three pueblo members, Picuris must have appreciated the assistance of some Hispanos at the pueblo who helped repel the attack.[91] What began as a mixed blessing became more of a curse when the Comanche threat ceased with the 1786 peace treaty and as the Spanish settlements near Picuris continued to increase in size.

Governor Vélez Cachupín made the Las Trampas grant in 1751 to twelve residents of the Analco barrio in Santa Fe. The grantees were a mixed group of Genízaros, Indians with family origins in New Spain, and people of Spanish ancestry. Like the Picuris people, the settlers of Las Trampas had the unenviable task of defending their homes, fields, livestock, and horses from Comanche raiders. Genízaros were among the best warriors, adept at fighting Indians with whom they shared bloodlines from such tribes as the Apaches, Kiowas, Pawnees, Jumanos, and Utes.[92] The Las Trampas grant was bounded on the west by the Sebastián Martín grant and on the east by Picuris. Since the Picuris league had probably not been measured, it is likely that there was some encroachment on Picuris land by the Las Trampas grant. The first marriage of someone from the area of Las Trampas/Santa Bárbara took place on 22 April 1754, as recorded in the Picuris marriage register, when Juan Antonio Leyba from Las Picuris married Rosalía Madrid, a *coyota* from Santa Bárbara.[93]

Much of the encroachment on Picuris land came from the south and southeast as the Las Trampas and Santa Bárbara grants were being settled, but encroachment nearer the center of the pueblo seems to have lacked the authority of any land grant as justification. It appears that communities such as Río Lucío grew up within the Picuris league during the period of all-out Comanche warfare, when the presence of Hispano settlers living near the pueblo may have been welcomed to augment the defense against Comanche attack.

Settlement at Santa Bárbara began in the early 1740s, as more and more land was being privatized under the relatively liberal land policies of Governor Codallos y Rabal. As the governor made grants in the Abiquiu, El Rito, and Ojo Caliente areas, available land was quickly snapped up, so men from these areas sought land near Picuris. Several of them were turned down in other locations because the land they sought was too close to other pueblos, so they turned to land near Picuris, believing that there would be little protest from the pueblo. Several settlers from Santa Bárbara and from Rio Arriba and Santa Cruz requested a grant "about a league" from the pueblo in 1739. Jacinto Martín was the leader of the settlement together with Santa Bárbara residents Felipe Bustamante, Antonio Martín, and Juan Francisco Martín.[94]

While the latter three grantees tried to settle the land by building houses and planting fields and gardens, none was a year-round resident except Jacinto Martín. Martín was the lieutenant alcalde of Picuris and realized the importance of year-round residency in providing some security against attack from the nomadic tribes such as the Comanches and the Apaches. One of the reasons Martín gave for requesting the grant was "for the protection and guarding of [Picuris] Pueblo." Martín was living at Santa Bárbara in 1743, for we know from the Picuris marriage records that he appeared as a witness in that year. It is likely that the Santa Bárbara settlement dates from at least then.[95]

Martín's three cograntees did little toward establishing permanent year-round settlement right after the grant was made, so Martín asked Governor Gaspar Domingo de Mendoza (1739–1743), who apparently made the grant, to compel Martín's companions to settle or lose their interest in the land. This forced Bustamante and the other two Martíns to build log huts on the land, but they still did not live there year round. Instead they came for two weeks in the spring to plant, then came back for a similar period in the fall to harvest what they grew, and then left until the next spring. Martín petitioned Governor Codallos y Rabal to force the other grantees to live year-round at Santa Bárbara. Before rendering his decision, Governor Codallos asked Alcalde Nicolás Ortiz to inspect the community and report on the extent of the improvements there. The information he gathered provides the first specific glimpse of the settlement of Santa Bárbara situated partially within the Picuris league. Jacinto Martín had a six-room house and fields with five fanegas and three *cuartillas* of wheat (about eight acres), one and a half fanegas of maize (four and a half acres), and one fanega of vegetables. Antonio Martín had a house with one room measuring nine varas, and he planted four fanegas of wheat (six acres), two almudes of maize, and one and a half fanegas of vegetables. Juan Francisco Martín also had a house of one room nine varas wide, and he planted one fanega and three cuartillas of wheat and one cuartilla of fava beans (habas).[96]

This indication from Ortiz's report of a substantial amount of work having been performed on the land was enough to convince Governor Codallos y Rabal to allow the Santa Bárbara grant to stand, but no new settlers were allowed. Those who were there were encouraged to continue their efforts at permanent settlement "so that they may shelter and protect one another with their weapons each time they are ordered and the necessity occurs."[97] The importance of establishing a settlement near Picuris to help defend the pueblo from attack outweighed the need to comply with the strict requirements for securing title to the land as argued for by Jacinto Martín. Martín believed that his cograntees would settle permanently if ordered to by the governor, but Codallos was not as strict as Governor Vélez Cachupín was when it came to the resettlement of Abiquiu less than a decade later.[98]

The Picuris Indians had mixed feelings when the settlement on the Santa Bárbara grant began encroaching on the Picuris league. They were apparently not consulted regarding the Santa Bárbara settlement either in the early stages or when the Santa Bárbara community grant was requested in 1796.[99] The fact that the Hispano Jacinto Martín was the lieutenant alcalde of Picuris should have meant that he would not intentionally try to obtain a land grant for himself that overlapped the Picuris league, although in fact Spanish officials regularly sought property on Indian land. In the decades following the first settlement on the Santa Bárbara grant, population increases coupled with a decrease in Comanche and Ute raids led to a marked expansion of the population, causing Picuris to protest other encroachments on the Picuris league.

The relationship between the Picuris people and the priests assigned to the pueblo had improved somewhat since the incident in 1621 when Father Arvide was beaten and the Pueblo Revolt when the priest was killed, but it was always a bit testy. The Picuris Indians were slow to convert to Christianity, and they performed labor for the priests somewhat grudgingly. Father Juan Nepomuceno Trigo reported in 1754 that while the Picuris people did not pay any parochial fees, they had the obligation to plant two fanegas of wheat and one almud of maize for the priest, who, Trigo said, "gets on badly enough." Other Picuris Indians serving the priest were "a boy for the cell, a bell ringer, a porter, two sacristans, a cook, two wood-cutters, and two women each week [to grind grain]." Twenty-two years later, when Father Claramonte was the priest at Picuris, the number of Indians serving had increased, but Claramonte still had difficulty finding Picuris to help with farming the Picuris land assigned to the mission.[100]

In 1776 Father Domínguez reported that the complement of Indians attending to the needs of the Picuris priest were a fiscal mayor, three subordinates, eight sacristans, four cooks, four bakers (who were allotted weekly), a stable boy, a shepherd, and a woman to care for the hens. Although this was a substantial number of servants, they were not all full time. Some, such as cooks and bakers, rotated to other pueblos. When it came to farming pueblo land assigned to the mission, Father Claramonte had to do much of the work himself. Although pueblo members did part of the sowing, cultivation, and harvesting, Claramonte told Father Domínguez that he had to thresh the wheat himself with six of his own animals. He also reported that he had some difficulty getting people from the pueblo to help with a maize field at Embudo that was owned by Picuris.[101]

The Picuris people's land at Embudo was apparently the same land mentioned at the time of the Picuris protest in 1725 when the Embudo grant was made. Although Picuris was not successful in preventing the Embudo grant, Spanish officials acknowledged that Picuris owned farmland at Embudo, three leagues from Picuris. The pueblo needed this land because it was at a lower elevation than the farmland near the pueblo and was capable of growing crops that could not be grown at Picuris because of the short growing season there. Father Domínguez reported that "frijol and chile do not yield a crop in the Picuris lands because of the cold. Maize usually freezes, but not consistently. There is a very pretty harvest of everything else. The Embudo lands yield a crop of everything sown in them (this is proven by the harvest of its settlers)."[102]

At the time of Domínguez's visitation, the mission at Picuris had a tract of land 200 varas long by 60 varas wide as part of the land at Embudo owned by Picuris. According to the priest, this land was "the best of all," for you could grow beans on it and you could not grow beans at Picuris. Father Claramonte was having difficulty getting the Picuris Indians to work this prime plot of land, however, even when he offered them half the harvest if they would irrigate the field. Finally Claramonte had to make an arrangement with a Hispano settler at Embudo to farm the land in return for one and a half fanegas of beans. This episode demonstrates the continuing recognition by the Spanish government, the Franciscans, and by Hispano settlers of land owned by Picuris outside of its Pueblo league.[103]

Both Picuris and Taos had a long and varied relationship with the Apaches, particularly the Cuartelejo and the Jicarilla Apaches. As one might expect, there were a substantial number of Picuris-Apache marriages and liaisons as a result of their contact with one another.[104] Trade between Plains Apaches and both Taos and Picuris existed prior to the Spanish conquest of New Mexico and continued thereafter. Although some warfare between Pueblos and Apaches before Spanish contact has been documented, for the most part "there was considerable commerce and friendly contacts between the two peoples."[105]

The Jicarilla Apaches may have been living in the Picuris area at the time of Oñate's arrival. Oñate indicated that he had some knowledge of Apaches living to the northeast of Picuris when he assigned "to Father fray Francisco de Zamora the province of the Picuries, together with all the Apaches from the Sierra Nevada toward the north and east."[106] In 1706, when Juan de Ulibarrí went to Cuartelejo to bring back the Picuris people who had gone there ten years earlier, he met peaceful Apache farmers cultivating their crops along the headwaters of the Canadian River. In 1719 the ill-fated Valverde expedition came across villages of Apache farmers living in clusters of from one to eight adobe houses, irrigating their crops with "many ditches and canals."[107]

The Jicarillas were apparently living somewhere north of Taos in 1733, for in that year the Franciscan custodian, José Ortíz de Velasco, founded a mission for them "and began to assemble and instruct them." Governor Cruzat y Góngora, however, "ordered the soldiers of the presidio to put them out, and they feared to return, although some of them come to seek the fathers of the mission." It is not clear where the Jicarillas were living, but the mission was apparently at or near Taos. Apparently, Governor Cruzat y Góngora did not want the Apaches living near or coming to visit Taos too frequently, since, like the Utes and the Comanches, they were alternately at peace and at war with the Hispanos.[108] Fifty years later, the settlers on the Cieneguilla grant had a similar reaction to living with or near the Jicarillas. The Cieneguilla settlers to the northwest of the Picuris league told Governor Melgares that if the Jicarilla were to be settled there, they would abandon their grant.[109]

The Jicarilla Apaches had several camping sites in the Picuris area concentrated to the northwest near Pilar (or Cieneguilla) and to the north along the northern slopes of the Picuris Mountains. The Jicarilla Apache site called Rocks Standing Up could be near the site referred to in 1854 by Indian Agent Christopher "Kit" Carson when he reported that there were about a hundred Jicarilla warriors with their families living near Picuris and making pottery to trade with the Hispanos for provisions. Carson recommended that a special agent be appointed to live with the Jicarillas to help them get provisions, for there was little game in the region and they were starving. Carson implied that they might take some desperate action.[110] A few days after Carson's report his prediction came true. On 30 March 1854 the Jicarillas moved away from their camp and lured a company of U.S. dragoons out of Camp Burgwin under Lieutenant Davidson into a trap. The U.S. troops were greatly outnumbered by the Jicarilla Apaches, joined by some Utes. The combined Indian forces defeated the U.S. military at the Battle of Cieneguilla at Embudo Mountain. Davidson lost thirty-five to forty of his sixty men and brought in seventeen wounded, a crushing defeat. In a report the day after the battle, Governor Messervy described the Jicarillas as composed of "a band of about 100 lodges or 500 souls. They have no permanent residence but roam the northern settlements of New Mexico." Messervy noted that the Jicarillas "manufacture a species of pottery ware capable of tolerable resistance to fire and much used by them and the Mexicans for culinary purposes. These they barter with the Mexicans." The government quashed the initial military reports about the Battle of Cieneguilla lest the resounding defeat of the U.S. military—almost all the troops were killed or wounded—be celebrated as a major Indian victory as was the Battle of Little Bighorn two decades later.[111]

Picuris claimed land to the east of the Pueblo league as common land, which would become an issue when the pueblo objected to the Río de Picurís grant in the late 1820s. During the early 1820s, some pueblos suffered substantial encroachment within their Pueblo leagues as the result of grants made to Hispanos by the Mexican government. A new governmental policy encouraging the privatization of "unused" pueblo land was enacted into law and put into effect in New Mexico, particularly at pueblos whose populations were shrinking. This policy was reversed by 1829.[112] It was during this period, when the sanctity of the Pueblo league was reestablished in theory, that Picuris filed a strong objection to the Río de Picurís grant, which lies east of the Picuris league along the Río de Picurís (today's Rio Pueblo).

Twenty-four citizens from Santa Cruz de la Cañada (including six members of the Fernández family) requested the Río de Picurís grant, bounded on the north by the Fernando de Taos grant, on the south the Río de Picurís, on the east by the hill of Lo de Mora, and on the west by the Picuris league. The petitioners repeated a formula found in many 1820s grant documents when they referred to "the sovereign decrees and laws in force that support the development of agriculture and also for pasturage for our animals" in asking for the land.[113] The territorial deputation referred the petition to the ayuntamiento of Santa Cruz de la Cañada, which recommended that the grant be made, as long as the pastures remained open to those who were using them and the fields were securely fenced.[114]

Before the territorial deputation could act on the recommendation of the Santa Cruz ayuntamiento, the Taos ayuntamiento received a protest petition from Indian representatives of Picuris, together with Hispanos living at Picuris and the alcalde of the pueblo and district of San Lorenzo de Picurís. Picuris argued that the land in question was within the jurisdiction of Taos and not that of the Santa Cruz ayuntamiento and was already being used by the pueblo as its ejido to pasture and water its animals in the summer. Picuris also claimed that the pueblo was surrounded by the settlements of Santa Bárbara, Llano, and Chamisal on the south and west and by the mountains on the north, and if the Río de Picurís grant was made the pueblo would be completely surrounded. Picuris argued further that the establishment of a farming community upstream from Picuris would diminish the water available to the pueblo for its own agriculture. Finally, the pueblo argued that the Santa Cruz citizens admitted that the requested land belonged to the jurisdiction of Taos when they refused to perform guard duty there against Plains Indian raids because the area was within the jurisdiction of the alcaldía of Taos.[115]

In addition to this protest by Picuris, the territorial deputation received protests from the Taos ayuntamiento claiming the Río de Picurís grant was within its jurisdiction, not that of the ayuntamiento of Santa Cruz de la Cañada. The Taos ayuntamiento agreed with Picuris that the land in question was within its jurisdiction and was not unoccupied as the grant petitioners alleged. It was being used for common pasturage and rights of way and should not be granted to the Santa Cruz de la Cañada petitioners.[116]

The territorial deputation made the Río de Picurís grant anyway on 2 May 1829 because it wanted to give the petitioners the opportunity to plant their fields during the current season before the expected smallpox epidemic arrived. In this emergency situation it was important that the Hispanos have an adequate food supply that would carry them over to the next year if possible. But the grant was for just one year, until the jurisdictional dispute could be resolved. The deputation described the grant as closer to Picuris than the petitioners indicated, saying the grant was "in the immediate area of Picuris Pueblo." The petitioners put their western boundary at the Picuris league, 5,000 varas from the center of the pueblo.[117]

The petitioners for the Río de Picurís grant must have planted soon after the early May grant, for by the time Picuris protested for the second time the fields were in existence. This must be what triggered the second protest, for once Picuris saw Hispanos planting and irrigating upstream they knew both their land and their water were in jeopardy. As mentioned in chapter 1, Mariano Rodríguez filed the protest, claiming that the Río de Picurís grant encroached on Picuris common land. Initially, the territorial deputation sided with Picuris, holding in 1831 that the Río de Picurís grant should not be made permanent, and the settlers at Vadito should be evicted. Two years later, however, when the Vadito settlers still had not moved, a new commission of the territorial deputation reversed the earlier decision, ruling that the Río de Picurís grant was valid and should be made permanent. The implied holding of the 1829 and 1831 decisions was clear: the settlement at Vadito was encroaching on the common lands of Picuris Pueblo, but this point was not addressed in the 1833 decision, giving credence to the view that that decision was based on political expediency. A new commission simply approved the status quo. By staying on the land, González and associates proved that they were not requesting the grant only to sell it. By ordering that "the pastures, watering places, and roads remain open and common" in the Río de Picurís grant, the territorial deputation presumably meant to suggest that the settlers and Indians at Picuris could still use these common grazing lands as they had before. Distributions of agricultural land were made that probably reflected the location of existing farmland.[118] The 1831 allotments established the Spanish settlement of Vadito, which was within the Pueblo league on the east as finally surveyed by the surveyor general. Thus, Picuris became almost completely surrounded when the Río de Picurís grant was finally made and the community of Vadito was established.

Additional allotments were made in 1841 when a group of nineteen settlers asked Alcalde Juan Antonio Martín to assign land to them for house lots. Apparently the settlers were farming their fields and had built houses around a plaza but had not received *hijuelas* (deeds) for their house lots. In addition to the house lots, 20 varas of *chorreras* were designated on the north and south. Furthermore, the nineteen settlers were admonished that unless they fortified the plaza, continued to cultivate their fields, and occupied "their settlement they [would] be banned from the land that was granted to them." It seems that Plains Indian raids were still a problem in the area northeast of the Picuris league and that the resettlement of the area that became Vadito was meant to provide a buffer zone against those raids. Alcalde Juan Antonio Martín completed the act of possession, reestablishing the plaza of Vadito, as he listed the names and the amount of land received by each of the Hispano citizens who were given land around the plaza at Vadito.[119] It is possible that some of the settlers wanted to sell their interest in the Río de Picurís grant and needed hijuelas in order to do that. Usually the sale of an interest in a community grant was accomplished by selling a private tract of land coupled with the use rights in the common lands. An example of the hijuela that was given out at the time the allotments were made to the nineteen settlers is that granted to José Miguel Argüello for a house lot $50^{4}/_{5}$ varas long by 12 varas wide. The Argüello tract was bounded by the Río de Picurís grant boundary on the north, the Río de Picurís on the south, the plaza on the east, and the land of Juan Miguel Tafoya on the west. Presumably all nineteen settlers receiving land at the time of the 1841 act of possession received similar hijuelas.[120]

In 1845 a land transfer between Antonio Benito Lucero and José Benito Salas indicated that the settlement of Vadito was still in existence and growing.[121] The large increase in population in the Taos Valley in the first three decades of the nineteenth century is probably the main reason the Taos ayuntamiento reversed itself and allowed the Río de Picurís grant within its jurisdiction. Taos Pueblo was more aggressive about protecting its league (even though there was a substantial amount of encroachment within its boundaries), and the amount of land and water available in the Taos Valley was diminishing. It made sense to Hispano officials to allow the settlement of the Río de Picurís grant where water and land was more plentiful, even though the effect of this policy was prejudicial to Picuris.[122] The Picuris league was mentioned in the Río de Picurís grant proceedings, but the league was not measured. Had Picuris requested that its league be measured in 1829, the pueblo might have had another argument against the Río de Picurís grant, but it was not until 1833 that the Picuris league was measured.[123]

Population figures in the 1820s are a clear indication of the extent of Hispano encroachment on Picuris land. In an 1821 census, 320 individuals were counted at Picuris, and 1,047 people were enumerated at nearby communities. By 1850 the Picuris population had declined to 222, while surrounding Hispano communities continued to grow.[124] Reference to measurement of the Picuris league came in a protest to increased settlement at Santa Bárbara filed by four Picuris Indians in 1845. The pueblo said that Hispanos were settling so far within the league that it felt surrounded.¹²⁵ In 1833 the pueblo asked the judge at Taos to measure the league to the south and erect boundary markers that would divide pueblo land from the land of José Andrés Martin. Doing this resolved the encroachment problem until 1837, when Picuris again complained about the encroachment of Santa Bárbara residents on the Picuris league. Between 1833 and 1837 the pueblo sold some land near their southern boundary to Hispanos, and it was to protect these purchasers that a second measurement was made of the Picuris league in a southerly direction. Again Picuris was satisfied that a clear division had been made between the southern boundary of Picuris and the settlers at Santa Bárbara, but that peace of mind lasted only a few years. In March 1845 pueblo members complained that they had been dispossessed of their land when the local justice evicted them from lands the Santa Bárbara settlers were claiming.¹²⁶ A response to this petition has not been found, but it seems likely that there was no response, because the Santa Bárbara settlers remained on the land.

As population increased around New Mexico pueblos in the latter part of the Mexican period, New Mexico governors and local officials seldom measured Pueblo leagues. Instead these officials were often more concerned with protecting their own interests through the making of new land grants to Hispanos as a U.S. invasion began to seem certain.¹²⁷ As a result, the community of Santa Bárbara continued to grow further into the Picuris league, later combining with several other communities to form the present-day settlement of Peñasco.

Soon after the United States acquired New Mexico following the end of the U.S.-Mexican War, Picuris officials began to register complaints about problems with their land and water with U.S. officials. In April 1852 eight Picuris came to Santa Fe to complain to Assistant Superintendent of Indian Affairs John Greiner that "Mexicans of Mora [were] taking all of the water and ruining the pueblo lands." The Picuris people were also concerned about a tract of land that a man named Solis was claiming. Greiner wrote to the prefect of Taos, asking him to settle the matter because he knew Picuris had little faith in the courts and he feared they might take matters into their own hands. In September 1852, Picuris again complained, saying Solis claimed land on which they planted and would not let them harvest. Greiner wrote directly to Solis, advising him to give the Picuris Indians the wheat they planted "to keep them quiet until the court decided who owned the land."¹²⁸

In June 1856 Picuris filed a Cruzate grant with the surveyor general (see chapter 8). The document purported to give Picuris four square leagues measured from the church on the west side of the pueblo. In December 1858 Congress confirmed the Picuris grant. In July 1859, John Garretson, deputy surveyor, surveyed it, finding it to contain 17,460 acres.[129]

Garretson surveyed the Pueblo league of Picuris from 13 to 18 July 1859. He started at the Picuris church and measured a line due west from the northwest corner of the church, a distance of 2 miles and 48⅓ chains to the western boundary of the Picurís grant. He then proceeded in a clockwise direction and surveyed the west, south, and east boundaries of the Picuris grant. The southern boundary passed through the town of Santa Bárbara just before reaching the 5 mile point. Garretson's field notes describe Santa Bárbara as containing "perhaps 50 houses."[130] The Garretson survey party did not measure the northern part of the grant because "the piñon trees are so thick on the ground that it is impossible to see a flag for any considerable distance—to the top of the mountain it is utterly impossible." Garretson's field notes do include a brief comment at the end of the survey of the west boundary, which supplies information about Hispano occupation within the Pueblo league while also providing a gratuitous assessment of how industrious the Picuris people were: "There are 3 considerable valleys from 20 to 39 chains wide and from 1 mile to 1½ mile in length with several smaller valleys within the boundaries of Picuris but mostly occupied by Mexicans. The Pueblo contains 12 dilapidated houses besides the church and the Indians have the appearance of poverty the sure consequence of idleness and improvidence." This comment probably reflected the general views of many Anglos toward the Picuris Indians and other pueblos.

The Picuris grant survey was tied into the nearest public land survey, since the northern boundary of Picuris grant met the southern boundary of Township 25N, Range 12E.[131] When the Garretson survey was complete, the Picuris grant was found to contain 17,460.69 acres. The survey was used to describe the Picuris grant in the patent for the grant, which was issued to Picuris on 1 November 1864. Not all the land within the Picuris grant was available for use by the pueblo, however, for it was later determined that more than 2,500 acres of the best land was covered by the settlements of non-Indians within the grant. This land was lost to the pueblo through the Pueblo Lands Board proceedings, although some compensation was paid to Picuris.[132]

The Pueblo Lands Board findings regarding the Picuris investigations were filed on 20 October 1928. A total of 674 private adverse claims were included on 2,691 acres within the recognized boundaries of the Picuris grant. Of these encroachments, 1,550 acres were located in the Peñasco area along the Río Santa Bárbara, 659 acres in the Chamisal area, and 481 acres in the Vadito area and along the Rio Pueblo. The board approved 549 claims totaling 2,068 acres and rejected 129 claims for 623 acres. The value of the approved claims was estimated to be $71,898.14, of which the loss to Picuris was set at $47,132.90. This amount was placed in an account within the U.S. Treasury for use by Picuris, accumulating interest at the rate of 4 percent. Of this $47,132.90 compensation, $7,684.50 was set aside to purchase land adjacent to the Picuris-owned land from the non-Indian residents.[133]

On 2 October 1930, the U.S. District Court for the District of New Mexico reversed 102 claims earlier rejected by the Pueblo Lands Board and continued to reject all or part of only 27 claims. The decision resulted in a further loss of 504 acres by the pueblo. When the U.S. attorney general failed to appeal this decision, the pueblo attempted an appeal to the Tenth Circuit Court of Appeals with a private attorney. The court of appeals refused to hear the case because the federal attorney would not file an appeal. An additional award of $15,625.59 compensation money was awarded to Picuris for this additional loss and an award of $11,464.73 was provided for the twenty-seven unsuccessful non-Indian claimants for their loss of 119 acres. The initial award to Picuris amounted to about $23 per acre lost. The supplemental award amounted to about $31 per acre lost. The award to the non-Indian claimants for loss amounted to about $96 per acre.[134]

Two years after the rulings of the U.S. District Court, additional lands for use by the residents of the pueblo had yet to be purchased. Landowners either refused to sell the land or the price of the land was considerably higher than the earlier appraisal. The commissioner of Indian affairs, Charles Rhoads, suggested in a memorandum concerning the status of the monies awarded to the various pueblos dated 11 February 1932 that Picuris be abandoned and the residents moved to San Juan: "We cannot condemn the non-Indian lands for the benefit of the Indians. It is difficult to know what is best to do with this little remaining group of Picuris Indians. But I suggest that if a high-line ditch can be built at San Juan bringing under cultivation there a large additional acreage, that arrangements might be made to move these Picuris Indians away from their pueblo to the San Juan district. This is a possibility, which has never been suggested, but it is one which should be given careful consideration."[135]

Fortunately for Picuris, this proposal was never seriously considered, but its mere mention shows how little the U.S. government's attitude toward the Pueblo Indians had changed since the U.S. Supreme Court in the 1913 Sandoval case declared them to be "a simple, uninformed and inferior people."[136] Finally, in 1938 the acquisition of additional land for the residents of Picuris was completed. A total of 1,258.19 acres was purchased with compensation money, and the title was vested in Picuris Pueblo.[137]

As with other pueblos, Picuris' aboriginal lands—lands that it used exclusively over a long period of time, outside of its confirmed grant—were never acknowledged by the United States, and eventually the Carson National Forest was expanded to extend right to the pueblo's grant boundary, presumably including a significant area that was most certainly aboriginal lands of the pueblo. In the 1990s, various persons filed mineral locations within the Carson National Forest for commercial deposits of mica, under the provisions of the 1872 Mining Act. These locations included an area known to the Picuris people as Mowlownan-á (pot-dirt place), an area just a few miles from the pueblo's grant lands that was the traditional area from which generations of Picuris potters gathered micaceous clay to make their famous clay pots, which were prized as cooking vessels throughout northern New Mexico. Pueblo potters continued to gather their clay from this locale, but when commercial mica mining began, it obliterated their clay pits, and the mining company eventually excluded Picuris members from their clay-gathering area, which deeply upset them. As pueblo governor Gerald Nailor put it, "The land belongs to Picuris. It is our heart and we have never given it away. The mine is like a knife in our heart and as long as it remains, our people will bleed because we cannot practice our traditions and cannot protect the earth."[138]

In 2004 Picuris brought suit against the mining companies, claiming that Mowlownan-á remained part of the pueblo's aboriginal lands, to which it retained unextinguished aboriginal title.[139] Within a year, Oglebay Norton Company, the company that had most recently conducted mining operations there, ceased its operations and entered into an agreement by which it conveyed clear title to the entire mining area to the pueblo. Picuris recovered its aboriginal clay-gathering area and was subsequently able to obtain grant money to undertake a complete reclamation of the mined area. Picuris potters are once again able to take their potting clay from Mowlownan-á.

Making the Sandia Pueblo grant. Drawing by Glen Strock.

CHAPTER 4

Sandia Pueblo

In 1983 Sandia and its history became front-page news when the pueblo requested a resurvey of its 1748 grant, especially the eastern boundary, which was the crest of Sandia Peak. This soon became a high-stakes confrontation involving the U.S. Forest Service, Sandia, private landholders on the slope of the mountain, and other pueblos supporting Sandia's claim. The ensuing court battle raised questions regarding improper alterations of the grant documents, an incompetent survey, and the special characteristics of the Sandia grant, which consisted of a hybrid of the Pueblo league and natural boundaries. Uncovering the complete story required journeys to the official archives of Spain and Mexico and pitted expert historians and anthropologists against one another. Pueblo leaders had to travel to Washington, D.C., to explain the spiritual importance of Sandia Mountain. Out of this litigation came a new appreciation of Sandia's history. This chapter tells the story of the land of Sandia Pueblo.

Potsherds from present-day Sandia indicate that the site was occupied from at least 1300 CE, but the precise location of the pueblo was not known to Coronado at the time of his expedition in 1540. Oñate's "Napeya" of 1598 was probably a corruption of the Southern Tiwa "Na-fiat," meaning "at the dusty place," the native name of the pueblo. Another traditional name for the place is "T'uf Shurn Tia" or "Green Reed Place." It is easy to see how "Shurn Tia" could have become "sandía," Spanish for "watermelon." As was often the case with Spanish corruptions of Indian place names, there is no relationship between the two meanings, nor is it true, as is often mentioned, that the Spanish named the mountain Sandia because it looked like a watermelon.[1]

Little is known of pre-Revolt Sandia. In an early mention, fray Isidro Ordóñez, newly returned to New Mexico in 1612, announced at Sandia that he had been named father commissary.[2] A 1641 report on the missions of New Mexico noted that the church at Sandia was "excellent."[3] The pueblo became the center of the so-called Sandia District during the administration of Governor López de Mendizábal, with Juan Domínguez de Mendoza serving as alcalde mayor of the district.[4] Lieutenant Governor Alonso García owned a large ranch in the Sandia-Isleta area and served as alcalde mayor of the district on at least two occasions, once before 1661 and then again in 1680 at the time of the Pueblo Revolt.[5]

The encomenderos entitled to receive tribute of a fanega of corn and a cotton blanket from each household in the pueblo were Francisco Gómez Robledo I and Francisco Gómez Robledo II, the latter inheriting the encomienda when his father died in 1656 or 1657. The Gómez Robledos were supporters of Governor López de Mendizábal. The Inquisition later charged the son with "Judaizing," but he was acquitted. None of the Gómez Robledos returned to New Mexico after the Pueblo Revolt. During this time, with López de Mendizábal's encouragement, the Indians of Sandia and Isleta resumed public performances of their kachina dances, much to the consternation of the Franciscans. The Audiencia of Mexico City later charged López de Mendizábal with numerous offenses, and he was sentenced in May 1662. He was cleared of permitting the kachina dances at Sandia but was convicted of the charge that he sold the office of alcalde of Sandia to Juan Domínguez de Mendoza in 1659 after removing his brother Tomé Domínguez de Mendoza from the office, for which López de Mendizábal was fined three thousand pesos.

Sandia was one of the most aggressively anti-Spanish pueblos during the events of 1680, for which its people paid dearly. During his retreat from Santa Fe following the Pueblo Revolt, Governor Otermín passed through the area, arriving at Sandia on 26 August 1680. He found the pueblo abandoned and the church door, which had arrow slits in it, closed. The porter's lodge was open, as were the doors providing access to the convento (priest's quarters), which was ruined. The doors to the cells were missing. The sacred images had been taken from the church, and a carved figure of St. Francis had been placed on the main altar, its arms hacked off with an axe.[6] The church was filled with straw to facilitate burning it. All the sacred vessels and vestments had been removed from the sacristy. A search of houses in the pueblo turned up some images and items of silver. Suddenly, at a distance of half a league from the pueblo, many Indians appeared on the heights, both mounted and on foot. They immediately attacked the Hispanos, a skirmish ensued, and the Indians fled for the hills. As they escaped the pursuing Hispanos, Governor Otermín noticed that the church was in flames, at which point he ordered the pueblo burned.[7]

Otermín returned in the winter of 1681–1682 to find the Southern Tiwa pueblos reinhabited.[8] He attacked Isleta and forced the pueblo to surrender. The people of Alameda, Puaray, and Sandia fled to the nearby sierra. Otermín looted the pueblos of their considerable stores of maize and put them to the torch. For Sandia and Isleta, it was the second time the pueblos were burned in a year. There is no indication that the people returned to Sandia after the Hispanos again withdrew to El Paso. Governor Pedro Reneros Posada (1686–1689) attempted to reconquer New Mexico in 1688, marching as far as Zia, which was apparently the southernmost occupied pueblo at the time. When Vargas conducted his ceremonial reconquest of New Mexico in 1692, he discovered Sandia abandoned and in ruins. Therefore it seems certain that between the time after Otermín burned Sandia in 1681 and the time Reneros visited in 1688, the inhabitants of Sandia had moved.[9]

Sandia oral tradition denies that the people ever left the pueblo, and there may well have been Sandia people who remained in the area or found refuge among other pueblos in New Mexico.[10] Nevertheless, most Tiwas from Sandia moved to Hopi country, where they constructed a pueblo called Payupki on Second Mesa.[11] While these Sandia people were in Hopi country, Hispanos began moving in or expanding their holdings north and south of the old pueblo, which would cause problems when the Sandia people returned to the pueblo from Hopi in 1748. A serious attempt to resettle Sandia took place in 1733, when a group of a hundred mostly Plains Indians who identified themselves as "los Genízaros" petitioned Governor Cruzat y Góngora for a land grant that would encompass the abandoned site of Sandia Pueblo. The governor responded by demanding that each Genízaro identify himself by name and tribe. Only twenty-five responded, and the governor denied their petition without stating his reasons.[12]

In the early 1740s, Franciscan priests traveled to Hopi country with the aim of repatriating Christianized Tiwas, bringing 441 individuals back to

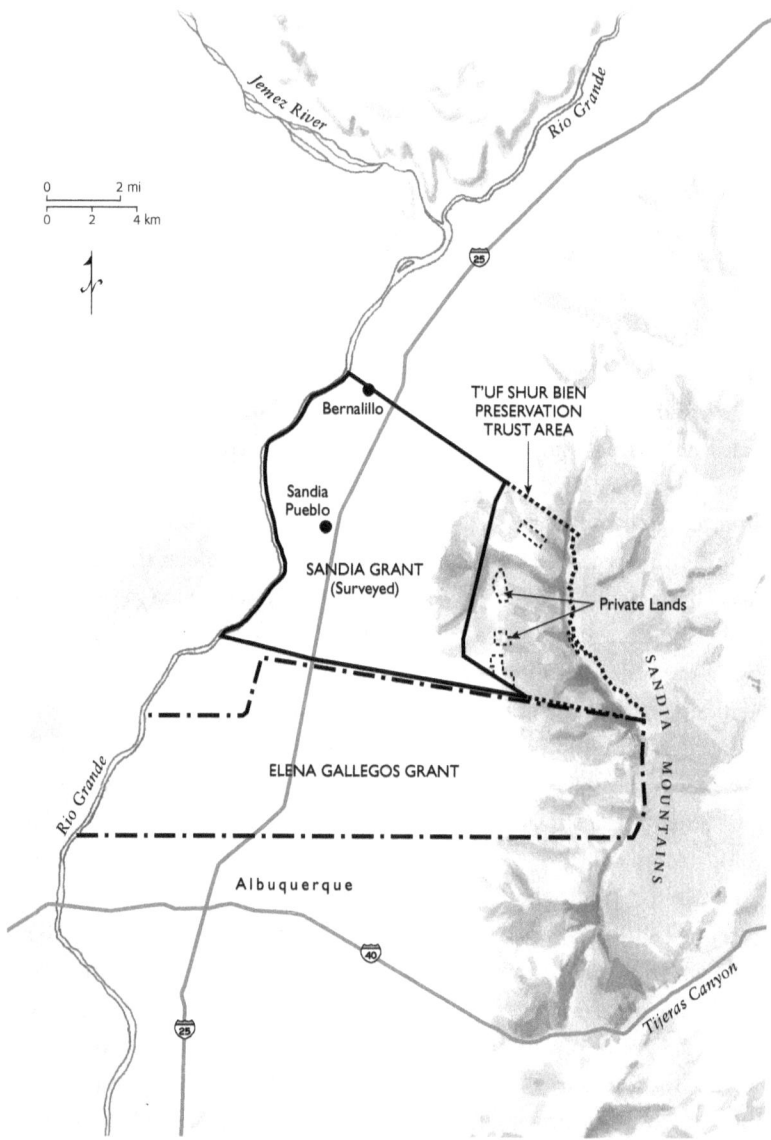

The Sandia Pueblo grant. The solid line shows the 1858 survey. The area within the dotted line (now the T'uf Shur Bien Preservation Trust Area) is what the pueblo contended should have been included within the grant boundaries. Map by Molly O'Halloran.

Jemez and Isleta. Among the group were some from Sandia who asked to be resettled in their own pueblo.[13] In 1748, on the viceroy's instructions and on the urging of Franciscan priest Juan Miguel Menchero, a group of around 350 mostly Sandia Indians and their offspring relocated to the vacant site of the old Sandia Pueblo. On 5 April Governor Codallos y Rabal ordered Lieutenant General Bernardo Bustamante to go to the old pueblo with ten soldiers from the presidio at Santa Fe and "examine the site, carrying out the allotment of lands . . . which should pertain to a formal pueblo of Indians in accordance as the royal regulations prescribed . . . as to the statement of their boundaries."[14] The governor was leaving Bustamante wide discretion in determining the boundaries, partly because Spanish settlers were already crowding in on Sandia land.

Bustamante established the boundaries in several stages, first dealing with the Spaniards on the west side of the pueblo's land and then with those on the north and south. On 14 May Bustamante ordered the three Hispanos with land to the west of Sandia to appear before him. Antonio Salazar, José Jaramillo, and Salvador Jaramillo owned land on the west bank of the Rio Grande that would have been well within the league to the west of the pueblo had the full measurement of 5,000 varas been made in that direction. Although measurements were made on the fourteenth, it seems clear that Bustamante had decided by that time on a variation of the standard Pueblo league, such that Sandia would not receive a full league to the west. As Bustamante put it, "I also informed them [the three Hispanos] that they were relieved from giving the Indians the league to the west, which as the law provides is one league in each direction." Bustamante did not say how this compromise was reached, or who, if anyone, represented the newly established Sandia Pueblo Indians when they gave up this important land within their league. In return for the pueblo's concession, the three Hispanos would allow the Sandia people to cross their land to take the pueblo's animals to pasture. It seems that Bustamante was negotiating the pueblo's boundaries one direction at a time. He had already determined that on the west the Rio Grande would be the boundary. Two days later Bustamante gathered the 350 resettled Sandia Indians and their newly appointed priest, fray Juan José Hernández, and performed a more formal act of possession in which the boundaries were determined to the north, south, and east as follows:

The leagues conceded for a formal pueblo were measured... and extended to the west wind as far as the Rio del Norte, which is the boundary, having no more than 12 cordeles of 120 Castilian varas each, which came to 1,440 varas, and in order to complete those which were lacking in this direction it was necessary to increase the leagues which pertain to the north and south winds equally so that the Spanish settler grantees would not be injured.... The land which is encompassed in these three winds [directions] is all irrigated land... and... I ordered them to place monument markers, mounds of mud and stone of the height of a man, with wooden crosses on top, these being on the north... of the cañada... called "del Agua," and on the south facing the mouth of the Cañada de Juan Tabovo, and on the east the Sierra Madre called Sandia, with which boundaries are the conveniences of pastures, woods, waters and watering places... in order to maintain their stock, both large and small, and a horse herd.[15]

Thus, the Sandia grant boundaries were a combination of natural landmarks (the Sandia Mountain) and a modified Pueblo league. The original of the grant proceedings was placed in the governor's archives, a certified copy was delivered to the pueblo, and a certified copy was sent to the Franciscan archive in Mexico City.

The ink was scarcely dry on the Sandia grant documents when one of Sandia's Spanish neighbors filed a strong protest to one of the boundaries. Salvador Martínez was at his home in Albuquerque when the Sandia grant was made, but he made clear in his petition that he did not renounce title to certain land near the pueblo that he claimed. Martínez asked that this land be restored to him or that he be paid its appraised value. He said being dispossessed of his land left him in "total ruin, because there does not remain one handful of ground for me, in which I can sow seed or pasture my livestock."[16] On the other hand, argued Martínez, the Indians of Sandia had more land than they needed and, in any case, "no law can permit that they take from some to give to others."[17] None of this rhetoric, however, made any impression on Governor Codallos y Rabal. He dismissed Martínez's petition out of hand, countering that Martínez was a trespasser, since his land was only one-quarter of a league from the pueblo's church. Having made the Sandia grant a few months earlier, Codallos y Rabal ruled in favor of the pueblo in this first challenge to one of its boundaries by a neighboring Hispano. Since Martínez had a house and land in Albuquerque, and since his Sandia ranch was so close to the center of the pueblo, the governor had little sympathy for his claim.

A few years after Martínez's protest was laid to rest, the seed of a dispute over Sandia's southern boundary was planted when a tract of land changed hands whose northern boundary was described as "the leagues of the Pueblo of Sandia." That transfer in 1753 was from María López del Castillo to five individuals, one of whom was Julián Rael de Aguilar, the grandson of Alfonso Rael de Aguilar, the protector of Indians in the early 1700s.[18] By 1764 the land had been consolidated into the hands of Julián Rael de Aguilar, who passed it on to his son Eusebio in his will. In the early 1800s Eusebio Rael de Aguilar complained to Governor Joaquín del Real Alencaster (1805–1808) that Sandia was using land outside of its league to the south, thus usurping land that Eusebio claimed.[19] The governor ordered Alcalde Anacleto Miera y Pacheco, son of the cartographer Bernardo Miera y Pacheco, to measure "the league that pertained to the Indians of the said pueblo, according to what the other pueblos of the province enjoy."[20] Miera y Pacheco died before he could execute the order, and nothing came of Rael's complaint, but this was the first of many times when the boundaries called for in the Sandia grant document were ignored in favor of boundaries determined as they were for other pueblos, that is, a league of 5,000 varas in each direction.

By 1821 the dispute was still unresolved, so Eusebio Rael de Aguilar filed another complaint with his local ayuntamiento, or town council, claiming that his land extended "up to the leagues that are conceded to the Indians, as is the case with the other pueblos."[21] The ayuntamiento ruled in Rael's favor, stating that as to "the excess of the league that Sandia Pueblo has . . . the Indians are not showing anything that proves it is theirs."[22] Accordingly, the ayuntamiento was of the opinion that Sandia should "be given their leagues and Rael should be returned what belongs to him."[23] Sandia appealed this ruling to the commanding general in Durango, where Ignacio María Sánchez Vergara, the former protector of Indians, argued on Rael's behalf. Sánchez Vergara was personally interested in land within the Sandia league and was later accused of fraud, "bad faith[,] and crookedness [when he] tore a hole in the title of ownership with the aim of obtaining half the land for himself."[24] In 1821 he also wrote to Governor Melgares asking whether he could petition the ayuntamiento for a grant "within the confines of the league of the pueblo of Sandia."[25] Melgares answered that it would not be proper for Sánchez Vergara to submit such a petition. There is no record that he did, but he continued to be involved in litigation over Sandia land throughout the 1820s. In later litigation it appears that Sánchez Vergara did acquire land within the boundaries of Sandia Pueblo, but in two cases in the late 1820s his role was to advocate on behalf of others who claimed land inside Sandia's boundaries.[26]

Sánchez Vergara argued in Durango that Rael's land was "outside of the leagues that by law belong to the pueblos."[27] He was confusing the issue by claiming that Sandia was entitled only to a standard 5,000 vara league rather than the augmented league to the north and south as called for in the Sandia grant. Without hearing Sandia's position, the lawyer advising the commanding general recommended in favor of Rael, stating his opinion "that the judge of the pueblo should proceed directly to measure the league" and then place Rael "in possession of the land that may be surplus."[28] Governor Narbona ordered Alcalde Miera y Pacheco to remeasure a standard league and to give any additional land to Rael. Rael died soon after the order was issued, and the remeasurement of the league did not take place at that time. Had the governor's order been followed to the letter at that point, Sandia would have lost at least the 1,780 varas added to the southern boundary.[29] The southern boundary was eventually remeasured in 1825, but only 5,000 varas of a league were measured. At that point, the additional 1,780 varas granted to Sandia in 1748 were declared to be the property of the heirs of Eusebio Rael de Aguilar.[30]

Sandia could not let this decision stand and appealed to the Supreme Court in Mexico City. Representatives of the pueblo traveled to Mexico City and filed a petition claiming "the league and a half of land, the most useful land that unquestionably pertains to us on our southern boundary."[31] In addition, the Sandias argued that the "land granted to them already should be expanded."[32] The pueblo members also introduced affidavits from Hispano settlers at Bernalillo, who testified about the history of the making of the Sandia grant, stating that in the years since the making of the grant "the land in the course of litigation had no other owners than . . . [Sandia] pueblo." The witnesses mentioned the Rio Grande as the west boundary but did not discuss the other boundaries. One witness, Rafael Miera, testified that he was present at a meeting between Sánchez Vergara and Eusebio Rael during which he saw the former altering the Sandia grant documents by removing certain words and inserting other ones.[33] The Supreme Court remanded the case to New Mexico.

The mutilation of the Sandia grant documents and the existence of documents showing a chain of title for Rael was a recurring theme in litigation between the pueblo and its neighbors. In February 1826 Sandia petitioned Governor Narbona through its advocate, Francisco Miera y Pacheco, to require Rael's heirs and Sánchez Vergara to produce the documents on which they were relying.[34] There was no response to this petition, but four months later Narbona turned down a request from Rael's heirs, speaking through their attorney, Juan González, to build a house on the contested land. Narbona said that Sandia still claimed the land and suggested that the pueblo and Rael's heirs work out a settlement.[35] Narbona made several requests to the central authorities in Mexico City for clarification of the laws of the Spanish Cortes dealing with pueblo land and would not rule against Sandia as long as the pueblo still claimed the land and was not overruled by higher authority.

On 13 February 1841 in Mexico City, José María Moquino, Andrés de la Candelaria, and Antonio de la Cruz, who were all from Sandia Pueblo, alleged that Sánchez Vergara removed two pages from the grant document and appropriated one and a half leagues of the best land.[36] The alcalde of Sandia, Juan Ramón Rael, stated that Sánchez Vergara tore the grant document in an effort to obtain half of the pueblo's land, adding that Sánchez Vergara was shiftless, lived by intrigue, and was unable to pay his expenses. These charges, although probably true, were not substantiated because the case of *Rael v. Sandia* was never resolved. On 20 July 1841 Governor Manuel Armijo (1837–1844) assigned the case to "the appropriate judge," but there is no record of a decision.

Sandia received the first grant to a resettled pueblo north of El Paso. It differed from the four-square-league measurements in several respects. First, it was based on an order from the viceroy through the intermediary of a priest. The thrust of the viceroy's order was to assess the needs of the resettled pueblo and then to give the Indians "water, land for pasture and cultivation in abundance . . . [as well as] oxen, seeds, tools, and other things . . . in a commodious place."[37] The act of possession by Bustamante y Tagle complied with the viceroy's order by giving the Indians of Sandia irrigable land as well as "pastures, woods, water, and watering places in abundance to raise cattle, small livestock, and horses."[38] The interpretation of such orders specifying the amount of land a Sandia was entitled to had to be flexible in order to try to balance the land needed with the land available. It was important to the Spanish government that the Indians of Sandia have an abundance of land to fulfill their needs so that they would stay at their new location and provide protection from Apache and Comanche attacks for the settlements in the Albuquerque area.

When the bishop of Durango, Pedro Tamarón y Romeral, visited Sandia in 1760 he noted the presence of both Hopis and Tiwas at the pueblo.[39] When fray Francisco Atanasio Domínguez visited in 1776, he recorded a description of the principal landforms that has particular relevance to the question of the eastern boundary of the Sandia grant, especially with respect to nomenclature.[40]

> From Santo Domingo one travels south some 7 leagues downstream along the whole meadow of the Rio del Norte, which is on the east, in sight of the said river. The ridge of hills, which I mentioned in the aforesaid pueblo, is always to the left, and at this point the hills run along below the foot of the sierra and in front of it. At the end of the said 7 leagues one finds the pueblo and mission of Nuestra Señora de los Dolores de Sandia. It is 16 good leagues from Santa Fe and is south, quarter south-southwest, of the villa, on the highway like the foregoing mission.
>
> The mission is new, founded for the Indians of the province of Moqui who were reduced by Father Menchero in the year 1746. It stands in the middle of the plain on the same site as the old mission, which was destroyed in the general uprising of this kingdom. To the east is a sierra called Sandia because there is a pueblo and mission of this name here. Although it does have a connection with the sierra of Santa Fe very high up (via some little hills and mounds), we cannot properly take it to be a continuation of the latter in view of the great distance and few indications; rather we shall call it a Sierra Madre, since it spreads down for a long way with the characteristics of a mother range. The Río del Norte is about half a league to the west among poplar groves.

Describing the prominent ridge located to the west of and below the Sandia Mountains, Father Domínguez clearly distinguished between a ridge of hills (the *cerros* forming the lower ridge) and the sierra (the Sandia Mountains). Domínguez specifically stated that "to the east is a sierra called Sandia" and more precisely delineated what he intended to convey by further defining it, saying "we shall call it a Sierra Madre, since it spreads down for a long way with

Sandia Pueblo grant with lines "pinched out" by Ignacio María
Sánchez Vergara (SANM I, SGP, Sandia Pueblo, image 008).
Courtesy New Mexico Records Center and Archives.

the characteristics of a mother range." Given this contemporary example, there can be no doubt that this usage was current during the eighteenth century or that these terms were applied in any other way to these physical features with respect to the limits of the Sandia grant. Domínguez noted that the Indian population of Sandia was made up of two nations. Most were Tiwa, and there were also a very few Hopis. Each group spoke its own language and communicated through interpreters. Despite their differences, as far as the Franciscan was concerned, they had the same customs. The main body of the pueblo consisted of three house blocks east of the church and two small plazas to the south. The Hopis lived apart from the Tiwas north of the church. Their location left them exposed to raiders, and in 1775 Comanches attacked them and killed around thirty.[41]

In 1846 the invasion of New Mexico by troops under the command of Stephen Watts Kearny brought a new regime under which Sandia was to be administered. A few years later, when the surveyor general of New Mexico was established to adjudicate all land grants, including Pueblo grants, Sandia submitted its 1748 grant to Surveyor General William Pelham for confirmation. The document filed contains damaged and altered portions, but two other copies of the Sandia grant documents are more complete.

The first copy is in the New Mexico State Records Center and Archives, which houses a series of documents referred to as the "Proceedings in the Concession of the Pueblo of Sandia grant, 1748," found in the Spanish Archives of New Mexico and assigned the number 848. The proceedings consist of the following documents: (1) an undated petition from fray Juan Miguel Menchero to the governor of New Mexico at the time (Joaquín Codallos y Rabal) asking him to order the repopulation of Sandia; (2) Governor Codallos y Rabal's proceedings of 5 April 1748 commissioning Bernardo Antonio de Bustamante y Tagle to carry out the granting of land for Sandia Pueblo; (3) Codallos y Rabal's certification of having returned a viceregal dispatch to Father Menchero; (4) and the proceedings of 14–16 May 1748 by the officiating justice, Bernardo Antonio de Bustamante y Tagle, granting possession of the land to Sandia through fray Juan Hernández, as its minister, and setting forth the boundaries for Sandia Pueblo.[42]

On 20 May 1748, the first certified copy of these four documents was prepared, signed by Bernardo Antonio de Bustamante y Tagle, and witnessed by Isidro Sánchez de Tagle and Pedro Tafoya. Sandia retained this copy until it was presented to the office of the surveyor general of New Mexico, on 16 October 1856. It is now found in the New Mexico State Records Center and Archives in the Surveyor General of New Mexico Records, Pueblo of Sandia, Report P. This certified retained copy includes the last line of Father Menchero's undated petition, the rest of the text, which would have been on a previous page, having been lost. This sentence is followed by the complete text of the remaining three documents. Portions of this copy have become illegible and torn at significant places, apparent evidence of Sánchez Vergara's malicious altering of the document. This suggests that this copy was the one the pueblo retained and delivered to U.S. authorities in Santa Fe in 1856.[43]

A second certified copy was also made on 20 May 1748. It too is signed by Bustamante y Tagle and witnessed by Sánchez de Tagle and Tafoya.[44] As a matter of course, a copy was sent to authorities in Mexico City, a fact noted on the last page of the original grant documents.[45] Today this certified copy can be found in the *fondos reservados* (special collections) of the Biblioteca Nacional de México at the Universidad Nacional Autónoma de México in Mexico City. It forms a part of the Archivo Franciscano and has been assigned the number 28/547 (caja 28, documento 547).[46] This is a verbatim copy of the original series of documents found in Spanish Archives of New Mexico, and is, therefore, more complete than the copy found in the Surveyor General of New Mexico Records. It contains the entire text of Father Menchero's initial petition, as well as the complete texts of the other three documents, including all of the proceedings related to the Sandia grant. Since no date of receipt was recorded on the document, it has not been possible to determine exactly when it arrived in Mexico City. It is possible, however, to closely approximate the time the documents were received at the Archive of the Holy Gospel Province of the Franciscan Order, of which the Custody of New Mexico was a dependent.

Fray Francisco Antonio de la Rosa Figueroa was named archivist of the Holy Gospel Province in 1753. His first inventory of the contents of the archive was completed in 1755 and included the first 119 *cajas* (boxes).[47] Father Rosa Figueroa made several annotations directly on this copy. Across the top of the document, he indicated that it was a copy and where it was to be filed.[48] He also indicated that it dealt with documents executed in the Custody of New Mexico on 20 May 1748. A longer annotation runs vertically along the length of the right margin:

Papers and legal instruments relating jointly and severally to the new repopulation of the mission called Sandia; they are arranged by date of their execution and all belong in Box 70 of this Archive of this holy province, in File 2, in number 47.

This suggests that the Mexico City copy arrived at the Franciscan archive and was filed by 1755. This copy is in the same hand as the certified retained copy in the Surveyor General of New Mexico Records. It is in far better physical condition, however, and has not suffered the same deterioration from excessive handling. Those few damaged portions in the surveyor general's copy are clear in the Mexico City copy and are verbatim copies of the original in the Spanish Archives of New Mexico.

Also of note in regard to these three sets of documents is that all of them that were executed before and signed by Bustamante y Tagle were written in the same blue ink. Moreover, all three documents were written on plain paper (with no tax stamp) bearing the same watermark.

The Surveyor General Records also contain the transcription of the original Spanish in modern handwriting and David V. Whiting's English translation. In preparing his transcript, Whiting worked from the copy Sánchez Vergara had altered (SG Report P), which further bolsters the idea that this was the copy of the grant that Sandia presented as proof of ownership. The unaltered original was probably still undisturbed in the archives. Whiting found it very difficult to reconstruct the missing text. Sometimes he guessed at missing words, and sometimes he indicated lacunae with asterisks. There is no evidence that he consulted the unaltered copy from the archives to fill in the gaps.

While Whiting's transcription is essentially faithful to the altered copy from which he worked, his translation differed considerably from the original Spanish and from his own transcription. On several occasions he changed the measurements recorded in the original document. For example, where his English translation reads "two lines of fifty and twenty castilian varas," the correct translation of the original is "twelve cords of 120 Castilian varas each." He also added geographical references that did not appear in the original such as, "the Maygua hill, opposite the spring of the Carrisito," which should have read "facing the mouth of the Cañada de Juan Tabovo." A particularly significant addition reads "two boundaries amounting to seven thousand three hundred and eighty castillian varas, the league toward the west being four thousand seven hundred and sixty varas less." This passage did not appear in the unaltered original. Whiting's translation indicated that the distance from the center of the pueblo to the river was 240 varas leaving a shortfall (from a standard league) of 4,760 varas. Following the procedure of adding land to the north and south would have added 2,380 varas in each direction instead of the 1,780 varas implied in the original grant document, a difference of 600 varas in each direction. Whiting's motivation for deviating so much in the translation of his transcription is unclear. Hordes presented information from a fragment of a document that was part of a complaint by Miguel Antonio Lovato on behalf of Sandia against its Hispano neighbors at the end of the Mexican period.[49] This document appears to be unique in its mention of the "loma de Maygua" and "Ojo del Carrisito," which suggests that someone familiar with these place names influenced Whiting to alter his translation in the pueblo's favor. Had Whiting compared the damaged copy of the document with the original in the archives, it would have been a relatively simple matter to supply the missing text.[50] The grant documents state that the leagues to the north and south (5,000 varas) were to be increased to complete those lacking to the west. Measuring only 1,440 varas to the west left a shortfall of 3,600 varas. If that figure was divided equally as called for in the document, it was necessary to measure and add 1,780 leagues each to the north and south. This means that the measurement to the north and south would have been 6,780 varas in each direction, but this adjusted figure is not mentioned in the grant document.

Surveyor General William Pelham forwarded the Sandia claim to the General Land Office in Washington, D.C., on 30 November 1856 with his recommendation that the grant be confirmed. Congress confirmed the grant to Sandia on 22 December 1858 on the basis of Whiting's translation. Deputy Surveyor John W. Garretson was selected to survey the Sandia grant. Garretson surveyed the northern pueblos of Tesuque, Pojoaque, San Ildefonso, and Santa Clara before he began the Sandia survey. Unlike his successor, Reuben Clements, Garretson had extensive experience surveying Indian pueblos. Pelham selected Garretson "because of his long experience and faithful fulfillment of earlier contracts awarded him."[51] The two were friends in Arkansas and became in-laws when Garretson married Pelham's wife's sister in September 1846. When Pelham became surveyor general of New Mexico in 1854 he invited Garretson to work for him, and from 1855 to 1858 Pelham contracted with no one else. A Santa Fe newspaper accused Pelham of nepotism, but Garretson's marriage ended in divorce in January 1858, so there was no need for an investigation. Garretson initiated a survey of Sandia, and his field notes are on record, but on 20 September 1859 he asked to be relieved of his duties. When Garretson first contracted to survey Sandia it was one of seventeen pueblo surveys and five community grants he agreed to complete.

Garretson's surveys were to be performed according to instructions from Thomas A. Hendricks, General Land Office commissioner, issued on 23 April 1859, which called for copious field notes and specified a method for locating natural objects such as Sandia Mountain. The surveyor was to attempt to have these boundaries pointed out to him, and if there was any doubt about the location of the natural features he was to report this to the General Land Office and await further instructions. To obtain help in locating boundaries and "to protect [the Indians] in their rights while the boundaries are being run," Pelham requested that the New Mexico Indian Affairs superintendent assign an agent to accompany the surveyor. Diego Archuleta was appointed, and he accompanied Garretson on the survey of fourteen pueblos. They started surveying Sandia but had to postpone it because of overlaps with "the settlement of Corrales and Bernalillo and the overlap of Mr. Miguel A. Lovato." Their instructions told them "to advise the citizens who may be found . . . occupying any portion of Indian lands that the government intended to remove them," but it does not appear that they were compensated for this work. Garretson did not mention this in his resignation, stating simply that "I shall not be able to finish my contract before winter sets in." Besides his concern about not having time to finish the Sandia survey, Garretson must have been deeply affected by the tragedy that struck his surveying crew in September 1859 when his compass man, William Drew, drowned while attempting to cross the Rio Grande near Cochiti.[52]

Surveyor General Pelham attempted to involve the Pueblo Indians in the surveying of their grants, even suggesting that one of his clerks be assigned to the deputy surveyor to take testimony on the ground during a survey. The acting general land office commissioner, Joseph S. Wilson, turned down this proposal, however, and the arrangement with Archuleta to accompany the deputy surveyor expired by the time Clements was hired to complete the Sandia grant survey. Clements, known as Colonel Clements from his Civil War service, had minimal experience surveying Indian pueblos, but he had had encounters with Plains Indians, mostly unpleasant. While Garretson was surveying the northern pueblos in New Mexico, Comanches who were driven from Texas captured Clements and a fellow surveyor with whom he was surveying in the Canadian River area. The Comanches must have taken umbrage when they saw government agents surveying territory they considered theirs. Clements was eventually released on condition that he leave the area, but he had "lost [his] enthusiasm for working in risk-filled areas." He was the perfect candidate to complete the Sandia survey in record time without any contact with Sandia Indians that might slow him down.[53]

The Sandia survey was carried out in only four days. Clements took few field notes and made numerous mistakes in locating the boundaries called for in the grant document. The troubles that beset Sandia for the next 130 years stemmed mostly from the incompetent Clements survey of November 1859. In contrast to Garretson, who talked to adjoining and encroaching landowners and had Archuleta with him to help locate the boundaries and protect the rights of the Sandia Indians, Clements performed the survey without giving notice to or seeking help from the pueblo. Clements reported that he and his crew walked the north boundary on 8 November, the west boundary on 9 November, and the south boundary on 10 November. The east boundary of Sandia Mountain was likewise surveyed in one day, 12 November 1859. Clements was surveying the boundaries set forth in the grant: a straight line on the north, the Rio Grande on the west, another roughly straight line with a slight angle on the south, and the Sierra Madre called Sandia on the east. While there were many errors in the surveys of the north, west, and south boundaries, the location of the east boundary was downright inept. Surveying practice has always called for the crest or summit of a mountain to be surveyed unless specific reference is made to some other part of the feature, such as the foothills. Clements, however, did not survey the foothills or the crest, although the line he surveyed was closer to the foothills. He did not even say he was surveying the foothills, calling it instead "the meanders of the Sandia Mountains." In fact, it appears that the eastern boundary was not surveyed at all; it seems to have been little more than a line drawn on paper, not a survey on the ground.[54]

Clements did not survey a meander line, since a meander line is not a boundary line and is almost always associated with a river, such as the western boundary in this case, which was the Rio Grande. In surveying parlance a meander line is run "for the purpose of defining the sinuosities of the shore or bank of a body of water [like a river]."[55] The meander line is not the boundary; rather, the river is the boundary. Clements's line was an almost straight line (after a slight lip on the north and a more pronounced lip on the south) almost due north. The east boundary line was not surveyed as part of a four-square-league grant, as would be argued later, or Clements would have said so. It was simply a crude method of completing a survey. It was as if Clements merely drew a line connecting the northeast corner and the southeast corner. The difference between Clements's incompetent survey and an accurate survey of the crest was, as Earl G. Harrington's survey of the Sandia grant in 1915 shows, about 10,000 acres.[56]

Evidence that Clements simply drew a line connecting the northeast and southeast boundaries rather than surveying the eastern boundary comes from Harrington's resurvey. Harrington found that Clements failed to monument his survey correctly, failed to follow the surveying instructions given to Garretson, and, most important, failed to survey the eastern boundary accurately so that it could be located on the ground.[57] An error of closure is an error in accuracy when a survey is rerun on the ground. Harrington discovered that Clements's error of closure was approximately 2,000 feet. Today an acceptable error of closure is a 1-foot error for every 7,500-foot run. In fact, Clements's survey was wholly incompetent, because the east line could not be located on the ground.[58]

Nevertheless, Pelham certified Clements's field notes on 12 January 1860 and sent the field notes and sketch maps to the Commissioner of the General Land Office later that month. The field notes were approved in October 1860, and a plat was submitted to the General Land Office in June 1861, which called for Sandia Mountain to be the eastern boundary but surveyed the boundary near the foothills rather than the summit. The Clements survey showed the Sandia grant contained 24,034 acres, which was the basis of a patent issued to Sandia in November 1864.[59]

◆ ◆ ◆ ◆

The Clements survey of the Sandia grant, the Whiting translation of the grant document, and the three versions of the 1748 grant document all came under intense scrutiny when Sandia sought a legal remedy for its eastern boundary dispute, claiming the crest rather than the foothills of the Sandia Mountain. During most of the twentieth century, the U.S. Forest Service administered the disputed area as a wilderness that had substantial inholdings of private land. In 1983 Sandia requested that the Department of the Interior resurvey the grant, especially in regard to the eastern boundary. The request set off two decades of legal actions that eventually drew in the U.S. Department of the Interior and the U.S. Department of Agriculture, Bernalillo and Sandoval counties, the Sandia Mountain Coalition (private landowners), Sandia Peak Tramway Company, the U.S. District Court for the District of Columbia, and the U.S. Congress. For five years the simple request to resurvey the eastern boundary of the Sandia grant was handled administratively.[60]

Unfortunately, Sandia's claim that its eastern boundary was the crest of Sandia Peak was discussed in the press as much as in the interior and agriculture departments. The Department of the Interior issued a draft opinion in 1986 stating that Sandia's claim was meritorious. The secretary of the interior sent the opinion to the Department of Agriculture, requesting that the matter be kept confidential until the paperwork was completed. Instead, the Albuquerque office of the Forest Service improperly released the draft opinion favoring Sandia to the public with a press package claiming the pueblo intended to eject private landowners. The opposition that was generated and the political pressure placed on the secretary of the interior caused him to reverse his position and issue an opinion rejecting the pueblo's claim in December 1988. That opinion, prepared by the solicitor of the Department of the Interior, Ralph Tarr, became known as the Tarr Opinion. It concluded that the secretary of the interior had no power to undertake a resurvey of the Sandia grant.[61]

The government then began a publicity campaign in support of the Tarr Opinion, which raised fears that if Sandia regained title to Sandia Mountain, private landowners in the area would be evicted or lose access rights to their land. Sandia tried to allay the fears of private landowners by putting forth its side of the story:

> The pueblo realizes non-Indians now live on the 600 acres of private land within the claim, and "we are not claiming those lands," [Sandia governor, Joseph] Lujan said. The pueblo is willing to issue legal deeds or guarantees of access that sign away Indian control of private homes in the claim area, he said. . . . The pueblo will not interfere with the access to

the private properties [and] the pueblo will not impose any property taxes on privately owned lands. The pueblo *is* seeking title to the 8,800 acres of National Forest and Wilderness within the claim. The Indians have asked the federal government to continue managing the lands as Wilderness and National Forest, but with the understanding that ultimate title rests with the pueblo. Lujan said the surveying error illegally deprived the Sandias of land granted the pueblo by the king of Spain in 1748.[62]

Dismayed by the publicity and political pressure surrounding the Tarr Opinion's rejection of Sandia's claim to Sandia Peak, the pueblo filed suit in federal court in Washington, D.C., on 7 December 1994. The pueblo asked the court to reverse the Tarr Opinion and require the Department of the Interior to resurvey the grant, so as to locate the eastern boundary on the crest of the mountain. Bernalillo County, the Sandia Peak Tramway Company, and a large coalition of private landowners all intervened (even though the pueblo repeatedly made it clear that it was making no claim to ownership of any private landholdings within the area that it contended had been wrongfully excluded from its grant). The suit became a case of dueling experts, involving many of the leading scholars of the Spanish colonial period in New Mexico, each of whom offered his or her interpretation of the original land-grant documents, Spanish law of the period pertaining to pueblo lands, and the intent of the Spanish authorities in setting aside land for Sandia in 1748.

Much attention was focused by the historical experts on the eastern boundary call: "on the east the Sierra Madre called Sandia" and, more particularly, on the meaning of "Sierra Madre." An examination of the meaning of this term outside of the context of the grant results in battling etymologies. No early modern Spanish etymological dictionary treats "sierra madre" as a single term. Francisco del Rosal's *Diccionario etimológico: Alfabeto primero de origen y etimología de todos los vocablos originales de la lengua castellana* (1601) glosses "sierra" as "montaña" (mountain).[63] John Stevens's 1706 Spanish-English dictionary defines "sierra" by its most obvious metaphorical relationship: "*Sierra*, a Saw, Lat. *Serra*. Also a Mountain, so call'd, because of its Ridges rising and falling like a Saw."[64] By contrast, 1737 *Diccionario de autoridades*, the forerunner of the dictionary of the Real Academia Española, explains that "sierra" refers to "la cordillera de montes, ó peñascos cortados" (the range of mountains or broken crags), so called "por lo que se semeja à los dientes de la sierrra" (because of their similarity to the teeth of a saw). Del Rosal glosses "madre" as coming from the Latin "matre," ablative of "mater" (mother).[65] Stevens gives both mother from the Latin "mater" and "matrix" (womb) as meanings of "madre."[66] The *Diccionario de autoridades* gives the same meanings as Stevens.

No etymological dictionary examined to date defines "sierra madre" as "main ridge," but Whiting was interpreting the term within the context of the grant rather than merely translating words. Whether one believes that "sierra madre" means "mountain" or "mountain range," one only needs to stand at Sandia to fully comprehend why Whiting chose the term "main ridge." From the vantage point of the pueblo, directly in one's line of sight is a not inconsiderable ridge rising to 8,000 feet in elevation. Looming above this feature and rising to an elevation of 10,400 feet is the crest of the Sandia Mountains. It seems logical that Whiting was simply making a clear distinction between the lower mountain and the higher, main ridge of the Sandia Mountains.

Understanding what Hispanos meant in New Mexico in 1748, then, becomes a question of knowing how they described geographical features employed as boundary calls.

> Under Spanish and Mexican legal custom, when a mountain was a boundary the summit was taken as the dividing line, unless otherwise indicated. If this had not been true, two land grants bounded by the same mountain range would not adjoin one another but would be separated by the land comprising the mountain range. Since the mountainside was needed by both the grants for summer grazing and for gathering wood, the granting authorities intended to include the mountain lands within each grant.[67]

The 1766 Piedra Lumbre grant is a case in point of a mountain serving as a boundary between two adjoining grants. Pedro Martín Serrano received this grant located in present-day Río Arriba County with the Cerro Pedernal as its southern boundary. A subsequent grant (the Polvadera grant) cited the boundary of Martín Serrano's grant as its northern grant without specific reference to the mountain. Only by extending the boundaries of each grant to the top of the Cerro Pedernal would each grantee have access to the resources of the mountain. Otherwise, neither grant would include the mountain, a situation clearly not intended by the granting authorities.[68]

Most grants with mountains as boundaries were surveyed to the crest, such as Gervasio Nolan, Vigil, St. Vrain, Maxwell, and Sangre de Cristo grants. In his interpretation of the eastern boundary of the Sandia grant, Luis Navarro García (then *catedrático* in the Departamento de Historia de América at the University of Seville and one of the leading experts on the history of Spain in the Americas) concurred that when a mountain was a boundary call its crest was taken to be the demarcation of the boundary. He added that how such a boundary was demarcated was particularly significant in areas of scarce water sources because rainfall flowed downward from the crest.[69] Writing about the Elena Gallegos grant, which adjoins the Sandia grant on the south, historian Marc Simmons (a noted expert on Spanish institutions in colonial New Mexico) stated that the "eastern limit of the grant was identified only as the Sandia Mountains, by which the colonial settlers understood, the summit of the range."[70] Anthropologist Peter Whiteley made a similar observation, stating that "unless these boundaries specify '*el pie*' (the foot), or another specific locale on a mountain, they have always been interpreted to refer to the crest."[71]

There are numerous examples in grant documents of something other than the summit of a mountain being intended as a grant boundary. In each such instance the delimiting language is quite specific, as Whiteley pointed out. Among the terms commonly used were "ceja" (brow), "falda" (skirt), and "pie" (foot). The 1767 Bartolomé Fernández grant established boundaries "por la parte del oriente la orilla de una mesa montuosa y por el poniente la ceja de una mesa corta" (on the east the edge of a timbered mesa and on the west the brow of a low mesa).[72] The 1744 Peñasco Largo grant gave the boundaries as "por la parte del norte y sur con las faldas de ambos sierras" (on the north and south the lower slopes of both mountains).[73] The 1793 Ojo Caliente grant called for boundaries "por el oriente el pie de las lomas y por el poniente el pie de las otras lomas de la otra banda del río" (on the east the foot of the hills and on the west the foot of the other hills on the other side of the river).[74] Thus the boundary call, "the Sierra Madre called Sandia," refers to the main ridge of Sandia Mountain and should have been surveyed to the crest.

District judge Harold Greene first ruled that the secretary did in fact have the authority to correct the survey if it were found to be erroneous.[75] Then, in a second, unpublished opinion, he concluded that the Tarr Opinion placed an unreasonably high burden on the pueblo and gave short shrift to the well-established legal doctrine that federal statutes affecting rights of Indian tribes (such as the 1858 act by which Congress confirmed the Sandia grant) should be interpreted such that any ambiguities (as, in this case, the question of where the east boundary of the grant should be located) are resolved in favor of the tribes. He ordered the matter remanded to the Department of the Interior for reconsideration of the survey issue.[76] The United States, Bernalillo County, and the Sandia Mountain Coalition appealed Judge Greene's decision, but while the appeal was pending the pueblo entered into settlement negotiations with the parties that lasted for two years. Ultimately, on 4 April 2000, the pueblo reached an agreement with the Justice Department, the Department of Agriculture (the pueblo's main adversary within the federal government), and the Sandia Peak Tram Company (although the county and the coalition dropped out of the negotiations) that required congressional ratification by 15 November, 2002. The settlement provided that the Forest Service would continue to have management responsibility over the disputed federal land and would continue to manage it under the laws applicable to wilderness areas. The pueblo would have special access privileges and the authority to regulate traditional and cultural uses of the land. The United States then asked the court of appeals to dismiss the appeal, arguing that the district court decision sent the survey issue back to the Department of the Interior and was thus not a final appealable decision. The court of appeals agreed.[77]

On 19 January 2001, the last day of the Clinton administration, Department of Interior solicitor John Leshy issued an opinion entitled "Eastern Boundary of the Sandia Pueblo Grant," in which he rejected the Tarr Opinion's determinations as to the correctness of the survey of the Sandia grant eastern boundary and concluded that the boundary should have been located on the crest of the mountain. Leshy said, however, that rather than move forward with a resurvey, the Department of the Interior should wait to see if Congress would act on the proposed settlement. It was not until April 2002 that a joint hearing on a bill to approve the settlement was held before the Senate Committee on Energy and Natural Resources, chaired by Senator Jeff Bingaman of New Mexico, and the Committee on Indian Affairs, chaired by Senator Daniel Inouye of Hawaii and vice-chaired by Senator Ben Nighthorse Campbell of Colorado. The extensive hearings were prompted by the settlement agreement and by the Leshy Opinion; Leshy, who had since become a law professor, was one of the main proponents of the settlement agreement. Leshy stated that there is precedent in settling Indian claims for giving Indian tribes outright title. Congress did this at the Blue Lake for Taos 20 years ago. There is precedent for giving Indians in disputed claims some sort of joint management responsibility. Congress did that with the Havasupi Indians in the Grand Canyon in 1975. Congress did that 2 years ago with the Timbashaw Indians in Death Valley National Park.... Congress has a golden opportunity before it to resolve a long-festering issue in a wholly satisfactory way.[78]

Testifying in opposition to the settlement agreement was Stanley M. Hordes, hired by the Forest Service in 1995 to investigate the Sandia Pueblo boundaries. In his opinion the Spanish government intended Sandia to receive only four square leagues of land (about 17,350 acres) and no more. This put him at odds with Judge Greene's decision, with former solicitor Leshy, and with most of the historical witnesses. The members of the joint committees and, in particular, Chairman Inouye seemed to agree with former solicitor Leshy that the 1859 Clements survey was incorrect with respect to the eastern boundary. As Sandia governor Stewart Paisano pointed out, after the courts held that Sandia owned the mountain, signing the settlement agreement required some "painful concessions." For Paisano it was the spiritual value of the mountain that was most important: "[The mountain] is central to our beliefs, practices and prayers. It is the only source of resources needed for religious ceremonies. Our spiritual leaders routinely make pilgrimages to the shrines on the mountain and leave offerings. These shrines are located on the mountain from the foothills all the way up to the crest."[79] It was these traditional cultural and religious uses of the mountain that would be protected by the settlement agreement.

As a result of the hearings and the mostly favorable testimony on the bill, Congress passed the T'uf Shur Bien Preservation Trust Area Act in September 2002, contradicting earlier predictions.[80] The act provides for protection in perpetuity of "the Wilderness and National Forest character of the Area and prohibits gambling of any kind, mineral production, timber production, and new uses . . . to which the Pueblo objects," as well as uses prohibited by the Wilderness Act. Sandia was given "free and unrestricted access to the Area for traditional and cultural uses," the right most important to the pueblo.

But exactly how the phrase "cultural uses" was to be defined was not entirely clear.[81] The act definitely covered ceremonial uses, such as pilgrimages to place offerings on the many shrines on the mountain. It definitely covered the gathering of herbs and other resources needed in Sandia religious ceremonies, but hunting rights were not spelled out and were understood differently by the parties. From the pueblo's point of view, "hunting is not a sport. . . . Hunting is part of our culture and our tradition. . . . It bears a source of food and a sense of healing."[82] The New Mexico Department of Fish and Game took a different view; it wanted to regulate hunting on the mountain and to be abe to issue licenses to non-Indians if sufficient game was found to exist. This is one of the "painful concessions" the pueblo had to make. By agreeing to relinquish its title to the mountain as determined by Judge Greene, Sandia had to subject itself to regulation by the New Mexico Department of Fish and Game.

In addition to wanting to protect the mountain for cultural and traditional uses, Sandia also sought to preserve the mountain's wilderness character. To make this possible, the act gives the pueblo "the right to consent or withhold consent to new uses, the right to consultation regarding modified uses, and the right to consultation regarding the management and preservation of the area." Most important, if for some reason the government wished to allow uses that had been prohibited or attempted to deny the pueblo access for traditional and cultural uses, it would have to "compensate the Pueblo as if the Pueblo had held a fee title interest" in the land. With this strong provision Sandia hoped, in Governor Paisano's words, "to protect and preserve what has been rightfully ours for centuries. That is important to us as a people so that we can continue in existence for future generations."[83]

Congress approved the settlement in 2003. Known as the T'uf Shur Bien Preservation Trust Area Act, the legislation calls for the area to remain undeveloped.[84] The act implies that Sandia Pueblo previously owned the mountain and that its ownership has been relinquished. Although the Forest Service still manages the land, Sandia is a comanager of it and has special-use privileges there.[85]

Santa Clara People protesting survey of Cañada de Santa Clara grant. Drawing by Glen Strock.

CHAPTER 5

Santa Clara Pueblo and Its Struggle to Protect Santa Clara Canyon

With an estimated current membership of over one thousand, Santa Clara is one of the largest of the six northern Tewa-speaking pueblos.[1] Historically, its population has varied—its low point was 134 in 1790 just after a smallpox epidemic killed more than 500 Indians in the Santa Clara and San Juan vicinity, and its high point was 1,204 in 1974, according to U.S. Bureau of Indian Affairs records. The population typically remained under 325 until the late 1920s, when it began to gradually increase.[2] The ancestors of the Santa Clarans are said to have lived in the abandoned pueblos of Puyé and Shufinné, clusters of caves dug into the pumice stone cliffs west of the Rio Grande. Drought and hostile attacks by nomadic Indians are said to have caused the abandonment of these sites.[3]

When Oñate arrived at Santa Clara in July of 1598 he recorded its name as Caypa, a name at first mistakenly identified with San Juan. Santa Clara soon began to raise livestock. In 1601 Ginés de Herrera Horta testified as part of Francisco Valverde's investigation of Oñate that there were about a thousand head of sheep and goats "at a pueblo named Santa Clara ... in the care of a certain Naranjo."[4] Fray Alonso de Benavides established the first church at Santa Clara when he visited the pueblo in 1629, but at the time of the Pueblo Revolt of 1680, when Santa Clara had a population of about three hundred, the pueblo had no resident priest and was a *visita* (charge) of San Ildefonso.[5] Santa

Clara was a vigorous participant in the Pueblo Revolt. It immediately joined the rebellion on 10 August 1680 and attacked an escort led by Captain Francisco de Anaya Almazán, killing two men and capturing Anaya's wife and children.[6] Santa Clara warriors were part of the massive reinforcements that turned the tide of battle against the Hispanos on 16 August. The church at Santa Clara was destroyed by the Indians in the Pueblo Revolt.

After the second Pueblo Revolt of 1696, a group of Santa Clarans accompanied the Picuris who journeyed to the plains in present-day Kansas to live with the Cuartelejo Apache for ten years, as discussed in chapter 3. They returned to New Mexico in 1706, accompanied by Juan de Ulibarrí, who led an expedition from Santa Fe to escort the Picuris and Santa Clarans back to New Mexico. The chief scout on this expedition was José Naranjo, who was probably from Santa Clara.[7]

Another group of Santa Clarans left their pueblo after the reconquest of 1692–1696 and helped establish the pueblo of Hano on the Hopi First Mesa. In the early 1700s, Naranjo, the same veteran scout who went to Cuartelejo, went to Walpi and brought back some Santa Clarans and other Tanos to the Santa Fe area, but Hano remained a Tewa-speaking pueblo on First Mesa and is still there today.[8]

Land at Santa Clara was assigned to families, not individuals, just as it was at other New Mexico pueblos. After the family selected a plot of land it applied for the land, and the governor and the tribal council visited the land to determine whether there were any prior claims, probably relying on signs of usage or lack thereof. If there were none, the land was assigned to the family requesting it. House sites were acquired in the same way as were farm lots. All other land was communally owned. All important sites such as "gathering plots, clay deposits, grazing rights or hunting, fishing, and wood-gathering areas" were usually communally owned, never privately owned.[9]

◆ ◆ ◆ ◆

During the late 1700s and early 1800s, Santa Clara was involved in two major lawsuits regarding its Pueblo league. The first was the dispute with San Ildefonso that concerned Hispano rancher Marcos Lucero and others, whose land between the two pueblos may have been encroaching on both pueblos and definitely overlapped San Ildefonso.[10] To determine the extent of the encroachment of Lucero and other Hispanos on the leagues of both Santa Clara and San Ildefonso, league measurements of the pueblos were made, first in 1763 under Governor Vélez Cachupín and then in 1786 under Governor Anza. The first measurements showed Lucero and the other Hispanos to be encroaching on the San Ildefonso league, but they were allowed to remain while San Ildefonso was given land in another direction, much like Sandia Pueblo in 1748. As a result of the second measurement in 1786 under Governor Anza, when Santa Clara took a more active part, a gap of only 236 varas was found between the two pueblos and Marcos Lucero was ordered to confine himself to this land. If he failed to do so, or attempted to move the boundary markers, he was subject to a one hundred–peso fine.[11]

The second suit had to do with a Santa Clara Indian named Roque Canjuebe, who became Christianized, attempted to leave the pueblo and be treated as a Spaniard, and received a grant within the Santa Clara league in 1744. He and his grandson Antonio mounted an attack on the Pueblo league from within, using some of the same arguments that Lucero had used to weaken the Pueblo league from outside. It was not until 1816 that Spanish authorities reversed this violation of the Santa Clara league, after a contingent of Santa Clara Indians traveled to Durango to argue their case.

Canjuebe called himself an *indio ladino*, or Spanish-speaking Indian. In late August 1744 he filed an unusual petition with Governor Codallos y Rabal seeking to be emancipated (although he did not use that word) from Santa Clara and assigned a tract of land on the edge of Santa Clara's league. Canjuebe told the governor that he owned more than one hundred head of cattle, eighty mares, and other livestock he was unable to care for. He thought that if he could get out of the pueblo and acquire land in his own name, his problems would be solved. The land requested was said to be located between the pueblo and Francisco Luján's ranch. In truth, Canjuebe was within the Santa Clara league.[12]

When Governor Codallos y Rabal sent Santiago Roybal, a vicar and ecclesiastic judge, to examine Canjuebe on the "rudiments of our holy Catholic faith," he passed with flying colors.[13] This was persuasive to Governor Codallos y Rabal, leading him to grant Canjuebe's petition so that he would be an "example to the other Indians of his tribe."[14] Alcalde Francisco Ortiz placed Canjuebe in possession of the land after notifying the leaders of Santa Clara and the adjoining landowner, Francisco Luján. Surprisingly, neither the pueblo nor Luján voiced objections to the grant. Luján was less likely to object than the pueblo because Canjuebe had agreed to give him an amount of land equal to the portion of Luján's ranch that was covered by Canjuebe's grant. More surprising was Santa Clara's failure to protest the grant at the time, but the pueblo strenuously objected seventy years later.[15]

In 1815 Canjuebe's grandson Antonio was living on the tract of land that was the subject of the 1744 grant, which was well within the Santa Clara league. This was so obvious to Antonio that he felt compelled to file a petition in Durango, more than a thousand miles from Santa Fe, to protect himself from Santa Clara. His petition was even stronger than his grandfather's was because as a Pueblo Indian he was making the same arguments against the Pueblo league that Hispanos had made in the case of Taos when Governor Máynez ruled against them.[16] Canjuebe stated that he had inherited his grandfather's grant, that he and his family had possessed the land for seventy years, and that therefore it should be protected. Canjuebe further argued that he deserved special protection as an Indian, even though he was opposing Santa Clara Pueblo. Canjuebe informed the commanding general that the *Recopilación* contained an entire title devoted to the protection of Indians that should apply to him.[17]

Unfortunately for Canjuebe, the commanding general referred the case to Governor Máynez for a decision. Six months after ruling that the Taos league should be inviolate, Máynez was just as firm about the land Santa Clara owned. Employing almost identical language as in the Taos decree, Máynez referred to Santa Clara's land as "the league that the king gave as patrimony to the Pueblos for them and their descendants."[18] He said that the pueblo could neither sell that land nor give it to an Indian who left the pueblo. According to Máynez, a dissatisfied Indian such as Antonio Canjuebe had two choices: he could leave the pueblo, become a tithe-paying citizen, and lose the property he had as a pueblo member, or he could remain a member of the pueblo and retain the property. In any case, having chosen vecino status, as had his grandfather Roque, Antonio could not also claim the benefits of Spanish laws protecting Indians—laws that protected Santa Clara.[19]

Canjuebe filed two petitions and made many cogent arguments, but he was getting nowhere. He must have been pleased when commanding general Bernardo Bonavía y Zapata ordered an attorney, don José Matos, appointed to represent him. Licenciado Matos lost no time. He filed a petition the day after he was appointed, making some of the same arguments Canjuebe had made, as well as some new ones. Matos may have gotten his facts wrong when he said Canjuebe was evicted from the pueblo or he may have been speaking rhetorically, but by so doing, he injected a note of urgency into the proceedings sufficient to turn the tide, at least temporarily. Matos also brought a new legal argument to bear as a companion to the argument that the grant to Roque Canjuebe should prevail over Santa Clara's league. Under the *Siete Partidas*, possession of land for thirty years without objection formed sufficient basis to claim title. That being the case, Matos argued, seventy years of unchallenged possession must be that much more persuasive. Now the matter was in the hands of the provisional solicitor general, who agreed completely with Matos. Solicitor Ángel Pinillas believed that the simple answer to the problem was to grant additional land to Santa Clara. In any case, wrote Pinillas, "the descendants of Roque Canjuebe must be protected and supported in a possession so ancient."[20]

Bonavía returned this opinion to New Mexico, and a new governor convened a meeting of Santa Clara people to notify them of the decision. Governor Pedro María de Allande (1816–1818) met with the governor and officials of the pueblo and the alcalde of Santa Cruz de la Cañada in mid-April 1816. On hearing the solicitor general's opinion, the Santa Clarans told Governor Allande they disagreed with the ruling and began making plans to go to Durango to appeal.[21]

Juan Tomás García, Juan de la Cruz Naranjo, Marcos Naranjo, and Francisco Naranjo from Santa Clara were ready to travel to Durango by 11 June 1816. Allande told Bonavía that these Indians were on their way, despite his attempts to persuade them to accept the ruling of 21 January 1816. Their appearance in Durango seems to have been an important factor in the provisional solicitor general's reversal of his earlier opinion in Canjuebe's favor. When the matter was again referred to him, Solicitor Pinillas came out strongly in favor of Santa Clara's position. He seemed to know all about the Pueblo league when he ruled that the land in question should be awarded to Santa Clara "to whom [it] has always belonged, as it is embraced within the league that by the law cited has been assigned to the Indian pueblos."[22] No specific law was cited, but Pinillas demonstrated his thorough knowledge of the laws protecting Indian land and made it clear that he was disposed to enforce those statutes when representatives of an Indian pueblo were willing to travel all the way to Durango to argue their case.

As with nearly all of the other pueblos, no specific document from any Spanish or Mexican official confirmed that Santa Clara was entitled to a league surrounding its village; that was simply recognized as legal practice in New Mexico by the Mexican authorities. The U.S. officials who assumed governmental authority over New Mexico in 1848, however, were under the impression that each pueblo had a paper grant for its lands.[23] William Pelham, who arrived in Santa Fe at the end of 1854 as the first surveyor general of New Mexico, came to share that belief, and he was presented with what purported to be grant documents for many of the pueblos, which he duly reported to Congress for confirmation.[24] That Santa Clara, like several other pueblos, had no such documents presented a problem, since Pelham was under direction to make addressing the issue of the Pueblo Indians' lands his priority.[25] Pelham devised a means to resolve the problem. With Santa Clara, as with each of the other pueblos that had no grant document, he had the governor of the pueblo and other leaders come to his office and respond to certain questions put to them through an interpreter. By this procedure, Pelham sought to establish that the pueblos had once had a document that had granted each pueblo a league, as provided by Spanish law, but that the document had been lost.[26]

The Santa Clara officials, who included Pascual, the governor; José María, the lieutenant governor; and José Pablo, the "chief" (probably meaning the cacique, or religious leader), appeared before Pelham and Indian agent Abraham Mayers on 16 June 1856 and gave what has the appearance of fairly carefully scripted "testimony" regarding their lost "grant." Pelham submitted a transcript of the brief exchange to the secretary of the interior with his recommendation for confirmation of the grant. The Santa Clara officials were asked whether they had once had a grant "from the government of Spain." They answered that "the old men of the pueblo say that they had a grant from the King" but that the document had been lost before the present officials "arrived at years of discretion." They were then asked whether the pueblo's lands were "considered to extend one league from the church to the four cardinal points of the compass." They responded, "The grants made to all the pueblos called for the same amount of land, and we claim the same amount that the others pueblos contain." They were then asked how old the pueblo was, a question they could not answer, and whether they survived solely on their agricultural pursuits, which they answered in the affirmative, saying, "Our support is derived entirely from the products of the soil. When our crops are not good we suffer for the necessaries of life."[27]

In December 1858 Congress confirmed the grant to Santa Clara Pueblo, and in July 1859 Deputy Surveyor John Garretson surveyed the grant at 17,368 acres, roughly the typical size of a four-square-league grant. The grant was patented on 1 July 1864, based on the Garretson survey.[28] Pelham was apparently unaware that Santa Clara had a valid Spanish grant and that at least some of the documents relating to it were evidently in its possession. Santa Clara Creek is a perennial stream that runs through one of the most prominent of the many narrow, deep, steep-sided canyons that drain the Pajarito Plateau, on the west side of the Rio Grande. Santa Clara's main village sits on Santa Clara Creek, beyond the mouth of the canyon and just upstream from its confluence with the Rio Grande. The creek is an important source of irrigation water for the pueblo. Equally important, the canyon is the pueblo's ancestral homeland. Its ancestral village, Puyé, the largest Classic Pueblo Period site on the Pajarito Plateau, includes a large surface structure on a high mesa on the edge of the canyon and hundreds of habitations carved into the soft tuff cliff, stretching for nearly a mile just below the surface pueblo. The Santa Clara people have used the canyon for millennia for religious and traditional purposes, hunting, gathering plants for various purposes, and farming.

Beginning in 1724, however, they faced increasingly aggressive efforts by Hispano settlers to settle in the canyon, and the pueblo's struggle to protect and retain control of its homeland spanned the next three centuries. In that year, brothers Juan and Antonio Tafoya petitioned Governor Juan Domingo de Bustamante for a grant of lands in the canyon, stretching from the lands of the pueblo (referring, presumably, to the Pueblo league) to the high mountains on the west (which was the rim of the huge collapsed volcanic crater known as the Valles Caldera).[29] Bustamante agreed, but when Alcalde Cristóbal Torres attempted to place the Tafoyas in possession, the officials of the pueblo protested, urging that the water supplied by the creek was barely sufficient for their needs. They threatened to take their protest to the governor, but the Tafoyas (through their father, Cristóbal) agreed that they would not engage in any agriculture on the tract but would merely pasture some cattle and horses. The Santa Clara leaders agreed to those terms, and possession was thus given based on that condition. But the Tafoyas evidently had no intention of keeping their word.

In 1733 the brothers approached Governor Cruzat y Góngora to revalidate the grant, stating that they had settled there and had cultivated the land for eight years but had lost their title papers. Cruzat y Góngora directed Alcalde Antonio de Ulibarrí to take testimony from witnesses concerning the grant, which revealed that the grant had been made on the condition that the grantees not cultivate any land. Cruzat y Góngora therefore reaffirmed the grant but only for ranching, not agriculture.[30] The Tafoya brothers were unhappy with this decision, and a few months later they approached the governor again with a petition that they be allowed to irrigate their fields in the canyon.

They told Governor Cruzat y Góngora that they were not irrigating upstream from Santa Clara by diverting water from the river because there were springs in the area that made irrigation from Santa Clara Creek unnecessary and that they also engaged in dry farming. The Tafoyas suggested that the governor should appoint experts to verify the truth of their statements, but, unfortunately for them, the expert who was appointed issued a report that showed the facts to be contrary to the Tafoya brothers' assertion.[31]

In early March 1734, Juan Páez Hurtado was commissioned to inspect the land and report to the governor regarding the assertions contained in the Tafoya brothers' petition. Páez Hurtado notified the Indians of Santa Clara and brought seven of them with him: five of the principal Indians, Roque the governor, and Bartolomé Quitoyo the interpreter. Also present were the Tafoya brothers, who commented on the physical evidence that Páez Hurtado found.[32]

Páez Hurtado found the spring the Tafoyas mentioned; it was "sixty paces from the river" and from there emptied "into a marsh and the latter into the river." Thus, the Tafoyas' use of the spring for irrigation reduced the amount of water flowing down to Santa Clara for irrigation.[33] Regarding the issue of dry-farmed land, Páez Hurtado allowed the Tafoyas to testify that the ditches were used "only when crops cannot be grown under dry-farming conditions" and "only to irrigate some places." Santa Clara's governor, on the other hand, argued strongly that the prohibition against irrigation above the pueblo had been violated "because there were some lateral ditches across the dry farms," suggesting all the land was under irrigation.[34] After receiving the report from Páez Hurtado, Governor Cruzat y Góngora denied the Tafoya brothers' petition, but they were apparently undaunted.[35]

Twenty-three years later the pueblo complained again that the Tafoya's cattle were damaging the crops at Santa Clara and that the problem of the upstream irrigation by the brothers, their heirs, and their successors was continuing.

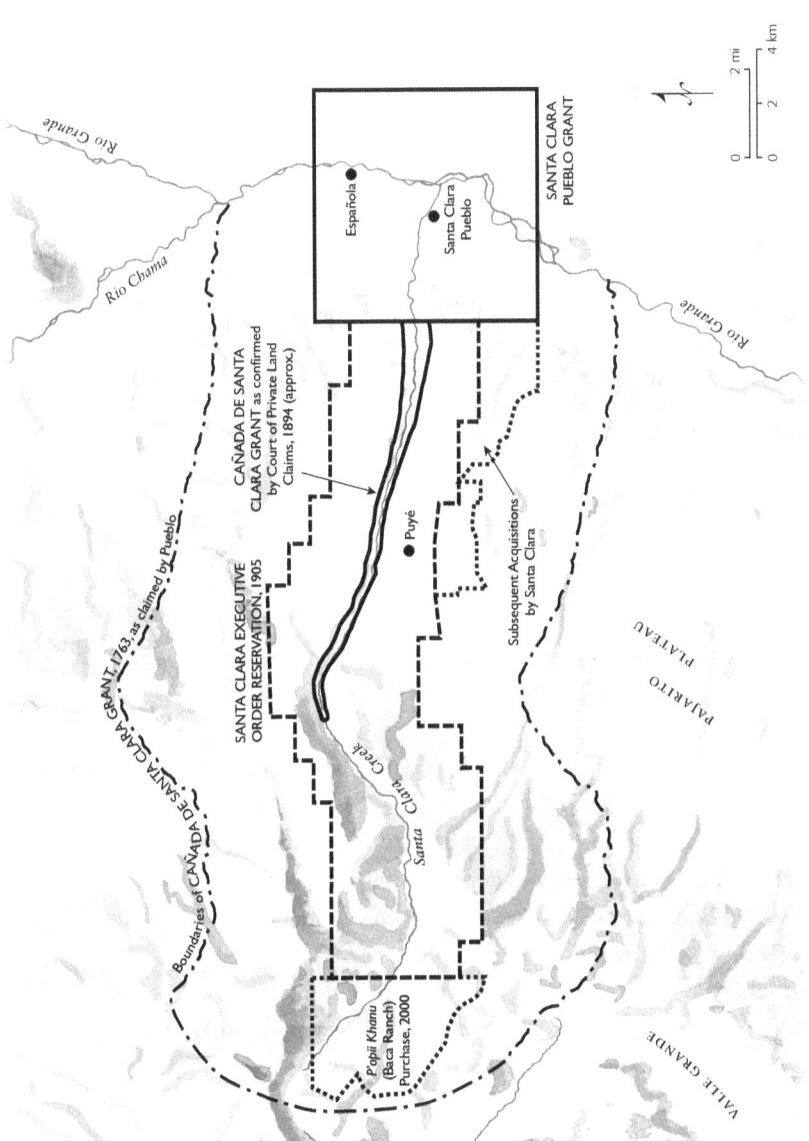

Santa Clara Pueblo and its Cañada de Santa Clara lands. Map by Molly O'Halloran.

Governor Marín del Valle became aware of Santa Clara's complaint when pueblo representatives approached him during a general tour of inspection. They protested that the Tafoyas were "shutting up their cattle and cutting off their water." The pueblo presented Marín del Valle with copies of the Tafoya grant containing the no-farming prohibition, which Governor Bustamente and Governor Mendoza had certified, as well as another protest the pueblo lodged with Governor Mendoza regarding the Tafoyas' upstream irrigation.[36]

Governor Marín del Valle, whose decrees regarding Indian pueblos were not always this forceful, fined the Tafoyas sixty pesos for their deliberate fraud in farming and irrigating land that was supposed to be used only for grazing and notified them that the lands they were surreptitiously irrigating should be left uncultivated. Marín del Valle noted that Santa Clara had suffered great damage because of the Tafoyas' irrigation upstream from the pueblo on the Rio Santa Clara, "on account of which water the pueblo was founded." Marín del Valle did not revoke the grant or eject the Tafoyas, however, a failure that would later cause more problems for Santa Clara.[37]

In the meantime, some of the Tafoya heirs decided to sell their interests in the grant because of Santa Clara's continued protests, the restrictive nature of Governor Marín del Valle's decree, and an increase in Ute raiding. Carlos Mirabal, the son-in-law of Juan Tafoya, sold half of the rancho to Joaquín Mestas for a thousand pesos and a good horse, a price Mestas would have paid only if the property included irrigated land. Mestas may have been justified in thinking he was buying irrigated land because the deed referred to a *sitio* (site) with a large house, several pieces of irrigated land, and some apricot trees. The deed was executed prior to the first Marín del Valle decree, and Mestas apparently did not know about the no-irrigating prohibition on the original grant, although a copy of the grant was apparently attached to the deed.[38]

It was not long before Mestas found out that although he paid for irrigable land, he was being told he had no right to irrigate. He sent a petition to Governor Marín del Valle asking that the prohibition against upstream irrigation be removed or that the Tafoya heirs be ordered to return the purchase price. Mestas made several arguments to support his petition. He suggested that Santa Clara might have waived its right to object to the Tafoyas' upstream irrigation because it had allowed such irrigation for seventeen or eighteen years without opposition. This was untrue. Santa Clara had protested several times about upstream water diversions and continued to complain. Mestas then tried a corollary of that argument, claiming that since Santa Clara did not protest, this meant it was not being harmed and had plenty of water. This argument failed because Santa Clara had protested.[39]

Mestas's pleas did not persuade Marín del Valle. Although the governor's decree is torn and an important part of the text is missing, subsequent events and later testimony indicate that Marín del Valle ruled against Mestas and in favor of Santa Clara. Again, the grant was not revoked, nor were the Tafoyas and their heirs and successors ejected from the land, which meant that these Hispanos kept irrigating on the Tafoya grant.[40]

By 1763 a new governor of New Mexico, more sympathetic to Pueblo land and water rights, was in office. Governor Vélez Cachupín heard about the claims of Santa Clara and the Tafoya heirs through a petition by Prudencia Gonzales, the widow of Antonio Tafoya. Gonzales asked the governor for a declaration regarding the nature of her title to the unsold part of the Tafoya grant. She said that her father-in-law, Cristóbal Tafoya, had received a grant from Governor Bustamente and that the land was settled, but in view of the recent Marín del Valle decree she was unsure of the extent of her rights to the land. She asked Governor Vélez Cachupín to take testimony from several people who could provide a history of the Cristóbal Tafoya grant.[41]

Domingo Vigil, Luis Archuleta, and Juan Archuleta were subsequently questioned. Their testimony noted that although the grant to the Tafoyas prohibited irrigation, the Tafoya family had settled and irrigated the land as early as 1724. The declaration of Juan Archuleta was particularly revealing. He stated that he went to the Tafoya rancho in 1731 to collect the tithe in the form of grain produced on the ranch and that on another occasion he again received the tithe on the vicar's orders. According to Archuleta, this grain assigned to the tithe was produced on irrigated land upstream from Santa Clara in violation of the initial Tafoya grant and of the governors' subsequent orders.[42]

Domingo Vigil, who was a teniente alcalde when Bustamente was governor, provided additional testimony, noting that Bustamente had ordered the arrest of Antonio Tafoya and the forfeiture of the grant to his father, Cristóbal Tafoya, when the two objected to a nearby grazing grant to Juan Esteban García de Noriega. Vigil implied that the grant was abandoned at that time, stating that the grant was resettled during the term of Governor Codallos y Rabal.[43] Luis Archuleta testified that Cristóbal Tafoya was given possession of his grant by Alcalde Francisco Montes Vigil and that he remained in possession continuously until the 1758 decree of Governor Marín del Valle. This statement regarding continuous possession (and presumably continuous irrigation) coincided with the testimony of Juan Archuleta.[44]

Once Vélez Cachupín read these statements regarding the history of the Tafoya grant, he solicited Santa Clara's side of the story. Vélez Cachupín directed that the entire proceedings be forwarded to Santa Clara's parish priest so that he could explain what rights the pueblo might have in regard to the Cañada de Santa Clara grants.[45] Father Mariano Rodríquez de la Torre did an excellent job advocating for the pueblo's position.

He pointed out that Santa Clara planted only one crop of corn per year, not two as in other places. If the crop failed because of lack of irrigation water the pueblo would be destitute. Accordingly, Father Rodríquez requested that the Indians of Santa Clara be granted the land at Cañada de Santa Clara covered by the Tafoya grant; such a grant would, in his view, resolve this long-standing problem. Even though a succession of governors had ruled in favor of Santa Clara, the Tafoyas had neither moved nor stopped irrigating. Moreover, these Hispanos, who were farming and irrigating in violation of the terms of their grant, went so far as to complain that Santa Clara cattle were eating their crops. Father Rodríquez pointed out that the Santa Clara Indians needed land to graze their own herds and again asked Governor Vélez Cachupín to grant the land covered by the Tafoya grant in the Cañada de Santa Clara to Santa Clara.[46]

Governor Vélez Cachupín accepted and embraced Father Rodríquez de la Torre's petition on behalf of Santa Clara. The governor reiterated the history of the Tafoya grant, pointing out that it was restricted to pasturage and that Santa Clara had opposed the grant from the beginning. Vélez Cachupín noted Marín del Valle's decree restricting the Tafoyas' rights and emphasized that Santa Clara "did not have all the area of cultivable lands it needs and ought to be allowed according to law and the royal will of his majesty."[47] Vélez Cachupín held that the Tafoya grant was null and void because the *Recopilación* directed that grazing grants to Hispanos should be at least a league and a half from a pueblo.

Governor Vélez Cachupín made the grant to Santa Clara in very specific terms, which were later ignored by some of the American surveyors who determined the boundaries of the Cañada de Santa Clara grant. The governor described the grant as covering "the whole of the valley of Santa Clara, which runs westward as far as the mountains and in which was situated the tract granted to Juan and Antonio Tafoya." Vélez Cachupín noted that the land was available to Santa Clara "as cultivable and common lands . . . for its flocks and horses with all its pastures and waters." The governor further declared the Tafoya grant was revoked, and he prohibited any new grants or land usage in the area of the Cañada de Santa Clara. Thus, Prudencia Gonzales had no rights to the land in question.[48]

Even with grant of the Cañada de Santa Clara land, the revocation of the Tafoya grant, and the prohibition of new grants or land usage in the area of the Cañada de Santa Clara, Santa Clara was not free from Hispanos irrigating upstream from the pueblo on the Rio Santa Clara. In early April 1780 another parish priest at Santa Clara complained about another Hispano irrigating upstream from Santa Clara, a matter addressed in a 1780 decree by Governor Anza. Anza noted that the priest at Santa Clara, Father Sebastián Antón, had complained on behalf of the pueblo about damages caused by Diego Borrego, a Hispano irrigating land in the Santa Clara canyon. Anza said that all the previous decrees, and in particular Vélez Cachupín's, had prohibited this sort of upstream irrigating and that the local alcaldes should not allow any Hispanos to take possession of land and irrigate crops upstream from the pueblo. Governor Anza imposed a one hundred–peso fine on alcaldes and their lieutenants who failed to enforce this restriction. In addition, Anza ordered that Borrego be notified of his decree, which listed all the previous decrees in favor of Santa Clara, and that he be made to comply with it.[49] On 24 April 1780, Alcalde José García de la Mora notified Borrego of Anza's decree, and Borrego agreed to comply with it, but eight years later a new governor, Fernando de la Concha (1788–1794) was still receiving complaints regarding Hispanos in the Cañada de Santa Clara.

In early August 1788, de la Concha received a memorial from Santa Clara complaining about the Hispanos who were grazing cattle upstream along the Rio Santa Clara and identifying these individuals as residents of Santa Cruz. Although upstream irrigation continued at the Cañada de Santa Clara, the grazing of livestock by Santa Cruz residents bothered the pueblo more. Since Santa Cruz residents had no ejido or grazing lands of their own, they were accustomed to pasturing their herds wherever they could, not only at the Cañada de Santa Clara but also north of the Truchas grant.[50] Governor De la Concha directed the alcalde assigned to the pueblo to go to Santa Clara, examine the documents in its possession, and proceed to enforce the restrictions former governors imposed. De la Concha was being far less proactive than Governor Vélez Cachupín, because his main concern was the one-and-one-half-league grazing restriction rather than the provisions of the Cañada de Santa Clara grant prohibiting any Hispanos or their livestock in the area.[51] The alcalde (whose name was cut off from his report), examined Santa Clara's documents, focusing in on the 1763 Vélez Cachupín grant. According to the alcalde, the grant covered the land "as far as the slopes of the mountains." The unnamed alcalde ordered the Hispanos to completely remove their cattle from the Cañada de Santa Clara grant, which he described as "the common lands of the said Indians."[52]

Spanish and Mexican records do not reflect further encroachments on Santa Clara lands, but the pueblo's efforts to confirm its title to the Cañada de Santa Clara grant after the United States assumed sovereignty over New Mexico turned out to be even more challenging than the problem of Spanish trespassers. During a time when Santa Clara had few allies and no lawyers to represent it, the Indian agent at the Santa Fe office of the Pueblo Indian Agency, Benjamin Thomas, filed a petition with the surveyor general on behalf of Santa Clara, seeking confirmation of the Cañada de Santa Clara grant. The petition claimed that the grant encompassed 90,000 acres, measuring 18 miles long and 7½ miles wide. The pueblo interpreted Marín del Valle's 1757 decree, which prohibited the Tafoyas from grazing their cattle within one and one-half leagues from the pueblo, as fixing the limits of the grant on the theory that if no one could graze there, the boundaries must be one and one-half leagues from the river on both sides.[53]

Surveyor General Clarence Pullen, who succeeded Atkinson, found that Spanish law authorized the granting of additional lands to a pueblo if its original grant was not sufficient to meet the needs of the community. After a hearing at which several pueblo members testified, Pullen decided to approve the grant. But he limited it to the boundaries set forth in the Vélez Cachupín grant of 19 July 1763, which granted the whole Valley of Santa Clara to the pueblo, extending to the west as far as the mountains.[54] Congress took no action on Pullen's recommendation for confirmation.

When George W. Julian took office as surveyor general, he reexamined the Cañada de Santa Clara grant. Julian concluded that Governor Vélez Cachupín had made a valid grant to Santa Clara of the lands covered by the Cañada de

Santa Clara grant, but he was convinced that the northern and southern boundaries of the grant should be confined to the narrow valley floor of the Santa Clara Canyon. Julian noted that the pueblo's population had declined from approximately five hundred in 1849 to fewer than two hundred in 1885 and that only one family was then living on the Cañada de Santa Clara grant. He pointed out that the inhabitants of the pueblo owned and grazed only 150 head of livestock on the grant. Julian thought that the pueblo no longer needed the land encompassed by the Cañada de Santa Clara grant for grazing and recommended that the Indians be paid a fair consideration for a release of their claim and that the land be opened for settlement.[55] José Dolores Romero, an agent for the Pueblo Indian Service, realized the canyon's importance to the pueblo. He protested Julian's recommendation on 28 November 1885, on the grounds that if the lands embraced within the grant were opened to settlement, the pueblo would again be deprived of its water supply. No action was taken on Julian's recommendation.[56]

The Court of Private Land Claims afforded Santa Clara another opportunity to seek recognition of its claim, and on 18 June 1892 a suit was filed.[57] The principal issue raised at the trial concerned the location of the boundaries of the grant, since there was no question about the grant's validity. The government contended that the northern and southern boundaries should be located along the edge of the narrow canyon bottom; the pueblo countered that the boundaries were located one and one-half leagues north and south of the stream. The government also argued that the western boundary should be located at the foot of the mountains, while the pueblo argued that it was located at the headwaters of Santa Clara Creek.[58]

The court's decision of 29 September 1894 held that the grant papers were genuine but fixed the grant's boundaries in accordance with the government's contentions. The decree confirmed the claim of Santa Clara to all the lands located in the canyon floor, between the cliffs on each side of the Santa Clara Creek, westward from the west boundary of the Santa Clara grant as far as the foot of the mountains.[59] As surveyed the area the court confirmed turned out to contain a mere 490 acres. A later survey by Francis Joy in 1914 reduced the acreage to 473 acres.[60]

The pueblo leaders saw that they had been cheated out of their land and began working to get the government to restore it, or at least to restore what Vélez Cachupín had granted them. George Hill Howard, who was appointed special attorney for the Pueblos shortly after the Court of Private Land Claims decision, set out to have those lands returned to Santa Clara and began working with Edgar Lee Hewett, the controversial head of the Museum of New Mexico. As it turned out, Hewitt wanted to create a national park on the Pajarito Plateau, an area that included much of Santa Clara's aboriginal lands and the Vélez Cachupín grant. He gained the trust of a Santa Clara leader who later became governor, Santiago Naranjo. Naranjo showed Hewett the sacred sites around Santa Clara, including the Puyé Cliffs. Although Hewett tried to emulate the respect for the land and secrecy that he saw in his guide, he was faced with the same paradox as all the early anthropologists: "He sought to convey the knowledge [and] . . . healing power of a culture not yet debased by civilization—and to protect that culture from encroachment. Yet these two ends were mutually exclusive."[61]

The plan to set aside lands for Santa Clara proceeded in tandem with the proposals for a national park and for including the area within a national forest, but only the reservation concept would benefit Santa Clara. Hewett tried to drum up federal support for a national park with the aid of John Lacy, chairman of the House Public Lands Committee, and Binger Hermann, commissioner of the General Land Office. As the two proposals proceeded, the entire Pajarito Plateau, including Santa Clara Canyon, was investigated. Lawyers such as Howard and his successors and the Indian agent drove the reservation proposal, while Hewett and his allies in the federal bureaucracy supported the park proposal. Both plans were resisted by westerners in general, "who long resented the power of the federal government over what they felt was their land."[62] In spite of the resistance to removing land from the public domain to create a national park or a reservation, in July 1905 President Roosevelt established the Santa Clara Reservation, a tract centered on Santa Clara Canyon, extending from the western edge of the Santa Clara league westward to the Baca Location No. 1, a grant the United States had made to the heirs of Luis María Cabeza de Baca in settlement of their claim arising out of their unsuccessful attempt to establish ownership of the Las Vegas Town grant. The reservation consisted of approximately 33,000 acres, making it about half as large as the original Cañada de Santa Clara grant.[63]

The Bureau of Indian Affairs managed the Santa Clara Reservation in a manner that was not always to the liking of Santa Clara. Although pueblo members could graze their livestock on the reservation, non-Indian stock was also allowed there under an agreement between the Bureau of Indian Affairs and the Department of Agriculture. Santa Clara was allowed to graze a specified number of animals on the Jemez Forest Reserve in return for allowing non-Indian livestock to graze on the Santa Clara Reservation. Such agreements were not in Santa Clara's best interest because of the greater number of non-Indian cattle grazers, which led to continuing conflicts between Santa Clara and Bureau of Indian Affairs officials in the period between 1905 and the late 1920s and early 1930s, when the Pueblo Lands Board's deliberations took place.[64]

Santa Clara soon realized that the Santa Clara Reservation did not even include all of the pueblo's ancestral lands and vowed to try once again to obtain trust title to the land. In 1917 Santa Clara governor Juan José Gutierrez wrote the Bureau of Indian Affairs commissioner asking for a reexamination of its claim of ownership of the entire Santa Clara Canyon in light of the 1763 Vélez Cachupín grant and Santa Clara's long-standing traditions. Part of those traditions, which John Peabody Harrington documented, involved Puyé Cliffs, which the pueblo maintained "belong to the Santa Claras" even though they were within the Santa Clara Reservation.[65] When the commissioner of Indian affairs received the petition from Governor Gutiérrez for recognition of the original Cañada de Santa Clara grant, he initially agreed with the pueblo but then quickly reversed himself, saying the Court of Private Land Claims had adjudicated the matter. Eventually Puyé came under the control of Santa Clara after the pueblo resisted attempts by the National Park Service to establish Puyé as a national monument. Today Santa Clara manages Puyé, holding feast days there and charging visitors fees for visits to the dramatic ruin where Santa Clara's ancestors once resided.[66]

With the establishment of the Indian Claims Commission in 1946, Santa Clara believed it had one more chance to reacquire its ancestral homelands, much of which was then held by the Forest Service and the Bureau of Land Management. The commission was set up to hear claims from Indian tribes who believed the United States had failed to carry out its treaty obligations, properly account for tribal funds it was holding, and adequately compensate Indian tribes for their land. The commission was empowered to award monetary compensation for land improperly taken but not to order a return of lands to a tribe, even if the U.S. government held those lands. This would become a sticking point with Santa Clara, which, although divided on other matters, was united in its desire for the return of its ancestral lands. No amount of money would compensate the pueblo for the loss of its sacred shrines, which under Forest Service management were often desecrated.[67] Santa Clara filed a petition in August 1951, but it would be twenty-two years before the claims commission rendered a decision. Initially hearings were held in July 1953 and September 1954, at which Santa Clarans testified about the boundaries and uses of their aboriginal lands. Even though the Indian Claims Commission was not empowered to return lands, Santa Clara announced its intention to try to regain its land through Congress, stating that it would not accept monetary compensation.[68]

While the Indian Claims Commission case was pending, Santa Clara had the opportunity to recover about 7,000 acres it was claiming before the commission from an unlikely source—the Atomic Energy Commission. The Manhattan Project, for which about 50,000 acres had been withdrawn from the public domain to create the Los Alamos National Laboratory, decided it no longer needed about 27,000 acres. Thus began a competition among the Forest Service, the newly created Los Alamos County, and the pueblos of Santa Clara and San Ildefonso for the land. Santa Clara and San Ildefonso had little bargaining power when dealing with the Forest Service or with Los Alamos County, but in June 1969 the Bureau of Indian Affairs proposed a compromise whereby the 27,000 acres would be divided between the pueblos and the Forest Service. The competition for the land was fierce, and Senator Clinton P. Anderson, the Forest Service, and Los Alamos County all came out against returning any of the land to the pueblos. It was argued that the pueblos were not entitled to the land for their exclusive use, which would be the result if the land were granted to the Indians, since then the area would no longer be open to the non-Indians who were accustomed to using the land for recreation. The pueblo's long history of use and ownership under a Spanish land grant was never brought into the discussion. Santa Clara was in the same position it was when the Pueblo Lands Board made its decision. The Atomic Energy Commission decided that the land would be put to better use if the Forest Service managed it. In the end the Bureau of Indian Affairs compromise was rejected and the entire tract was transferred to the Forest Service.[69]

Thus, the Indian Claims Commission was the only avenue left to Santa Clara for redress. A few months after the transfer to the Forest Service, Santa

Clara's attorney stipulated that the area of the pueblo's aboriginal claim was almost 32,000 acres. The claims commission valued this land at between three and six million dollars. Rather than take the money, Santa Clara decided to fire its attorney and to fight for a return of the land. When the Indian Claims Commission was dissolved in 1968, the case was transferred to the U.S. Court of Claims, where, in another stipulation, Santa Clara agreed to accept compensation for about 5,300 acres east of its grant lands, if the earlier agreement relinquishing its claim to more than 26,000 acres on the Pajarito Plateau was voided. Although the pueblo's members were still divided on whether to accept compensation for any of the land, the majority hoped that this new plan would help the pueblo muster support in Congress for restoration of lost land the pueblo had been trying to regain control of for more than a century.[70]

Over time, the pueblo was able to purchase several hundred acres along the south side of the area it contended it had been granted in 1763, but it was not until 2000 that the pueblo was able to acquire any substantial additional portion of the lands it had lost within Santa Clara Canyon. A tract of about 2,400 acres of BLM land within the grant but south of the canyon was transferred to it in 2003.[71] In 2000 the United States, pursuant to congressional authorization, entered into an agreement to purchase Baca Location No. 1 from the heirs of Pat Dunnigan, a Texas oilman who had acquired the 98,000-acre ranch in 1962.[72] The tract, which encompasses essentially all of the Valles Caldera, including vast meadows and several resurgent volcanic domes, also takes in most of the headwaters of Santa Clara Creek, an area known to the pueblo as P'opii Khanu. Pueblo representatives were able to persuade the federal negotiators to allow the pueblo to acquire that portion of the ranch, and they were also able to obtain critical financial support for the acquisition from a Santa Fe–based charitable foundation.[73] Thus, on 25 July 2000, the pueblo regained title to approximately 5,045 acres, consisting of P'opii Khanu, the pristine headwaters of Santa Clara Creek.[74] Santa Clara's efforts to regain its ancestral homeland are not ended, and it continues the fight, undaunted by the long odds.

Cochiti Dam flooding shrines and agricultural land during construction.
Drawing by Glen Strock.

CHAPTER 6

Cochiti Pueblo

Cochiti is the northernmost Keresan-speaking pueblo in New Mexico.[1] Many Cochiti tribal members believe that the tribe lived at Tyuonyi, the great ruin on the floor of Frijoles Canyon in Bandelier National Monument, before it moved to its current location, which it did before the arrival of the Spaniards. Not all Spanish expeditions mention Cochiti. In 1581 the Rodríguez-Chamuscado expedition visited Cochiti, describing the pueblo as having "230 houses of two and three stories."[2] In 1582 the Espejo expedition noted that "the [Cochiti] people were very peaceful. [They] gave us maize, tortillas, turkeys, and *pinole*. We bartered very fine buffalo skins for sleigh bells and small iron articles."

With the arrival of Oñate, Cochiti fell under the sway of the first Spanish colonists to settle permanently in New Mexico, but like other pueblos, it became less friendly toward Hispanos as forced Christianization proceeded. The first priest assigned to Cochiti was Father Rosas, who was headquartered at Santo Domingo. For the first part of the seventeenth century, Cochiti was a visita of Santo Domingo, but by 1637 a friar resided at the pueblo. Even though Cochiti was considered secondary to Santo Domingo in the early 1600s, its population was the larger of the two pueblos until after the 1680 Revolt. This reversal of fortune was due to Cochiti's losses during the revolt and an influx of Tanos into Santo Domingo.[3]

Cochiti took an active part in the Pueblo Revolt. When the Cochiti people learned of Governor Otermín's 1681 attempt to reconquer New Mexico, they moved to the mesa top known as the Potrero Viejo, or the Cieneguilla de Cochití. There they remained off and on with their allies from San Felipe, Santo Domingo, San Marcos, and other pueblos, until Vargas, aided by a strong contingent of pueblo warriors from Santa Ana, San Felipe, and others, attacked and dislodged the Cochitis from their stronghold in 1693.[4]

◆ ◇ ◆ ◇

During the eighteenth and nineteenth centuries, Cochiti was subjected to grants to local Hispanos that overlapped its Pueblo league and its common grazing lands northeast of the pueblo. These overlapping grants included the 1728 Cañada de Cochití grant and the overlap of Miguel and Domingo Romero, whose claim stemmed from a 1739 grant to Andrés Montoya. Partly because of these overlapping grants, Governor Vélez Cachupín gave Cochiti its own grazing grant in 1766. In each of these cases of overlaps and new grants, Cochiti lost the lands it claimed.[5] Cochiti also received land between its Pueblo league and that of Santo Domingo in 1722 when Alfonso Rael de Aguilar measured the two leagues, found about 1,600 varas between the two, and awarded 800 varas of additional land to Cochiti and Santo Domingo. Eventually Cochiti also lost this land to encroaching Hispanos. This case is discussed in more detail in chapter 1.

In 1718 Cochiti filed a complaint with the cabildo of Santa Fe against alcalde Manuel Baca and his lieutenant, Antonio Baca, who was his son. Governor Antonio de Valverde Cosío (1716, 1718–1721) decided in favor of the pueblo, removing Antonio Baca from office, ordering him to remove his animals from Cochiti lands, and directing him to go on the next two campaigns "against the enemy who invade this kingdom." Nevertheless, Baca was in office again in the 1750s and 1760s until Governor Vélez Cachupín removed him in response to a petition signed by forty-five residents of his jurisdiction, complaining of bribery, persecution, and various other offenses—some against the pueblos.[6]

Luis María Cabeza de Baca, a descendant of Manuel Baca, was part of another generation of Bacas who fought with Cochiti over the mistreatment of pueblo members and encroachment on Cochiti lands. In 1815 Cochiti initiated a lawsuit against Baca after a series of incidents in which Cochiti claimed that Baca was oppressing the pueblo both by physical abuse and encroachment.[7]

Another Hispano involved in this litigation was Antonio Ortiz, whose Rancho de Sile, south of Cochiti, overlapped Cochiti and Santo Domingo, prompting Santo Domingo to intervene in the lawsuit, claiming its league had been incorrectly measured. The litigation bounced around among New Mexico, the general command in Durango, and the Audiencia of Guadalajara.[8]

The case began in the spring of 1815 when Felipe Sandoval, the protector of Indians, brought to Governor Máynez's attention the many complaints the Indians of Cochiti had against Cabeza de Baca. During Governor José Manrique's administration (1808–1814), Alcalde José Mariano de la Peña measured the Cochiti league, demonstrating that Baca was indeed encroaching on Cochiti land. Instead of abiding by this decision, Baca removed some of the boundary markers the alcalde put in place, whereupon Peña ordered Baca neither to remove any marker nor plant on land within the Cochiti league. Nevertheless, Baca moved a boundary marker, which resulted in "taking a considerable amount of land away from the Indians." Cochiti was so concerned that it offered to repurchase the land at double the amount Baca had paid for it in the first place.[9] Sandoval also brought Santo Domingo's involvement in the case to Governor Máynez's attention in March 1815. Santo Domingo complained to Sandoval about Antonio José Ortiz's measurement of its league, which differed from Peña's measurement. It is no wonder Ortiz's measurement was questioned, for he was the Hispano allegedly encroaching on Santo Domingo land.[10]

Meanwhile, Cochiti's case against Cabeza de Baca was moving through New Mexico's judicial system. After receiving Sandoval's report, Governor Máynez ruled that the Cochiti league "must always remain free" and that Baca's houses and corrals were encroaching on Cochiti's land. Beyond that, Máynez held that Baca's purchase from Cochiti was void because it was coerced against the will of the pueblo's representatives. When Cabeza de Baca was informed of Governor Máynez's ruling, he agreed to leave after his crop was harvested and to accept the return of the purchase price from the pueblo.[11] As in the past, however, Baca did not abide by this agreement and again refused to leave.

Frustrated with the legal process in New Mexico, Cochiti representatives journeyed to Durango, as others did before them, and got the protector of Indians in that city, José Joaquín Reyes, to argue their case before the commanding general. Reyes presented new facts to establish that the sale of

Rancho de Peña Blanca from Cochiti to Baca was invalid. To impose his will on the Indians, Baca had allegedly imprisoned some of them and placed others in the stocks. In addition, Reyes alleged that Baca illegally used the pueblo's water. Reyes cited *Recopilación* 4-12-9, 12, and 18 in support of his argument that the sale to Baca was illegal because the protector of Indians and a competent judge had not approved it. Reyes also made a strong argument for the Pueblo league, but he did not demand a full league, stating that "it is well known that Indians in these provinces have a league, divided in half in each direction," although he cited no authority for this proposition. Reyes asked the commanding general to return the Peña Blanca land to Cochiti and to require Baca to pay court costs.[12]

Although Baca agreed on several occasions to return the Peña Blanca land to Cochiti, by August 1816 he had decided to fight the pueblo by hiring his own lawyer in Durango, Rafael Bracho. Bracho repeated the statement made by Reyes about the Pueblo league being half a league in each direction rather than a full league, citing *Recopilación* 6-3-8. Under this argument, which Bracho twisted out of Reyes's misleading statements, Baca's land would be outside of Cochiti's league because the "league" would be much smaller—one-fourth the size of a standard Pueblo league. Rather than making a decision on the arguments of Reyes and Bracho, the commanding general sought the opinion of Ángel Pinella, the general counsel, who recommended returning the matter to New Mexico and contacting a lawyer in Durango who would consult with the New Mexico governor.[13]

Commanding general Bonavía appointed Dr. Francisco Antonio de Landa to be the consulting lawyer, but Landa informed Bonavía that he was too busy, asking that another *letrado*, or jurist, be assigned to the case.[14] The commanding general would hear none of it, however, notifying Landa that his affairs were not more important than what the government asked of him. This procedural maneuvering compelled Landa to formulate an opinion, which he directed to Governor Pedro María de Allande (1816–1818) in Santa Fe. He stated that the Cochiti and Santo Domingo leagues had to be remeasured because Alcalde Peña marked off a full league in each direction, even though "according to the spirit of the laws of the Indies and the testimony of the protector of Indians, don José Joaquín Reyes, the league should be divided in half in each cardinal direction."[15] Landa further suggested that Cabeza de Baca, the protector of Indians, the other adjoining property owners, and "a government attorney who will be named so that he can make the required claims on behalf of the royal treasury" be present at the measurement by a knowledgeable individual.[16]

Landa's suggestions apparently became an order, although there is no record of Bonavía having adopted either them or Landa's opinion that the Pueblo league should be half a league rather than a full league in each direction, and the case was returned to New Mexico. Landa based his opinion on Reyes's statement that only half a league should be measured, but Bracho perverted the thrust of Reyes's argument. Reyes argued that Cochiti's sale to Baca was illegal because it was coerced and did not receive the approval of the protector of Indians and of a competent judge. Presumably, the requirement of such approval was designed to uncover the fraud and coercion that Baca was alleged to have engaged in in effecting the purchase from Cochiti. Since Reyes was arguing that the purchase was invalid and should be set aside, the measurement of the Cochiti league was irrelevant in determining the validity of the Cochiti purchase. Baca's lawyer picked up on the measurement of the league as the sole determination of the validity of the Baca purchase, conveniently forgetting the issue of Baca's fraud and coercion in inducing the sale. Bracho referred to *Recopilación* 6-3-8 as justifying the half a league measurement, but the law cited applied only to resettled pueblos and provided for an ejido of a league in length, without specifying how it was to be measured.[17]

Based on these legal arguments by the Durango lawyers, Governor Allande ordered the Cochiti and Santo Domingo leagues measured, appointing Pedro Bautista Pino to make the measurements. Since the office of protector of Indians was vacant, the governor appointed Vicente Villanueva to the post, at least for the duration of the proceeding. Ignacio María Sánchez Vergara was there as well, not as protector of Indians, but as *promotor fiscal*, an official charged with looking after the crown's financial interests. Landa suggested the appointment of the promotor fiscal, but in the hands of Sánchez Vergara, such an appointment could only lead to mischief.[18] Also present at the measurement were Alcalde Juan José Gutiérrez, who measured Santo Domingo league in 1815, and former alcalde Salvador Montoya, who was involved with the Jemez league. Pino planned to measure the Santo Domingo league first, but when he went to the pueblo, the Indians resisted another measurement, perhaps having learned that he was only planning to measure half a league.[19]

Pino proceeded to carry out the measurement anyway. As New Mexico's only delegate to the Spanish Cortes, Pino fully embraced the idea that the privatization of Indian land would encourage the growth of New Mexico's economy. Here was an opportunity to put that philosophy into effect as he measured what might be called the short league of Santo Domingo. The pueblo lost land to encroaching Hispanos in every direction. South to north José Miguel de la Peña's property bounded the pueblo's land; east to west Antonio José Ortiz's property bounded the pueblo's land. Presumably, these Hispanos had been encroaching on the Santo Domingo league, as Gutiérrez measured it. Now, with the tables turned, they became adjoining owners rather than encroachers.[20] The half-league measurement to the south took away the full league measured in 1770, when Governor Mendinueta made the grant to San Felipe and Santo Domingo. At Sánchez Vergara's request, Pino continued measuring until he reached the boundary of the Mendinueta grant, another 3,750 varas. A few days later, it became clear why Sánchez Vergara was so eager to have this land measured.[21]

Meanwhile, Pino measured the short Cochiti league, using the same cordel he used at Santo Domingo. Again, the measurement ended at land belonging to Hispanos, including that of Nerio Antonio Montoya, whose property was also adjacent to the Santo Domingo league. On the north the measurement ended at the boundary of the Cañada de Cochití grant. By this time the only Hispano whose land had not been measured was Luis María Cabeza de Baca. The way the measurements were going for the other Hispanos in the Cochiti–Santo Domingo area, it appeared that Baca had no concerns. Before Pino could make the measurement in the direction of Baca's land, Villanueva, who was representing Cochiti, stepped forward and conceded that the pueblo had no basis for its claim against Baca, arguing that a previous protector persuaded Cochiti to file its claim.[22]

It seems clear that what really happened is that Baca found a way to induce Villanueva to take his side, even though Villanueva's responsibility was to represent Cochiti's interests. Baca, Villanueva, and Sánchez Vergara then worked out a compromise whereby Baca promised to pay for damages his cattle caused to Cochiti's land and to keep his cattle off their meadows unless he had permission. No Cochiti representative was present to sign this so-called compromise. In fact, Baca made this promise before and refused to keep it. All Cochiti had after this litigation, which included trips to Durango and Mexico City, was Baca's empty promise.[23]

Villanueva betrayed the interests of his Cochiti clients because he knew that the proper way to measure a Pueblo league was a full 5,000 varas in each direction (he measured such a distance in each direction at Pecos). He even noted that "the ancient custom practiced with the other pueblos . . . is to measure a league in each direction."[24] He also knew Baca was encroaching on Cochiti land. Yet Villanueva's betrayal of Cochiti came at a price. Whether his death came at the hands of hostile Apaches, Pecos Hispanos unhappy with his measurement of the league, or Cochitis who remembered his betrayal of their interests, Villanueva's body was discovered near Los Trigos around 1822.

Pino's performance of his duties in measuring the league also left something to be desired. Instead of measuring the half league in Baca's direction as Governor Allande ordered, Pino accepted the statement of the protector of Indians on behalf of Cochiti that the sale to Baca was legal, adding that eighteen additional families also owned land in the area. These others who might have purchased land from Cochiti or were simply trespassing made up the community of Peña Blanca, which would have been found to be encroaching on Cochiti's league had it been measured properly. These individuals, along with Baca, must have put pressure on Pino, Villanueva, and Allande to arrive at a decision allowing Baca and the other Peña Blanca residents to remain. Fortunately for Cochiti, its case and that of Santo Domingo still required the Audiencia of Guadalajara's approval. It was there that Cochiti would finally get a fair hearing.[25]

In advance of the Cochiti and Santo Domingo cases being returned to Guadalajara, Villanueva and Sánchez Vergara continued to hatch schemes to deprive Cochiti and Santo Domingo of land they owned. On 14 May 1817, Villanueva suggested to Pino that the Cochiti measurement should treat land Cochiti purchased from neighboring Hispanos as though it were part of the Cochiti league. According to Villanueva, this idea originated with Cochiti's late protector of Indians, Felipe Sandoval, who told the people of Cochiti that "they could defend their land better by saying it was from their patrimony than by saying they had purchased it." Fortunately for Cochiti, it does not appear this proposal was adopted.[26]

In another communication to Pino, Villanueva said that Sánchez Vergara wanted the land between Santo Domingo and San Felipe that was the subject of the 1770 Mendinueta grant to be declared royal domain because it was neither cultivated nor settled. In addition, Sánchez Vergara wanted the land between the Mendinueta grant and the recent half-league measurement of Cochiti's league to be declared public domain, as well as the land bordering Santo Domingo's half-league measurement. Sánchez Vergara was trying to cement the half-league measurements of the Cochiti and Santo Domingo grants by declaring the land to be public domain. It was not just the interest of the royal treasury that Sánchez Vergara was worried about: he soon petitioned on his own behalf for the land Mendinueta granted between Santo Domingo and San Felipe.[27]

On 16 May Governor Allande directed Villanueva to respond to Sánchez Vergara's claim. Villanueva answered that he agreed that the land should be public domain.[28] In the long history of advocates who spoke for the Pueblo Indians of New Mexico, this was obviously one of the low points, because Villanueva's concession was completely contrary to the interests of both pueblos. Certainly, eighteenth-century advocates such as Bartolomé Fernández, Felipe Tafoya, and Rael de Aguilar would have made the argument that the Pueblo league, as it was always measured in New Mexico, was inviolate. They could have cited an entire page full of reasons why the earlier measurements of the Cochiti and Santo Domingo leagues should prevail. As recently as 1815, Governor Máynez referred to the 5,000 vara league as a patrimony or inherited estate, such that "no judge or governor has the authority to sell all or part of the aforesaid league."[29] Villanueva did not even make a perfunctory defense of the full Pueblo league or of the 1770 Mendinueta grant to San Felipe and Santo Domingo. Such a breach of the trust bestowed on him must have surprised Governor Allande, who appointed Villanueva protector of Indians. It must have also shocked the protector in Guadalajara, who was much more vigorous in his defense of the indigenous peoples in his jurisdiction.

The *Cochiti v. Cabeza de Baca* file was sent to Guadalajara where it was received on 30 July 1817. By 11 August the protector of Indians, Mariano Mendiola, had submitted a lengthy report that provided a concise summary of the case up to that point. Mendiola concluded with the recommendation that Baca's Rancho de Peña Blanca be returned to Cochiti and Ortiz's Ojo de Santa Cruz land be returned to Santo Domingo. Mendiola based his recommendation on *Recopilación* 4-12-18, which provided restrictions and conditions on the sale of Indian land, and 4-12-9, which provided that if land was given to Hispanos in a manner prejudicial to Indians, the land must be returned to its rightful owner. In addition, the protector of Indians focused on the price Baca paid for the Peña Blanca land. Not only was it less than half of the fair price, but the entire Cochiti sale to Baca was riddled with errors, given that none of the formalities were followed. In fact, Mendiola observed, Baca should not even get the purchase price back because of the Instruction of 23 February 1781.[30]

The audiencia adopted Mendiola's recommendation but was reluctant to issue a final ruling without giving Baca one last opportunity to be heard. The audiencia directed Governor Allande to inform Baca that he must appear in Guadalajara either in person or through a legal representative. Baca responded that because of his advanced age and poor health he could not appear in person but would have Licenciado Bracho of Durango appear on his behalf, the same lawyer who had represented him in 1816.[31] On this occasion, Bracho informed the audiencia that since he did not have a written power of attorney from Baca, he was naming a lawyer in Guadalajara, Ladislao Jáuregui del Castillo, to handle the case. Bracho also argued that Cochiti could not challenge the Baca sale because of the law declaring that defective titles issued before 1700 could not be challenged, but he did not clarify why that law applied to the Baca purchase, which occurred much later. Bracho suggested one reason (besides not wanting to represent Baca again) why he did not want to be involved further in this case: he was highly critical of the New Mexico legal system, saying that the people of New Mexico were a simple folk with little education and therefore did not pay sufficient attention to legal formalities in their transactions.[32]

Jáuregui also refused to accept the power of attorney from Bracho, citing his heavy workload with the ecclesiastical curia. Growing impatient, Mendiola seemed to bristle in response. He argued that since Baca agreed to leave the Peña Blanca land, the Cochiti Indians should be given the land in accordance with *Recopilación* 6-1-27 and the law of 23 February 1785, which the Audiencia of Mexico City had cited previously. Since Jáuregui refused the appointment, Mendiola believed it would be contrary to the spirit of the law to delay any longer in giving Cochiti back its land. Almost two months later the audiencia ruled that it had sufficient information to rule as Mendiola suggested. Cochiti won its almost four-year-long legal battle with Baca. It seemed that all that remained was to collect the court costs assessed against Cabeza de Baca.[33] Yet in spite of his promises and the audiencia's decision, Luis María Cabeza de Baca never left Peña Blanca. His professed poor health notwithstanding, he lived more than a decade longer and probably died there in 1833.

Cochiti's paper victory was not for naught. The vicissitudes of litigation before the Audiencia of Guadalajara and the commanding general in Durango revealed a distortion and a misunderstanding of the Pueblo league, followed by a vindication of the full Pueblo league. Protector of Indians Mendiola never mentioned the measurement of the Cochiti league in his recommendations and opinions, but the ruling for which he argued assumed that Cochiti owned a full 5,000 vara league in each cardinal direction. The most applicable law Mendiola cited was *Recopilación* 6-1-27, which provided a detailed procedure for Spanish approval of sales of Indian land. He said that these provisions were not followed in Cochiti's sale of the Peña Blanca land to Baca. Mendiola was assuming that the land in question was Indian land, which was true only if the 5,000 vara league rather than the half-league measurement was used.[34] The half-league measurement was never again proposed as a standard in New Mexico. The persistence of the custom of measuring the 5,000 vara league from the cross in the cemetery or center of the pueblo was stronger than the statements to the contrary by a few Durango lawyers.

Cochiti traveled a long road through the Spanish judicial system before the Audiencia of Guadalajara established the pueblo's right to four square leagues. Pueblo members first journeyed to Durango where Protector of Indians José Joaquín Reyes represented them. Although Reyes was forceful in arguing for a Pueblo league and claiming that Baca's purchase from Cochiti was illegal, he stumbled when he asked for only a half league in each direction. This was the first of several instances when Cochiti was ill served or betrayed by lawyers who were supposed to advocate on the pueblo's behalf. Another such instance came when Vicente Villanueva conceded Cochiti's claim to its Pueblo league without consulting the pueblo. Finally, there was Ignacio María Sánchez Vergara, who tried to acquire Cochiti land by asserting the validity of the half-league measurement when he knew better, having measured the full Pueblo league for other pueblos. Fortunately for Cochiti, their advocate in Guadalajara presented a compelling argument, which the audiencia approved when Luis María Cabeza de Baca failed to appear in court. Although Cochiti won, it failed to preserve the document recording the audiencia's decision and present it to U.S. authorities.

◆ ◇ ◆ ◇

In 1856 Cochiti submitted a claim to the surveyor general of New Mexico, based on its Cruzate grant dated 25 September 1689, that purported to make a grant to the pueblo having the following description: on the north, a point one league north of the pueblo; on the east, a point one league east of the pueblo; on the south, the point of a barren hill near a stream of water that is running in the direction of the rising sun and that empties into the Rio Bravo (the Rio Grande); and on the west, a point one league west of the pueblo.[35] Surveyor General William Pelham, in his annual report of 30 September 1856, reported that Cochiti had received a grant from Spain and recommended that Congress confirm it.[36] Based on this favorable report, in 1858 Congress confirmed the grant and directed the commissioner of the General Land Office to have the grant surveyed and patented.[37] In 1859, with this description, deputy surveyor John W. Garretson surveyed the grant and found that it contained 24,256 acres. The east and west boundaries were located about one league from the pueblo. Contrary to the calls in the grant, Garreston located the south boundary one league from the pueblo and the north boundary at the confluence of the Rio Chiquito (which flows east, off the Pajarito Plateau) and Rio Grande, approximately one and three-quarters leagues north of the pueblo. The grant was patented to Cochiti Pueblo on 1 November 1864.

In 1951 Cochiti filed a petition with the Indian Claims Commission seeking compensation for the loss of about 25,000 acres of land the pueblo purchased in 1744 from Juan Fernández de la Pedrera and his son Bartolomé Fernández for 1,500 pesos. The pueblo claimed compensation both under the 1744 deed to Cochiti and by virtue of its aboriginal title to the land. Aboriginal title, which the Indian Claims Commission recognized as the basis for compensation for lost land, is based on exclusive use and occupation of land over a long period of time, but it seems that Cochiti relied primarily on the deed from the Fernándezes, father and son. The pueblo was in a strong position since it had paid dearly for the land, but it was hampered by not having presented the deed in any earlier proceedings, particularly those for confirmation of the Cochiti pasture grant. This failure by attorney N. B. Laughlin was one of many that saw Cochiti either not represented by a lawyer or represented by an advocate who failed to protect the pueblo's interests. Cochiti was not well protected regarding this tract east of the pueblo, because after purchasing the land, two overlapping land grants were made in the area covered by the 1744 deed—the Caja del Río and La Majada grants—and the Court of Private Land Claims confirmed both of those grants. The Indian Claims Commission used these two overlapping grants as the main reason for denying Cochiti any compensation for the loss of the land covered in the Bartolomé Fernández et al. deed.[38]

Governor Mendoza made the Caja del Río grant northeast of Cochiti to Captain Nicolás Ortiz in 1742. The land was bounded by lands of San Ildefonso on the north and by the Santa Cruz spring on the south. Cochiti was not mentioned in the description of the land and was not notified of the Caja del Río grant, even though it encroached on Cochiti land. San Ildefonso was notified, but since it did not object, Governor Mendoza made the Caja del Río grant on 18 June 1742. The Court of Private Land Claims confirmed the grant to the heirs of Nicolás Ortiz on 30 August 1893, but since Cochiti was not a party to that proceeding, the overlap with the Bartolomé Fernández purchase was not considered. This failure to object, either when the grant was first made or when it was confirmed, proved fatal to Cochiti's claim before the Indian Claims Commission.[39]

The other overlapping grant conflicting with the land described in the 1744 deed to Cochiti was the La Majada grant. Governor Vargas made that grant in 1695 to Jacinto Peláez, but since Peláez never took possession, he sought revalidation of the grant from Governor Rodríguez Cubero. In December 1698, Rodríguez Cubero revalidated the grant, but Peláez died before taking possession. Thereafter, the land within the La Majada grant was regranted to Jacinto Sánchez and Nicolás Ortiz, the latter being the grantee of the Caja del Río grant. The ownership of the La Majada grant became more confused as the heirs of Jacinto Peláez, including Juan Fernández de la Pedrera, claimed an interest in it. In July 1744 Bartolomé Fernández, son of Juan, stated that his father gave him possession of the premises and asked Governor Codallos y Rabal for permission to sell his interest in the grant. Yet no sale to the Indians of Cochiti was recorded in the La Majada grant proceedings; rather, the sale was documented as having been made to Paulina Montoya. It seems that Fernández was executing several deeds for the same land in 1744, but the deed to Cochiti did not surface until the early 1900s in a suit to partition the La Majada grant.[40] Cochiti was not a party to the trial of the La Majada grant before the Court of Private Land Claims, and the plaintiffs did not produce the 1744 deed, although it was allegedly in their possession. It seems that Cochiti always claimed the land within the La Majada grant and had several of their sacred shrines in the area. As early as 1728, there were complaints by members of the family of Bartolomé Fernández of "trespass" on the lands of the La Majada grant. Fernández must have recognized Cochiti's legitimate claim to a portion of the La Majada grant (less than a third) and deeded that portion to the pueblo while retaining the remainder of the grant. Since the plaintiffs did not produce the deed to Cochiti, the Court of Private Land Claims confirmed the entire La Majada grant to the heirs of Jacinto Peláez in September 1894. When the grant was surveyed in October 1895, it was found to contain 54,404 acres.[41]

In 1904 a suit to partition the La Majada grant was filed in the Sandoval County District Court. For the first time in the La Majada grant proceeding, Cochiti was represented by an attorney: Francis C. Wilson, special attorney for the Pueblo Indians of New Mexico. Also for the first time, Cochiti introduced the 1744 deed, but the court found that Cochiti had no interest in the La Majada grant, and it was partitioned to the heirs of Jacinto Peláez, the most prominent of whom was Benjamin Pankey, owner of a large ranch on the San Cristóbal grant. The district court found an overlap between the La Majada grant and the Cochiti grant as patented by Congress in 1858, and the area was awarded to Cochiti because the Cochiti grant (a Cruzate grant) was considered to be older than the 1704 La Majada grant. The court did not give any reason, however, for denying Cochiti's claim for the roughly 25,000 acres conveyed in the 1744 deed from Bartolomé Fernández.[42] When Cochiti's claim for this land was submitted to the Indian Claims Commission in 1959, the judgment in the 1904 partition suit denying the claims based on the 1744 deed was urged on the commission as a bar to the claim. Cochiti responded that claims for Indian land were a matter for federal courts, which had exclusive jurisdiction over matters of Indian land. The U.S. government responded that the partition suit was binding on Cochiti because the pueblo had been represented in the case by Wilson, the special attorney for the Pueblo Indians of New Mexico. The Indian Claims Commission agreed with this position and found against Cochiti, primarily on the ground that the partition suit had already adjudicated the issues against Cochiti.

However, rather than rest its decision solely on the narrow ground of prior adjudication in the partition suit, the Indian Claims Commission examined the issue of Cochiti's possible aboriginal title to the lands partially covered by the 1744 deed. Cochiti offered proof that it used the land in question and had several shrines there, arguing that it should have been notified and given the right to object to both the Caja del Río and the La Majada land grants. By granting land to non-Indians the Spanish government of New Mexico might have wronged Cochiti, but the Indian Claims Commission decided that it had no jurisdiction to correct such a wrong:

[The United States] acquired the ceded lands from Mexico subject to the titles of the grantees of the two grants and under the treaty we were required to recognize their validity under Mexican law, as we did. If Spain or Mexico perpetrated a wrong on the Cochiti, we are under no obligation to right it under international law, the Treaty of Guadalupe Hidalgo, or under the Indian Claims Commission Act. The record is devoid of proof showing any duty or obligation of defendant to the Cochiti that makes defendant liable in any way for the action of the Spanish government in granting Cochiti lands to non-Indians.[43]

An act of Congress in 1984 superseded this narrow ruling of the Indian Claims Commission and awarded the land conveyed in the 1744 deed to Cochiti.

◆ ◆ ◆ ◆

Less than five years after the Indian Claims Commission ruling, plans were being made that would forever change Cochiti and result in the destruction of numerous sacred sites. When the idea of a huge dam and a lake near the pueblo were first presented to Cochiti, the tribal council rejected it, but a few years later pressure from the U.S. Army Corps of Engineers and even the Bureau of Indian Affairs led some in the pueblo to agree that economic development might be the answer to some of Cochiti's problems.[44] Although some tribal members accepted the plan, the council was divided and pressured by the threat of condemnation of their land. No one was aware of the extent of the development that was planned or the massive loss of agricultural land and sacred sites that the plan entailed. Pueblo members were in for a rude shock. Not only was a dam going to flood Cochiti's sacred sites, but a development called the Town of Cochiti Lake was going to be built.[45] When younger pueblo leaders saw what was happening they fought back, seeking "to slay the two-headed monster," to use the vivid metaphor of pueblo leader Regis Pecos. The pueblo soon learned that it was a three-headed monster, the third head being the threat to use the dam to generate hydroelectric power.

Soon after completion of the dam, the extent of the devastation became apparent. Pecos spoke of the effect on Cochiti elders:

They spoke with a deep sense of hurt that they had failed as the stewards and the protectors of this incredible, beautiful, and sacred place to our pueblo people. It was the heart of what gave meaning to our lives. . . . One of the most emotional periods in our history was watching our ancestors torn from their resting places, removed during excavation. The places of worship were dynamited, destroyed, and desecrated by the construction. When the flood gates closed and waters filled Cochiti lake, to see the devastation to all of the agricultural land upon which we had walked and had learned the lessons of life from our grandfathers destroyed before our eyes was like the world was coming to an end. And all we could do was watch.[46]

Although Cochiti farmlands were downstream from the dam, its construction raised the water table dramatically, and the earthen dam seeped, which resulted in the fields becoming seriously waterlogged. This eventually led to a lawsuit against the Corps of Engineers. The lawsuit was filed against an initially uncooperative Corps of Engineers in November 1985.[47] After the corps denied responsibility for the seepage problem, Congress held hearings in March 1988, at which pueblo representatives testified that the construction of Cochiti Dam and subsequent seepage under the dam caused serious damage. Former governor Fred Cordero testified that the shrine where Whirlpool Rock used to sit was desecrated in violation of an agreement with the Corps of Engineers. Construction of the dam destroyed the shrine, which was sacred to all Pueblo Indians.[48] The governor of Cochiti, John Bowannie, then presented a moving statement noting that flooding destroyed 615 acres out of the total of 800 acres suitable for farming. Governor Bowannie worried that the seepage would affect the pueblo, flooding homes and kivas and further threatening its traditional way of life. As a result of the hearings and the efforts of Senators Jeff Bingaman and Pete Domenici, Cochiti reached a settlement with the Corps of Engineers that helped minimize the seepage problem and provide reparations.[49]

The dam and lake were devastating to Cochiti lands and culture, but the planned development, the second head of the monster, was even worse. In the late 1960s, a company called Great Western Cities persuaded Cochiti that a housing development near the lake would bring prosperity to the tribe. The pueblo, again under pressure from the Bureau of Indian Affairs and Corps of Engineers, approved a ninety-nine-year lease of nearly a third of Cochiti's grant lands to the development company, which then sublet lots to people who could construct homes on them. The plan called for Cochiti Lake City to have an eventual population of fifty thousand with restaurants, schools, businesses, and all the amenities associated with a typical non-Indian community. With opposition to the plan from the pueblo and its allies, the development sputtered and never really gained momentum. In 1984, with only a few lots sold and fewer than 150 houses built, Great Western Cities filed for bankruptcy.[50]

At this point the pueblo leaders decided to fight back with a combination of lawsuits and prayer. Cochiti formed the Cochiti Community Development Corporation and devised a plan to invest several million dollars in the project. The pueblo petitioned the bankruptcy court, asking to take over as developer. Cochiti's development company purchased the lease out of the bankruptcy proceeding and took over the development. Cochiti planned to scale down the development, but the pueblo's new master plan was primarily a way of giving Cochiti control, of becoming "the landlord of our own land as a way to force the developers out" and "to reduce the size of . . . the Town of Cochiti Lake to a manageable size."[51]

Unfortunately, just as Cochiti began to take control of the development of the Town of Cochiti Lake and began to work with the Army Corps of Engineers to reduce the effect of flooding on agricultural lands and on sacred sites, the third head of the monster appeared and attacked even more fiercely than the other two. The Corps of Engineers began pushing a proposal to construct a hydroelectric facility at the dam, and an application was made to the Federal Energy Regulatory Commission to issue a license for such a facility. Meeting the threat of hydroelectric power generation meant more litigation and more prayer. The location of this planned development was one of the most sacred Cochiti sites. In the words of one elder, to further desecrate this site in return for income to the pueblo "would be like throwing the sacred cornmeal with one hand and reaching out with the other hand for cash." Cochiti had to fight the developer in court but soon realized that to make its case the pueblo would have to disclose secret religious information. This would violate "one of the most fundamental tenets . . . of pueblo religion," the prohibition against divulging any aspect of that religion.[52] The pueblo was on the horns of an impossible dilemma: either divulge secret sacred information or lose the battle to protect a very sacred site.

The Cochiti Tribal Council came to the realization that anyone who made the arguments in court that were needed to meet the burden of proof about the religious nature of Cochiti sacred sites would have to be "excommunicated," because that person would have broken a sacred vow in order to protect the site.[53] In the end, the tribal elders decided that they could not ask that sacrifice of anyone. Thus, the elders would once again fail in their sacred trust to protect Cochiti places of worship. Rather than sacrifice a pueblo member, it seemed that Cochiti would have to walk away from the fight and allow the hydroelectric project to proceed, but Congressman Bill Richardson introduced legislation at the last minute to prevent hydroelectric power generation at the Cochiti Dam site. Opponents of the bill argued that such an accommodation to Cochiti would set a dangerous precedent and that other tribes would marshal the same arguments to delay or prevent similar water projects. Nevertheless, Richardson's bill passed just before adjournment, an answer to Cochiti's fervent prayers.[54]

Now that the third head of the monster had been lopped off through the efforts of Cochiti and its allies, a huge effort got under way to study the history, archeology, ethnobotany, and legal history of the pueblo. Funding of a large number of studies brought forth experts from many disciplines. The National Park Service, the U.S. Army Corps of Engineers, the U.S. Forest Service, and the University of New Mexico were among those who funded research. Some of these studies were salvage archeology, whose practitioners explore and document important sites before they are inundated and lost forever. Similar studies were done at other large dams and lakes, such as Abiquiu Dam. Lawyers, historians, and surveyors reviewed the history of Cochiti's land dealings to determine whether another attempt could be made to regain lost land.[55]

Investigations focused on the Indian Claims Commission's decision regarding the 1744 Bartolomé Fernández purchase. The commission rejected the claim because it was held that the La Majada and Caja del Río grants superseded it. In neither case was Cochiti afforded an opportunity to object to the grant, but while acknowledging that this might have been a violation of Spanish law, the commission decided that it did not have the power to correct this injustice. By the 1980s U.S. Forest Service held this land east of the pueblo, and a new attempt was launched to return it to Cochiti. The Forest Service described the land as the Santa Cruz spring tract, and Cochiti questioned its size and the fairness of the decision. The Indian Claims Commission said it was about 25,000 acres, but the survey submitted to the commission showed a much smaller tract.

In 1980 the Bureau of Indian Affairs conducted a field trip and survey with about eight pueblo elders. They found Mark Radcliffe's survey, which was submitted to the Indian Claims Commission, to be in error by more than 10,000 acres. The leader of this field trip and survey, Milford Keene, was of the opinion that Cochiti had been misled. His new survey amounted to approximately 24,000 acres, which was much closer to the 25,000 acres referred to in the testimony than the 13,440-acre survey Radcliffe submitted to the Indian Claims Commission. Keene added that Radcliffe had made numerous land-description and surveying errors at other pueblos, which resulted in multiple problems. Finally, Keene stated that he thought Radcliffe's version of the Santa Cruz spring tract was in error.[56] Armed with this new survey, Cochiti and its allies, which by now included the Army Corps of Engineers and local ranchers, introduced a bill in Congress to transfer to the pueblo the approximately 24,000 acres in the newly surveyed tract to be held in trust. The bill passed, and Cochiti was finally able to regain a good portion of the lands it had lost.

Throughout its legal history Cochiti fought to retain its lands from encroachment from all sides: on the north, from Antonio Lucero and the Cañada de Cochití grant; on the south, from Luis María Cabeza de Baca; on the east, from the Caja del Río and La Majada grants; and the west, from Miguel and Domingo Romero and the family of Antonio Lucero. In its extensive court battles, Cochiti was almost uniformly unsuccessful in the nineteenth and early twentieth centuries, partly because it lacked effective advocacy and partly because the powerful Hispanos with whom the pueblo fought often influenced the outcome or refused to comply with court orders and decrees when they lost in court. Particularly outrageous was the treatment Cochiti received at the hands of officials whose job it was to protect the pueblo's rights during the 1815 litigation with Luis María Cabeza de Baca. Protector of Indians José Joaquín Reyes in Guadalajara and protectors of Indians Vicente Villanueva and Ignacio María Sánchez Vergara all made legal arguments contrary to Cochiti's interests. Most egregious was Sanchez Vergara, who claimed some of the land in dispute. Cochiti suffered from poor representation throughout most of its history, but ultimately, in the aftermath of Cochiti Dam, Cochiti Lake, and the Town of Cochiti Lake and following numerous studies of the pueblo and its sacred sites lost to flooding, Cochiti Pueblo has gained some of the land it lost and taken control of its destiny.

Jemez Pueblo commemorating the return of remains of its ancestors.
Drawing by Glen Strock.

CHAPTER 7

Jemez Pueblo

According to Jemez oral history as historian Joe Sando recounted it, the Towa-speaking people of Jemez originated at Wá˙vinatɨ˙tá (also Hua-na-tota), a lake in the north, which is said to be Stone Lake on the Jicarilla Apache reservation, south of Dulce, New Mexico. By 1300 CE they were living in the mountains and on the mesas above the present-day village of Walatowa.[1] Other Jemez people locate their place of origin in the Four Corners area.[2]

In the fifteenth and sixteenth centuries, the Jemez people "developed a distinctive material culture and settlement system in the upper Rio Jemez, Rio Guadalupe, and Rito Vallecito drainages."[3] When the Spaniards explored the Rio Jemez valley in 1541, they found seven pueblos whose inhabitants referred to themselves as "Hemes" and who were clearly distinct from their Tewa neighbors.[4] Franciscans probably established a mission at Giusewa not long after fray Alonso de Lugo arrived in 1601. The mission did not last long and was likely abandoned by 1610.[5] Seventeenth-century Spanish documents name five missions: San José de los Jémez, San Diego de la Congregación, San Diego de los Jémez, San Diego del Monte, and San Juan de los Jémez.[6] In 1621 fray Gerónimo de Zárate Salmerón founded San José de los Jémez and San Diego de la Congregación in an attempt to get the Jemez people to come down off their mesas and settle in the two mission villages.[7]

The residents of San Diego de la Congregación rebelled in 1623, burning the mission and returning to the mesa tops. Three years later fray Martín de

Arvide reestablished the San Diego mission. San José was permanently abandoned in the period from 1632 to 1639, after which time San Diego de la Congregación was the only functioning Franciscan mission among the Jemez people until the Pueblo Revolt of 1680. Jemez played a very significant role in the Revolt and killed fray Juan de Jesús, one of the two Franciscans assigned to the mission of San Diego de la Congregación.[8] As Hispanos were leaving New Mexico, the inhabitants of Santa Ana, Zia, and Jemez (among others) were not touched because they were outside the direct line of march, but they were reported to be openly hostile to Hispanos.

When Vargas returned to New Mexico during his ceremonial reconquest in 1692, he took possession of the Jemez pueblo located on San Diego Mesa. The following year when Vargas came back with colonists and an obvious intention to remain, Jemez continued to rebel and attacked neighboring pueblos, such as Zia, which were allying themselves with the Hispanos. Vargas then punished Jemez by attacking Astialakwa, the refugee village atop Guadalupe Mesa, in July 1694. The defeated Jemez Indians were forced to fight against Tewa rebels on Black Mesa. In order to secure the return of pueblo members who were prisoners of the Spaniards, the Jemez people rebuilt San Diego de la Congregación, which received the new name San Juan de los Jémez. The site of the mission was Walatowa, the present-day pueblo on the east bank of the Jemez River, about 20 miles northwest of Bernalillo.[9]

In June 1696 the Jemez people revolted again and killed fray Francisco de Jesús at San Diego del Monte mission. Vargas retaliated by launching punitive expeditions against the pueblo. Later in the month of June, the Jemez people were defeated in the Battle of San Diego Canyon, but even then many of them moved west to live among the Navajos, the Hopis, and possibly other tribes. Others took refuge in the Jemez Mountains.[10] By 1703 some Jemez refugees had reoccupied their village at Walatowa.[11] In 1706 they rebuilt the mission church there.[12] A contingent of Jemez Indians who were living among the Hopis came back to their homeland in 1716.[13]

◆ ◇ ◆ ◇

Early in the eighteenth century, several pueblos began to demand that Spanish authorities measure the four square leagues surrounding the pueblo to which they were entitled. Invariably, the Pueblo league was measured in response to the claim by the pueblo that a Hispano was encroaching on pueblo land. Often a Spanish land grant was proposed or made adjacent to pueblo land that overlapped the Pueblo league. For example, measurements made in response to requests by local land owners, such as that of Rafael García in 1833, partially defined the Jemez league.[14]

Several grants encroached on the Jemez league, particularly the San Isidro grant and others to be discussed later. The Jemez league was nevertheless measured and was eventually confirmed and patented to the pueblo. In September 1855 Jemez submitted a claim to the surveyor general of New Mexico based on its Cruzate grant, which granted the pueblo four square leagues of land measured from the church in the center of the pueblo, one league in each direction.[15] Congress confirmed the Jemez grant in 1858, and Deputy Surveyor John Garretson surveyed it at 17,510 acres. The grant was patented in 1864.[16]

In addition to its pueblo league, Jemez, along with Zia and Santa Ana, received the Ojo del Espíritu Santo grazing grant west of the pueblo. This grant represented an attempt to protect these pueblos' traditional grazing lands by preventing grants to Hispanos that would encroach on those lands. This grant from Governor Vélez Cachupín was eventually overrun by the very Hispano grants it was designed to prevent and was rejected by the Court of Private Land Claims. The Ojo del Espíritu Santo grant (subsequently surveyed at more than 382,000 acres), encompassed the traditional hunting ground and grazing land that all three pueblos shared as well as numerous sacred sites (including the Espíritu Santo spring).[17] Vélez Cachupín was well aware of the problem of encroachment and the need to protect Pueblo land, having made some of the adjacent land grants to Hispano settlers and similar grazing grants to other pueblos and Hispanos.[18]

In June 1766 Felipe Tafoya filed a petition on behalf of Zia, Jemez, and Santa Ana for the Ojo del Espíritu Santo grant in the name of Cristóbal, the governor of Zia, and Tomás, the war captain of Zia. Acting on behalf of the three pueblos, Tafoya alleged that they had used the land as common pastures for grazing sheep, cattle, and horses since "the time of the foundation" of each pueblo. He added that the presidial horse herd also pastured on the land. Since Hispanos had petitioned for land grants in the area, the three pueblos asked Governor Vélez Cachupín to declare the Ojo del Espíritu Santo tract as *pastos concejiles* (common pasture) of the three pueblos. The boundaries requested were La Ventana on the north, where some Navajo Apaches resided, the pueblos of Zia, Santa Ana, and Jemez on the east, the lands of the settlers of the Rio Puerco on the south, and the rim of the bank (ceja) of the Rio Puerco on the west.[19]

Governor Vélez Cachupín ordered Alcalde Bartolomé Fernández to go to the Espíritu Santo tract, examine the boundaries, measure the distance from north to south and east to west, and determine whether the three pueblos had sufficient livestock to justify the amount of land requested. Even though there was no notice of the petition given to the adjoining landowners at this time, Fernández was to determine whether the grant would prejudice the rights of third parties.[20] Fernández determined that the distance from La Ventana on the north to the stone ford (where the settlers of the Rio Puerco were located) was about eight leagues (about 21 miles), and the distance from Zia (the nearest pueblo to the land) was about six leagues (about 15½ miles). According to Fernández there was very little water on the land, making the tract suitable only for grazing. Since the three pueblos had many cattle and sheep and no place else to pasture them, and given that the proposed grant would not prejudice the rights of any third party, Governor Vélez Cachupín decided to make the grant.[21] On 6 August 1776 he granted the land to the three pueblos for grazing their livestock on the condition that the stallions of the presidial horse herd could be pastured there if necessary. With the exception of this condition, the land granted was to be considered the property of the three pueblos and not subject to any other grant or use by Hispanos. Vélez Cachupín added that the pueblos "own the land with legitimate right by means of this royal grant."[22]

Present when the three pueblos took possession of the land were Alcalde Fernández; several Hispanos from the settlement of San Fernando del Río Puerco; and the governors, caciques, and war captains from each pueblo. Fernández fulfilled his mandate of determining whether there were any conflicting claims by having the Rio Puerco settlers present. It turned out, however, that the threat of encroachment on the Ojo del Espíritu Santo grant came not from the east, where the Rio Puerco settlers were located, but from the west. There being no objection by the Rio Puerco settlers, the grantees completed the act of possession of the Espíritu Santo grant by throwing stones and pulling up grass, thereby proving their ownership of the property. The land described was north to south from La Ventana to the stone ford and east to west from the boundary of Zia to the bank (orilla) of the Rio Puerco.[23]

The Court of Private Land Claims rejected the Jemez, Zia, and Santa Ana grazing grant, as will be seen, but now we turn our attention to two grants that encroached to the greatest extent on Jemez and the 1766 Ojo del Espíritu Santo grant: the San Isidro grant and the 1815 Ojo del Espíritu Santo grant. In 1786 Antonio Armenta, alcalde of the Keres Pueblos, and Salvador Antonio Sandoval, a presidial soldier, requested from Governor Anza a tract of land that became known as the town of San Isidro grant, east of the Ojo del Espíritu Santo grant. This was similar to several other grants in the area made to alcaldes or Spanish officials who learned about available land in their capacity as Spanish officials. Both Bartolomé Fernández and Felipe Tafoya, the officials involved with the Ojo del Espíritu Santo grant, received similar grants.[24] Since the proposed San Isidro grant was bounded by Jemez on the north and Zia on the south, Governor Anza agreed to grant the request of the petitioners on the conditions that the grant would not overlap with the lands of those two pueblos and that the two pueblos' preemption and use of the water would not be interfered with.[25]

When Alcalde Nerio Antonio Montoya of Alameda met with the grantees to place them in possession of the grant, representatives of both Zia and Jemez appeared to object because of encroachment of the grant on their lands. Alcalde Montoya was not exactly a disinterested party, for he owned land to the east of the San Isidro grant. Nevertheless, he did notify both Jemez and Zia and listen to their objections. Jemez claimed to have planted some land within the boundaries of the proposed San Isidro grant, so Alcalde Montoya extended the boundaries of the Jemez league by 262 varas to include the contested land. Alcalde Montoya also extended the boundary of the Zia league by 1,000 varas to encompass two tracts of land Zia had purchased from Hispanos: the Juan Galván and Miguel Montoya tracts. Besides encroaching on the Pueblo leagues of both Jemez and Zia, the town of San Isidro grant encroached on the western part of the Ojo del Espíritu Santo grant. But Alcalde Montoya found that a 2,900-vara tract between the two pueblos was still available and made the grant with the following boundaries: Jemez on the north; Zia on the south; Nerio Antonio Montoya's land on the east; and the mountain of the Ojo del Espíritu Santo at the place called Los Blancos on the west. Even though the San Isidro grant encroached on Zia, Santa Ana, and Jemez land (including the 1766 Ojo del Espíritu Santo grant), Spanish government officials were clearly protective of the rights of the pueblos and did everything they could to adjust the boundaries of pueblo land to accommodate them.[26]

The main grant to Hispanos that overlapped the Ojo del Espíritu Santo grant was the 1815 Ojo del Espíritu Santo grant made to Luis María Cabeza de Baca, grandfather of Diego Baca.[27] In 1815 Luis María Cabeza de Baca and his family received their own grant, also called the Ojo del Espíritu Santo grant, covering similar boundaries, a fact that has confused historians and mapmakers. We distinguish the two by prefacing the name of the grant with the date it was granted, either 1766 or 1815. In spite of the encroachments on the 1766 Ojo del Espíritu Santo grant, all three pueblos grazed their cattle there, except during times of hostility with the Navajos, when they moved the stock to a safer place.[28]

◆ ◆ ◆ ◆

Zia, Santa Ana, and Jemez submitted a claim for the 1766 Ojo del Espíritu Santo grant to the surveyor general of New Mexico in 1856, but there was no action until 1874, when the pueblos hired attorney Samuel Ellison. Ellison petitioned Surveyor General James Proudfit for confirmation of the grant, and the claimants submitted the certified copy of the 1766 grant proceedings. Proudfit took extensive testimony about the use of the land.[29] One witness testified that the three pueblos used the grant for grazing their livestock and that no one claimed an adverse interest in the grant except "Diego Baca [who] has resided at the spring for the last three or four years and has been cultivating the land and has some livestock there."[30] On 2 February 1874, Proudfit recommended the 1766 Ojo del Espíritu Santo grant for confirmation by Congress, noting that the three pueblos proved "an absolute grant and full possession under it."[31] The 1877 survey of the grant found it to contain 382,849 acres.

By the time that Proudfit recommended the confirmation of the 1766 Ojo del Espíritu Santo grant, however, the entire surveyor general system for land-grant confirmation had broken down, and Congress looked askance at every grant recommended. Not until the establishment of the Court of Private Land Claims in 1891 were Zia, Santa Ana, and Jemez able to file suit for confirmation of their grant.[32]

In the meantime, Hispano encroachment on the Ojo del Espíritu Santo grant was taking place at a rapid rate. Indian agent M. C. Williams brought the issue of encroachment of other grants on the Ojo del Espíritu Santo grant to the attention of John D. C. Atkins, commissioner of Indian Affairs, on 18 June 1888. Williams listed several grants as lying wholly or partially within the 1766 Ojo del Espíritu Santo grant, including the 1815 Ojo del Espíritu Santo grant and the 1786 San Isidro grant. Williams said he was completely frustrated in his attempts to protect the Espíritu Santo grant from encroachment.

> No steps have been taken to protect the land from being encroached upon save [for] notices posted forbidding parties to occupy Indian lands. The greater part of the parties who are occupying the said land have been there for many years [and] cannot be ousted from said land save by legal process.... [I]t is utterly impracticable for me to attempt to remove any of them [even] if I had the power.[33]

The only suggestion that Williams had was for the Indian Department to "prevent the confirmation and patenting of anymore [overlapping] grants ... until the grant to the Indians is confirmed and patented." Although this was a good suggestion, it fell on deaf ears. There was little inclination for the Indian Service to become involved in the adjudication of pueblo lands, and in any case Congress never confirmed the Espíritu Santo grant after Surveyor General Proudfit's initial approval.[34]

In their petition to the Court of Private Land Claims, George Hill Howard and Henry Earle represented the plaintiffs, claiming that the three pueblos had received "a formal and final grant, in fee absolute, coupled with no conditions" except that the presidial horse herd could also use the grant when necessary.[35] The three pueblos noted that there were several nearby or overlapping grants in the area but that the Ojo del Espíritu Santo grant was senior to them all. Of the overlapping or potentially overlapping grants, the San Isidro and the 1815 Espíritu Santo grants were the most problematic because in both cases there had been occupation of the 1766 Ojo del Espíritu Santo grant by claimants under those grants, and their heirs and successors were making claims in this lawsuit before the land claims court. Mariano Otero had a ranch on the Ojo del Espiritu Santo grant, and Pedro Perea, Mariano Otero, and Charles Gildersleeve were claiming that interest, while Diego Baca claimed an interest under the 1815 Ojo del Espíritu Santo grant, and Thomas B. Catron was claiming that interest. The petition for confirmation of the Ojo del Espíritu Santo grant referred to these conflicting grants and alleged that all were subsequent to the original 1766 Ojo del Espíritu Santo grant. If they were confirmed (as was the 1815 Ojo del Espíritu Santo grant), this was done without notifying Zia, Santa Ana, or Jemez, making these grants void.[36]

After a lengthy trial dominated by Catron, whose questions sought to belittle Indian witnesses in an attempt to prove that the three pueblos did not have exclusive possession of the land, the Court of Private Land Claims rejected the original 1766 Ojo del Espíritu Santo grant. The court held that Zia, Santa Ana, and Jemez did not receive an absolute grant that vested title in the three pueblos. Instead, they enjoyed a "possessory right which could be revoked by the Spanish or Mexican authorities at any time and was liable to be forfeited by abandonment or nonuse, [and] that the re-granting of various portions of the grant . . . evidenced its forfeiture."[37]

Governor Vélez Cachupín had made it clear that the 1766 Ojo del Espíritu Santo grant was the absolute property of the three pueblos and was not subject to another grant or even use by Hispanos. Clearly the intent of the 1766 Ojo del Espíritu Santo grant was for it to be permanent and irrevocable, not temporary and revocable. Nevertheless, the Court of Private Land Claims entered its decree rejecting the 1766 Ojo del Espíritu Santo grant on 18 August 1893.[38]

Dissatisfied by the decision of the Court of Private Land Claims, Zia, Santa Ana, and Jemez appealed to the U.S. Supreme Court. The same lawyers who argued the case in the lower court, Earle for the three pueblos (Howard was no longer involved) and Matthew Givens Reynolds for the U.S. government, briefed and argued the case in the Supreme Court. Right at the beginning of the short opinion rendered by Justice Henry Billings Brown, the court opined that the 1766 Ojo del Espíritu Santo grant established "a right somewhat akin to the right of common under the English law."[39] The justices were unable to apply the principles of Spanish law to determine Vélez Cachupín's true intent and affirmed the decision of the Court of Private Land Claims rejecting the grant.

◆ ◆ ◆ ◆

By the early 1800s, the population of Jemez Pueblo was growing steadily, while Pecos Pueblo was losing members in a gradual attrition due in large part to several factors, including disease, enemy raiding, and declining birth rate.[40] By 1837 or 1838, as the population dwindled to a handful of Pecos Indians, the remnants of Pecos Pueblo decided to accept the invitation of the linguistically related Jemez Pueblo to abandon its ancestral home and move to Jemez. Stories differ as to how many and which Pecos Indians moved to Jemez. Mariano Ruiz told Adolph Bandelier one of the best-known accounts in the fall of 1880. Ruiz, who claimed to have come from Jemez to Pecos in 1837, told Bandelier that after an invitation from a delegation from Jemez, the Pecos remnants, numbering only five individuals, appeared before Governor Manuel Armijo and declared their intention to abandon Pecos Pueblo and move to Jemez. No documentation of this meeting has surfaced, but Ruiz also said that he received a deed from the remaining Pecos Indians to the land he was occupying.[41]

Jemez historian Joe Sando listed twenty-one immigrants from Pecos to Jemez, whose families were living in the pueblo in 1982 when *Nee Hemish* was published. These individuals could have been the descendants of the five or so heads of families said to have journeyed to Jemez in 1838. Several of the families Sando listed included his own ancestors, and several of the members of these families adopted the surname "Pecos." Many Jemez leaders came from this pool of Pecos immigrants. Among those who served as governors of Jemez were Juan Antonio Toya, the governor of Pecos who brought his people to Jemez in 1838, and Agustin Cota Pecos, who served in 1888. José Romero, who was governor of Jemez in the late 1890s, was also from Pecos.[42]

The Pecos faction at Jemez still claimed ownership of Pecos Pueblo, although Ruiz stated he had a deed from Pecos officials to the land he was occupying when Bandelier interviewed him in 1880, and a Pecos Indian named José Cota deeded the ciénega of Pecos to Juan Estevan Pino on behalf of the entire Pecos Pueblo.[43] Most of the land comprising the Pecos grant was sold, but the remaining Pecos Indians at Jemez still wanted to file a claim for their lost Pueblo league. Even though the Pecos grant was submitted to the surveyor general, approved by Congress, and patented to Pecos Pueblo, title to all the land passed into non-Indian hands either before the patent was issued in 1864 or soon thereafter. In 1859 representatives of Pecos Pueblo living at Jemez asked their Indian agent to either restore their Pecos lands to them so they could be sold or leased for their benefit or to purchase additional land for them in the Jemez area. When this and other similar requests came to nothing, several of the remnants of Pecos living at Jemez took action. Unfortunately for them, they signed a document that led to the complete loss of Pecos land to members of the pueblo.[44]

In 1868 eleven Pecos emigrants living at Jemez executed a power of attorney to John Ward, a former Indian agent, expecting him to provide them with legal representation and obtain some compensation for their lost land. But instead of representing Pecos, Ward sold the land. Thereafter, a long series of transactions and several parallel chains of title finally ended in a suit by Gross, Kelly and Company to quiet title to the entire Pecos Pueblo grant. Gross, Kelly and Company then sold the Pecos grant to a San Diego investment company. During this long and intricate chain of title, money passed hands at just about every transaction, but none of it went to the surviving Pecos Indians living at Jemez.[45]

Still refusing to give up, in April 1921 three Pecos descendants living at Jemez asked Leo Crane, the Southern Pueblos superintendent, to inquire about the possibility of regaining their lost land. Crane wrote a long history of Pecos, which amounted to "an appeal to the people of the United States in the Pueblo Indian nation's fight against the proposed Holm Bursum Bill of 1922."[46] When the Pueblo Lands Board (discussed in chapter 10) heard the Pecos case, it concluded that the Pecos descendants living at Jemez no longer had an interest in Pecos lands, but it nevertheless recommended

> that if possible suitable lands be purchased near Jemez, and that such lands be assigned for the specific use of Pecos descendants living in the Pueblo of Jemez; or if such lands could not be segregated for the specific use of Pecos descendants, that they be added to those of Jemez Pueblo generally. The board was informed that according to church records there were then about two hundred and fifty people at Jemez with Pecos blood, and that it would be difficult to divide lands between Indians of the two backgrounds.

Instead of returning land, the Pueblo Lands Board recommended payment of $1.50 per acre, based on "approximate average value from the occupancy of this territory in 1846 to the present time," which amounted to an award of $28,145.[47] Congress appropriated the money on 14 February 1931, and on 19 June 1936 passed an act to consolidate Pecos and Jemez pueblos. This made it possible for Pecos to "spend the meager amount awarded to Pecos by the Pueblo Lands Board." In 1937, after the consolidation, the sum of $28,145, together with a payment of $2,385 for Jemez land held by non-Indians, was transferred to the Jemez trust fund account in Washington, D.C.[48]

On 1 September 1906, Jemez also received a tract of almost 15,000 acres to the west of the pueblo. This land, together with several additional purchases at tax sales and transfers from the government, brought the current total of Jemez land to 89,957 acres. In addition to this land, Jemez had use rights in the form of grazing leases to the Ojo del Espíritu Santo and the San Isidro grants, both of which the U.S. government purchased.

◆ ◆ ◆ ◆

In the mid-1930s the federal government instituted a program of acquisition of former Spanish land grant lands in order to make them available for grazing to neighboring Hispano communities and Indian pueblos. This was part of a Depression-era program designed by John Collier, the commissioner of Indian Affairs. The government bought land grants at tax sales or from speculators who had acquired the land under questionable circumstances, as was the case with the Ojo del Espíritu Santo and the San Isidro grants.

In July 1936 the Rural Resettlement Administration was in the process of acquiring the San Isidro grant for grazing use by the neighboring pueblos. This brought the matter of the patent and final survey of the San Isidro grant to a head. On 28 July 1936, the Grant Lands Office chief C. G. Tudor issued an opinion on the points raised earlier by the surveyor general George Washington Julian, holding that the act of possession did not show that the additional lands granted to the Jemez Indians were located south of their league. Therefore, he held that the south line of the Pueblo of Jemez grant should be common with the north line of the San Isidro grant. In fact, it was not true that the act of possession of the San Isidro grant did not award additional land south of the Jemez league to the pueblo. But it seems that the dead hand of Julian prevailed, coupled with forty years of inaction. To add insult to injury, Tudor pretended that Jemez made no claim to these lands when he stated that "it appears from the records of this office that no lands are claimed by the Indians south of the south boundary." This was so only because the government made a point of not contacting Jemez. Tudor's opinion concluded by holding that the 1877 survey by Daniel Sawyer and Stephen McElroy should not be set aside, because all the interested parties had accepted it as being correct for more than sixty years. In addition, he recommended patenting the grant according to that survey. Although the grant was finally patented on 14 November 1936, it soon became apparent that Jemez was an interested party and did not recognize the northern boundary on the Sawyer and McElroy survey as the proper boundary line of the grant.[49]

In the late 1930s and 1940s the San Isidro grant was administered by the Bureau of Indian Affairs to provide grazing land for both Zia and Jemez. The two pueblos differed, however, on the question of the proportion of the grant that would be allotted to each pueblo. In 1940, when the northern boundary of the San Isidro grant began to be fenced, Jemez Governor George Toledo immediately protested to General Superintendent Sophie Aberle, in a letter dated 23 January 1940. He questioned the authorization for the fence, stating that the three pueblos (Jemez, Zia, and Santa Ana) were entitled to use the same grazing land, and that prior to the fencing of the northern boundary, Jemez had had free access to the San Isidro grant. By this time about 3 miles, or approximately half of the northern boundary, were fenced. On 26 January United Pueblos Agency director Dan T. O'Neill stated that it would be impossible to pull up and move the fencing already in place and suggested that Jemez and Zia agree on some division of the remaining area.

Jemez officials asked that the grant be divided through the center, east to west; Zia officials demanded that the grant be fenced within their grazing area. They finally asked O'Neill to decide the location, which he agreed to do if they would sign a statement accepting his decision. O'Neill established a line providing for about 1,000 acres for Jemez and more than 4,000 acres for Zia. This land was eventually established as trust lands for the two pueblos. The Jemez Indians protested the division, but since they had signed the agreement, they were bound to its terms. They believed that "they were entitled to as much land as Zia. Acting Superintendent Alan Laflin told them that they would be issued permits to enter the Zia portion of the grant to hunt rabbits, collect firewood, and conduct ceremonies at their sacred areas, but that the agency could do little else, in view of the signed agreement." Thus, the Jemez people regained the use of land that they once considered theirs. This establishment of trust lands on contested land was a pattern established for other pueblos as well.[50]

Cochiti also secured grazing leases as a result of Collier's land reform program that acquired land grants to provide grazing lands to both Hispanos and Indians. Initially, the U.S. government purchased the 1815 Espíritu Santo grant from Charles C. Catron for the use of the Jemez, Zia, and other Pueblo Indians. Jemez and Zia sheepmen began using the grant in April 1935.

Collier, however, had approved the transfer of the Ojo del Espíritu Santo grant from pueblo to primarily Hispano use "at a time when he still hoped to mobilize the Hispano rancher behind his land reform program."[51] Jemez sent a protest petition to Secretary Collier, which made a strong plea for the pueblos to be allowed to continue using the Espíritu Santo grant.

> Our friends, please look over this matter again and think of all the times that we have wondered why we lost the Espíritu Santo grant, why we couldn't use it when old Catron had it, . . . and think about how helpless we were in any old court proceedings, and when you think about these things, try your very best to let us keep the Espíritu Santo grant which, no matter what the papers say, actually in spirit belongs to us.[52]

Upon receipt of the petition, Commissioner Collier wrote a memorandum to Secretary of the Interior Ickes recommending that the department seek a revision of the 1938 agreement between Interior and Agriculture in order to give Jemez and Zia Pueblos continued-use rights to the portion of the Espíritu Santo grant they then occupied.[53] Collier admitted that he had recommended the removal of all Indian sheep from the Espíritu Santo grant to the Montaño grant without seeking clearance from the tribes or the superintendent. Secretary Ickes then wrote to the governors of the three pueblos of Zia, Santa Ana, and Jemez, noting that their "recital of the history of the Espíritu Santo grant is very interesting and persuasive. . . . In the light of the record I am instructing Commissioner Collier to negotiate for a revision of the agreement."[54] Soon thereafter a modification of the 1938 agreement was signed, providing that Jemez and Zia be given permanent use privileges on the Espíritu Santo grant.

Vindication of Jemez's traditional rights to the Ojo del Espíritu Santo grant on paper did not translate to exclusive grazing by Jemez and the other pueblos in practice. There were just too many large-scale, mostly Anglo, stockmen with large herds of animals from adjacent communities without sufficient grazing lands. In January 1938 the stockmen from the neighboring communities of Cabezon, La Ventana, Guadalupe, San Luis, and Casa Salazar threatened to trespass on Indian grazing land, and in February 42 men with 458 cattle and horses and 1,200 sheep grimly marched through the gates onto the grassy lands of the grant.[55] The Soil Conservation Service ordered the removal of animals owned by the Hispano stockmen from neighboring communities without delay.

The order was ignored, however, and by 1940 the stockmen from surrounding communities "were officially allowed to graze their stock within the Espíritu Santo grant that had been set aside for the exclusive use of Jemez and the other Indian Pueblos." Having lost the Espíritu Santo grazing grant and then gained the right to exclusive grazing on the grant when they produced a copy of the 1766 Espíritu Santo grant, Jemez again lost these exclusive grazing rights.

After losing the battle to regain possession or use of the land, Jemez resubmitted its claim for compensation for the loss of the Ojo del Espíritu Santo grant to the Indian Claims Commission in 1946.[56] The commission was authorized to hear claims by Indian tribes against the U.S. alleging that the government had not "carried out its treaties, had failed to pay them adequately for their land, or had not been 'fair and honorable' in their dealings with them."[57] Zia, Jemez, and Santa Ana Pueblos accordingly filed a petition with the Indian Claims Commission seeking damages for the 298,634 acres covered by the grant. Although the commission recognized that no other Indians permanently occupied the area, it rejected the claim. Jemez appealed the decision to the U.S. Court of Claims, which reversed the Indian Claims Commission on 17 April 1964 and remanded the claim for a determination of the value of the land at the time of the taking, which the parties agreed was in 1848. Eventually, an award of approximately $750,000 was agreed to, which was divided equally among the three pueblos.[58]

In the early 1980s Jemez recovered an acre of prime land near the heart of Jemez village that the pueblo had leased to the Presbyterian Board of Home Missions to operate a school. When the school closed in 1924, the pueblo sued unsuccessfully to have the land returned. Stung by this loss, pueblo historian Joe Sando began researching the history of the lease and hired Boulder, Colorado, Native American Rights Fund attorney John Echohawk to help negotiate a return of the property. The Presbyterians relinquished the property to the pueblo in 1984.[59]

Although Jemez managed to get some of its land back, most of its lost land was never returned; nevertheless the pueblo persevered in its quest to have sacred objects and human remains repatriated to the pueblo. In 1993 Jemez brought many ceremonial objects home from the Smithsonian Museum in time for its 12 November feast day.[60] Anthropologist Elsie Clews Parsons had removed the objects, including altar figurines and ceremonial leather shields, in the early 1930s. They were part of the collection of the Smithsonian Institution, which acquired them from the collection of the Heye Foundation. At the time of the return of Jemez Pueblo's ceremonial objects, Governor Paul Tosa explained why the pueblo considered them as important as pueblo land: "They are living breathing tribal members, ... not just objects. ... They're the protectors, ... they're the fertility, not only to us, but to the whole world."[61] Then, in 1999, Jemez participated in the repatriation of almost two thousand Pecos human remains from Harvard's Peabody Museum to their place of reburial at the Pecos National Historic Park. The importance of the occasion was underscored by a large group of primarily Jemez and other pueblo members who, over the course of three days, walked all the way from Jemez to Pecos Pueblo to honor and pay their last respects at the reburial. By the time they reached Pecos to meet the truck carrying the ancestral remains, the group, which included delegates from Cochiti and other pueblos, as well as Navajos, Kiowas, Comanches, and Mescalero and Jicarilla Apaches, was more than five hundred strong. As the reburial was completed, the spiritual connection with the Pecos land was reinforced. Although the four square leagues of Pecos Pueblo were lost, the "traditional values of Jemez remain 100% strong," said Jemez governor Ruben Sando.[62] With some setbacks and some victories, Jemez has seen some land returned, has received some monetary compensation, and through it all has retained its traditional beliefs and ceremonies.

Governor Domingo Jironza Pétriz de Cruzate interrogating Bartolomé de Ojeda.
Drawing by Glen Strock.

CHAPTER 8

The Surveyor General and the Cruzate Grants

The core landholdings of nine New Mexico pueblos—Picuris, San Juan (Ohkay Owingeh), Cochiti, Santo Domingo, San Felipe, Jemez, Zia, Acoma, and Zuni—are based on documents dated 20 or 25 September 1689, purporting to be grants to those pueblos from Governor Domingo Jironza Pétriz de Cruzate (1689–1691).[1] Congress confirmed most of these grants in 1858, so they are conclusively presumed to be valid from a legal standpoint.[2] Yet all scholars of New Mexico history who have studied the Cruzate grants believe them to be fraudulent.[3] There is substantial evidence demonstrating that these documents, most of which are now kept in the New Mexico State Records Center and Archives, were created no earlier than the mid-1800s. This chapter provides an overview of the evidence that has been proffered to show that these documents are not authentic, including the facts that the paper used was not produced until the 1840s and was certainly not used in 1689 and that some of the language in two of the Cruzate documents came from a book published in 1832. That the documents are not authentic 1689 documents is beyond dispute, but the possibility that these documents were somehow derived from authentic originals that are now lost cannot be entirely ruled out. Yet who created the existing documents, and when, and with what motive are questions that remain unanswered. There are clues in the documentary record as to who might have been involved, but the evidence is scant and entirely circumstantial, and the origin of the Cruzate documents remains one of the most extraordinary mysteries of New Mexico history. This chapter provides a close reading of the Cruzate-grant documents to elucidate and possibly come closer to the heart of that mystery.

The story of the Cruzate grants must start with William Pelham, whose job was seemingly made much easier when these documents appeared. Pelham arrived in Santa Fe on 28 December 1854 as the first surveyor general of New Mexico, a position Congress created by the Act of 22 July 1854.[4] Charged with ascertaining the character, nature, and extent of all private claims to land in New Mexico and with making recommendations to Congress about those claims he thought merited confirmation, Pelham might not have been the best-suited person for the task before him. By all accounts a decent and conscientious public servant, Pelham formerly served as surveyor general of Arkansas, where his job was primarily surveying the public domain and processing claims under U.S. public land laws. In New Mexico, however, he faced problems almost without precedent for a U.S. land official. Spanish and Mexican officials made land grants in the territory, and those grants changed hands, for more than two hundred years. The official records of those transactions were recorded in Spanish, and the documents were bundled and stacked in the rambling, adobe-walled Palace of the Governors in Santa Fe. Pelham neither spoke nor read Spanish and was a surveyor, not a lawyer. He knew nothing of Spanish or Mexican land law or legal history. He repeatedly asked the Department of the Interior to provide him with advice or information on these subjects, but he received none.[5] He was expected to review and base his decisions on the official Spanish and Mexican archives of the territory, which were in disarray, and was provided with few resources with which to organize or analyze them. To make matters worse, hostile Comanches or Apaches repeatedly menaced and occasionally captured his surveying teams.[6] Under these circumstances, that he accomplished as much as he did is remarkable.[7]

Soon after he arrived and set up his office, Pelham hired David V. Whiting as a clerk and translator. Whiting was born in Caracas, Venezuela, in 1827, the son of an American furniture maker, and he was raised there until he was seventeen or eighteen.[8] He then moved to Baltimore and soon afterward became secretary to the Venezuelan legation in Washington. In 1849 he was sent to Santa Fe to settle the estate of a member of a Philadelphia mercantile house with which he was associated who was killed in an Apache and Ute raid on a wagon train near Wagon Mound, New Mexico. Although that trip lasted only a few months, Whiting was back in Santa Fe in October 1850, apparently intending to open a school.[9] James S. Calhoun arrived in Santa Fe on 22 July 1849 as the first Indian agent in New Mexico and was made governor in January 1851. By February 1851, Whiting was working as Calhoun's private secretary and translator.[10] Whiting and Calhoun were accompanying a delegation from Tesuque Pueblo that was traveling to Washington, hoping to meet with President Fillmore, when Calhoun died, near Independence, Missouri, in June 1852. Whiting accompanied the Pueblo members on to Washington and back to Santa Fe.[11] Hired by Pelham three years later, he worked in the surveyor general's office until 29 August 1860.[12]

Pelham also hired David J. Miller, a native of Alabama who was raised and learned Spanish in San Antonio, Texas, while living in the home of Tejano patriot José Antonio Navarro. Miller served as translator in the General Land Office in Austin, Texas, from 1850 to 1854 and then moved to Santa Fe to go to work for Pelham.[13]

Pelham needed to examine documents that purported to establish land titles in the territory, and he asked territorial governor David Merriwether to provide him with any such documents in the archives left from the Spanish and Mexican regimes. Merriwether did not offer to separate out the land documents, having no funding for such a task, but he invited Pelham to tackle the 168 bundles of documents himself. Each bundle held about one thousand separate pages. Miller and Whiting had gone through them by the end of July 1855, identifying 1,715 documents pertaining to grants, conveyances, and other matters related to land titles.[14] Pelham also began to ask New Mexicans, and especially the Pueblo Indians, to bring him any documents in their possession on which they based their claims to land. Procuring documents from New Mexicans turned out to be even more difficult than combing through the archives. Pelham's letters reveal that many New Mexicans, particularly the Pueblo Indians, were highly suspicious of the new government and were entirely unconvinced that it would deal with their claims fairly or that they would ever see their documents again if they brought them to Pelham's office.[15]

Pelham persisted, however, and enlisted the assistance of the agents appointed to deal with the Pueblos, and by late 1856 documents were delivered to him concerning twelve pueblos. The pueblos on whose behalf documents were delivered to Pelham and the dates they were received are as follows: San Juan, 18 August 1855 (two documents); Jemez, 14 September 1855 (two documents for Jemez, and apparently two documents for the then-abandoned Pecos Pueblo); San Felipe, 18 February 1856 (two documents); Acoma, 3 March 1856 (two documents and a third document submitted at a later date, possibly in 1863); Santo Domingo, 12 March 1856 (eight documents); Cochiti, 12 March 1856; Picuris, 12 June 1856; Taos, 2 August 1856; Sandia, 16 October 1856 (two documents); Zia, 16 October 1856; Laguna, 27 June 1857 (two documents). A document was also submitted for San Cristóbal Pueblo, but the surveyor general's docket book gives no filing date, nor does it identify who submitted it. On 3 July 1875, Zuni submitted a Cruzate grant to Surveyor General Henry M. Atkinson.[16]

Sandia brought in its 1748 grant from Governor Codallos y Rabal.[17] Taos Pueblo submitted a letter dated 15 April 1815 from Governor Máynez stating that Taos was entitled to a four-square-league grant.[18] All the grant documents submitted by or for the other pueblos were dated 20 or 25 September 1689, and all were very similar.[19] In a highly irregular form, they purported to be land grants to those pueblos made by then Governor don Domingo Jironza Pétriz de Cruzate. These documents became known as the "Cruzate grants." Pelham eventually submitted nine Cruzate documents (along with the Sandia grant and the Taos document) to the secretary of the interior, with his recommendation for confirmation, by his annual report to the secretary dated 30 September 1856, and Congress confirmed them two years later.[20]

Each Cruzate document is handwritten in the same legible hand on both sides of sheets of paper that measure approximately 8½ × 13 or 8½ × 14 inches. Most consist of a single sheet comprising two pages of text, but a few are in folio and contain three or four pages of text. Although they are supposed to be substantial grants of land to the Pueblos, none is in the typical form of a land grant made in New Mexico in the Spanish or Mexican periods.[21] In that standard form, the documentation typically began with the grantee's petition for the land (whose boundaries were usually described by reference to natural monuments) and offered some justification for why the petitioner sought the grant. There was often a record of investigation by the governor, who commonly referred the task to the alcalde of the place where the lands were located, and then a declaration of the making of the grant, in highly formalized language, setting forth the boundaries, followed by the delivery of possession of the land.

The Cruzate documents follow none of these conventions; rather, each document appears to be a transcription of an interrogation of a Zia Pueblo man who at the time was Governor Jironza Pétriz de Cruzate's prisoner.[22] All purport to have been made at a time when the Spanish colony of New Mexico was in exile in El Paso del Norte. None of the pueblos to whom these grants were supposedly made requested a grant, nor could they have known that such grants were being issued. Most of the documents have marginalia written sideways in the left-hand margin of the first page that reference terms associated with land grants, but other than that, there is no indication that a land grant is intended until the end of the document. Some say, "merced concedida a," or "grant made to," followed by the name of the pueblo. Others have the word "miras," a surveying term meaning "sights." The Santo Domingo Cruzate grant has the phrase "lineas y miras" (lines [or boundaries] and sights; this is possibly the equivalent of today's "metes and bounds").[23]

Jironza was first appointed governor in 1683, succeeding Antonio de Otermín, who vainly tried to defend Santa Fe against the 1680 Revolt and then led the Spanish survivors in their retreat from the capital. Despite several attempts, Otermín was unable to reestablish a foothold in the province. Jironza hoped to retake New Mexico, but native uprisings closer to El Paso del Norte sapped his meager resources. Moreover, the crown showed little interest in supplying the soldiers or equipment such a campaign would require.[24] Pedro Reneros Posada replaced Jironza as governor in 1686 and apparently made an expedition in 1688 as far as the Keres pueblos of Santa Ana and Zia, but otherwise he accomplished little.[25]

Reappointed governor in February 1689, Jironza immediately made plans to reconquer New Mexico. His strategy consisted of a series of fast, decisive assaults intended to destroy Pueblo morale and resources. He planned to begin on 10 August, the ninth anniversary of the Pueblo Revolt. He spent the summer assembling and equipping a company of well-disciplined, well-trained troops and collecting supplies, and on the appointed day he moved rapidly north from El Paso, with about 80 soldiers and about 120 Indian allies, mounted and heavily armed.[26] Apparently learning that a strong Indian force was assembled 15 miles northwest of Bernalillo on the Rio Jemez at Zia, Jironza marched his troops there. On 29 August they attacked the strongly fortified pueblo and engaged in a ferocious battle, lasting from dawn until 8 p.m. Reportedly, as many as 600 Zia warriors and their allies were killed, either in the fighting or in the burning of the pueblo that followed, and approximately 70 were taken prisoner.[27] Adolph Bandelier called this "the most bloody engagement in the wars for the reconquest of New Mexico."[28] Hispanos also suffered heavy casualties, with 50 soldiers injured and 1 killed. Jironza and his men quickly withdrew to El Paso.[29] He intended to resume the campaign the following year, but renewed Apache uprisings around El Paso kept his attention and his forces focused there.[30]

The Zia war captain whose interrogation forms the substance of each of the Cruzate documents was Bartolomé de Ojeda, twenty-one or twenty-two years of age, who was one of the defenders captured in the battle. Documents once in the Spanish archives in Santa Fe confirm that Ojeda distinguished himself by his bravery in battle until he was wounded by gunshot and arrow and surrendered, as the Cruzate documents say. The Hispanos treated his wounds, and after he arrived in El Paso he recovered from his injuries.[31] It is also well documented in the letters, journals, and reports of Diego de Vargas (who succeeded Jironza as governor of New Mexico in 1691), that Ojeda was fluent in spoken and written Spanish (apparently having been raised by priests). Ojeda underwent a transformation in El Paso, where he remarried and became the leader of a community of Pueblo Indians who had returned to the Catholic faith. Ojeda also resolved to assist Vargas's reentry to New Mexico. When Hispanos returned to New Mexico under Vargas's command, Ojeda acted as Vargas's interpreter with the Keres pueblos, and Vargas used Ojeda's influence to keep Santa Ana, Zia, and San Felipe allied with the Hispanos throughout the violent period from 1694 to 1696. Vargas wrote that Ojeda provided "invaluable" service to him as he struggled to overcome Pueblo resistance to the resumption of Spanish rule in the province.[32] Ojeda emerged as a prominent leader of the Keres pueblos of Santa Ana, Zia, and San Felipe.

Although there are important differences among the Cruzate documents, they are mainly notable for their marked similarities. Each document takes the form of a narrative of Ojeda's interrogation, told by Jironza's secretary of government and war, who is identified as "don Pedro Ladrón de Guitara." Each begins by stating that the interrogation took place in "El Paso del Río del Norte" on either 20 or 25 September.[33] The opening paragraphs of nearly all the documents are practically identical. Typically, the text explains that Governor Jironza stated that in the fight with the Keres, Tewas, and Tanos and the fighting with all the other pueblos, Ojeda distinguished himself in battle, was wounded, surrendered, and was interrogated under oath about the conditions of the pueblos who had abandoned the Catholic faith and took part in the wars of New Mexico.

In most of the documents, Jironza asks Ojeda whether he thought a named pueblo would rebel in the future. Each time, using almost identical language, Ojeda responds that even though the pueblo had allied itself with the people of Zia in the events of the previous year, he thought it would now give its allegiance to the Spaniards. In the Jemez, Pecos, Laguna, and Cochiti Cruzate documents, Ojeda adds that the Indians of those pueblos "were very much intimidated."

Most of the documents state that Jironza "granted" the named pueblo certain lands. Six Cruzate documents presented to the surveyor general—those pertaining to Jemez, Zia, Pecos, Picuris, San Cristóbal, and Zuni—called for standard league grants, that is, grants of one league in each cardinal direction, to be measured from the four corners of the church in the middle of the pueblo in the cases of Jemez, Zia, and Picuris, and from the four corners of the pueblo in the cases of Zuni, Pecos, and San Cristóbal.

Three other Cruzate documents purport to make grants defined by a combination of leagues and natural monuments or landmarks. The San Juan and Cochiti Cruzate documents make grants of one league in each of three directions that are bounded by natural features in the fourth direction. For San Juan, the north boundary was the Río Bravo del Norte (the Rio Grande), which does in fact curve to the east and runs northeasterly just north of San Juan and thus could serve as a northern boundary.[34] For Cochiti, the south boundary was described as "the point of a barren hill, near a stream of water, running in the direction of the rising sun, and which empties into the Río Bravo."[35]

The San Felipe Cruzate document grants a tract one league to the east and one league to the west but bounded on the north by the "bosque grande" (a large grove of cottonwoods) and on the south by "a small grove in front of a hill called Culcura, opposite the fields of the Santa Ana Indians." The word "culcura," appears in Whiting's translation as printed in the surveyor general's report, but his Spanish transcription and his handwritten translation give the word as "culenra."[36] This appears to be a misreading of the original, which almost certainly is "culevra" or "culebra," meaning "snake." A prominent landmark in the vicinity of the south boundary of the San Felipe grant, on the west side of the Rio Grande, is known to the Indians as "Culebra," and there is a cottonwood grove

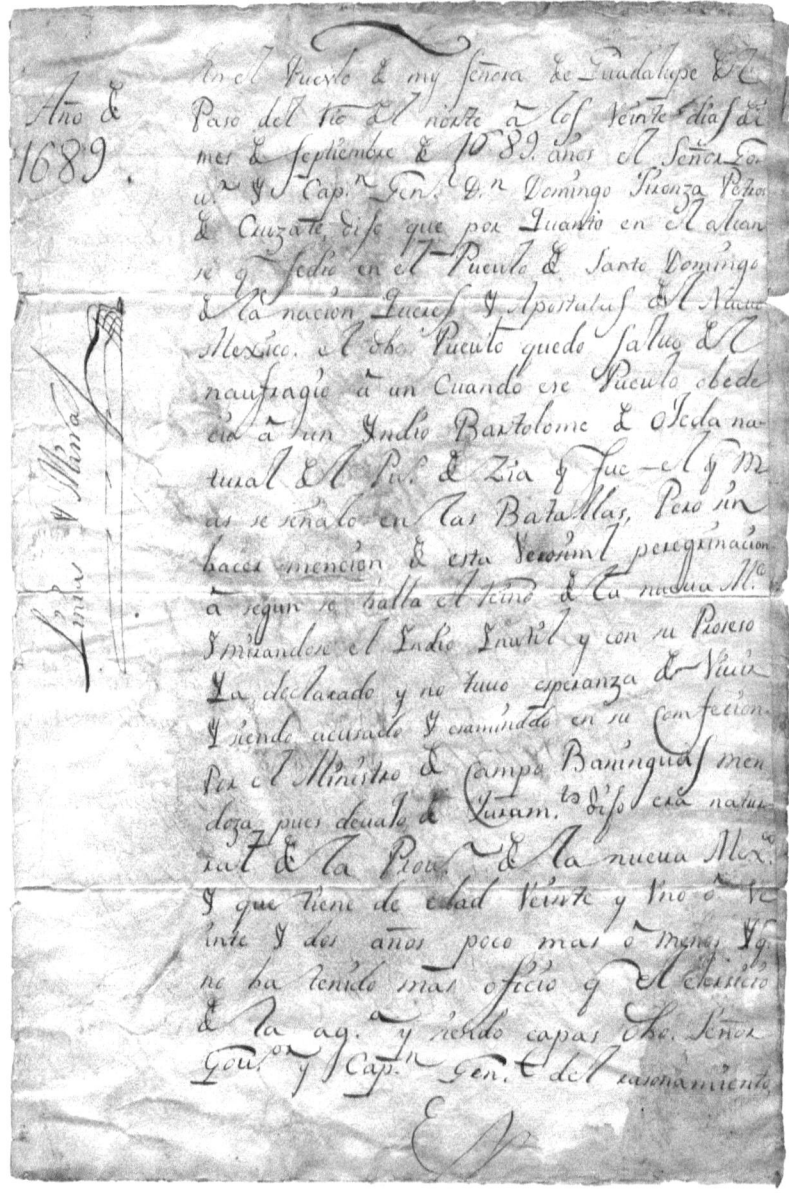

First page of the Santo Domingo Cruzate Grant. Note the inscription "Lineas y Miras" (lines and sights) in the left margin. On the eighth and ninth lines is the strange phrase "quedo saluo del naufragio" (escaped shipwreck) (SANM I, SG Report H, Santo Domingo Pueblo, image 003). Courtesy New Mexico Records Center and Archives.

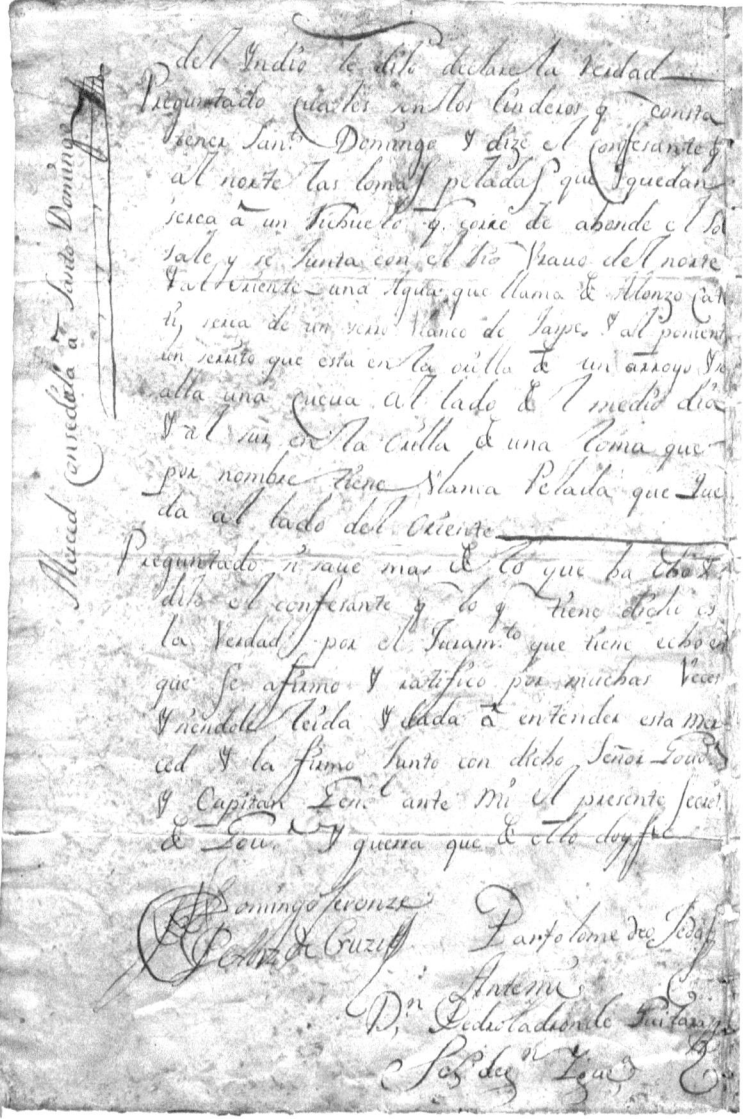

Second page of the Santo Domingo Cruzate Grant. Note the rather scrawled initial "D" in "Domingo" in the governor's signature and the unique spelling of his matrilineal name, "Jironze." What purports to be Bartolomé de Ojeda's signature appears just to the right of Jironza's, and below it is the signature "Pedro Ladron de Guitara," identified by the title below as secretary of government and war (SANM I, SG Report H, Santo Domingo Pueblo, image 004). Courtesy New Mexico Records Center and Archives.

just to the north of that hill (and thus, "in front of" it, as viewed from San Felipe Pueblo) that is presumably the "small grove" referred to.

The Cruzate documents for Santo Domingo, Acoma, and Laguna are especially noteworthy in that they describe those pueblos' lands as being bounded on all four sides by natural features rather than by league measurements. Unlike the other Cruzate documents, in none of these three documents does Jironza say he granted lands with these boundaries; rather, in each case Ojeda supplied the boundary calls when queried about them. The final paragraph states that after "this grant" was read to Ojeda, he signed it in the presence of the governor and the secretary of government and war.[37]

Rueben Clements surveyed the Santo Domingo grant in 1858 and found that it contained 78,743.11 acres. In the late 1800s, surveys of adjacent grants were unable to locate evidence of Clements's survey, and the General Land Office consequently ordered a resurvey, which Wendell Hall eventually carried out in 1907–1908.[38] Members of the pueblo accompanied Hall, and they seemed to know the natural landmarks described in the grant document. The resurvey increased the grant area to 92,398.4 acres. Congress confirmed Hall's survey as part of the settlement of Santo Domingo's claims under the Indian Claims Commission Act.[39]

There are two known Cruzate documents pertaining to Acoma.[40] One was delivered to Pelham's office on 3 March 1856. This is the document Pelham approved and submitted to the General Land Office in 1856 and that Congress confirmed in 1858 as the Acoma grant.[41] It is noteworthy for its distinctive text, which for the most part resembles none of the other Cruzate documents. In it Governor Jironza interrogates Ojeda, not about whether Acoma is likely to rebel against the Hispanos, but about its disputes with neighboring Laguna Pueblo over water. At the time this document was submitted to Pelham, Acoma and Laguna had been disputing and litigating their respective rights to land and water for more than a century.[42] Asked why Laguna and Acoma disagreed so much and why the Acoma people had relocated to the great mesa on which the pueblo's main village was located, Ojeda said that they moved because of the frequent wars between the two pueblos. He added that Laguna moved near Acoma because of "the abundance of water" but that it was established that Acoma had the first right to the water and that Laguna was entitled only to "the surplus." Finally, Jironza asked Ojeda to describe Acoma's boundaries, which he did.[43]

The other Acoma Cruzate document is unique in that it is dated 28 (not 20 or 25) September 1689. This document was the subject of a lawsuit Acoma filed in Socorro County in 1854 against a Mexican named Victor de la O and two others. In the suit the pueblo claimed that De la O and the other defendants had possession of a document dated 28 September 1689 that confirmed Acoma's title to its lands and that he demanded that Acoma pay six hundred dollars for the document. The court ruled in Acoma's favor, a matter this chapter will return to, ordering De la O to surrender the document to the pueblo. The surveyor general files do not contain the original document; there is only a transcription and Miller's translation dated 30 September 1863.[44]

The Laguna document, which Pelham did not receive until 29 June 1857, is a more typical Cruzate document. Pelham approved it and forwarded it to the General Land Office with a recommendation for confirmation on 1 September 1859, but Congress took no action on it.[45] Laguna hired Santa Fe attorney (and former territorial supreme court justice) John S. Watts, to press its claim. On 22 November 1872, a little over a month after Watts wrote him urging confirmation, James K. Proudfit, the surveyor general, approved the claim and sent it on to the secretary of the interior for transmittal to Congress.[46] Proudfit had the grant surveyed for what turned out to be approximately 125,000 acres. Congress again failed to act, however, and in 1893 Laguna filed suit for confirmation of the grant in the Court of Private Land Claims. In the course of that lawsuit, Will Tipton, the government's translator and handwriting expert, first expressed the view that the Laguna grant was not authentic. Tipton is primarily responsible for the modern view among historians that the Cruzate documents are, to use his oft-repeated but somewhat unusual term, "spurious," and his analysis of the documents bears further discussion.

Tipton arrived in Santa Fe in 1875 and found a job as a surveyor in the General Land Office under Surveyor General Henry M. Atkinson, who was married to Tipton's sister. Tipton married Felipita Gallegos, a Santa Fe native and the daughter of a former priest, José Manuel Gallegos, who had served as president of the New Mexico legislative assembly and as a territorial delegate to Congress. Tipton's marriage to Felipita, although tragically cut short by her early death, was a happy one, as testified to by letters of Adolph F. Bandelier, the acclaimed ethnologist, who became a close friend of the Tipton family.[47] With his wife's help and encouragement, Tipton learned Spanish, and while working under David Miller in Atkinson's office, he became a skilled translator.[48] When Miller left the General Land Office in the mid-1880s, Tipton became custodian of the Spanish archives, and it was said that he came to know them better than any other living person. He also became an expert in colonial Spanish handwriting and was frequently called upon to testify in court as to the authenticity of Spanish and Mexican documents.⁴⁹

After Congress created the Court of Private Land Claims in 1891, Matthew G. Reynolds was hired to represent the United States in cases before the court. At Reynolds's urging, the attorney general named Tipton as special agent assigned to cases before the court. He served in that capacity until 1901, when he resigned to go to the Philippines, which the United States had acquired as a result of the Spanish-American War, to oversee land investigations. Tipton returned to Santa Fe to work for the General Land Office in 1907, and in 1912 he went to work for the newly established office of the New Mexico State Land Commissioner.

Although Tipton is cited as the originator of the proposition that the Cruzate documents are frauds, this thought might have first occurred to Bandelier, who spent much of his time reading and copying documents in the surveyor general's office. An entry in his journal dated 4 September 1887 noted his very strong suspicion that the Laguna grant document was a forgery. He concluded that either the author of the *Relación anónima* was in serious error or the Laguna Cruzate document could not have been created in 1689.⁵⁰

The title *Relación anónima* was given to a partial copy of fray Silvestre Vélez de Escalante's *Extracto de noticias*, a lengthy summary of documents in the official government archives in Santa Fe that the young Franciscan prepared in 1778.⁵¹ Because the only known copies of that work (the original of which was in the Franciscan archives in Mexico City) at the time were incomplete and lacked the title page, it was referred to as the "anonymous report," but Bandelier concluded that Vélez de Escalante was the author.⁵² Thomas B. Catron somehow acquired a copy of the third series of the *Relación*, produced in 1856, which Bandelier read and copied.⁵³

Bandelier offered no further explanation for his conclusion that the *Relación* proved that the Laguna grant was not authentic. Another journal entry in late November 1891 describes Bandelier copying a copy of the San Felipe Cruzate document, but he is silent as to its authenticity.⁵⁴ In his *Final Report*, Bandelier mentions the Cruzate documents but says nothing about them being fraudulent.⁵⁵ Bandelier probably read in the *Relación* the description of Governor Rodríguez Cubero's trip to the western pueblos in 1699 and the formal recognition granted to the pueblo of San José de la Laguna during that excursion.[56] The apparent fact that Laguna did not formally exist until 1699 might have led him to conclude that the Laguna grant could not have been made in 1689.

Given their close personal relationship and Bandelier's awareness of Tipton's involvement with the Spanish and Mexican land records, it seems probable that Bandelier mentioned his suspicions about the Laguna Cruzate document to Tipton. Tipton was working for the Court of Private Land Claims in 1893 when Laguna filed its petition, basing its claim entirely on its Cruzate grant.[57] Tipton would no doubt already have been alerted to concerns about that document. Upon reviewing it, he noted three substantial features of it, besides the date, that he thought proved its lack of authenticity. Presumably Tipton reported his findings to Matthew Reynolds, who told Laguna's attorney, Edwin B. Seward, that he intended to disprove the authenticity of the grant.[58]

On 8 October 1896 Seward filed an amended petition in the Court of Private Land Claims, in which he modified the claim based on the Cruzate document, saying only that Laguna had received a grant but that the pueblo no longer had the original document and that Laguna had been in possession of the lands described in the grant for at least three hundred years.[59] The amended petition also alleged that in a *second* Cruzate document, Governor Jironza promised grants to all New Mexico pueblos.

The pueblo offered both Cruzate documents at trial on 17 September 1897, but its new attorney, George Hill Howard (who replaced Seward shortly before the trial), acknowledged to the court that he was not offering them as "authentic documents bearing authentic signatures."[60] The court issued its decision on 2 October 1897, finding that because the signatures of Jironza and his secretary of government and war on the two Cruzate documents were not genuine, the documents could not be admitted into evidence.[61] That left the pueblo with no evidentiary basis for its claim of title. The court went further, however, and concluded that Spanish law of the period would have accorded Laguna the right to a tract measuring one league in each direction from the center of the village and that the pueblo was entitled to have title to such a tract confirmed. A decree entered the same day confirmed a four-square-league grant to Laguna.[62] This is the only case in which a court was called on to consider the authenticity of a Cruzate grant, and the document was rejected after a concession by the party offering the grant that the document was not authentic.

The second Cruzate document Laguna introduced at trial, which the court characterized as a "treaty" between Jironza and Bartolomé de Ojeda in which the governor stated he would grant land to each pueblo, was presented to the surveyor general's office, possibly on 3 March 1856, with the first Acoma Cruzate grant.[63] Never submitted to Congress and not previously discussed in the scholarly literature, this unusual document, to which we will return, is directly related to the Cruzate-grant documents.

There are four aspects of the Laguna Cruzate document on which Tipton based his conclusion that the document was "spurious." First, the text and the signatures appeared to have been written by the same person, and Jironza's signature differed from those on documents believed to be authentic. Second, the name of the secretary of government and war, the supposed author of the document, "don Pedro Ladrón de Guitara" (don Pedro the guitar thief), was plainly wrong, No such person ever held that position; Jironza's secretary of government and war was Pedro Ladrón de Guevara. Third, Laguna Pueblo was not formally established until 1699, ten years after the date of the alleged grant. And, last, attached to the three-page grant document was a fourth page, written in the same handwriting as the main document, containing a twisted account of matters related to the early history of New Mexico derived from the opening passages of an 1832 Mexican publication, *Ojeada sobre Nuevo México* (*Glance over New Mexico*), by Antonio Barreiro. The first two factors are common to all the Cruzate documents, which led Tipton to conclude that "it is also true that all the Indian grants in New Mexico, purporting to have been made in 1689, were written by the same hand which wrote this so-called grant to Laguna, and are equally spurious."[64] Tipton's opinions, which have been frequently cited and relied on, merit further examination.

The characteristics and authenticity of the handwriting of the Cruzate documents is a matter for experts. Tipton wrote that "the signature of the governor, his secretary and the Indian witness, Bartolomé Ojeda, are in the same handwriting" and that the governor's signature, when compared with his signature on other documents in the archives or at the Library of Congress, is "clearly shown to be spurious."[65] Allan Keown, a handwriting expert based in El Paso, Texas, submitted an affidavit dated 18 August 1988 that was filed in the case of *United States v. Thompson*, a suit seeking to quiet the title of Santo Domingo Pueblo to certain lands within its surveyed Cruzate grant. Keown examined the Santo Domingo and Cochiti Cruzate documents, along with seven other documents from the Spanish Archives of New Mexico that contained what are believed to be authentic signatures of Governor Jironza and Secretary Ladrón de Guevara. Keown concluded that the signatures on the Cruzate documents were not made by the same persons who signed the presumably authentic documents and that the "grant" documents were "bogus."[66]

Although Jironza's signatures on the Cruzate documents appear to differ in significant ways from his authentic signature, there is little doubt that whoever made the Cruzate documents had seen and attempted to copy a real Jironza signature. Similarly, notwithstanding the consistent misspelling of the name, the signatures of the secretary of government and war in the Cruzate documents, including the flourish that immediately follows the signature, look very much like the authentic examples of Guevara's signature and rubric. It is unlikely that Tipton had an authentic exemplar of Ojeda's signature to compare with those on the Cruzate documents, but various letters from Ojeda to Vargas, written from 1694 to 1696, have since come to light.[67] Ojeda's handwriting and signature on these documents bear no resemblance to the signatures on the Santo Domingo, Acoma, Laguna, Cochiti, and San Juan Cruzate documents. There are also other examples of misspelled names, such as Jironza's *maestro de campo*, Juan Domínguez de Mendoza, who appears consistently in the documents as "Baninguas Mendoza."[68]

Tipton's assertion that the Laguna Cruzate grant was spurious because it was made ten years before the pueblo was "founded" is less compelling. Official recognition of the pueblo occurred on 4 July 1699, when it was formally designated as "San José de la Laguna" during Governor Pedro Rodríguez Cubero's trip to the western pueblos, in the course of which he visited Acoma and Zuni.[69] But Laguna did not suddenly come into existence on that date. Evidence suggests that soon after the Pueblo Revolt of 1680, if not before, members of a faction from Acoma settled at Laguna, and Vélez de Escalante's *Extracto* states that refugees from Cieneguilla, Santo Domingo, and Cochiti, among others, likewise went there to settle during that period.[70] The text of the Laguna Cruzate document acknowledges the fact that the community was recently settled by members of various pueblos, mostly Keres. Ojeda states in the document that at the time of the Pueblo Revolt, Laguna was in the process of "*becoming inhabited* but that the Pueblo of Acoma *had settled upon it sometime before.*"[71]

Tipton's fourth ground for his conclusion focuses on what is often referred to as the "appendix" to the Laguna Cruzate document. Evidently when the three-page Laguna document was filed with Pelham's office on 29 June 1857, it was accompanied by a fourth page that textually bears practically no relationship to the supposed 1689 grant document but is indisputably in the same hand, appears to be on the same type of paper, and is signed "Pedro Ladrón de Guitara."[72] Presumably recognizing that this appended document had nothing to do with the grant, David Whiting did not include it as part of his translation of the Cruzate document itself.[73] When attorney John Watts wrote Surveyor General Proudfit in 1872 seeking consideration of the grant, he did not refer to the appendix in his letter or in the translation of the Cruzate document he enclosed. Proudfit did not mention it when he approved the grant and sent it on to Congress. Laguna's complaint filed in the Court of Private Land Claims simply ignored this embarrassing appendage, but it was in the surveyor general's files, and Tipton could hardly have failed to take note of it. He wrote, "The contents of this fourth page of document 'B' has nothing to do with a grant to the pueblo of Laguna; the handwriting establishes the fact that it was written by the same person who wrote the so-called grant of 1689; its contents show that it contains statements taken bodily from a book published in 1832."[74]

The appendix begins with the phrase "ojeada sobre Nuevo México." Tipton knew this to be the title of a volume published in 1832 in Puebla, Mexico, by Antonio Barreiro, a Mexican attorney who was sent to New Mexico in 1831 as territorial *asesor* (legal advisor), possibly to help establish a judicial system.[75] The *Ojeada sobre Nuevo México* was intended as a report to the Mexican government on the state of affairs in this remote territory. The Laguna appendix repeats bits of the opening passages of the *Ojeada Sobre Nuevo México* but adapts them to New Mexico and changes the text in odd, ungrammatical, and, in places, nonsensical ways. For example, following Barreiro, the appendix refers to the disastrous 1528 expedition of Pánfilo de Narvaez, which is recounted in the *Ojeada*, but alters the story so that after being shipwrecked, Álvar Núñez Cabeza de Vaca and other survivors wander through the southwest before arriving in New Mexico rather than New Spain, which is where they actually ended up.

The appendix refers to "Domingo Jironza Petroz de Cruzate" and "Pedro Renero de Possada." It is worthy of note that "Petroz" and "Possada" are misspellings that appear frequently in the Cruzate documents. The document contains what can only be characterized as Spanish gibberish, such as "luego que los Yndios conbalesieron del prestigio Y la bujerias buse misisipe" (as soon as the

Indians had recovered from the spell and witchcraft *buse misisipe* [an untranslatable phrase]).[76] The document is signed "Don Pedro ladron de Guitara." There is no denying Tipton's observation that the extensive duplication of passages from the opening of the *Ojeada* in the appendix cannot be coincidental. Tipton also noticed that the Laguna document is not the only Cruzate document in which shards of the *Ojeada sobre Nuevo Mexico* appear.[77] The Santo Domingo document also contains two brief passages that derive from the *Ojeada*.

A far more consequential factor weighing against the authenticity of the documents, which Tipton did not comment on and may not have recognized, is the fact that all the Cruzate documents presented to the surveyor general that are in the New Mexico State Records Center and Archives today were written on paper that bears the watermark "MARIANO" in block letters on the first sheet, and a flowery letter "M" on the facing folio. Although the origin of this watermark has yet to be identified, it appears to date these documents to the 1840s.

During the seventeenth, eighteenth, and early nineteenth centuries, virtually all the paper used in New Mexico was manufactured in Europe. The sheets bear watermarks featuring myriad designs, including floral figures, fleur-de-lis, figures of bulls, coats of arms, and names, such as "NOTARO."[78] Once the Santa Fe Trail opened in 1821, paper from the eastern United States undoubtedly found its way to Santa Fe, and after 1824, when the first Mexican paper factory opened, paper bearing identifiable Mexican watermarks gradually came into use in the territory.

Stanley M. Hordes, who served as New Mexico state historian from 1981 to 1985, submitted an affidavit in the *United States v. Thompson* litigation, dated 23 August 1988, in which he stated that he had never seen a Spanish or Mexican document in the Spanish Archives of New Mexico with the "MARIANO" watermark that was dated earlier than 1845, although he had seen several such documents dated between 1845 and 1849.[79] Mathews-Lamb, in the course of working on her doctoral dissertation on the Cruzate documents in the late 1990s, examined hundreds of nineteenth-century documents from New Mexico and found that "MARIANO"-marked paper was apparently scarce in New Mexico but that it was occasionally used by Donaciano Vigil, Manuel Armijo y Mestas (nephew of Governor Manuel Armijo), Francisco Sarracino (who served as governor during Mexican rule and in 1850 was named a "substitute" delegate to Congress from the territory), and a few others. One letter written by Surveyor General John A. Clark, in 1862, turned up on "MARIANO"-marked paper.[80] The fact that no example exists of paper bearing this mark prior to the 1840s, in any event, must be considered strong evidence that the Cruzate documents in the archives were created in the mid-1800s.

It has been suggested that the Cruzate documents could be copies of presumably authentic documents that are now lost.[81] It is certainly true that many of the errors in the Cruzate documents—the misspellings and occasionally garbled text—are of the sort that would be made in copying. An excellent example of scribal dittography, the mechanical repetition of text, is found on the second page of the first Acoma Cruzate document, where the phrase "siendo unos Indios tan Avilantados habían dejado su Pueblo Y responde que se habían mudado al Peñol" (because they were such insolent Indians that they left their pueblo. He responded that they had moved to the Peñol) is repeated, almost verbatim immediately afterward in the document.[82] That so much of the text in nearly all the "standard form" Cruzate documents is practically identical suggests that most of the documents were copied from a master. It is one thing to say that the documents appear to be copies, but it is another matter to suggest that they were official or authorized copies that thereby partook of the authenticity of presumed originals. The Cruzate documents do not appear to be that sort of document; rather, they are clearly intended to look like original, seventeenth-century documents, not copies. Apart from the fact that there is nothing on any of the documents indicating they are copies of originals, that they were intended to be taken for originals may be inferred from the appearance of the dates and titles in the margins, the characteristics of the penmanship and orthography, and, most importantly, the signatures. The signatures unquestionably reflect an effort to forge the signatures and *rubricas* (signature flourishes) of the persons whose names are affixed to the documents. By contrast, authorized copies of Spanish colonial documents record only the names of the original signatories and do not bear their rubrics.

Although the Acoma Cruzate document surfaced in a lawsuit in Socorro in 1854, it is evident that these documents were largely unknown in New Mexico before they began to be presented to the surveyor general in 1855. In June 1856, after Pelham received a number of Cruzate documents and was preparing to recommend the confirmation of eight of them, Donaciano Vigil signed an affidavit stating that, having been in charge of the public archives of the territory since 1840, he knew the contents of the archives and that they contained no land grants to any Indian pueblos. Vigil served as secretary to Governor Manuel Armijo, the last Mexican governor of New Mexico, and General Stephen Watts Kearny appointed him territorial secretary after the Army of the West brought U.S. rule to New Mexico in August 1846. Vigil served as secretary until 1851, except for the period 1847–1848, during which he was acting governor after Governor Charles Bent (1846–1847) was killed in the Taos uprising in 1847. Although he was implicated in some shady dealings involving the Preston Beck grant, the Pecos grant, and perhaps others, his familiarity with the archives is undeniable.[83] After being appointed territorial secretary Vigil had an inventory of the archives made, now known as the Vigil Index, which is a listing and description of more than ten thousand individual items and groups of documents.[84] He surely exaggerated somewhat in his 1856 affidavit; he might have known of the 1748 grant to Sandia by Governor Joaquín Codallos y Rabal, the 1763 grant to Santa Clara for the Cañada de Santa Clara, the 1770 grant to Santo Domingo and San Felipe of the land between their leagues, or a few others.[85] Vigil's indisputable point, however, was that the Cruzate documents were not previously part of the official archives of the territory.

Notably, Governor Jironza, in his report to the king of his accomplishments during his terms as governor, made no mention of the making of grants to the pueblos.[86] There is also no indication that he communicated to his successor, Vargas, that he made such grants. Although the surviving correspondence between Ojeda and Vargas is fragmentary, it is worth observing that in none of the surviving documents does Ojeda refer to grants by Jironza to the pueblos. Moreover, there are scores of documents in the Spanish Archives of New Mexico concerning land disputes involving one or more of the pueblos that invariably record Spanish officials asking the pueblos to produce their documents relative to their lands. There is no evidence that any pueblo ever produced a document bearing any resemblance to a Cruzate document. Numerous documents in the archives relate to land disputes and land transactions involving Santo Domingo, Acoma, Laguna, and San Felipe, whose Cruzate documents specified natural monuments as boundary calls. In each of those instances, the documents show that the pueblo claimed a league, or a boundary specified in a deed of purchase.[87] The apparent fact that none of the Pueblos possessed, or at least revealed to anyone, any such grant until shortly before U.S. authorities called on them to produce their documents in 1855 suggests that they did not have them.

Among the Cruzate documents presented to Pelham's office in 1855 and 1856 were two that purported to be league grants to pueblos that no longer existed, one of which was abandoned by its Indian inhabitants for probably a century and a half. Pecos, which was one of the two Towa pueblos of New Mexico (Jemez is the other), had long been at the time of the Revolt and for some time thereafter one of the most powerful and prosperous of the New Mexico pueblos. It was the gateway for commerce between the Indians and Hispanos in New Mexico and the powerful tribes of the Great Plains. Its warriors fought in the Revolt and helped expel the Hispanos from Santa Fe, but by the early nineteenth century, as a result of disease, the influx of Hispano settlers onto its lands, the opening of the Santa Fe Trail to wagon-borne commerce with the United States in 1821, and other factors, the pueblo was in a state of rapid decline. By 1838 its last score or so of survivors packed up their belongings and moved to Jemez Pueblo, the home of their nearest linguistic relatives.[88] Nothing is heard from Pecos as a separate and distinct pueblo thereafter.

Yet, on 14 September 1855, the same day that a Cruzate document for Jemez arrived at the surveyor general's office, a very similar grant for Pecos Pueblo was also filed. In all likelihood, the Jemez representatives brought both documents, but Pelham's docket book identifies the claimants as "inhabitants of Pecos Pueblo."[89] Two weeks later, in his first annual report to the General Land Office, Pelham stated that he had received and approved grant documents for five pueblos, including Pecos, for which he noted ten inhabitants.[90] Congress confirmed the Pecos grant in 1858.[91]

Far more puzzling is the Cruzate grant to San Cristóbal. The surveyor general's docket book shows the filing of that document, a standard league grant, by "inhabitants of San Cristobal Pueblo," although it gives no date on which the document was submitted to Pelham's office. Pelham never submitted the grant for confirmation, probably because he was aware that San Cristóbal had not existed as a pueblo for at least a century and a half. In addition, he already had before him and eventually approved and submitted to Congress a claim for confirmation of a Mexican land grant that included the entire four-square-league area of the San Cristóbal Cruzate grant.[92]

When the Hispanos arrived in New Mexico, the Tano pueblo of San Cristóbal, located about 20 miles southeast of the future site of Santa Fe, was one of the largest pueblos in the Galisteo Basin. The Tanos were part of the first assault on Santa Fe during the Pueblo Revolt.[93] After the Revolt the residents of San Cristóbal abandoned the Galisteo Basin and moved to Santa Fe, where they occupied the former residences of the Spanish citizens.

By the time Vargas returned Spanish rule to Santa Fe in 1693, San Cristóbal had reestablished itself on the Río Santa Cruz, about 20 miles north of Santa Fe, just south of San Juan Pueblo.[94] The Santa Cruz valley was home to a large number of Spanish settlers prior to the Revolt, and Vargas was determined to restore them to their lands. Therefore, in 1695 he decreed the establishment of the town of Villa Nueva de Santa Cruz and ordered the relocation of San Cristóbal, which was on land formerly belonging to Hispanos.[95] Vargas resettled the people of San Cristóbal to the site of Chimayo, on the Río Santa Cruz about 6 miles east of Santa Cruz.[96] The people of San Cristóbal moved, but during the subsequent pueblo uprising of 1696, in which the Tanos rebelled along with many of the Tewa pueblos, most of them moved again, this time westward to the Hopi villages in what is now Arizona.

In 1822 Santa Fe resident Domingo Fernández petitioned Governor Melgares for a grant that included the land formerly occupied by San Cristóbal.[97] He, along with Donaciano Vigil, was perhaps the most knowledgeable about the official Spanish and Mexican archives in Santa Fe, having been hired by Vigil to prepare the Vigil Index. While working for the government as a keeper of the archives, Fernández was also acquiring land grants himself.[98] On 8 August 1827, Governor Armijo finally made the grant Fernández had requested at San Cristóbal.[99] Fernández conveyed his rights to the grant to Ethan Eaton and Alexander Reynolds in 1851 for five hundred dollars. Eaton subsequently acquired Reynolds's interest and then submitted a claim for the entire grant to Pelham on 11 October 1855.[100] Pelham approved the claim in 1857, and Congress confirmed it in 1860.[101] As ultimately surveyed, the grant, generally rectangular in shape, encompassed more than 81,000 acres, extending from the village of Galisteo on the northwest to White Lakes on the southeast. It included not only the entirety of the San Cristóbal lands but also several other major Galisteo Basin pueblo ruins. It is today known as the San Cristóbal grant. Intriguingly, the San Cristóbal Cruzate document, which is practically indistinguishable from the other Cruzate documents, contains the following notation, written in a light and more modern script that appears to be in pencil, below the signatures on the second page: "De donde vendrá?" (Where did this come from?).

The documents Pelham recorded in his docket book as Cruzate documents, which he sent on to the commissioner of the General Land Office, were not the only documents turned over to Pelham that were part of the 1689 Cruzate opus, nor, indeed, did Pelham or his successors receive all the Cruzate documents that existed. We will probably never know how many such documents there were.

Zuni waited until 3 July 1875 to bring its Cruzate document to the surveyor general's office in Santa Fe.[102] The document purported to be a standard league grant, which was preliminarily surveyed for approximately 17,580 acres. The Zuni Cruzate document, based on the extant transcription and translations in the State Record Center and Archives, is generally typical of standard Cruzate documents.[103] It includes an unusual reference to the murder of the priests at Zuni during the Pueblo Revolt, but otherwise it is unremarkable.

On 25 September 1879, Surveyor General Henry M. Atkinson issued his opinion that the grant was valid and entitled to be confirmed, and he duly forwarded it on to Washington.[104] By then, however, Congress was so weary of the tales of corruption and fraud in the grant confirmation process in New Mexico that it had ceased confirming land grants in the territory. No action was taken on the Zuni grant, but President Rutherford B. Hayes had issued an executive order on 16 March 1877 (later amended by executive order of 1 May 1883) creating a reservation for the pueblo of more than 250,000 acres. Subsequent executive orders and legislation enlarged the reservation to more than 340,000 acres.[105]

In the course of the Pueblo Lands Board proceedings in the 1920s, the board examined Zuni's Cruzate document, along with Surveyor General Atkinson's recommendation for its confirmation. The board recommended that Congress confirm the grant, even though the area embraced within it (and much more) was already set aside in trust for the pueblo. Congress complied, and by the Act of 3 March 1931 it authorized the survey and patenting of the grant.[106] The pueblo now owns those lands in fee simple, comprising 17,636 acres, although as with the rest of its reservation, it is subject to the full array of federal law restrictions against alienation.

Sandia presented documentation of its 1748 grant from Governor Codallos y Rabal to Pelham on 16 October 1856.[107] Pelham approved the grant, and Congress confirmed it in 1858.[108] As surveyed, the grant comprised more than 24,000 acres. In the 1990s the pueblo raised an issue with the United States over the location of the east boundary of its grant as established by the

U.S. survey.[109] In the course of the historical research prompted by the dispute, the pueblo produced two original Cruzate documents, whose existence was previously unknown. It allowed them to be copied, but the pueblo retained the originals.[110]

The documents show significant tears but are otherwise in good condition. They are in the typical Cruzate handwriting. One of them (the grant document) has the "MARIANO" watermark, and the other has the flowery "M" countermark, suggesting that they were originally parts of a single sheet. Both are dated 20 September 1689, and both contain the signature "Ladrón de Guitara." Following the standard Cruzate-document opening, Ojeda recounts the fact that the Sandia people were among the most rebellious Indians during the Revolt and that the pueblo was burned and that he understood that more than four hundred people, adults and children, were killed.[111] This piece of information is significant because Otermín's after-action report does not recount the deaths of so many Sandia Indians. How such an account would have come to a non-Indian creating a fraudulent document in the mid-1800s in New Mexico is an open question.

The other Sandia Cruzate document looks very similar to other typical Cruzate documents, but it is peculiar textually and is grammatically challenging. Jironza seemed to be saying that he had asked for information about the boundaries of all the rebellious pueblos at the time of the uprising when they "surrendered" to General Reneros Posada.[112] Reneros, who served as governor from 1686 to 1689 (between Jironza's two terms), acted as Jironza's general in the campaign of August 1689 that ended in the battle at Zia, but no pueblos ever surrendered to him. Nevertheless, the document lists eighteen pueblos by name, and it seems to imply that the Tano pueblos of San Lázaro and San Cristóbal were abandoned. Jironza stated that he made the grants to all the pueblos of New Mexico—the first going to Sandia—at Ojeda's request.[113] This document, unlike the "grant" document, contains a signature purporting to be that of Ojeda, which looks identical to the other Ojeda signatures on the other Cruzate documents, in addition to bearing the signatures of Jironza and Ladrón de Guitara.

These documents add credence to the possibility that the Cruzate documents were based, to some extent at least, on lost originals. As we have seen, the documents contain bits of historical information that would have been difficult to access in mid-nineteenth-century New Mexico. It is hard to imagine why someone simply trying to create fake grants would go to the effort required to dress the documents up with these pieces of history. The second document, curious when considered in isolation, takes on new and striking significance when viewed in conjunction with the "generic" Cruzate document and the apparently lost second San Juan document, both of which we will return to. It must also be noted that the fact that Sandia apparently had these documents in its possession but never turned them over to the surveyor general, although it did produce its 1748 grant documents, raises other questions. Perhaps Sandia realized that there was something wrong with its Cruzate documents.

When Laguna Pueblo went to trial in the Court of Private Land Claims on 17 September 1897 in an attempt to prove its entitlement to the lands embraced by its Cruzate document, it introduced into evidence another document that the court characterized as a "treaty" between Jironza and Ojeda. By the terms of this treaty, the governor stipulated that if the Indians ceased hostilities and resumed their allegiance to the Spanish crown, he would grant land to each pueblo.[114] The document the court was referring to is a Cruzate document dated 20 September 1689, which was included with the Acoma Pueblo documents when the records constituting the Spanish Archives of New Mexico, Series I were microfilmed.[115] The court's decision in the Laguna case stated that both the Cruzate document and the "treaty" were in Laguna's possession "from time immemorial."[116] The surveyor general's docket book shows that on 27 June 1875, Laguna brought two Spanish documents to Pelham's office, but the same is true of the entry regarding Acoma, dated 3 March 1856.[117] It is thus uncertain how the second document came into the possession of the surveyor general's office, but it is present today in the archives. Because this document describes Jironza's decision, at Ojeda's request, to make grants to all the pueblos without singling out any one of them specially, we refer to it as the "generic" Cruzate document.

The document, dated 20 September 1689, looks like the other Cruzate documents in handwriting and overall appearance. It contains, however, a remarkable passage wherein Ojeda asks Jironza to make grants to all the pueblos so that they will remain in possession of their land and within the boundaries the governor considers appropriate. Jironza agreed to make the grants and to give a copy to each pueblo for safekeeping, noting that the originals would remain in the archive of the government.[118]

This document makes no grant; rather, the text purports to identify Ojeda as the originator of the plan to make grants to all the pueblos, to which Jironza accedes. Significantly, it indicates that the intention was that a copy of each grant document would be delivered to each pueblo and that the originals would remain in the Spanish archives in El Paso. No other known Cruzate document contains similar information.[119]

Among the documents in the surveyor general files for San Juan is a Whiting translation of a document dated 11 November 1855.[120] Neither the original nor a Spanish transcription of the document is in the file. The document is dated 20 September 1689, and the translation of the first of its two pages indicates that that portion is practically identical to the second Sandia document and quite similar to the generic Cruzate document. The document states that Jironza "confided" to Ojeda grants to all the pueblos of New Mexico.

The surveyor general's docket book shows that on 18 August 1855, San Juan representatives brought in "Spanish title papers A & B," but there is only one original Spanish document in the San Juan file—the Cruzate document.[121] The original of document "B," which most likely was the document Whiting translated on 11 November 1855, is missing, although its translation remains in the file. Moreover, in a few other instances, the docket book shows that pueblos brought in two documents, but only the Cruzate document remains. This is true for Acoma, Jemez, and San Felipe.[122] None of these files contain translations of lost documents, as does the San Juan file. It may be significant that San Juan was the first pueblo to submit its documents to the surveyor general. It would have been normal for both San Juan documents to be translated. It is at least conceivable, however, that when other pueblos brought in documents like the second San Juan document, the surveyor general chose to disregard them, leave them untranslated, and perhaps destroy them. Interestingly, the translation of the second (missing) San Juan document, which is neatly written in ink, has on its second page a note, apparently written in pencil, that reads "not to be copied," triple underlined.[123]

◆ ◆ ◆ ◆

On 21 June 1856, Pelham sent a letter to Abraham G. Mayers, one of the Indian agents appointed to work with the Pueblo Indians in New Mexico, in which Pelham stated that he had received information from former governor Donaciano Vigil that a Mexican residing in Socorro had some Pueblo grants in his possession. Vigil learned this from a Santo Domingo Indian named Juan Esteban, who informed him that Santo Domingo, Sandia, and Jemez had obtained land-grant documents from that individual. Pelham urged Mayers to investigate the matter at his earliest convenience, noting that obtaining the Indian grants was of the utmost importance to the Indians and the government. Should he find the person mentioned and determine that he had any such Pueblo grants in his possession, Mayers was to acquire them and deliver them to Pelham as soon as possible.[124]

There is no response from Mayers to this urgent request in the surveyor general's files, but the identity of the Mexican living in Socorro was already known by virtue of a lawsuit that Acoma had filed in district court in Socorro County in August 1854. It is surprising that Pelham was apparently unaware of this case, which by 1856 had already been appealed to the territorial supreme court in Santa Fe and which resulted, in February of the following year, in a dramatic decision in favor of the pueblo.

Attorney Spruce M. Baird filed Acoma's petition against defendants Vicente Ariluead, Victor de la O, and Ramón Sanches on or about 26 August 1854.[125] Acoma governor Juan José Lovato verified the petition, which alleged that the defendants had somehow acquired title documents for lands granted to Acoma "by the King of Spain or by his Viceroy" and that they were threatening to take the documents back to Mexico unless Acoma paid them "the enormous sum of six hundred dollars." The petition further alleged that the Acomas were engaged in litigation over the boundaries of their pueblo with Laguna and that without the documents the defendants were withholding, "it is wholly impossible for them to defend their rights to [their] lands."[126] Judge Kirby Benedict, who was an associate justice of the territorial supreme court and judge of the Third Judicial District, immediately entered an order restraining and enjoining the defendants from doing anything with the documents referred to in Acoma's petition.[127]

John Watts, who until a few months earlier was a member of the same territorial supreme court on which Justice Benedict sat, represented the defendants. On 6 November 1854, Watts filed separate verified answers by each of the three defendants. Sanches stated that he had nothing to do with the affair and that he merely delivered a letter to Acoma on one occasion for Ariluead and De la O. Ariluead acknowledged that he assisted De la O in dealing with the Acoma document, but only as his agent, because De la O was totally illiterate. Both defendants were dismissed from the case.

De la O did not deny any of the allegations of Acoma's petition, although he did deny that he threatened to take the document back to Mexico. He asserted that Acoma had agreed to pay six hundred dollars for the document in May 1850 during a meeting at the home of Manuel Trujillo in Polvadera in Socorro County and that Acoma had made an earnest money payment of eight dollars to seal the deal.[128] De la O insisted that the transaction was fair and aboveboard and demanded that the court enforce his contractual right to the balance of the money from Acoma or auction off the document and pay him the proceeds of the sale. He added that he sold a similar document pertaining to the lands of the Laguna to General Manuel Armijo for two hundred dollars and that Armijo sold it to an Indian named Sarracino, who then sold it to Laguna.[129]

De la O claimed to have acquired the documents from his father, Gregorio de la O, a former lieutenant in the Spanish dragoons in the city of Chihuahua, who died in 1810, when Victor was only ten. He said that his father was an educated man who possessed many books and official papers but that he himself was illiterate and had squandered much of the collection because he had no idea of the papers' contents or worth. Victor came to Socorro in 1833, and in 1836 his wife joined him, bringing the documents remaining in their possession from his father's collection. De la O signed his answer with an "X."[130] Vicente Ariluead stated that in 1849 he came into contact with De la O, who asked him to examine the documents and assist in negotiations for their sale.[131]

De la O's claim that he had a valid contract did not impress Justice Benedict. Following the hearing in November 1854, he ordered the document to be delivered to Acoma so that it could be recorded in the records of Valencia County, where the pueblo's land was situated.[132] De la O appealed to the territorial supreme court.

The appeal was finally decided in January 1857.[133] It must have been dismaying to the appellant to find that the court's decision was authored by the same justice—Kirby Benedict—who decided the case in the district court.[134] His opinion quotes at length from the document at issue in the case and clearly identifies it as the Cruzate document Acoma presented to the surveyor general's office prior to 30 September 1863.[135] Without explaining the legal basis for his conclusion, Benedict appeared to assume that a title document belonged to the party to whom the title was conveyed. He concluded that De la O had no right to do anything but restore the document freely to Acoma (and likewise to restore the Laguna document that he sold to General Armijo to that pueblo). Benedict affirmed his own district court ruling in favor of Acoma.

Nothing more is known about Victor de la O or his father, Gregorio, but his account cannot simply be dismissed. What is important is that De la O plainly had possession of at least several of the Cruzate documents, including the second Acoma document. Acoma and the other pueblos who purchased their "grant" documents from De la O clearly believed that the documents were authentic and important. De la O's apparent connections with persons who are known to have utilized paper bearing the "MARIANO" watermark raises the intriguing possibility that he was involved with General Armijo's nephew, Francisco Sarracino and/or Donaciano Vigil, in the creation of the documents, who perhaps worked from original documents that were in De la O's collection.

◆ ◆ ◆ ◆

In short, while there seems to be little doubt that the Cruzate documents are not authentic seventeenth-century documents and in fact were probably created in the mid-nineteenth century, why they were created at all, and by whom, remains a mystery. The account of Victor de la O as to the documents' origin, although apparently not truthful in and of itself (since he implicitly claimed, though he did not say it directly, that the documents came from his father's collection and that they were authentic), together with the evidence as to other use of paper bearing the "MARIANO" watermark, are highly suggestive of the possibility that Donaciano Vigil or Manuel Armijo's nephew and De la O colluded in the creation of the documents. Vigil's familiarity with and access to the Spanish archives in Santa Fe significantly enhance the likelihood that he played a part, as only someone who was familiar with documents from the Pueblo Revolt period and knew more than a little of New Mexico's history from that period could have fabricated these documents. It also appears that he was the person who informed Pelham that De la O was peddling grant documents, but this makes the affidavit Vigil gave Pelham, insisting that no grants to Indian Pueblos were ever in the archives, extremely puzzling: if he went to the extraordinary effort to produce the Cruzate grants, or even to assist in their production, presumably with the intention of passing the documents off as genuine, why would he then seek to impeach them?

There is also the question of motive for such an undertaking. Having apparently authentic Spanish land grants of considerable antiquity would plainly be of enormous benefit to the pueblos when the United States began trying to sort out land-ownership matters in New Mexico. That Donaciano Vigil, or any other Hispano citizen in mid-nineteenth-century New Mexico, would go out of his way to assist the pueblos in asserting claims to land seems incredible. From all that appears in the historical record, the former Mexican citizens of the territory were far more interested in taking pueblo land than they were in helping the pueblos hold onto it, and Vigil was never known as a friend of the pueblos.

Some historians have suggested that, to the contrary, the grants were intended to *limit* pueblo land claims under the U.S. regime, not to substantiate their claims, but this view is hard to reconcile with what we know of how the United States treated pueblo land claims. As chapter 9 explains in greater detail, had the United States understood the pueblos to be holding their lands by aboriginal title, like Indian tribes elsewhere, the pueblos might well have laid claims to vast swaths of the territory. But from the beginning of U.S. rule, officials expressly assumed that the pueblos held their lands pursuant to paper grants from Spain or Mexico. The Cruzate grants appeared to confirm that belief, and for those pueblos lacking any document, the surveyor general helped create stories of "lost grants."[136] It is true that those pueblos whose Cruzate documents merely conveyed standard four-square-league grants might have ended up with the same quantity of land even without the documents, but others, such as Cochiti, Santo Domingo, San Felipe, and Acoma, ended up with much larger confirmed grants than the standard league measurement would have yielded. For them, at least, the Cruzate documents were a huge benefit, but those pueblos cannot have had any involvement in the creation of the documents, having none of the skills or resources that the undertaking required (and Acoma, of course, had to sue to get possession of one of its Cruzate grants). So, who was their mysterious benefactor? And why did he or she go to all of the trouble?

Finally, one can only wonder at the extraordinary peculiarity of how its authors designed this enterprise, seen in its totality. Had someone of this period set out to fabricate old Spanish grants, it is most difficult to imagine that such a person would have gone about it in the way the creators of the Cruzate documents did; rather, such a person would have no doubt produced more conventional-looking grant documents. The utilization of the format of the interrogation of Bartolomé de Ojeda, the inclusion of little-known historical details, the creation of grants to no-longer-existent pueblos, the invention of subsidiary documents, all of this and much more, leave one with more questions than answers in trying to make sense of it all, especially given the historical context. It seems inconceivable that someone engaged in a simple land-fraud scheme, however motivated, would have gone about it in this way. The only explanation that seems moderately plausible is that these documents were at least partially based on authentic documents in which, at least to some extent, the events recounted in the extant Cruzate documents were set forth. Unfortunately, there is simply no direct evidence to support that explanation, and so we are left with a fascinating conundrum. Perhaps it is better to have some mysteries still to solve.

Pueblo Indians petitioning Brigadier General Stephen Watts Kearny in Santa Fe. Drawing by Glen Strock.

CHAPTER 9

The Pueblos Come Under U.S. Rule

In the course of more than two centuries of Spanish rule, the Pueblos enjoyed some benefits from the special status the Hispanos accorded them. The institution of protector of the Indians, the fairly consistent respect shown to the Pueblo league, at least in theory, and the occasional willingness to rule against conflicting non-Indian claims that infringed on Pueblo lands all reflected a well-intentioned policy of protection of Pueblo rights. That policy grew out of the early debates about the nature of the indigenous peoples of the Americas, the reforms initiated by the writings of Bartolomé de las Casas, and the favorable laws protecting Indian lands in the *Recopilación*, although admittedly the Spanish policy of defining and protecting Indian land was often not followed in practice.

Whether that policy of protection of Indian land remained in place after Mexican independence beginning in 1821 is uncertain. The doctrine of citizenship and equality of all persons embodied in the Mexican Plan of Iguala, which Agustín de Iturbide proclaimed on 24 February 1821, and the 9 February 1811 laws of the Spanish Cortes, arguably meant that pueblos no longer enjoyed special status.[1] Whether due to a change in the law or simply the ineptitude and corruption of local officials, however, it seems clear that the pueblos began to experience increased intrusions onto their lands by non-Indians for which they had little or no remedy. It may have been for that reason that the Pueblos appeared to welcome the advent of U.S. rule in New Mexico, first manifested by the arrival in Santa Fe of General Stephen W. Kearny and his Army of the West in 1846 and then by the 1848 ratification of the Treaty of Guadalupe Hidalgo, by which Mexico ceded to the United States what is now the American Southwest.[2]

As it happened, the Pueblos' hope that the United States would protect their lands proved to be ill founded. Although the U.S. government had legal doctrines and policies in place that should have provided security for the Pueblos' lands, they lost far more valuable land at the hands of the U.S. government, and especially the U.S. courts, within eighty years of the establishment of U.S. rule than they had under a quarter of a millennium of Spanish and Mexican rule.

U.S. legal doctrines regarding relations with the native peoples within its borders or that lay in the path of its westward expansion were based in part on international law that reflected teachings of thinkers such as the sixteenth-century Spanish Dominican philosopher, theologian, and jurist Francisco de Vitoria. Vitoria laid down several key principles that soon became incorporated into international law: (1) that Indian nations possessed both rights of property in their lands and sovereign powers over them; (2) that lands could be acquired from Indian tribes only with their consent or as a result of a "just war"; and (3) that acquisition of Indian lands was a right reserved to the governments of the colonial powers and could not be undertaken by private individuals.[3] (An important implication of these principles, which Vitoria also proclaimed, is that a European power's mere discovery of lands did not give that government title to the lands discovered. The Indians retained their titles unless the lands were lawfully acquired from them.) Some of these principles are reflected in three early and seminal decisions of the U.S. Supreme Court: *Cherokee Nation v. Georgia*, *Worcester v. Georgia*, and *Johnson v. M'Intosh*, known as the "Marshall trilogy" for their author, Chief Justice John Marshall of Virginia.[4]

In *Cherokee Nation*, the tribe brought an original action in the Supreme Court seeking to prevent the state of Georgia's aggressive effort to abolish the huge Cherokee Reservation within that state and to subject the Cherokee people to state jurisdiction and control. The first issue the court had to address was whether the Cherokee Nation could bring an original action against Georgia in the Supreme Court, based on the provision of article 3, section 2, of the Constitution that gives that court original jurisdiction over controversies "between a State . . . and foreign States." The court ultimately rejected the

Cherokee claim that it was a "foreign State" for purposes of that provision, with Marshall writing that the Cherokee should more properly be seen as a "domestic dependent nation," but the opinion nonetheless emphasizes the distinct governmental character of the Indian tribes.[5]

The *Worcester* case, a continuation of the struggle between Georgia and the Cherokees, was an appeal by a white missionary from his conviction in a Georgia court of entering Cherokee territory without obtaining a state license. Samuel Worcester was imprisoned because of his advocacy against forced removal of the Cherokees. Marshall's decision firmly rejected the notion that a state had any authority over Indian lands or people, declaring that the Constitution made federal jurisdiction exclusive in the area of Indian affairs.[6]

The doctrine of "discovery," and the principle of governmental monopoly on land transactions with the Indian tribes that follows from it, were the bases of the decision in *Johnson v. M'Intosh*.[7] That case was a title dispute between settlers who purchased land in Illinois in 1773 and 1775 from the Illinois and Piankeshaw Indians and another party whose title derived from a patent from the United States, which acquired the lands by a *later* cession from the same tribes. The Supreme Court held that their "discovery" of the New World gave the European powers an exclusive right to treat with the native inhabitants for land; the United States succeeded to this right upon achieving its independence. Thus the conveyances by the tribes to the settlers were void, and the party whose title derived from the United States prevailed.

Lofty language in early federal legislation manifested an intention that Indian tribes would be treated in accordance with the highest standards of international law. The Northwest Ordinance of July 1787, which established the framework for the surveying, settlement, and organization of the Northwest Territories (later the states of Ohio, Indiana, Illinois, Michigan, and Wisconsin), declared in article 3, section 14 that

> the utmost good faith shall always be observed towards the Indians; their land and property shall never be taken from them without their consent; and in their property, rights and liberty, they shall never be invaded or disturbed, unless in just and lawful wars authorized by Congress; but laws founded in justice and humanity shall from time to time be made, for preventing wrongs being done to them, and for preserving peace and friendship with them.

One of the earliest enactments by the new Congress created by the Constitution was the Act to Regulate Trade and Intercourse with the Indian Tribes.[8] The act set forth a system of regulating commerce with the various tribes, provided for punishment of non-Indians who committed crimes and trespasses against Indians and their lands, and codified the principle that Vitoria first articulated and that was later embodied in the decision in *Johnson v. M'Intosh*, namely, that no sale of any interest in Indian lands to any state or person would have any validity unless done under the authority of the United States.[9] Originally enacted with a three-year lifespan, Congress periodically reenacted the Trade and Intercourse Act with various additions and modifications until it was made permanent in 1802. The last such act was passed in 1834.[10]

These legal rules, however, as solicitous of Indian interests as they might have seemed (at least, from the white man's point of view), did not assure that in practice Indian rights would be inviolably respected.[11] The young nation made numerous treaties with the various tribes, most of them primarily aimed at establishing peace and obtaining cessions of land. Invariably, the government would make promises of permanent peace, provision of financial and material assistance, protection from non-Indian incursions, and assurance that the lands remaining to the tribe would never be taken. Just as invariably, those assurances turned out to be hollow. The rapidly expanding population's incessant need for more land for settlement was most often the factor that caused the federal representatives to return to the tribes demanding further cessions. Moreover, the cessions were typically for consideration amounting to pittances, the tribes rarely having any awareness of the real value of their lands in U.S. dollars or, much less, the value of the mineral wealth those lands might contain.[12]

Eventually, as the tribes began to resist the increasingly insistent demands for further and larger cessions of land, the United States set out on a policy of forced removal of the eastern tribes from their lands, pursuant to treaties that the tribes were simply given no option to reject. For the most part, the tribes were forced to move to a newly designated area within the Louisiana Purchase, directly north of Texas, called "the Indian Territory." This was to become a permanent homeland for those tribes that moved there, although in 1889 the government reneged on that promise, too, opening the Indian Territory to the first Oklahoma land rush and eventually abolishing the reservations in the Indian Territory to make way for the state of Oklahoma.[13] By 1850 hardly any organized tribes remained east of the Mississippi.[14]

In 1849 Congress created the Department of the Interior and transferred authority over Indian affairs from the War Department to this new cabinet-level department.[15] The Indian Office had been a civilian bureau since 1830, so this transfer did not herald any major change in its operations, but the shift nonetheless was an acknowledgment on the part of Congress that Indian policy was no longer a matter of external relations with often-hostile foreign sovereigns. Instead it increasingly involved dealing with what Marshall described as "domestic dependent nations," separate nations that would continue to exist within U.S. borders and to which the United States would have certain special obligations. With the acquisition of New Mexico by the Treaty of Guadalupe Hidalgo, moreover, the United States acquired a score or so of largely "civilized" Pueblo Indian tribes, and federal Indian policy eventually found itself in knots over the exact status of the Pueblos. The government was more accustomed to dealing with roaming bands of "savage" Indians and found it difficult to adjust its policies to the village-oriented, agricultural, industrious, and generally peaceful Pueblos. Worse, non-Indians who wanted Pueblo land eventually found ways to use the Pueblos' more "civilized" character to the Pueblos' grave disadvantage.

There was considerable uncertainty in the courts about the status of the Pueblos under the Treaty of Guadalupe Hidalgo. The Plan of Iguala stated that all inhabitants of Mexico, regardless of race, were citizens of the new Republic of Mexico and thus possessed equal rights and responsibilities under the law.[16] Many historians (although not all) contend that the Plan of Iguala thus erased all legal distinctions between the Pueblo Indians and the Mexicans and that the Pueblo people understood this.[17] This issue bears directly on the effect of the treaty, which in articles 8 and 9 provided that "Mexicans" residing in the area ceded to the United States who did not affirmatively declare their intention to remain Mexican citizens within one year after the treaty was ratified would become citizens of the United States.[18] No Pueblo Indians are known to have made such a declaration, but whether they thus became U.S. citizens is, like the effect of the Plan of Iguala, disputed. Although article 11 of the treaty discusses the handling of depredations of the "savage tribes," the treaty makes no specific mention of the pueblos, and Supreme Court decisions left the question undetermined.[19]

The New Mexico territorial courts insisted that the Pueblo Indians succeeded to all the rights of U.S. citizenship by virtue of the treaty, but the New

Mexico territorial legislative assembly in 1854 passed a law specifically prohibiting Pueblo Indians from voting in territorial elections.[20] And the first state constitution, adopted in 1912, carefully excluded "Indians not taxed" from the categories of persons entitled to vote.[21] Only in 1924 did Congress finally confirm the applicability of section 1 of the 14th Amendment to the U.S. Constitution to Indians by enacting the Indian Citizenship Act (43 Stat. 253), which declared all "non-citizen Indians born within the territorial limits of the United States" to be U.S. citizens. The right of Indians in New Mexico to vote, however, was not established until 1948, at the earliest, when the federal court in New Mexico decided in an unreported opinion that the phrase "Indians not taxed" in the state Constitution violated the 14th Amendment.[22] Five years later, the legislature amended what was then section 3-1-1 of the New Mexico statutes, the statute that set forth the qualifications for voters, by deleting the "Indians not taxed" language (although that phrase was not removed from the state constitution until 1967).[23]

Despite this roller coaster of judicial and legislative expressions on the status of the Pueblos, the executive branch of the federal government appeared to have no doubt, from the ratification of the treaty onward, that the Pueblos were entitled to the same attention and protection as the government was obliged to extend to all other Indian tribes within its jurisdiction. Nor was there any question that the Pueblos desperately needed federal protection for their lands.

The first Indian agent for New Mexico, James S. Calhoun, was appointed relatively quickly after the Treaty of Guadalupe Hidalgo was ratified, arriving in Santa Fe on 22 July 1849.[24] In his first official report to the commissioner of Indian Affairs, William Medill, dated 29 July 1849, Calhoun stated that "the Pueblo Indians . . . are entitled to the early, and especial consideration of the government of the United States. They are the only tribe in perfect amity with government, and are an industrious, agricultural and pastoral people, living principally in villages."[25] On 1 October 1849, reporting at length on the circumstances of a number of the tribes in the territory, Calhoun noted that the pueblos "complain of many encroachments upon their boundaries, and hope the U.S. government will restore them their ancient rights."[26] Three days later Calhoun reiterated that "the protection of these [Pueblo] Indians, in their persons and property, is of great importance."[27] On 7 October Calhoun traveled to Jemez, where he stayed until 10 October, meeting with leaders of most of the pueblos. His report to Commissioner Medill on that meeting, dated 13 October

1849, emphasized the Indians' concerns about protection of their lands.[28] In a much longer report sent two days later, Calhoun exhibited considerable admiration for the Pueblos (observing, for example, that "their houses, are superior to those of Santa Fe" and praising their agricultural skills), and he noted that their lands were held "by Spanish and Mexican grants [although] to what extent is unknown."[29] He made clear, however, his great uncertainty as to whether the general laws and policies of the United States regarding the "savage" Indians should be applied equally to the Pueblos. Calhoun believed that the Pueblo Indians should be considered citizens entitled to vote, but he also recognized that they required the continuing protection of the government from the depredations of non-Indians in the territory.[30]

Representatives of sixteen pueblos came to Calhoun in mid-November 1849, asking Congress to extend to New Mexico the laws regulating trade and intercourse with the Indians, especially the law commonly referred to as the "Nonintercourse Act," which prohibits the transfer of any interest in Indian lands except as provided by Congress.[31] Calhoun fully endorsed that request.[32] Congress responded to that recommendation the following year, extending "the laws now in force, regulating trade and intercourse with the Indian tribes, . . . over the Indian tribes in the territories of New Mexico and Utah," and authorizing the appointment of four Indian agents for New Mexico.[33] It would be another seventy-five years, however, before the question of whether Pueblo lands were protected by that legislation was finally settled.[34]

Calhoun continued to complain to Washington that the Pueblos' lands were threatened and that the government should confirm their titles and survey their boundaries.[35] He wrote to Commissioner Orlando Brown on 25 January 1850, stating that "the wrongs to which the Pueblo Indians are subjected, are inconceivable, and ought to be remedied without a moment's delay." In the same letter, Calhoun requested authority to negotiate a treaty with the Pueblos.[36] Commissioner Brown finally responded on 24 April 1850, authorizing Calhoun to negotiate a treaty.[37] Calhoun acted quickly. In July 1850 he negotiated a treaty that ten of the pueblos signed, by which the United States promised that the boundaries of the pueblos "shall never be diminished, but may be enlarged" whenever the government deemed it advisable.[38] Congress failed to act on that treaty, however, and Calhoun, who was appointed the first governor of the territory in early January 1851, died near Independence, Missouri, in June 1852, while on his way to Washington, escorting a group of five Tesuque Pueblo leaders who wished to meet President Millard Fillmore and to lobby for the treaty's ratification. David Whiting, who was then Calhoun's private secretary, continued on to Washington with the Tesuque delegation, which spent six weeks in the capital and met with President Fillmore and Secretary of State Alexander Stuart, among other dignitaries. They made a sensation in the local press and among Washington society, but apart from receiving some polite assurances that the president would look into the treaty, they came back essentially empty handed.[39]

The Pueblo treaty was never ratified, but in 1854 Congress finally got around to attempting compliance with article 8 of the Treaty of Guadalupe Hidalgo, which imposed on the United States the duty to assure that "property of every kind belonging to Mexicans... shall be inviolably respected... as if the same belonged to citizens of the United States."[40] That obligation was owed to the citizens of the newly acquired New Mexico Territory not only by virtue of the treaty but also pursuant to generally accepted principles of international law recognized in decisions of the U.S. Supreme Court.[41] The 1854 act of Congress created the Office of Surveyor General of New Mexico, who was to ascertain "the origin, nature, character and extent of all claims to land under the laws, customs, and usages of Spain and Mexico" within the territory and to recommend, first to the secretary of the interior and then to Congress, whether the United States should honor the claim. In the act Congress specified that the surveyor general was to "make a report in regard to all pueblos existing in the Territory, showing the extent and locality of each, stating the number of inhabitants in the said pueblos, respectively, and the nature of their titles to the land."[42] That instruction was reiterated in the written directions that William Pelham, the first surveyor general, received from General Land Office commissioner John Wilson before Pelham left Washington for Santa Fe.[43]

Pelham eventually submitted to Congress for confirmation land grants for the pueblos of Jemez, Acoma, San Juan, Picuris, San Felipe, Cochiti, Santo Domingo, and Zia, as well as for Pecos, which no longer existed. All these claims were based on documents dated 1689 that purported to be grants (referred to as Cruzate grants) made by Governor Domingo Jironza Pétriz de Cruzate, which are discussed in chapter 8.[44] Pelham also submitted, and Congress confirmed, the Sandia grant and the Taos grant.[45] In his report to the secretary of the interior in 1856, by which he conveyed his recommendation for confirmation of the pueblo grants, Pelham, echoing Calhoun's pleas of six years earlier, urged prompt action on the grants, noting that

> the Pueblo Indians are constantly encroached upon by Mexican citizens, and in many instances the Indians are despoiled of their best lands; I therefore respectfully recommend that these claims be confirmed by Congress as speedily as possible, and that an appropriation be made to survey their lands, in order that their boundaries may be permanently fixed.[46]

Several pueblos—Santa Clara, San Ildefonso, Nambe, Pojoaque, Tesuque, Santa Ana, and Isleta—had no grant documents. U.S. officials operated on the assumption that all the pueblos had at one time received written land grants from Spanish and Mexican authorities, a view possibly based on Calhoun's reports. The U.S. authorities also seemed to be aware, as a result in part of Donaciano Vigil's sworn testimony, that "all recognized that the pueblos were entitled to four square leagues, with or without documents."[47] This minimum entitlement was usually defined as a tract consisting of a square, each of whose sides was one league (approximately 2.605 miles) in each of the cardinal directions from the center of the village and thus two leagues on each side.[48]

Pelham devised a proceeding that provided a basis for recommending confirmation of grants for those pueblos without documents. Pelham brought the governor and other headmen of each such pueblo into his office and asked them a brief series of questions—most of them leading—about their lands. Each pueblo's leaders responded that the pueblo once had a grant document that was lost or taken from them and that the lost document proved that the pueblo was entitled to a four-square-league grant. Pelham included transcripts of these "depositions" in his report to the secretary of the interior, along with his recommendation that the pueblo's league grant be confirmed. Although the questions and answers tended to vary in detail from one pueblo to the next, they are quite similar and have the distinct appearance of having been carefully scripted. In any event, the exchanges all went through an interpreter who plainly knew the required answers.[49]

For example, Carlos Vigil, the governor of Tesuque, was asked, "Have you the original title-deeds to the pueblo lands granted by the Spanish government?" The interpreter translated Vigil's response, which was, "They have not." Asked whether the pueblo ever had such a document, Vigil answered it did but that the Mexican authorities took it to have it "copied and revalidated" because the original was torn and that the pueblo had not seen the document since. He was then asked, "Do the lands of the pueblo extend one league from the church in the direction of the four cardinal points of the compass?" (This question is asked in almost identical words of each governor.) Governor Vigil confirmed that the pueblo lands extended one league in each direction from the church, but he added, interestingly, that "the distance from east to west only has been measured." The interrogatory concluded with one or two questions intended to confirm that the pueblo had been in its present location for a very long time.[50] San Ildefonso's governor stated that its grant was lost when the priest took it to Santa Fe to have it copied.[51] Santa Clara said simply that its grant was lost many years before.[52] Pojoaque reported that it presented its document to an alcalde in connection with a land dispute but had not seen it since.[53] Congress confirmed all these claimed lost grants in the 1858 act.[54]

Due to a mix-up in the surveyor general's records, Santa Ana's claim for lands around its old village of Tamaya on the Jemez River, for which it had no grant document, did not receive the surveyor general's official attention until October 1866.[55] Surveyor General John A. Clark followed essentially the same course that Pelham had set for such situations, with slight differences. Rather than put the information in the form of a series of questions, Clark took statements from the pueblo's governor and lieutenant governor and from a non-Indian. These statements noted that Santa Ana had a grant for these lands but that the document had been lost. Interestingly, the governor and lieutenant governor gave boundaries for the pueblo's lands based on natural monuments (mountains, rivers, arroyos, and so forth), not league measurements (although they did not agree on what the monuments were). Disregarding those claims, Clark recommended, and Congress confirmed, a regular Pueblo league grant to Santa Ana centered on the mission at Tamaya.[56]

Although it is conceivable that some or all of these accounts of lost grant documents were true, of the pueblo grants actually supported by documents, the only one that was unquestionably in the pueblo's possession for more than a few years was that of Sandia, which received its grant in 1748, as discussed in chapter 4. Apparently, the Cruzate-grant documents were sold or otherwise transferred to their grantee pueblos by a Mexican named Victor de la O and his confederates, starting in around 1850, as discussed in chapter 8. The claim that the other pueblos had lost their grant papers many years earlier or had lost them when they were taken to be copied because the originals were worn sounds contrived. Especially in the case of Santa Ana, the contention that the pueblo mislaid its grant document is extremely difficult to credit, given the extraordinary care with which the pueblo kept the documents pertaining to its land purchases along the Rio Grande dating from 1709, which are discussed in detail in chapter 2.[57]

Of particular interest is the Isleta grant that Pelham recommended for approval. Isleta representatives insisted that they had had a grant from the Spanish governor that was in the Spanish archives in Santa Fe but that a man named Miguel Antonio Lobato subsequently told them that he saw the document in the possession of a man in Polvadera, near Socorro, New Mexico. They had not seen it since. They insisted, however, that although it was for a league to the north and to the south, the grant reached eastward to the Manzano Mountains and west to the Rio Puerco. Pelham upheld the claim, and the Isleta grant was surveyed for more than 110,000 acres. Congress confirmed it in 1858, making it the largest pueblo grant in New Mexico confirmed by the U.S. Congress.[58]

The manner in which these claims were handled tells a great deal about U.S. assumptions as to the extent and nature of Pueblo landholdings—specifically, the apparently unshakeable conviction that each pueblo's lands were defined by a specific grant from Spanish authorities, or by the four-square-league entitlement. John Marshall's landmark Supreme Court opinion in *Johnson v. M'Intosh* first described in U.S. law the relative rights of Native Americans throughout the United States and their European conquerors.[59] Marshall stated that the "original inhabitants" of the continent "were admitted to be the rightful occupants of the soil, with a legal as well as just claim to retain possession of it" but that the conquest of the land by the European powers, to whom the United States was successor, gave the conqueror title to the land, subject only to *the Indian right of occupancy* and the exclusive power to extinguish that right by purchase or by conquest of the Indians.[60] This was a bedrock principle of U.S. policy toward the Indian tribes, and it was the basis on which virtually all of the treaties of cession with the Indian tribes of North America were entered into.

When Anglo-Americans came to the Rio Grande valley, they found villages of Indian people living relatively close to, and relatively in peace with, villages of non-Indians, along with a European-derived system of land titles in which some Indians participated extensively. Most Anglo-Americans did not realize that while these Pueblo Indians managed to adapt their customs and economies to the necessity of living amid communities of Europeans who brought with them a completely different approach to land ownership, the Pueblos steadfastly maintained their traditional attachments to the landscapes surrounding their villages through hunting, herding, agriculture, gathering of plant and mineral materials, and myriad traditional cultural uses that had remained largely unchanged since long before the arrival of the Spaniards. The status of aboriginal title claims in the lands acquired under the Treaty of Guadalupe Hidalgo was not firmly established in U.S. law until the 1942 Supreme Court decision in *United States v. Santa Fe Pacific Railroad Co.*[61] The court found that the Hualapai tribe of Arizona held aboriginal title to its lands, which title was not extinguished by the issuance of patents over tracts of those lands to the railroad or by the Indian Department's settlement of the tribe on a reservation against its wishes.[62] The proposition that pueblos that had confirmed grants could also claim land by aboriginal title was not settled until 1964, by the decision of the U.S. Court of Claims (in an appeal from the Indian Claims Commission), in *Pueblo de Zia, Pueblo de Jemez and Pueblo de Santa Ana v. United States.*[63] Legal recognition of these claims, which the pueblos always understood that they possessed, came so late because they were simply ignored by U.S. authorities throughout the nineteenth and early twentieth centuries. The statements taken from the Santa Ana officials by Surveyor General John Clark, for example, manifested Santa Ana's views of the limits of the lands it used and occupied for its economic and cultural purposes, but Clark disregarded that information completely and recommended only a league grant. The only claims for confirmation of titles that the surveyor general submitted to Congress on behalf of the pueblos were those based on actual documents (the Cruzate grants and the Sandia and Taos documents) or claims for Pueblo league grants for which the pueblos said they once had documents.[64]

The 1858 act confirming the Pueblo grants expressly directed the commissioner of the General Land Office to "cause a patent . . . to issue as in ordinary cases to private individuals" to each pueblo for its grant according to the grant's survey.[65] Upon the issuance of the patents, the pueblos owned the lands embraced by the surveys in fee simple, that is, like other private landowners. Thus, Pueblo ownership of Pueblo grant lands is distinct from the ownership of the lands of tribes throughout most of the rest of the country, who were placed on "reservations." Reservation lands are owned by the United States but were "reserved" from the public domain and are held in trust for the tribes. Pueblo grant lands are owned by the Pueblo Indians, pursuant to patents issued by the United States. However, given that Congress had extended the provisions of the Nonintercourse Act to New Mexico in 1851, the fact that the pueblos held their lands in fee should have made no difference, since that act should have made Pueblo lands fully subject to federal-law protections against alienation.[66] But fairly quickly the territorial courts of New Mexico began issuing a series of decisions that had the effect of stripping the Pueblos of the protection the Nonintercourse Act afforded.

The first such case was *United States v. Lucero*, one of thirty similar cases the United States brought to challenge the growing problem of non-Indian trespass on Pueblo lands. *Lucero*, which dealt with the lands of Cochiti, was heard in the district court by Justice John P. Slough. In 1862, during the Civil War, Slough led a contingent of Colorado Volunteers down to New Mexico to oppose invading Confederate forces at the Battle of Glorieta Pass, southeast of Santa Fe.[67] He returned to New Mexico in 1864 and two years later was appointed to the territorial supreme court, replacing Kirby Benedict, who was removed from the bench in 1866. Two years later, when U.S. attorney Stephen B. Elkins filed the Pueblo lands cases, Benedict appeared as counsel for the defendants. In each of the cases the United States asserted that the defendants were settled unlawfully on Pueblo lands in violation of the terms of section 11 of the 1834 Trade and Intercourse Act, which made it a federal offense to settle on the lands of "any Indian tribe."

Benedict moved to dismiss the complaints, arguing that the 1834 act had no applicability to Pueblo lands. Judge Slough agreed, and in a fairly lengthy opinion he concluded that the Trade and Intercourse Act was never intended to apply to "civilized Indians," and that since the Pueblos were citizens of Mexico and had become citizens of the United States under the terms of the Treaty of Guadalupe Hidalgo, the treaty protected their rights to their lands. He thus held that the law under which the actions were brought had no applicability to the Pueblos, warranting dismissal of the cases.[68] The decision essentially meant that Pueblo lands enjoyed no protection under federal law. The United States appealed to the territorial supreme court, partly on the urging of John Ward and others in the Indian Agency who believed that the Slough decision would "open the doors ... for such individuals as may think it proper to take advantage of these [Pueblo] people."[69]

Chief Justice Watts's opinion in the New Mexico Territorial Supreme Court begins with a blistering characterization of the "savage" Indians for whom, the court insisted, the Trade and Intercourse Acts were passed, referring to them as "a handful of wild, half-naked, thieving, plundering, murdering savages" and expressing indignation that the United States should accord them the status of "*quasi* nations."[70] In contrast, Watts describes the Pueblo Indians whom the Hispanos found inhabiting the Rio Grande valley as "civilized, peaceful and kind," and thus "easy victim[s] of [the Hispanos'] cupidity and despotic rule."[71] The opinion offers a lengthy analysis of the Pueblos' status as of the date of the Treaty of Guadalupe Hidalgo, concluding, as had Slough, that "[the Indians] were in fact Mexican citizens at the date of the Treaty ... and are entitled to the benefit of all of the articles in said treaty designed to protect the life, liberty and property of Mexicans under the new sovereign."[72] Largely on that basis, the court concluded that Congress's purported assumption of control over Pueblo lands was beyond its authority, stating that it "does not consider it proper to assent to the withdrawal of eight thousand citizens of New Mexico from the operation of the laws, made to secure and maintain them in their liberty and property, and consign their liberty and property to a system of laws and trade made for wandering savages and administered by agents of the Indian department." Consequently, the court held that the statute under which Lucero was charged did not apply to Cochiti's lands, and it affirmed the district court's dismissal of the complaints the United States had filed.[73]

The district court and the territorial supreme court carefully calculated the extravagant praise that they heaped on the Pueblos to establish that they were so completely unlike the "savage Indians" that there was no legitimate basis for the assertion of federal authority over them or their lands. If federal-law protections were not applicable to Pueblo lands, those lands, which included some of the most valuable irrigated land in the territory, could be bought and sold, acquired by adverse possession, and taxed (and then sold at tax sales for nonpayment). Justice Watts's observation that the "civilized, peaceful and kind" demeanor of the pueblos made them "easy victims" of the Hispanos' "cupidity and despotic rule" is ironic. The "cupidity" of the Hispanos, if that was a fair characterization, was nothing compared with that of the Anglo-Americans. The court seized on the Pueblos' civilized and peaceful qualities to justify the claim that they were not protected by federal law and were therefore fully exposed to the cupidity of their new Anglo-American neighbors.

Indian agents in New Mexico saw the disastrous potential for the Pueblos of this ruling and urged their superiors in Washington to take the case to the U.S. Supreme Court, but no appeal was made. Elkins resigned as U.S. attorney in 1870, and Thomas B. Catron was appointed to replace him. The United States then determined to bring a new round of lawsuits that it hoped would clearly establish the status of the Pueblos and their lands as being under the full protection of federal law. In 1873 Catron identified 204 persons believed to be trespassing on Pueblo lands and began preparing new trespass suits.[74]

The cases Catron selected to be the lead cases in this array pertained to Taos Pueblo and the defunct Pecos Pueblo. Taos was obviously a vital and important pueblo, but Pecos was abandoned, and the status of its lands was uncertain. Regardless, Catron pursued suits against Manuel Varela, a member of the territorial assembly from San Miguel County, and Martin Koslowski, a Polish immigrant who settled in Pecos in 1858 and whose ranch was an important staging ground for federal troops in the Civil War battles of Apache Pass and Glorieta Pass. Catron's complaints alleged that both were trespassing on Pecos land.[75] Catron also sued Juan Santistevan and Antonio Joseph for trespassing on Taos land.[76] Justice Joseph G. Palen, sitting as district judge, quickly dismissed all four suits, and Catron appealed to the territorial supreme court.

Santistevan was treated as the lead case in the Supreme Court, and Justice Johnson's opinion affirming the district court was relatively brief. It did not mention the *Lucero* decision, but the reasoning was similar, with one additional factor: Johnson noted that the section of the Trade and Intercourse Act under which the cases were brought referred to persons who settled on "any lands belonging, secured or granted by treaty with the United States to any Indian tribe." By applying some grammatically questionable rules of interpretation, the court concluded that the terms "belonging," "secured," and "granted" were each modified by the clause, "by treaty with the United States" and that since there was no treaty in place with Taos, the section was inapplicable to that pueblo's lands.[77] Justice Johnson went on to set forth the more general proposition that congressional power over the property and affairs of the Indians was intended to reach only "the wild tribes" and that any assertion of federal authority over the lands of the Pueblos would violate their rights as Mexican citizens under the Treaty of Guadalupe Hidalgo.[78]

The cases of Varela, Koslowski, and Joseph were reported separately with a one-paragraph statement by Johnson referencing the decision in *Santistevan* and noting that the same reasoning warranted affirming these decisions as well.[79]

Catron wasted no time appealing the *Joseph* and *Santistevan* cases to the U.S. Supreme Court, where ironically the defendants were represented by none other than Stephen B. Elkins, the former U.S. attorney for New Mexico who had brought the *Lucero* case. In May 1877 the Supreme Court issued its decision in an opinion by Justice Samuel Miller.[80] It should be noted that there was no factual record in the case; there was only the United States' complaint and the defendants' motion to dismiss (called a "demurrer" in the legal nomenclature of the day). Miller's opinion, although avoiding the hyperbole of Watts's opinion in *Lucero*, nonetheless relied for its rationale on characterizations of the Pueblos as peaceful, industrious, law-abiding, and devout peoples, just as both the district court and the territorial supreme court in *Lucero* had done. Oddly, Miller included a long quotation that he said was from "the opinion of the chief justice of the court whose judgment we are reviewing," as if it came from Justice Johnson's opinion in the case. But the passage Justice Miller quotes, a lengthy description of the pueblos emphasizing the "peaceful, civilized" qualities that supposedly set them apart from the "savage Indians," is taken directly from the opinion written by then chief justice Slough sitting as the *district* judge in what became the *Lucero* case, twelve years earlier. Although it presented identical issues, this was not the case before the Supreme Court.[81] The qualities of the Pueblos that the court described in the quoted passage, Miller said, "all forbid the idea that they should be classed with the Indian tribes for whom the intercourse acts were made." At the same time, however, the court declined to determine that the Pueblos were citizens, either of the United States or of New Mexico, deeming that question to be not properly before it and thus leaving the pueblos in legal limbo.[82]

Justice Miller went on to consider the tenure by which pueblo lands were held. He observed that the land rights of tribal Indians—that is, aboriginal title—had always been viewed as subject to the ultimate title held by the United States and that it was that superior right that warranted the government's assertion of control over conveyances of and occupancy on Indian lands.[83] The Pueblos' lands, however, were held by them "by a right superior to that of the United States," and by its confirmation of those titles, the United States disclaimed any right of control over those lands.[84] The court concluded with the observation that if the defendant (trespasser) was on the pueblo's lands wrongfully, he could be ejected by suit in the territorial court, adding that "we know of no injury which the United States suffers by his presence, nor any statute which he violates in that regard."[85] In short, the Supreme Court completely embraced the theory that the Pueblos were "too good to be Indians" and thus did not need protection. To be sure, the flattering descriptions of the Pueblos set forth in the *Joseph* opinion were not untrue, so far as they went, but they did not by any means negate the indisputable fact that the Pueblo people were Native Americans, just like the "wild tribes" and "savage Indians" with whom they were so sharply contrasted. Ironically, none of these opinions ever makes any reference to the bloody Pueblo Revolt.

The effect of the *Joseph* decision was that the U.S. attorney for New Mexico was thereafter legally barred from acting to deal with the growing problem of trespass on Pueblo lands because the United States no longer had a trust responsibility toward the Pueblo Indians. The stream of incursions by non-Indians onto Pueblo lands—some with claimed titles, many without— became a flood, and the territorial courts facilitated the purported transfers of title.[86] The *Joseph* decision encouraged further alienation of Pueblo lands and subjected the determination of title to the territorial courts, which nearly always upheld the claims of non-Indians. By allowing and even encouraging further loss of Pueblo lands, the *Joseph* decision signaled a period of benign neglect by the federal government. This left the field open to land speculators such as Catron and Antonio Joseph himself to continue their speculation in Pueblo lands. Joseph, whose political and business rivalry with Catron probably led to his being sued in the first place, was able to keep his holdings near Taos Pueblo; Catron, who lost the *Joseph* case on behalf of the Pueblos, soon began using it to prove the validity of his own claims to Pueblo lands.[87]

Neither the Indian Service nor Congress seemed affected by the dramatic change the *Joseph* decision wrought in the technical legal status of the pueblos. Indian agents continued to represent the government in dealings with the Pueblos, federal Indian schools were established for the education of Pueblo youth, and in virtually every other respect the administration continued to act as if the United States had the same relationship with the pueblos as it did with other tribes. As the Supreme Court explained in its next occasion to examine the status of the pueblos, following the decision in *Joseph*, public moneys have been expended in presenting them with farming implements and utensils, and in their civilization and instruction; agents and superintendents have been provided to guard their interests; central training schools and day schools at the pueblos have been established and maintained for the education of their children; dams and irrigation works have been constructed to encourage and enable them to cultivate their lands and sustain themselves; public lands ... have been reserved for their use and occupancy where their own lands were deemed inadequate; a special attorney has been employed since 1898 ... to represent them and maintain their rights.[88]

The attitude of Congress was made clear in 1904 when the territorial supreme court ruled for the first time that Pueblo lands were subject to taxation.[89] The brief opinion of the court, relying primarily on *Lucero* and *Joseph*, simply held that the Pueblos were not wards of the United States, that they owned their lands in fee simple, that they were not subject to any federal restrictions on alienation, and that they therefore were liable for property taxes on their lands. It was apparent to the officials of the Indian Service in New Mexico that taxation of Pueblo lands would inevitably lead to the complete loss of those lands, and urgent pleas were sent to Washington. Barely a year later, on 3 March 1905, Congress included in the appropriations bill for the Indian Department a paragraph stating

> that the lands now held by the various villages or pueblos of Pueblo Indians, or by individual members thereof, within Pueblo reservations or lands, in the Territory of New Mexico, and all personal property furnished said Indians by the United States, or used in cultivating said lands, and any cattle and sheep now possessed or that may hereafter be acquired by said Indians shall be free and exempt from taxation of any sort whatsoever, including taxes heretofore levied, if any, until Congress shall otherwise provide.[90]

In New Mexico, the territorial supreme court remained unconvinced. In 1907 it decided *United States v. Mares*, a federal prosecution of a non-Indian for selling whiskey to members of Taos Pueblo in violation of an 1897 law that made it a crime to sell alcoholic beverages "to any Indian a ward of the government under the charge of any Indian superintendent or agent, or to any Indian . . . over whom the government . . . exercises guardianship."[91] The court affirmed the dismissal of the charges by the district court, holding that Pueblo Indians were not under the government's superintendence or guardianship. It viewed the matter as beyond dispute, saying that "the stipulation that the Indians in question were Pueblos places them as a matter of law beyond the protection of the statute."[92]

Congress parried that thrust as well in a manner unmistakably designed to permanently undo the effect of the *Joseph* decision and all of its progeny in the territorial courts. In 1910, in preparation for New Mexico's admission to the Union as the forty-seventh state, Congress passed the New Mexico Enabling Act, which set forth the procedures by which the people of the territory could adopt a new constitution and form a state government.[93] But it imposed certain conditions, first among which was that the constitutional convention had to provide, "by an ordinance irrevocable without the consent of the United States and the people of said State," that "the sale, barter, or giving of intoxicating liquors to Indians and the introduction of liquors into Indian country, *which term shall also include all lands now owned or occupied by the Pueblo Indians of New Mexico*, are forever prohibited." The act also required that the constitution provide that

> the people inhabiting said proposed State do agree and declare that they forever disclaim all right and title . . . to all lands lying within said boundaries owned or held by any Indian or Indian tribes the right or title to which shall have been acquired through or from the United States or any prior sovereignty, and that until the title or titles of such Indian or Indian tribes shall have been extinguished the same shall be and remain subject to the absolute jurisdiction and control of the Congress of the United States . . . that no taxes shall be imposed by the State upon lands or property therein belonging to or which may hereafter be acquired by the United States or reserved for its use; but nothing herein, or in the ordinance herein provided for, shall preclude the State from taxing, as other lands and other property are taxed, any lands and other property outside of an Indian reservation owned or held by any Indian, save and except such lands as have been granted or acquired as aforesaid or as may be granted or confirmed to any Indian or any Indians under any Act of

Congress, but said ordinance shall provide that all such lands shall be exempt from taxation by said State so long and to such extent as Congress has prescribed or may hereafter prescribe.[94]

Although perhaps not worded in the most felicitous language, this passage clearly manifested Congress's determination to maintain federal guardianship over the Pueblos and to preserve their immunity from state authority. As federal officials would quickly learn, however, the New Mexico courts were not prepared to take that language at face value. The prospective state of New Mexico grudgingly incorporated language into its constitution consistent with the Enabling Act's commands, but the status of the Pueblos was years away from being settled.

New Mexico was admitted to the Union on 6 January 1912.[95] The ink was barely dry on the proclamation when Francis Wilson, special U.S. attorney for the Pueblo Indians, brought an indictment against one Felipe Sandoval for introducing liquor into the lands of Santa Clara, contrary to the 1897 statute.[96] A. B. Renehan, who faced off against Wilson ten years later in the raging controversy that developed over the Pueblo Lands Act, represented Sandoval in the federal district court. Renehan moved to dismiss the indictment, arguing that the 1897 law did not apply and that the provisions of the Enabling Act were invalid, as violative of the "equal footing" doctrine, which requires that each state admitted to the Union must be admitted with the same rights and degree of sovereignty as every other state. Renehan argued that for Congress to assert power over and restrict commerce with the Pueblos in the New Mexico Enabling Act as a condition of New Mexico's admission to the Union diminished New Mexico's police power over its citizens. This, Renehan argued, constituted the attempted exercise of a power that Congress could not constitutionally impose on one state.

Federal judge John H. Pope agreed with Renehan. He ruled that "the Pueblo Indians are not tribes within the meaning of the Constitution" and that the provisions of the Enabling Act (and presumably, the provisions of the state constitution enacted in compliance with that act) barring sales of alcoholic beverages to Pueblo Indians amounted to "a detraction from the police power properly belonging to the state" and were thus invalid.[97] While that ruling dealt only with the prohibition against sales of liquor, its logic would necessarily apply equally to the other provisions of the Enabling Act intended to make clear the federal guardianship over the Pueblos and their land. Wilson persuaded the government to take the case to the U.S. Supreme Court. Ralph Emerson Twitchell later testified that "there was not a living soul in New Mexico, lawyer or layman, who ever believed Judge Pope would be reversed in the Sandoval case."[98] Those souls were to be surprised. In *United States v. Sandoval* (1913), in an opinion by Justice Willis Van Devanter, a unanimous court held that Congress had the power to assert federal guardianship over the Pueblos, that it had done so, and that that decision was not subject to judicial scrutiny.[99]

The opinion rejected the argument that the equal footing doctrine precluded the assertion of federal authority, reasoning that as long as Congress is simply exercising a power it possesses under the constitution and not imposing a new condition on the state as a "term of admission," there can be no objection to the congressional action. The sole question in the court's view was "whether the status of the Pueblo Indians and their lands is such" that Congress could competently regulate the introduction and sale of alcohol on such lands (and, by implication, impose the full array of federal law restrictions on alienation of Pueblo lands).[100] In answering that question, the court found it necessary to reexamine the character of the Pueblo Indians and (without expressly saying so, until the very end of the opinion) to revisit the view taken of them in the *Joseph* decision. It is an ironic and regrettable feature of the opinion that in order to establish the foundation for its conclusion, namely, that Congress could legitimately assert federal authority over the pueblos, the court seemed to feel that it was necessary to describe the Pueblos in demeaning terms. Thus, Van Devanter wrote that the Pueblo people,

> although sedentary rather than nomadic in their inclinations, and disposed to peace and industry, are nevertheless Indians in race, customs and domestic government. Always living in separate and isolated communities, adhering to primitive modes of life, largely influenced by superstition and fetishism, and chiefly governed according to the crude customs inherited from their ancestors, they are essentially a simple, uninformed and inferior people.[101]

Van Devanter quoted extensively from reports of Indian Service superintendents, who made similarly uncomplimentary observations about their

Pueblo charges, to support the conclusion that the pueblos were "dependent on the fostering care and protection of the government, like reservation Indians in general."[102] More to the point, the opinion demonstrated that from the time New Mexico became part of the United States, Congress had been treating the Pueblos like other Indian communities entitled to "special care and protection," by providing them with numerous services and amenities and appointing federal agents and other officials to assist them and deal with their needs. It also noted that both Spanish and Mexican colonial regimes accorded the Pueblos special legal protection.[103]

The critical consideration was that "long continued legislative and executive usage and an unbroken current of judicial decisions have attributed to the United States . . . the power and the duty of exercising a fostering care and protection over all dependent Indian communities within its borders" and that "in respect of distinctly Indian communities the questions whether, to what extent and for what time they shall be recognized and dealt with as dependent tribes . . . are to be determined by Congress, and not by the courts."[104] Inasmuch as Congress consistently treated the Pueblos "as dependent communities entitled to its aid and protection, like other Indian tribes," the court held, "this assertion of guardianship over them . . . must be regarded as both authorized and controlling."[105] The court dismissed both the arguments that the Pueblos were citizens and therefore could not be made subject to Congress's authority ("whether they are citizens is an open question," Van Devanter said, adding that even if they were, that would not preclude a finding of federal guardianship) and that since they owned their lands in fee, those lands could not be brought under federal control. The court noted that in this respect the Pueblos' situation was essentially the same as that of the so-called Five Civilized Tribes of Oklahoma, whose lands, although also held in fee simple title, "were adjudged subject to the legislation of Congress enacted in the exercise of the government's guardianship over those tribes and their affairs."[106]

The court acknowledged that its ruling was at odds with the views expressed in *Joseph*, a fact it attributed to the territorial court having been given inaccurate information about the Pueblos. Without expressly overruling that decision, the court said simply that *Joseph* "cannot be regarded as holding that these Indians or their lands are beyond the range of congressional power under the Constitution."[107] That, of course, was what that case *had* held. The resolution of that conundrum would have to wait another thirteen years.

Although the *Sandoval* decision brought about a sea change in the legal status of the Pueblos under federal law, it initially had far less impact in New Mexico than one might have expected. Two days after the opinion was issued, the *Santa Fe New Mexican* of 22 October 1913 carried a front-page interview with Francis Wilson in which he explained his view of the significance of the decision. He also responded to an article that appeared in the *Albuquerque Morning Journal* the previous day by A. B. Renehan, who argued the case for Sandoval. Neither Wilson nor Renehan had read the full decision. Nevertheless, Renehan predicted its effect: "Some several thousand Mexican and American citizens residing within Pueblo grants have been disfranchised."[108] In the *New Mexican* article Wilson vigorously disputed Renehan's claim that the decision seriously impacted the titles of non-Indians residing within Pueblo grants, calling such a contention "too ridiculous to need much discussion."[109] Two days later, the *New Mexican* ran an editorial on the decision, entitled "The Question Settled," saying that the only question settled was whether the United States could regulate the sale of alcoholic beverages to Pueblo Indians. For several years after the decision, the case was generally regarded as "that liquor case."[110] Leo Crane, who arrived in Albuquerque in 1919 to take his position as the new Pueblo superintendent for the Indian Service, found that many New Mexicans were "studiously blind to the *Sandoval* decision of 1913."[111]

By demolishing the factual rationale of the *Joseph* decision, as the Supreme Court later observed, *Sandoval* "cast a pall" over the titles of the twelve thousand non-Indians, who by then had moved onto Pueblo land, by raising the likelihood that without federal approval none of their titles were valid.[112] In 1913 the United States hired surveyor Francis Joy to survey all the lands that non-Indians claimed within pueblo grants. In 1919 Richard H. Hanna, a former New Mexico Supreme Court justice, was hired as special attorney for the Pueblos (replacing Wilson) and began filing ejectment suits against hundreds of those non-Indians. With Hanna's action the "pall" became a firestorm of outrage and controversy that brought the question of the pueblos and their lands right back before Congress. The story of the years of tortuous congressional proceedings that resulted in the Pueblo Lands Act of 1924 is related in chapter 10.

In the meantime, the Supreme Court finally had occasion with its 1926 decision in *United States v. Candelaria* to wrap up the unfinished business left by the *Sandoval* decision and to make clear that *Sandoval* was not just a "liquor case." *Candelaria* began in 1922 as a suit by the United States to quiet the title of Laguna Pueblo against José Candelaria and others, who were alleged to be occupying and fencing Laguna's grant lands under a false claim of title. The United States brought the action on the theory that it was the guardian of the Indians and their lands and that it had a duty to protect those lands. The defendants asserted that a previous decree of the state court upheld their claims to the land and that that decree should be accorded res judicata effect in federal district court (meaning that the matter had been decided and could not be relitigated) when the pueblo tried to assert its title in a new suit in 1916. The United States responded that it had not been party to either of those cases and was not bound by either decree, but the district court held that the prior decrees barred the United States' suit and dismissed the complaint. The United States appealed to the Tenth Circuit Court of Appeals, and that court, uncertain as to whether the *Joseph* decision was still good law, certified two questions to the U.S. Supreme Court. The first question was whether the Pueblo Indians were subject to federal guardianship with respect to their lands, such that a decree affecting pueblo lands in a case to which the United States was not party would not bar the United States from pursuing its own action with regard to those lands. The second question was whether the state court had jurisdiction to enter a judgment concerning pueblo land that would be res judicata as to the United States.

Justice Van Devanter again wrote the Supreme Court's opinion in *United States v. Candelaria*. He began by quoting several lengthy passages from the *Sandoval* opinion, affirming Congress's power to assert federal authority over Indian tribes within its territory. He noted that Congress had unequivocally asserted authority over the Pueblo Indians of New Mexico such that their lands were subject to the federal guardianship.[113] The court then referred to the provisions of the Nonintercourse Act that provided that "no purchase, grant, lease, or other conveyance of lands, or of any title or claim thereto, from any Indian nation or tribe of Indians, shall be of any validity in law or equity, unless the same be made by treaty or convention entered into pursuant to the Constitution."[114] This was the statute whose applicability to Pueblo lands was squarely at issue in *Joseph*. In *Candelaria*, Van Devanter noted that the statute was extended "over 'the Indian tribes of New Mexico' in 1851" and, using language drawn from *Sandoval*, he explained why that act should be understood to have included the pueblos:

While there is no express reference in the provision to Pueblo Indians, we think it must be taken as including them. They are plainly within its spirit, and, in our opinion, fairly within its words, "any tribe of Indians." Although sedentary, industrious, and disposed to peace, they are Indians in race, customs, and domestic government, always have lived in isolated communities, and are a simple, uninformed people, ill-prepared to cope with the intelligence and greed of other races. It therefore is difficult to believe that Congress in 1851 was not intending to protect them, but only the nomadic and savage Indians then living in New Mexico. A more reasonable view is that the term "Indian tribe" was used in the acts of 1834 and 1851 in the sense of "a body of Indians of the same or similar race, united in a community under one leadership or government, and inhabiting a particular though sometimes ill-defined territory." ... In that sense the term easily includes Pueblo Indians.[115]

Although the court made no reference to *Joseph*, its holding that the Nonintercourse Act "easily includes Pueblo Indians" left nothing standing of the 1877 decision. The court sent the case back to the court of appeals, making it clear that since the United States had not been involved in the earlier cases, it could not be barred by those decrees. "The Indians of the pueblo are wards of the United States, and hold their lands subject to the restriction that the same cannot be alienated in any wise without its consent."[116]

The task of restoring the Pueblos to the full protection of the federal guardianship was still not quite complete. It would take a cattle-rustling case from Isleta to complete the process. In 1932 the United States indicted Gregorio Chávez and José María Chávez for stealing cattle belonging to members of Isleta Pueblo on pueblo lands. The defendants moved to dismiss, arguing that Isleta land was not Indian country and that even if it were the United States could not punish a nonmember of the pueblo. The district court granted the defendants' motion, ruling that under the Enabling Act a crime by a non-Indian on Pueblo land, even against Indian-owned property, could only be dealt with under the laws of the state. The United States took a direct appeal to the Supreme Court, and Justice Van Devanter took up his pen for the third time in *United States v. Chávez* to set the lower courts of New Mexico straight as to the relationship between the Pueblo Indians and the federal government. The justice restated the reasoning and holdings of *Sandoval* and *Candelaria* as to the character and status of the Pueblos and the actions of Congress manifesting the existence of the federal guardianship. He also pointed out that the statute under which the indictments for cattle theft were brought was originally enacted as part of the same 1834 Trade and Intercourse Act that contained the Nonintercourse Act, which in *Candelaria* was expressly held to apply to the Pueblos. There could be, he noted, no basis for making any distinction between the meaning or scope of "Indian country" as between the two statutes. "It follows from what has been said," the opinion stated,

> that the people of the pueblo of Isleta are Indian wards of the United States; that the lands owned and occupied by them under their ancient grant are Indian country in the sense of section 217; that the United States, in virtue of its guardianship, has full power to punish crimes committed within the limits of the pueblo lands by or against the Indians or against their property, even though, where the offense is against an Indian or his property, the offender be not an Indian.[117]

The opinion concluded by noting that to the extent the district court's decision relied on the equal footing doctrine, "the principle of equality [among the states] is not disturbed by a legitimate exertion by the United States of its constitutional power in respect of its Indian wards and their property." The *Chávez* decision left no further room for argument that the Pueblo Indians and their lands lay outside of federal guardianship. Still, the "facts on the ground" of non-Indian encroachment on Pueblo land during the fifty years of judicial confusion as to the Pueblos' status (and before) proved to be nearly impossible to undo, as chapter 10 explains.

◆ ◆ ◆ ◆

Until 1891 Congress's sole means of determining private titles in the New Mexico Territory was through the review of claims by the surveyor general, who referred to Congress those claims he believed merited confirmation. Over time, this process became tainted by conflicts of interest within the surveyor general's office. It is clear that several of the incumbents in that position were heavily invested in land-grant claims.[118] Congress became so skeptical of the recommendations it received from that office that it virtually stopped considering recommendations from the surveyor general by the late 1860s. During the period Congress confirmed 18 Pueblo grants covering 566,579 acres and 45 Hispano grants (and purchases made by Laguna) covering 8,636,673 acres.[119] Finally, in 1891, Congress created the Court of Private Land Claims.[120] The court was a 5-judge tribunal that considered claims of private titles to lands in New Mexico (although it also heard a few claims to lands in Colorado and Arizona) in adversary proceedings in which the United States was the defendant, seeking to disprove the validity or at least to minimize the extent of the claims presented. Matthew G. Reynolds, the U.S. attorney representing the government, was effective in defeating many claims, partly because "he had assembled a superb team of experts to assist him in fashioning a defense to each claim," including Will Tipton, Henry Flipper, and several assistant U.S. attorneys.[121] Two hundred and eighty-two claims were filed with the court during its 15-year existence, claiming a total of 34,653,340 acres. The court confirmed 82 claims, for a total of 1,934,986 acres.[122] Many claims were confirmed only to have their acreage reduced by questionable surveys or the operation of the 1897 Sandoval case that rejected the common lands of non-Indian community grants.

Although Congress indicated in the act creating the court that preference was to be given to Indian claims, the several pueblos that brought claims before the court fared no better than anyone else; in most cases they did much worse.[123] Seven Pueblo claims were filed.[124] Of those, two—the claim of Jemez, Zia, and Santa Ana to their jointly held, 276,000-acre Ojo del Espíritu Santo grant and Cochiti's claim to the 20,000-acre Juana Baca grant and the Cochiti pasture grant—were rejected entirely. Santa Clara filed a claim for its Cañada de Santa Clara grant, which it contended amounted to approximately 90,000 acres, embracing the full extent of Santa Clara Canyon. The court confirmed the Cañada de Santa Clara grant but determined that it consisted solely of the narrow riparian strip at the bottom of the canyon, amounting to just 490 acres. A later survey reduced the area to 473 acres.[125]

Santo Domingo and San Felipe filed a claim to the joint grant that Governor Mendinueta made to them in 1770, which they contended embraced about 40,000 acres. The court ruled similarly to the way it had ruled in the Cañada de Santa Clara case, confirming the grant, but only for 1,070 acres, three quarters of which was already included within the surveyed Cruzate grants of those two pueblos. The grant was expressly made to the two pueblos to accommodate their herds, but as the two dissenting justices of the court noted, the area allowed by the court's decision "would only support one small goat."[126] In 1902, at the urging of the Indian Service, President Theodore Roosevelt set aside by executive order a reservation for San Felipe of about 12,000 acres to correct this miscarriage of justice. Due to an apparent belief on the part of the Indian Service that Santo Domingo already had enough land, the reservation was set aside solely for San Felipe, with no land given to Santo Domingo.

Laguna Pueblo filed a claim with the Court of Private Land Claims after being thwarted by the surveyor general process. Laguna Pueblo's Cruzate grant (whose boundaries encompassed an estimated 125,000 acres) was presented to Surveyor General Pelham in 1857, but although he recommended it for confirmation in 1859, Congress did not act on it.[127] In 1872 Laguna retained former New Mexico Territorial Supreme Court justice John S. Watts to press once again for confirmation of the grant. Surveyor General James K. Proudfit approved the grant and sent it to Interior, but Congress again refused to act. Finally, Laguna filed a claim for the grant in the Court of Private Land Claims. The filing of this claim led Will Tipton, a translator and handwriting expert in the court's employ, to examine the Laguna Cruzate document carefully and to conclude that it, and consequently all of the pueblo Cruzates, were "spurious." U.S. attorney Reynolds advised Laguna's counsel of this, and at trial Laguna abandoned any reliance on the document, instead claiming that it used and occupied the land under a claim of right for a long time and that the document was based on an authentic original that was lost. The court rejected that claim, although it concluded that Laguna was at least entitled to a standard Pueblo league grant as a matter of Spanish law, and it confirmed such a grant, amounting to 17,330 acres.[128]

As described in chapter 2, Santa Ana possesses extensive original documentation of its purchases from Spanish settlers of its Ranchiit'u lands along the Rio Grande just north of Bernalillo. Although it presented those documents to U.S. officials soon after they took up residence in Santa Fe, the surveyor general's office never took any action to have the land surveyed or confirmed. Therefore, in 1893 Santa Ana retained George Hill Howard to file an action in the Court of Private Land Claims to confirm its titles. A letter from U.S. attorney Reynolds to the attorney general in Washington, written on 19 June 1897, just two weeks after the court issued its decree in the case, explains what happened.[129] Reynolds carefully listed each of the five major transactions by which Santa Ana acquired these lands, giving the dates and boundaries of each.[130] Reynolds stated that the genuineness of the "voluminous" documentation "was beyond dispute" and showed that Santa Ana had purchased the various tracts over a century ago, for what was then large sums of money, and that Spanish authorities had approved all the purchases. He said that the lands the purchases embraced comprised "about 95,360 acres."[131] Reynolds admitted that the United States "had no special defense to offer," except for its claim that "the boundaries claimed were excessive." In response, at the end of the trial of the claim Howard agreed to amend the petition to reduce the area claimed to what Reynolds thought was about 8,000 acres. Based on that, Reynolds recommended that the United States not appeal the decision. Later, when the area was surveyed, it came to only 4,945 acres. Why Howard agreed to such a reduction in the Pueblo's claim is not addressed in Reynolds's letter.

Santa Ana received only about one-twentieth of the land for which the pueblo had paid and for which it had deeds. Santa Clara's grant to the Cañada de Santa Clara was confirmed but for an even smaller fraction of the land to which they were entitled. Santo Domingo and San Felipe had their joint grant confirmed but for only a small amount of the land they claimed. Finally, the joint grant to Zia, Santa Ana, and Jemez, as well as the grazing grant to Cochiti, were rejected. Only Isleta succeeded in obtaining confirmation of the full extent of its claim to the 50,000-acre Lo de Padilla grant. The often confusing and contradictory decisions of the New Mexico and U.S. Supreme Courts led to further non-Indian encroachment on Pueblo land, a situation that was difficult to undo when the U.S. government attempted to sort out Indian and non-Indian titles under the Pueblo Lands Act, the subject of chapter 10.

The Pueblo lands board. Drawing by Glen Strock.

CHAPTER 10

The Pueblo Lands Board

When special attorney for the Pueblos Richard Hanna began filing ejectment actions in federal court against non-Indians residing on Pueblo lands in 1919, the issue of non-Indian trespass on Pueblo lands was finally brought into full focus. An understanding of the interplay of litigation, legislative activity, administrative intrigue, and pressure-group lobbying that led to the enactment of the Pueblo Lands Act and the subsequent proceedings of the Pueblo Lands Board is essential to an understanding of how the Pueblos came to lose approximately 45,000 acres of their grant lands to non-Indian settlers and thousands more due to the misconduct of the Pueblo Lands Board itself.[1]

After the *Sandoval* decision in 1913, "every possible means to evade the consequences of the . . . decision was utilized by those non-Indians who were in possession of Pueblo lands."[2] Tensions were growing, especially after Francis Joy completed his surveys of the non-Indian claims at each pueblo. Although only intended to show the extent of the claims, the non-Indians viewed Joy's surveys as confirming their titles, and they began erecting fences on the boundaries shown on his plats. The Pueblos began tearing the fences down. One such incident at Tesuque Pueblo, when a "band of Tesuque Indians dismantled about 2 miles of fence recently erected" by a new resident of the area, nearly led to bloodshed.[3] The first efforts to legislate a solution to the growing conflict came in the closing weeks of the 66th Congress in early 1921. John B. Payne, the outgoing Democratic secretary of the interior, forwarded a proposed bill that would invalidate any non-Indian claim to Pueblo lands not approved by the secretary of the interior (that is, effectively all of them) to Senator Charles Curtis, chairman of the Senate Indian Affairs Committee. The bill would also have imposed a patronizing regime of secretarial authority over the Pueblos' internal affairs. At about the same time, retiring New Mexico congressman Benigno C. Hernandez introduced a bill in the House that would have provided for the *validation* of nearly all non-Indian claims to Pueblo lands, without compensation to the Pueblos, and the creation of a three-member commission empowered to issue patents to every non-Indian who could show occupancy of Pueblo land for at least ten years prior to New Mexico statehood. Although neither bill was acted on, they set the stage for the fight to come. Interestingly, two concepts embodied in Hernandez's bill—the three-member commission and the occupancy requirement of a number of years—became part of the final act.[4]

When the new Congress convened on 4 March 1921, Republicans controlled both Houses and the White House as well, marking a change in the political lineup that became critical for the outcome of the Pueblo land issue. Former New Mexico senator Albert B. Fall became secretary of the interior and in his place, New Mexico governor Merritt Mechem (1921–1923) appointed Fall's political rival, Holm O. Bursum of Socorro, as senator. Fall previously had little involvement in the Pueblo land issue, but Bursum saw it as a potent weapon in the special election for the Senate seat he faced in the fall against Richard H. Hanna; he therefore made himself the champion of the non-Indian settlers. Soon after taking office, on 1 June 1921, Bursum introduced a bill that would confirm the titles of all non-Indians who could show continuous occupancy of tracts of pueblo lands of 160 acres or less for ten years prior to the passage of the act and would bar the United States or the Pueblos from taking any legal action intended to recover such lands. The Pueblos were to receive no compensation for their loss of lands. This bill was seen as blatantly one-sided and went nowhere.[5] Six weeks later Bursum tried again with a bill more similar to Hernandez's proposal, under which a three-member commission would review the non-Indian claims and those claimants who could show occupancy during the ten-year period prior to statehood would receive clear titles. Even those whose occupancy commenced after statehood could obtain title if they had deeds or the "implied consent" of the Pueblo, or if they had made improvements on the land.

That, too, failed to garner support in the Senate, but these efforts were getting results for Bursum back in New Mexico.[6]

At the Republican convention that nominated Bursum to run against Hanna in the special election, A. B. Renehan made the keynote speech, in which he condemned Hanna's role in filing the ejectment suits and praised Bursum's efforts to support the settlers; his remarks drew loud applause. Bursum lost the vote in the southern part of the state, which was his home territory, but he piled up a huge margin in the north, where emotions were building over the Pueblo land fight to come; this gave him a comfortable victory.[7]

The bills Bursum introduced, along with the reintroduction of Secretary Payne's bill by Representative Homer Snyder, finally forced Secretary Fall to involve himself in the Pueblo land controversy. His first act was to hire Ralph Emerson Twitchell to advise him on the complex legal and historical issues involved.[8] Twitchell delivered his report to Fall in late December 1921. Twitchell extensively reviewed the Pueblos' history under Spanish and Mexican rule and acknowledged that most, if not all, of the non-Indian occupants of Pueblo land had no valid titles to back up their claims. He added that since the establishment of U.S. sovereignty, illegal encroachments on Pueblo land had been even worse than under the Mexican regime. He criticized Bursum's two bills as "clearly anti-Indian," but Twitchell plainly sympathized with the settlers nonetheless. The following April he produced his own draft bill, one that would have validated the titles of those settlers who could show that they had occupied Pueblo land since before the 1848 Treaty of Guadalupe Hidalgo; those whose occupancy was pursuant to an overlapping grant from the government of Spain, Mexico, or the United States; and those who could show continuous occupancy for at least ten years prior to statehood, with or without color of title. The Pueblos would receive no compensation for lands lost to the claims of the first group. As to the claims of the second and third groups, however, the Pueblos would be compensated for the loss of their lands by grants of adjacent federal "agricultural" lands (as was later pointed out, a nonexistent category) or cash payments. He also included a provision concerning water rights, which Bursum and others felt was far too favorable to the Indians.[9]

Circulation of Twitchell's draft bill aroused new controversy in the state, and at the urging of Indian Affairs commissioner Charles Burke, Fall brought Twitchell and Renehan (representing Bursum) to his office on 11 July 1922 in an effort to come up with acceptable legislation. They hammered out what would become known as "the infamous Bursum bill." The bill incorporated Twitchell's proposals regarding the confirmation of titles of all claimants who could prove occupancy before 1900, but it added a provision allowing claimants who commenced occupancy after 1900 to try to persuade the federal court, or the secretary of the interior, to validate their claims regardless. This provision, insisted on by Renehan, was perhaps the most outrageous of all, since the Pueblos would have no opportunity to challenge the valuation or forced sale of their lands. The bill also used the 1914 surveys by Francis C. Joy, which only meant to demarcate areas that were claimed, as prima facie evidence of the *validity* of those claims. The Pueblos would be compensated (with adjacent federal lands or, if there were none, cash) only for those lands the occupancy of which began after 1900 without color of title. All grant overlaps would be resolved in favor of the non-Indian grants. Twitchell's water rights language was thrown out and a new section was inserted that made Pueblo water rights, as well as contested land titles, subject to state-court jurisdiction. It limited the Pueblos' water rights to the amount they were using at the time the bill was enacted.[10] The bill also established federal-court jurisdiction over suits involving internal Pueblo matters, including claims to land within Pueblo grants and even issues regarding internal affairs of governance of a pueblo. All in all, the bill would have been catastrophic for the Pueblos had it been enacted.[11]

Bursum introduced the bill nine days after the meeting in Fall's office. He and Fall falsely told Senator Irvine Lenroot, chairman of the Public Lands Committee, that the bill was a compromise and that all parties to the controversy supported it.[12] The Pueblos, who were completely left out of the process, were apparently not considered "parties" to this dispute. On 11 September 1922, after no public hearings and only a few routine questions from Senator William Borah of Idaho to Bursum, the Senate unanimously approved the Bursum bill. Then came the firestorm.[13]

To understand how the Bursum bill became the focus of nationwide controversy requires some background. John Collier was an idealistic young social worker and community organizer when, in 1920, he accepted the invitation of his friend, New York socialite Mabel Dodge, to visit her at her new home in Taos, New Mexico. The five-month visit, and the introduction to Pueblo society and culture that made up so much of it, literally changed Collier's life. Collier would bring the Pueblos to national attention and ultimately bring about major and lasting changes in federal Indian policy. Dodge (later Mabel Dodge Luhan, after her marriage to Taos Indian Tony Luhan) initiated Collier into the intricacies of the Pueblo land dispute, which Collier soon adopted wholeheartedly as his all-consuming cause. He then brought Stella Atwood of California into the dispute. She was chairwoman of the national committee on Indian welfare of the General Federation of Women's Clubs (GFWC). Although she was somewhat familiar with problems of the California Indians, she had practically no knowledge of or personal experience with the Pueblos. The information with which Collier constantly supplied her, along with his prodding, turned her into a dogged and persistent advocate for Pueblo land rights as against the non-Indian settlers.[14] She was also able to influence some wealthy members of the California GFWC to donate money to pay Collier as a "field investigator" for her committee in New Mexico.[15]

Atwood began sending a steady stream of letters to Indian Affairs commissioner Burke in the fall of 1921, complaining about the early bills Senator Bursum had introduced to resolve the Pueblo land issue. Burke, and at his urging even Twitchell and Fall, wrote Atwood assuring her that Bursum's proposals were unacceptable and that the Indian Office was working to ensure that Pueblo rights would be fully protected. In early August 1922, however, just a month after she had met with Burke in Washington and discussed the Pueblo land situation, Atwood received a copy of the latest bill that Senator Bursum had introduced—the bill produced at the meeting in Fall's office—and she became indignant, charging Burke with having deliberately deceived her. She and Collier quickly began to organize a campaign to defeat the bill.[16]

It is difficult today to imagine that this legally complicated and obscure issue, which concerned only a small segment of one of the nation's poorest and least known states, would suddenly become an object of national notoriety, but that was exactly what happened. By October 1922, deploying the letter-writing resources of the two million–strong GFWC and the extraordinary influence of the artist communities in Taos and Santa Fe, and with help from wealthy collectors of Indian art in New York and California (many of whom owned homes or land in or around Santa Fe) and others, Atwood and Collier had stirred up a storm of furious controversy. Their efforts generated thousands of angry letters, resolutions of various national professional associations, and editorials and columns in the *New York Times*, the *New York World*, the *Christian Science Monitor*, and other respected newspapers and journals. All generally denounced the injustice the Bursum bill threatened to the Pueblo Indians, especially the likely loss of up to 60,000 acres of the best Pueblo land, largely without compensation. Atwood retained Francis C. Wilson, a prominent Santa Fe attorney, who had served as special attorney for the Pueblos from 1909 to 1914, to prepare an analysis of the bill. Wilson's memo was published in Santa Fe and promptly circulated to every member of Congress. Mabel Dodge even persuaded British author D. H. Lawrence, who had recently arrived in Taos and soon became enamored of New Mexico, to write a series of articles about the Pueblo situation, which were then published in the *New York Times*.[17]

In the meantime, Collier began meeting with the leaders of each pueblo, patiently explaining to them how the Bursum bill would affect them. These efforts culminated in a two-day meeting at Santo Domingo Pueblo, which began on 5 November 1922 and was attended by 121 delegates representing all the New Mexico pueblos, as well as Collier, Francis Wilson, and other Pueblo advocates from Santa Fe. The attendees heard detailed explanations of the bill's provisions, after which the whites were excused while the Pueblo delegates decided what to do. After the Pueblo delegates allowed the whites back in, they read them a memorial they had drafted, entitled "An Appeal by the Pueblo Indians of New Mexico to the People of the United States," in which they stated that the Bursum bill would destroy "everything we hold dear—our lands, our customs, our traditions." They also agreed to raise money to travel to Washington to testify before Congress. News of the meeting traveled quickly across the country, making headlines in Santa Fe, New York, and elsewhere, and the text of the memorial soon appeared in the *New York Times*.[18]

Collier and Atwood's campaign succeeded in blocking the Bursum bill. Congress went into its summer recess before the House was able to act on the bill, but the day after it reconvened on 21 November 1922, Senator Borah, in a move almost without precedent, moved the Senate to recall the bill from the House. He said that the bill was passed in the hectic final days before the recess, when the Senate was "under a misapprehension as to what its terms were." Collier, Atwood, and the other Pueblo supporters were jubilant. As it turned out, however, the defeat of the Bursum bill did not necessarily mean victory for the Pueblos, as the tortuous path that led over the next two years to the Pueblo Lands Act demonstrated.[19]

Secretary Fall took the repudiation of the Bursum bill extremely badly. He announced that he would immediately seek the ejectment of all twelve thousand non-Indians on Pueblo lands, a fairly transparent attempt to create a backlash against the Pueblo supporters that fell flat. He also sent Senator Borah a scathing, thirty-five-page defense of the Bursum bill, which Renehan probably authored, lashing out at the "propagandists" who attacked it. Fall's importunate overreaction left him more alienated than ever from the Harding administration, and in January 1923 he announced that he would resign in March.[20] In the meantime, Representative Snyder, chairman of the House Indian Affairs Committee, introduced a watered-down version of the Bursum bill in the House. Shortly afterward, Senator Andrieus Jones of New Mexico introduced a strongly pro-Pueblo bill that Francis Wilson drafted. Hearings were set on the Bursum bill and the Jones bill before the Senate Public Lands Subcommittee in January. Hearings before the Indian Affairs Committee on Snyder's bill and on the Wilson-drafted bill, which was introduced by Representative E. O. Leatherwood of Utah, were heard in February. All of the key players testified at the hearings—Collier, Atwood, Wilson, Twitchell, Renehan, Burke, Pablo Abeita of Isleta, and even Secretary Fall, who took the occasion once again to lash out at Pueblo supporters and at the Jones pro-Pueblo bill.[21] Pablo Abeita, the only Pueblo delegate allowed to testify before the Senate subcommittee, expressed regret that the Pueblos were so willing to accommodate and accept white rule, and he told the senators that "it has come to a point, to a time, where we Pueblo Indians have to raise our voices and demand justice." Senator Bursum interjected that the only land title the Pueblos had was given to them by the United States, to which Abeita replied, "the government has simply given us the papers, but the land was always ours."[22] Although the lengthy hearings demonstrated the blatant unfairness of the Bursum bill, the Pueblo supporters were unsuccessful in their effort to persuade either committee that Francis Wilson's bill, which would have had a commission decide on the non-Indian claims based on vague notions of "good conscience and justice," was at all workable.

Collier left Washington once the hearings ended, unaware that on 18 February 1923 Senator Irvine Lenroot of Wisconsin, chairman of the Public Lands Subcommittee, had convened a subcommittee session that Commissioner Burke attended to hammer out a compromise bill. Francis Wilson was not allowed to attend, but Lenroot let him submit suggested provisions. The bill that emerged, known as the Lenroot Substitute but still bearing the number of Bursum's bill (S. 3855), was the basis for what was finally enacted a year later as the Pueblo Lands Act. It was a substantial improvement over the Bursum bill, although it had several serious flaws. It called for the establishment of a three-member land board that would consider all claims by non-Indians to tracts of land within Pueblo grant lands. Persons who could show "open, notorious, actual, exclusive, continuous possession" for more than twenty years prior to the enactment of the act with color of title or for thirty years without color of title would receive patents to their lands. Those whose claims the board rejected could present their claims to the federal district court in a quiet-title suit to be brought on behalf of each Pueblo. No compensation to the Pueblos was specifically provided for, but the secretary of the interior was to make recommendations to Congress for compensation. Provisions of the original Bursum bill granting federal court jurisdiction over internal Pueblo matters and state court jurisdiction over Pueblo water rights, limiting the Pueblos' water rights to amounts they were using at the time, and making the Joy surveys evidence of the validity of the claims, were deleted.[23]

Without consulting Collier or any other Pueblo advocate, Wilson informed Lenroot that he would support this bill. Wilson clearly had some sympathy for the non-Indian settlers, and the Eastern Association on American Indian Affairs and the New Mexico Association on Indian Affairs concurred in his views. With Wilson's endorsement, the Lenroot Substitute passed the Senate on 28 February 1923, but on 3 March, the day before the 67th Congress adjourned, it failed to garner unanimous consent for passage in the House and died. Thus the issue was not yet settled. This development caused a deep and permanent rift between Collier and Wilson.[24]

The fundamental difference between these two men and the groups for whom they spoke was over how to view the legality of non-Indian settlement. Collier believed that the *Sandoval* decision established that no non-Indian could validly obtain title to Pueblo land without federal authorization. Therefore the non-Indians were all trespassers and should be dealt with as such. He felt that there should be a lofty burden on those seeking to legitimize their claims and that the adoption of an adverse-possession standard, derived from state law, did not fairly protect the Pueblos. Collier believed that the Pueblos should have to give up only that land they voluntarily decided they did not need. Wilson, in contrast, considered *Sandoval* to have marked an abrupt change in the law—a not unreasonable conclusion—and thought that the non-Indians who purchased property and settled on Pueblo land in good-faith reliance on the law as reflected in the *Joseph* decision, which condoned the alienation of Pueblo land, should not be unduly punished for having done so. There was no meeting of the minds between those two positions, and after an angry exchange of telegrams and letters and an acrimonious meeting in Santa Fe, Collier simply cut Wilson off from any further involvement in his work on Indian issues. He managed to stir up the Pueblos against Wilson as well. With his followers he formed the American Indian Defense Association, with himself as executive secretary, to pursue the goal of redirecting United States Indian policy away from the assimilationist strategy that had held sway since the Dawes (General Allotment) Act of 1888 and toward an approach aimed at protection and preservation of Indian culture, religion, land base, and welfare.[25]

Collier's somewhat high-handed approach to the Pueblo land issue, as well as his eventual repudiation of the efforts of the New Mexico Association on Indian Affairs on behalf of the Pueblos, caused new rifts even within his own organization. His unwillingness to compromise and his insistence on the complete removal of non-Indians from Pueblo lands left many feeling that he was creating an unrealistic sense of entitlement among the Pueblos; defections from the American Indian Defense Association board increased as 1923 drew to a close. As it turned out, the American Indian Defense Association's most significant accomplishment regarding the Pueblo land dispute was to retain New York lawyer Adolf A. Berle in May 1923 to replace Francis Wilson. Berle was a prodigy who had graduated from Harvard Law School at twenty-one, making him the school's youngest graduate, and who had clerked for Supreme Court justice Louis Brandeis before accompanying President Woodrow Wilson to the Versailles peace negotiations concluding World War I. He had experience dealing with Spanish colonial law as a result of his wartime work in the Dominican Republic in the army's military intelligence branch and promptly plunged into the Pueblo land issue. Berle visited Santa Fe in August and was taken around by Collier to meet with the Pueblos, and he even had a chance meeting with Wilson. His firsthand exposure to the issues eventually stood him in good stead.[26] With input from Collier and others, Berle drafted a bill setting forth the Pueblo position that no lands should be taken from them without their consent and full compensation. Senator Charles Curtis of Kansas (who happened to have significant Indian ancestry) introduced the bill in mid-January 1924, and shortly afterward Lenroot created a special subcommittee whose members included Bursum and Jones of New Mexico and was chaired by Senator Alva Adams of Colorado. This subcommittee was to meet with Berle and Wilson in a final effort to draft a bill that could achieve passage. This group worked through March and April, and from its efforts emerged the bill that became the Pueblo Lands Act. Collier, who fell ill and had to go to California for surgery, was unable to take part in the process at all except through occasional correspondence with Berle.

The primary debate within this group was over the inclusion of statute-of-limitations standards by which the non-Indian claims would be judged, something that Collier fought against throughout the legislative process. Eventually Berle agreed to the language of Wilson's draft, allowing claims based on possession since 6 January 1902 under color of title and since 16 March 1889 without it. This happened only after the others agreed to the inclusion of a provision Berle proposed that allowed any Pueblo to reject the procedures of the act at any time prior to the patenting of any non-Indian claim and file suit in federal court to eject the non-Indians. Also included was a requirement that to succeed on his claim a claimant had to show continuous payment of taxes on the land claimed from the specified dates of occupancy. Berle thought the independent-suit provision resolved the problem of the constitutionality of retroactively granting the settlers rights in Pueblo land. He believed that the language requiring payment of taxes would be most crucial in defeating the vast majority of the claims, as it was widely assumed that few, if any, of the settlers paid any taxes on the lands on which they were living. But this critical language was later effectively nullified by the Pueblo Lands Board and the courts.

Berle also got the subcommittee to require both the Pueblos and the unsuccessful non-Indian claimants to be compensated for the lands and improvements they lost in the process of reviewing the claims. A section included in the bill specified that the Pueblos would retain all land covered by any grant overlap, even in those cases in which the overlapping Spanish or Mexican grant had been made before the Pueblo grant. Another section authorized the Pueblos to use the compensation paid to them to repurchase lands they lost in the proceedings under the act.[27] Finally, the bill also included a section that Wilson apparently drafted that was supposedly intended to confirm the federal guardianship over Pueblo lands and to apply the provisions of the Non-intercourse Act to those lands. If it did indeed confirm federal guardianship, however, it was only by a decidedly peculiar grammatical construction that the Supreme Court much later interpreted as having accomplished almost the opposite.[28] With these changes and additions and the eventual concurrence of Collier and Berle, the bill easily passed both houses and was signed by President Coolidge on 7 June 1924.

As enacted, the Pueblo Lands Act called for the creation of a three-member Pueblo Lands Board, one of whose members was to be appointed by the president, one by the secretary of the interior, and one by the attorney general. The board was to review all claims by non-Indians occupying Pueblo grant lands as shown by the Joy surveys and conduct hearings during which the claimants could submit testimony and documentary evidence in support of their claims. Each claim was numbered sequentially and was designated "private claim" (or "PC"). The board was to determine whether each non-Indian claim met the requirements of section 4, that is, whether the claimant showed continuous occupancy under color of title since 6 January 1902 or without color of title since 16 March 1889 and had in either case paid the taxes "lawfully assessed and levied thereon." Following its ruling on all of the claims at a specific pueblo, the board was to issue a report setting forth by metes and bounds a description of the lands granted to that pueblo the title to which had not been extinguished by non-Indian claims. Also included, as exceptions, were non-Indian claims within the Pueblo grant that the board had upheld.[29]

The United States was to then file a quiet-title action on behalf of the pueblo in federal district court, naming as defendants each claimant whose claim the board had rejected. In this way, those claimants got a second opportunity to have their claims upheld—this time by the court. At the conclusion of the quiet-title proceeding, field notes and plats of all of the claims upheld by the board or by the district court were to be filed in the "office of the surveyor general of New Mexico"—actually, by then, the General Land Office—and that filing was to constitute conclusive evidence of the extinguishment of "all the right, title and interest of the Indians in and to the lands so described in said plat and field notes and of any claim of the United States in and to the same." Subsequently, patents for the successful claims would be issued by the secretary of the interior to the claimants.[30]

Section 4 contained an important provision inserted at Berle's insistence stating that nothing in the act "shall be construed to impair or destroy any existing right of the Pueblo Indians of New Mexico to assert and maintain unaffected by the provisions of this act their title and right to any land by original proceedings . . . at any time prior to the filing of the field notes and plats." This critical savings provision meant that any pueblo that felt that the proceedings under the act were unfair or otherwise unsatisfactory could simply sue the non-Indian settlers in ejectment, an option that later turned out to be of crucial importance in giving the Pueblos the only leverage they would have to force changes in the board's compensation awards.

Under section 6, the board was to file a report setting forth the fair market value of the land and of any appurtenant water rights, the Indian title to which was extinguished, and the Pueblos could challenge that determination in federal court. The court was to determine the amount of compensation due each pueblo. The board was also to determine the fair market value of the lands claimed by unsuccessful non-Indian claimants and improvements thereon, under section 7. Under section 14, all conflicts between Pueblo grants and other Spanish or Mexican grants, even those superior to the pueblo grant in time, were to be resolved in favor of the Pueblos. Section 17 intended to apply the terms of the Nonintercourse Act specifically to Pueblo grant lands.

Pueblo advocates believed that the final form of the act included important modifications and additions to the bill that greatly improved the chances that many of the settlers' claims would have to be rejected. In any event, the Pueblos were supposed to receive fair compensation for the land they lost. As it happened, however, the implementation of the act was far worse for the Pueblos than the process by which the bill had been patched together. The board, supported by the federal court, saw to it that nearly all of the non-Indian claims prevailed, despite the language of the act, and that the compensation to the Pueblos fell far short of the amounts to which they were legally entitled.

Collier's hope that he could somehow influence the appointments to the Pueblo Lands Board proved to be in vain. None of the initial appointments seemed favorable to the Pueblos. The attorney general named Charles Jennings, a Maryland lawyer who knew nothing at all about the Pueblos or the act. President Coolidge, over Collier's strong objection, appointed his old Amherst College friend, Roberts Walker, a New York lawyer and one of the founders of the Eastern Association on Indian Affairs, who had developed a strong aversion to Collier's positions in the proceedings leading to the Pueblo Lands Act's enactment. Walker was at least familiar with the debates that led to the act, but he endorsed interpretations of the act that were decidedly unfavorable to the Pueblos. His tenure on the board, however, turned out to be brief. Interior secretary Hubert Work named Herbert Hagerman, a former territorial governor of New Mexico whom Fall had recently appointed as the secretary's special commissioner to the Navajos. Fall appointed Hagerman "to ensure that anticipated oil development on the Navajo Reservation would be conducted efficiently and quickly," which should have alerted Collier to Hagerman's prodevelopment, anti-Indian views, which he shared with Fall. Despite Hagerman's connection with Fall, Collier initially approved of the appointment but later had cause to regret that decision.[31]

With this lineup, there was no one on the board sympathetic to the Pueblo position. Twitchell, who Walker suggested should serve as the board's attorney, suffered a severe stroke in 1925 and died shortly afterward in California. The department brought in George A. H. Fraser, an assistant U.S. attorney in Denver, to replace him. Walter Cochrane, a young New Mexico attorney fresh out of law school, was named special attorney for the Pueblos to represent the pueblos before the board. Neither of these men had any familiarity with what went into the crafting of the act. Collier got Hanna to agree to serve as independent counsel for the Pueblos under a retainer with Collier's American Indian Defense Association, a move that deeply irritated Hagerman, who insisted that Cochrane could serve the Pueblos perfectly well.[32]

During the board's first set of hearings in August and September 1925, which involved claims against Tesuque, its true feelings about Pueblo land issues surfaced. The question raised was whether the requirements of section 4 regarding possession of lands claimed by non-Indians were the exclusive defenses the settlers could raise or whether they could also assert a state law adverse-possession defense, which required only ten years' possession with color of title. Both Cochrane and Fraser advised the board that section 4 set forth the exclusive grounds on which a claim could be upheld, but Walker prevailed on Jennings and Hagerman to allow claims based on the state adverse-possession statute; by October even Fraser had been persuaded to back down on this critical issue. The cavalier manner in which the board made this important decision about how it would interpret the law under which it was operating, and its failure to hold a formal hearing or to provide an opportunity for all advocates from the pueblos to present their argument, presaged future opaque deliberations. These were often led by the imperious Herbert Hagerman and usually resulted in harm to the interest of the pueblos.[33]

At its meeting on 15 May 1925 the board decided that it would not reveal publicly the grounds for any of its decisions on non-Indian claims. Thus, it was a long time before the Pueblo advocates realized why so many dubious claims were being allowed. Hanna, the independent counsel for the Pueblos, complained about not having any information explaining the board's decisions and asked to see the evidence the board considered in its deliberations, such as deeds and appraiser's reports. Not only did the board reject that request, it also stated cavalierly that thereafter the Pueblo's lawyer would not even be provided with transcripts of the hearings, as he was for the Tesuque hearings. The board asserted that to provide transcripts would place unreasonable burdens on its resources. Hanna complained to the U.S. attorney general about this unconscionable decision, and his letter led to the board being summoned to a meeting in Washington on 18 January 1926. John Sargent, the attorney general, and Work, the secretary of the interior, along with Collier, were present, although Hagerman begged off, claiming he was "unwell and needed a few weeks rest in California." Four days later the board was directed to make all evidence considered by it available to Hanna, but it still was not required to provide a transcript of its hearings.[34]

The board's decision to continue to allow non-Indian settlers to prevail in their claims based on the state statute of limitations was left standing in the face of George A. H. Fraser's strong opposition. Not until July 1928 was the board's position on that issue corrected. Federal district judges Orie Phillips and Colin Neblett, sitting together, ruled in the Nambe quiet-title action that non-Indian claims could only be upheld if the section 4 standards were met; state statutes of limitations were ruled to be completely inapplicable.[35] Characteristically, Hagerman wrote Indian Affairs commissioner Burke that the court's decision on the adverse-possession issue was "in general agreement, it is believed, with the view of the Board."[36] The Supreme Court's 1926 *Candelaria* decision case plainly foreshadowed this ruling, and Hagerman was presumably prepared for it. Although accepting this ruling for future cases, the board made no effort to reexamine the cases that had already been decided favorably for the claimants based on its legally erroneous position on section 4.

Another key issue on which the board adopted a position contrary to the language of the act and the interests of the Pueblos was that of the requirement in section 4 that claimants show that they paid all taxes "lawfully assessed" on their lands during the required periods of occupancy. In November 1926, responding to Indian Affairs commissioner Burke's request for clarification of the board's view of the tax issue, Hagerman wrote that if claimants were required to show payment of taxes in every year of occupancy, "not 2% of the claimants whose cases are otherwise good could possibly meet such requirements." The board satisfied itself in every case, he added, that taxes were paid "to the extent required by the Act," but he did not try to reconcile those two conflicting statements.[37]

Hagerman elaborated on his views of the tax payment issue in a March 1928 memo in response to the position that Commissioner Jennings and new appointee Louis Warner were proposing to take in the San Felipe hearings: to reject the claims of every claimant who could not produce receipts for all of the required tax payments.[38] In past proceedings the board had asked for tax receipts, but it accepted evidence of payment of taxes after passage of the Pueblo Lands Act as proof that taxes were paid before the act. Hagerman acknowledged that no claimant ever produced records showing payment of taxes all the way back to 1889 or 1902, but the board accepted as proof sworn testimony that the taxes were paid. As to the charge by the Collier forces that this explanation showed the board was engaging in liberal interpretations of section 4's requirements so as to favor the non-Indians, Hagerman noted that while the Pueblos had two lawyers present to speak for them, the non-Indians usually had none, and he suggested that the board itself should therefore act on behalf of the non-Indians. Hagerman added that the settlers' land would probably be worth less to the Pueblos than the money they would get as compensation for its loss. If true, this would have obviated the need for evaluating the non-Indian claims, but it failed to take into account the views of the Pueblos themselves.[39] This revealing memo reflected Hagerman's magisterial attitude that the board could—and should—do pretty much as it pleased with the claims, regardless of the strict language of the act. He based this on the board's own sense of "equity," which primarily translated as sympathy for the plight of the non-Indians. As it happened, the federal courts' rulings on the tax issue, although not as oblivious to the statutory language as Hagerman's position, ended up achieving about the same result.

Judges Neblett and Phillips ruled in the Nambe case that proof of payment of taxes was required to support the non-Indians' claims but that such proof was needed only for those years in which taxes "were lawfully assessed and levied."[40] Two years later the Tenth Circuit Court of Appeals squarely addressed the tax issue in *United States v. Wooten*, an appeal from the district court in the quiet-title suit brought on behalf of Taos Pueblo. The court rejected the settlers' arguments that no taxes could ever have been "lawfully assessed" on their lands, either because they were Pueblo lands that could not be taxed under federal law or because of a state statute that (unlike the general adverse-possession statute) contained no tax-paying requirement in the case of adverse possession of lands acquired by grant from Spain, Mexico, or the United States. Those arguments were also made in the Nambe case, and the court of appeals specifically approved the district court's ruling that in requiring payment of taxes in section 4 "to the extent required by the statutes" of New Mexico, Congress could not reasonably have intended to refer to a nonexistent requirement. But it went on to hold that the burden the act placed on the settlers should not be more onerous than the requirement facing ordinary landowners, such that as long as all unpaid taxes, penalties, and interest due were paid in full before any tax sale of the property occurred, section 4's requirement of payment of taxes was satisfied, regardless of whether any such taxes were actually paid during the required period of occupation. That ruling effectively nullified the taxpaying requirement in section 4.[41]

Property taxes in New Mexico in the first half of the twentieth century were at best a nominal burden, and the non-Indian claimants working with cooperative county tax assessors could usually find ways to pay off outstanding tax bills on the lands they claimed. More than any other single event, this decision guaranteed that losses of land by the Pueblos to non-Indian settlers under the act, although not amounting to the 60,000 acres originally feared by Collier, would nonetheless be huge. George Fraser began working on a petition asking the U.S. Supreme Court to review the *Wooten* decision, but in July the attorney general instructed him to drop it, apparently out of concern that if the government prevailed, this would cause substantial additional work for the board, which would then have to revise decisions it had made in many cases, an astonishing show of callous indifference to the Pueblos' interests.[42] Thus, the Supreme Court had no opportunity to review any decision involving interpretation of the Pueblo Lands Act until fifty years after the board had concluded its work, when a case was brought in the mid-1980s by Santa Ana.[43]

One of the board's most egregious actions concerned the Santo Domingo grant and certain Spanish land grants that overlapped it. Santo Domingo had a Cruzate grant that, unlike most of the Cruzates, defined the pueblo's boundaries by natural monuments in all four directions.[44] The grant was supposedly surveyed in 1859 by Deputy Reuben E. Clements and found by him to comprise about 78,000 acres, but Wendell Hall resurveyed it in 1907 because none of Clements's boundary monuments could be located. That survey, which encompassed approximately 93,000 acres, revealed that the Santo Domingo grant overlapped the 1704 La Majada grant and the 1782 Mesita de Juana López grant by 26,320 acres (as well as the tiny Sitio de Juana López Grant by a small amount). No non-Indian made any claim before the board for any land within the area of any grant overlap based on the conflicting grants, on the section 4 criteria, or for any other reason. For unstated reasons, however, in its report on Santo Domingo the board held that the pueblo was entitled to the lands within its surveyed grant boundaries except for certain private claims of 550.71 acres, "and except the lands over-lapped by the La Majada, Sitio de Juana Lopez and Mesita de Juana Lopez grants." The area thus confirmed to the pueblo by the board amounted to 66,081.81 acres.

The fact that the non-Indian grants were issued later than the Santo Domingo grant should have resolved those conflicts in favor of the pueblo, but section 14 of the Pueblo Lands Act also specified that even in the case of an earlier grant, the Pueblo title would prevail, and the non-Indian grant claimant would be entitled to compensation. It was the federal court, moreover, not the board, that was to make this determination.[45] A few days after issuing its decision on Santo Domingo, in a letter to Interior secretary Hubert Work transmitting the Santo Domingo documents, Hagerman said that the board "after full investigation, found that the Indians are not entitled to the areas included in these [grant] conflicts."[46] This was untrue: the board conducted no such investigation and had no authority to do so. No one challenged this action, even though the board made no effort to determine any compensation to Santo Domingo for this loss of nearly one-third of its grant. The quiet-title action the United States filed on behalf of Santo Domingo sought no relief as to the overlap area. Nearly fifty years later, when the United States brought suit seeking to recover these lands for the Pueblo, the federal district court and the court of appeals concluded that the board had plainly acted with no authority whatsoever, but both courts held that the suit by the United States came too late.[47] Ironically, in proceedings involving Cochiti, whose Cruzate league grant was also overlapped substantially by the La Majada grant, the board barely mentioned the overlap and confirmed the entire area to Cochiti.[48]

The board's practices regarding the amount of compensation to be provided to the Pueblos for land lost to settlers also reflected an indifference to Pueblo rights, leading to vigorous criticism by Collier and his forces. The board consistently awarded the Pueblos compensation well below the appraised amounts, often as little as one-third of the appraisal, while compensation awarded to the non-Indians was routinely at the amounts appraised. For example, in March 1931, the board decided to award compensation of $86,821 to Santa Clara, the pueblo that had lost more land to non-Indian settlers than any other, a little over one-third of the amount determined by appraisal, and Judge Neblett upheld that award without change. By then, Pueblo lawyer Richard Hanna was seriously ill, and his partner Dudley Cornell, who was handling much of the Pueblo work, was appointed an assistant U.S. attorney. The firm essentially ceased acting on behalf of the Pueblos at a time when the board's work and the cases before the district court were piling up.[49]

Collier finally was able to get back to New Mexico to see what could be done to salvage something from the disasters looming for the Pueblos, but because of the lack of Pueblo representation in the quiet-title cases over the preceding year, there was little to be done even with new counsel engaged.[50] Collier therefore decided to resort to the only significant weapon the Pueblos had under the Pueblo Lands Act: the ability to file independent ejectment suits that would circumvent the act's procedures entirely. Although some of Collier's supporters were concerned that such a tactic would inflame local opinion, he prevailed by arguing that there was no alternative and that the suits were the only tactic left that might persuade the Justice Department, or even Congress, to begin to correct the injustices the Pueblos were suffering. At the end of 1930, a lawsuit was quietly filed for Taos and one was prepared for Picuris. "No publicity was given . . . in the hope of perfecting the new strategy before the furor began."[51]

At the same time, Collier laid the groundwork for a congressional committee to review the actions of the board. On 30 January 1931 a subcommittee of the Senate Indian Affairs Committee, which Collier supplied with extensive documentation supporting his claims of inadequate compensation awards and mistaken interpretations of the act, opened hearings in Washington. Unfortunately for the pueblos, Collier opened his presentation with attacks on Hagerman, most of which had to do with Hagerman's work at Navajo, not with the work of the board. This generated expressions of support for Hagerman from New Mexico's legislature and senators. The subcommittee was receptive, however, to Collier's explanation of the substandard compensation awards (although he acknowledged that he had no idea whether Hagerman's water-rights theory would be upheld in court). When Hagerman finally testified in his defense, he propounded a complicated theory of how the interplay between non-Indian claims and Pueblo water rights determined the board's compensation awards. But Collier was able to show that this view had never been accepted by the board or any court and that the board had not even mentioned water rights in most of its decisions on compensation since the Tesuque report.[52]

The Senate subcommittee resumed its hearings on the work of the Pueblo Lands Board in May in Albuquerque, but this time Hagerman did not attend, pleading illness and a need to attend to other business. The hearings opened with Hanna's lengthy report in which he documented the board's persistent minimization of the amount of land returned to the Pueblos and the low compensation for lost land. He laid the responsibility squarely at Hagerman's feet (Hagerman had, at one time, blamed low compensation awards on "President Coolidge [who] insists on economy"). Hanna pointed out that notwithstanding the federal court ruling that the state statute of limitations could not be used to uphold a claim, at least 848 claims totaling 10,701 acres were upheld on this theory prior to the court ruling and that the board had done nothing to reopen those cases. He hammered at the board's refusal to award more than thirty-five dollars an acre to the Pueblos as compensation, even after Judge Phillips increased the award to Nambe to sixty-five dollars an acre and after it was disclosed that the government was unable to purchase any replacement lands for the Pueblos at the thirty-five-dollar-an-acre valuation. Although Jennings, Warner, and even Wilson tried to defend Hagerman and the board's record, Senator Burton K. Wheeler brought the first day of the hearings to a close with the observation that the board "had construed every provision [of the act] against the Indian and in favor of the Government.... Now, if there is anything just about that situation, I am unable to see it."[53]

The hearings accomplished some good, for at their conclusion it was announced that a bill would be submitted to Congress to increase the compensation levels for the Pueblos. Despite Hagerman's last-ditch effort to block it, the bill went forward in early 1932, with New Mexico senators Sam Bratton and Bronson Cutting as its sponsors.[54] Largely the work of Richard Hanna, the bill included significantly increased compensation for the Pueblos, equaling more than the total that had been awarded by the board. The bill was boosted by the release of the Indian Affairs Subcommittee report on its earlier hearings in which it charged that the board had materially and substantially departed from appraised valuations of lands lost by the Pueblos, while setting the awards to non-Indians at the appraised values.⁵⁵

Hearings on the compensation bill before the Senate Committee on Indian Affairs began with Hanna's presentation explaining the board's reduction of the appraised amounts in its awards to the Pueblos.⁵⁶ Then Hagerman tried yet again, this time with some help from Commissioner Rhoads, to assert his theory about primary-versus-secondary water rights to justify the reduced awards. Under tough questioning from Bratton and Wheeler and clearly confused by his own illogic and grasping at false depictions of what the board said in its reports, Hagerman was ultimately forced to concede that the board had no idea whether the Pueblos kept or lost water rights with the lands they lost to non-Indians. Thus, the board's compensation awards could not be squared with any consistent theory about water. Both Hagerman and Rhoads had to concede that the entire water rights issue had been turned over to the Justice Department and that there had been no action to resolve it. When Bratton and Wheeler suggested that the board had avoided dealing with the issue, Hagerman insisted that the board lacked authority to settle it, a response that, as Wheeler quickly pointed out, was totally at odds with Hagerman's insistence that the water-rights theory was the basis for the reduced awards.⁵⁷

On the third day of hearings Northcutt Ely, the executive assistant to the secretary of the interior and someone quite knowledgeable about Indian water rights, testified that the Department of the Interior felt strongly that the Pueblos retained superior priority to water with respect to all of the lands that remained in their possession and that the rights that passed to non-Indians with the land they were awarded were junior rights. For that reason, Ely explained, the department was concerned that increasing the compensation awards might imply that the Pueblos had lost their superior priority to water. This was a more coherent version of the theory that Hagerman had claimed motivated the board's awards, although Ely did acknowledge that the Pueblos had lost some water rights with the land; it was the priority of their remaining rights that the department wanted to protect.⁵⁸

The next day, John Collier presented the committee with a chart that explained that even if Hagerman's water-rights theory were correct, the fact that the Pueblos lost water rights that had a superior priority appurtenant to the lands that were patented to the non-Indians meant that the value of their losses equaled the full appraised value of the land with the rights intact. Collier, who strongly supported the bill, called Hagerman's theory a "fantastic fiction," concocted solely as a post hoc justification for the low compensation awards, but he also forcefully showed that it did not justify any reduction in the awards.[59]

A few weeks later the whole pageant was played out again before the House Committee on Indian Affairs, with the players having rehearsed their roles somewhat more thoroughly. New Mexico Congressman Dennis Chavez introduced a new version of the Pueblo compensation bill, and again Ely was a key witness. He provoked a fierce response from Representative Chavez when Ely insisted that if the Pueblos wanted all the water in their stream systems they were "entitled to it all." Does this mean that "my folks who have lived there for a hundred years" should just "move out?" Chavez demanded. Ely responded, "Those Indians have been there for a thousand years."[60] Ely, whose primary concern throughout the hearings had been that there should be no implication by the award of additional compensation that the Pueblos were losing their water-rights priority for their retained lands, then produced a proposed new section for the bill (that became section 9 in both Senate and House bills). The bill stated that "nothing herein shall . . . be construed to deprive any of the Pueblo Indians of a prior right to the use of water . . . for lands remaining in Indian ownership" and that such rights would not be subject to loss by nonuse or abandonment.[61] With that change, the bill seemed headed for passage, until Bratton and Senator Lynn Frazier of North Dakota succeeded in amending the Interior Appropriations bill to delete any salary for Hagerman, thereby fulfilling one of Frazier's most cherished goals. That move provoked Interior secretary Ray Lyman Wilbur to announce that the administration would not support the Pueblo bill; it died at the end of the 72nd Congress.[62]

In the fall of 1932, with the nation wracked by the Great Depression, Franklin D. Roosevelt was elected president, and the Democrats achieved huge majorities in both houses of Congress. On 21 April 1933, Collier reached the apex of his extraordinary journey that began with his visit to Mabel Dodge's Taos home in 1920, having been appointed commissioner of Indian Affairs. He soon set in motion what was to amount to a total transformation of federal policy in Indian affairs. The Pueblo compensation bill was soon reintroduced and passed, and President Roosevelt signed it into law on 31 May. It added nearly $800,000 to the $621,000 in Pueblo compensation that the board previously approved—not enough to bring the awards up to appraised value, but enough to result in Collier's acquiescence in the dismissal of the independent suits filed in December 1930.⁶³

In the end, the board approved adverse claims totaling more than 36,150 acres of Pueblo grant lands, and the federal court allowed claims amounting to another 8,320 acres, for a total of approximately 44,500 acres lost by the Pueblos to non-Indian settlers.⁶⁴ While a few pueblos, such as Acoma, Zia, Santa Ana, and Jemez, lost little or no land, some, such as Santa Clara, San Juan, Picuris, and Taos, lost significant portions of their grant lands. At Picuris, whose grant encompasses the Hispano communities of Rio Lucio, Peñasco, and Vadito, and at Taos, whose grant includes most of the town of Taos, the losses amounted to approximately 15 percent of those pueblos' grants. Santa Clara and San Juan, whose grants embrace significant portions of the town of Española, each lost about 25 percent of their grant lands.⁶⁵

One unintended outcome of the Pueblo Land Board's proceedings arose from the fact that there was no provision in the act for dealing with claims for easements or other types of interests covering roadways, railroads, or electric lines and similar facilities. The board usually commented in its reports that such-and-such pueblo's lands were "burdened" with existing roadways, but those statements had no legal effect under the terms of the Pueblo Lands Act. The roads remained pueblo property even though all the land on both sides might have been patented to non-Indians.⁶⁶ This problem led to another instance of creative interpretation of the Pueblo Lands Act, although in this case it was by the U.S. regarding the White Pine Lumber Company. The ruling held that the lumber company had the rights to take timber from the Jemez Mountains via its wholly owned subsidiary, the Santa Fe Northwestern Railway, which constructed a narrow-gauge railroad down San Diego Canyon along the Jemez River and across the lands of Jemez, Zia, and Santa Ana to take the cut logs to the Atchison, Topeka, and Santa Fe Railway line at Bernalillo. The company acquired rights-of-way across the pueblos' lands from the secretary of the interior, under the Act of 2 March 1899 (now codified at 25 U.S.C. §312), which provided authority for railroad rights-of-way "through any Indian reservation."⁶⁷ When George A. H. Fraser was preparing the quiet-title suit on behalf of Jemez, however, following the completion of the Pueblo Lands Board's work there, he looked into the Santa Fe Northwestern right-of-way and concluded that the 1899 act was inapplicable. Pueblo grant lands, Frasier reasoned, could not be characterized as Indian "reservations," inasmuch as the pueblos owned the grant lands in fee simple (whereas nearly all Indian reservation lands are owned by the United States in trust for the tribes). He therefore believed that the railroad was trespassing, and he named it as a defendant in the quiet-title suit.

White Pine was just then in the process of negotiating the refinancing of $1.25 million in debt with a Chicago bond house. When the bond house's attorneys learned of the suit, the refinancing ground to a halt and put the company in considerable distress. The company's lawyers and the bond house lawyers immediately set up a meeting in Santa Fe on 26 February 1926 with Fraser, Hagerman, and Cochrane. Hanna was also present, although not on behalf of the Pueblos; he was there representing the railroad, as well as other companies that had lines across Pueblo lands and wanted to avoid being sued.[68]

Fraser insisted that the inapplicability of the 1899 act was clear on its face, but he also focused on the first clause of section 17 of the Pueblo Lands Act, which stated that "no right, title or interest in or to the lands of the Pueblo Indians of New Mexico to which their title has not been extinguished as hereinbefore determined shall hereafter be acquired or initiated by virtue of the laws of the State of New Mexico, or in any other manner except as may hereafter be provided by Congress." As Fraser read that language, until Congress enacted authority for grants of interests in Pueblo lands, none existed. Judge Melvin Hawley, the Chicago lawyer who represented the bond house, proposed focusing instead on the second clause of that section, which read, "and no sale, grant, lease of any character, or other conveyance of lands, or any claim thereto, made by any pueblo as a community . . . shall be of any validity in law or in equity unless the same be first approved by the Secretary of the Interior." That language, Judge Hawley suggested, could be interpreted to mean that a grant of an interest in Pueblo land, in any form, *would* be valid if it were made by the pueblo itself and was approved by the secretary of the interior. The first half of the section, Hawley asserted, could be seen as prohibiting any adverse acquisition of an interest in Pueblo land (as, for example, by adverse possession), while the second half appeared to deal with consensual grants. Fraser was unconvinced, believing that the second clause was simply intended to be an elaboration of the requirements set forth in the first clause, but he was ultimately persuaded that the dire consequences the railroad would suffer justified indulging this unusual construction of the language.[69] Eventually, both the Department of the Interior and the Justice Department accepted this new interpretation, and when the railroad approached the Zia and Santa Ana tribal councils, offering "a carload of lumber" as compensation for a right-of-way agreement, both pueblos agreed. The secretary of the interior promptly approved the agreements under section 17 of the act.[70]

Jemez Pueblo refused to agree to any terms, however, being opposed to the railroad's presence on its lands. Hanna's law partner, Fred Wilson, who was then serving as New Mexico attorney general, therefore drafted a bill allowing condemnation of Pueblo lands for "public purposes." In marked contrast to what happened with the Pueblo Lands Act, the bill sailed through Congress and was signed into law on 10 May 1926. Yet in the first suit to be filed under that act, a suit by the New Mexico state highway department to acquire a highway right-of-way over San Felipe lands, Judge Colin Neblett ruled that the United States, as trustee of the Pueblos' lands, was a necessary party to any such suit and that the statute contained no provision for joining the United States.[71] That ruling seemed to gut the condemnation act, and in 1928, acting on Fraser's recommendation, Congress passed a bill that simply extended to the lands of the Pueblos the general right-of-way statutes that applied to other Indian lands. (That law is now codified at 25 U.S.C. §322.) The Santa Fe Northwestern soon got its right-of-way across Jemez lands (the 1899 railroad right-of-way act did not require tribal consent), but to little avail: within a few years the company was out of business, and the line was abandoned.[72]

Even after the enactment of the 1928 act, section 17 of the Pueblo Lands Act continued to be utilized off and on as authority for easements over Pueblo lands, usually to avoid some restriction that applied under the general right-of-way statutes.[73] In the 1980s Santa Ana Pueblo challenged the validity of those rights-of-way, prevailing in federal district court and the Tenth Circuit Court of Appeals, but the Supreme Court reversed, holding that the language of the second clause of section 17 appeared to give the secretary unbridled authority to approve any grant of an interest in Pueblo lands to which a pueblo agreed.[74]

Thus, despite the extraordinary exertions of John Collier and his supporters, the Pueblo Lands Act turned out to be nearly as bad for the Pueblos as the passage of the Bursum bill would have been. At every turn the courts and the Pueblo Lands Board interpreted the Pueblo Lands Act so as to favor the non-Indian claimants and seemed to go out of their way to arrive at policies and interpretations that were disadvantageous to the Pueblos. Although the Pueblos received some monetary compensation and preserved their guardian-ward relationship with the federal government, they lost tens of thousands of acres of land, including much of their best irrigable lands. Several pueblos ended up with substantial non-Indian populations living in their midst, bringing with them complex jurisdictional and social problems. The act left the status of Pueblo water rights entirely unclear, and that conundrum has yet to be resolved legally. The confused status of the Pueblo Indians resulting from the *Lucero* and *Joseph* decisions led to problems that the Pueblo Lands Act did not resolve. The legacy of those decisions turned out to be far more lasting and consequential for the Pueblos than anyone would have imagined. From the Pueblos' point of view, the Pueblo Lands Act was just another in a long string of broken promises.

Taos Pueblo Cacique and traditional leaders celebrating congressional approval of the return of Blue Lake. Drawing by Glen Strock.

CHAPTER 11

Taos Pueblo and the Return of Blue Lake

Blue Lake, formed in a glacial cirque of the Sangre de Cristo Mountains at over 11,000 feet, sits in natural grandeur behind Taos Pueblo. The most sacred of Taos's natural shrines, it is considered to be the source of the pueblo's life, both spiritually as the place of emergence of the pueblo and literally as the principal source of the Rio Pueblo, which provides irrigation and drinking water to the pueblo. Not only the lake but the entire watershed is considered sacred by the pueblo and is dotted with shrines where regular religious observances have been held for centuries. These ceremonies are secret and not open to outsiders, but beginning around 1890 the lake and the watershed began to be invaded when rumors of gold and silver deposits in the area brought prospectors and, in their wake, hunters, campers, and fishermen. Over the next quarter century, the pristine character of the lake and surrounding watershed was violated, making it difficult for the pueblo to continue its religious observances. Regaining control of Blue Lake and its surroundings became the pueblo's highest priority. This is the story of how Taos Pueblo was able to achieve that long-sought-after goal.

The story involves all the important political figures in Washington and New Mexico from the 1930s to 1970 including, to name a few, Robert F. Kennedy, Stewart Udall, Fred Harris, Clinton P. Anderson, and Richard Nixon, the pueblo leaders, both religious and secular, who interacted with these politicians and kept the momentum going through difficult times and two major congressional hearings, and the pueblo supporters who, although they did not always agree among themselves, helped to gradually move nationwide sentiment in favor of Taos Pueblo. Included among the Taos leaders were Paul Bernal, Seferino Martinez, John Rainer, Querino Romero, and Juan de Jesús Romero. Pueblo supporters included John Collier, Oliver La Farge, and Frank Waters, to name just a few. But it was the determination and persistence of the people of Taos Pueblo that ultimately won the day.[1]

The saga of the twentieth-century struggle of Taos over Blue Lake began in 1906, when the United States appropriated Blue Lake and made it part of Carson National Forest. The process that led to this move began three years earlier when the secretary of agriculture petitioned the Department of the Interior to temporarily prevent settlement in the Blue Lake area and nearby communities until an examination of its suitability as a forest reserve could be undertaken. Although Taos Pueblo was exercising exclusive use of the Blue Lake area, it had title to roughly 5,700 acres in the Tenorio tract, which it purchased in 1818, and the approximately 17,350 acres contained in its Pueblo league patented in 1864.[2] From a legal standpoint, the United States considered the rest of the area to be vacant public land, a part of the public domain. The Interior Department complied with the secretary of agriculture's request and withdrew the Blue Lake area from settlement while a feasibility study was conducted. Upon learning of the department's actions, Taos wrote to the secretary of the interior asking him to issue an exclusive-use permit for the Blue Lake area when the contemplated forest reserve was created.[3]

Theodore F. Rixon of the U.S. Geological Survey submitted a report favoring the creation of a forest reserve, noting that the Blue Lake area was in such excellent condition because of the land stewardship of Taos Pueblo. Forest Service chief Gifford Pinchot also supported the creation of a forest reserve as soon as possible. On 7 November 1906 President Theodore Roosevelt signed a proclamation creating the Taos Forest Reserve, to be administered by the U.S. Forest Service.

Gilford Pinchot believed in the application of science to forest management to maximize production of raw materials (usually timber). This concept was expressed in the policy of multiple use, which envisioned three uses of forest reserves: recreation, production and extraction of raw materials (timber and minerals), and grazing. Advancement of these uses implied construction of roads and buildings when required. The concept of multiple use contrasted dramatically with the world view of the people of Taos Pueblo, who believed themselves to be linked to the land in a sacred union. For Taos, the Blue Lake area was to be honored through prayer and ceremony and kept inviolate. Essential for the practice of their religion was the secrecy of tribal religious knowledge.

In 1916 Elliot Barker, who believed that Indian land should be treated like national forests, became supervisor of Carson National Forest. At Barker's direction trails were cut into the Blue Lake area to facilitate access for recreation, trout were released into the lake, and fishermen ventured to the lake. Citing the exigencies of World War I, Barker pushed Taos Pueblo to allow non-Indian cattle to graze on the east side of the Blue Lake watershed. Barker's tenure at Carson National Forest lasted only three years, but in that short time Taos lost its unfettered access to Blue Lake after centuries of uninterrupted, exclusive use.[4]

Beginning in 1921, the religious practices of Taos came under attack by commissioner of Indian Affairs Charles Burke, who vilified Pueblo religion as part of the government's aggressive campaign to abolish all Native religion. Burke even went to Taos and intruded on the tribal council, denouncing tribal elders as "half human" because of their religious beliefs. Burke insisted that the tribal council renounce their religion within a year and also demanded that it end the practice of withdrawing the youth from school temporarily for religious instruction at the pueblo. When the council refused to comply with Burke's demands he had pueblo members transported to Santa Fe, where they were jailed and subsequently released.[5]

Congress passed the Pueblo Lands Act in 1924 to establish a process by which non-Indians who settled on Pueblo land could make claims to the lands they occupied and be given good title if it were found that their claims met certain criteria set forth in the act. In 1926 the Pueblo Lands Board initiated its investigations at Taos. The pueblo appeared before the board and proposed dropping any opposition to the two hundred–odd claims made by claimants in the town of Taos and forgoing any monetary compensation, on condition that the Blue Lake watershed be transferred from the Forest Service to the Department of the Interior as an executive order reservation for the pueblo. The tribe was aware that the board lacked authority to return Blue Lake, but it hoped that a recommendation from the board would help its cause. It was also the case that current law prohibited the president of the United States from creating executive order reservations in New Mexico, so that Taos would need congressional action to make the proposed transfer a reality. The Pueblo Lands Board accepted Taos Pueblo's relinquishment of any claims to land in the town of Taos but ignored the request for the transfer of the Blue Lake watershed. The pueblo thus found itself subject to the dishonorable dealings of the U.S. government, which distorted a conditional offer by accepting the beneficial part and refusing to deliver the quid pro quo.[6]

Having failed with the Pueblo Lands Board, Taos took its case to Commissioner Burke, appealing to him to help it gain trust title to the Blue Lake watershed. Beginning a long bureaucratic paper chase, Burke forwarded the tribe's request to the secretary of the interior, Hubert Work, who passed it along to the secretary of agriculture and asked whether there was any objection to removing the Blue Lake area from Carson National Forest and adding it to the land of Taos Pueblo. The Department of Agriculture objected to the idea of a transfer, saying that it was against the policy of the department to withdraw land previously set aside as national forest and donate it for "private" purposes.[7]

Many in the pueblo were wary of dealing with any branch of the U.S. government after these setbacks, which occurred during a time when the government's avowed policy was to terminate all Pueblo religious ceremonies. However, the tribe had no choice but to continue negotiating politically, while religious leaders like Juan de Jesús Romero continued praying for the day when the Blue Lake watershed would be returned to the pueblo to be used without restrictions. In 1927 and 1928 two initiatives were passed that seemed intended to address Taos's concerns. The first had to do with limiting mining. After some negotiations, President Calvin Coolidge issued an executive order on 7 July 1928 withdrawing 30,000 acres in the Rio Pueblo basin from mining entry, which seemed to end the threat mining posed to the Blue Lake watershed. The second initiative was less propitious and would begin a four-decade-long relationship with the Forest Service that would range from difficult to hostile. After some one-sided negotiations with the Forest Service, Taos and the Forest Service signed a cooperative-use agreement on 28 September 1927 that called on the pueblo to patrol the Blue Lake area, report violations to the Forest Service, and assist in fire suppression. The Forest Service was required to protect the water supply and allow non-pueblo members into the watershed only with written permits. The Forest Service reserved the right to construct roads and trails and carry out timbering operations. The agreement was flawed at the outset and suggested "that the Forest Service thought of the sacred watershed as its domain" and "that the Indians had no rights to it and should be grateful for any Forest Service concessions." The government attorney representing the pueblo recommended the agreement as "the most [the tribe] could hope for." Many in the pueblo wanted to obtain the Blue Lake area with no restrictions, and the disrespectful treatment of the pueblo by the Forest Service in the years to come would strengthen that desire.[8]

As the cooperative-use agreement was put into effect in the fall of 1927, problems between the Forest Service and Taos grew. The main point of contention was the issuance of visitor permits. In order to streamline the permitting process, the Forest Service allowed tour operators to issue visitor permits, which were then mailed in. The effect of this practice was that Taos Pueblo had no foreknowledge of the arrival of visitors, who could potentially disrupt religious activities. The Forest Service dismissed a request from Taos to countersign visitor permits as unnecessary, although Taos continued to assert this right under the concurrence clause of the use agreement. This openly disrespectful treatment of Taos religion reached new levels when the Forest Service constructed a cabin, outhouse, refuse dump, and corrals at Blue Lake, allowing a forest manager to live there. The use agreement should have meant that the pueblo could expect privacy for its August ceremonies at Blue Lake, but instead it now had to deal with a forest ranger who was in residence in the cabin for at least thirty days during the summer months, and during 1928 alone almost a hundred permits were issued for recreational uses. This meant that practically every day during the summer an outsider was camped on or near Blue Lake.[9]

Just as the pueblo's fortunes seemed hopeless, John Collier, soon-to-be commissioner of Indian Affairs and a passionate reformer, appeared on the scene. In 1923 he helped form the American Indian Defense Association to protect the rights of Native people and to push for his version of what would become the Pueblo Lands Act. As the organization's executive secretary, he traveled throughout the United States seeking to learn firsthand about the living conditions of Native Americans. In 1927 he persuaded Congress to create the Indian Investigating Committee, which issued a report about the conditions of Indian life that shocked many people. In 1931 the Senate Committee on Indian Affairs held hearings regarding the Pueblo Lands Board's fairness in resolving Indian land claims, as discussed in chapter 9. The committee determined that while non-Indian claimants were paid fair market value for their land, Indian claimants were paid only about one-third of the appraised value. Even at this lower rate Taos was awarded almost $460,000, of which only about $76,000 was paid. The remaining amount of about $384,000 was never paid to the pueblo, because the Pueblo Lands Board deemed that the pueblo had waived its right to the money. Yet Taos Pueblo had agreed not to oppose claims in the town of Taos on condition that the board would recommend that Blue Lake would be returned to the pueblo. The committee concluded that Taos should either be paid the money owed it or that Blue Lake should be returned to it, which was the bargain Taos Pueblo thought it had made. In response to this clear-cut recommendation, Congress authorized payment of about $84,000 to the pueblo, and in lieu of the remaining nearly $300,000 the secretary of agriculture was authorized to grant the pueblo a fifty-year use permit for the Blue Lake sacred area. This was the genesis of the use permit, which would replace the cooperative agreement with little change in the restrictions on pueblo usage.[10]

As commissioner of Indian Affairs, John Collier took a personal interest in Taos's struggle to regain the Blue Lake watershed through the course of the 1930s. In his position as commissioner, Collier attempted to craft the use permit in such a way that it would "give exclusive use of the land to the Indians, together with all the natural resources of the area." Unfortunately for the pueblo, it took seven years to hammer out the terms of the use permit so that it would be satisfactory to Taos, and even then joint administration of the area with the Forest Service left bad feelings with Taos Pueblo. The breaches of trust over the joint administration of the Blue Lake area gradually led the pueblo to the firm conviction that only unrestricted ownership by the pueblo through trust title would protect its sacred, secret religious character.[11]

Soon after the 1933 act was signed authorizing the use permit, the pueblo discovered that about 7,000 acres that were part of the Blue Lake watershed were not covered by the use permit. With the help of Collier, efforts were made to include this additional acreage under the use agreement with the Forest Service. But after all the work that went into drafting the 1933 act, its exact terms relating to the use permit turned out not to be clear. The pueblo had the impression that it would have exclusive use of the Blue Lake area "not by any grace, but because the pueblo relinquished very valuable claims it had," as Bureau of Indian Affairs superintendent Sophie Aberle put it. The Forest Service, however, still believed it had the ultimate administrative jurisdiction over the land and therefore the right to limit Taos's use of the land according to its interpretation of the use permit. By the summer of 1940 Collier and the Department of Agriculture had crafted a revised permit to protect Taos's use rights. The permit, issued on 24 October 1940, gave the pueblo limited use rights to 30,000 acres surrounding Blue Lake for fifty years. The permit covered grazing, water use, wood and timber extraction, and religious ceremonial use. The tribe gained exclusive use of the Blue Lake area for three days in August and the exclusive right to wood, timber, and grazing for personal use. The Forest Service was to manage the forest, and the tribe was to patrol the watershed for violations and to ensure fire suppression.[12]

Almost as soon as the new use permit went into effect there was disagreement about its implementation. The Taos Pueblo leader Seferino Martinez, who had served for many years as governor and council member, "did all he could to make life miserable for Forest Service personnel employed in the watershed." Martinez and other pueblo leaders chafed at any restrictions of their rights to use the Blue Lake area at any time. Through the 1940s and early 1950s "the various difficulties between the tribe and the Forest Service—over grazing, timbering, fishing, tourists, litter, and boundary disputes—made the Indians wary of continued outside control." Even as the Taos Indians sought legislation to add acreage to the permit area, they "insisted that they wanted to get a patent to the whole area," as they "didn't like [the] permit."[13]

During the 1950s, as the pueblo was growing utterly frustrated in its attempts to deal with the Forest Service, some new allies joined the growing ranks of supporters for the return of Blue Lake to the pueblo: the writers Frank Waters and Oliver La Farge. Frank Waters's most famous book, *The Man Who Killed the Deer*, published in 1942, is a fictionalized dramatic rendering of the struggle of Taos for the return of its sacred lake (named Dawn Lake in the book); it was called—with some exaggeration—the "single most potent outside force in Taos's achieving its ultimate victory."[14] Oliver La Farge, whose book *Laughing Boy*, which is set on the Navajo Reservation, won the Pulitzer Prize in 1929, worked with John Collier in the 1930s in organizations that assisted Native Americans, such as the Association on American Indian Affairs. By the mid to late 1940s La Farge had moved into a direct relationship with Taos Pueblo, advising the pueblo on the best means of getting Blue Lake back and sometimes mediating between different factions within the pueblo. Perhaps more important than outside support was the dedication of Taos leaders such as Seferino Martinez, Paul J. Bernal, John Reyna, and the cacique, or spiritual leader, Juan de Jesús Romero, who helped maintain the faith of Taos so that it would ultimately be successful in its quest.[15]

Among the thorniest of issues was how to deal with the Indian Claims Commission and the lawyers representing the pueblo before that body. The Indian Claims Commission Act of 1946 authorized the creation of the Indian Claims Commission, a court before which Indian tribes could present claims for lost land for which they did not receive adequate compensation. Taos filed suit before the Indian Claims Commission in 1951, and during 1953 and 1954 the tribal council provided testimony about the tribe's claim to the Blue Lake watershed. The 1950s were a particularly inauspicious time for American Indian tribes, because in August 1953 the official policy of the U.S. government became the pursuit of the rapid termination of the special legal status of all Native Americans. An aspect of termination was an end to the trust arrangements that provided for federal government protection of Indian land held in communal ownership and an opening of that land to private entry and settlement. Although numerous tribes in California, the Northwest, and elsewhere were stripped of their lands and the protection of the federal government by this policy, the Pueblos were spared. No effects of termination were ever felt in New Mexico.[16]

Despite this unfavorable political climate, the Taos tribal council, led by Seferino Martinez, pursued a strategy whereby the pueblo would seek a judgment from the Indian Claims Commission that would establish the pueblo's rights to the Blue Lake watershed and then use that ruling as leverage with Congress for legislation that would grant the pueblo trust title to the land. This dual effort was at least partly motivated by Martinez's suspicion that the tribe's lawyers would seek a financial settlement before the Indian Claims Commission rather than insist on the return of the sacred land, or that an Indian Claims Commission judgment would force the tribe to accept money. In 1955 the tribe prepared a draft bill seeking trust title to the entire Blue Lake watershed for submission to the leader of the New Mexico congressional delegation, Senator Clinton P. Anderson.[17] Anderson had served as secretary of agriculture in the Truman administration from 1945 to 1948, and while at the Department of Agriculture he had become an admirer of the philosophy of Gifford Pinchot; this made him disinclined to remove land from the national forests. He believed it would be more in the interest of Taos to accept a monetary settlement than to pursue the return of the Blue Lake watershed, and he refused to take any action on behalf of the pueblo.[18]

Faced with Senator Anderson's opposition to the legislation, Taos Pueblo decided to take its case to the American people. In the spring of 1955 the tribe produced a petition asking Congress for ownership rights of the Blue Lake watershed. This document focused on the religious importance of Blue Lake to the pueblo. Although the petition received widespread public notice, the attempt to bring about a legislative remedy for Taos's pursuit of trust title got nowhere. Instead, New Mexico congressman Antonio Fernandez introduced H.R. 7758, which called for including all 50,000 acres of the Blue Lake watershed in an expanded version of the pueblo's use-permit agreement, adding 20,000 acres. The tribe was not in favor of this attempt, but La Farge persuaded them that it would help their case before the Indian Claims Commission if Congress granted them the use permit requested in Fernandez's bill. In turn, a favorable judgment from the Indian Claims Commission would help persuade Congress to grant trust title at some future date. Meanwhile, Martinez cajoled members of the tribal council into firing claims attorney Darwin Kingsley for his handling of the Indian Claims Commission case, charging him with seeking only a cash settlement to increase his fee. Only by means of La Farge's intervention was the firing reversed.[19]

Early in 1956 the Taos Pueblo Tribal Council announced its support for Fernandez's bill and repudiated a second attempt by Martinez to have Kingsley removed from the Indian Claims Commission case. In early January 1957, Senator Anderson submitted S. 48, which added 20,000 acres to Taos's use permit, as did Fernandez's bill, H.R. 7758. The Forest Service opposed both bills and the Department of Agriculture effectively blocked action on them. Anderson introduced the bills again in 1958 and 1959 at Taos's behest. The Department of Agriculture again blocked action in 1958. In 1959, however, Taos changed tactics. Having failed to make progress on the use-permit legislation, it sought again to acquire trust title to the Blue Lake watershed. The tribal council consulted with Roger Ernst, assistant secretary of the Bureau of Indian Affairs, who agreed to work with Interior to draft a bill to secure trust title to the entire 50,000-acre watershed. When the draft bill was ready, Taos would ask Senator Anderson to withdraw his latest bill proposing an expanded use permit, S. 903. The tribe formally took this step in March 1960. With the Department of Agriculture still expressing strong opposition to

Interior's efforts on behalf of Taos Pueblo, Interior sought to enlist the support of the Department of Justice, but no progress was made through the course of 1960.[20]

In the spring of 1961 Martinez and Bernal met with Richard E. McArdle, chief of the Forest Service, who surprised them by saying that he was prepared to transfer the Blue Lake watershed to Taos Pueblo. When McArdle reneged on this promise two months later, Martinez threatened to stop signing visitor permits under the concurrence clause of the special-use permit, and in July he made good on his threat. The Forest Service continued to maintain that the current arrangement was the best for all parties. George Proctor, supervisor of Carson National Forest, declared that he alone would continue to issue visitor permits to the Blue Lake watershed, a serious violation of tribal rights. The effective closure of the area to non-Indians caused a firestorm of protest against what was construed as the unlawful seizure of federal land by the pueblo. Late in 1961 the tribe shifted its focus once again and took up in earnest the matter of non-Indians entering the Blue Lake watershed. John Collier, by this time a resident of Taos, intervened on the tribe's behalf and prepared an affidavit stating that the intent of the 1933 use-permit agreement was "to insure to the pueblo the exclusive use of the Sacred Area, the year-round exclusive use, identical with that which a trust patent might insure." The issue of the pueblo signing off on visitor permits continued to be contentious, and eventually the Department of Agriculture agreed not to issue permits without a tribal signature.[21]

In the summer of 1963 events took an unexpected turn when Collier became convinced that the quest for trust title was not really in Taos's best interest. This put Collier at odds with La Farge, who maintained that obtaining trust title was always the true goal. Collier came around to the view that if an exclusive-use permit were strictly enforced, it would be more desirable than trust title. The disagreement between Collier and La Farge was marked by some personal enmity, which was unfortunate at this critical juncture of the Blue Lake struggle. Collier believed that the trust-title initiative was being imposed on the tribal council by the pueblo's legal counsel; it seems that he had more trust in the Forest Service's good faith in implementing the use permit than was justified. La Farge saw no contradiction on the pueblo's part in desiring trust title over the permit, stating that he believed "the Indians were right in desiring outright title," because of the numerous unfortunate occurrences that the use permit had given rise to. La Farge's death in August 1963 and Collier's newfound opposition to trust title delayed any progress for two years. It also led Taos Pueblo to reevaluate the merits of trust title versus use permit. Collier urged the pueblo to force the Forest Service to manage the Blue Lake watershed in such as way as to be exclusively advantageous to the pueblo under the terms of the 1940 use permit. Notwithstanding Collier's assurances, however, the pueblo was determined not to abandon its efforts to achieve trust title, believing it had always owned Blue Lake and the surrounding land and that it should not be forced to continually ask permission to use it on terms dictated by the Forest Service.[22]

After La Farge's death, Corinne Locker filled his role as the chief advocate for trust title in the pueblo. She was La Farge's secretary during his tenure as president of the Association on American Indian Affairs and became the association's southwest field secretary after his death. Locker strongly encouraged the tribe to continue its pursuit of trust title. She also took on the role of keeping the association in New York and the tribe's attorneys in Washington informed of local developments. What was most important was that she helped induce William Schaab, a prominent partner in the Rodey firm, the largest in New Mexico, to take on the Blue Lake cause. In addition, over the course of 1964 and 1965, Taos Pueblo took measures to improve its relationship with the town of Taos, permitting, for example, a local ditch association to enter Taos Pueblo land to make repairs on the ditch and allowing the town to construct a dam on Pueblo land. Another move that favored the tribe was the transfer of Carson National Forest supervisor George Proctor to Arizona. Finally, a change in editors at the *Taos News* promised less opposition from the local newspaper.[23]

Another significant development was the hiring of Rufus Poole as Association on American Indian Affairs attorney. The executive director of the association, William Byler, and Locker joined the tribal council at a meeting in September 1964 during which it was revealed that Taos was ready to begin a new effort to obtain trust title. Byler believed it was crucial to get church and conservation organizations on board to assist in the pueblo's fight. Early in 1965 both Collier and Seferino Martinez dropped their opposition to the pursuit of trust title.[24]

Meanwhile, the Indian Claims Commission finally ruled on 11 September 1965 that Taos held aboriginal title to a large area covering approximately

300,000 acres, which included the Blue Lake basin, relying heavily on testimony by Taos elders and expert witnesses such as Florence Hawley Ellis and Myra Ellen Jenkins. The commission held that the United States had extinguished the pueblo's title without payment of compensation in November 1906 by the creation of the Taos National Forest, which included the entire Blue Lake region.[25] The pueblo felt that this decision—confirming that Blue Lake belonged exclusively to the pueblo and that it had been taken by the United States—was just what it needed to bolster its case in Congress. With this victory in hand, Taos began preparations to have the New Mexico congressional delegation draft legislation that would give the Pueblo trust title to the watershed.[26]

From 1966 to 1968 the pueblo pursued a three-pronged approach to securing trust title to the Blue Lake watershed. First, the tribe focused its efforts on building local support for its position. Second, the Association on American Indian Affairs concentrated on developing support among national religious and conservation groups. Third, the tribe's attorneys worked in concert to further legislative efforts in the nation's capital. The legislative effort faced a thorny problem from the outset related to perceptions as to the pueblo's ability to conserve the Blue Lake watershed. Don Seaman, supervisor of Carson National Forest, stated publicly that he did not believe the tribe could handle the conservation issues connected with the area and that the Forest Service would oppose any effort to reduce its authority. This was ironic because the pueblo had preserved Blue Lake, while the Forest Service wanted to expand use of the land and to develop it. The matter caused a rift among the pueblo's advisors: some argued for inserting a clause that would delegate the responsibility for conservation to the Forest Service, while others doubted that the pueblo and the Forest Service could ever work out a mutually acceptable policy. In the end, the parties put aside their differences and opted for a clause that gave the pueblo exclusive use and benefit of the watershed and provided for the secretary of agriculture to supervise the conservation of the watershed. The tribal council approved the draft trust-title bill and sent it to Senator Anderson. He introduced the pueblo's bill as S. 3085 on 15 March 1966.[27]

Although there was opposition to Taos Pueblo's bill on the part of the Taos County Board of Commissioners, local cattlemen, and the New Mexico Wildlife and Conservation Association, this was balanced by the support of the New Mexico Council of Churches and James P. Davis, archbishop of Santa Fe.

A booklet the tribe prepared spelling out the religious significance of Blue Lake was particularly effective, attracting the attention of the national media, notably the *New York Times*, which urged the enactment of S. 3085. The effort was helped by the fact that the pueblo steadfastly refused to accept monetary compensation for the loss of its most sacred land. The pueblo carried the message of its quest for religious freedom to the annual Association on American Indian Affairs meeting, held in New York City in May 1966. There they met the U.S. attorney general, Robert Kennedy, who offered the tribe his support. Interior secretary Stewart Udall, who spoke at the meeting, also became an important backer of S. 3085.[28]

While the Senate hearing for S. 3085 was scheduled for 18 May 1966, Udall learned that opponents of the bill were going to claim that it was an economically motivated piece of legislation cloaked in religious garb. To counter this smear tactic, Udall suggested amending the bill to place all 50,000 acres of the Blue Lake watershed under the protection of the Wilderness Act. With the tribe's approval, Udall and his staff set to work on the amendment. Senator Lee Metcalf of Montana chaired the Senate Subcommittee on Indian Affairs. Udall testified first for the pueblo and stressed the need for privacy to protect the religious freedom of the tribe. The practice of Taos's religion required the exclusion of people who were not members of the pueblo. As long as the Forest Service patrolled and managed the sacred Blue Lake watershed, the tribe would never be truly free to practice its religion. Trust title would ensure that the land was preserved in its natural state as befitted such a holy place.[29]

Testifying in opposition to S. 3085, Arthur W. Greeley, associate chief forester of the Forest Service, advanced a number of arguments. He expressed concern for downstream water users in the event that Taos mismanaged the Blue Lake watershed. Tribal control of the area would prevent the timbering of hundreds of millions of board feet of trees that in Greeley's estimation were ready to be harvested. The bill would remove 2,000 acres from the Wheeler Wilderness, leaving only 3,000 acres, which would be below the 5,000-acre minimum cited in the Wilderness Act. Greely claimed that the Forest Service was well aware of the pueblo's religious concerns and that it acted so as to protect its rights by limiting visitors. He advanced the idea that if Taos received land instead of a monetary settlement as a result of the ruling of the Indian Claims Commission it would set a precedent, and other tribes would follow suit and threaten millions of acres of land currently in national forests. Greeley noted that the bill placed the trust title under the Department of the Interior and left the Forest Service, a division of the Department of Agriculture, in charge of conservation and management, creating a jurisdictional conflict. Finally, Greeley said that the bill would allow the tribe to buy grazing permits then in force, which he suggested was a privilege and not a vested interest.[30]

The tribe was very pleased with the way the hearing went and by what it assumed was Senator Anderson's support for the bill he introduced. What went unnoticed, however, was that Anderson introduced the bill "by request," a signal to his fellow congressmen that he introduced the bill only because his constituents requested the legislation, not because he personally supported it. In fact, as soon became apparent, Anderson was very much opposed to granting Taos any control over the Blue Lake watershed. On one level, Anderson's opposition was philosophical: he was a believer in Pinchot's multiple-use doctrine. On quite another level, Anderson had a less lofty motive for trying to thwart the pueblo: he was attempting to facilitate a deal that lumberman Robert Le Sage was negotiating with the Forest Service to harvest timber on 20,000 acres of the Blue Lake watershed.[31]

Far from supporting the pueblo, Senator Anderson launched his offensive against Taos in July 1966 when he announced that he had prepared a new bill that would give the pueblo trust title only to Blue Lake and its immediate surroundings, a total of approximately 3,100 acres. The bill would place 27,000 acres under the Wilderness Protection Act and would not remove the 2,000 acres from the Wheeler Wilderness. No mention was made of the 18,000 acres remaining in the Blue Lake watershed. When he met with the tribe, Anderson informed them that his reasons for opposing S. 3085 were the ten million dollars worth of timber in the 18,000-acre parcel and the issue of the 2,000 acres from the Wheeler Wilderness. Despite several attempts at compromise, in the end the senator and the pueblo remained at odds, and no legislation went forward. In late April 1967 Senator Anderson again introduced legislation that would give the tribe only 3,100 acres instead of the entire 48,000-acre watershed. That summer the long-standing relationship between the Association on American Indian Affairs and Taos Pueblo ended, largely over differences between Corinne Locker and the claims attorneys and the association's board of directors about how to deal with the Anderson proposal. Countering Anderson's proposal, which would take trust title for the Blue Lake watershed off the table and leave 18,000 acres open to timbering, the claims attorneys prepared a counterproposal that would place 3,100 acres surrounding Blue Lake in trust title and give the pueblo a perpetual use permit for the remaining 45,000 acres, on which non-Indian visitation would be permissible only with Pueblo consent.[32]

Taos did not like the counterproposal. Fearing a repeat of the continuing conflict with the Forest Service over non-Indian visitation, the pueblo informed Anderson that they were "prepared to wait for years if necessary to obtain satisfactory legislation." Anderson responded bitterly, "I have wasted a good many years of my life trying to get a decision that could be implemented by legislation." The claims attorneys advised the pueblo that its only hope for acquiring Blue Lake was to negotiate with Senator Clinton P. Anderson, while Corinne Locker of the Association on American Indian Affairs believed the claims attorneys were pressuring the pueblo to further their own financial interests, although this was not the position of the association itself, which supported the claims counsel. The bitter dispute between the association and Locker ended with Locker's firing and with the tribe's determination to proceed in the Blue Lake quest "without consulting further with AAIA."[33] The National Council of Churches soon emerged as the primary advocate for the pueblo, a role that the Association on American Indian Affairs had played for so long. Reverend Dean Kelley, director of the National Council of Churches' Commission on Religious Liberty, took a leading role in preparing testimony for the upcoming Senate hearing. He published an article in the spring of 1967 explaining the sanctity of the Blue Lake watershed to Taos. His eloquent writing proved very influential in the hearings and debates that followed.[34]

The participation of the National Council of Churches in support of Taos became crucial when Senator Anderson expressed doubts that religion was really the motive behind the pueblo's efforts to secure trust title to the Blue Lake watershed. Instead, he suspected an economic motive. Anderson's suspicions had no factual basis, but they seemed to be supported by the opinions of George L. Tragar, a linguist from Southern Methodist University, and M. E. Smith of Florida State University, who told the National Council of Churches that "the annual Blue Lake pilgrimage had become popular only recently when it seemed that pilgrimages would help them establish a right to the [land]."[35] Anderson was willing to accept that the 3,100-acre parcel represented a truly religious area, but he could not accept the idea that the entire watershed was sacred. Anderson considered the pueblo's claim as being nothing more than a land grab that would favor the tribe and its attorneys and deny the rest of the public.

Taos Pueblo responded to Anderson's accusations by issuing a public statement reaffirming that it considered the entire Blue Lake watershed to be its religious sanctuary. The statement further reiterated the pueblo's support for Udall's wilderness proposal. At Kelley's suggestion, the pueblo formed a national committee of influential individuals who supported the Taos claim to Blue Lake. Also at Kelley's insistence, the pueblo sought and obtained the support of the New Mexico Council of Churches, whose representatives were convinced "how important it was," having seen "what was happening to the land" and "what the Forest Service had allowed to happen with the timber industry there" when they were taken on a trip to Blue Lake and the areas Le Sage had clear-cut. The pueblo began to meet privately with New Mexico governor David Cargo (1967–1970), who began to work behind the scenes to help the cause of obtaining trust title to the Blue Lake watershed. All of these groups and individuals worked to put more political pressure on Senator Anderson.[36]

During this period Poole became gravely ill, and Albuquerque attorney William Schaab replaced him in January 1968. In March Schaab drafted a legal memo detailing for the first time the complete history of the pueblo's claim, which became a significant piece of evidence in the coming hearings. A new entity, the National Committee for Restoration of the Blue Lake Lands to the Taos Indians, was formed to raise money for a tax-exempt fund at the National Council of Churches. Consuelo La Farge, widow of Oliver, was the chairwoman of the committee, which included important religious figures such as Russell Carter and Dean Kelley of the National Council of Churches; Archbishop James Davis of Santa Fe; New Mexico Council of Churches president Lee Hobert; Howard Squadron, chair of the Commission on Law and Social Action of the American Jewish Congress; the photographer Eliot Porter; and John Collier.[37]

In early May 1968, Representative James Haley opened hearings on H.R. 3306, a bill to give Taos trust title to the entire 48,000-acre Blue Lake watershed. The Department of the Interior would support the bill if it were amended to include all the land returned to Taos under the Wilderness Act. Agriculture opposed H.R. 3306 and supported the Anderson bill, which would award only 3,100 acres to the tribe. Udall repeated his 1966 testimony on the religious significance of the Blue Lake watershed. Edward P. Cliff, chief of the Forest Service, stated that although he believed the 1940 use permit provided all the religious protection the pueblo needed, he was amenable to granting an exclusive-use permit for the Blue Lake area but not to granting trust title, because of the fear of an adverse precedent. After hearing more testimony, the subcommittee began to mark up the bill. It removed the 2,000 acres in the Wheeler Wilderness from the area to be returned. Language was added to clearly indicate that non-Indians would be allowed in the Blue Lake watershed only with tribal consent. The entire watershed was placed under the Wilderness Act and under the administrative authority of Interior. With the markup completed, the subcommittee voted to pass H.R. 3306. The jubilation felt in Taos was soon deflated when it was learned that the House Agriculture Committee had blocked action on the bill. Haley then had the bill withdrawn from that committee and got it scheduled for debate on the floor in mid-June. Wayne Aspinall, chairman of the House Committee on Interior and Insular Affairs, introduced the bill and spoke in favor of it. John Saylor of Pennsylvania, ranking minority member on the committee, then spoke in support of the bill. No one rose to oppose it, and the House approved H.R. 3306 by unanimous consent.[38]

In the wake of the victory in the House, Taos was buoyed on a rising tide of public support, both local and national, including editorial support in the *New York Times*. Yet another attempt to negotiate with Senator Anderson, who was feeling the weight of the mounting public support for the Blue Lake claim, ended in acrimony. When the *Washington Post* learned of the failed negotiations, the paper slammed Anderson for refusing to right such an old wrong. Senator George McGovern, chairman of the Senate Interior Committee's Subcommittee on Indian Affairs, where the bill was bottled up, called for a public hearing in the Senate on the Blue Lake bill.[39]

The hearings took place on 19 and 20 September. Udall again repeated his earlier testimony, but on this occasion he added an important new wrinkle. He noted that Senator Anderson's bills and Representative Haley's bill all recognized that a wrong had been done to Taos Pueblo. The only difference among the bills was how much land they proposed to be returned to the pueblo. Addressing the precedent issue, Udall stated that if other tribes could prove the religious significance of their land as Taos had done, then Congress should see that they received justice too. When Seferino Martinez and Governor Querino Romero testified before the committee, Montana senator Lee Metcalf launched into a line of aggressive inquiry that questioned the religious motives of the pueblo's claim. As it turned out, the opposition was just getting warmed up, and an embittered Senator Anderson orchestrated a harsh line of testimony. Jon Little, president of the New Mexico Wildlife and Conservation Association, testified that he accompanied two Forest Service employees to Blue Lake after the August ceremonials and found extensive littering. He bolstered his testimony with photographic evidence. Preston Gunter of the Sportsmen's Legislative Action Committee of New Mexico followed with additional criticism, stating that the proposed legislation would leave Taos in possession of the land and leave the taxpayer paying for it without the right to visit the area. Gunter openly accused the pueblo of practicing an immoral and obscene religion, in fact, a peyote cult, which he argued was the real explanation for the pueblo's need for secrecy. Although the tribe took what steps it could to refute the allegations, the testimony before the Subcommittee on Indian Affairs was damaging, and the subcommittee took no action on any of the proposed Blue Lake legislation.[40]

Then, in the fall of 1968, Taos's struggle to regain Blue Lake was transformed by a number of positive developments. In September, presidential candidate Richard Nixon announced a proposal for what he called "self-determination," by which he meant that the federal government would transfer responsibility for Indian affairs to tribal governments. As it happened, photographs of Taos elders appeared in Nixon's campaign literature. Taos native John Rainer, the first tribal member to graduate from college, became chairman of the All-Indian Pueblo Council and the Governors' Interstate Indian Council, as well as first vice president of the National Congress of American Indians. From his position of power in these organizations, Rainer was able to get their support for the Blue Lake claim and make the issue significant to all Indians across the country. In addition, New Mexico governor David Cargo appointed Rainer director of the New Mexico Commission on Indian Affairs. Cargo was a supporter of Taos Pueblo and conveyed this to Nixon's running mate, Spiro Agnew. After the Nixon-Agnew ticket was victorious in the November election, Cargo met with them along with other governors and used the opportunity to speak in support of the Blue Lake claim.[41]

Despite the support of the new administration, Taos's nemesis, Senator Clinton P. Anderson, was heartened by his victory in the recent subcommittee hearings. He introduced S. 750, a new proposal that reduced the amount of land to be transferred to the pueblo from 3,100 acres to 1,600 acres. The senator was not the only problem the pueblo had to confront, however. Pueblo leaders Seferino Martinez and Paul Bernal, who had disagreed in the past, found themselves at odds again. Financial woes were an ongoing concern as legal fees and the expenses of getting the tribal delegation to Washington mounted. Most troubling was the appointment of Alaska governor Walter Hickle as secretary of the Department of the Interior to replace Stewart Udall. Whereas Udall was a steadfast supporter of Taos, Hickle was something of an unknown to the pueblo, and what was known about him did not augur well.[42]

On the first day Congress was in session in 1969, Representative Haley introduced H.R. 471, which was identical to H.R. 3306 of the previous year. Haley called another hearing on the Blue Lake claim for mid-May. The undersecretary of the interior department, Russell Train, informed Representative Aspinall that the department still supported Haley's bill. Secretary of Agriculture Clifford Hardin reaffirmed his department's opposition to the proposed legislation. These two positions represented the status quo, but a surprise statement of opposition from the Bureau of the Budget greatly disappointed the pueblo. This was because the bureau's position was taken to be a reflection of the view of the Nixon administration, which was reported to view most legislation from a budgetary point of view.[43]

In two days of testimony for and against Taos's Blue Lake claim, the basic arguments presented in previous hearings were again aired. What was notably different on this occasion, however, was the rhetorical virtuosity reached by Schaab and Bernal. Schaab made the salient point that the Department of Agriculture, which was dedicated to a multiuse policy, would always be in conflict with the pueblo, which required privacy in the practice of its religion. That was all the more reason to transfer administrative responsibility to the Department of the Interior, he said. Moreover, Interior's Bureau of Indian Affairs would have its Forestry Division oversee the land, and it would not contemplate harvesting timber in the Blue Lake watershed and would not "encourage tourists and recreationalists to come into the area." "They will manage it as if it were truly trust land held for the benefit of the Indians and in accordance with [the] desires of the Indians."[44]

Bernal made the most powerful statement regarding the conflict between multiple use and his religion. He stressed that religious ceremonial activity took place in the Blue Lake watershed at various times throughout the year but noted that the times and places were secret. Therefore, the Forest Service could not know when it interfered with Taos religious practice. Bernal also made the point that the Forest Service's multiuse policy was predicated on the idea of human superiority over nature, but the religion of Taos required the people to adapt to their natural surroundings. Rather than harvest trees, the Indians had a religious requirement to preserve the trees in their primordial state. Bernal went on to make a crucial point that zeroed in on the different world views at the heart of the conflict: "The idea that man must subdue nature and bend its processes to his purposes is repugnant to our people.... Any outside interference with natural conditions of the watershed interferes with our religion." Also helpful to the pueblo's cause was a petition that 364 youths of Taos signed. The document indicated their support for the struggle to regain Blue Lake and stated that their continued participation in the Indian way of life depended on the pueblo regaining possession of Blue Lake.[45]

After the hearings, New Mexico congressman Manuel Lujan announced his support for the Blue Lake claim. During the hearings he appeared to be clearly in opposition, but the weight of the testimony changed his mind. Lujan was an important convert to the cause. This gave Taos the support of two powerful New Mexico politicians, since it already had Governor Cargo's. Haley's committee passed H.R. 471 in June and got debate in the full House scheduled for September. The bill then passed the House with only two members voting against it.[46]

Seeking an issue to improve his image among the Indians, Secretary Walter Hickle embraced Taos's claim to Blue Lake. When he announced his support, he followed Udall's lead in placing Interior squarely behind the pueblo. Senator Anderson expressed his dismay that Hickle took that position and that the Nixon administration was apparently now backing Taos. He urged the Republicans to take another look at the issue. Rather than reassess its position, however, the Republican Party provided additional support. The Republican National Committee took an interest in the Blue Lake claim and expressed its support.

Early in 1970 the National Congress of American Indians called on the Nixon administration to announce a new Indian policy. Among the issues it brought forward was the return of Blue Lake, and it asked the administration to support the bill. Rainer and Strauss met with Hickle and were doubtless relieved to hear that Anderson's urging had not moved the secretary to change his position. Hickle suggested that he thought he could get President Nixon to make a statement in support of Taos's claim. It became clear that enlisting the president's support was the key to the passage of the bill. It happened that a young woman named Bobbie Greene Kilberg, a Yale Law School graduate and White House fellow with an interest in Indian education, who became friends with LaDonna Harris, the Comanche wife of Senator Fred Harris of Oklahoma, went to work for John Erlichman, President Nixon's domestic affairs advisor. Aware of Greene Kilberg's experience with Indians, Erlichman asked her to help formulate a new Indian policy for the Nixon administration. Greene Kilberg, with Harris's help, put together a report containing policy recommendations that was presented to the administration. It concluded with a proposal that Vice President Agnew and others in the administration should speak in favor of H.R. 471 at every opportunity.[47]

Erlichman viewed Taos's claim as an opportunity for the Nixon White House to deal positively with a minority issue. Therefore he gave Greene Kilberg the go-ahead to work with others in the White House on the Blue Lake issue. Senator Harris became an important supporter of the Blue Lake cause after a visit from a pueblo delegation in January. Harris was deeply impressed with the Taos leaders and told them he would help them. After the tribal delegation left his office he said to his assistant, "If we don't do another damn thing while we're here in the Senate, let's help these people get back their land." Harris wrote to Senator George McGovern to ask him to do what he could to bring the bill before the Senate. Vice President Spiro Agnew also began to take a personal interest and worked to get the Department of Agriculture to cease its opposition to the bill. In March he informed Nixon that after a thorough review of the issue, he believed that the administration should support H.R. 471. In the vice president's opinion, the bill would be an important symbol of Nixon's intention to redress the wrongs done to Indians. It would also improve the chances of having Indians eventually take responsibility for programs designed to assist them. Beginning in April 1970, Clifford M. Hardin, the secretary of agriculture, under pressure from Agnew, began to back down from his staunch opposition to the Blue Lake claim. After the addition of language about the uniqueness of Taos's case, Hardin finally came out in support of the bill. Next to change its position was the Bureau of the Budget, whose acting director, James R. Schlesinger, eventually agreed to support the bill after attempting unsuccessfully to alter some of the language in the bill by adding a reversion clause under which title would revert to the government if the pueblo ever stopped using the land for religious purposes.[48]

As the Nixon administration was gradually falling into line in support of the bill, Senator Fred Harris was promoting H.R. 471 among his Senate colleagues. Greene Kilberg became alarmed that the work of Harris, a Democrat, was going to detract attention from the Republican Nixon administration, and she got Erlichman to persuade the president that he needed to issue a statement supporting Taos before the Democrats got all the credit. The statement was set to be released on 16 April 1970, but concern over the possibility of losing Anderson's and Senator Henry Jackson's backing on an Anti-Ballistic Missile treaty, which both senators were threatening, led the White House to hesitate. When Nixon asked Erlichman to explain the political costs and the meaning of Blue Lake in simple terms, Erlichman replied "that it was like cowboys and Indians and that we were on the side of the Indians. [Nixon] indicated that he was more of a John Wayne man himself and . . . thought we [might have] made a serious mistake [politically]." As a result, Nixon delayed issuing his statement of support, fearing the political consequences.[49]

To break this impasse Taos turned to its most powerful member and spiritual leader, Cacique Juan de Jesús Romero. Through all the years of struggle, Romero watched over the spiritual needs of the pueblo but remained out of the public eye, behind the scenes. His devotion to the Blue Lake quest was described by his grandson, William Martinez: "Every night and every day . . . he used to pray in our way about getting it back. Every day he used to go to the river at five o' clock in the morning . . . even if it was cold, ice. . . . [H]e used to take a morning bath . . . and pray [for the return of Blue Lake]." Since Senator Anderson was now the major obstacle to the Blue Lake claim, the pueblo decided to take the ninety-year-old cacique to Washington: "The only way to make Anderson believe us is to take him [Romero] to look at him face to face." So the cacique came forward to warn that if Blue Lake was not returned to Taos, the people would scatter because their religion was what held them together.[50]

The words and presence of the cacique appeared to have an immediate effect. McGovern announced that Senate hearings on H.R. 471 would commence on 9 July 1970. Nixon finally decided to voice his support, and in a press conference on 8 July 1970 with Taos elders in attendance, the president declared his support for their claim to the Blue Lake watershed. At the same time, the president produced a silver-headed ceremonial cane inscribed with his name and the date, which was later presented to Taos Pueblo governor Querino Romero. This highly symbolic gesture helped the pueblo maintain its focus and commitment in the difficult days before a final vote was taken on H.R. 471. The next day, with Nixon on the front page of the *New York Times* and his message of support printed inside, the Senate opened hearings on the bill. The polarization between Anderson and Fred Harris and the tense political battle between the two sides at the time of this important hearing is illustrated by an exchange between the two senators in which Anderson said, "Fred, I don't mess with your Indians in Oklahoma and you don't mess with my Indians in New Mexico," to which Harris responded, "Senator, they aren't our Indians."[51]

The odds in this hearing were very favorable to Taos, with the support of the Department of the Interior, the Department of Agriculture, and the White House. Moreover, it became obvious that Senator Metcalf was inebriated and that Anderson was quite ill. Many old backers were there to testify. An important addition was Myra Ellen Jenkins, whose testimony before the Indian Claims Commission had been so effective. Jenkins testified that

> perhaps no tribe of Indians has more tenaciously resisted absorption by its non-Indian neighbors than has the Pueblo of Taos. Since Spanish occupation in 1598 its history has been characterized by a constant attempt to preserve its tribal identity and to stop encroachment on lands which the Taos Indians consider their ancestral heritage for farming, grazing, or religious practices.[52]

The most powerful testimony came from Taos leaders, including Paul Bernal and Governor Querino Romero. Romero testified that "we are fighting for our own land; we are fighting to have our own land returned to us for our own particular use."[53]

Senator Metcalf's drunkenness likely explains his aggressive, insulting, and abusive conduct, especially his dismissive line of questioning about Indian religion. At one point, Metcalf added gratuitously that "maybe passage of this bill would be an encouragement and inspiration for a whole lot of Indian religions and medicine men would spring up all over the country," implying a lack of serious spirituality in a religion he did not understand and certainly did not respect. Observers were appalled at Metcalf's behavior and the Taos Indians were particularly incensed. Bernal accused Metcalf "of being under the influence of firewater" and said that his remarks were an insult to all American Indians. Most upset of all was the ninety-year-old cacique. "The night they got back he spent most of the night in the kiva," reported his grandson, "and the next morning when he came down he was changed altogether. After that, he started really praying . . . He put everything, all his whole life into it from that time on." Metcalf's insulting behavior backfired, building more sympathy for Taos and galvanizing leaders, both spiritual and political, for the final push.[54]

In the face of the momentum in favor of the Blue Lake Bill, Clinton Anderson remained intransigent, using his political skills in a last-ditch attempt to prevent a vote on H.R. 471. During the autumn of 1970 the maneuvering intensified: as the Blue Lake bill crafted by Senator Haley (H.R. 471) was finally released from the bureaucratic bottleneck, so was Anderson's substitute bill, S. 750, which provided protection for only 1,600 acres around Blue Lake. Under enormous pressure from Senator Harris, Anderson and McGovern moved H.R. 471 out of the Indian Affairs Subcommittee where they had kept it bottled up, but McGovern also reported Anderson's 1,600-acre bill, S. 750, out of the subcommittee. Jackson's Interior committee then had to decide between Anderson's and Haley's bills. Nixon and Agnew personally lobbied Republican members of the committee, and it began to look like Taos was destined to win. At this point Anderson indicated that he was preparing a new bill that would create a new ranger district encompassing the entire Blue Lake watershed. The new district would be staffed by Taos Pueblo members as rangers. In this way, the precedent of giving the Indians title to Forest Service land would be avoided. The White House informed the Republican committee members that it was opposed to Anderson's substitute bill, because it would appear to set a bad precedent by taking a parcel of national forest land and giving exclusive control of it to a single group. The best way of dealing with the Blue Lake issue, the administration insisted, was to transfer title to Taos. Despite the administration's pressure, the following day the Senate Interior Committee reported Anderson's substitute bill out of committee, with four Republicans going against the president's wishes.

Countering Anderson's move Harris and Senator Robert Griffin attached H.R. 471 to Anderson's substitute bill. It was like a high-stakes chess match with Anderson, visibly weak and ailing, fighting his last major political battle, as the pueblo's luck finally turned. Minority Whip Griffin approached Harris about cosponsoring H.R. 471 as an amendment to Anderson's substitute bill, which became known as the Griffin-Harris amendment. This maneuver gave the supporters of the pueblo the opportunity to get their bill on the Senate floor for debate even though Anderson's substitute was reported out of committee.[55]

Senate debate on Blue Lake began on 1 December 1970. Harris, McGovern, and Edward Kennedy opened testimony. Kennedy offered a different take on the precedent issue, arguing that it would be unjust to deny a valid claim on the grounds that it might encourage other Indians to seek the return of their sacred land. Each bill should be examined on its merits. He said that Congress had the ability to judge future claims should they arise. On the second day of the hearings, Jackson and Metcalf repeated their previous concerns about precedent and the transfer of land from Agriculture to Interior. Next to speak was Senator Barry Goldwater, generally considered to be one of the Senate's most knowledgeable members on Indian affairs. Goldwater focused his remarks on the nature of Indian religion and its relationship to the land. Central to his argument was that land was sacred to the Indians. If an Indian tribe claimed land for its religious significance, the government should be prepared to give the land to the tribe, especially when it was government land once used and owned by the Indians. Momentum was building in favor of Taos's six-decade-long quest for the return of Blue Lake. When the Senate voted, it defeated Anderson's substitute bill fifty-six to twenty-one. The next matter before the Senate was the Griffin-Harris amendment. Griffin observed: "Cathedrals, mosques, and temples are generally respected as structures of sanctity and significance. What the Indians of Pueblo de Taos are asking is that equal consideration—no more and no less—be extended to the shrine where they have performed their religious obligations for at least as long as the famed cathedrals of Europe have been in use." Griffin's stirring statement won the day and the Griffin-Harris amendment was approved, preparing the way for the final roll call vote on H.R. 471.[56]

As the roll was called and the senators announced their yeas or nays, the old cacique, Juan de Jesús Romero, Governor Querino Romero, James Mirabal, and Paul Bernal sat in the top row of the Senate gallery listening to the vote. "They huddled together chanting softly, making medicine, and communicating with the spirits. . . . They asked for strength, not to punish the government, which had taken their sacred land, but to achieve justice by recovering the sacred area. After so many years of work, so many trips to Washington . . . [the voting had begun]." The vote was seventy in favor of Blue Lake, twelve opposed, eighteen absent. The interminable quest was at an end; the Blue Lake victory had been decisively won.[57]

Upon completion of the vote, the cacique, Juan de Jesús Romero, stood up very quietly and in a gesture of triumph held the Pueblo canes aloft—one from the Spanish government, one from President Lincoln, and one from President Nixon—in the Senate chambers. "He didn't say a word . . . and there was a silence. Then all 100 senators turned and looked at the cacique . . . who nodded and then sat down. Then the place burst into applause."[58]

The signing ceremony took place in the State Dining Room in the White House. There, on 15 December 1970, President Nixon signed into law Public Law 91-550, returning the 48,000 acres of the Blue Lake watershed to Taos. After signing the law with a flourish, President Nixon gave the pen to Cacique Romero. The signing ceremony, the culmination of a sixty-four-year struggle, was "unlike any other signing that anybody had ever been to," for "the [Taos] people showed that they were so directly affected by the return [of Blue Lake] . . . that it captured everyone." Even President Nixon "was really choked up" when he spoke after the signing. He said, in words that warmed the heart of the cacique and all others present, that "for 700 years the Taos Pueblo Indians worshipped in this place. We restore this place of worship to them for all years to come."[59]

It took a while for the news of the signing of the Blue Lake law to sink in at Taos. The day of the signing the mission bell in the pueblo church was rung, but the celebration was subdued. A *New York Times* reporter found a man in the plaza and told him the news, which he already knew. "Our ancestors came out of Blue Lake long ago," he said. "Blue Lake nourishes everything. It is the source of our wisdom, of our life." The reporter was moved by this simple statement and by "the tear which swelled slowly out of his eye, curved around his broad shallow nose before dropping into the mud. 'I am very, very happy,' he said quietly."[60] Later, a day of celebration was chosen: "Amid laughter and tears, people crowded the rooftops, poured through the streets and filled the church to offer thanks. It was a day never to be forgotten." Every twenty years since then, the pueblo has commemorated the great day when Blue Lake was returned. Pueblo leaders not only give thanks and express gratitude to their own leaders who dedicated their lives to the return of Blue Lake, but also express their thanks to their many supporters, from John Collier to Fred Harris, from Oliver La Farge to David Cargo and Manuel Lujan, among many others.[61]

Since the passage of Public Law 91-550, hundreds of thousands of acres of land have been returned to Indian tribes, based in part on the precedent set by Blue Lake and because these claims were considered valid on their merits. In 1986 Taos received another small high-mountain lake called Bear Lake into trust status and an area of about 700 acres, protecting Taos's access to its sacred sites. And in 1997 Taos Pueblo won back the disputed Bottleneck tract, a 764-acre strip leading to the Blue Lake watershed. Other pueblos have successfully fought for the return of lost land and received additional lands either by act of Congress or by purchase, including Picuris, Santo Domingo, and San Ildefonso, among others.[62] It was not only the Blue Lake bill that made this possible but also the greater public sympathy for the return of sacred sites to Indian pueblos and other tribes, which was generated in part by the Blue Lake struggle. R. C. Gordon-McCutchan's book *The Taos Indians and the Battle for Blue Lake* concludes with an apt encapsulation of the Blue Lake struggle: "It shows that the impossible can be made possible by even a small group when its members are spiritually inspired, politically determined and individually brave."[63]

Epilogue

Across much of the United States, the history of Indian land tenure is a sad tale of treaties broken, homelands lost, and forced migration to federally designated reservations far from the sacred sites of the ancestral homelands of the tribes, the places sung about and recounted in myths and origin stories. In New Mexico, the story of Pueblo land tenure was different. Although many Pueblo villages that existed at the time of the arrival of the Spanish in New Mexico disappeared within the next century, those that survived generally managed to maintain their control of lands surrounding their villages. A policy developed of respecting Pueblo rights to a "league"—an area of four square leagues, centered on the Spanish mission church in the village—a policy unknown elsewhere in Spain's dominions.

In writing this book, we have attempted to discover the origin of the concept of the Pueblo league and how it was put into practice in New Mexico. Among the questions we have sought to answer were whether these grants of four square leagues represented a minimum or a maximum entitlement to each pueblo and how those land grants relate to Pueblo landholdings today. In order to respond to such queries, we have examined thousands of pages of the documentary record over the last twenty years. The case studies presented in this book are the result of this research.

We now believe that evidence exists that before the Pueblo Revolt of 1680, at least some Pueblo lands were delineated and monumented, a fact recalled by village elders in later years. After the reconquest of New Mexico in the early 1690s, as Pueblos and their Hispano neighbors came into conflict over land, the practice of measuring a Pueblo league was recorded over and over again throughout the eighteenth and nineteenth centuries. From the outset, Pueblos were actively involved in measuring and monumenting their land. They participated in the process of verifying the accuracy of the cordel, measuring the land, and setting their own boundary markers. Pueblo Indians taught their children where the boundary monuments were, even hiding some of them underground so they could be found if the other, more visible markers were removed, as they sometimes were.

It is also now clear that Spanish authorities occasionally granted more land to Pueblo Indians, in small tracts between pueblos, for example, and in very large tracts as grazing grants. Such a picture emerges only because the Pueblo league was tested in court on numerous occasions, most often in the case of Pueblos trying to defend themselves against encroachment by their Hispano neighbors. Several pueblos were also able, even during the Spanish period, to enlarge their recognized landholdings through purchases of additional land from Hispano settlers.

In a remarkably short period of time, some Pueblos became adept at maneuvering within the Spanish system of land tenure, engaging with their Hispano neighbors in the business of buying and selling land under the rules of the Spanish legal system. In the main, Pueblos defined their ownership of the land as communal, so that no individual Indian could sell it, although there were occasional exceptions, some of which resulted in conflict between adjoining pueblos or with non-Indians. There can be no doubt that some Pueblos grasped the complexities of the Spanish and Mexican legal systems, and some, notably Cochiti, Santa Ana, and Santa Clara, went to extraordinary lengths to pursue justice. When the situation required it, Pueblo Indians traveled to Chihuahua, Durango, Guadalajara, and Mexico City to present their cases in courts of appeal in an effort to establish ownership of their Pueblo league or of land they purchased from Hispanos. Pueblos usually won these legal battles, especially when a protector of Indians represented them, but their victories won in courts of appeal were not always respected in New Mexico, and favorable rulings were not necessarily implemented. Encroaching Hispanos often flatly refused to leave Pueblo land, invoking the time-honored privilege accorded all Spanish citizens to obey but not comply with orders (*obedesco pero no cumplo*).

Under Mexican rule, the Pueblos faced new challenges as their land came under attack by Hispano settlers and government officials who asserted that the 1812 Cortes of Cadiz sanctioned privatization of "unused" Indian land within the Pueblo league. Pueblos again filed petitions with the government in Santa Fe or Mexico City and achieved legal victories that were not always respected in practice. To the extent that Mexican law conferred citizenship with equal rights to all Mexicans—including Indians—Pueblos found themselves in a dilemma. Mexican citizenship promised the Pueblos equal rights to those of their Hispano neighbors, but it also implied the loss of their status as wards of the state, which they enjoyed under Spanish rule. This meant, at least theoretically, that as citizens of Mexico, individual Indians could sell plots of land to non-Indians who wanted their irrigated fields. In this way, more non-Indian settlers found their way inside the limits of the Pueblo leagues as they purchased or claimed to have purchased land from individual Indians.

After the United States acquired New Mexico, settling the issue of land grants to Hispanos and Pueblos was given a priority, and government officials asked the Pueblos to bring in land-grant documents for examination. Some pueblos, Santa Ana in particular, had carefully guarded documents relating to their land acquisitions. Others did not. Although they had obtained a favorable ruling in 1815 in Mexico City in a suit about its Pueblo league, Santa Clara Pueblo officials did not submit the supporting documentation to the Surveyor General or the Court of Private Land Claims. Even when pueblos submitted documentation, it sometimes came to naught. Laguna (a pueblo we did not deal with in this book) went to great lengths to define and keep a written record of the lands it owned. In 1813 Alcalde José Manuel Aragón prepared a declaration at the pueblo's request listing the lands in addition to its pueblo league that were granted by New Mexico governors Chacón, Alencaster, Máynez, and Manrique during visits to Laguna in the early nineteenth century.[1] Governor Narbona approved the declaration in 1826, but it was rejected as evidence of the pueblo's ownership of land when the document was introduced in evidence in the Court of Private Land Claims. Thus, even though the pueblo obtained recognition from Spanish and Mexican government officials of land it purchased and used, the U.S. courts rejected the documentation. This may explain why more pueblos did not submit similar documents to the U.S. government officials.

In addition to rejecting some documents that pueblos submitted, government officials apparently made no attempt to examine the extensive documentation in the archives in Santa Fe that would have provided definitive proof that the practice in New Mexico during the Spanish and Mexican periods had been to grant each Pueblo at least four square leagues of land. This should have been readily apparent to researchers in the middle of the nineteenth century, just as it was to us. Rather than rely on the documentary record—the case law—available in the archives, U.S. officials accepted the Cruzate-grant documents as the legitimate basis for recommending congressional approval of Pueblo land claims.

The Pueblo Indians lost tens of thousands of acres of land to non-Indian encroachment for which they received compensation at less than market value by virtue of the Pueblo Lands Board decisions. Often they were poorly represented. Court decisions that determined whether they would receive government protection often turned on the old debate over whether they were civilized. As Emlen Hall aptly declared, "[In the sixteenth century] Indians had proved their humanity and had won crown protection for their lands. In the *Joseph* decision the court had rewarded their civilization by removing that protection. In the *Sandoval* appeal the Pueblo won back that protection only by proving their inferiority."[2] It seems that the more favorably the Pueblo Indians were portrayed in the courts, the less protection they received. But the Pueblo Indians rallied in the face of adversity. With the help of individuals such as John Collier, they organized to fight and defeat the Bursum bill, which would have legitimated non-Indian encroachment on Pueblo land. With the assistance of historians, anthropologists, and other experts the Pueblos have reclaimed sacred lands, with perhaps the best example being Taos Blue Lake, and secured the return of sacred objects such as the Jemez artifacts and Pecos human remains.

◆ ◆ ◆ ◆

Although we are finished with this volume, our pursuit of this story will continue. Malcolm Ebright will be publishing another volume on land grants with the University of New Mexico Press, which he is calling *Advocates for the Oppressed: Hispanos, Indians, Genízaros, and Their Land in New Mexico*, in the fall of 2014. Richard Hughes and Rick Hendricks are still on the trail of the crafters of the Cruzate-grant documents and hope to publish their findings in the near future.

In the course of the research for this book, we were privileged to be given access to a trove of documents—the earliest from 1709—preserved by the Pueblo of Santa Ana. These documents record the land purchases made by the pueblo, but they also provide a rare window into the past. The description of the 1763 Contreras purchase, with pueblo members lining up to pay for land with whatever livestock they had, is one of the most evocative accounts we have ever seen in a New Mexico colonial document. In a rather remarkable and unprecedented development, the pueblo recently agreed to place this documentary record on loan at the New Mexico State Records Center and Archives in Santa Fe. We can only hope that other pueblos will consider a similar arrangement.

This book is the story of land lost and land regained. It is also, more importantly, a story of Pueblo resilience and cultural survival in the face of repeated and persistent efforts by non-Indians to encroach on Pueblo land. Pueblo traditional practices and rituals, although diminished from the time before the arrival of the Spaniards, remain vital and important in the day-to-day lives of the people. This is very likely attributable, in large measure, to the fact that during more than four centuries of pervasive presence of non-Indians throughout their lands, the Pueblos have managed to retain control over much of their homeland, including their villages and fields. Today the Pueblos maintain one foot in the sacred world of their ancestors and the other in the modern world of U.S. law, commerce, and government, and in doing so they continue to protect their long-held and much-cherished land.

ACKNOWLEDGMENTS

An earlier version of chapter 1 appeared in volume 4 of *Ysleta del Sur Pueblo Archives* (El Paso, TX: Sundance Press, 2001). Funding for the research and writing of chapters 5, 6, and 7 was provided by grants from the New Mexico Historical Records Advisory Board.

Malcolm is grateful for the research and word-processing assistance of Margaret McGee. The authors wish to thank the staff of the University of New Mexico Press, especially W. Clark Whitehorn, editor-in-chief; Maya Allen-Gallegos, managing editor and production manager; James Ayers, production editor; and Zoya Lozoya, marketing associate. They also thank Beth Hadas, former director of the press. Finally, they thank their copyeditor, M. J. Devaney.

APPENDIX 1

Confirmed Pueblo Grants

Name of Pueblo	Cruzate Grant?	League or Natural Monuments?	When Submitted to Surveyor General	When Confirmed	Acres Confirmed
Acoma	Yes	Natural	23 Oct. 1855 or 3 Mar. 1856	22 Dec. 1858	95,792
Cochiti	Yes	League and natural	12 Mar. 1856	22 Dec. 1858	24,256
Isleta	No	League and natural	8 Nov. 1856	22 Dec. 1858	110,080
Jemez	Yes	League	14 Sept. 1855	22 Dec. 1858	17,510
Laguna	Yes	Natural	29 June 1857	Cruzate grant rejected; CPLC confirmed league grant, 2 Oct. 1897	17,329
Nambe	No	League	29 Sept. 1856	22 Dec. 1858	13,586
Ohkay Owingeh (San Juan)	Yes	League and natural	18 Aug. 1855	22 Dec. 1858	17,546
Pecos	Yes	League	14 Sept. 1855	22 Dec. 1858	18,763
Picuris	Yes	League	2 June 1856	22 Dec. 1858	17,461
Pojoaque	No	League	28 June 1856	22 Dec. 1858	13,520
Sandia	No (Cruzate grant not submitted)	Natural	16 Oct. 1856	22 Dec. 1858	24,187
San Felipe	Yes	League and natural	18 Feb. 1856	22 Dec. 1858	34,767
San Ildefonso	No	League	16 June 1856	22 Dec. 1858	17,293
Santa Ana	No	League	3 Oct. 1866	9 Feb. 1869	17,361
Santa Clara	No	League	16 June 1856	22 Dec. 1858	17,369
Santo Domingo	Yes	Natural	12 Mar. 1856	22 Dec. 1858	92,398
Taos	No	League	2 Aug. 1856	22 Dec. 1858	17,361
Tesuque	No	League	14 June 1856	22 Dec. 1858	17,471
Zia	Yes	League	16 Oct. 1856	22 Dec. 1858	17,515
Zuni	Yes	League	3 Jul. 1875	3 Mar. 1931	17,636

APPENDIX 2

Documents Relating to the New Mexico Pueblo League

Date	Source	Summary
1687	Borah, *Justice by Insurance*, 136	The *fondo legal* (minimum endowment of land for an Indian village) in central New Spain was 600 varas in four directions measured from the outermost house in the town (cedula of 4 June 1687). Spaniards complained that Indians extended their boundaries by building new houses in the fields, so a new cedula established the fondo legal as 600 varas measured from the church in the center of the town (cedula of 12 July 1695).
1693	Kessell and Hendricks, *By Force of Arms*, 386	When Vargas found La Ciénega Pueblo abandoned he ordered that "should some Keres Indians return to settle there, they will be limited to 500 varas from the door of the church in the four directions and no more."
1697	Kessell, Hendricks, Dodge, and Miller, *That Disturbances Cease*, 85	Lázaro de Mizquía's proposals to reorganize New Mexico (which were not adopted) "provide [that] each pueblo will be given one league in length."
1704	SANM I:78	Petition for lands adjacent to San Felipe. Protector of Indians Alfonso Rael de Aguilar objects to the petition, referring to the Pueblo league as "granted by royal law to the Pueblo Indians."
1704	SANM I:1339	*Ignacio Roybal v. San Ildefonso*. Rael de Aguilar argues that San Ildefonso is entitled to four square leagues, and acting Governor Páez Hurtado orders Alcalde Cristóbal Arellano to measure a league in each direction from the center of the pueblo.
1716	SANM I:500	Petition by Antonio Montoya for the sobras (excess lands) between the pueblos of Santo Domingo and San Felipe. Alcalde Manuel Baca reported that the Indians wanted their league measured so they would know what belonged to them.
1722	SANM I:1343	Proceedings concerning land between Santo Domingo and Cochiti. Rael de Aguilar (no longer serving as protector of Indians) measures 5,000 varas from the cemeteries of the church of each pueblo.
1724	SANM I:1344	Land between Santa Clara and San Ildefonso. Juan Páez Hurtado investigates claim of Mateo Trujillo.

Table continued

Date	Source	Summary
1734	SANM I:1345	Baltazar Romero petitions to sell Spanish lands in the Bernalillo area to Santa Ana Pueblo; Governor Cruzat y Góngora denies the request, maintaining that lands should be sold to Hispanos, not Indians.
1736	SANM I:1039	José de Riaño asks for measurement of the lands of Santa Clara and San Ildefonso so he can see where his lands between the two pueblos are. Governor Cruzat y Góngora appoints Juan Páez Hurtado to measure the two leagues. Although these measurements from the center of the pueblo to the Riaño land fall short of a full league, Páez Hurtado claims that Riaño has 84 varas between the pueblos.
1744	SANM I:213	Roque Canjuebes receives a grant from Spanish authorities of land within the Santa Clara Pueblo league, without objection from pueblo officials, according to Alcalde Francisco Ortiz (see 1815 for appeal).
1748	SANM I:531	Fray Juan Miguel Menchero asks Governor Codallos y Rabal to authorize property confiscated from Pueblo Indians charged with a crime to be paid to him so he can improve the church at Sandia and thereby settle the Hopis there, who are scattered among the different pueblos.
1748	SANM I:848; SANM I:347	Sandia grant is made by Governor Codallos y Rabal of abandoned pueblo of Sandia to Indians living at Hopi. Governor orders Alcalde Bustamante Tagle to examine the site and allot "the lands, waters, pastures, and watering places which pertain to a formal pueblo of Indians." Litigation subsequently ensues in the Spanish and Mexican periods over the northern and southern boundaries (SANM 1:1375) and in the American period over the eastern boundary Sandia Peak.
1754	Abiquiu grant, PLC 52 38/884	Vélez Cachupín makes grant to Genízaro Pueblo of Abiquiu citing *Recopilación* 6-3-8. The governor himself measured from the center of the pueblo, 5,000 varas to the south, 2,400 varas to the north, 2,550 varas to the east, and 2,550 varas to the west, and an ejido of a league for grazing south of the pueblo.
1763–1764	SANM I:1351	Measurement of San Ildefonso's league in light of possible encroachment by Francisco Gómez del Castillo and the heirs of Juana Luján. Carlos Fernández cites several cases upholding the right of a pueblo to four square leagues, and Governor Vélez Cachupín orders the alcalde to measure San Ildefonso's league.
1765	SANM I:1269	Petition for land adjacent to Jemez. Sánchez Vergara says the grant would not prejudice "the Indian league of the Pueblo of Jemez."

Date	Source	Summary
1770	SANM I:1376	Santo Domingo and San Felipe request a grant of the land between them, which is the surplus of each pueblo. Governor Mendinueta makes the grant. Bartolomé Fernández places the pueblos in possession of the grant, measuring the league, which belongs to each one of the pueblos, dividing the excess land between the Pueblo leagues equally, and placing landmarks on the boundary.
1776	Adams and Chávez, *Missions of New Mexico*, 89–90	The lands of San Juan "extend for a league above the pueblo and a league below it, and the same distance along the other bank," according to fray Francisco Atanasio Domínguez.
1786	SANM I:1354	Measurement of the Pueblo leagues of Santa Clara and San Ildefonso. Alcalde Carlos Fernández argues that the "league[s] which the king our lord . . . grants to each pueblo" should be measured.
1808	SANM I:1269	Ignacio Sánchez Vergara, alcalde of Jemez, forwards a petition for land adjacent to Jemez to Governor Máynez recommending that the grant be made, although the settlers at Vallecito[s] object. Sánchez Vergara tells Máynez that the grant "does not harm, in any way, the Indian league of the Pueblo of Jemez."
1812	SANM I:1355	The sale of land at Jemez is illegal because it "belongs to the league which they have by grant which they ask shall be measured." Protector of Indians Felipe Sandoval presents to Governor Manrique a protest by Jemez against a sale to Alcalde Antonio Armenta, made by an Indian named Cumpa, of land which "belongs to the league, which they have by grant." The pueblo does not consent to this sale and offers to return the purchase price to Armenta. Governor Manrique forwards the petition to Rafael Bracho, the assesor in Chihuahua.
1813	SANM I:1234; SANM I:1356	*Santa Ana v. San Felipe* (dispute over land at Angostura). Purchasers, who bought land from San Felipe that was determined to be owned by Santa Ana, were given land at Las Lemitas, measured from the boundary line of the league of the Santa Ana Pueblo.
1815	SANM I:1280	Bernardo Bonavía at Durango to governor of New Mexico about lands claimed by Roque Canjuebes's grandson Antonio within "lands ceded by his majesty to the pueblo of Santa Clara." Roque Canjuebes received a grant within Santa Clara's league and was emancipated from the pueblo. Bonavía decided that Canjuebes could not leave Santa Clara and still own land there.

Table continued

Date	Source	Summary
1815	SANM I:1357	Dispute between Taos Pueblo and its Hispano neighbors. Governor Alberto Máynez decrees that the pueblo's "right to the league which his majesty has granted them is incontestable."
1816	SANM I:668	*Juan Pino v. Laguna* (dispute over occupation of land at El Rillito). The pueblo needs the land because "to confine themselves to their league is impossible for [it contains] only sandy ground."
1817	SANM I:1361	Decree of the Audiencia in Guadalajara nullifying the sale of the Peña Blanca rancho located within the Cochiti league.
1821	SANM I:1195	Ignacio María Sánchez Vergara asks Governor Melgares whether he could petition the ayuntamiento for a grant of land "in the lower part of the league of the Pueblo of Sandia." Melgares says he can see no obstacle to granting the request.
1821 21 Apr.	SANM I:1133	Proclamation of the 1813 decree of the Spanish Cortes ordering the privatization of up to half of the common lands, except the necessary ejidos of towns. (This would later be applied to Indian pueblos.)
1821 11 Oct.	SANM I:1367	San Juan complains to the commanding general in Chihuahua about a proclamation stating that lands of the pueblos should be decreased. San Juan says its land "is so little that it does not make a league in any direction [unlike] other pueblos who own a full league."
1823	SANM I:896	Six soldiers from the presidio request a grant between Santo Domingo and San Felipe of the surplus land of the leagues of each pueblo. Governor Bartolomé Baca refers the matter to provincial deputation for decision, despite the earlier grant to both pueblos.
1824 14 Feb.	SANM I:134	Manuel Baca, Santiago Abréu, and two others also request land between the Pueblo leagues of Santo Domingo and San Felipe. Governor Baca refers the petition to the territorial deputation.
1824 14 Feb.	SANM I:1065	Ignacio María Sánchez Vergara also asks Governor Baca for a grant between the leagues of the pueblos of Santo Domingo and San Felipe. Governor Baca refers the matter to the provincial deputation for decision.

Date	Source	Summary
1825	SANM I:807	Miguel Ribera and five others request a grant within Pecos's Pueblo league. In their first petition, which was granted, they asked for adjacent lands but this was ignored by the pueblo, which sold the lands. The dispute is referred to the territorial deputation, which characterizes the land as "the ejidos of the Pecos Pueblo, now uncultivated."
1829	SANM I:1375	*Sánchez Vergara v. Sandia*. Contains testimony that Sánchez Vergara altered the boundaries of the Sandia grant to the north, south, and west.
1829–1831	SANM I:1374	Mariano Rodríguez, for himself and on behalf of the Indians of Picuris, protests against granting of lands within the Pueblo league to Rafael Fernández and Miguel González.
1830	SANM I:1369	José María Paredes, Mexico, communication to Ramón Abreu, secretary of the provincial deputation, regarding the lands granted to Domingo Fernández and the counterclaim made by Pecos Pueblo.
1844	SANM I:1380	Miguel Antonio Lobato, on behalf of Santo Domingo Pueblo, requests measurement of their Pueblo league. Governor Mariano Martínez approves.

ABBREVIATIONS

AASF	Archives of the Archdiocese of Santa Fe
AGI	Archivo General de Indias
AGN	Archivo General de la Nación
AHAD	Archivos Históricos del Arzobispado de Durango
ARAG	Real Audiencia de Guadalajara, Biblioteca del Estado de Jalisco
BLM	Bureau of Land Management
BNM	Biblioteca Nacional de México
JSC	Julius Seligman Collection
MANM	Mexican Archives of New Mexico
NARA	National Records and Archive Administration
PLC	Records of the Court of Private Land Claims
SA	Santa Ana Land Documents
SANM	Spanish Archives of New Mexico
SG	Records of the Office of the Surveyor General
SRCA	New Mexico State Records Center and Archives
TBL	The Bancroft Library

NOTES

Preface

1. Hall, "Pueblo Grant Labyrinth," 127.
2. Ibid. Among the important books dealing with Pueblo land are Hall, *Four Leagues of Pecos*, Minge, *Acoma*, and Sando, *Nee Hemish*. See also Brayer, *Pueblo Indian Land Grants of the "Rio Abajo," New Mexico*.
3. Hall, "Pueblo Grant Labyrinth," 126.
4. Baxter, *Spanish Irrigation in Taos Valley*; Baxter, *Spanish Irrigation in the Pojoaque and Tesuque Valleys During the Eighteenth and Early Nineteenth Centuries*; Tyler, "Land and Water Tenure in New Mexico"; Meyer and Deeds, "Land, Water, and Equity in Spanish Colonial and Mexican Law."
5. Levine, *Our Prayers Are in this Place*, xvi.
6. Eusebio Mairo to Felipe Sandoval, petition, Santa Ana, 5 May 1813, SANM I:1356.

Introduction

1. Oñate conducted a ceremony of taking possession of all of New Mexico for the king of Spain on 30 April 1598 at a place a few miles south of present-day El Paso. In 1598 there were many more pueblos in New Mexico than today—at least forty-six and possibly as many as eighty-one (Hammond and Rey, *Don Juan de Oñate*, 16; Barrett, *Conquest and Catastrophe*, 55–58; Sando, *Pueblo Nations*, x, 274, 275).
2. Land and agriculture were central to Pueblo religion. "To Pueblo people, large harvests of corn . . . stand as irrefutable evidence that the movement of life energy, as it flows between the natural and supernatural worlds of their cosmos, is unimpeded. In this sense, agricultural work stands as the day-to-day practice of Pueblo religion" (Anschuetz, "Not Waiting for Rain," 10). See also Riley, *Kachina and the Cross*, 77; Sando, *Nee Hemish*, 15–17; Gutiérrez, *When Jesus Came the Corn Mothers Went Away*, 103.
3. Enote, introduction to *Mapping Our Places*. On a hill in the Valley of Sonora, there is a petroglyph map showing landholdings and irrigation patterns in the valley below (Gortner, "Evidence for a Prehistoric Petroglyph Trail Map in the Sierra Nevada"; Doolittle, *Pre-Hispanic Occupancy in the Valley of Sonora, Mexico*; Montgomery, "Corn Shrine of the Tanos").
4. Enote, introduction to *Mapping Our Places*, 12; Scott, Warren, Enote, et al., *Mapping Our Places*, 71.
5. Prechtel, *Toe Bone and the Tooth*, xii–xvi.

6. Seed, *Ceremonies of Possession*, 2-15.
7. A pueblo's land and the people, cattle, and crops raised on it were often subject to raids by nomadic tribes such as the Utes, Navajos, Jicarilla Apaches, and especially the Comanches (Forbes, *Apache, Navajo, and Spaniard*, 270, 281-85; Ortiz, *A Tewa World*, 20-23).
8. The Zunis have mapped their traditional plant and mineral collection areas, their hunting and grazing areas, and their agriculture and religious-use areas (Ferguson and Hart, *A Zuni Atlas*, 37-51).
9. Walker, "American Indian Sacred Geography," vil, cited in Gulliford, *Sacred Objects and Sacred Places*, vii.
10. Seed, *Ceremonies of Possession*, 95.
11. Ibid., 70. Seed analyzes the background of this ritual of speech known as the requerimiento (requirement) and goes back to the presence of Islam in Spain, showing the influence (although not completely direct) of Islam in the requirement to prove her point that this ritual was the sole province of the Spanish. See also Seed, "Taking Possession and Reading Texts." For a different interpretation of this topic, specifically related to the Ordinances of Discovery of 1573 and their shared origins with other European nations, see Herzog, "La política espacial y las tácticas de conquista."
12. Todorov, *Conquest of America*, 147.
13. Ibid., 148.
14. For the requerimiento at Santo Domingo and other pueblos, see Hammond and Rey, *Don Juan de Oñate*, 1:337-62.
15. Weber, *Spanish Frontier*, 125.
16. Juan Manso, inventory, Santa Fe, 4 May, 1662, AGN, Tierras, 3268, and Pedro Lucero de Godoy, statement, Pecos, 29 June 1663, AGN, Tierras, 3268, cited in Kessell, *Kiva, Cross, and Crown*, 186-88.
17. Weber, *Spanish Frontier*, 410n12. Weber notes that Scholes states that the number of encomiendas was limited in 1639 but that he provides no source. Weber's reading of the trial of Governor Diego de Peñalosa (1661-1664) suggests that the limit was placed on the number of encomiendas in New Mexico between 1640 and 1642.
18. The Hispano population of New Mexico in 1660, including individuals of mixed blood, was approximately 2,500 (Scholes, "Civil Government and Society," 96).
19. Barrett, *Spanish Colonial Settlement*, 70-71. Paul Kraemer concluded that by 1675 there were more than a hundred estancias that "can be identified by location and family name, and indeed by this time every pueblo was completely blanketed by Spanish estancias" (Kraemer, *Perfect Crystals*, 67, 71n8).
20. Barrett, *Spanish Colonial Settlement*, 26.
21. Certain Indians, such as unmarried men and widows, might have been exempt from paying encomienda tribute. Governor Alonso Pacheco (1642-1644) calculated tribute on a per capita basis, which was impractical in such a poor province (Scholes, *Troublous Times in New Mexico*, 91).

22. Many of the encomenderos also received one fanega of corn per year, worth four reales. Hence the total values of the encomienda payments may have been ten to twelve reales per year per household. New Mexico encomenderos were generally far more interested in obtaining shawls, skins, and other articles of trade through their encomienda tribute (Hackett, *Historical Documents*, 3:110).
23. Lockhart, "Encomienda and Hacienda," 416.
24. Ebright, *Advocates for the Oppressed*, chap. 5.
25. Weber, *Spanish Frontier*, 125.
26. Scholes, *Troublous Times in New Mexico*, 41.
27. After his untimely death in 1704, Vargas's four thousand–peso encomienda was converted into a pension for his daughter (Kessell, *Remote Beyond Compare*, 68–69, 119n158, 263–74, 210n4; Gerhard, *North Frontier of New Spain*, 316).
28. Snow, "Note on Encomienda Economics"; Weber, *Spanish Frontier*, 410n12.
29. John, *Storms Brewed*, 149.
30. Brown, *Pueblo Indians*, 77.
31. Kessell, Hendricks, and Dodge, *Blood on the Boulders*, 44, 70, 73, 823, 912, 989.
32. Kessell, Hendricks, Dodge, and Miller, *Settling of Accounts*, 92.
33. Carlos Fernández to Juan Bautista de Anza, petition, Santa Fe, [May] 1786, SANM I:1354; petition of San Juan objecting to the diminishment of their land and to payment of tithes, San Juan, n.d., SANM I:1367; Fernández, [29] May 1786, SANM I:1354. Although the San Juan petition is undated, the response to the petition is dated 11 October 1821.
34. "La legua de cinco mil varas medidas desde la cruz del cementerio para todos rumbos, que su majestad hizo merced a cada pueblo de indios desde el principio de su establecimiento es para que se conserve para mantenerse los hijos de él de modo que tienen el uso y no pueden dar ni vender sin licencia del rey por ser patrimonio o mayorazgo que ningún juez ni gobernador tiene facultad para vender parte ni el todo de la citada legua" (Alberto Máynez, decree, Santa Fe, 15 Apr. 1815, SANM I:1357).
35. Hall, "Pueblo Grant Labyrinth," 67–138, 97; Hall, *Four Leagues of Pecos*, 82.

Chapter 1

1. An example of a vara from New Mexico that was used between 1835 and 1846 is in the Museum of New Mexico. It is a heavy oak stick and measures 33.07 inches (Boyd, "Vara," 46; Tórrez, "Vara"). New Mexico surveyor general William Pelham examined varas in use in New Mexico and found them to be very uniform but varying in length from 32.3 to 33.3 inches. He accepted the California definition of 33 inches.
2. On standard maps of New Mexico that depict Indian lands, the squares that demarcate many pueblos' lands represent U.S. surveys of the Pueblo league. The areas of these surveys typically varied from the norm because of surveying errors, topography, neighboring grants, and other factors.

3. Cutter agrees that both the rationale and the date of origin of the league entitlement in New Mexico "remains hazy," but he acknowledges that it was established by the early eighteenth century (*Legal Culture of Northern New Spain*, 38).
4. Taylor, "Colonial Land and Water Rights," 18–19.
5. Wagner, *Life and Writings of Bartolomé de las Casas*, 178–82; Hanke, *Spanish Struggle for Justice*; Las Casas, *In Defense of the Indians*; Las Casas, *Tears of the Indians*.
6. The New Laws of 1542 were the first laws adopted to protect Indians in New Spain. They provided for Indian slaves to be set free and for advocates to be named for the Indians at royal expense. But Spanish colonists and religious alike fiercely resisted the laws, and they were repealed in 1545. Las Casas returned to Spain and spent the rest of his life advising King Charles V on matters related to the native peoples of the Indies (Wagner, *Life and Writings of Bartolomé de las Casas*, 114–16; Las Casas, *Devastation of the Indies*).
7. See "Disposiciones sobre fundo legal y ejidos de los pueblos."
8. Borah, *Justice by Insurance*, 136–37.
9. Gibson believed that nineteenth-century lawyers coined the term "fundo legal" (*Aztecs Under Spanish Rule*, 285). The term is found in Audiencia of Guadalajara, decree regarding Cochiti, Guadalajara, 16 Jan. 1817, SANM I:1361.
10. *Xocotipac Province of Teposcolula vs. don Manuel Dionisio Güenduláin, vecino of Oaxaca*, Mexico City, 28 Feb. 1800, cited in Borah, *Justice by Insurance*, 137–38. See also Hall, *Four Leagues of Pecos*, 72–73, and Kessell, Hendricks, and Dodge, *To the Royal Crown Restored*, 125–26n15. According to William Taylor's study of land in colonial Oaxaca, Indian villages fought more with each other over land than with Spaniards; see *Landlord and Peasant in Colonial Oaxaca*, 83–89, 108–9.
11. Simmons, "Primer on Rope-Making."
12. Hall describes his own fairly excruciating experience measuring the Pecos league in 1980, with a ten-year-old boy, using a 100-vara-long rope (*Four Leagues of Pecos*, xiii–xvii).
13. Chardon, "Elusive Spanish League," 294–95, 299; Galván Rivera, *Ordenanzas de tierras y aguas*, 157–58.
14. Barrett, "*Jugerum* and *Caballería* in New Spain," 424; Perez, "Locating the Ysleta Grant," maps 368a–b.
15. For a succinct account of the problem Vargas faced as he tried to recolonize New Mexico, see Kessell, Hendricks, and Dodge, *Blood on the Boulders*, 1:603–4.
16. Diego de Vargas to the Conde de Galve, El Paso, 12 Jan. 1693, cited in Kessell, Hendricks, and Dodge, *To the Royal Crown Restored*, 111.
17. Greenleaf, "Land and Water in Mexico and New Mexico," 94.
18. "una legua de largo a cada pueblo" (Kessell, Hendricks, Dodge, and Miller, *That Disturbances Cease*, 85).
19. "un ejido de una legua de largo" (*Recopilación* 6-3-8).
20. "pasé a medir la legua que según ordenanzas y leyes reales goza cada pueblo.

Y echando cordeles se midieron treinta de a cien pasos que hace tres mil más otros seiscientos pasos que la parte les dio a dichos indios de Cochití a petición suya" (Diego Montoya and Juana Baca, granting of possession, Cochiti, 22 Feb. 1703, ARAG, Ramo Civil 261-15, folder 51, 1818, f. 26–28). When measured by paces, a league equaled three *millas* (a Roman mile), each of which was one thousand paces (Barrett, "*Jugerum* and *Caballería*," 432; Galván Rivera, *Ordenanzas de tierras y aguas*, 157–58).

21. "tienen más de lo que manda la ley y no es razón . . . [que] nosotros no tengamos nada" (Cristóbal and Juan Varela Jaramillo to Diego de Vargas, petition, Bernalillo, Feb. 1704, SANM I:78).
22. "desde su fundación" (Alfonso Rael de Aguilar, report, San Felipe, 23 Feb. 1704, SANM I:78).
23. "tiene concedido por ley real a los pueblos de dichos naturales" (Alfonso Rael de Aguilar to Diego de Vargas, San Felipe, 23 Feb. 1704, SANM I:78). Hall suggests that until the mid-1700s the Pueblo league was simply a means of assuring that Spanish and Pueblo settlements were adequately separated rather than serving to demarcate an area owned by the Pueblos (*Four Leagues of Pecos*, 13). But Rael de Aguilar clearly understood, as had Diego Montoya in the Cochiti–Juana Baca matter the previous year, the Pueblo league to be an area granted to and thus owned by the pueblo, not just a buffer zone.
24. "dicha legua es y se entiende en la circunvalación de dicho pueblo. Esta no se le puede dar al dicho pueblo de San Felipe por la parte del poniente por estar la mesa inmediata al dicho pueblo con que precisamente se le ha de agregar todas las cuatro leguas por donde les fuere de más conveniencia a dichos naturales" (Rael de Aguilar to Vargas, SANM I:78).
25. The protector of Indians was a Spanish official appointed to advocate on behalf of Christianized Indians in New Spain, including the Pueblo Indians of New Mexico. The position was created largely as the result of the advocacy of Bartolomé de las Casas, and he was the first person appointed to the post in New Spain. A protector served in New Mexico beginning in the mid-1600s, but in 1717 the office became vacant and remained so until the end of the first decade of the nineteenth century (Cutter, *Protector de Indios*; Borah, *Justice by Insurance*; Ebright, "Advocates for the Oppressed").
26. Diego de Vargas to Ignacio Roybal, land grant, Santa Fe, 4 Mar. 1704, SANM I:1339. This rather summary procedure was common in the early 1700s.
27. *San Ildefonso v. Ignacio Roybal*, San Ildefonso, Sept. 1704, SANM I:1339.
28. "los nueve pregones en el término de nueve días" (Alfonso Rael de Aguilar on behalf of San Ildefonso to Juan Páez Hurtado, petition, Santa Fe, 16 Sept. 1704, SANM I:1339).
29. Rael de Aguilar on behalf of San Ildefonso to Páez Hurtado, petition, SANM I:1339; Diego de Vargas to Ignacio Roybal, land grant, Santa Fe, 4 Mar. 1704, SANM I:1339.

30. Rael de Aguilar on behalf of San Ildefonso to Páez Hurtado, petition, SANM I:1339; *Recopilación* 4-12-12 and 6-3-20 (Spanish ranches not to be located near Indian communities) and 4-7-1 (Spanish communities not to be established where Indians' rights would be prejudiced).
31. "la suya según la voluntad de su majestad" (Rael de Aguilar on behalf of San Ildefonso to Páez Hurtado, petition, SANM I:1339).
32. Juan Páez Hurtado, order, Santa Fe, Sept. 1704, SANM I:1339.
33. Páez Hurtado, order, SANM I:1339. One of Vargas's trusted lieutenants, Páez Hurtado served as acting governor following Vargas's abbreviated second term. He supervised the settlement of Santa Cruz de la Cañada in 1695 and filled various important posts in government service. He had two more stints as interim governor, in 1717 and again in 1724 (Kessell and Hendricks, *By Force of Arms*, 300n3; Kessell, Hendricks, and Dodge, *Blood on the Boulders*, 1:450n67).
34. "por no haber tierra de labor en que apuntar por todos vientos la legua que es lo que dicen los naturales piden y no montes, lomas, ni aún de [adonde] no se pueda sembrar" (Cristóbal de Arellano, measurement, San Ildefonso, 9 Oct. 1704, SANM I:1339).
35. "los primeros españoles y justicias señalarnoslos por nuestros" (San Ildefonso, petition for reconsideration, Santa Fe, 28 Sept. 1704, SANM I:1339).
36. San Ildefonso, petition for reconsideration, SANM I:1339.
37. "las cuatro leguas por cada viento la suya según la voluntad de su majestad, amojonándose el dicho pueblo de San Ildefonso con cuya diligencia cesaran disputas y pleitos" (Rael de Aguilar on behalf of San Ildefonso to Páez Hurtado, petition, SANM I:1339).
38. For a list of many of the cases in which the four-square-league concept is mentioned in the Spanish archives of New Mexico, see Taylor, "Colonial Land and Water Rights," 44. Cutter argues that "it was the repeated insistence that Spaniards live up to the 'rules of the game' that helped inscribe this territorial dimension as the norm in New Mexico" (*Legal Culture of Northern New Spain*, 38–39).
39. Kessell, *Kiva, Cross, and Crown*, 303–4.
40. Francisco Cuervo y Valdés, decree, Santa Fe, 25 Aug. 1705, SANM I:1340.
41. Antonio Montoya, petition, Bernalillo, n.d., SANM I:500.
42. Félix Martínez, order, Santa Fe, 8 Mar. 1716, SANM I:500.
43. Manuel Baca, report, 13 Mar. 1716, SANM I:500. At the time, Santo Domingo was located on the Río Galisteo, half a mile or so north and about 3 miles east of where it sits today. That village, called Guypuy, was destroyed by a flood later in the 1700s, and the pueblo rebuilt its village along the Rio Grande (Twitchell, *Spanish Archives of New Mexico*, 1:472).
44. Diego Montoya and Juana Baca, granting of possession, Cochiti, 22 Feb. 1703, ARAG, Ramo Civil 261-15, folder 51, 1818, f. 26–28.
45. Alfonso Rael de Aguilar, report, Santo Domingo, 8 June 1722, SANM I:1343.
46. Like the 1704 San Felipe case, this one is entirely in Rael de Aguilar's handwriting, except for the petition (Rael de Aguilar, report, SANM I:1343).

47. Alfonso Rael de Aguilar, declaratory judgment, Santo Domingo Pueblo, 8 June 1722, SANM I:500. To be sure, the records of this adjudication were not presented to the U.S. surveyor general, and thus, under U.S. rule, Cochiti and Santo Domingo lost the additional land that Rael de Aguilar awarded to them.
48. Felipe de Sandoval, 17 Mar. 1815, ARAG, Ramo Civil 261-15.
49. Juan José Gutiérrez, measurement of land, Santo Domingo, 19 Apr. 1815, ARAG, Ramo Civil 261-15, f. 8–9; Antonio Ortiz to the commanding general in Durango, Santa Fe, 4 Sept. 1815, ARAG, Ramo Civil 261-15, f. 12–14.
50. "como lo manifiesta una acequia que está en dicho sitio" (Juan Páez Hurtado to Juan Domingo de Bustamante, Santa Cruz de la Cañada, 10 June 1724, SANM I:1344).
51. Páez Hurtado to Bustamante, SANM I:1344.
52. José Riaño's importance and wealth can be measured by the size of his estate when he died in 1743. The inventory showed his assets, which included a house and lands at El Álamo valued at two thousand pesos, to amount to some twenty-one thousand pesos (José Riaño Tagle, will and estate inventory, Santa Fe, 1743, SANM I:963–94; Joaquín Codallos y Rabal, administration of the estate of José Riaño, Santa Fe, 1744, SANM I:762).
53. "presenten los instrumentos que tienen para el reconocimiento de su pertenencia" (José Riaño to Gervasio Cruzat y Góngora, petition, Santa Fe, [Mar. 1736], SANM I:1039).
54. "pidiendo se midan las dos leguas que pertenecen a los dos pueblos de San Ildefonso y de Santa Clara una legua por cada pueblo" (Gervasio Cruzat y Góngora, order, Santa Fe, 15 Mar. 1736, SANM I:1039).
55. Juan Páez Hurtado, measurement of Pueblo leagues, Santa Clara, 17 Mar. 1736, SANM I:1039.
56. Gervasio Cruzat y Góngora, decree, Santa Fe, 18 Mar. 1736, SANM I:1039.
57. Inventory of documents in government archives, Santa Fe, 20 Nov. 1736, SANM I:1159.
58. Joaquín Codallos y Rabal, decree related to the Sandia grant, Santa Fe, 5 Apr. 1748, SANM I:848.
59. Joaquín Codallas y Rabal, order, Santa Fe, 13 Mar. 1748, SANM I:28.
60. Tomás Vélez Cachupín, decree and act of possession, Abiquiu, 10 May 1754, PLC 52, r. 38, f. 889–907; Abiquiu grant, SG 140, r. 26, f. 279.
61. Ebright and Hendricks, *Witches of Abiquiu*, 89–105.
62. Tafoya alleged that San Ildefonso had suffered intrusions within its boundaries since the administration of Governor Rodríguez Cubero (petition, Santa Fe, Feb. 1763, SANM I:1351).
63. "sin admitirle el más leve recurso" (Tomás Vélez Cachupín, order, Santa Fe, 4 Feb. 1763, SANM I:1351).
64. Vélez Cachupín, order, SANM I:1351.
65. Measurement of the Pueblo leagues of Santa Clara and San Ildefonso, Santa Clara and San Ildefonso, May–June 1786, SANM I:1354.

66. "la legua que según ley deben tener los pueblos por cada viento" (Juan Gómez Castillo, statement, 28 Feb. 1763, SANM I:1351).
67. Gómez del Castillo, statement, SANM I:1351.
68. "sin abrir la puerta a muchos ejemplares que resultaran a los demás pueblos en iguales términos" (Fernando de Torija y Leri, opinion, Chihuahua, 27 Oct. 1764, SANM I:1351).
69. Tomás Vélez Cachupín, order, Santa Fe, 12 Nov. 1763, SANM I:1351.
70. "la legua que el rey nuestro señor ... concede a cada pueblo" (Carlos Fernández to Juan Bautista de Anza, petition, Santa Fe, [May] 1786, SANM I:1354). It was not true that Santa Clara's league was never measured. The records of the José Riaño dispute show that both pueblos' leagues were measured in 1736 (Páez Hurtado, measurement of Pueblo leagues, Santa Clara, SANM I:1039).
71. "un cordel encerado que contenga cien varas" (Juan Bautista de Anza, order, Santa Fe, 6 May 1786, SANM I:1354).
72. Anza, order, SANM I:1354.
73. José Campo Redondo, measurement proceedings, Santa Clara, 10 May 1786, SANM I:1354; Juan Bautista de Anza to Carlos Fernández, referral, Santa Fe, 13 May 1786, SANM I:1354.
74. Carlos Fernández, statement, Santa Fe, 13 May 1786, SANM I:1354.
75. Marcos Lucero, statement, [18] May 1786, SANM I:1354.
76. Juan Bautista de Anza, order, Santa Fe, 19 May 1786, SANM I:1354.
77. "por el encerado no da de sí, y el no encerado da mucho" (José Campo Redondo, measurement, Santa Clara, 23 May 1786, SANM 1:1354).
78. Juan Bautista de Anza, decree, Santa Fe, 10 June 1786, SANM I:1354. It might be recalled that when the San Ildefonso and Santa Clara leagues were measured in 1736, at the request of José Riaño, the gap between the two was 84 varas (Juan Páez Hurtado, measurement of Pueblo leagues, Santa Clara, 17 Mar. 1736, SANM I:1039).
79. This is evidence that there was a copy of the *Recopilación* in New Mexico at this time, for Anza refers to his "having before me the royal laws" (decree, Santa Fe, 10 June 1786, SANM I:1354).
80. *Recopilación* 6-3-8; Anza, decree, SANM I:1354.
81. Anza, decree, SANM I:1354.
82. Carlos Fernández, statement, [29] May 1786, SANM I:1354.
83. Marcos Lucero, statement, [Santa Fe], [2] June 1786, SANM I:1354.
84. Santiago Fernández de la Pedrera, petition on behalf of Santo Domingo and San Felipe, 1770, Pueblo of Santo Domingo, SG Report H, r. 7, f. 110 (trans. David Miller).
85. Fernández de la Pedrera, petition on behalf of Santo Domingo and San Felipe, 1770, Pueblo of Santo Domingo, SG Report H, r. 7, f. 110.
86. Fernández de la Pedrera, petition on behalf of Santo Domingo and San Felipe, 1770, Pueblo of Santo Domingo, SG Report H, r. 7, f. 111.
87. Antonio Caballero, petition on behalf of Santo Domingo Pueblo, 14 Aug. 1808,

SANM 1:1232. A copy of this letter was submitted by the pueblo to the surveyor general in 1856, along with several other documents (including the pueblo's Cruzate grant; see chapter 7). One of those documents was a 1748 deed by which the pueblo purchased a large tract of land granted in 1730 to Diego Gallegos. (A copy of the grant was also included in the documents the pueblo submitted to the surveyor general.) Santo Domingo bought the grant from Gallegos's widow, Maria Josefa Gutiérrez, for four hundred pesos. Its eastern boundary was described as "the lands of the Pueblo of Santo Domingo," presumably referring to the pueblo's league (Pueblo of Santo Domingo, SG Report H, r. 7, ff. 120–25, 128–35). See Jenkins, "Title of the Pueblo of Santo Domingo to the Diego Gallegos Land Grant." The surveyor general, however, ignored all the Santo Domingo documents except the Cruzate grant. Twitchell mistakenly identified the lands referred to in Caballero's letter as the Cañada de Cochití grant, which was made to Antonio Lucero in 1728 and was confirmed by the Court of Private Land Claims in 1898 (Twitchell, *Spanish Archives of New Mexico*, 1:357). Brayer, probably relying on Twitchell, made the same mistake (*Pueblo Indian Land Grants*, 110–11). The Gallegos grant was never submitted to that court.
88. Mora, *México y sus revoluciones*, 179, cited in Hall and Weber, "Mexican Liberals and the Pueblo Indians," 6. A strikingly similar rationale was advanced by proponents of the General Allotment Act of 8 February 1887 (24 Stat. 388), by which Congress authorized the president of the United States to "open" selected Indian reservations to allotment—that is, to allocate tracts of 80 or 160 acres to each tribal member, with the balance of the lands being made available for white settlement. It was claimed that the example of their neighboring white farmers would turn the Indians into productive "yeoman farmers" and end their dependence on federal handouts. This disastrous policy (never applied to the Pueblo Indians in New Mexico) resulted in the loss of 100 million acres of tribal land, the further impoverishment of tribal members, and the utter disruption of tribal communal societies where it was applied. It was finally ended in 1934.
89. Dublan and Lozano, *Legislación mexicana*, 1:396.
90. José Francisco Luján, petition, Taos, 11 Apr. 1815, SANM I:1357.
91. "estar distante de la legua de los indios" (Nerio Sisneros, petition, Taos, 27 Mar. 1815, Arroyo Hondo grant, PLC 5, r. 33, f. 652).
92. Sisneros, petition, Arroyo Hondo grant, PLC 5, r. 33, f. 652.
93. José Francisco Luján, petition, Taos, 11 Apr. 1815, SANM I:1357.
94. "La legua de cinco mil varas medidas desde la cruz del cementerio para todos rumbos, que su majestad hizo merced a cada pueblo de indios desde el principio de su establecimiento es para que se conserve para mantenerse los hijos de él de modo que tienen el uso y no pueden dar ni vender sin licencia del rey por ser patrimonio o mayorazgo que ningún juez ni gobernador tiene facultad para vender parte ni el todo de la citada legua" (Alberto Máynez, decree, 15 Apr. 1815, SANM I:1357). See also Taylor, "Colonial Land and Water Rights," 45–46.

95. Alberto Máynez, decree, SANM I:1357.
96. "agregaban a los españoles para que les ayudaran a la defensa de ese pueblo contra las naciones bárbaras" (José Romero, statement, Taos, 15 May 1815, SANM I:1357).
97. Pedro Martín, statement, Taos, 3 May 1815, SANM I:1357.
98. *Citizens of Taos v. Pedro Martín*, Santa Fe, 14 Mar.–27 June 1816, SANM II:2655. This case is discussed in Tórrez, "Taos Tax Revolt of 1816," 3–6.
99. "los indios están sobrantes de tierra y además de estar posesionados . . . no son capaces" (José Benito Pereyro and Pedro Martín, statement, Taos, 20 May 1815, SANM I:1357).
100. José Romero, statement, Taos, 15 May 1815, SANM I:1357.
101. "puede resultar una grande sensación entre vecinos e indios" (Pedro Martín and José Benito Pereyro to Alberto Máynez, Taos, 13 May 1815, SANM 2:2596).
102. "sus derechos a la legua que su majestad le mercenó, son incontestables" (Alberto Máynez, decree, Santa Fe, 22 May 1815, SANM I:1357). As it happened, the settlers remained on Taos land. When the Pueblo Lands Board conducted its proceedings at Taos in the late 1920s, nearly all the non-Indian claims were upheld, accounting for the fact that today, much of Taos lies inside the boundaries of the Taos Pueblo league. See chapter 10.
103. Alejo García to Facundo Melgares, [Chihuahua], 21 Apr. 1821, SANM I:1133.
104. "habernos leído un bando en que dice que se recorten las tierras de los pueblos" (San Juan to García Conde, [San Juan], 1821, SANM I:1367).
105. "tan poca que por ningún rumbo tiene legua, pues así se mandó desde los antiguos reyes" (San Juan to García Conde, [San Juan], 1821, SANM I:1367).
106. "tienen su legua completa" (San Juan to García Conde, [San Juan], 1821, SANM I:1367).
107. "pues los otros pueblos fueron bajados a fuerza de guerra" (San Juan to García Conde, [San Juan], 1821, SANM I:1367).
108. "por cuya gracia nos hizo [el rey] caballeros, más que a los otros pueblos" (San Juan to García Conde, [San Juan], 1821, SANM I:1367). This was a bit of revisionist history. None of the pueblos violently resisted Oñate's original assertion of Spanish authority, as far as is known, but San Juan (now known as Ohkay Owingeh) was one of the leaders of the very violent Pueblo Revolt of 1680. Popé, one of the acknowledged leaders of the revolt, was from San Juan.
109. "manteniéndoles en la posesión que disfrutan desde que le[s] fueran concedidas" (García Conde, order, Chihuahua, 11 Oct. 1821, SANM I:1367).
110. Félix Guerra and Demetrio Ontiveros to the deputation, [San Lorenzo], Feb. 1823, MANM, r. 2, f. 709–11.
111. Schroeder, "Pecos Pueblo," 432.
112. Francisco Trujillo, Bartolomé Márquez, and Diego Padilla, petition, Santa Fe, 21 Aug. 1813, SANM I:1005.
113. Francisco Trujillo, Bartolomé Márquez, and Diego Padilla, petition, Santa Fe, 21 Aug. 1813, SANM I:1005; Hall, *Four Leagues of Pecos*, 17–21.

NOTES TO PAGES 34-38

114. Alberto Máynez, order, Santa Fe, 22 June 1815, SANM I:1357; Los Trigos grant, SG 8, r. 13, f. 310.
115. Juan de Dios Pena, Francisco Ortiz, and Juan Bautista Aguilar, petition, Santa Fe, 1814, SANM I:703.
116. Felipe Sandoval, report, Santa Fe, 28 Mar. 1815, SANM I:1357; Alejandro Valle grant, SG 18, r. 14, f. 683.
117. Hall explains that Ortiz's measurement clearly prejudiced Pecos, because he began at the cross in the middle of the cemetery, which was well to the south of the village (*Four Leagues of Pecos*, 23–24). When Alcalde Vicente Villanueva subsequently remeasured the league, he began in the center of the village to avoid this unfairness.
118. Juan de Aguilar, petition, Santa Fe, [Aug. 1818], SANM I:56.
119. "en que hacía costumbre (y yo lo he practicado) el comenzar de la cruz del cementerio y esta ha sido no por regla fija sino es porque todos [menos este] poco más o menos tienen la iglesia en su centro" (Vicente Villanueva, response, San Miguel del Bado, 15 Aug. 1818, SANM I:56).
120. Villanueva, response, SANM I:56. For a drawing of Pecos Pueblo as it might have appeared at about this time, see Kessell, *Kiva, Cross, and Crown*, 345.
121. "tierra arrugada y doblada" (Villanueva, response, SANM I:56).
122. Villanueva, response, SANM I:56.
123. Esteban Baca, petition, Santa Fe, 10 Feb. 1821, SANM I:130; Facundo Melgares to Juan Rafael Ortiz, Santa Fe, 12 Feb. 1821, SANM I:130; Juan Rafael Ortiz, report, Santa Fe, 10 Apr. 1821, SANM I:130.
124. Weber, *Mexican Frontier*, 26–27.
125. The previous year, Fernández successfully petitioned the governor for a grant that included all of the abandoned Pueblo of San Cristóbal (Ethan Eaton grant, SG 19, r.14, f. 787–1100).
126. Domingo Fernández et al., petition, Santa Fe, 1 Sept. 1823, SANM I:283.
127. Bartolomé Baca to the alcalde of El Bado, Santa Fe, 1 Sept. 1823, SANM I:283.
128. Ayuntamiento of San Miguel del Bado to Bartolomé Baca, San Miguel del Bado, 18 Sept. 1823, SANM I:283.
129. Domingo Fernández and Rafael Benavídez to Bartolomé Baca, Santa Fe, 21 Sept. 1823, SANM I:283.
130. "los naturales del pueblo de Pecos decían que el terreno que tienen de labor apenas les facilitaba la subsistencia y que se obligaban a labrarlo todo" (Fernández and Benavídez to Baca, SANM I:283).
131. Fernández and Benavídez to Baca, SANM I:283.
132. Minutes of the deputation meeting, Santa Fe, 16 Feb. 1825, MANM, r. 42, f. 257, cited in Hall and Weber, "Mexican Liberals and the Pueblo Indians," 15n40.
133. Minutes of the deputation meeting, Santa Fe, 3 Mar. 1825, MANM, r. 42, f. 261, cited in Hall and Weber, "Mexican Liberals and the Pueblo Indians," 15n41.
134. "que así como se cesaron sus antiguas cargas han terminado sus privilegios

quedando igual unos y otros a todos los demás ciudadanos que con ellos forman la gran familia mexicana" (minutes of the deputation meeting, Santa Fe, 3 Mar. 1825, MANM, r. 42, f. 261, cited in Hall and Weber, "Mexican Liberals and the Pueblo Indians," 15n41).

135. Hall and Weber, "Mexican Liberals and the Pueblo Indians," 16n43; minutes of the deputation meeting, Santa Fe, 19 Mar. 1825, MANM, r. 42, f. 272–73.
136. Hall and Weber, "Mexican Liberals and the Pueblo Indians," 16; minutes of the deputation meeting, Santa Fe, 16 Jul. 1825, MANM, r. 42, f. 284.
137. "aquellos naturales que su excelencia puede disponer de aquellas tierras y procurar el progreso de la decadente agricultura de este vasto territorio" (minutes of the deputation meeting, Santa Fe, 16 Feb. 1824, MANM, r. 42, f. 170–71).
138. Minutes of the deputation, Santa Fe, 12 Mar. 1824, MANM, r. 42, f. 174–75.
139. "el terreno sobrante en los pueblos de San Felipe y Santo Domingo" (minutes of the deputation, Santa Fe, 12 Mar. 1824, MANM, r. 42, f. 174–75).
140. Minutes of the deputation, Santa Fe, 12 Mar. 1824, MANM, r. 42, f. 174–75.
141. "se resolvió no tomar en consideración esta u otras solicitudes de su tenor hasta tanto no se consulte al supremo gobierno de la federación solicitando una resolución general en materia de tanta trascendencia" (minutes of the deputation, Santa Fe, 15 Sept. 1825, MANM, r. 42, f. 298).
142. "los naturales de Pecos solicitan se les declare como propiedad inmemorial una legua de terreno que por cada rumbo han considerado corresponderle a cada un pueblo de los de este territorio" (minutes of the deputation, Santa Fe, 17 Nov. 1825, MANM, r. 42, f. 313–14).
143. Minutes of the deputation, Santa Fe, 17 Nov. 1825, MANM, r. 42, f. 313–14.
144. Rafael Aguilar, Lucas Domingo Vigil, and José Manuel Armenta on behalf of Pecos Pueblo, petition, Pecos, 12 Mar. 1826, SANM I:1370. This document is discussed in Hall, *Four Leagues of Pecos*, 49–50, and Kessell, *Kiva, Cross, and Crown*, 445–46.
145. Aguilar, Vigil, and Armenta on behalf of Pecos Pueblo, petition, SANM I:1370.
146. Unsigned response of the deputation, [Santa Fe], 21 Mar. 1826, SANM I:1370.
147. Sebastián Camacho, Mexico City, 31 May 1826, MANM, r. 5, f. 29–32.
148. Antonio Narbona to the secretary of the interior and foreign relations, Santa Fe, 14 Oct. 1826, SANM I:1371.
149. "antigua inmemorial posesión que se les dio ... ocupa una legua por cada viento ... Con igualdad de derechos en pastos, abrevaderos y siembras" (Antonio Narbona to the secretary of the interior and foreign relations, Santa Fe, 14 Oct. 1826, SANM I:1371).
150. "no se auxilian unos a otros para la manutención y adelanta ... Todos los de su clase siempre han resistido el familiarizarse con los vecinos" (Antonio Narbona to the secretary of the interior and foreign relations, Santa Fe, 14 Oct. 1826, SANM I:1371).
151. Minutes of the deputation, Santa Fe, 21 Oct. 1826, MANM, r. 42, f. 438–39.

152. Hall and Weber, "Mexican Liberals and the Pueblo Indians," 18.
153. Rafael Aguilar and José Cota on behalf of Pecos Pueblo to the deputation, petition, Santa Fe, 9 Mar. 1829, SANM I:288.
154. Antonio Narbona, Santa Fe, 14 Oct. 1826, SANM I:1371; Aguilar and Cota on behalf of Pecos Pueblo to the deputation, petition, SANM I:288.
155. "toda su tierra a los naturales del pueblo de Pecos, pues su excelencia en aquel tiempo para este violento despojo no tuvo sin duda presente las leyes que habla sobre respetar las propiedades de todo individuo" (Pino, Arce, and Baca Commission, report, Santa Fe, n.d., Pueblo of Pecos , SG Report F, r. 7, f. 81).
156. "se les devuelva toda la tierra a los naturales del pueblo de Pecos de cuanto se les despojó" (Pino, Arce, and Baca Commission, report, Santa Fe, n.d., Pueblo of Pecos, SG Report F, r. 7, f. 81, f. 81–82).
157. "a los vecinos posesionados en ellas se les avisa el alcalde de aquel partido el ningún derecho que han adquirido en dicha posesión por haber sido dicha merced dada en tierras con dueños" (Pino, Arce, and Baca Commission, report, Santa Fe, n.d., Pueblo of Peco, SG Report F, r. 7, f. 81, f. 81–82).
158. "las tierras que se han de volver a los hijos de Pecos son las donadas y no las vendidas por ellos" (minutes of the deputation, Santa Fe, 24 Mar. 1829, MANM r. 42, f. 605–6, transcription from Hall, *Four Leagues of Pecos*, 30n68).
159. For a good discussion of the effect of the deputation's ruling of 24 Mar. 1829, see Hall, *Four Leagues of Pecos*, 56–57; for the San Felipe–Santa Ana audiencia decision, see *Cuentas*, 27 Mar. 1818, SANM I:1363.
160. Domingo Fernández et al. to José Antonio Chávez, Santa Fe, 7 May 1829, SANM I:288; José Antonio Chávez to the deputation, Santa Fe, 8 May 1829, SANM I:288. See also Hall, "Juan Estevan Pino, 'Se les coma,'" 27.
161. Pino, Ortiz, and Sarracino Committee, report, Santa Fe, 13 June 1829, SANM I:288.
162. "una propiedad inmemorial de dichos naturales" (minutes of deputation meeting, 29 Nov. 1829, MANM, r. 42, f. 631).
163. José María Paredes to Ramón Abréu, Mexico City, 17 Feb. 1830, SANM I:1369.
164. "dentro del derecho y propiedad de los ejidos del pueblo de mi residencia" (Mariano Rodríguez to Santiago Abréu, petition, Picuris, 14 May 1829, SANM I:1374).
165. "en los márgenes del río de dicho pueblo en la parte de arriba fuera de la legua que por derecho pertenece a los indios" (Martínez, Salazar, and Quintana Committee, report, Santa Fe, 14 Apr. 1830, SANM I:1374).
166. Martínez, Salazar, and Quintana Committee, report, SANM I:1374; Sarracino and Baca Committee, report, Santa Fe, 4 Mar. 1830, SANM I:1374; deputation, decree, Santa Fe, 5 June 1829, SANM I:1374; deputation, decree, Santa Fe, 4 Mar. 1830, SANM I:1374.
167. "estuviera la república del pueblo metido a salir dentro o él a la tierra del pueblo" (Salvador Montoya to [Francisco Sarracino], petition, Jemez, 18 Apr. 1833, SANM I:1245).

168. Montoya to [Sarracino], petition, SANM I:1245.
169. Ibid.
170. "latías añadidas" (Montoya to [Sarracino], petition, SANM I:1245).
171. "decirme en la manera por menor en la manera qué deberé hacer, en qué vara, ¿de qué deberé ser el cordel, desde qué iglesia, desde la que se fundó primero o la que esta ahora o desde la mediación de ambas?" (Montoya to [Sarracino], petition, SANM I:1245).
172. Santiago Abréu, decree, Santa Fe, 21 Apr. 1833, SANM I:1245.
173. "se practiquen las medidas necesarias de una legua que por los cuatro vientos les fue adjudicada por el gobierno español" (Miguel Antonio Lobato to Mariano Martínez, petition, Santa Fe, 23 Aug. 1844, SANM I:1380).
174. Lobato to Martínez, petition, SANM I:1380.
175. "sobre una varilla de madera perfectamente asemblada, que al propósito se mandó construir en el tamaño expresado" (Francisco Sarracino, measurement of the northern part of the Santo Domingo league, Santo Domingo, 3 Sept. 1844, SANM I:1380).
176. "como cada de ellas contenga cincuenta varas, resultan medidas cinco mil varas que componen una legua es la que tiene señalada como ejidos el referido pueblo de Santo Domingo" (Sarracino, measurement of the northern part of the Santo Domingo league, SANM I:1380).
177. "se pusiese . . . una mojonera firme de piedra en el punto donde concluyeron las cinco mil varas antedichas" (Sarracino, measurement of the northern part of the Santo Domingo league, SANM I:1380).
178. Sarracino, measurement of the northern part of the Santo Domingo league, SANM I:1380.
179. "se encontraron señales ciertas y seguras de haber existido allí mismo mojoneras que en otros tiempos debieron haberse puesto . . . según y como se anunció por algunos naturales de edad avanzada" (Sarracino, measurement of the northern part of the Santo Domingo league, SANM I:1380).

Chapter 2

1. Kessell, Hendricks, and Dodge, *Blood on the Boulders*, 90, 321–22, 366–67.
2. Bayer, with Montoya and the Pueblo of Santa Ana, *Santa Ana*, 77–95.
3. The Santa Ana collection consists of many original documents the pueblo has kept for which there are no copies. It also contains copies of some documents found in SANM. Some Santa Ana documents cited here can only be found in SANM or in ARAG. During the preparation of this book, the pueblo entered into an agreement with the New Mexico Commission of Public Records to place the entire collection at the New Mexico State Records Center and Archives on a long-term loan. The documents were formally transferred on 3 December 2013. The references that follow, in the form "SA" plus a number, use the identifiers assigned to the

documents in the official inventory that was attached to the loan agreement. That inventory, which gives a brief description of each document, can be found on the SRCA website, at nmcpr.state.nm.us/archives/gencat_cover.htm.
4. Ellis, "Anthropological Evidence Supporting the Land Claim of the Pueblos of Zia, Santa Ana, and Jemez." Bayer, Montoya, and the Santa Ana Pueblo relate the prehistory and early history of Tamaya according to Pueblo tradition. There is a difference of opinion among anthropologists as to the migration routes of the Eastern Keres. Florence Hawley Ellis agrees with Richard Ford, Stewart Peckham, and Albert Schroeder (1972) about migration from the San Juan Anasazi region, while Erik Reed (1949) locates the beginning of the migration from the Upper Little Colorado region near the Hopi area. A map of these three possible migration routes is in Bayer, Montoya, and the Pueblo of Santa Ana, *Santa Ana*, 257.
5. Bayer, Montoya, and the Pueblo of Santa Ana, *Santa Ana*, 73–80. The name "ranchiit'u" is presumably a Keres corruption of the Spanish term, "ranchito," suggesting that it probably attached no earlier than the eighteenth century. The Court of Private Land Claims case that adjudicated Santa Ana's titles to the area, although formally captioned *Pueblo of Santa Ana and the Inhabitants Thereof v. United States*, No. 137, was informally referred to as the "El Ranchito case." The tract as confirmed by the court and surveyed became known as the "El Ranchito grant," even though there was no such grant.
6. Manuel Baca to Santa Ana, deed, Bernalillo, 27 June 1709, SA 1, 2. There is an original and a contemporaneous copy in the Santa Ana collection.
7. Inventory of Archives of Cabildo of Santa Fe, SANM I:1136. The Pueblo Indians probably destroyed the archives in Santa Fe at the time of the Pueblo Revolt. In 1713, apparently in an effort to reconstruct the records of land titles in the province, Governor Flores Mogollón ordered that all extant documents relative to land titles be presented to the cabildo of Santa Fe. The inventory of the documents was evidently completed two years later. The Manuel Baca grant is listed in Twitchell, *Spanish Archives of New Mexico*, 1:338.
8. SG, Register of Land Titles, Day Book C, r. 11, f. 213–17; Kessell and Hendricks, *By Force of Arms*, 221n87.
9. Kessell and Hendricks, *By Force of Arms*, 221n87.
10. Fernando Durán y Chaves, a favorite of Governor Vargas, was appointed royal standard-bearer for the entrada into Santa Fe in December 1693 and soon became alcalde at Bernalillo and war captain of San Felipe. Although he was somewhat more prestigious than his neighbor and rival, Manuel Baca, their careers ran a parallel course for several years. Durán y Chaves received his grant from Vargas in 1692; Baca received his in 1695. He was placed in possession of his land in 1700, and Durán y Chaves was placed in possession of his land in 1703 (Manuel Baca to Fernando Durán y Chaves, Bernalillo, gift deed, 5 May 1701, SANM I:230).
11. SG, Register of Land Titles, Day Book C, r. 11, f. 213–17; Baca to Durán y Chaves, 5 May 1701, SANM I:230.

12. *Manuel Baca v. Fernando Durán y Chaves*, SG, Register of Land Titles, Day Book C, r. 11, f. 213–17.
13. *Baca v. Durán y Chaves*, SG, Register of Land Titles, Day Book C, r. 11, f. 230–32. Vargas died in Bernalillo, probably at the home of Durán y Chaves (who witnessed Vargas's will), on 4 April, just six weeks after settling this dispute (Twitchell, *Spanish Archives of New Mexico*, 1:301–10; Chávez, *Origins of New Mexico Families*, 161).
14. Chávez, *Chávez*, 68–69.
15. *Baca v. Durán y Chaves*, SG, Register of Land Titles, Day Book C, r. 11, f. 233–37.
16. In 1700 Vargas granted a group of settlers led by Durán y Chaves the Atrisco land grant on the west bank of the Rio Grande, south of Bernalillo. The resulting settlement helped give rise to the establishment of Albuquerque. Governor Pedro Fermín de Mendinueta enlarged the grant by means of a subsequent grant in 1768, extending the area to the west to the Rio Puerco. The Court of Private Land Claims confirmed the combined grants, which measured about 82,728 acres. See *Armijo v. Town of Atrisco*, 56 N.M. 2, 239 P.2d 535 (1952).
17. Manuel Baca to Juana Baca, deed, Santa Fe, 23 Aug. 1713, SA 3.
18. Manuel Baca to Cristóbal Martínez, deed, Bernalillo, 3 June 1733, El Ranchito case, PLC 157, r. 49, f. 633.
19. Juan González Bas to Santa Ana, deed, SA 4.
20. "pertenece al puesto de Bernalillo población muy antigua de españoles" (Gervasio Cruzat y Góngora, annulment of sale of land to Santa Ana by Baltasar Romero, Santa Fe, 1 Mar. 1734, SANM 1:1345).
21. In 1778 Father Morfi reported that "although royal laws prohibit Spaniards . . . from living in Indian pueblos, they have never been obeyed with any strictness" (Simmons, *Father Juan Agustín Morfi's Account of Disorders in New Mexico*, 26–27).
22. Josefa Baca was engaged in assembling a modest amount of land in this area during the same period. In 1713 she acquired a small tract east of the Rio Grande from Juan González Bas (SA 5). Although no boundaries are specified in the deed, by 1739 she managed to expand her holdings to cover a tract of land stretching from the Rio Grande on the west all the way to the Sandia Mountains on the east, which she conveyed to Cristóbal Martín for three hundred pesos. See SA 9. Martín consolidated this expanded tract with two others he purchased from the Bacas (SA 8, 10). Santa Ana later acquired all this land from his widow (SA 15).

The 1713 deed to Josefa Baca contained no boundaries or other description of the tract. Manuals for *escribanos* of the day, which provided the model for alcaldes who wrote up deeds, showed the property description as the first item that should be included after the names of the parties and the place where the deed was signed. Baca's deed states only that the property was on the east side of the Rio Grande. When Josefa sold the property to Martín in 1739, the boundary descriptions were quite specific: on the east by the Sandia Mountains, on the west by the Rio Grande, on the north "below the house of Doña Ana where there is a bushy-topped cottonwood" (*un álamo coposo*), and on the south the house of the elder Montoya. By then the price had increased from the 110 pesos she paid in 1713 to 300 pesos. The 1739 deed also makes clear that at that time, the Rio Grande flowed *east* of Bernalillo (Josefa Baca to Cristóbal Martín, deed, Albuquerque, 20 Dec. 1739, SA 9 [this document is a copy of the original, made in 1748]; Juan González Bas to Josefa Baca, deed, Bernalillo, 14 Oct. 1713, SA 5). See also González de Villarroel, *Examen y práctica de escribanos*.

23. Josefa Baca to Santa Ana, deed, Bernalillo, 4 June 1742, SA 6. Although a literal translation of the northern boundary described as "la salida de la Angostura" is "the exit of the narrows," we have rendered the phrase throughout as "the place where the narrows widens" because this is the best physical description of the location of this boundary.
24. Manuel Baca to Santa Ana, deed, Bernalillo, 27 June 1709, SA 1, 2.
25. *Cristóbal and Nerio Montoya vs. Antonio Baca*, Santa Fe, 9–25 Aug. 1763, SANM II:570.
26. Chávez, *Origins of New Mexico Families*, 141.
27. *Montoya vs. Baca*, SANM II:570.
28. LeCompte, "Independent Women of Hispanic New Mexico"; Jenkins, "Some Eighteenth-Century New Mexico Women of Property," 335.
29. Proceedings against Juan Márquez and Francisco Javier for the death of María Magdalena Baca II, Santa Fe and Albuquerque, 22 Feb.–19 May 1741, SANM II:437.
30. Born in the Spanish region of Cantabria in 1713, Miera y Pacheco arrived in New Mexico in the early 1740s. Although little is known of his early life and career, in New Mexico he gained reknown as a true Renaissance man. Miera is most celebrated as the cartographer who produced a series of maps, notable for their artistic flair and ethnographic precision, for Governor Marín del Valle over a twenty-year period, beginning in 1758. Miera was also an artist, district official, engineer, explorer, merchant, mine owner, rancher, and sculptor. With the patronage of the governor and his wealthy wife, doña María Ignacia Martínez, Miera produced the carved stone altarpiece for the *Castrense*, the military chapel in Santa Fe, which is widely considered the most spectacular piece of art from the Spanish colonial period in New Mexico, as well as many other works of art. Miera was also the cartographer of the 1776 expedition led by fray Francisco Atanasio Domínguez and fray Silverste Vélez de Escalante to the Great Basin (Kessell, *Miera y Pacheco*, xiii, 34–40, 47, 91–118, 121).
31. Tomás Vélez Cachupín, order, Santa Fe, 9 Aug. 1763, SA 15; *Montoya vs. Baca*, SANM II:570; José de Jesús Montaño and Mariano Martínez Gallegos on behalf of Quiteria Contreras to Santa Ana, sale of land, SA 15.
32. Bernardo Miera y Pacheco, report, Santa Ana, 13 Aug. 1763, SANM II:570.

33. Antonio Baca, statement, Santa Fe, 16 Aug. 1763; *Montoya vs. Baca*, SANM II:570.
34. Isidro Sánchez, statement, Albuquerque, 27 Jul. 1763, SA 15; *Montoya vs. Baca*, SANM II:570.
35. "están muchos expersos en varios pueblos, buscando donde sembrar" (Antonio Baca, list of goods with which the Indians paid, Santa Ana, May 1753, SA 11).
36. Alejandro Mora to Santa Ana, deed, Santa Ana, 24 May, 1753, SA 11. The claim that the lands Mora sold extended westward to the Rio Puerco (which is actually stated in the deed by which Feliciano Miranda's father, Javier de Miranda, acquired the land from Pedro Romero [Pedro Romero to Javier de Miranda, deed, Bernalillo, 20 Nov. 1739, SA 11]) must be taken with a grain of salt. That river lies nearly 30 miles west of the Rio Grande (the eastern boundary of the tract being sold) in this vicinity, and Zia and Santa Ana's old village of Tamaya lie in between the two rivers. In 1766 Governor Vélez Cachupín made a joint grant to the three pueblos of Santa Ana, Zia, and Jemez, which would become known as the Ojo del Espíritu Santo grant, that extended from the lands of Zia Pueblo on the east to the Rio Puerco on the west, plainly including most of the lands purportedly embraced by the Mora deed. The pueblos' claim to the grant was eventually rejected by the Court of Private Land Claims (Zia, Santa Ana, and Jemez grant, PLC 50, r. 38, f. 575-55). The lands Mora conveyed to the pueblo, however, unquestionably extended all the way westward to Tamaya.
37. See McKnight's discussion of *Recopilación* 5-9-2 and 5-9-3 in "Texas Community Property Law," 74.
38. Proceedings against Alejandro Mora for mistreatment of his wife, Albuquerque, 23 Sept.–6 Nov. 1750, SANM II:515.
39. "continuados azotes, palos . . . y encerrada" (Feliciana Miranda, testimony, proceedings against Alejandro Mora, SANM II:515).
40. "a que desnuda del todo la colgaba y azotaba con una cuarta" (Miranda, testimony, proceedings against Alejandro Mora, SANM II:515).
41. "ni ahora ni nunca se quiere juntar con su esposo, Alejandro Mora, por la mala vida que le da" (Miranda, declaration, proceedings against Alejandro Mora, Albuquerque, Oct. 1751, SANM II:515).
42. "por que le había perdido todo su ganado y que se iba a los pueblos" (Alejandro Mora, declaration, proceedings against Alejandro Mora, Santa Fe, 25 Nov. 1751, SANM II:515).
43. "un Indio del Pueblo de Santa Ana" (Mora, declaration, proceedings against Alejandro Mora, SANM II:515).
44. "se convinieron y ajustaron maridablemente abrazándose y haciendo otros demonstraciones de palabras de carino" (Tomás Vélez Cachupín, decree, proceedings against Alejandro Mora, Santa Fe, 7 Nov. 1752, SANM II:515).
45. Not until the Mexican period was it established that "none who had contracted matrimony should be forced to live together if there was sufficient cause for divorce" (LeCompte, "Independent Women of Hispanic New Mexico," 30n4).

46. "personas desinteresades e inteligentes" (Tomás Vélez Cachupín, decree, Santa Fe, 13 May 1753, SA 11). For the final approval, see Tomás Vélez Cachupín, decree, Santa Fe, 28 May, 1753, SA 11.
47. "tasaron y avaluaron según se les mando en cristiandad" (Antonio Baca, list of goods with which the Indians paid, Santa Ana, SA 11).
48. Heirs of Cristóbal Baca to San Felipe, deed, Santa Fe, 24 Apr. 1753, SANM I:1348.
49. "los naturales del pueblo de San Felipe . . . no pueden ni deben celebrar compras ni ventas de bienes raíces" (Tomás Vélez Cachupín, decree, Santa Fe, 1753, SANM I:1348).
50. Heirs of Cristóbal Baca to San Felipe, deed, SANM I:1348.
51. Pedro Romero, deed of sale, Bernalillo, 20 Nov. 1739, SA 11.
52. The deeds by which at least some of these lands were acquired were transferred to Santa Ana as part of the Contreras transaction and remain in the Santa Ana archive (Josefa Baca to Cristóbal Martín, deed, 30 Dec. 1739, Albuquerque, SA 9; heirs and wife of Diego Manuel Baca to Cristóbal Martín, deed, 12 Jul. 1748, Sandia, SA 8; Antonio Baca to Cristóbal Martín, deed, 8 Feb. 1749, Bernalillo, SA 10).
53. José de Jesús Montaño and Mariano Martínez Gallegos on behalf of Quiteria Contreras to Santa Ana, sale of land, Jul. 1763, Bernalillo, SANM I:1349.
54. Montaño and Martínez Gallegos on behalf of Contreras to Santa Ana, SA 15.
55. See the following documents in SA 15/SANM 1:1349: Bernardo Miera y Pacheco, order, Santa Ana, 5 Jul. 1763; Bernardo Miera y Pacheco, naming of appraisers, Santa Ana, 6 Jul. 1763; Bernardo Miera y Pacheco, record of payment made by Santa Ana, 7 Jul. 1763; Bernardo Miera y Pacheco, deed prepared for Santa Ana, Santa Ana, 7 Jul. 1763.
56. "pongan mojoneras estables y subsistentes que sirvan de señal a los linderos que se prescriben en la escritura de venta" (Tomás Vélez Cachupín, decree of confirmation of purchase, [Santa Fe, 1763], SA 15/SANM I:1349).
57. Bernardo Miera y Pacheco, order, Santa Ana, 5 Jul. 1763, SA 15/SANM I:1349.
58. "un hombre de ciencia y conciencia" (Miera y Pacheco, order, SA 15/SANM I:1349).
59. "de obrar fial y legalmente según su leal saber y entender" (Bernardo Miera y Pacheco, naming of appraisers, SA 15/SANM I:1349).
60. Francisco Pablo Salazar and Juan Bautista Montaño, appraisal, Santa Ana, 7 Jul. 1763, SA 14/SANM 1:1349.
61. "magua, el caballo tordillo, en cincuenta pesos" (Bernardo Miera y Pacheco, record of payment made by Santa Ana, 7 Jul. 1763, SA 15/SANM I:1349).
62. Miera y Pacheco, record of payment, SA 15/SANM I:1349.
63. Miera y Pacheco, record of payment, SA 15/SANM I:1349; Minge, "The Pueblo of Santa Ana's El Ranchito Purchase," 8.
64. Miera y Pacheco noted that the tract bordered the land "the Indians purchased that belonged to Miranda," referring to the Mora tract, directly across the river (Bernardo Miera y Pacheco, deed prepared for Santa Ana, SA 15/SANM I:1349).
65. Miera y Pacheco, deed prepared for Santa Ana, SA 15/SANM I:1349.

66. Quiteria Contreras, authorization, Nuestra Señora de la Luz, San Fernando, and San Blas, 5 Jul., 1763, SA 13. When Contreras executed her will, on 19 March 1778, the document reaffirmed that she had sold these lands to Santa Ana and that the pueblo had received a copy of the will (Quiteria Ávalos Contereras, will, El Sauzal, 19 Mar. 1778, SA 17).
67. Pedro Garcia to Santa Ana, deed, 25 Oct. 1777, Bernalillo, SA 16.
68. *Santa Ana v. San Felipe*, SANM II:1356; Audiencia of Guadalajara proceedings, SANM II:1363, SANM II:2715; proceedings implementing the audiencia's decision, SANM I:1234.
69. Like Juan José Gallegos, Andrés Montoya was also a resident of Cieneguilla and had many land interests throughout New Mexico (Angostura grant, SG 84, r. 21, f. 749–842; Gerónimo Gonzáles grant [Angostura grant], SG 76 r. 31, f. 154–72; Angostura grant, PLC 229, r. 52, f. 1240–1307; Juan José Gallegos to Joaquín Codallos y Rabal, petition, Angostura grant, PLC 229, r. 52, f. 1249–50; Joaquín Codallos y Rabal, grant, Santa Fe, 4 Nov. 1745, Angostura grant, PLC 229, r. 52, f. 1249–50).
70. As early as 1704, San Felipe claimed the Angostura area when the Hispanos Cristóbal and Juan Varela Jaramillo sought a land grant there. Alfonso Rael de Aguilar, acting on behalf of San Felipe as protector of Indians, told Governor Vargas that the grant should not be made because San Felipe had possessed the land since the pueblo was founded and had planted grain and cotton there. San Felipe did not want the Hispanos to receive this grant because they believed it was within their four square leagues and if the grant was made the Hispanos would bring their cattle and sheep, resulting in damage to pueblo crops. The grant was not made, and San Felipe's Pueblo league was not measured. This is the earliest surviving document in the SRCA that mentions the Pueblo league (Ebright, "Advocates for the Oppressed," 308–9; Rael de Aguilar to Diego de Vargas, San Felipe, 23 Feb. 1704, SANM 1:78; Juan José Gallegos to San Felipe, sale of land, 5 Dec. 1752, SG 84 r. 21, f. 756–59).
71. Andrés Montoya to Juan José Gallegos, act of possession of the Angostura grant, San Felipe, 10 Nov. 1745, PLC 229, r. 52, f. 1250.
72. Rafael Antonio García and Bautista Garviso to José Leandro Perea, sale of land, Peña Blanca, PLC 229, r. 52, f. 1294–96.
73. Joseph R. Reed, decree of confirmation, Angostura grant, Santa Fe, 28 Jan. 1898, SG 84 r. 21, f. 792–94.
74. Final decree, *United States, as Guardian for the Indians of the Pueblo of San Felipe, v. Algodones Land Co., et al.*, No. 1870, Equity (D.N.M., 22 Apr. 1930).
75. "partiendo la mitad del río viejo" (settlement between Santa Ana and San Felipe, Santa Ana, 14 Jul. 1779, SA 18).
76. "enterrar piedras desde donde el río se mudó hasta volvió a entrar" (settlement between Santa Ana and San Felipe, SA 18).
77. The original of the settlement document is part of the Santa Ana Archive (SA 18).

At the bottom of the document, below the signature of Nerio Antonio Montoya and the two witnesses, is a declaration written by José María de Arce, the alferez of the Santa Fe presidial company, whom Governor José Manrique appointed to adjudicate the Santa Ana–San Felipe dispute in 1813 after San Felipe appealed José Pino's original decision. Arce's declaration fills the back side of the document and is signed by him, the alcaldes, the protector, and various witnesses. It describes his view that the 1779 settlement was the only authoritative document he had seen that established this portion of the boundary between the two pueblos, which he determined to be "taking the middle to be where the river was in ancient times" (tomando la mediación centro por donde antiguamente venía el río). He ordered the reestablishment of the north–south line of stones that Montoya originally established in 1779.

78. Ellis, "Anthropological Evidence Supporting the Land Claim of the Pueblos of Zia, Santa Ana, and Jemez," 16, 30.
79. See, for example, *María Victoria Gutiérrez v. Pedro Miguel Gutiérrez*, 1820, SANM I:383.
80. Cutter, *Protector de Indios*, 81–83.
81. In his petition to the protector, Mairo stated that five years earlier the pueblo complained to the governor of New Mexico about San Felipe's incursions onto land that Santa Ana had purchased. Apparently there was no response to that petition (Eusebio Mairo, petition, 5 May 1813, SANM I:1356).
82. "se determine quién es el legítimo dueño según los documentos que tengamos" (Mairo, petition, SANM I:1356).
83. "pues demorándose más cuando se llegue a declarar ya no habrá un álamo que quede a favor del sitio y siendo nosotros incapaces de hacer ver nuestro derecho" (Mairo, petition, SANM I:1356).
84. José Manrique, order, Santa Fe, 10 May 1813, SANM I:1356.
85. "el tronco que cita en su escritura" (José Pino, order, Angostura, 13 May 1813, SANM I:1356).
86. "el cual no existe ni hubo en los circunstantes quien diera razón de él" (Pino, order, SANM I:1356).
87. Pino, order, SANM I:1356.
88. Pino, order, SANM I:1356.
89. José Manrique, order, Santa Fe, 3 June 1813, SANM I:1356.
90. José María de Arce left no direct descendants, but his adopted son, José María de Arce II, enlisted as a soldier in 1831 at age fourteen (Chávez, *Origins of New Mexico Families*, 128).
91. In the fall of 1818, Arce led a detachment of troops sent north to impede an impending Pawnee attack, although the attack never materialized. This is documented in the diary of José María Arce's expedition "to . . . destroy or detain a force of foreign enemies approaching" (Thomas, "Documents Bearing upon the Northern Frontier of New Mexico").

92. The fact that Arce had a liaison with a Taos Pueblo woman, with whom he had a daughter, María Josefa, might have made him sympathetic to the pueblos' plight (Chávez, *Origins of New Mexico Families*, 83–88, 342–43).
93. José María de Arce, report, Angostura, 5 June 1813, SANM I:1356.
94. "ninguna que cite en toda forma los linderos" (Arce, report, SANM 1:1356).
95. Heirs of Cristóbal Baca to San Felipe, deed, SANM I:1348.
96. "la mitad de la Angostura donde está puesta una cruz confinando con las pertenencias del pueblo de San Felipe" (Quiteria Contreras, José de Jesús Montaño, and Mariano Martínez Gallegos to Santa Ana, deed, Santa Ana, 7 Jul. 1763, SA 15/SANM I:1349; Arce, report, SANM I:1356).
97. "de las tierra que el río les había quitado" (Arce, report, Angostura, 6 June 1813, SANM I:1356).
98. por donde antiguamente venía el río arrimado a las lomas del oriente ... señañándoles una línea curva según torcía el río, partiéndole por donde se gradúo el centro de él" (Arce, report, 6 June 1813, SANM I:1356).
99. "cercanas y lindantes unas con otras que se pusieron enterradas en la tierra y visibles de piedra y lodo para que no vuelvan a perderse ni puedan quitarse con facilidad, mandándoles las reconozcan a menudo hagen saber de ellas hasta a los más inferiores de sus respectivos pueblos" (Arce, report, 6 June 1813, SANM I:1356). It was not uncommon for Spaniards with land adjacent to or overlapping Indian pueblos to remove boundary markers and threaten to harm any Indian who tried to replace them. Luis María Cabeza de Baca threatened Cochiti Indians who opposed his removal of Cochiti's boundary markers (ARAG, Ramo Civil 261-15-3564, el común del Pueblo de Cochití, f. 69, cited in Cutter, *Protector de Indios*, 89).
100. Jóse Manrique, order, Santa Fe, 18 June 1813, SANM I:1356.
101. The Audiencia of Guadalajara was established on 15 February 1548 with a president, four *oidores* (judges), and a fiscal. It was initially called the Audiencia of Nueva Galicia and was inaugurated in what Haring called the "squalid little village of Compostela." In 1560 this audiencia relocated to Guadalajara. For about twenty-five years the Audiencia of Guadalajara was subordinate to the Audiencia of Mexico City. During this early period, civil cases of importance could be appealed from Guadalajara to the Audiencia of Mexico City. Thereafter, the Audiencia of Guadalajara was of equal authority with the other audiencias, each of which was the highest colonial judicial tribunal for their jurisdictions (Haring, *Spanish Empire in America*, 74, 121–22; Cunningham, *Audiencia in the Spanish Colonies*, 17; see also Parry, *Audiencia of New Galicia in the Sixteenth Century*).
102. *Cochiti and Santo Domingo v. Luis María Cabeza de Baca*, Guadalajara, 26 Sept. 1816, ARAG, Ramo Civil 261-15-3564; Cutter, *Protector de Indios*, 81–93.
103. Cutter, *Protector de Indios*, 93–94.
104. According to Sánchez Vergara, Santa Ana's leaders were "making sacrifices to the Devil" (haciendo sacrificios al Demonio) (Ignacio María Sánchez Vergara to Alberto Máynez, Santa Fe, 10 Aug. 1808, SANM II:2140).

105. Máynez's order is in the form of a corrected draft. Besides making the claim for personal services, the Indians stated that they gave Sánchez Vergara a mule as payment for his preparation of a legal document. Governor Máynez ordered the mule returned. Although the people of Santa Ana objected to being forced to cultivate a field for Sánchez Vergara, they did not mind doing it for their priest. As late as 1940, Santa Ana still set aside and farmed a plot for the missionary (Frank, *From Settler to Citizen*, 25; Alberto Máynez, order, Santa Fe, [28 Jul.] 1808, SANM II:2140).
106. "del estado de los Indios tratamiento que reciben, si les falta doctrina, o se hayan sirviendo de esclavos en algunas casas, o sin las tierras que corresponden a sus pueblos conforme a las reales prevenciones que tan estrechamente se hacen en las leyes 12 y 14 del expresado título y libro" (Mariano Mendiola Velarde, appointment of Ignacio María Sánchez Vergara as protector of Indians, Guadalajara, 21 June 1817, SANM II:2692).
107. "submergidos en la ignorancia conservando aquellas máximas gentilicas de idolatría y vida privada" (Ignacio María Sánchez Vergara, report, Jemez, 13 Jan. 1818, AHAD, r. 237, f. 779).
108. "cultivar todo el terreno de que necesiten sin dejar partes de que no benefician . . . libre y desembarazado todo terreno sobrante" (Sánchez Vergara, report, AHAD, r. 237, f. 779).
109. "tan escasas que apenas se pueden matener" (Sánchez Vergara, report, AHAD, r. 237, f. 779).
110. "tierra que con grave perjuicio les usurparon los indios del pueblo de San Felipe y vendieron a tres or cuatro vecinos" (Sánchez Vergara, report, AHAD, r. 237, f. 779).
111. "se les reemplace a dichos vecinos en terrenos baldíos y realengos o que se les devuelva lo que han dado" (Sánchez Vergara, report, AHAD, r. 237, f. 779).
112. Sánchez Vergara, report, AHAD, r. 237, f. 779.
113. Mariano Mendiola Velarde, petition, Guadalajara 27 Mar. 1818, SANM II:2715; *Recopilación* 2-31-13. "Que los visitadores vean si las estancias situadas están en perjuicio de los Indios, y hagan justicia" deals with the problem of Spanish livestock damaging Indian fields; it does not discuss reimbursement from royal land of either Spaniards or Indians.
114. See, for example, *Cochiti and Santo Domingo v. Luis María Cabeza de Baca*, Guadalajara, 26 Sept. 1816, ARAG, Ramo Civil 261-15-3564, copy in SRCA; Cutter, *Protector de Indios*, 81–93.
115. Mariano Mendiola Velarde, petition, Guadalajara, 27 Mar. 1818, SANM II:2715.
116. Rafael Cuentas, copy of the proceedings of the Audiencia of Guadalajara of 27 Mar. 1818, Guadalajara, 14 Jan. 1819, SANM I:1363.
117. Ignacio María Sánchez Vergara to Facundo Melgares, Jemez, 14 Apr. 1819, SANM I:1364.
118. José Mariano de la Peña to Facundo Melgares, Rancho Anaya, 8 May 1819, SANM I:1365.

119. De la Peña to Melgares, SANM I:1365; Ignacio María Sánchez Vergara to Facundo Melgares, Santa Ana, 9 May 1819, SANM I:1365.
120. Pedro Fermín de Mendinueta, grant to San Felipe and Santo Domingo of the land between them, Santa Fe, 10 Sept. 1770, SANM I:1376.
121. José Gutiérrez to Alberto Máynez, Santo Domingo, 29 Aug. 1815, SANM 1:281.
122. Alberto Máynez, grant to Domingo Fernández, Juan de Abrego, Santiago Fernández, Buenaventura Esquibel, and Santiago Rodríquez Santa Fe, 29 Aug. 1815, SANM I:281.
123. In August 1819 San Felipe and Santo Domingo still owned the land between the two pueblos except for the area the 1815 Domingo Fernández grant encompassed. That did not stop Sánchez Vergara from seeking a grant of that land. In 1824 he requested the land from Governor Bartolomé Baca, who was willing to grant land within the Pueblo league to Hispanos. There is no record that the grant was made, but Sánchez Vergara's action shows his moral and ethical laxity when it came to protecting Indian land (José Mariano de la Peña, land exchange at Cubero, Angostura, 3 Aug. 1819, SANM II:2843; Ignacio María Sánchez Vergara, petition for a grant between Santo Domingo and San Felipe, [Santa Fe, Feb. 1824], SANM I:1065).
124. *San Felipe Pueblo vs. the Protector of Indians*, case 54, Index of Judicial cases, 5 Aug. 1818–17 Feb. 1824, SANM II:2738.
125. José Mariano de la Peña and Ignacio María Sánchez Vergara to Facundo Melgares, Angostura, 5 Aug. 1819, SANM I:1234.
126. "como que todos compraron tierra airosa y ahora la entregan de beneficio" (De la Peña and Sánchez Vergara to Melgares, SANM I:1234).
127. De la Peña and Sánchez Vergara to Melgares, SANM I:1234.
128. Ibid.
129. The land San Felipe proposed trading with Juan Bautista González was said to be north of the "league of Santa Ana Pueblo," but presumably the alcalde was using that language simply to refer to the pueblo's lands, since Santa Ana had no "league" in that vicinity (Bowden, "Private Land Claims in the Southwest," 5:1224).
130. "no admite y decide que no le acomoda así; se retiraron a sus casas a las seis y media de la tarde en cuya hora tuve que volver a pasar el río, con los de mi asistencia" (José Mariano de la Peña and Ignacio María Sánchez Vergara to Facundo Melgares, Angostura, 12 Aug. 1819, SANM I:1234).
131. Ignacio María Sánchez Vergara, proceedings, Santa Ana, 1 Oct. 1819, SA 20.
132. "quedando y gozando los preferidos dueños del dicho pueblo de Santa Ana" (Juan Bautista González, receipt, n.p., 20 Sept. 1821, SA 22).
133. Juan Bautista González, receipt, n.p., 20 Sept. 1821, SA 22.
134. Ignacio María Sánchez Vergara to Joaquín Montoya, n.p., 28 Feb. 1821, SA 21.
135. "Los citados Santa Anas no haber vendido a don Pablo Montoya las tierra de estas escrituras" (Vicente Baca to Facundo Melgares, documents relating to land claims of Santa Ana, Jemez, 27 Apr. 1821, SA 25).

136. Bartolomé Baca, order, Santa Fe, 27 Apr. 1824, JSC, 1.
137. Pedro José Perea, order, Bernalillo, 18 Jul. 1829, JSC, 2.
138. Salvador Montoya et al. to Francisco Sarracino, Santa Fe, 11 Jul. 1834; Francisco Sarracino, decree, Santa Fe, 1 Aug. 1834, JSC, 3.
139. José Andrés Sandoval, order, San Isidro, 30 June 1836, JSC, 4.
140. "le de el agua al enunciado Montoya pues usted sabe que aún cuando no tuviera derecho la necesidad es la suprema de todas las leyes" (Salvador Montoya, order, Jemez, 1 Aug. 1838, JSC, 5).
141. Montoya, order, JSC, 5.
142. To avoid losing the ranch to Pino, Pedro Miguel Gutiérrez paid his sister the eight hundred sheep and as a result claimed an interest in the land that was rightfully Santa Ana's (*María Victoria Gutiérrez v. Pedro Miguel Gutiérrez*, Santa Fe, 16 Mar. 1820–28 Apr. 1820, SANM I:383). During his testimony, Pedro Miguel Gutiérrez stated that Juan Esteban Pino would devour his sister and her family ("se los coma") if the mortgage of eight hundred sheep was not paid (Hall, "Juan Estevan Pino, '*Se Los Coma*,'" 27–42).
143. Pedro Bautista Pino to Facundo Melgares, statement, Santa Fe, 5 Apr. 1820, SANM II:383.
144. Bayer, Montoya, and the Pueblo of Santa Ana, *Santa Ana*, 113.
145. Ibid.
146. King Fernando VII abolished the position of protector of Indians on 11 January 1821 as part of what Cutter describes as a philosophical revolution sweeping through early nineteenth-century Europe, dictating equality for all persons and bringing to an end the special wardship that the Indians of New Spain enjoyed (*Protector de Indios*, 98–100). Although it is doubtful that news of the cedula could have reached New Mexico for several months, Sánchez Vergara seemed aware of the fact that it was coming. He was reported to have stated in a document dated 20 February 1821 that the "Indians have emerged from their minority and that they now have no need of a protector" (Facundo Melgares, draft message to the provincial junta, Santa Fe, 18 Apr. 1821, SANM II:2974). There can be little doubt that Sánchez Vergara knew he was out of a job by February of the following year when the confrontation at Angostura occurred.
147. Andrés Maygua to Facundo Melgares, [Santa Ana, Apr.] 1822, SA 23.
148. "que ha habido sobre la materia" (Facundo Melgares to Pedro José Perea, Santa Fe, 27 Apr. 1822, SA 23).
149. "informado yo de una presentación que traía en su mano decretada de la real provisión, procedió el dicho protector haciendo su entrega de tierra a la república de San Felipe despojando de suyas a la república de Santa Ana" (Pedro José Perea to Facundo Melgares, Bernalillo, 4 May 1822, SA 23).
150. Perea to Melgares, SA 23.
151. "con todo lo que haya operado y [el] decreto del excelentísimo senor Comandante General para el despojo a la tierra a los de Santa Ana" (Facundo Melgares to the alcalde of Alameda, Santa Fe, 9 May 1822, SA 26). The commanding general was

a high Spanish, then Mexican official, based in Durango or Chihuahua, Mexico, with jurisdiction over the *provincias internas*, such as New Mexico (Simmons, *Spanish Government in New Mexico*, 22–25).

152. These events are detailed in a document in the Santa Ana archive (SA 23). The document starts with Santa Ana governor Maygua's petition to Melgares, dated April 1822, describing the history of the dispute with San Felipe, Santa Ana's recovery of its lands, and the meeting at Angostura ordered by Sánchez Vergara. Melgares replied with an order of 27 April, directing Alcalde Perea to report to him on the meeting. Perea's reponse is dated 4 May 1822. Melgares's further directive, of 9 May 1822, was for Perea to order Sánchez Vergara to appear before him, with the decree of the commanding general that he claimed to be holding. The document ends there, suggesting that Sánchez Vergara did not appear and that there was no such decree. In 2001 and 2002, historian Thomas Merlan conducted extensive research in archival repositories in the United States and Mexico, searching unsuccessfully for the order Sánchez Vergara claimed to possess (Merlan, report in support of final brief San Felipe Pueblo).

153. Santa Ana's governor, Miguel Lucero, was correct that Jemez was the proper jurisdiction in which to bring the lawsuit, at least prior to 1837; after that date the districts were redrawn and the prefect at Algodones was given legal responsibility for Santa Ana (Miguel Lucero to Albino Chacón, 17 Jan. 1846, in *Santa Ana v. Ramón Gurulé*, Santa Ana and Santa Fe, 17 Jan.–3 June 1846, SA 28; Bayer, Montoya, and the Pueblo of Santa Ana, *Santa Ana*, 111; Jenkins and Schroeder, *Brief History of New Mexico*, 34, 41; leaders of Santa Ana to Miguel Lucero, power of attorney, Santa Fe, 5 May 1846, SA 30).

154. Chacón is referred to both as Albino Chacón and José Albino Chacón in this document (José Albino Chacón, decision, Santa Fe, 3 June 1846, SA 31).

155. See, for example, SA 15, the extensive record of the 1763 sale by Quiteria Contreras of her late husband's rancho to Santa Ana, at the end of which is inscribed, in Spanish but in a completely different hand than the main document (and plainly with a steel nib pen), "registered in Book D, folios 58, 59, 60, 61, and 62, which I certify for the record. Santa Fe, September 25, 1850. Donaciano Vigil, Registrar."

156. Titles of Santa Ana Pueblo, SA 37.

157. Act of 9 February 1869, c. 26, 15 Stat. 438.

158. Final decree, El Ranchito grant, SG 239, r. 30, f. 100–7; Matthew G. Reynolds to attorney general, 19 June 1897, NARA, Department of Justice Records, RG 60, file 9865–1892, ltr. 9472–1897.

159. Act of 28 June 1934, 48 Stat. 1296 (43 USC §315 et seq.).

160. Act of 14 September 1961, Pub. L. 87–231, 75 Stat. 500. That act also placed various federal lands into trust for Zia, Jemez, San Felipe, Santo Domingo, Cochiti, Isleta, and San Ildefonso.

161. Act of 21 October 1978, Pub. L. 95–498, 92 Stat. 1672. The act also authorized the United States to acquire approximately 2,000 acres of state trust lands within the area, also to be held in trust for the pueblo, which was subsequently done.

162. HR Rep. No. 95-1219 at 7 (1978).
163. Act of 28 October 1986, Pub. L. 99-575, 100 Stat. 3243.
164. White predicted "this movement in the direction of individualism is probably weakening the solidarity of the pueblo as an organization, and by relaxing pueblo supervision and discipline over behavior, is conducive to a loss of Indian culture and to the acquisition of American culture"; "it may be confidently expected," he noted, "that when the history of Santa Ana is written ... the migration to Ranchitos will loom large in the story of disintegration of their culture" (White, "Pueblo of Santa Ana, New Mexico," 41, 79).

Chapter 3

1. Hammond and Rey, *Don Juan de Oñate*, 1:320-21.
2. A gold or silver strike that would justify Oñate's colonization of New Mexico never took place (Hammond and Rey, *Don Juan de Oñate*, 1:21).
3. Shroeder, *Brief History of Picuris Pueblo*, 1.
4. Schroeder and Matson, *Colony on the Move*, 123-24.
5. Ibid.
6. Brown, "Picuris Pueblo"; memorial of fray Francisco de Velasco, 9 April 1609, cited in Hammond and Rey, *Don Juan de Oñate* 2:1094.
7. Zamora was assigned to Picuris and to "all the Apaches from the Sierra Nevada toward the north and east, and the province of Taos, with its neighboring pueblos and those that border upon it and those of that cordillera on the bank of the Río del Norte" (Hammond and Rey, eds., *Don Juan de Oñate*, 1:345).
8. Arvide was then assigned to two other rebellious pueblos, Jemez and then Zuni, and was killed at Zuni in 1626 (Benavides, *Fray Alonso de Benavides' Revised Memorial of 1634*, 78).
9. Scholes, "Church and State in New Mexico," 315-16, 320, 324, 324n48.
10. Benavides, *Memorial of Fray Alonso Benavides*, 25-26, 108-11.
11. Hackett, *Historical Documents*, 3:188.
12. Pedro Nanboa of Alameda Pueblo, declaration, El Alamillo, 6 Sept. 1680, cited in Hackett, and Shelby, *Revolt of the Pueblo Indians*, 1:60-62.
13. Sando, "Pueblo Revolt."
14. Knaut, *Pueblo Revolt of 1680*, 3-15; Hackett, and Shelby, *Revolt of the Pueblo Indians*, 1:xxiv-xxx. Picuris had about 2,000 inhabitants in 1630 according to fray Alonso Benavides and that population probably dropped somewhat and then rebounded to around 2,200 in the fifty-year period between 1630 and 1680. Kessell gives complete population figures for Taos showing a similar pattern (*Kiva, Cross, and Crown*, 489-92). For the population of New Mexican pueblos and a discussion of the controversial "rebound effect" that would have brought Pueblo population to a peak in 1680, see Zubrow, *Population, Contact, and Climate*, 12-14.
15. Hackett, and Shelby, *Revolt of the Pueblo Indians*, 1:xxix-xxxi; Hackett, *Historical Documents*, 3:330, 332, 337.

16. Antonio de Otermín to fray Francisco de Ayeta, 8 Sept.1680, cited in Hackett, *Historical Documents*, 3:327–35; Hackett, and Shelby, *Revolt of the Pueblo Indians*, 1:xxxi, xxxvi, xiii; Forbes, *Apache, Navaho, and Spaniard*, 178–79.
17. Antonio de Otermín to Francisco de Ayeta, 8 Sept. 1680, cited in Hackett, and Shelby, *Revolt of the Pueblo Indians* 1:98–101.
18. Hackett, and Shelby, *Revolt of the Pueblo Indians*, 1:101–5.
19. In 1680 Luis Tupatú was said to be a brother-in-law of Lorenzo Tupatú, but in 1692 they were called brothers. Vargas always referred to Luis Tupatú as don Luis, "El Picurí," and never used don Luis Tupatú (Espinosa, *Pueblo Indian Revolt*, 36; Espinosa, "Governor Vargas in Colorado," 186; Espinosa, *First Expedition*, 112, 148; Schroeder, *Brief History of Picuris Pueblo*, 4, 21n23; Folsom, *Indian Uprising on the Rio Grande*, 86; Hackett, and Shelby, *Revolt of the Pueblo Indians*, 1:clv–clx, 2:294–96).
20. Kessell and Hendricks, *By Force of Arms*, 404.
21. Ibid., 406–7.
22. Ibid., 406–7, 485–86n53.
23. Ibid., 408–15; 446–48.
24. Ibid., 448–52.
25. Ibid., 412–25.
26. Kessell, Hendricks, and Dodge, *To the Royal Crown Restored*, 416.
27. Ibid., 431–32, 501; Kessell, Hendricks, and Dodge, *Blood on the Boulders*, 1:34–36.
28. Kessell, Hendricks, and Dodge, *Blood on the Boulders*, 1:254.
29. Ibid., 1:581–82.
30. Ibid., 2:674–75, 1083; Chávez, *Archives of the Archdiocese of Santa Fe*, 19.
31. Knaut, *Pueblo Revolt of 1680*, 183; Kessell, Hendricks, and Dodge, *Blood on the Boulders*, 2:753.
32. Kessell, Hendricks, and Dodge, *Blood on the Boulders*, 2:844–46, 1001–2, 1032–33.
33. Ibid., 1036–37.
34. Ibid., 1039.
35. Ibid., 1042, 1050–53; Thomas, *After Coronado*, 14–15.
36. Kessell, Hendricks, and Dodge, *Blood on the Boulders*, 2:1042, 1050–53; Thomas, *After Coronado*, 14–15.
37. Kessell, Hendricks, and Dodge, *Blood on the Boulders*, 2:1,054–57; Espinosa, *Pueblo Indian Revolt*, 54–55; Thomas, *After Coronado*, 14–16.
38. Kessell, Hendricks, and Dodge, *Blood on the Boulders*, 2:1062.
39. Fray Juan Álvarez, statement, 12 Jan. 1706, translated in Hackett, *Historical Documents*, 3:374.
40. Juan de Ulibarrí, diary of expedition to El Cuartelejo, Jul. and Aug. 1706, translated in Thomas, *After Coronado*, 72–73.
41. Brooks, *Captives and Cousins*, 60–61.
42. Francisco Cuervo y Valdés to Duque de Albuquerque, [Santa Fe], n.d., translated in Thomas, *After Coronado*, 77; Diego de Vargas to Conde de Moctezuma, Santa Fe,

NOTES TO PAGES 99–103

24 Nov. 1696, translated in Kessell, Hendricks, and Dodge, *Blood on the Boulders*, 2:1062.
43. Thomas, *After Coronado*, 61–62.
44. Williston and Martin ("Some Pueblo Ruins," 124–30) and Dunbar ("Massacre of the Villazur Expedition," 397–423) placed Cuartelejo in Scott County, Kansas, but Thomas argued that Cuartelejo was further west, in Kiowa County, Colorado ("Massacre of the Villasur Expedition," 67-81; *After Coronado*, 270–71). Edgar Lee Hewett examined pottery found at the site of Cuartelejo and was of the opinion that the pottery "had been introduced from New Mexico, and had not been made in the vicinity of the . . . village [of Cuartelejo]" (Twitchell, *Old Santa Fe*, 468–69).
45. Thomas, *After Coronado*, 69–73.
46. Ibid., 71–74.
47. Francisco Cuervo y Valdés to Duque de Alburquerque, Santa Fe, 23 Sept. 1706, translated in Thomas, *After Coronado*, 79.
48. Governor Cuervo y Valdés had misled the viceroy before. In 1706 Cuervo reported that he had founded a new villa in accordance with the strict requirements of the *Recopilación* and named it Albuquerque after the viceroy. The report was largely untrue since Albuquerque was nothing more than a scattering of farms spread along the Rio Grande (Simmons, *Albuquerque*, 81–94).
49. Thomas, *After Coronado*, 82–84, 89.
50. Ibid., 79.
51. Ibid., 25, 89–93, 98.
52. Juan Páez Hurtado, diary of campaign, 30 Aug. 1715, translated in Thomas, *After Coronado*, 98.
53. Hendricks and Wilson, *Navajos in 1705*, 103–4; Jones, *Pueblo Warriors and Spanish Conquest*, 71–72.
54. Sebastián Martín grant, SG 28, r. 16, f. 443; Bowden, "Private Land Claims in the Southwest," 4: 1202–4.
55. Ebright, *Land Grants and Lawsuits*, 147.
56. Sebastián Martín grant, SG 28, r. 16, f. 443; Bowden, "Private Land Claims in the Southwest," 4:1202–4.
57. Bowden, "Private Land Claims in the Southwest," 4:1204–5.
58. *Recopilación* 4-12-18.
59. "fuera . . . desde unas milpas que los naturales de él siembran fuera de su pertenencia" (Juan Márquez, Francisco Martín, and Lázaro Córdoba, petition, Puesto de Río Arriba [n.d.], 20, Embudo grant, SG 91, r. 31, f. 285–86).
60. Juan Márquez, Francisco Martín, and Lázaro Córdoba, petition, Puesto de Río Arriba [n.d.], 20, Embudo grant, SG 91, r. 31, f. 285–86. For a more complete discussion of the Embudo grant and its adjudication by the Court of Private Land Claims, see Ebright, *Land Grants and Lawsuits*, 127–42.
61. Juan Domingo de Bustamante, decree, Santa Fe, 17 Jul. 1725, Embudo grant, SG 91, r. 31, f. 286.

62. José de la Vega y Coca, report, Embudo de Picurís, 19 Jul. 1725, Embudo grant, SG 91, r. 31, f. 287–88.
63. *Recopilación* 4-12-18.
64. "unas diligencias que dicho alcalde mayor ejecutó sobre que los Indios de la nación Tiguas . . . en dichos pueblos de Taos y Picurís, salieren y se poblarsen en el de San Agustín de la Isleta" (José de la Vega y Coca, investigation and act of possession, Embudo de Picurís, 19 Jul. 1725, Embudo grant, SG 91, r. 31, f. 287–88).
65. "echaban a comer sus caballos cuando venían a sembrar" (José de la Vega y Coca, investigation and act of possession, Embudo de Picurís, 19 Jul. 1725, Embudo grant, SG 91, r. 31, f. 287–88).
66. José de la Vega y Coca, investigation and act of possession, Embudo de Picurís, 19 Jul. 1725, Embudo grant, SG 91, r. 31, f. 287–88.
67. Ibid.
68. Ibid.
69. Picuris was one of the first pueblos Oñate visited. He called it "the great pueblo of Picuris" (Hammond and Rey, *Don Juan de Oñate*, 1:320–21). Benavides estimated the population of Picuris population at two thousand (*Benavides Memorial of 1630*, 25).
70. "en que claramente manifestaban impeder la poblazón de los españoles" (José de la Vega y Coca, investigation and act of possession, Embudo de Picurís, 19 Jul. 1725, Embudo grant, SG 91, r. 31, f. 288).
71. "muy notorio no haberles conocido desde que este reino se conquistó ningunas milpas en este sitio" (José de la Vega y Coca, investigation and act of possession, Embudo de Picurís, 19 Jul. 1725, Embudo grant, SG 91, r. 31, f. 288).
72. "a sus caballadas tiene bastante ejido en las lomas montuosas; tienen suficientes tierras de labor en este embudo que dista a su pueblo más de tres leguas" (José de la Vega y Coca, investigation and act of possession, Embudo de Picurís, 19 Jul. 1725, Embudo grant, SG 91, r. 31, f. 288).
73. For the Picurís protest of the Río de Picurís grant, see Juan de Jesús Martínez et al., petition, San Lorenzo de Picurís, 11 Apr. 1829, SANM I:625, and Mariano Rodríguez, petition, San Lorenzo de Picurís, 14 May 1829, SANM I:1374.
74. For campaigns on which Picuris auxiliaries accompanied Spaniards, see Jones, *Pueblo Warriors and Spanish Conquest*, 90–94, 128.
75. Thomas, *Plains Indians and New Mexico*, 16.
76. Proceedings relating to a sale of lands by Luis Romero to Pedro Montes Vigil, Santa Fe, 17–28 Feb. 1732, SANM I:1038. Governor Cruzat y Góngora was less liberal when it came to approving land purchases by pueblos. He denied Santa Ana's request to purchase property it claimed as traditional land from Baltasar Romero in 1734 (SANM I:1345). This case is discussed in Ebright, "Advocates for the Oppressed," 317; see also chapter 2.

77. The charges against New Mexican priests stemmed from a jurisdictional dispute between the Franciscans and the bishop of Durango who insisted on his right to appoint a vicar and to control ecclesiastic matters in New Mexico. When Bishop Crespo visited New Mexico in August 1730, some of the Franciscans, following instructions from the Franciscan custodian, fray Andrés Varo, refused to allow him to confirm them. Crespo sued the Franciscans and Varo authored a report in their defense. This ecclesiastical dispute spawned a series of charges and countercharges that had the effect of weakening the position of the Franciscans vis-à-vis the Spanish colonial government. By 1750 the civil authorities led by Governor Tomás Vélez Cachupín had completely eclipsed the Franciscans in the long-standing power struggle between church and state. In 1730, and during an earlier visit in 1725, Bishop Crespo's position was strengthened by the fact that heavy rains fell during these visits with great benefit to the province (Bancroft, *History of Arizona and New Mexico*, 240–41; Norris, "Franciscans Eclipsed").
78. Schroeder, *Brief History of Picuris Pueblo*, 8.
79. The six priests who recorded thirty-one marriages at Picuris between 10 July 1729 and 18 October 1739 were José Irigoyen, Juan Antonio de Ezeiza, Juan José Pérez Mirabal, Manuel de Sopeña, Caetano de Otero, and Juan Antonio Sánchez (Vigil, *Picuris, N.M. Marriages*, 7–17).
80. Miguel Palacios to Marqués de Casa Fuerte, Mexico City, 20 Oct. 1724, translated in Thomas, *After Coronado*, 209.
81. Schroeder, *Brief History of Picuris Pueblo*, 9.
82. Jefferson, Delaney, and Thompson, *Southern Utes*, 5–7.
83. Fray Juan Miguel Menchero, declaration, Santa Bárbara, 10 May 1744, AGN, Historia, 25, translated in Hackett, *Historical Documents Relating to New Mexico, Nueva Vizcaya, and Approaches Thereto to 1773*, 3:395, 403.
84. Entries 50 and 51 (ASSF 28:205) and entry 69 (ASSF 28:210), Vigil, *Picuris, N.M. Marriages*, 18, 22.
85. See, for example, entry 86, marriage of Juan Antonio de Leyba from Las Trampas and Rosalía Madrid, *coyota*, from Santa Bárbara (Vigil, *Picuris, N.M. Marriages*, 26).
86. Jones, *Pueblo Warriors and Spanish Conquest*, 137.
87. An attempt was made to pursue the Comanches, but "no pursuit could be carried five leagues beyond that district" (Thomas, *Plains Indians and New Mexico*, 166).
88. Adams and Chávez, *Missions of New Mexico*, 92.
89. Thomas, *Plains Indians and New Mexico*, 43–44, 51.
90. Brown, "Structural Change at Picuris Pueblo," 37–38.
91. The teniente alcalde informed Governor Mendinueta that many Comanches were wounded in battle (Pedro Fermín de Mendinueta to Antonio Bucareli, Santa Fe, 23 Jul. 1773, AGN, Provincias Internas, 103).

92. These tribes along with the mysterious Aa tribe, were all represented in a Genízaro petition for a land grant in April of 1733 (SANM I:1208). For more on the Aa, see Simmons, "Mysterious A Tribe of the Southern Plains."
93. See entry 86 in Vigil, *Picuris, N.M. Marriages*.
94. Jacinto Martín, petition, Jul. 1744, SANM I:529.
95. Martín is listed as a witness in entry 50, Mateo Fernández and María Guadalupe, marriage, 3 Nov. 1743 (Vigil, *Picuris, N.M. Marriages*, 18).
96. A fanega varied from one and a half to two and a half bushels and an almud varied from three to twenty-three liters according to the locality (Simmons, *Spanish Government in New Mexico*, 219–20; Nicolás Ortiz, report, Santa Bárbara, 23 July 1744, SANM I:529).
97. Joaquín Codallos y Rabal, decree, Santa Fe, 24 Jul. 1744, SANM I:529.
98. In 1750 Vélez Cachupín ordered the settlers from Abiquiu, Ojo Caliente, and Embudo to resettle their lands or lose their rights to them. When the Valdez family protested, Vélez Cachupín accused them of "seeking frivolous pretense as [an] excuse," and told them they would not only lose their land but also be assessed a fine of a hundred pesos to be taken from the best of their property if they did not resettle. The Valdezes reluctantly agreed to resettle rather than suffer this harsh penalty (SANM I:1100).
99. Bowden, "Private Land Claims in the Southwest," 4:993; Santa Bárbara grant, SG 114/PLC 96. The John W. Garretson survey of 1859 shows the settlement of Santa Bárbara just south of the Pueblo league boundary and another settlement right on the southern boundary of the Picuris league (Garretson survey, Aug. 1859, BLM, Santa Fe).
100. Juan Nepomuceno Trigo, letter, Istacalco, 23 Jul. 1754, translated in Hackett, *Historical Documents*, 3:467. For Father Arvide, see note 8.
101. Adams and Chávez, *Missions of New Mexico*, 94.
102. Ibid., 98.
103. Ibid., 94–95.
104. The first book of Picuris marriages (1726–1775) includes the following marriages involving Apaches: 7 May 1741, Giego Pituse (Apache) married María Antta (Apache), and 29 June 1741, Antonio (Picuris?) married Rosa (Apache). It is likely that there were many more Picuris-Apache marriages (AASF 28, f. 204–5; Vigil, *Picuris, N.M. Marriages*).
105. Forbes, *Apache, Navaho, and Spaniard*, 24.
106. Hammond and Rey, *Don Juan de Oñate*, 1:345.
107. Thomas, *After Coronado*, 62–64, 110–33.
108. Juan Miguel Menchero, declaration, Santa Bárbara, 10 May 1744, translated in Hackett, *Historical Documents*, 3:403.
109. Town of Cieneguilla grant, SG 62, r. 19, f. 668–72.
110. Kit Carson to William Messervy, 21 Mar. 1854, NARA, Records of the Bureau of Indian Affairs, r. 547, Letters Received by the Office of Indian Affairs, 1824–81, New Mexico Superintendency, 1854–55.

111. William Messervy to George Manypenny, NARA, Records of the Bureau of Indian Affairs, r. 547, Letters Received by the Office of Indian Affairs, 1824–81, New Mexico Superintendency, 1854–55. For an apparent firsthand account of the battle that differs from the military's, see Bennett, "Notes and Documents"; see also Taylor, "Campaigns Against the Jicarilla Apache."
112. Ebright and Hendricks, "Pueblo League and Pueblo Indian Land," 150–52.
113. "los soberanos decretos como leyes vigentes que tanto reencarga el formento de agricultura y también para hacer uso de pasteo para nuestros animales" (Rafael Fernández et al., petition, Santa Fe, 6 Mar. 1829, SANM I:287; Río del Pueblo grant, PLC 65, r. 41, f. 7).
114. Ayuntamiento of Santa Cruz de la Cañada, report, Santa Cruz de la Cañada, 5 Apr. 1829, Río del Pueblo grant, PLC 65, r. 41, f. 8.
115. Juan de Jesús Martínez, Juan Vicente Campos, Antonio Simbolo, Mariano Rodríguez, and Juan de los Reyes Rodríguez on behalf of Picuris, petition to the Ayuntamiento of San Jerónimo de Taos, San Lorenzo de Picurís, 11 Apr. 1829, SANM I:625. For a rough approximation of the alcaldías in northern New Mexico, see the 1779 Miera y Pacheco map in Adams and Chávez, *Missions of New Mexico*, 2–3, and on the cover of White, Koch, Kelley, McCarthy, and the New Mexico State Planning Office, *Land Title Study*. This map suggests that the southern line of the Taos Alcaldia was north of Picuris.
116. Ayuntamiento of Taos to the governor, San Jerónimo de Taos, 12 Apr. 1829, SANM I:625.
117. "en las inmediaciones del pueblo de Picurís" (territorial deputation to the governor, Santa Fe, 2 May 1829, SANM I:219).
118. Martínez, Tenorio, and Quintana committee, report, Santa Fe, 18 Jul. 1832, SANM I: 396. This report was found in the José Dolores Fernández grant (SG 71).
119. The settlers who were placed in possession of lots around the plaza of Vadito and the amount of land they received are as follows:

Manuel Fernández	twenty varas
Pedro Fernández	fifteen varas
Vicente Fernández	twenty varas
José Rafael Espinosa	twenty varas
Francisco Fernández	twelve varas
Antonio Santisteban	fifteen varas
José Rafael Medina	twelve varas
Manuel Valdez	twelve varas
Antonio de Herrera	twenty varas
Felipe Medina	ten varas
Ramón Ronquillo	twelve varas
José Miguel Argüello	twelve varas
José Ignacio Tafoya	twelve varas
Juan Miguel Tafoya	twenty varas

Blas Casillas	fifteen varas
Victor Gallegos	fifteen varas
José Dolores Fernández	twenty varas
Juan Fernández	twelve varas
Juan Antonio Vigil	twelve varas

120. Act of possession establishing the plaza of the Río de Pueblo de Picurís, 11 Dec. 1841; José Miguel Argüello, hijuela, Río de Picurís, 4 Dec. 1841, SRCA, Taos County Deed Book A-1, 248–51.
121. Antonio Benito Lucero to José Benito Salas, sale of land, 21 Aug, 1845, SRCA, Taos County Deed Book A-1, 248–51.
122. Ebright, "Sharing the Shortages," 20–22.
123. The Río de Picurís grant was rejected on 15 September 1894 by the Court of Private Land Claims for lack of authority of the territorial deputation to make grants under Mexican law. The Court of Private Land Claims was established by Congress in 1891 to complete the task of determining valid titles to land grants in the Southwest derived from Spanish and Mexican law (Bowden, "Private Land Claims in the Southwest," 4:1001–4).
124. Schroeder, *Brief History of Picuris Pueblo*, 13.
125. Juan Domingo Simbolo, Parcita, Juanito, and Juan de Jesús Simbolo, petition to Manuel [Armijo], Picuris, 6 Apr. 1845, box 3, folder 99, Donanciano Vigil Collection, SRCA. The petition was written and signed by Miguel González as holder of a power of attorney from the petitioners. The petitioners or their agent mistakenly referred to "una legua de tierra cuadrada" (a league of land squared) rather than to four square leagues, the amount of land recognized for all New Mexico pueblos.
126. Juan Domingo Simbolo, Parcita, Juanito, and Juan de Jesús Simbolo, petition to Manuel [Armijo], Picuris, 6 Apr. 1845, box 3, folder 99, Donaciano Vigil Collection, SRCA.
127. Stoller, "Grants of Desperation, Lands of Speculation," 22–23.
128. Abel, "Journal of John Greiner," 199, 203, 241.
129. Bowden, "Private Land Claims in the Southwest," 4:1009.
130. Garretson, field notes, survey of Pueblo de Picurís, 3, BLM.
131. Garretson, field notes, survey of Pueblo de Picurís, 4, 6–8, BLM.
132. Bowden, "Private Land Claims in the Southwest," 4:1009.
133. Aberle, *Pueblo Indians of New Mexico*, 69–83.
134. Brown, "Structural Change at Picuris Pueblo," 181–221.
135. Ibid.
136. *United States v. Sandoval*, 231 U.S. 28 (1913).
137. Brown, "Structural Change at Picuris Pueblo," 206–8. An interesting footnote to the land acquisition occurred in 1944 when the Bureau of Indian Affairs used compensation money still held in the trust account for Picuris and Pojoaque to purchase land from the New Mexico and Arizona Land Company that it leased

to the Ramah Navajos. A total of 26,727.28 acres was purchased with Picuris funds and 29,526.16 acres with Pojoaque funds. The lease money was placed in the U.S. Treasury for use by the Pueblo Indians. In 1956 the land was purchased by the Navajo Nation. Picuris was not consulted about these transactions nor did it receive funds from leasing or sale of these lands. It is presumably owed compensation for this misuse of its compensation funds by the United States.

138. Schiller, "Picuris Pueblo Files Claim to Aboriginal Lands."
139. *Pueblo of Picuris v. Oglebay Norton Co., et al.*, Civ. No. 04-0475 (D.N.M. 2004); Neary, "Picuris Reclaims Clay Site"; Schiller, "Picuris Pueblo Files Claim to Aboriginal Lands."

Chapter 4

1. Brandt, "Sandia Pueblo," 344-45. Tiwa language instructors at Sandia indicate that the preferred spelling is "Tuf Sh<u>eu</u>r Teui", with "e" and "u" underlined for linguistic notation for the pronunciation of the word, which is considered part of the spelling of the word (email to authors, 11 Dec. 2012). For the folk etymology of "Sandia," see Julyan, *Place Names of New Mexico*, 322.
2. Kessell, *Kiva, Cross, and Crown*, 96. The commissary was the superior of the Franciscans in New Mexico.
3. Ibid., 169.
4. Scholes, *Troublous Times in New Mexico*, 247-48.
5. Ibid., 6-7; Chávez, *Origins of New Mexico Families*, 35-36; Riley, *Kachina and the Cross*, 168, 180-81; Snow, "Note on Encomienda Economics," 346-47.
6. The hacking off of the arms of St. Francis has been seen as a symbolic crippling of the friars. In addition, "a crucifix had been whipped with such ferocity that all the paint and varnish was removed" (Liebmann and Preucel, "Archaeology of the Pueblo Revolt," 198).
7. Hackett, and Shelby, *Revolt of the Pueblo*, 1:26.
8. Barrett, *Conquest and Catastrophe*, 93.
9. Kessell and Hendricks, *By Force of Arms*, 383.
10. Brandt, "Sandia Pueblo, New Mexico," 37.
11. Preucel and Liebman, *Archaeologies of the Pueblo Revolt*.
12. Ebright and Hendricks, *Witches of Abiquiu*, 28-29.
13. Ibid.; Kelley, "Franciscan Missions of New Mexico," 43-44.
14. Bernardo Bustamante y Tagle, act of possession, Sandia, 16 May 1748, SANM I:848.
15. Ibid.
16. "total destrucción porque no me queda ni un palmo de tierra en que poder sembrar" (Salvador Martínez, petition, Albuquerque, n.d., SANM I:532).
17. "ningún derecho lo permite que se quite a unos para dar a otros" (Salvador Martínez, petition, Albuquerque, n.d., SANM I:532).
18. Chávez, *Origins of New Mexico Families*, 263.
19. Ibid., 230.

20. "la legua que pertenecía a los naturales del citado pueblo según disfrutan los demás pueblos de la provincia" (SRCA Land Grants Miscellany, Pueblo Indians, Sandia Pueblo, Dispute over encroachment by settlers who had purchased lands originally granted to Juan de Ulibarrí, folder 18 [1712–1826]).
21. "hasta las leguas que le[s] es concedidas a dichos naturales como los demás pueblos" (SRCA, Land Grants Miscellany, Pueblo Indians, Sandia Pueblo, Dispute over encroachment by settlers who had purchased lands originally granted to Juan de Ulibarrí, folder 18 [1712–1826]).
22. "demasía de la legua que goza el pueblo de Sandía ... dichos naturales manifiestan nada satisfacen a ser de ellos" (SRCA, Land Grants Miscellany, Pueblo Indians, Sandia Pueblo, Dispute over encroachment by settlers who had purchased lands originally granted to Juan de Ulibarrí, folder 18 [1712–1826]).
23. SRCA, Land Grants Miscellany, Pueblo Indians, Sandia Pueblo, Dispute over encroachment by settlers who had purchased lands originally granted to Juan de Ulibarrí, folder 18 (1712–1826).
24. "mala fe y picardía ... rompió el título de propiedad con el objeto de hacerse de la mitad de las tierras" (AGN, Justicia, 48:24).
25. Ignacio María Sánchez Vergara to Facundo Melgares, Jemez, 5 Jul. 1821, SANM I:1195.
26. In 1827 Sánchez Vergara sent a stack of thirty-two documents to Governor Manuel Armijo relating to the claim of Julián Rael to lands adjacent to or overlapping the pueblo's boundaries. Instead of taking a neutral position on the case befitting a former protector of Indians, Sánchez Vergara wrote a lengthy letter in support of Julián Rael and against Sandia. Sánchez Vergara claimed that Rael had a deed describing land bounded by "the league belonging to Sandia Pueblo" (Ignacio María Sánchez Vergara to Manuel Armijo, Alameda, 7 Jul. 1827, SANM I:1298).
27. "fuera de las leguas que por ley corresponde a los pueblos" (Ignacio María Sánchez Vergara to commanding general, Durango, 9 Sept. 1823, SRCA, Land Grants Miscellany, Pueblo Indians, Sandia Pueblo, Dispute over encroachment by settlers who had purchased lands originally granted to Juan de Ulibarrí, folder 18 [1712–1826]). It is worthy of note that in the original document, the "s" in "leguas" was altered to make the word read "legua" and that an attempt was made to change the date.
28. "que el juez del referido pueblo proceda luego a la medida de la legua susodicha, de los terrenos que resulten sobrantes" (Licenciado Elorriaga to commanding general, Durango, 13 Sept. 1823, SRCA, Land Grants Miscellany, Pueblo Indians, Sandia Pueblo, Dispute over encroachment by settlers who had purchased lands originally granted to Juan de Ulibarrí, folder 18 [1712–1826]).
29. *Pueblo of Sandia v. Babbitt*, Civ. No. 94-2624 (D.D.C. 18 Jul. 1998); Eusebio Rael de Aguilar, copy of petition, Alameda, 1 Sept. 1821, SRCA, Land Grants Miscellany, Pueblo Indians, Sandia Pueblo, Dispute over encroachment by settlers who had purchased lands originally granted to Juan de Ulibarrí, folder 18 (1712–1826).

NOTES TO PAGES 130–135

30. See the following documents in SRCA, Land Grants Miscellany, Pueblo Indians, Sandia Pueblo, Dispute over encroachment by settlers who had purchased lands originally granted to Juan de Ulibarrí, folder 18 (1712–1826): copy of transfer of land from Juan González to Julián Rael de Aguilar, Villa de San Felipe de Albuquerque, 18 June 1753; copy of transfer of land from José Garcia de Noriega to Julián Rael de Aguilar, Villa de San Felipe de Alburquerque, 19 Apr. 1764; José Petronilo Gutiérrez, copy of a declaration, Puesto de Bernalillo, 5 Sept. 1821; Eusebio Rael, will, 29 Mar. 1826.
31. "de legua y media de tierras de las más útiles que incuestionablemente nos pertenecen por el rumbo del sur" (José María Moquino, Andrés de la Candelaria, and Antonio de la Cruz, petition, [Sandia, 1829], AGN, Justicia, 48:24).
32. "tierras deben ampliársenos las ya concedidas" (José María Moquino, Andrés de la Candelaria, and Antonio de la Cruz, petition, [Sandia, 1829], AGN, Justicia, 48:24).
33. Andrés Romero, Juan José Gutiérrez, and Rafael Miera, depositions regarding land ownership in the vicinity of Sandia, Bernalillo, 18 May 1829, AGN, Justicia, 48:24.
34. Mariano Montoya and Francisco Miera y Pacheco on behalf of Sandia, petition, Bernalillo, 14 Feb. 1826, SANM I:623.
35. Juan González on behalf of the heirs of Eusebio Rael, petition, Corrales, 1 June 1826, SANM I:1210.
36. José María Moquino, Andrés de la Candelaria, and Antonio de la Cruz, and Juan Ramón Rael, statements, Mexico City, 13 Feb. 1841, AGN, Justicia 48.
37. "con abundancia, agua, tierras, para pastos y labores . . . buyes, semillas, herramientas y demás . . . en paraje cómodo" (Juan Francisco de Güemes y Horcasitas, decree, Mexico City, 16 Mar. 1747, SANM I:1347).
38. "pastos, montes, aguas y abrevaderos en abundancia para mantener ganados mayores y menores y caballada" (Bustamante y Tagle, act of possession, Sandia, 16 May 1748, SANM I:848).
39. Adams, "Bishop Tamarón's Visitation of New Mexico, 1760," 203.
40. Adams and Chávez, *Missions of New Mexico*, 138.
41. Ibid.
42. Proceedings in the concession of the Sandia grant, 1748, SANM I:848.
43. Pueblo of Sandia, Report P.
44. Joaquín Codallos y Rabal, certification of the proceedings of the resettlement of the mission of Sandia, Santa Fe, May 1748, BNM, Archivo Franciscano, 28/547, Fondos Reservados.
45. SANM I:848.
46. Hendricks examined this copy on 27 and 29 November 1995.
47. del Río, *Guía del Archivo Franciscano*, 1:lxix, lxxi–ii.
48. Rosa Figueroa paid special attention to the documents related to New Mexico and used them in preparing a report for the viceroy of New Spain, the Marqués

de Cruillas, in 1761. It is possible that some of the annotations in Rosa Figueroa's hand that appear on the certified copy date from that time.
49. Hordes, "History of the Boundaries of the Pueblo of Sandia," 21.
50. Former state historian Stanley M. Hordes, who served as a historical expert for those who opposed Sandia's effort to have its boundary reestablished on the crest of Sandia Mountain, argues convincingly that a document prepared by Miguel Antonio Lovato on behalf of Sandia could have been the source of the terms Whiting added. The Lovato document gives the Loma de Maygua as landmarks at the southern limit of the Sandia grant and Ojo del Carrisito. Neither term occurs in the original (Hordes, "History of the Boundaries of the Pueblo of Sandia," 20–21).
51. William Pelham to Thomas A. Hendricks, 1 Sept. 1859, SG, Letters Sent, r. 56, vol. 1, f. 212-17; Westphall, *Mercedes Reales*, 115; Morgan "'And on the East....'" John Wesley Garretson was born on 19 May 1812 in Tennessee and died on 7 May 1895 in San Antonio, Texas. After completing his work in New Mexico he settled in Texas where he surveyed for the New York and Texas Land Company (Roeder, "John W. Garretson").
52. Thomas A. Hendricks to William Pelham, 23 Apr. 1859, SG, Letters Received, r. 60, f. 217-21; William Pelham to John W. Garretson, 10 June 1859, SG, Letters Sent, r. 56, vol. 1, f. 193-95; William Pelham to James C. Collins, 10 June 1859, SG, Letters Sent, r. 56, vol. 1, f. 192; James C. Collins to Diego Archuleta, 11 June 1859, SG, Letters Received, r. 60, f. 228-29; Jenkins, "The Pueblo of Sandia and Its Lands," 59-63; Roeder, "John W. Garretson."
53. John Wilson to William Pelham, 26 Sept. 1859, SG Letters Received, r. 60, f. 259; John W. Garretson to William Pelham, 20 Sept. 1859, SG, Letters Received, r. 60, f. 258; Jenkins, "The Pueblo of Sandia and Its Lands," 61-64; William Pelham to Thomas A. Hendricks, 22 Aug. 1859, SG, Letters Sent, r. 56, vol. 1, f. 209; William Pelham to Thomas A. Hendricks, 1 Sept. 1859, SG, Letters Sent, r. 56, vol. 1, f. 212-17; Collins to Pelham, 7 Jul. 1859, SG, Letters Received, r. 60, f. 245; Morgan, "'And on the East...,'" 38. Reuben Clements was born in Tennessee and came to Texas in 1848, settling in Brownsville. He was city engineer and a state legislator there (Olson, "GLO Surveyor Personal Notes").
54. Clements, "Field Notes of the Pueblo of Sandia Survey," BLM; Pueblo of Sandia plat, BLM; Jenkins, "Pueblo of Sandia and Its Lands."
55. Grimes, *Treatise on the Law of Surveying and Boundaries*, 308-9.
56. Cited in Keene, "Report of the Sandia Pueblo East Boundary."
57. Cited in Keene, "Report of the Sandia Pueblo East Boundary."
58. In the case of *Santa Ana v. Baca*, 844F.2d 708 (10th Cir. 1988), Clements's survey of the San Felipe Grant was described as "inept" (Keene, "Report of the Sandia Pueblo East Boundary," 18).
59. Bowden, "Private Land Claims in the Southwest," 5:1319-20.
60. Politically, the pueblo's task was made more difficult by the fact that in 1978,

Congress designated most of the land Sandia was claiming as the Sandia Mountain Wilderness Area. The area was a favorite recreation spot for hikers and climbers in the Albuquerque region (Berthier-Foglar, "Sandia's New Buffalo Ideology").
61. Pueblo of Sandia Boundary, 96 Interior Decisions 331, 9 Dec. 1988. The Tarr opinion's decision that the secretary lacked authority to correct erroneous surveys of Pueblo grants was reversed by a decision entitled "Boundary Dispute between Santa Ana Pueblo and San Felipe Pueblo" (M-37010, 5 Dec. 2000). The opinion's decision that the Sandia Mountain was not the eastern boundary of the grant was reversed in "Eastern Boundary of the Sandia Pueblo Grant" (19 Jan. 2001).
62. Ebright, "What History Has to Say."
63. Del Rosal, *Diccionario etimológico*, 279v [562].
64. Stevens, *New Spanish and English Dictionary*.
65. Del Rosal, *Diccionario etimológico*, 214v [432.]
66. Stevens, *New Spanish and English Dictionary*.
67. Ebright, *Land Grants and Lawsuits*, 329.
68. Ebright, "What History Has to Say."
69. Luis Navarro García to Rick Hendricks, personal communication, Seville, 14 Nov. 1996.
70. Simmons, *Albuquerque*, 393.
71. Whiteley, "Law, Fact Legitimize Claim Up to Crest."
72. Bartolomé Fernández grant, PLC 61, r. 40, f. 113–62/SG 78, r. 20, f. 139–208.
73. Peñasco Largo grant, PLC 122, r. 44, f. 1222–83.
74. Ojo Caliente grant, SG 77, r. 20, f. 6–138.
75. *Pueblo of Sandia v. Babbitt*, 1996 WL 808067 (D.D.C. 1996).
76. *Pueblo of Sandia v. Babbitt*, No. 94-2624 (D.D.C., 20 Jul. 1998).
77. *Pueblo of Sandia v. Babbitt*, 231 F.3d 878 (D.C.Cir. 2000).
78. Ibid.
79. Testimony and statement of Stanley Hordes and testimony and statement of Sandia governor Stewart Paisano, in U.S. Senate, *Joint Hearing before the Senate Committee on Energy and Natural Resources and the Committee on Indian Affairs on Senate Bill 2016*, 47–49.
80. Representative Heather Wilson said in April 2000 that "it's never going to be approved by Congress, I can tell you that" ("Sandia Plan Gets Rocky Reception").
81. T'uf Shur Bien Preservation Trust Area Act, Pub. L. 108–007, Division F, Title 4.
82. The compromise reached would delineate a specific area for tribal hunting for traditional cultural purposes, leaving the remainder subject to fish and game jurisdiction (testimony of Governor Paisano in response to questions from Senators Dominici and Campbell, in U.S. Senate, *Joint Hearing before the Senate Committee on Energy and Natural Resources and the Committee on Indian Affairs on Senate Bill 2016*, 53–54).
83. Testimony of Governor Paisano in response to question from Senator Inouye,

in U.S. Senate, *Joint Hearing before the Senate Committee on Energy and Natural Resources and the Committee on Indian Affairs on Senate Bill 2016*, 52–53.
84. The T'uf Shur Bien Preservation Trust Area Act, Pub. L. 108-007, Division F, Title 4.
85. Berthier-Foglar, "Sandia's New Buffalo Ideology," 19.

Chapter 5

1. The other five Tewa pueblos are San Juan (now known by its Tewa name of Ohkay Owingeh), San Ildefonso, Nambe, Pojoaque, and Tesuque (cubitplanning.com/city/23781-santa-clara-pueblo-cdp-census-2010-population).
2. Cited in Arnon and Hill, "Santa Clara Pueblo," 298. See also Swentzell, "Architectural History of Santa Clara Pueblo," 97. These figures are estimates and should be used cautiously, especially in the pre-1854 period. Moreover, Santa Clara's membership numbers have been restricted by a membership law the pueblo adopted in 1939. See *Martinez v. Santa Clara Pueblo*, 540 F. 2d 1039 (10th Cir. 1976), *reversed*, 436 U.S. 49 (1978). Changes to that law currently being considered by the tribal council could increase the pueblo's membership by 50 to 100 percent.
3. Naranjo, "Thoughts on Migration by Santa Clara Pueblo," 248; Harrington, *Ethnogeography of the Tewa Indians*, 237. Other Tewas probably occupied these cliff lodges as well (Arnon and Hill, "Santa Clara Pueblo," 296).
4. Naranjo has been a common name at Santa Clara since the seventeenth century (Hammond and Rey, *Don Juan de Oñate*, 1:320, 2:651).
5. Benavides, *Fray Alonso de Benavides' Revised Memorial of 1634*, 69.
6. Antonio de Otermín to fray Francisco de Ayeta, 8 Sept. 1680, cited in Hackett and Shelby, *Revolt of the Pueblo Indians*, 98–101; Knaut, *Pueblo Revolt of 1680*, 7–8.
7. Thomas, *After Coronado*, 72–73. For a Naranjo genealogy, including many José Naranjos, see Hill and Lange, *Ethnogeography of Santa Clara Pueblo*, 356–63.
8. Dozier, *Hano*.
9. Hill and Lange, *Ethnogeography of Santa Clara Pueblo New Mexico*, 19–21.
10. See chapter 1 for the story of the overlap with San Ildefonso.
11. Tomás Vélez Cachupín, order, Santa Fe, 12 Nov. 1763, SANM I:1351; Juan Bautista de Anza, decree, Santa Fe, 10 June 1786, SANM I:1354.
12. Roque Canjuebe to Joaquín Codallos Rabal, petition, [Santa Fe, Aug. 1744], SANM I:213.
13. Santiago Roybal, report, Santa Fe, 24 Aug. 1744, SANM I:213.
14. Joaquín Codallos y Rabal, decree, Santa Fe, 1 Sept. 1744, SANM I:213.
15. Francisco Ortiz, act of possession, Santa Fe, 15 Dec. 1744, SANM I:213.
16. Antonio Canjuebe et al., petition, Durango, 15 Oct. 1815, SANM I:213. The Taos case is fully discussed in chapter 1.
17. Canjuebe et al., petition, SANM I:213.

18. "la legua que el rey dio al pueblo para él y sus descendientes como patrimonio" (Alberto Máynez, decree, Santa Fe, 22 Sept. 1815, SANM I:213).
19. Máynez, decree, SANM I:213.
20. Ángel Pinillas, Opinion, Durango, 21 Jan. 1816, SANM I:213. Under the Spanish doctrine of prescription (similar to the rules for adverse possession under U.S. law), title to land could be acquired by possession that went unchallenged for a sufficient period of time. If the period was at least thirty years, title could be acquired, even to stolen property (*Siete Partidas*, book 3, title 29, law 21).
21. Pedro María de Allande and José Miguel López, proceedings with the Indians of Santa Clara, Santa Fe, 30 Apr. 1816, SANM I:213.
22. "a quien siempre ha pertenecido por estar comprendido dentro de la legua que por la ley esta señalada a los pueblos de indios" (Ángel Pinillas, opinion, Durango, 8 Aug. 1816, SANM I:213).
23. See, for example, a 1 October 1849 letter from James S. Calhoun, first Indian agent in New Mexico, to the commissioner of Indian Affairs, saying that the Pueblos' lands "are held by Spanish and Mexican grants" (Abel, *Official Correspondence*, 53).
24. See chapter 8.
25. Act of July 22, 1854, c.103, § 8, 10 Stat. 308, 309.
26. Chapter 9 contains a more thorough discussion of this "fix" for pueblos that had no grant documents.
27. *Annual Report of the Surveyor General of New Mexico, 30 Sept. 1856, Executive Documents, Senate of the United States, 3rd Session, 34th Congress* (Washington: 1857), 514.
28. Bowden, "Private Land Claims in the Southwest," 2:552–53.
29. Juan and Antonio Tafoya, petition for use of water in the Cañada de Santa Clara, Santa Fe, 10. June 1724, SANM I:942.
30. Juan and Antonio Tafoya, petition for revalidation of grant of lands in the Cañada de Santa Clara, Santa Fe, 12 Sept. 1733, SANM I:952.
31. Juan Tafoya Altamirano and Antonio Tafoya, petition for lands in the Cañada de Santa Clara, Santa Fe, Mar. 1734, SANM I:949.
32. Juan Páez Hurtado, report, Cañada de Santa Clara, 8 Mar. 1734, SANM I:949.
33. Ibid.
34. Ibid.
35. Gervasio Cruzat y Góngora, decree, Santa Fe, 13 Mar. 1734, SANM I:949.
36. Francisco Antonio Marín del Valle, decree, Santa Fe, [Aug. 1757], Cañada de Santa Clara grant, SG 138, r. 25, f. 1530–32.
37. Ibid.
38. Joaquín Mestas from Carlos Mirabal and Juan Tafoya, deed certified by Francisco Gómez del Castillo, Santa Fe, 6 Mar. 1757, Cañada de Santa Clara grant, SG 138, r. 25, f. 1534–37.
39. Joaquín Mestas, petition, [Santa Fe] [early Apr.] 1758, Cañada de Santa Clara grant, SG 138, r. 25, f. 1537–40.

40. Francisco Antonio Marín del Valle, decree, Santa Fe, 24 Apr. 1758, Cañada de Santa Clara grant, SG 138, r. 25, f. 1540.
41. Prudencia González, petition, [Santa Fe, early May] 1763, Cañada de Santa Clara grant, SG 138, r. 25, f. 1541–42.
42. Juan Archuleta, declaration, [Santa Fe], 10 May 1763, Cañada de Santa Clara grant, SG 138, r. 25, f. 1545–46.
43. Domingo Vigil, declaration, Santa Cruz de la Cañada, [10 May] 1763, Cañada de Santa Clara grant, SG 138, r. 25, f. 1543–45.
44. Luis Archuleta, declaration, Santa Cruz de la Cañada, 10 May 1763, Cañada de Santa Clara grant, SG 138, r. 25, f. 1544–45.
45. Tomás Vélez Cachupín, order, Santa Fe, 1 Jul. 1763, Cañada de Santa Clara grant, SG 138, r. 25, f. 1548.
46. Mariano Rodríquez de la Torre, declaration, [Santa Clara, mid-Jul.] 1763, Cañada de Santa Clara grant, SG 138, r. 25, f. 1548–52.
47. "no tiene toda la extension de tierras de labor que necesita y debe considerassele segun derecho y es la real voluntad de su majestad" (Tomás Vélez Cachupín, decree, Santa Fe, 19 Jul. 1763, Cañada de Santa Clara grant, SG 138, r. 25, f. 1552–55).
48. "toda la Cañada de Santa Clara que corre al poniente hasta la sierra y en la que se hallaba el sitio mercenado a Juan y Antonio Tafoya" (Tomás Vélez Cachupín, decree, SG 138, r. 25, f. 1552–55).
49. Governor Anza cited *Recopilación* 6-3-20 to the effect that Spaniards who settled within one and one-half leagues of an Indian pueblo were subject to losing their farmlands (Juan Bautista de Anza, decree, Santa Fe, 19 Apr. 1780).
50. Governor Vélez Cachupín noted the lack of grazing lands for the town of Santa Cruz de la Cañada in his grant to Francisco Montes Vigil (grant, Santa Fe, 16 May 1754, Francisco Montes Vigil grant, PLC 14, r. 34, f. 1208).
51. Fernando de la Concha, decree, Santa Fe, 7 Aug. 1788, Cañada de Santa Clara grant, SG 138, r. 25, f. 1561–62.
52. De la Concha, decree, SG 138, r. 25, f. 1561–62.
53. Benjamin Thomas, petition on behalf of Santa Clara, 13 Dec. 1882, Cañada de Santa Clara grant, SG 138, r. 25, f. 1498–99.
54. Clarence Pullen, opinion, Cañada de Santa Clara grant, SG 138, r. 25, f. 1636–39.
55. George W. Julian, opinion, Santa Fe, 10 Oct. 1885, Cañada de Santa Clara grant, SG 138, r. 25, f. 1640–51.
56. S. Exec. Doc. No. 26, 49th Cong., 2nd Session, 2 (1887), 2–6, 33–34.
57. D. H. Smith on behalf of Cañada de Santa Clara Pueblo, petition, Santa Clara grant, PLC 17, r. 34, f. 1391–1395. Although dealing with the Cañada de Santa Clara grant, the Court of Private Land Claims file is entitled "Santa Clara Pueblo Grant" (PLC 17); this should not be confused with the surveyor general file covering the claim for Santa Clara's Pueblo league (SG Report K).
58. United States, answer, Santa Clara grant, PLC 17, r. 34, f. 1391–95.
59. Court of Private Land Claims, decision, Cañada de Santa Clara grant, SG 138, r. 25, f. 1654–55.

60. "Plat showing the Pueblo of Santa Clara Grant . . . Surveyed 28 Sept. to 8 Oct. 1914," General Land Office, Washington, D.C., Nov. 1917, BLM.
61. Warren, "Defining a Homeland," 147–49; Rothman, *On Rims and Ridges*, 49–50.
62. Rothman, *Bandelier National Monument*, 4.
63. Baklini, "Land Claims of Santa Clara Pueblo," 47–48; Aberle, *Pueblo Indians of New Mexico*; Rothman, *Bandelier National Monument*, 8.
64. Warren, "Defining a Homeland," 162–64.
65. Harrington, *Ethnogeography of the Tewa Indians*, 237; Warren, "Defining a Homeland," 171–73.
66. Arnon and Hill, "Santa Clara Pueblo," 306; Rothman, *On Rims and Ridges*, 171–73.
67. Wolf, "The Los Utes Case," 66.
68. Barney, "Indian Claims Commission"; "Battle to Preserve Ancient Pueblo Ruins."
69. Warren, "Defining a Homeland," 201–3; Rothman, *On Rims and Ridges*, 289.
70. Warren, "Defining a Homeland," 203–10.
71. Act of July 30, 2003, Pub. L, 108-66, 117 Stat. 876.
72. Act of July 25, 2000, Pub. L. 106-248, 114 Stat. 598.
73. See Act of July 25, 2000, Pub. L. 106-248, § 104(g), 114 Stat. 598, 602.
74. Unfortunately, in the disastrous Las Conchas fire of 2011, much of the forested lands within upper Santa Clara Canyon were destroyed, and the pueblo faces a long, difficult, and expensive battle to restore those lands.

Chapter 6

1. The other Keresan-speaking pueblos are Santo Domingo, San Felipe, Santa Ana, Acoma, Zia, and Laguna.
2. Hammond and Rey, *Rediscovery of New Mexico*, 15–27, 232–34.
3. Lange, *Cochiti*, 8–11.
4. Hodge, *Handbook of American Indians North of Mexico*, 1:317–18.
5. For a discussion of the Cañada de Cochití grant, the Miguel and Domingo Romero overlap, and the Cochiti pasture grant see Ebright, *Advocates for the Oppressed*, chap. 4.
6. Proceedings for the Santa Fe cabildo against Manuel Baca and Antonio Baca for mistreatment of Indians, Pinart Collection, PE 52:11, TBL.
7. Early in the litigation, Cabeza de Baca is referred to as simply Baca. He changed his name to Cabeza de Baca based on the mistaken belief that he was a descendant of the famous Álvar Núñez Cabeza de Baca (Chávez, "Valle de Cochiti").
8. *Cochiti v. Cabeza de Baca* is discussed in Cutter, *Protector de Indios*, 88–93, and Brayer, *Pueblo Indian Land Grants of the "Rio Abajo," New Mexico*, 116–23.
9. Felipe Sandoval to Alberto Máynez, Santa Fe, 5 Apr. 1815, ARAG, Ramo Civil 261-15, f. 40–41.
10. José Martínez, Baltasar Domínguez, Antonio Alonso, Juan Ignacio Montoya, and Juan Diego Coris to Felipe de Sandoval, Santo Domingo, 14 Mar. 1815, ARAG,

Ramo Civil 261-15, f. 6; Felipe Sandoval to Alberto Máynez, Santa Fe, 17 Mar. 1815, ARAG, Ramo Civil 261-15, f. 6-7.
11. Alberto Máynez, order, Santa Fe, 5 Apr. 1815, ARAG, Ramo Civil 261-15, f. 41-42; Alberto Máynez, oral ruling, Santa Fe, 26 Apr. 1815, ARAG, Ramo Civil 261-15, f. 42-43.
12. José Joaquín Reyes to Bernardo Bonavía, Durango [10 Aug. 1816], ARAG, Ramo Civil 261-15, f. 44-48; José Joaquín Reyes to Bernardo Bonavía, Durango [25 Sept. 1816], ARAG, Ramo Civil 261-15, f. 49-55.
13. Rafael Bracho to Bernardo Bonavía, Durango, [1816], ARAG, Ramo Civil 261-15, f. 59-70; Ángel Pinillas to Bernardo Bonavía, Durango, 3 Oct. 1816, ARAG, Ramo Civil 261-15, f. 71-73.
14. The term "letrado" was restricted in usage to mean a jurist, a lawyer who had completed university studies and attained the title of *bachiller, licenciado,* or doctor in civil law, canon law, or *in utroque iure,* which included both types of law (Icaza Dufour, *La abogacía en el reino de la Nueva España,* 54).
15. "según el espíritu de las leyes de Indias y confesión del mismo protector de los naturales, don José Joaquín Reyes, debe disfrutarse el to[do de una] legua de terreno repartida en media por cada viento" (Francisco Antonio de Landa to Pedro María de Allande, Durango, 31 Dec. 1816, ARAG, Ramo Civil 261-15, f. 2-5).
16. "y de un promotor fiscal que se nombrare para que pueda hacer los reclamos debidos en favor del real fisco" (Francisco Antonio de Landa to Pedro María de Allande, Durango, 31 Dec. 1816, ARAG, Ramo Civil 261-15, f. 2-5).
17. *Recopilación* 6-3-8.
18. In the seventeenth century, the official representing the crown's interest (the fiscal) appeared "especially in cases affecting the exchequer, the Church, and the rights of the Indians." It is ironic that in Sánchez Vergara's hands, the office of promotor fiscal opposed the interests of the Pueblo Indians (Pedro María de Allande, order, Santa Fe, 10 May 1817, ARAG, Ramo Civil 267-19, f. 1-2; Haring, *Spanish Empire in America,* 120).
19. Pedro Bautista Pino, measurement of the Santo Domingo league, Santo Domingo, 12-13 May 1817, ARAG, Ramo Civil 267-19, f. 2-14.
20. Ibid.
21. Ibid.
22. Ibid.
23. Ibid.
24. "la costumbre antigua y practicada con los demás pueblos ... es medir una legua a cada rumbo" (Domingo Fernández, testimony, 27 Jul. 1857, Los Trigos grant, SG 8, r. 13, f. 34-36; see Hall, *Four Leagues of Pecos,* 29, 296n58).
25. Pedro Bautista Pino, measurement of the Santo Domingo league, Santo Domingo, 12-13 May 1817, ARAG, Ramo Civil 267-19, f. 2-14.

26. Vicente Villanueva to Pedro Bautista Pino, Cochiti, 14 May 1817, ARAG, Ramo Civil 267-19, f. 16–19.
27. Vicente Villanueva to Pedro Bautista Pino, Cochiti, 16 May 1817, ARAG, Ramo Civil 267-19, f. 20–21.
28. Vicente Villanueva to Pedro Bautista Pino, Cochiti, 16 May 1817, ARAG, Ramo Civil 267-19, f. 21–22; Vicente Villanueva to Pedro Bautista Pino, Cochiti, 17 May 1817, ARAG, Ramo Civil 267-19, f. 22.
29. "ningún juez ni gobernador tiene facultad para vender parte ni el todo de la citada legua" (Alberto Máynez, decree, Santa Fe, 15 Apr. 1815, SANM I:1357). The eighteenth-century advocates for the pueblos are discussed in Ebright, *Advocates for the Oppressed*, chap. 1.
30. Francisco de Mendiola, opinion, Guadalajara, 11 Aug. 1817, ARAG, Ramo Civil 267-19, f. 23–33.
31. Rafael Cuentas, issuance of Francisco de Mendiola's opinion, Guadalajara, 30 Mar. 1818, ARAG, Ramo Civil 267-19, f. 34; Audiencia of Guadalajara to Pedro María de Allande, 30 Mar. 1818, ARAG, Ramo Civil 267-19, f. 34–35; Luis María Cabeza de Baca to Pedro María de Allande, Peña Blanca, 14 June 1818, ARAG, Ramo Civil 267-19, f. 36–37.
32. Rafael Bracho to the Audiencia of Guadalajara, Durango, 18 June 1818, ARAG, Ramo Civil 267-19, f. 54-58.
33. Francisco de Mendiola to the Audiencia of Guadalajara, Guadalajara, 6 Nov. 1818, ARAG, Ramo Civil 267-19, f. 60–65; Audiencia of Guadalajara, notification, Guadalajara, 17 Nov. 1818, Ramo Civil 267-19, f., 66; Ladislao Jáuregui to the Audiencia of Guadalajara, Guadalajara, 19 Nov. 1818, Ramo Civil 267-19, f. 67; Francisco de Mendiola, opinion, Guadalajara, 3 Dec. 1818, Ramo Civil 267-19, f. 68–72; Audiencia of Guadalajara's ruling, Guadalajara, 26 Jan. 1819, Ramo Civil 267-19, f. 73; Lázaro Negrete, calculation of court costs, Guadalajara 13 April– 3 July 1819, Ramo Civil 267-19, f. 75–81.
34. Francisco de Mendiola, 3 Dec. 1818, ARAG, Ramo Civil 267-19, f. 68-72. *Recopilación* 6-1-27 is titled "Que los Indios puedan vender sus haciendas con autoridad de justicia."
35. Bowden, "Private Land Claims in the Southwest," 5:1245–46; HR Exec. Doc. No. 1, 34th Cong., 3rd Sess., 508 (1856).
36. Pueblo of Cochiti, SG Report G, r. 7, f. 89-98; *Annual Report of the Surveyor General of New Mexico*, 411.
37. An Act to Confirm the Land Claims of Certain Pueblos and Towns in the Territory of New Mexico, Chap. 5, 11 Stat. 374 (1858).
38. *Pueblo de Cochiti v. United States*, in Horr, ed., *Pueblo Indians* 5:9–44.
39. Bowden, "Private Land Claims in the Southwest," 3:530–34.
40. Bartolomé Fernández was the grandson of Juan Fernández de la Pedrera and the son of Juan Fernández de la Pedrera II. Juan Fernández de la Pedrera I came

from the province of Galicia but at the time he left for the Americas he was living in Madrid. He married María Jurado de García of Albuquerque in 1695, who bore a son, Juan Fernández de la Pedrera II. After María died, Captain Juan moved in with the Ignacio Roybal family, who lived near San Ildefonso. In 1710 he married María Peláez, daughter of Jacinto Peláez, one of the grantees of the La Majada grant. Ignacio Roybal later appeared in court attempting to have the regranting of the La Majada grant to Jacinto Sánchez and Nicolás Ortiz set aside in favor of María Pálaez, for whom he was acting as guardian. Bartolomé Fernández was one of the two children of Juan Fernández de la Pedrera II (Chávez, *Origins of New Mexico Families*, 174–75; Bowden, "Private Land Claims in the Southwest," 3:524).

41. La Majada grant, SG 224, r. 30, f. 387.
42. *Trinidad Baca, et al., v. Unknown Heirs of Jacinto Paláez*, Civ. No. 26, District Court of Sandoval County, SRCA, Santa Fe, 1909.
43. *Pueblo de Cochití v. United States*, 7 Ind. Cl. Comm. 422, 454 (1959).
44. Pecos, "History of Cochiti Lake," 642.
45. Pinel, "Stopping the Flood of Damages from Cochiti Dam."
46. Pecos, "History of Cochiti Lake," 645.
47. *Pueblo of Cochiti, et al. v. U.S.A. and the Army Corps of Engineers, et al.*, U.S. District Court for the District of New Mexico, Civil Cause No. 85–1552, Nov. 1985.
48. Fred Cordero, testimony, in U.S. Senate, *Cochiti Pueblo-Corps of Engineers Dam Project*.
49. John Bowannie, testimony, in U.S. Senate, *Cochiti Pueblo-Corps of Engineers Dam Project*. Governor Bowannie noted that Cochiti was able to maintain its traditions because "we still follow our ancient religion and we are still able to speak our native language, and also because our lives are strongly connected to the land."
50. Coleman, "Leased Town Didn't Meet Expectations for Pueblo."
51. Pecos, "History of Cochiti Lake," 647.
52. Ibid., 649–50.
53. Ibid.
54. Ibid., 650; Indian Arts and Crafts Act of 1989, §601, 27 Oct. 1990 (amendment of HR 3618, 15 Mar. 1985).
55. An example of a study of Cochiti funded by the National Park Service is Biella and Chapman, *Archeological Investigations in Cochiti Reservoir*. Similar studies were done at other large dams and lakes, such as Abiquiu Dam. See Hibben and Stallings, *Excavation of the Riana Ruin and Chama Valley Survey*. Some of these sites are discussed in Carrillo, "Oral History-Ethnohistory of the Abiquiú Reservoir Area." See also Jeançon, *Excavations in the Chama Valley, New Mexico*, 75–76.
56. Keene, "Report on the Boundaries of the Santa Cruz Tract."

Chapter 7

1. Sando postulated that the great drought of the years 1276–1299 prompted the Hemish people to leave the Gallina-Cuba area (Sando, *Nee Hemish*, 12; Sando, "Jemez Pueblo").
2. "History of the Pueblo of Jemez."
3. Elliott, "Mission and Mesa," 45.
4. Liebmann, *Revolt*, 20.
5. Elliott, "Mission and Mesa," 46.
6. Ibid., 45.
7. Ibid., 46.
8. Hackett and Shelby, *Revolt of the Pueblo Indians*, 1:31.
9. Elliott, "Mission and Mesa," 51.
10. Ibid., 51, 47.
11. Sando, "Jemez Pueblo," 298.
12. Elliott, "Mission and Mesa," 51.
13. Ibid., 47–48.
14. See chapter 1 for a full account of this case.
15. For a complete discussion of the Cruzate grant, see chapter 8.
16. Bowden, "Private Land Claims in the Southwest," 5:1347.
17. The Ojo del Espíritu Santo grant was submitted to the surveyor general as the Zia, Santa Ana, and Jemez grant, SG Report TT, r. 7, f. 341–90; and to the Court of Private Land Claims as the Zia, Santa Ana, and Jemez grant, PLC 50, r. 38, f. 575–755 (Dory-Garduño, "1766 Ojo del Espíritu Santo Grant").
18. An example of another grazing grant made to a pueblo is the Cochiti pasture grant–Juana Baca grant that Vélez Cachupín made to Cochiti (Bowden, "Private Land Claims in the Southwest," 5:1252).
19. Zia, Santa Ana, and Jemez pueblos, petition for the Ojo del Espíritu Santo grant, Zia, Santa Ana, and Jemez grant, SG Report TT, r. 7, f. 363–64.
20. Tomás Vélez Cachupín, decree, Santa Fe, 16 June 1766, Zia, Santa Ana, and Jemez grant, SG Report TT, r. 7, f. 374 (translation).
21. Bartolomé Fernández, report, Santa Fe, 16 June 1766, Zia, Santa Ana, and Jemez grant, SG Report TT, r. 7, f. 365.
22. "lo posean con derecho legítimo mediante esta real merced" (Tomás Vélez Cachupín, granting decree, Zia, Santa Ana, and Jemez grant, SG Report TT, r. 7, f. 364).
23. Bartolomé Fernández, act of possession, Paraje del Ojo del Espíritu Santo, 28 Sept. 1766, Zia, Santa Ana, and Jemez grant, SG Report TT, r. 7, f. 367–68 (translation).
24. For a discussion of the grants to Felipe Tafoya and Bartolomé Fernández, see Malcolm Ebright, *Advocates for the Oppressed*, chap. 4.

25. Petition for the San Isidro grant, and grant by Juan Bautista de Anza, Santa Fe, 4 May 1786, town of San Isidro grant, SG 24, r. 16, f. 8–9; Bowden, "Private Land Claims in the Southwest," 5:1341.
26. Act of possession of the San Isidro grant, petition for the San Isidro grant, and grant by Juan Bautista de Anza, Santa Fe, 4 May 1786, town of San Isidro grant, SG 24, r. 16, f. 9–10; Bowden, "Private Land Claims in the Southwest," 5:1340.
27. Bowden, "Private Land Claims in the Southwest," 5:1370, 1391; Cañón de San Diego grant, SG 25, r. 16, f. 69–72.
28. Bowden, "Private Land Claims in the Southwest," 5:1329.
29. Although the authenticity of the Vélez Cachupín-certified copy of the Ojo del Espíritu Santo grant was later questioned, its genuineness had been clearly established (Dory-Garduño, "1766 Ojo del Espíritu Santo Grant," 157–96).
30. Dory-Garduño, "1766 Ojo del Espíritu Santo Grant," 157–96.
31. Zia, Santa Ana, and Jemez grant, SG Report TT, r. 7, f. 386–88; Bowden, "Private Land Claims in the Southwest," 5:1329–30.
32. Congress did not confirm any land grants after 1879, and ten years later there was a backlog of 116 grants awaiting Congressional action (Ebright, *Land Grants and Lawsuits*, 45).
33. M. C. Williams to commissioner of Indian Affairs, Santa Fe, 18 June 1888, NARA, Records of the Bureau of Indian Affairs, Miscellaneous Letters Sent by the Pueblo Indian Agency, 1874–91.
34. The statute providing for the first congressional appropriation for a special attorney for the Pueblo Indians was not passed until 1898 (30 Stat 571 at 594). Although no evidence has been found of an earlier statute providing for appointment of a special attorney, Twitchell testified that the pueblos had had a special attorney "for a long time" before the Court of Private Land claims was established in 1891 (Hall, *Four Leagues of Pecos*, 340n12).
35. Petition for confirmation of the Ojo del Espíritu Santo grant, Zia, Santa Ana, and Jemez grant, PLC 50, r. 38, f. 576–84.
36. Petition for confirmation of the Zia, Santa Ana, and Jemez grant and the Ojo del Espíritu Santo grant, PLC 50, r. 38, f. 580–83.
37. Bowden, "Private Land Claims," 5: 1330–31.
38. In 1764 Vélez Cachupín granted the settlers of San Gabriel de las Nutrias a temporary grant or license to establish a settlement on the grant on the banks of the Rio Grande. When the settlers could demonstrate that the settlement was well established, the governor would make the grant permanent (SANM I:780; Ebright, *Advocates for the Oppressed*, chap. 9).
39. Henry Billings Brown served on the U.S. Supreme Court from 1890 to 1906. He authored the infamous opinion in the 1896 case of *Plessy v. Ferguson* upholding racially segregated railroad cars and providing a foundation for racially discriminatory laws until the mid-twentieth century (Hall, *The Oxford Companion to the Supreme Court*, 92–93).
40. Levine, *Our Prayers Are in This Place*, 71.

41. Ibid., 52–54.
42. Sando, *Nee Hemish*, 72, 150–53.
43. Hall, *Four Leagues of Pecos*, 58–9.
44. Sando, *Nee Hemish*, 154–57; Hall, *Four Leagues of Pecos*, 97–98
45. Hall, *Four Leagues of Pecos*, 91–109.
46. Sando, *Nee Hemish*, 159.
47. An Act to Consolidate the Indian Pueblos of Jemez and Pecos, New Mexico, cited in Levine, *Our Prayers Are in This Place*, 157–58.
48. Sando, *Nee Hemish*, 159–60.
49. C. J. Tudor, memorandum opinion regarding the San Isidro grant, 28 Jul. 1936, town of San Isidro grant, SG 24, r. 16, f. 45–52; Bowden, "Private Land Claims in the Southwest," 5: 1344–45.
50. Dan T. O'Niell, report, 27 Jan. 1940, cited in Sando, *Nee Hemish*, 39–40.
51. Forrest, *Preservation of the Village*, 143.
52. Sando, *Nee Hemish*, 46.
53. Ibid.
54. Ibid.
55. U.S. Criminal Code, 18 USC 110; *New Mexico Sentinel*, 2 Feb. 1938; Sando, *Nee Hemish*, 48-49.
56. Sando, *Nee Hemish*, 46–99; Horr, *Pueblo Indians*, 1:13.
57. Horr, *Pueblo Indians*, 13.
58. *Pueblo of Zia, Jemez, and Santa Ana v. United States*, 11 Ind. Cl. Comm. 131 (1962); *Pueblo of Zia, Jemez, and Santa Ana v. United States*, 165 Ct. Cl. 501 (1964); Jadrnak, "Feds Seek Dismissal of Land Suit."
59. Nauman, "Jemez Pueblo Regains Land Church Leased."
60. Jemez identified 161 objects in the Smithsonian Collection as belonging to the pueblo but was only able to persuade the museum to return eighty-six. The idea that Pueblo Indians owned their property communally and did not have the capacity as individuals to sell pueblo property is also a central issue in the cases dealing with the sale of pueblo land (Linthicum, "Long Way Home to Jemez"; Hall, *Four Leagues of Pecos*, 166).
61. Linthicum, "Long Way Home to Jemez."
62. Baca, "More Than 70 Years After Exhumation Pecos Pueblo Ancestors Are Reburied"; Walker, "Eight-Year Effort Pays Off for All."

Chapter 8

1. Proper regard for Spanish naming custom would require that a shortened reference to Domingo Jironza Pétriz de Cruzate would be "Jironza," the governor's patrilineal name. These documents, however, have become well known in historical circles as the "Cruzate grants." We therefore refer to the governor as "Jironza," and the documents as the "Cruzate grants," the "Cruzate documents," or the "Cruzates," following standard convention.

2. Act of 22 Dec. 1858, 11 Stat. 374. Laguna and Zuni submitted Cruzate grants to Congress for confirmation by the surveyor general in the 1870s, but Congress failed to act on them. Laguna filed a claim in the Court of Private Land Claims, seeking confirmation of its grant, which the court rejected (*Pueblo of Laguna v. United States*, Court of Private Land Claims, No. 133 [20 Apr. 20 1898]). Congress confirmed the Zuni Cruzate grant in 1931. That they are considered legally valid is established by cases such as *Astiazaran v. Santa Rita Land & Mining Co.*, 148 U.S. 80, 82–84 (1893); *United States v. Maxwell Land Grant Co.*, 121 U.S. 365, 365–69 (1887); and *Jones v. St. Louis Land & Cattle Co.*, 232 U.S. 355, 360–63 (1914).
3. Twitchell, *Spanish Archives of New Mexico*, 1:2, 4, 477; Brayer, *Pueblo Indian Land Grants*, 14–15, 32, 47–48; Jenkins, "Spanish Land Grants in the Tewa Area," 113, 116n7; Westphall, *Mercedes Reales*, 108–9; Minge, *Acoma*, 25nn31–32; Kessell, *Pueblos, Spaniards, and the Kingdom of New Mexico*, 140; Matthews-Lamb, "Designing and Mischievous Individuals"; Mathews-Lamb, "'Nineteenth-Century' Cruzate Grants"; Brescia, "Historical Assessment of Ohkay Owingeh's Water Rights," 18–19; Cutter, "'Spurious' Seventeenth-Century Pueblo Grants of New Mexico."
4. C. 103, §8, 10 Stat. 308, 309.
5. Donaciano Vigil removed the library of Spanish and Mexican law books that were kept in the territorial secretary's office. He was territorial secretary under the last Mexican governor, Manuel Armijo, and General Stephen Watts Kearny appointed Vigil to the same post when he took Santa Fe in 1846. David V. Whiting, who was then acting as secretary to territorial governor James Calhoun, wrote Vigil in early April 1851, requesting the return of the books, evidently in vain (David V. Whiting to Donaciano Vigil, 8 Apr. 1851, folder 283, Donaciano Vigil Collection, SRCA).
6. William Pelham to John Garland, 29 May 1858, SG, Letters Sent, r. 56, vol. 1, f. 129.
7. Hall, *Four Leagues of Pecos*, 78–79.
8. Duarte, "El mobiliario de la época republicana en Venezuela," 23, cited in Hendricks, "David V. Whiting."
9. David V. Whiting to Manuel Álvarez, 4 Oct. 1840, Benjamin Reed Collection, 313a, SRCA.
10. Abel, *Official Correspondence of James S. Calhoun*, 284.
11. Whitely, "Reconnoitering 'Pueblo' Ethnicity," 437, 461–64.
12. A. P. Wilbur to Joseph G. Wilson, 29 Aug. 1860, SG, Letters Sent, r. 56, vol. 1, f. 194.
13. Ebright has suggested that Miller mistranslated a key phrase in the Tierra Amarilla grant, which had the effect of changing the grant from a community grant to a grant to a single individual, Manuel Martínez. Pelham recommended confirmation of the grant in 1856, and Congress, acting on that recommendation, confirmed it in 1860, to Francisco Martínez, Manuel Martínez's heir (Ebright, *Tierra Amarilla Grant*, 7–8, 16–18; *Daily New Mexican*, 19 Oct. 1880, cited in Hendricks, "David J. Miller").

NOTES TO PAGES 207–209

14. Twitchell, *Spanish Archives of New Mexico*, 1:x–xi; William Pelham to commissioner, 30 Sept. 1855, SG, Letters Sent, r. 56, vol. 1, f. 78–81.
15. Pelham stated that "designing and mischievous individuals" were trying to persuade the Pueblos that the government was requesting their title documents in order to destroy their evidence of title and withhold patents. In fact, the opposite was true: were the Pueblos *not* to present their claims to the government, they could lose their lands. The letter indicates that efforts to undermine Pueblo land tenure were well underway when Pelham began his work (William Pelham to commissioner, 27 May 1856, SG, Letters Sent, r. 56, vol. 1, f. 54–55; Twitchell, *Spanish Archives of New Mexico*, 1:xii; Twitchell, *Leading Facts of New Mexican History*, 2:459–60).
16. Docket Book, PLC, r. 11, f. 732–44.
17. Sandia also submitted a subsequent decree issued in 1762 by Governor Vélez Cachupín (Pueblo of Sandia, SG Report P, r. 7, f. 224–31).
18. Pueblo of Taos, SG Report I, r.7, f. 173–74.
19. Santo Domingo delivered eight original Spanish documents to Pelham's office, but he seems to have ignored all of them except the Cruzate grant.
20. Act of 22 Dec. 1858, 11 Stat. 374. The Zia grant, which was not submitted to Pelham until 16 October 1856, was sent to the secretary on 30 November 1856 but it was also confirmed by the 1858 act (William Pelham to Thomas A. Hendricks, 30 Sept. 1856, SG, Letters Sent, r. 56, vol. 1, f. 93–94). The Laguna grant, submitted to Pelham in 1857, was not submitted by him to Congress until 1859 and was never acted on (11 Stat. 374; Docket Book, PLC, r. 56, f. 399).
21. Ebright, *Land Grants and Lawsuits*, 23–24; White, Koch, Kelley, McCarthy, and the New Mexico State Planning Office, *Land Title Study*, 10–11.
22. This format of interrogation of prisoners was not in itself unusual. See, for example, the transcripts of depositions of Pueblo captives by Governor Otermín and his staff, after the Hispanos were driven out of Santa Fe in the Pueblo Revolt. The distinctive feature of the Cruzate grants is the addition of purported grants to the various pueblos to the deposition transcripts (Twitchell, *Spanish Archives of New Mexico*, 2:51–68).
23. Pueblo of San Juan, SG Report C, r. 7, f. 42; Pueblo of Picuris, SG Report D, r. 7, f. 54; Pueblo of San Felipe, SG Report E, r. 7, f. 67; Pueblo of Cochiti, SG Report G, r. 7, f. 91; Pueblo of Santo Domingo, SG Report H, r. 7, f. 127; Pueblo of Zia, SG Report O, r. 7, f. 214; Pueblo of Laguna, SG Report S, r. 7, f. 251.
24. The viceroy issued a commission to Jironza in 1684 that has been cited by some as authorizing (even directing) Jironza to make grants to the pueblos of New Mexico. In fact, however, the king's charge was that Jironza could make grants to Hispanos in the El Paso area and establish reducciones of Indians living there, many of whom left New Mexico with the departing Hispanos in 1680 (Twitchell, *Spanish Archives of New Mexico*, 1:1338, 1394, 2:82–85 [translation]).
25. Twitchell, *Leading Facts of New Mexican History*, 1:379–80 and 385n; Bancroft, *History of Arizona and New Mexico*, 194.

26. Kessell, *Pueblos, Spaniards and the Kingdom of New Mexico*, 137. Terrell suggests that Jironza could not have had more than 100 or 120 troops (*Pueblos, Gods and Spaniards*, 312).
27. Some historians have disputed the date of this battle, saying it occurred in 1688 (Twitchell, *Leading Facts of New Mexican History*, 1:379–80, 385n, 454; Bancroft, *History of Arizona and New Mexico*, 194n35; Minge, *Acoma*, 25). Given that Jironza was not reappointed governor until February 1689 and the clear statement of the date of the battle in his service record, the proposition that the battle took place on 29 August 1689 should not be open to dispute (Mathews-Lamb, "'Nineteenth-Century' Cruzate Grants," 129n75; Terrell, *Pueblos, Gods and Spaniards*, 311–12). The confusion may arise from Reneros Posadas's inconsequential attack on Zia in 1688 (Domingo Jironza Pétriz de Cruzate, service record, 12 Jan. 1693, AGI, Indiferente, 133, N. 58; Kessell and Hendricks, *By Force of Arms*, 26).
28. Bandelier, *Final Report of Investigations Among the Indians of the Southwestern United States Carried on Mainly in the Years from 1880 to 1885*, 2:198.
29. Manje, "Diary of an Expedition," 286–87. Manje was Jironza's nephew and part of the force that attacked Zia.
30. Terrell, *Pueblos, Gods and Spaniards*, 313; Twitchell, *Leading Facts of New Mexican History*, 1:380.
31. Kessell, *Pueblos, Spaniards, and the Kingdom of New Mexico*, 138-40; Fray Silvestre Vélez de Escalante, *Extracto de noticias*, BNM, Archivo Franciscano, New Mexico Documents, legajo 3, no. 1 (1778) (trans. Eleanor Adams), 156.
32. Kessell, Hendricks, and Dodge, *To the Royal Crown Restored*, 519–20, 540, 552–53n61, 608.
33. Unless otherwise noted, quotes from the Cruzate grants are taken from Whiting's translations. He appears to have done the official translations of nearly all the Cruzate grants submitted to Congress. (David Miller translated the Zia Cruzate grant.) Whiting's handwritten translations are in SG, grants to Pueblo Indians, r. 7, but translations of the grants that were submitted to the secretary in 1856 were typeset with the *Annual Report of the Surveyor General of New Mexico*, 493–511.
34. Although Congress confirmed the grant, the survey appears to have ignored this northern boundary call. The grant was surveyed as a standard league grant comprising about 17,545 acres (White, Koch, Kelley, McCarthy and the New Mexico State Planning Office, *Land Title Study*, 223).
35. The U.S. survey of the Cochiti grant seems to have switched the north and south calls in the grant, locating the south boundary, like the east and west boundaries, one league from the church and locating the *north* boundary about 1¾ leagues (about 4½ miles) north of the pueblo, approximately intersecting the point where Peralta Canyon, running easterly from the Pajarito Plateau, meets the Rio Grande. The surveyed grant thus totaled about 24,256 acres (White, Koch, Kelley, McCarthy, and the New Mexico State Planning Office, *Land Title Study*, 223; Pueblo of Cochiti, SG Report G, r. 7, f. 94).

36. Senate Exec. Docs., 34th Cong., 3d Sess., 503; Pueblo of San Felipe, SG Report G, r. 7, f. 70.
37. It is notable that these three documents purport to be signed by Ojeda himself. Besides these three, of those grant documents presented to the surveyor general, only the Cochiti and San Juan documents bear a signature that is supposed to be that of Ojeda.
38. Clements surveyed several Pueblo grants during this period, but his surveys have been judicially declared "inept" (*United States v. Algodones Land Co.*, 52 F.2d 359, 361 [10th Cir. 1931]; *Pueblo of Santa Ana v. Baca*, 844 F.2d 708, 712 [10th Cir. 1988]).
39. *Santo Domingo v. United States*, Docket 355; 25 U.S.C. §1777a(4).
40. The Acoma entry in the surveyor general's docket book suggests that there may have been a third document. If so, it now may be lost (SANM I, r. 11, f. 734).
41. Pueblo of Acoma, SG Report B, r. 7, f. 20-22.
42. The documentation of disputes between the two pueblos over water—primarily over rights to the Rio San José—extends at least as far back as the mid-eighteenth century. In 1742 Governor Gaspar Domingo de Mendoza ruled in favor of Acoma in a dispute with Laguna over the right to irrigate at Cubero. Just fifteen years later, however, Governor Francisco Antonio Marín del Valle recognized Laguna's rights in the Rio San José but explicitly noted that those rights were subordinate to those of Acoma (Bibo Collection, no. 2 [copy of Marín del Valle's decision dated 25 Apr. 1832], SRCA). In 1827 three Laguna Indians petitioned the Mexican governor to order Acoma not to enlarge its farming lands at Cubero, as they were impeding the flow of water to Laguna, and claimed that "the Lagunas have always enjoyed the right of preference to the water" (Twitchell, *Spanish Archives of New Mexico*, 1:441; three Laguna Indians, petition, 15 June 1857, SANM I:1372).
43. As surveyed, the grant was found to contain about 96,000 acres (Twitchell, *Spanish Archives of New Mexico*, 1:478).
44. Pueblo of Acoma, SG Report B, r. 7, f. 29-30, 34-35.
45. Pelham noted that because Laguna and Acoma had a long-standing dispute over the location of their common boundary, he proposed to postpone the survey of the Acoma grant until the Laguna grant was confirmed (William Pelham to Thomas A. Hendricks, 1 Sept. 1859, SG, Letters Sent, r. 56, vol. 1, f. 168-70). Pelham previously approved and sent to the Department of the Interior for confirmation a group of five Laguna claims to lands it acquired by purchase in the eighteenth and nineteenth centuries, all of which were within the boundaries set forth in their Cruzate grant (Pueblo of Acoma, SG Report B, r. 46. 526-28).
46. Pueblo of Laguna, SG Report S, r. 7, f. 269-72. Watts first wrote Proudfit's predecessor, T. Rush Spencer (Pueblo of Laguna, SG Report S, r. 7, f. 256-68).
47. Bandelier's journals frequently mention visits to and from Tipton, and when Felipita fell mortally ill in June 1890, Bandelier was at their home almost every day until she died on 12 July (Bandelier, *Southwestern Journals of Adolph F. Bandelier, 1889-1892*, 109-11).

48. Tipton had occasion to review at least some of the Cruzate grants during this period; in the archives, for example, there is a translation of the first Acoma Cruzate grant, dated 14 November 1884, that is signed by him as "Assistant Translator" in the Office of the Surveyor General.
49. Bradfute, *Court of Private Land Claims*, 62.
50. Bandelier, *Southwestern Journals of Adolph Bandelier, 1885–1888*, 217.
51. Bandelier, *Southwestern Journals of Adolph Bandelier, 1889–1892*, 492n697.
52. Bandelier, *Southwestern Journals of Adolph Bandelier, 1889–1892*, 492n697; Twitchell, *Leading Facts of New Mexican History*, 1:370n378.
53. Bandelier, *Southwestern Journals of Adolph Bandelier, 1889–1892*, 492n697.
54. This entry suggests that at least some pueblos had copies made of their Cruzate grants, copies that the pueblos kept themselves (ibid.).
55. Bandelier, *Final Report*, 2:15 n3, 202n1, 313.
56. Vélez de Escalante, *Extracto de noticias*, BNM, Archivo Franciscano, New Mexico Documents, legajo 3, no. 1 (1778) (trans. Eleanor Adams), 284.
57. Pueblo of Laguna grant, PLC 133, r. 46, f. 410–12.
58. Twitchell, *Spanish Archives of New Mexico*, 1:482.
59. The claim of possession "for at least three hundred years" was clearly exaggerated, given the undisputed fact that Laguna was only established about two hundred years earlier, in 1699 (PLC, r. 46, f. 431–32).
60. Pueblo of Laguna grant, PLC 133, r. 46, f. 516.
61. Pueblo of Laguna grant, PLC 133, r. 46, f. 489–92.
62. The five purchased tracts, Laguna's title to which Congress previously confirmed, essentially surrounded the league. They were surveyed such that their outer boundaries more or less matched those of the Cruzate grant and such that their inner boundaries were the league boundaries. As a result, Laguna appears to have ended up with approximately the same area confirmed to it as the Cruzate grant described (Pueblo of Laguna grant, PLC 133, r. 46, f. 491–92, 543–45).
63. It is unclear how this document came to the surveyor general. It immediately precedes the Acoma grant in the microfilmed copies of the surveyor general's files. The surveyor general's docket book shows that two Spanish documents were submitted on behalf of Acoma on 3 March 1856 (although Twitchell, citing an unspecified work by Tipton, says that only one Spanish document was submitted, but the docket book also shows that Laguna submitted two documents on 29 June 1857) (Docket Book, PLC, r. 11, f. 734; Twitchell, *Spanish Archives of New Mexico*, 1:478; Pueblo of Laguna grant, PLC 133, r. 46, f. 490; SG, Letters Sent, r. 56, vol 1, f. 742; Pueblo of Acoma, SG Report B, r. 7, f. 16–18). For the typed translation of the second, "treaty" document, submitted as part of Laguna's case in the Court of Private Land Claims, see Pueblo of Laguna grant, PLC 133, r. 46, f. 530–31.
64. Will M. Tipton, "Memorandum in Regard to Indian Pueblo Grants in New Mexico," NARA, RG 75, Bureau of Indian Affairs, United Pueblos Agency, General Correspondence, 1935–43, entry 99, box 294, file 049, 7. This memorandum, which

Tipton apparently produced in 1911 or 1912, was unknown in modern times until it was located in the federal archives in the course of the preparation of this book. A copy is now at the SRCA. Twitchell quotes it at length (*Spanish Archives of New Mexico*, 1:482).

65. Tipton, "Memorandum in Regard to Indian Pueblo Grants in New Mexico," NARA, RG 75, Bureau of Indian Affairs, United Pueblos Agency, General Correspondence, 1935–43, entry 99, box 294, file 049, 7; Twitchell, *Spanish Archives of New Mexico*, 1:481–82.

66. Keown's opinion on this issue was of no legal consequence, since Congress confirmed the Santo Domingo grant years before, as it had nearly all the other Cruzate grants, and that confirmation precludes any attack on its validity. Nevertheless, the court hearing the *Thompson* case decided that the government's effort to undo a gross mistake by the Pueblo Lands Board had come too late. The court found that the pueblo's title to a portion of its grant that a later Spanish grant overlapped was extinguished, and the suit was dismissed (*United States v. Thompson*, 941 F.2d 1074 [10th Cir. 1991]).

67. According to former state historian Myra Ellen Jenkins, there was no authentic document signed by Ojeda in the archives (Myra Ellen Jenkins to Omar Bradley, 27 July 1982, unpublished letter in the possession of Richard W. Hughes). The William G. Ritch Collection at the Huntington Library in San Marino, California, contains a part of Vargas's campaign journal in which there is a four-page letter from Ojeda to Vargas. Presumably this document was part of the Spanish Archives of New Mexico prior to the 1880s, when Ritch, who served as New Mexico territorial secretary from 1873 to 1885, apparently removed it (along with several hundred other items, now at the Huntington). Translations of the extant Ojeda letters appear in Kessell, Hendricks, and Dodge, *Blood on the Boulders*, 1:32–33, 320–21, 396–98; 2:735–36, 740–41, 798–99.

68. See, for example, Pueblo of Acoma, SG Report B, r. 7, f. 20, Pueblo of Laguna, SG Report S, r. 7, f. 248, Pueblo of Santo Domingo, SG Report H, r. 7, f. 127

69. Vélez de Escalante, *Extracto de noticias*, BNM, Archivo Franciscano, New Mexico Documents, legajo 3, no. 1 (1778) (trans. Eleanor Adams), 284. The *Extracto* states that on that date "the Queres of the new Pueblo, which [Governor Pedro Rodríguez] Cubero named Señor San Joseph de la Laguna, rendered obedience" to the Spaniards.

70. Kessell and Hendricks, *By Force of Arms*, 26–27; Vélez de Escalante, *Extracto de noticias*, BNM, Archivo Franciscano, New Mexico Documents, legajo 3, no. 1 (1778) (trans. Eleanor Adams), 284.

71. Pueblo of Laguna, SG Report S, r. 7, f. 253 (emphasis added).

72. In the microfilm of the four-page Laguna submission, this is the third page, clearly out of order, as it precedes the last page of the grant document (Pueblo of Laguna, SG Report S, r. 7, f. 250.

73. Pueblo of Laguna, SG Report S, r. 7, f. 252–55.

74. Tipton, "Memorandum in Regard to Indian Pueblo Grants in New Mexico," NARA, RG 75, Bureau of Indian Affairs, United Pueblos Agency, General Correspondence, 1935-43, entry 99, box 294, file 049, 7; Twitchell, *Spanish Archives of New Mexico*, 1:481. The surveyor general's docket book shows that the two Spanish documents submitted to the office by or on behalf of Laguna on 29 June 1857 were labeled "A" and "B." Document B was the four-page grant, but Tipton said that *both* documents were dated 1689 (Pueblo of Laguna, SG Report S, r. 7, f. 742).
75. Barreiro later served in the Mexican national congress as delegate from New Mexico. He had the first printing press brought into the territory, and with it he founded the first periodical, *El crepúsculo de la libertad* (*The Dawn of Liberty*), a publication that was later taken over by the famous taoseño, Padre Antonio José Martínez. (For the complete text of the *Ojeada* in Spanish and English translation see Bloom, "Barreiro's *Ojeada sobre Nuevo-México*.")
76. Barreiro describes Vargas's return to New Mexico and explains that at about the same time, some Frenchmen explored "an arm of the Mississippi" (un brazo del Missisipi) but claimed to have found the Río Bravo del Norte. The meaningless phrase "buse misisipe," which clearly appears in the text of the Laguna document, appears to derive from that phrase.
77. Tipton, "Memorandum in Regard to Indian Pueblo Grants in New Mexico," NARA, RG 75, Bureau of Indian Affairs, United Pueblos Agency, General Correspondence, 1935-43, entry 99, box 294, file 049, 3; Twitchell, *Spanish Archives of New Mexico*, 1:479.
78. Dory-Garduño, "1766 Ojo del Espiritu Santo Grant," 157, 168-69.
79. Stanley M. Hordes, affidavit, *United States v. Thompson*, No. 84-314 (D.N.M.), filed 24 Aug. 1988, paras. 5-7.
80. Mathews-Lamb, "'Nineteenth-Century' Cruzate Grants," 97-99.
81. Cutter, "'Spurious' Seventeenth-Century Pueblo Grants," 7, 11.
82. Pueblo of Acoma, SG Report B, r. 7, f. 21.
83. Hall, *Four Leagues of Pecos*, 148-59.
84. The Vigil Index listed only one document involving Jironza, having nothing to do with these grants (Fernández, Vigil, and Vigil, *Vigil Index, Spanish Archives and Mexican Archives of New Mexico, 1681 to 1846*, ed. Julián Josué Vigil, SANM I, r. 10).
85. The Vigil Index does not specifically mention a grant to Sandia. It is possible that item 720, a petition from fray Juan Miguel Menchero, was related to the grant or included the grant document (Fernández, Vigil, and Vigil, *Vigil Index*, SANM I, r. 10; Sandia grant, SANM I:848). It also makes no mention of the Cañada de Santa Clara grant (*Vigil Index*, SANM I, r. 10, f. 20-21; Cañada de Santa Clara grant, SG 138) or the Santo Domingo-San Felipe grant (*Vigil Index*, SAMN I, r. 10, f. 23-24; Santo Domingo-San Felipe grant, SG 142).
86. Domingo Jironza Pétriz de Cruzate, service record, 12 Jan. 1693, AGI, Indiferente, 133, N. 58.

87. See, for example, the discussion of the extensively documented adjudication of the boundary between Santa Ana Pueblo and San Felipe Pueblo in chapter 2. The documents produced by San Felipe in the course of that adjudication were deeds by which it acquired lands abutting Santa Ana's lands from Spaniards. At no time did it produce anything like the San Felipe Cruzate grant.
88. Kessell, *Kiva, Cross, and Crown*, 413–63.
89. Two documents were submitted for Pecos: the Cruzate grant and an 1829 report to the Mexican territorial government on alleged encroachment by Hispano settlers onto Pecos lands (Docket Book, PLC, r. 7, f. 736; Hall, *Four Leagues of Pecos*, 80; Pueblo of Pecos, SG Report F, r. 7 f. 81–84).
90. Pelham to commissioner, 30 Sept. 1855, SG, Letters Sent, r. 56, vol. 1, f. 78–80.
91. Act of 22 Dec. 1858, 11 Stat. 374. The subsequent, convoluted ownership history of this grant is told in exhaustive but entertaining detail in Hall, *Four Leagues of Pecos*.
92. Ethan Eaton, petition for confirmation of the Eaton grant, 11 Oct. 1855, SG 19, r. 14, f. 787. What is commonly called the "San Cristóbal grant" is recorded in SG as the Eaton grant. For a brief history of the San Cristóbal grant, covering the Indian pueblo and the later Mexican period grant to Domingo Fernández, see Ebright, *Advocates for the Opressed*, chap. 6.
93. Schroeder, "Pueblos Abandoned in Historic Times," 247.
94. Jenkins, "Spanish Land Grants in the Tewa Area," 117–18.
95. Villa Nueva de Santa Cruz, settlement, 1695, SANM I:882; Twitchell, *Spanish Archives of New Mexico*, 1:243–44.
96. Twitchell, *Spanish Archives of New Mexico*, 1:246–47; Jenkins, "Spanish Land Grants in the Tewa Area," 117–18.
97. Fernández had a record of seeking grants of lands adjacent to or on top of pueblo lands; see petition for lands, 1815, SAMN I:281, seeking a grant at Rancho de Cubero, located between Santo Domingo and San Felipe (the grant was approved and was later confirmed under U.S. rule) and petition for lands, 1823–24 SANM I:283, seeking a grant of land at Pecos Pueblo (this grant was denied) (Hall, *Four Leagues of Pecos*, 35–45).
98. Fernández, Vigil, and Vigil, *Vigil Index*, i–ii.
99. Bowden, "Private Land Claims in the Southwest," 6:272–81.
100. A cover sheet with the San Cristóbal Cruzate grant indicates that Pelham originally filed the document with the Eaton grant claim file (SG 19) but later struck that and placed it with the other pueblo grant claims. That inscription indicates that the Eaton claim was already on file with Pelham when he received the San Cristóbal Cruzate grant.
101. Act of 21 June 1860, §1, 12 Stat. 71 (1860).
102. Docket Book, PLC, r. 7, f. 734.
103. The original document is not at the State Records Center and Archives; presumably, the pueblo reclaimed it after it was transcribed and recorded. There is a

Miller transcription and translation (although the text of the translation is not in his handwriting), both dated 31 December 1878. There is also a transcription of the grant dated 12 November 1895, which is signed by Surveyor General Charles F. Easley (Pueblo of Zuni, SG Report V, r. 7, f. 401–6, 408–13).

104. Pueblo of Zuni, SG Report V, r. 7, f. 398.
105. "Pueblo of Zuni, Land Status," Branch of Real Estate Services, Albuquerque Area Office, Bureau of Indian Affairs, Feb. 1, 1979, 56.
106. The grant as surveyed comprised 17,635.8 acres ("Pueblo of Zuni, Land Status," Albuquerque Area Office, Bureau of Indian Affairs, 1 Feb. 1979, 55).
107. Docket Book, PLC, r. 11, f. 741; Pueblo of Sandia, SG Report P, r. 7, f. 223.
108. Act of 22 Dec. 1858, 11 Stat. 374.
109. See chapter 4.
110. In the course of the preparation of this book, the pueblo allowed the authors to examine the originals and to have high-quality scans made of them for the State Record Center and Archives.
111. Sandia Cruzate grant (trans. Rick Hendricks).
112. Sandia Cruzate grant B (by Rick Hendricks).
113. Ibid.
114. Opinion, *Laguna v. United States*, No. 133, Court of Private Land Claims (undated), Pueblo of Laguna grant, PLC 133, r. 46, f. 490. A translation of the document, which was evidently used in the trial, appears at r. 46, f. 530–31.
115. Pueblo of Acoma, SG Report B, r. 7, f. 16–18. There is no translation of the document in the microfilmed records or currently existing files.
116. Opinion, Pueblo of Laguna, SG Report S, r. 46, f. 490. It seems more likely that Laguna acquired the document in the early 1850s from middlemen who acquired it from Victor de la O.
117. "Spanish Papers A & B Filed," Docket Book, PLC, r. 11, f. 734, 742.
118. "Spanish Papers A & B Filed," Docket Book, PLC, r. 11, f. 17–18.
119. The fate of the Spanish archives from the El Paso exile period has never been clear. There is no evidence that any significant number of post-Revolt, exile-period documents were returned to Santa Fe after the reconquest. For descriptions of some documents from the period that did survive in other archives, see Twitchell, *Spanish Archives of New Mexico*, 2:3–78.
120. Pueblo of San Juan, SG Report C, r. 7, f. 47–48, 50–51. Whiting's translation of the San Juan Cruzate grant is dated 18 November 1855, just a week later.
121. Docket Book, PLC, r. 11, f. 735.
122. Pueblo of Acoma, SG Report B, r. 7, f. 20–22; Docket Book, PLC, r. 11, f. 732, 734, 736. Although the generic Cruzate grant was microfilmed with the Acoma documents, it seems likely that Laguna submitted it. It is difficult to determine which of the eight documents that Santo Domingo submitted were designated as separate documents by Pelham's office and whether any are missing. Most of these documents were not translated.
123. Pueblo of San Juan, SG Report C, r. 7, f. 51.

124. SG, Letters Sent, r. 56, vol. 1, f. 395.
125. Acoma's original petition identified the defendants as "Vincenti Abilucia, Victor de Loba and Ramón Sánchez" (*Acoma v. Abilucia, et al.*, Case No. 11 [3d Dist. Ct.], petition filed 24 Aug. 1854).
126. *Acoma v. Abilucia, et al.*, Case No. 11, petition filed 24 Aug. 1854. As already noted, on 3 March 1856 Acoma presented to the surveyor general's office another Cruzate grant, which was apparently not the one at issue in this litigation. On the surveyor general's recommendation Congress confirmed this document as the Acoma grant. In light of the litigation, one must wonder how Acoma came by *that* document.
127. *Acoma v. Abilucia, et al.*, Case No. 11, order entered 26 Aug. 1854.
128. The reference to Polvadera (which Twitchell misspelled as "Polaverda"), an old but tiny, unincorporated community on the west bank of the Rio Grande between San Acacia and Socorro, brings to mind the claim that Isleta presented to Pelham in support of its request for confirmation of its "grant." Isleta had no grant document to present to the surveyor general, but its leaders testified that they had a document that was deposited in the Spanish archives, although a Mexican named Miguel Antonio Lobato had later told them that he had seen the document in the possession of a man in Polvadera or Socorro. They stated that the grant extended from the Manzano Mountains on the east to the Rio Puerco on the west. Pelham accepted the claim, and the grant was surveyed and confirmed by Congress for more than 110,000 acres, the largest confirmed pueblo "grant" in New Mexico. It seems at least possible that if there was a document underlying this claim, it was another Cruzate grant (Twitchell, *The Spanish Archives of New Mexico*, 1:481).
129. *Acoma v. Abilucia, et al.*, Case No. 11, Victor de la O, answer, 6 Nov. 1854. According to Mathews-Lamb, Donaciano Vigil and Manuel Armijo were among the few people in New Mexico who utilized paper bearing the "MARIANO" watermark, on which all the Cruzate grants are written. Another such person was Francisco Sarracino, a former governor of the territory whom Mathews-Lamb describes as a "close associate" of Armijo's. This may be the same Sarracino referred to in De la O's answer (Mathews-Lamb, "'Nineteenth-Century' Cruzate Grants," 98–99).
130. *Acoma v. Abilucia, et al.*, Case No. 11, Victor de la O, response, 6 Nov. 1854.
131. Ibid.
132. *Acoma v. Abilucia, et al.*, Case No. 11, order entered 6 Nov. 1854.
133. *De la O v. Pueblo of Acoma*, 1 N.M. 226 (Terr. Sup. Ct. 1857).
134. The apparent conflict of interest in Justice Benedict ruling on his own lower court opinion was simply a consequence of the structure of the courts in the new territory at that time (Rosen, "Acoma v. Laguna and the Transition from Spanish Colonial Law to American Civil Procedure in New Mexico," para. 72n57).
135. This second Acoma document is the only Cruzate grant dated 28 September 1689. The text as quoted in Benedict's opinion closely tracks Miller's

translation, which is dated 30 September 1863. The surveyor general file also includes a transcription of the Spanish (Pueblo of Acoma, SG Report B, r. 7, f. 29–30, 34–35).

136. See discussion in chapter 9.

Chapter 9

1. When Governor Melgares received the 1811 Law of the Cortes declaring "the juridical equality of Spaniard and Indians," he decreed the "'minority' of the Pueblo Indians ended," after which they "ceased to be wards of the State with a Special Protector of Indians, assigned to look after their interests" (Hall and Weber, "Mexican Liberals and the Pueblo Indians," 5–32, 7–8; Hall, *Four Leagues of Pecos*, 32–33). W. W. H. Davis (who served as U.S. attorney for the territory in 1853–1854 and was later secretary of the territory and, briefly, governor), among others, insisted that Mexican laws and official actions continued to treat the Pueblos as wards of the government (*El Gringo*, 149).
2. Treaty of Peace, Friendship, Limits and Settlement Between the United States of America and the Mexican Republic, 9 Stat. 922. The treaty was signed on 2 February 1848, in Guadalupe Hidalgo, now in the northwestern part of Mexico City. Within days of his arrival in Santa Fe, General Kearny was visited by several pueblo governors, who "expressed great satisfaction over the arrival of the United States forces while undoubtedly pressing their claims for protection of their lands against encroachment" (Calvin, *Lieutenant Emory Reports*, 58).
3. Cited in Newton et al., *Cohen's Handbook of Federal Indian Law*, 9–12.
4. *Cherokee Nation v. Georgia*, 30 U.S. 1 (1831); *Worcester v. Georgia*, 31 U.S. 515 (1832); *Johnson v. M'Intosh*, 21 U.S. 543 (1823). For a brief biography of John Marshall, see Newman, *Yale Biographical Dictionary of American Law*, 136–61.
5. This decision was the first to articulate the guardian-ward theory of the relationship between the United States and the Indian tribes (*Cherokee Nation v. Georgia*, 30 U.S. at 16).
6. Georgia ignored the decision, as it had the entire proceeding before the Supreme Court. The resulting political furor nearly brought the court to its knees in what has been referred to as "the most serious crisis in the history of the Court" (Warren, *Supreme Court in United States History*, 2:189). Worcester was eventually pardoned and released, but within five years the Cherokees were forced out of Georgia and onto the Trail of Tears, to the Indian Territory (modern-day Oklahoma) (Burke, "Cherokee Cases; Smith, *An American Betrayal*, 134–37; Perdue and Green, *Cherokee Nation and the Trail of Tears*, 78–83).
7. 21 U.S. 543 (1823).
8. Trade and Intercourse Act of 22 Jul. 1790, 1 Stat. 137.
9. Trade and Intercourse Act of 22 Jul. 1790, 1 Stat. 137, §4. Reenacted repeatedly until, with slight modifications in wording, it was made permanent in 1834, this

section remains in effect as a prominent feature of federal Indian law (codified at 25 U.S.C. §177). It is commonly referred to as "the Nonintercourse Act."

10. Trade and Intercourse Act of 1834, 4 Stat. 729. Much of this enactment remains in effect as various sections of the modern Title 25 of the U.S. Code.

11. Alexis de Tocqueville, the young French aristocrat who toured the United States from 1831 to 1833 ostensibly to observe the U.S. penal system for the French government, produced a trenchant and insightful collection of observations about American society and politics in the two-volume compilation of his journals and observations that he published on his return to France. He wrote that the United States managed to overcome the Indians and to acquire their lands "with singular felicity, tranquilly, legally, philanthropically ... without violating a single great principle of morality in the eyes of the world.... It is impossible to destroy men with more respect for the laws of humanity" (*Democracy in America*, 335).

12. The largest category of claims over which the Indian Claims Commission was given jurisdiction when Congress created it in 1946 in an effort to provide remedies for the many wrongs done to the Indian tribes over the years was that of inadequate compensation for cessions of land made by tribes by treaties and other agreements. See Act of 13 Aug. 1946, c. 959, §2, 60 Stat. 1050 (formerly codified at 25 U.S.C. §70a). Decisions of the Supreme Court required these claims to be valued as of the dates of the takings, which were almost always in the nineteenth century, without any payment of interest (see *Tee-Hit-Ton Indians v. United States*, 348 U.S. 272 [1955]). Yet by the time Congress terminated the commission in 1978, it had entered judgments in favor of the tribes totaling more than $818 million, and there were still sixty-eight cases remaining that were transferred to the Court of Claims (U.S. Indian Claims Commission, *Final Report*, 125).

13. See, generally, Prucha, *Great Father*, esp. 214–69.

14. To be sure, many eastern Indians remained on their original homelands, but they mostly kept a low profile, until by the latter half of the twentieth century the United States became willing to acknowledge their presence and resume their recognition as tribes subject to federal protection. See, for example, *United States v. John*, 437 U.S. 634 (1978) (affirming "Indian country" status of lands held by Choctaws within the state of Mississippi).

15. Act of 3 March 1849, §5, 9 Stat. 395.

16. Brayer, *Pueblo Indian Land Grants of the "Rio Abajo," New Mexico*, 17–19.

17. Hall, *Four Leagues of Pecos*, 32–33. Hall cites but rejects the contrary views of three other historians of New Mexico, including Brayer, though he agrees that "it took ten years" for this new legal regime to become manifest in New Mexico (*Four Leagues of Pecos*, 296n4). On the question of Pueblo citizenship see Hall and Weber, "Mexican Liberals and the Pueblo Indians," 5.

18. 9 Stat. 922, §§8, 9.

19. See *United States v. Sandoval*, 231 U.S. 28, 38 (1913) ("It remains an open question

whether they have become citizens"), and *United States v. Joseph*, 94 U.S. 614, 618 (1877) (leaving open the question whether Pueblos are citizens of United States or of New Mexico).

20. *United States v. Lucero*, 1 N.M. 422, 432 (1869). For other cases maintaining that the treaty had the effect of granting the rights of U.S. citizenship to the Pueblos, see, for example, *United States v. Santistevan*, 1 N.M. 583 (1874) and *Territory v. Delinquent Taxpayers*, 12 N.M. 139 (1904).
21. N.M. Const., Art. 7, §1 (since amended).
22. *Trujillo v. Garley*, No. 1350 (D.N.M., 11 Aug. 1948).
23. See the note following N.M. Const., Art. 7, §1; see also *Montoya v. Bolack*, 70 N.M. 196, 200 (1962).
24. Historian Howard Lamar has written that President Zachary Taylor intended Calhoun, a former Whig congressman from Georgia, to use his office to lobby to bring New Mexico quickly into the Union as a state. The effort very nearly succeeded, fueled largely by Texas's claim that New Mexico to the east bank of the Rio Grande was part of Texas. Taylor's death in June 1850 squelched the attempt, and the Mexican cession, excluding California, which achieved statehood in 1850, was organized into the territories of New Mexico and Utah (*Far Southwest*, 64–69).
25. Abel, *Official Correspondence of James S. Calhoun*, 18.
26. Ibid., 33. Calhoun added that some "wicked" men, including Mexicans and Americans, were awakening apprehensions among the Pueblos, suggesting to them that the Americans would take their lands and move them elsewhere (ibid.). Of course, given the Americans' record with other tribes, that warning would not have seemed at all farfetched, but there is no evidence that any such plan was ever considered with respect to the Pueblos.
27. Ibid., 40.
28. Ibid., 44–47.
29. Ibid., 52–53. In a much later report dated 29 March 1850, Calhoun acknowledged that "nothing is definitely known" regarding the Pueblos' landholdings but reiterated his belief that they were held by "Spanish and Mexican grants." He observed that the "general opinion" was that each pueblo had a square of not less than 8½ miles on a side (ibid., 173.). That "general opinion," of course, was off by nearly a factor of three in terms of the area encompassed; Pueblo league grants are about 5.2 miles on each side.
30. Ibid., 54.
31. Ibid., 78.
32. "I earnestly insist that should be done" (Abel, *Official Correspondence of James S. Calhoun*, 140).
33. Act of 27 Feb. 1851, §§5, 7, 9 Stat. 574, 587. In 1851 the New Mexico Territory included all of what is now Arizona and much of southern Nevada. The Utah Territory stretched from California (which became a state in 1850) to the front range of the Rocky Mountains. Nevada, Arizona, and Colorado did not yet exist.

34. *United States v. Joseph*, 94 U.S. 614; *United States v. Sandoval*, 231 U.S. at 40–44; *United States v. Candelaria*, 271 U.S. 432, 440–41 (1926).
35. See Abel, *Official Correspondence of James S. Calhoun*, 119, 132–34, 172–73, 187.
36. Ibid., 103.
37. Ibid., 191.
38. Ibid., 227–28, 238–46.
39. Whitely, "Reconnoitering 'Pueblo' Ethnicity," 437, 456, 462–70.
40. Treaty of Peace, Friendship, Limits and Settlement with the Republic of Mexico, 2 Feb. 1848, Art. 8, 9 Stat. 922, 929.
41. *United States v. Percheman*, 31 U.S. (7 Pet.) 51, 86–88 (1833); *Mitchell v. United States*, 34 U.S. (9 Pet.) 711, 734 (1835); *Ainsa v. New Mexico & Arizona Railroad Co.*, 175 U.S. 76, 79–83 (1899).
42. Act of July 22, 1854, c. 103, §8, 10 Stat. 308, 309.
43. John Wilson to William Pelham, 21 Aug. 1854, SG, Letter File, r. 60.
44. See the discussion of the Cruzate grants in chapter 8. Laguna Pueblo submitted a Cruzate grant to Pelham in 1857, but it was not submitted to Congress until 1859, and Congress never acted on it. Laguna tried to get it confirmed by the Court of Private Land Claims in 1893, but without success. Zuni waited until 1875 to present its Cruzate grant to the surveyor general, and fifty-six years later, in 1931, Congress confirmed it.
45. The Sandia grant was based on an actual grant document, and the existence of a league grant for Taos was inferred from an 1815 communication from Governor Máynez confirming that the pueblo was entitled to such a grant (Pueblo of Taos, SG Report I, r. 7, f. 173–75).
46. *Annual Report of the Surveyor General of New Mexico*, 411–12.
47. Hall, *Four Leagues of Pecos*, 82.
48. Such a tract consisted of approximately 27.14 square miles, or about 17,350 acres, although, as surveyed, the acreages of different grants varied due to terrain, surveying errors, or the proximity of other pueblo grants. See chapter 1.
49. The original handwritten transcripts remain in the surveyor general files in the New Mexico State Record Center and Archives (*Annual Report of the Surveyor General of New Mexico*, 514 [Santa Clara], 515 [Tesuque], 516–17 [San Ildefonso], 517–18 [Pojoaque]). Pelham submitted similar reports two months later for Nambe and Isleta, and in 1867 Surveyor General John A. Clark submitted a similarly based claim for Santa Ana.
50. *Annual Report of the Surveyor General of New Mexico*, 515; Pueblo of Tesuque, SG Report L, r. 7, f. 199–200.
51. *Annual Report of the Surveyor General of New Mexico*, 516; Pueblo of San Ildefonso, SG Report M, r. 7, f. 204.
52. *Annual Report of the Surveyor General of New Mexico*, 514; Pueblo of Santa Clara, SG Report K, r. 7, f. 191.

53. *Annual Report of the Surveyor General of New Mexico*, 517; Pueblo of Pojoaque, SG Report N, r. 7, f. 209.
54. Act of 22 Dec. 1858, c. 5, 11 Stat. 374.
55. In his report to the commissioner of the General Land Office dated 30 September 1855, Pelham stated that a Spanish grant to Santa Ana (among other pueblos listed) was "filed, examined and approved by this office," but that was plainly a mistake. There is no record of any such grant ever having been submitted to that office. In a letter to the commissioner dated 5 January 1867, then surveyor general Clark noted this discrepancy and confirmed that he found no record of any Santa Ana grant document in the office. He added that the Santa Ana Indians were complaining that no action had ever been taken to confirm their lands (John A. Clark to Joseph S. Wilson, SG Letters Sent, r. 56, vol. 2, f. 404-5).
56. Pueblo of Santa Ana, SG Report T, r. 7, f. 318-19, 330-39; U.S. House of Representatives, *Report on the Pueblo of Santa Ana*; Act of 9 Feb. 1869, c. 26, 15 Stat. 438.
57. It appears that for whatever reason, Santa Ana never presented those documents to the surveyor general. The documents themselves reflect that the pueblo took many of them to Donaciano Vigil in 1850 for recording when Vigil was serving as secretary of the territory, as he wrote on each one his certification that they were presented to him. Additionally, Santa Ana has a document that consists of a transcription of many of its old land documents that was prepared by John Greiner, Indian agent (although he signed the certification as secretary of the territory), on 6 December 1852. The surveyor general took no action on these documents, and they did not resurface until the pueblo filed suit in the Court of Private Land Claims for their confirmation in 1897.
58. Pueblo of Isleta, SG Report Q, r. 7, f. 233.
59. 21 U.S. at 574, 579-80.
60. *Johnson v. M'Intosh*, 21 U.S., at 574, 587, 758. Twelve years later, in *Mitchell v. United States*, 34 U.S. (9 Pet.) at 746, the court described it as "a settled principle, that [the Indian] right of occupancy is considered as sacred as the fee simple of the whites." It added that the tribes' "right to the lands as property" was "not merely of possession"; the right of alienation was, it maintained "concomitant": "both were equally secured, protected and guaranteed" by the colonial powers.
61. 314 U.S. 339 (1941).
62. *United States v. Santa Fe Pacific Railroad Co.*, 314 U.S., 347, 353-54. An earlier decision, *Barker v. Harvey*, 181 U.S. 481 (1901), apparently assumed that such rights existed in the lands ceded by Mexico, but given the court's disposition of the case, that was of no consequence. The case concerned Indian aboriginal title claims in California. In 1851, Congress enacted a statute, Act of 3 March 1851 (c. 41, 9 Stat. 631), intended to resolve private titles in that state, again in recognition of the obligation of article 8 of the Treaty of Guadalupe Hidalgo. In sharp contrast to the open-ended procedure adopted with respect to such claims in New Mexico, the law enacted for California created a three-member commission and *required* that any

person having any claim to land whatever, "by virtue of any right or title derived from the Spanish or Mexican government," had to present the claim to the commission within two years or else the land covered by the claim would be deemed to be part of the public domain of the United States. In *Barker*, the Supreme Court held that Indian claims of aboriginal title to lands were within the category of claims that had to be presented to the commission or be lost. Obviously, no tribe made any such claim; the effect of the ruling, thus, was that virtually *all* claims of Indian aboriginal title in California were extinguished as of 1854.

63. 165 Ct. Cl. 501 (1964). Originally this claim was for the Ojo del Espíritu Santo grant that Governor Vélez Cachupín made to the three pueblos in 1766, which the Court of Private Land Claims rejected as nothing more than a grazing permit (see chapter 7). The pueblos' experts, however, showed that the pueblos had an aboriginal claim to a much larger area, and the claim was later amended to include some of the additional land. But the claims attorneys sought only compensation, not land, and the pueblos' title was thus extinguished by payment of the judgment. See *United States v. Dann*, 470 U.S. 39 (1985). For a discussion of the Ojo del Espíritu Santo grant, see Ebright, Adv*ocates for the Oppressed*, chap. 4. In *United States v. Pueblo de San Ildefonso* (523 F.2d 1383 [Ct. Cl. 1975]), another Indian Claims Commission case, the Court of Claims specifically held that neither the Treaty of Guadalupe Hidalgo nor congressional confirmation of the pueblos' grants extinguished the pueblos' aboriginal titles to lands outside of their grants.

64. Additionally, the surveyor general recommended that Laguna's claims to land based on a series of purchases it had made from Spanish settlers in the eighteenth and nineteenth centuries be recognized, which Congress confirmed.

65. Act of 22 Dec. 1858, c. 5, 11 Stat. 374.

66. Act of 27 Feb. 1851, c. 14, §7, 9 Stat. 574, 587.

67. Colonel Slough's reputation as the leader of the Union forces at Glorieta was not unblemished: it was said that "his own men became so disgusted with him for keeping so far to the rear of the action that they turned a howitzer on him and opened fire. . . . [T]he colonel barely escaped with his life" (Sides, *Blood and Thunder*, 301).

68. Slough's opinion was actually rendered in the case of *United States v. Ortiz*, not *Lucero*, but it decided the outcome of all thirty cases. His opinion was appended to the Territorial Supreme Court's decision affirming Slough. See *United States v. Lucero*, 1 N.M. at 450–58.

Hall suggests that one of the reasons the Supreme Court accorded this unusual distinction to Slough (of publishing his district court opinion as part of the court's decision) was that Slough was murdered in a brawl at the La Fonda Hotel in Santa Fe in late 1867 while the pueblo land cases were pending in the Supreme Court. Slough was killed by William Logan Rynerson, a member of the territorial legislature, who was campaigning to have him removed from the Supreme Court (Hall, *Four Leagues of Pecos*, 116, 118–19).

69. Quoted in Hall, *Four Leagues of Pecos*, 119n23.
70. *United States v. Lucero*, 1 N.M. at 426.
71. *United States v. Lucero*, 1 N.M. at 427. Interestingly, Watts mentions that in 1689, the Hispanos issued to the Pueblos "their titles to their lands," obviously referring to the Cruzate grants (*United States v. Lucero*, 1 N.M. at 428).
72. *United States v. Lucero*, 1 N.M. at 432. The opinion relies in part on a decision of the United States Supreme Court, *United States v. Ritchie*, 58 U.S. 525 (1854), in which the court addressed a challenge to a claim to land in California. The claim was based on a conveyance from one Francisco Solano, a California Indian and chief of his tribe, who received the land by grant from the Mexican governor. The United States contended that Solano, as an Indian, was not competent to take, hold, or convey real property under Mexican law. The court concluded that by the Plan of Iguala and the other organic documents of the Republic of Mexico, Indians in the territory were fully invested with the "privileges of citizenship," including the right to hold and transfer titles to land. Yet in a passage not mentioned in the *Lucero* opinion, the court pointed out that while the Indians made considerable advancements under the Spanish and Mexican regimes, "they still, doubtless, required [the government's] fostering care and protection" (*United States v. Ritchie*, 58 U.S. at 540). In the final paragraph of the opinion, moreover, the court carefully noted that the lands at issue in the case "do not belong to the class called Pueblo lands, in respect to which we do not intend to express any opinion, either as to the power of the authorities to grant or the Indians to convey" (*United States v. Ritchie*, 58 U.S. at 541). The *Lucero* court noted that passage from *Ritchie* but disregarded it (*United States v. Lucero*, 1 N.M. at 455).
73. The opinion throughout engages in toadying praise of the virtues of the Pueblos, referring to them as "the most honest, industrious, law-abiding citizens of New Mexico," and so forth, and at one point, referring to the court's personal experience with them, indulges in this striking bit of hyperbole:

> We say without fear of successful contradiction, that you may pick out one thousand of the best Americans in New Mexico, and one thousand of the best Mexicans in New Mexico, and one thousand of the worst pueblo Indians, and there will be found less, vastly less, murder, robbery, theft, or other crimes among the thousand of the worst pueblo Indians than among the thousand of the best Mexicans or Americans in New Mexico. (*United States v. Lucero*, 1 N.M. at 441)

The court also had to acknowledge that one of the territorial legislature's earliest acts excluded these "honest, industrious, law-abiding citizens" from having the right to vote. The propriety of that action, it said, was "not properly before us" (*United States v. Lucero*, 1 N.M. at 438, 441).
74. Hall, *Four Leagues of Pecos*, 121.
75. Ibid., 121–26.

76. Hall explains that petty political quarrels plainly motivated Catron's choices of these two as the lead defendants in the Taos suits (*Four Leagues of Pecos*, 128–29).
77. *United States v. Santistevan*, 1 N.M. at 588.
78. *United States v. Santistevan*, 1 N.M. at 589.
79. *United States v. Varela*, 1 N.M. 593 (1874). Justice Bristol wrote a separate opinion in the *Joseph* case, expressing his own view, arrived at by reasoning somewhat different from Johnson's, that the Pueblos were not "Indians" within the meaning of federal Indian law (in his view their villages were little different from the Hispanic towns in New Mexico) and were never recognized as such by Congress and that their lands were not, in any event, within any category of lands referred to in the Trade and Intercourse Act (*United States v. Joseph*, 1 N.M. 593, 598).
80. *United States v. Joseph*, 94 U.S. 614.
81. *United States v. Joseph*, 94 U.S. at 616–17; cf. *United States v. Lucero*, 1 N.M. at 451–58 (setting forth opinion of district court in *United States v. Ortiz*).
82. *United States v. Joseph*, 94 U.S. at 617–18.
83. Although in a somewhat different context, ten years later the Supreme Court held that it was the federal guardianship over the Indians whence arose plenary federal authority over their affairs, saying that this proposition "has always been recognized by . . . this court, whenever the question has arisen." That opinion, too, was penned by Justice Samuel Miller (*United States v. Kagama*, 118. U.S. 375, 383–84 [1886]).
84. *United States v. Joseph*, 94 U.S. at 618–19.
85. *United States v. Joseph*, 94 U.S. at 619.
86. Philp, *John Collier's Crusade for Indian Reform*, 28; Kelly, *Assault on Assimilation*, 191. See also *Pueblo of Nambé v. Romero*, 10 N.M. 58 (1900), in which the territorial supreme court ruled that the pueblo lost its lands by adverse possession. That result would have been impossible had the federal guardianship over those lands been recognized.
87. Catron would use the *Joseph* case to prove the validity of his interest in the Gaspar Ortiz grant, which overlapped part of the Nambe grant (Hall, *Four Leagues of Pecos*, 138).
88. *United States v. Sandoval*, 231 U.S. at 39–40.
89. *Territory of New Mexico v. Persons* 12 N.M. 139.
90. Act of 3 March 1905, c. 1479, 33 Stat. 1048, 1069.
91. Act of 30 Jan. 1897, c. 109, 29 Stat. 506.
92. *United States v. Mares* 14 N.M. at 2. The court also noted that the pueblos "are now citizens of the United States," a proposition the Supreme Court deliberately avoided in *Joseph*.
93. Act of 20 June 1910, c. 310, 36 Stat. 557.
94. Act of 20 June 1910, c. 310, §2, 36 Stat. 559–60 (emphasis added). These requirements were complied with by their inclusion in the New Mexico Constitution (Art. 21, §§2, 8, 9, and 10).

95. Proclamation Admitting New Mexico as a State Into the Union, 6 Jan. 1912, 37 Stat. 1723.
96. Francis C. Wilson was born in Winchester, Massachusetts, in 1876. He graduated from Columbia Law School in 1903 and arrived in New Mexico in 1907. In 1909 he became special U.S. attorney for the Pueblo Indians and over a long and distinguished career became an authority on Pueblo land law. He died in 1952 (Miller, "The Papers of Francis C. Wilson").
97. *United States v. Sandoval*, 198 F. 539, 550, 551 (1912).
98. Hall, *Four Leagues of Pecos*, 204.
99. Van Devanter was an Indiana native who began his legal career in Wyoming and later went to Washington as an assistant attorney general representing the Department of the Interior. He successfully argued several cases in the Supreme Court, for the state and the United States, opposing tribal rights, such as *Ward v. Race Horse* (163 U.S. 504 [1896]), which held that the creation of Wyoming as a state abrogated the treaty right of the Bannock Indians of the Ft. Hall Reservation in Idaho to hunt freely on lands within the boundaries of Wyoming, and *Lone Wolf v. Hitchcock* (187 U.S. 553 [1903]), in which the court ruled that Congress had unqualified authority to abrogate Indian treaties. He was appointed to the Eighth Circuit Court of Appeals bench and then to the Supreme Court in 1910. He became known as one of the most conservative justices on the Supreme Court, but his opinions in a number of important Indian law cases marked a sharp turnaround from the positions he had taken previously as advocate for Wyoming and the United States. See, for example, *Alaska Pacific Fisheries v. United States*, (248 U.S. 78 [1918]), which held that a reservation that was established for the immigrant Metlakahtla Indians on the Annette Islands of Alaska included the adjacent waters and submerged lands, such that a large fish trap erected by the corporation offshore was trespassing on the Indians' lands, and *Lane v. Pueblo of Santa Rosa* (249 U.S. 110 [1919]), which established that Indian lands in the territory acquired from Mexico (in this case by the Gadsden Treaty; the pueblo was a village of the Papago Tribe, now known as the Tohono O'odham Nation) could not be treated by the United States as public lands and disposed of as such because such an act "would not be an exercise of guardianship but an act of confiscation" (249 U.S. at 113). In *United States v. Creek Nation* (295 U.S. 103 [1935]), in which the government wrongfully patented to third parties lands belonging to the tribe, Van Devanter's often-quoted opinion, a landmark in the law of the federal trusteeship over the tribes, declared that the United States' plenary authority over the Indian tribes "was subject to limitations inhering in . . . a guardianship and to pertinent constitutional restrictions," and the United States was ordered to pay the tribe just compensation, including interest from the date of the taking. His opinions in *United States v. Sandoval*, *United States v. Candelaria*, and *United States v. Chávez*

confirmed that the Pueblos and their lands were fully protected by federal laws enacted for the benefit of Indian tribes.
100. *United States v. Sandoval*, 231 U.S. at 38.
101. *United States v. Sandoval*, 231 U.S. at 39.
102. One such Indian Service report, whose author is not identified, railed against "the secret dance, from which all whites are excluded, [as] perhaps one of the greatest evils. What goes on . . . I will not attempt to say, but I firmly believe that it is little less than a ribald system of debauchery" (*United States v. Sandoval*, 231 U.S. at 40–44).
103. *United States v. Sandoval*, 231 U.S. at 39–40, 44–45.
104. *United States v. Sandoval*, 231 U.S. at 46.
105. *United States v. Sandoval*, 231 U.S. at 47.
106. *United States v. Sandoval*, 231 U.S. at 48. The five civilized tribes were the Choctaw, Chicasaw, Cherokee, Creek, and Seminole. They received land in Oklahoma after their forced removal from their homelands in the southern United States.
107. *United States v. Sandoval*, 231 U.S. at 49.
108. "Pueblo Indians of New Mexico Are Federal Wards Says Decision: Attorney A. B. Renehan Gives Review of Case," *Albuquerque Morning Journal*, 21 Oct. 1913.
109. "Wilson Replies to A. B. Renehan Interview."
110. Hall, *Four Leagues of Pecos*, 206–7.
111. Crane, *Desert Drums*, 170–71. Crane describes an incident that occurred shortly after his arrival in New Mexico during which a group of New Mexico State Mounted Police went to Santo Domingo Pueblo to execute a state search warrant, supposedly looking for evidence of cattle rustling, and provoked near-violent resistance by the pueblo's members. Crane, summoned by telegram, arrived at the pueblo and insisted to the state police colonel that they had no authority on Pueblo land. The colonel rejected such assertions until Crane hastily assembled a meeting in Santa Fe at the office of Francis Wilson. Present were the state attorney general, the colonel, the governor of Santo Domingo, and Richard H. Hanna, a former chief justice of the state supreme court, who had recently been appointed special attorney for the Pueblos. According to Crane, the attorney general "could not understand . . . that the Pueblo Indians were wholly under Federal control. That was the attitude of practically all New Mexicans" (ibid).
112. *Mountain States Tel. & Tel. Co. v. Pueblo of Santa Ana*, 472 U.S. 237, 243 (1985); Philp, *John Collier's Crusade for Indian Reform*, 29–30. As Philp notes, although the non-Indian claims encompassed only about 10 percent of the pueblos' lands, they included much of the most valuable irrigated land.
113. *United States v. Candelaria*, 271 U.S. at 439–41.
114. Then codified as section 2116 of the Revised Statutes; now 25 U.S.C. §177.
115. *United States v. Candelaria*, 271 U.S. at 441, citing the Act of 27 Feb. 1851, c. 14, 9 Stat. 574, 587, §7, quoting *Montoya v. United States*, 180 U.S. at 266.

116. *United States v. Candelaria*, 271 U.S. at 443.
117. *United States v. Chávez*, 290 U.S. at 364–65.
118. Westphall, *Mercedes Reales*, 95–105 (trans. David Miller). Both T. Rush Spencer and Henry M. Atkinson had land-grant holdings while serving as surveyor general (Ebright, *Land Grants and Lawsuits*, 40–41; Ebright, *Tierra Amarilla Grant*, 3n8, 18n50).
119. White, Koch, Kelley, McCarthy, and the New Mexico State Planning Office, *Land Title Study*, 222–23; Ebright, *Land Grants and Lawsuits*, 37–45.
120. Act of 3 Mar. 1891, c. 539, 26 Stat. 854.
121. Ebright, *Land Grants and Lawsuits*, 45–47, 134–36; Bradfute, *Court of Private Land Claims*, viii.
122. To be sure, three rejected grants, the Peralta grant (12.5 million acres in Arizona and New Mexico), the Las Ánimas grant (4 million acres in Colorado), and the Conejos grant (2.5 million acres in Colorado) comprised about 55 percent of the total area claimed. Even excluding those extravagant claims, the court confirmed only about 12 percent of the total acreage claimed in the cases that came before it (White, Koch, Kelley, McCarthy, and the New Mexico State Planning Office, *Land Title Study*, 225–34).
123. The second clause of section 13 provided that "no claim shall be allowed that shall interfere with or overthrow any just and unextinguished Indian title or right to any land or place."
124. Originally there were eight, but Santo Domingo's and San Felipe's separate claims to their joint grant were consolidated into one claim. The other claims were the joint Santa Ana, Zia, and Jemez grant; the Cochiti pasture grant; the Cañada de Santa Clara grant; the Laguna grant; the Isleta grant; the Lo de Padilla grant; and Santa Ana's claim to the Ranchito tract.
125. See chapter 5. In July 1905 President Roosevelt, at the urging of the Indian Service to correct an obvious injustice to the pueblo, created the Santa Clara Reservation by executive order, adding 33,000 acres, including the entirety of the canyon and much of the adjacent plateau, but westward only to the border of Baca Location No. 1 (part of a grant that the United States made to the heirs of Luis María Cabeza de Baca when their claim to the Las Vegas Town grant was unsuccessful). In 2000 the pueblo acquired by purchase the 5,045 acres of Santa Clara Canyon within Baca Location No. 1 (Act of 25 Jul. 2000, §104[g][2], Pub. L. 106-248).
126. Pueblos of Santo Domingo and San Felipe grant, PLC 134, r. 46, f. 547–612.
127. Pueblo of Laguna, SG Report S, r. 7, f. 248–51; William Pelham to commissioner, 1 Sept.1859, SG, Letters Sent, r. 56, vol. 1, f. 168–70.
128. *Pueblo of Laguna v. United States*, No. 133 (Court of Private Land Claims, 2 Oct. 1897), PLC, r. 46, f. 489–92. See the discussion in chapter 8.
129. Final decree, El Ranchito grant, SG 239, r. 30, f. 100–107.
130. Matthew G. Reynolds to attorney general, 19 June 1897, NARA, Department of

Justice Records, file 9865-1892, ltr. 9472-1897. These were the purchases from Captain Manuel Baca in 1709, Juan González Bas (date uncertain), Josefa Baca in 1742, Alejandro Mora in 1753, and Quiteria Contreras in 1763. Santa Ana has in its possession the original documents of each of these transactions. See chapter 2.

131. Matthew G. Reynolds to attorney general, 19 June 1897, NARA, Department of Justice Records, file 9865-1892, ltr. 9472-1897.

Chapter 10

1. In *The Assault on Assimilation*, Lawrence C. Kelly tells the story of the enactment of the act in fascinating and highly readable detail (see 163–254). Kelly has subsequently updated, broadened, and extended his research, in part based on archives not available when he first wrote the book, in three unpublished manuscripts: "History of the Pueblo Lands Board" (1984), a paper he submitted as an expert report in the case of *New Mexico v. Aamodt*, 618 F.Supp. 993 (D.N.M. 1985); "Section 17 of the Pueblo Lands Act" (1984), a paper that was submitted as an expert report and that Justice William Brennan relied on extensively in his lengthy, stinging dissent in *Mountain States Tel. & Tel. Co. v. Pueblo of Santa Ana*, 472 U.S. 237, 255-83 (1985); and "The Pueblo Lands Act and the Problem of Overlapping Pueblo and Non-Indian Grants" (1987), a paper submitted as an expert report in the case of *United States v. Thompson*, 708 F.Supp. 1206 (D.N.M. 1989), affirmed, 941 F.2d 1074 (10th Cir. 1991). See also Philp, *John Collier's Crusade for Indian Reform*, 26–54, and Long, "Senator Bursum and the Pueblo Indian Lands Act of 1924."
2. Brayer, *Pueblo Indian Land Grants*, 26.
3. The claim that the Indian agent "had incited the [Tesuque] Indians to violence" led to an investigation and a transfer of the agent, even though the investigation found that "the Indian claim to the land is probably right" (Kelly, *Assault on Assimilation*, 193, 205–6).
4. Ibid.
5. Ibid., 202; Kelly, "Pueblo Lands Act," 6.
6. Kelly, *Assault on Assimilation*, 202–3; Kelly, "Pueblo Lands Act," 6.
7. Kelly, *Assault on Assimilation*, 200–202.
8. Twitchell came to New Mexico in 1882, immediately after receiving his law degree from the University of Michigan, and went to work with Henry L. Waldo representing the AT&SF Railroad, which became a lifelong association for Twitchell. Twitchell became politically prominent, serving as mayor of Santa Fe, district attorney for Santa Fe County, and eventually as special U.S. attorney for the Pueblos (although in the struggle over Pueblo land titles, he clearly sympathized with the Hispanic settlers). He became deeply enamored of New Mexico history and eventually authored several seminal works on the subject, including the two-volume *Leading Facts of New Mexico History* (1911), *Old Santa Fe* (1925), and most importantly, *The Spanish Archives of New Mexico* (1914), the first

published index to the massive archives (which Twitchell had personally helped save from destruction when the territorial capital burned to the ground in 1892). Twitchell's numeric catalog of the documents is still commonly used.
9. Kelly, *Assault on Assimilation*, 204–7.
10. Ibid., 209–11; Philp, *John Collier's Crusade for Indian Reform*, 31–32; Kelly, "Pueblo Lands Act," 8.
11. Long, "Senator Bursum and the Pueblo Indian Lands Act of 1924," 13.
12. Albert Bacon Fall, who John Collier characterized as the "epitome of evil forces working against Indians," helped draft New Mexico's constitution, was elected to the U.S. Senate in 1912, became the secretary of the interior in the administration of President Warren Harding, and was eventually sentenced to federal prison for his involvement in the Teapot Dome Scandal (Clifford, "Albert Fall").
13. "Fall baldy lied [when he said] that 'by their own choice' the Pueblos had been represented by A. B. Renehan" (Kelly, *Assault on Assimilation*, 214–16).
14. Ibid., 124–30.
15. Ibid., 131.
16. Ibid., 133–34.
17. To be sure, some of Lawrence's columns made Dodge, Collier, and their coterie of supporters out to be little more than wild-eyed fanatics (Kelly, *Assault on Assimilation*, 217–19, 225–26; Philp, *John Collier's Crusade for Indian Reform*, 32–35; *New York Times*, 24 Dec. 1922).
18. Kelly, *Assault on Assimilation*, 218–21; Philp, *John Collier's Crusade for Indian Reform*, 35–36; Long, "Senator Bursum and the Pueblo Indian Lands Act of 1924," 18–22. The text of the memorial is reprinted in Kelly, *Assault on Assimilation*, 379–81.
19. *Congressional Record*, Senate, 67th Congress, 3rd sess., 1922, 63, 1:11; Kelly, *Assault on Assimilation*, 223.
20. Kelly, *Assault on Assimilation*, 230–31, 236; Philp, *John Collier's Crusade for Indian Reform*, 36–37. By then the facts surrounding the Teapot Dome oil-leasing scandal were beginning to be known, and that could have been a substantial factor in Fall's decision to leave public office.
21. *Hearings on S. 3855 and S. 4223 before the Subcommittee of the Senate Committee on Public Lands and Surveys*, 194; Long, "Senator Bursum and the Pueblo Indian Lands Act of 1924," 38–39.
22. Philp, *John Collier's Crusade for Indian Reform*, 39–45; Kelly, *Assault on Assimilation*, 238–45; Long, "Senator Bursum and the Pueblo Indian Lands Act of 1924," 33–44. Pablo Abeita was one of the most influential Pueblo Indians in New Mexico in his day. In the 1930s Abeita liked to remind people that he was the only living Indian who had met all the U.S. presidents, from Grover Cleveland in 1886 through Franklin D. Roosevelt. He was also a personal friend of many members of Congress, having made trips to Washington to argue on behalf of many Indian issues (Simmons, "Pablo Abeita").

23. Kelly, *Assault on Assimilation*, 253–54; Philp, *John Collier's Crusade for Indian Reform*, 45–46.
24. Kelly, *Assault on Assimilation*, 254; Philp, *John Collier's Crusade for Indian Reform*, 46.
25. Kelly, *Assault on Assimilation*, 256–69; Philp, *John Collier's Crusade for Indian Reform*, 46–49.
26. In his journal of the trip to New Mexico, Berle wrote, "It is no joke to evict the Mexicans; it goes against my grain to throw out a family whose land is tilled and whose house is surrounded by hollyhocks and larkspur. No help for it though. We must get them some compensation" (Kelly, *Assault on Assimilation*, 280–84). For a brief biography of Adolf A. Berle Jr., see Newman, *Yale Biographical Dictionary of American Law*, 39–40.
27. Kelly, *Assault on Assimilation*, 295–98. See also Act of 7 June 1924, c. 331, 43 Stat. 636.
28. Act of 7 June 1924, c. 331, 43 Stat. 636, 641, sec. 17; see also Kelly, "Section 17 of the Pueblo Lands Act" and *Mountain States Tel. & Tel. Co. v. Pueblo of Santa Ana*, 472 U.S. 237.
29. Each successful claim is thus typically identified on survey plats with both a PC number and an exception number.
30. Act of 7 June 1924, c. 331, 43 Stat. 636, 640, sec. 13. That the claimants' titles originate in patents from the United States, which previously patented the lands to the pueblos, is an interesting construct. The theory was apparently that the extinguishment of the pueblo's title to the claim, by the filing of the field notes and plats, restored the land to the public domain and made it patentable again. But in that case, the phrase stating that the filing of the field notes and plats extinguished "any claim of the United States" is puzzling. If the U.S. claims to these tracts had thus been extinguished, one can only wonder how the United States could thereafter patent those lands to the successful claimants.
31. Kelly, "History of the Pueblo Lands Board," 28–29. This report and Kelly's two subsequent unpublished reports (see chap. 10, n. 1) are the only known scholarly accounts of the work of the board relying on the original records of the board's proceedings. As special commissioner, Hagerman would negotiate oil leases on behalf of a new Navajo tribal council established by Fall to replace more democratic local tribal councils for the numerous Navajo jurisdictions. Though never its chairman, Hagerman exerted the most powerful influence over the board's deliberations, and not to the benefit of the Pueblos. "In time," Kelly notes, "the two men grew to hate each other" (*Assault on Assimilation*, 277–78, 299).
32. Berle resigned from the American Indian Defense Association after the Pueblo Lands Act was passed (Kelly, *Assault on Assimilation*, 326). He went on to become a professor at Columbia Law School and later a member of Franklin D. Roosevelt's "brain trust." In 1932 he authored, with Gardiner Means, *The Modern Corporation and Private Property*, which remains even today one of the most widely cited texts in the field of corporate governance.

33. Kelly, "History of the Pueblo Lands Board," 31–37.
34. Ibid., 37–41.
35. Order, *United States, as guardian of the Pueblo of Nambé, v. Herrera*, No. 1720 Equity (D.N.M., 24 May 1928). The court also issued a critical ruling on the interpretation of the "continuous payment of taxes."
36. Quoted in Kelly, "History of the Pueblo Lands Board," 85.
37. Ibid., 61.
38. Roberts Walker suffered a stroke in June 1926. The president eventually forced his resignation from the board and appointed a seventy-year-old political supporter, Lucius Embree, to replace him. Embree resigned in January 1928, and Coolidge named Louis H. Warner, a Washington, D.C., lawyer, to replace him. Warner was quickly made chairman of the board (ibid., 79–81).
39. Ibid., 81–83.
40. Order, *United States, as guardian of the Pueblo of Nambé, v. Herrera*, No. 1720 Equity (quoting Pueblo Lands Act, 43 Stat. 636, sec. 4).
41. *United States v. Wooten*, 40 F.2d 882, 884–89 (10th Cir. 1930). Interestingly, by then Judge Phillips had been elevated to the court of appeals bench, and he sat on the panel that decided *Wooten*. To be sure, the following year the same court (with Phillips writing the opinion) ruled that where the land claimed was sold at tax sale and only afterward redeemed by the claimant, the tax sale defeated the claim that taxes were paid, and the pueblo was entitled to recover the land (*Pueblo de Taos v. Gusdorf*, 50 F.2d 721 [10th Cir. 1931]).
42. The solicitor general, who made the decision not to pursue *Wooten*, added in his memo that "it is my understanding that the land in question is not valuable." He did not explain the factual basis for his "understanding," and it is highly doubtful that his view was shared by the pueblos themselves (Kelly, "History of the Pueblo Lands Board," 105–6).
43. *Mountain States Tel. & Tel. Co. v. Pueblo of Santa Ana*, 427 U.S. 237.
44. Pueblo of Santo Domingo, SGReport H, r. 7, f. 126–27. See chapter 8.
45. Kelly, "Pueblo Lands Act," 68; Bowden, "Private Land Claims in the Southwest," 1262–63.
46. Kelly, "Pueblo Lands Act," 72.
47. *United States v. Thompson*, 941 F.2d 1074.
48. Kelly, "Pueblo Lands Act," 90.
49. Ibid., 104.
50. Ibid., 106–10. See, for example, the decision in *Pueblo de San Juan v. United States* (47 F.2d 446 [10th Cir. 1931]), in which the court of appeals rejected the effort by Charles Fahy, whom Collier retained to handle the cases for the Pueblos, to get the district court's approval of the compensation award for San Juan overturned as inadequate, on the ground that no evidence was presented to the district court to

NOTES TO PAGES 284–287

support a higher award. In effect, the cases were being botched by the Pueblos' independent counsel. Fahy had previously represented a number of non-Indian claimants, and in proceedings leading up to the Pueblo Compensation Act, he represented a number of non-Indian residents of Taos who succeeded in having removed from the bill a provision that would have restored Blue Lake to Taos Pueblo. See U.S. Senate, *Survey of Conditions of the Indians throughout the United States* 20:11269.
51. Kelly, "History of the Pueblo Lands Board," 111–13.
52. U.S. Senate, *Survey of Conditions of the Indians*, 11:4366–4451, 4571–98.
53. Ibid., 20:10705–10858; Kelly, "History of the Pueblo Lands Board," 122–26. Wheeler was one of the sponsors of the Indian Reorganization Act of 1934 (also known as the Wheeler-Howard Act), the landmark piece of legislation Collier authored after he was appointed Roosevelt's commissioner of Indian Affairs that began a complete reversal of fifty years of federal Indian policy. That act rejected the assimilationist approach that had characterized federal policy since the 1880s and put into place a new policy of respect for and support of tribal governments, as well as protection and increase of the tribal land base.
54. As Kelly explains in some detail, Hagerman insisted in letters to Indian Affairs commissioner Charles Rhoads and others that the Pueblo compensation awards were justified by his theory of the Pueblos' water rights—that the Pueblos had not really lost any water rights with the land they lost, a frankly nonsensical proposition—and he tried to get Rhoads to push for litigation to establish his theory in court. For a variety of reasons, including the fact that those who understood Hagerman's theory did not accept it, that never happened (Kelly, "History of the Pueblo Lands Board," 127–40).
55. Ibid., 141.
56. U.S. Senate, *Survey of Conditions of the Indians*, 20:11096–11125.
57. Ibid., 20:11125–48; Kelly, "History of the Pueblo Lands Board," 142–46. Two days later, John Collier testified that in 1925 or early 1926, in his sworn testimony as a witness in the suit brought by San Juan Pueblo (now known as Ohkay Owingeh) challenging the board's award of compensation, Hagerman had testified at length about how the board arrived at its compensation figures but said not a word about this "primary-secondary water rights" theory (U.S. Senate, *Survey of Conditions of the Indians*, 20:11245–49).
58. Ibid. 20:11125–48; Kelly, "History of the Pueblo Lands Board," 147–49.
59. U.S. Senate, *Survey of Conditions of the Indians*, 20:11249–54. Collier's argument that Hagerman's theory could not justify the greatly reduced compensation awarded by the board was also correct. By losing the land, the Pueblos also lost the water rights with superior priority appurtenant to that land, regardless of the fact that they retained that priority for rights appurtenant to the lands they held. It turned out to be true that the non-Indians did not succeed to the Pueblo priority,

so that the value of the water rights they obtained was less than what the Pueblos lost, but that should have had no bearing on the calculation of the compensation due the Pueblos.
60. U.S. House of Representatives, *Authorization of Appropriations*, 116–26, 154.
61. Ibid., 126–29. Section 9 of the Pueblo Compensation Act was discussed extensively by the Tenth Circuit Court of Appeals in *New Mexico v. Aamodt*, 537 F.2d 1102, 1110, 1113 (10th Cir. 1976), an interlocutory appeal in the general stream adjudication of the Rio Tesuque–Rio Nambe–Rio Pojoaque stream system (ironically, Hagerman urged the United States to file suit to adjudicate the same river basin in 1932 in hopes of vindicating his theory of Pueblo water rights). The court viewed that section as the key to determining the character of the water rights retained by the Pueblos after that act, although in wondering how those rights were to be quantified, the court could only say that "we do not know" (*New Mexico v. Aamodt*, 537 F.2d at 1113). That issue was left to the district court on remand, but after holding three separate trials on different theories of the Pueblos' rights and receiving thousands of pages of briefs, expert reports, and special master's recommended findings and conclusions, the district court essentially rejected them all and came up with a ruling that no party ever proposed and that is seemingly refuted by all of the history of the Pueblo Lands Act, especially by the events leading to the Pueblo Compensation Act (which the court basically ignored in its ruling). In *New Mexico v. Aamodt* (618 F.Supp. at 1010), the district court held that the Pueblos' water rights were limited to as much water as was needed to irrigate lands irrigated by them between 1848 and 1924 and that their rights were "*fixed* [by the 1924 act] to acreage irrigated *as of that date*" (emphasis added). As has been noted, this was a concept that appeared in the Bursum Bill, which Congress eventually rejected, but nothing similar appeared in the Pueblo Lands Act, or much less the 1933 act. Unfortunately, the court of appeals declined to accept review of this bizarre interlocutory holding, and the *Aamodt* case was eventually settled. See Act of 8 Dec. 2010, Pub. L. 111–291, Title 6, 124 Stat. 3064, 3134. No other case considering Pueblo water rights has generated any rulings that shed light on, much less correct, this decision.
62. U.S. House of Representatives, *Authorization of Appropriations*, 151–58.
63. Pueblo Compensation Act, Act of 31 May 1933, 48 Stat. 108, c. 45.
64. U.S. Senate, *Survey of Conditions of the Indians*, 20:10914–15. To this number must be added the 26,300 acres Santo Domingo lost as a result of the board's unlawful exclusion from that pueblo's grant of land overlapped by junior non-Indian grants. Importantly, in 2006 the New Mexico Supreme Court ruled that lands patented to non-Indians under the terms of the act remained "Indian country" and thus subject to the special federal law jurisdictional rules that apply within Indian country (*State v. Romero*, 2006-NMSC-039, 140 N.M. 399, 142 P.3d 887).
65. The board also conducted proceedings with respect to the defunct Pecos Pueblo,

in the course of which it upheld every claim presented, covering all but a tiny sliver of the Pecos grant.
66. For an illustration of the complicated jurisdictional problems that arose from this situation, see *United States v. Arrieta*, 436 F.3d 1246 (10th Cir. 2006), in which a non-Indian, standing on a roadway on the Pojoaque grant that remained Pueblo land, although it was lined on both sides by tracts patented to non-Indians under the act, fired a gun and hit a pueblo member inside a house on one of the private claims. The court of appeals rejected the argument that the roadway lost its Indian country character because it was lined by privately owned land and affirmed the district court's ruling that the defendant could be prosecuted under the Indian Country Crimes Act (18 U.S.C. §1852). In 2005 Congress enacted an amendment to the Pueblo Lands Act, by the Act of 20 Dec. 2005 (Public Law 109-133, 119 Stat. 2753), that should resolve all such claims in the future. The amendment makes clear that the United States and the Pueblos continue to have exclusive criminal jurisdiction over crimes by or against Indians that occur "anywhere within the exterior boundaries of any grant from a prior sovereign, as confirmed by Congress or the Court of Private Land Claims to a Pueblo Indian tribe of New Mexico." That jurisdiction includes private claims, and while the enactment does not use the term, its effect fairly plainly is to establish that notwithstanding their having been patented to non-Indians, the private claims remain "Indian country" for jurisdictional purposes. That, indeed, was the holding of the New Mexico Supreme Court in *State v. Romero*.
67. Kelly, "Section 17 of the Pueblo Lands Act," 21-22.
68. Ibid., 23.
69. Ibid., 24-26.
70. Hanna quickly approached Sandia for a right-of-way for Albuquerque Gas & Electric Co., another of his clients, and that became the first right-of-way the secretary approved under section 17 (ibid., 27-30).
71. This ruling should have brought an end to suits under that act, but they continued to be brought and to result in condemnation decrees, until in 1976 the Tenth Circuit Court of Appeals ruled that the 1926 condemnation act was repealed by necessary implication by subsequent legislation enacted by Congress in 1928 (ibid., 32-34; *Plains Electric Generation and Transmission Cooperative v. Pueblo of Laguna*, 542 F.2d 1375 [10th Cir. 1976]).
72. Kelly, "Section 17 of the Pueblo Lands Act," 35-36.
73. Ibid., 38-44.
74. *Mountain States Tel. and Tel. Co. v. Pueblo of Santa Ana*, 472 U.S. 237.

Chapter 11

1. Gordon-McCutchan, *Taos Indians and the Battle for Blue Lake*, 11; Collins, "Battle for Blue Lake," 11.

2. U.S. Bureau of Indian Affairs, *1979 Land Status Report*, 30.
3. Rixon, *Report on an Examination of the Taos Forest Reserve*, 27–28; Gordon-McCutchan, *Taos Indians and the Battle for Blue Lake*, 12.
4. Gordon-McCutchan, *Taos Indians and the Battle for Blue Lake*, 15.
5. Ibid., 34; Sando, *Pueblo Indians*, 75; Nabokov, *Where the Lightning Strikes*, 79.
6. Pueblo of Taos to Pueblo Lands Board, Oct. 1926, Paul J. Bernal Papers, box 2, folder 26, SRCA; Gordon-McCutchan, *Taos Indians and the Battle for Blue Lake*, 17–18.
7. Gordon-McCutchan, *Taos Indians and the Battle for Blue Lake*, 18–19.
8. Pueblo of Taos to Pueblo Lands Board, Bernal Papers, box 2, folder 26, SRCA; Gordon-McCutchan, *Taos Indians and the Battle for Blue Lake*, 19–20.
9. Whatley, "Saga of Taos Blue Lake," 24; Gordon-McCutchan, *Taos Indians and the Battle for Blue Lake*, 21.
10. Bodine, "Blue Lake," 26–27; Gordon-McCutchan, *Taos Indians and the Battle for Blue Lake*, 26–28.
11. Bodine, "Taos Blue Lake Controversy," 45.
12. Sophie Aberle to William Zimmerman, 31 Oct. 1939, Bernal Papers, box 2, folder 26, SRCA; Gordon-McCutchan, *Taos Indians and the Battle for Blue Lake*, 28–33. Part of the problem with section 4 of the 1933 act was that it did not set forth the terms of the use permit, leaving that to be negotiated between the pueblo and the government.
13. Gordon-McCutchan, *Taos Indians and the Battle for Blue Lake*, 33–35.
14. Ibid., 39–47. The book not only brought the Blue Lake struggle to millions of readers but also portrayed the spiritual depths and conflicts of Pueblo Indians. On the jacket copy, Stephen Vincent Benet calls it "perhaps the best book . . . written about the American Indian."
15. Ibid.
16. Burt, *Tribalism in Crisis*, 5; Gordon-McCutchan, *Taos Indians and the Battle for Blue Lake*, 43–45.
17. Gordon-McCutchan, *Taos Indians and the Battle for Blue Lake*, 45–47.
18. Oliver La Farge to Clinton B. Anderson, 6 May 1955, Bernal Papers, box 2, folder 28, SRCA.
19. Gordon-McCutchan, *Taos Indians and the Battle for Blue Lake*, 51, 52.
20. E. T. Benson to James E. Murray, 24 Mar. 1958, Bernal Papers, box 2, folder 28, SRCA; Gordon-McCutchan, *Taos Indians and the Battle for Blue Lake*, 55.
21. Gordon-McCutchan, *Taos Indians and the Battle for Blue Lake*, 59.
22. Ibid., 62–65; La Farge, "Indians on the New Frontier," 1–2.
23. Stephen A. Mitchell to Richard Schifter, 3 Feb. 1961, Bernal Papers, box 1, folder 5, SRCA; Gordon-McCutchan, *Taos Indians and the Battle for Blue Lake*, 69–70.
24. Richard Schifter to Corinne H. Locker, 25 Sept.1964, Bernal Papers, box 1, folder 5, SRCA; Gordon-McCutchan, *Taos Indians and the Battle for Blue Lake*, 71–72.
25. *Pueblo of Taos v. United States*, 15 Ind. Cl. Comm. 666 (1965). The Indian Claims

Commission relied heavily on the testimony and reports of Ellis and Jenkins and the testimony of tribal elders, discounting the testimony of the government's witness, Harold H. Dunham. Dunham had argued that the Pueblo Indians did not have exclusive use of the area because of the six to one population imbalance in favor of the Spaniards, while Ellis and Jenkins pointed out that although both the Indians and the Spaniards used the low-lying agricultural lands, "the Spanish confined themselves to the bottom land, leaving the mountains to the Indians." Dunham's approach was ineffective because he dealt more in the theoretical realm, while Ellis provided specific instances of land use in the Blue Lake watershed by the Taos Indians. The complete reports of Florence Hawley Ellis and Harold Dunham and the complete Indian Claims Commission decision can be found in Ellis, "Anthropological Data Pertaining to the Taos Land Claim," 29–150; Dunham, "Spanish and Mexican Land Policies and Grants in the Taos Pueblo Region," 151–313; and "Historical Study of Land Use Eastward of the Taos Indians' Pueblo Land Grant," in Horr, *Pueblo Indians*, 313–44.

26. "Blue Lake Controversy," 13; Gordon-McCutchan, *Taos Indians and the Battle for Blue Lake*, 74–83.
27. William Byler on behalf of the Association on American Indians Affairs, 27 May 1966, Bernal Papers, box 1, folder 2, SRCA; Gordon-McCutchan, *Taos Indians and the Battle for Blue Lake*, 85, 87.
28. Taos Pueblo Council, *Blue Lake Area . . . An Appeal from Taos Pueblo*, vertical file, "Taos Blue Lake," Southwest Room, New Mexico State Library, Santa Fe. This booklet was mailed to the editors of one hundred leading newspapers throughout the country (Gordon-McCutchan, *Taos Indians and the Battle for Blue Lake*, 91, 90–94).
29. Richard Schifter to Lewis A. Sigler, 9 May 1966, Bernal Papers, box 1, folder 10, SRCA; Gordon-McCutchan, *Taos Indians and the Battle for Blue Lake*, 95–99.
30. Gordon-McCutchan, *Taos Indians and the Battle for Blue Lake*, 100.
31. Ibid., 103–4. Le Sage wanted to trade the Forest Service a 19,000-acre tract that he had clear-cut for timber rights on a comparable tract within the Blue Lake watershed.
32. Ibid., 110–11.
33. Ibid., 110–16.
34. Ibid., 115, 118–21.
35. Report of Harry Summers, 24 Aug. 1967, Bernal Papers, box 5, folder 38, SRCA; Gordon-McCutchan, *Taos Indians and the Battle for Blue Lake*, 121.
36. Graybill, "'Strong on the Merits and Powerfully Symbolic,'" 145–46; Gordon-McCutchan, *Taos Indians and the Battle for Blue Lake*, 124–25, 129.
37. Gordon-McCutchan, *Taos Indians and the Battle for Blue Lake*, 127–28.
38. Ibid., 130–35.
39. A 1968 *Washington Post* editorial stated that "if the senator [Anderson] has any legitimate objection to righting a wrong done more than 60 years ago, he ought

to lay his cards on the table. It seems inexcusable to suppress a bill of this kind, involving the national integrity." (ibid., 137–38)
40. Ibid., 140–41.
41. Aberle to Zimmerman, Bernal Papers, box 2, folder 26, SRCA; Gordon-McCutchan, *Taos Indians and the Battle for Blue Lake*, 148–50.
42. Gordon-McCutchan, *Taos Indians and the Battle for Blue Lake*, 152.
43. "Blue Lake Controversy," 14.
44. Gordon-McCutchan, *Taos Indians and the Battle for Blue Lake*, 156; "Blue Lake Controversy," 13.
45. Gulliford, *Sacred Objects, Sacred Places*, 159; Gordon-McCutchan, *Taos Indians and the Battle for Blue Lake*, 157–59.
46. Gordon-McCutchan, *Taos Indians and the Battle for Blue Lake*, 161, 163.
47. Ibid., 168.
48. Graybill, "'Strong on the Merits and Powerfully Symbolic,'" 146–47.
49. Gordon-McCutchan, *Taos Indians and the Battle for Blue Lake*, 177.
50. Ibid., 182–85; Graves, "Taos Leader."
51. Sherry, "I Interact Therefore I Am"; Gordon-McCutchan, *Taos Indians and the Battle for Blue Lake*, 186–87.
52. U.S. Senate, *Taos Indians Blue Lake*, 91st Congress, 68.
53. Gordon-McCutchan, *Taos Indians and the Battle for Blue Lake*, 160.
54. Ibid., 191–93. Anthropologist John Bodine expressed the difficulty in translating and explaining Pueblo religion: "The problem was truly one of translation.... The Taos themselves could not reveal sacred knowledge. To do so would have been contrary to everything they had learned as initiated members of their tribal religion. But to argue simply that Blue Lake is 'our church,' or that 'we worship all of nature' meant little to those not knowledgeable about Indian cultures" (Bodine, "Blue Lake," 30).
55. Gordon-McCutchan, *Taos Indians and the Battle for Blue Lake*, 197–204.
56. Ibid., 213.
57. Ibid.
58. Bobbie Greene Kilberg, quoted in Romancito, "Fighters for Blue Lake Return."
59. Gordon-McCutchan, *Taos Indians and the Battle for Blue Lake*, 216–18.
60. Griffith, "Taos Indians Have a Small Generation Gap."
61. Simmons, "Saving of Blue Lake."
62. Gulliford, *Sacred Objects and Sacred Places*, 161; Gordon-McCutchan, *Taos Indians and the Battle for Blue Lake*, 217–19. For Picuris, see chapter 3; for Santo Domingo, see Nauman, "U.S. Sues to Settle Santo Domingo Land Claim" and *Senate Report 106-506, To Settle the Land Claims of the Pueblo of Santo Domingo*, 106th Congress, 2nd session, October 18, 2000 [to accompany S. 2917]; and for San Ildefonso see Lezon, "Commission Questions Pueblo Land Acquisitions," and *Senate Report 109-252, to Resolve Certain Native American Claims in New Mexico, and for Other Purposes*, 109th Congress, 2nd session, May 3, 2006 [to accompany S. 1773].
63. Gordon-McCutchan, *Taos Indians and the Battle for Blue Lake*, 219.

Epilogue

1. José Manuel Aragón, declaration, [Laguna], 25 March 1813, Pueblo of Laguna, PLC 133, r. 46, f. 537–45. The declaration defines four sites beyond the pueblo that these governors had recognized, and which the Indians had purchased from Hispanos (Bowden, "Private Land Claims," 5:1556–63).
2. Hall, *Four Leagues of Pecos*, 205.

GLOSSARY

abrevaderos: Publicly accessible water sources

acequia: An irrigation ditch; from the Arabic "as-saquiya"

adverse possession: A means of acquiring title by possession, for a period of time provided for in a statute of limitations based on a deed that appears to convey title

alcalde: A local governmental official with judicial, executive, and police powers

alcaldía: The area governed by an alcalde or ayuntamiento

alferez: An ensign, standard-bearer

asesor: A legal advisor

audiencia: A judicial body, sometimes with legislative powers; the highest court of appeal in New Spain

ayuntamiento: A town council

bando: A proclamation, decree

caballería: A unit of agricultural land, about 105 acres

cabildo: A municipal council; also the meeting place of such a council

cacique: An Indian leader or local ruler

cedula: An order or decree, usually from the king

chorreras: A right-of-way or passage between adjoining properties

cordel: A cord for measuring land, usually 50 or a 100 varas long, usually made of a fiber like yucca but also of horsehair or leather

cortes: The senate or congress of deputies in Spain

commanding general: The official who administers the military-political district known as the *comandancia general* or general command

ejido: Common land owned by a community

encomienda: A grant of Indian tribute to a Hispano; its holder was an encomendero *escribano*: A notary, judicial assistant; an official with legal training

estancia: A ranch, usually of medium size

fanega: A unit of dry measure of one and a half to two and a half bushels

fee simple title: The highest form of ownership interest in real property

hijuela: A deed, often effecting the division of a larger tract

juez receptor: A temporarily appointed magistrate charged with collecting evidence

justice of the peace (*juez de paz*): The successor to alcaldes during the Mexican period

letrado: A lawyer; literally, a man of letters, a person trained in the law with a law degree

licenciado: A person with a university degree

merced: A grant of land or water

monte: Mountainous common lands used primarily for wood gathering

plaza de armas: A site where an army camps and musters in formation when it is on a campaign or where garrisoned troops muster and drill

prefect: A governmental official during the Mexican Period, subordinate to the governor, who administers a prefectura

puesto: An outpost

regidor: A member of an ayuntamiento

santo: A carved image of a saint

statute of limitations: A law providing a time period within which a claimant must sue or have the claim barred (see *adverse possession*)

teniente: An assistant

vara: A unit of measurement, approximately 33 inches

vecino: A landowning resident of a community entitled to vote, usually a Hispano.

villa: The largest of the Hispano municipalities in New Mexico; the three villas were Santa Fe, Santa Cruz de la Cañada, and Albuquerque

visita: A church that lacks a resident priest but is visited by a priest who conducts services

WORKS CITED

Archival Materials

Archives of the Diocese of Santa Fe, Santa Fe, NM (AASF)
Archivo de la Real Audiencia de Guadalajara, Biblioteca del Estado de Jalisco, Guadalajara, Mexico (ARAG)
    Ramo Civil
Archivo General de Indias, Seville, Spain (AGI)
    Indiferente
Archivo General de la Nación, Mexico City, Mexico (AGN)
    Audiencia of Mexico City
    Historia
    Justicia
    Provincias Internas
Archivos Históricos del Arzobispado de Durango, New Mexico State University Library, Microfilm, Archives and Special Collections Department, Las Cruces (AHAD)
Bancroft Library, University of California, Berkeley (TBL)
    Bolton Collection
    Pinart Collection
Biblioteca Nacional de México, Universidad Autónoma de México, Mexico City (BNM)
    Archivo Franciscano
Bureau of Land Management, Santa Fe, NM (BLM)
Center for Southwest Research, Zimmerman Library, University of New Mexico, Albuquerque
    Julius Seligman Collection (JSC)
National Records and Archive Administration, Washington, D.C. (NARA)
New Mexico State Records Center and Archives, Santa Fe (SRCA)
    Mexican Archives of New Mexico (MANM)
    Records of the Court of Private Land Claims (PLC)
    Records of the Office of the Surveyor General (SG)
    Spanish Archives of New Mexico (SANM)

Other Works

Abel, Annie Heloise, ed. "The Journal of John Greiner." *Old Santa Fe* 3, no. 11 (1916): 189–241.

———. *The Official Correspondence of James S. Calhoun While Indian Agent at Santa Fé and Superintendent of Indian Affairs in New Mexico, Collected Mainly from the Files of the Indian Office and Edited Under Its Direction*. Washington, D.C.: GPO, 1915.

Aberle, Sophie D. *The Pueblo Indians of New Mexico: Their Land, Economy and Civil Organization*. New York: Kraus Reprint, 1969.

Adams, Eleanor B. "Bishop Tamarón's Visitation of New Mexico, 1760." *New Mexico Historical Review* 28, no. 3 (1953): 192–221.

Adams, Eleanor B., and Angélico Chávez, trans. *The Missions of New Mexico, 1776: A Description by Fray Francisco Atanasio Domínguez, with Other Contemporary Documents*. Albuquerque: University of New Mexico Press, 1956.

Annual Report of the Surveyor General of New Mexico, 30 Sept. 1856, House Executive Documents, 3rd Session, 34th Congress. Washington, D.C.: GPO, 1857.

Anschuetz, Kurt. "Not Waiting for Rain: Integrated Systems of Water Management by Pre-Columbian Pueblo Farmers in North-Central New Mexico." PhD diss., University of Michigan, 1998.

Arnon, Nancy, and W. W. Hill. "Santa Clara Pueblo." In vol. 9 of the *Handbook of North American Indians: Southwest*, ed. Alfonso Ortiz, 296–307. Washington, D.C.: Smithsonian Institution, 1979.

Baklini, Joanne. "The Land Claims of Santa Clara Pueblo." Master's thesis, University of New Mexico, 1969.

Bancroft, Herbert Howe. *History of Arizona and New Mexico, 1530–1888*. San Francisco, CA: History Company, 1889.

Bandelier, Adolph F. *Final Report of Investigations Among the Indians of the Southwestern United States Carried on Mainly in the Years from 1880 to 1885*. 2 vols. Cambridge, MA: Archaeological Institute of America, 1892.

———. *The Southwestern Journals of Adolph Bandelier, 1885–1888*. Edited by Charles H. Lange, Carroll L. Riley, and Elizabeth Lange. Albuquerque: University of New Mexico Press, 1975.

———. *The Southwestern Journals of Adolph Bandelier, 1889–1892*. Edited by Charles H. Lange and Carroll L. Riley. Albuquerque: University of New Mexico Press, 1984.

Barney, Ralph. "The Indian Claims Commission." In *American Indian Ethnohistory: Indians of the Southwest*, edited by David Agee Horr, 13–16. New York: Garland, 1974.

Barrett, Elinore M. *Conquest and Catastrophe: Changing Rio Grande Pueblo Settlement Patterns in the Sixteenth and Seventeenth Centuries*. Albuquerque: University of New Mexico Press, 2002.

Barrett, Ward. "*Jugerum* and *Caballería* in New Spain." *Agricultural History* 53, no. 2 (1979): 423–37.

"Battle to Preserve Ancient Pueblo Ruins." *Indian Affairs: Newsletter of the Association of American Indian Affairs* 107 (Oct. 1984): 4.

Baxter, John O. *Spanish Irrigation in Taos Valley.* Santa Fe: New Mexico State Engineer Office, 1990.

———. *Spanish Irrigation in the Pojoaque and Tesuque Valleys during the Eighteenth and Early Nineteenth Centuries.* Santa Fe: New Mexico State Engineer Office, 1984.

Bayer, Laura, Floyd Montoya, and the Pueblo of Santa Ana. *Santa Ana: The People, the Pueblo, and the History of Tamaya.* Albuquerque: University of New Mexico Press, 1994.

Benavides, Alonso de. *Fray Alonso de Benavides' Revised Memorial of 1634.* Edited by Frederick Webb Hodge, George Hammond, and Agapito Rey. Albuquerque: University of New Mexico Press, 1945.

———. *The Memorial of Fray Alonso de Benavides, 1630.* Translated by Emma Burbank Ayer. Chicago: privately printed, 1916.

Bennett, James A. "Notes and Documents." *New Mexico Historical Review* 25, no. 4 (1950): 328–29.

Berthier-Fogler. "Sandia's New Buffalo Ideology: A Casino, an Old Land Grant, Compromises, and Conservationism." 26th American Indian Workshop, Munich Germany, 11–13 Apr. 2005.

Biella, Jan V. and Richard C. Chapman, eds. *Archeological Investigations in Cochiti Reservoir, New Mexico.* Vol. 1: *A Survey of Regional Variability.* Albuquerque: University of New Mexico Department of Anthropology, Office of Contract Archeology, 1977.

Bloom, Lansing B. "Barreiro's *Ojeada sobre Nuevo-México.*" Pt. 1. *New Mexico Historical Review* 3, no. 1 (1928): 75–96.

———. "Barreiro's *Ojeada sobre Nuevo-México.*" Pt. 2. *New Mexico Historical Review* 3, no. 2 (1928): 145–78.

"The Blue Lake Controversy." *New Mexico Review* (Nov. 1969): 13–14.

Bodine, John J. "Blue Lake: A Struggle for Indian Rights." *American Indian Law Review* 1, no. 1 (1973): 23–32.

———. "Taos Blue Lake Controversy." *Journal of Ethnic Studies* 6, no. 1 (1978): 42–48.

Borah, Woodrow. *Justice by Insurance: The General Indian Court of the Half-Real.* Berkeley: University of California Press, 1983.

Bowden, J. J. "Private Land Claims in the Southwest." 6 vols. Master's thesis, Southern Methodist University, 1969.

Boyd, Elizabeth. "The Vara, a Unit of Measurement." *El Palacio* 61, no. 2 (1954): 46–47.

Bradfute, Richard L. *The Court of Private Land Claims: The Adjudication of Spanish and Mexican Land Grant Titles, 1891–1904.* Albuquerque: University of New Mexico Press, 1975.

Brandt, Elizabeth. "Sandia Pueblo." In vol. 9 of the *Handbook of North American Indians Southwest*, edited by Alfonso Ortiz, 343–50. Washington, D.C.: Smithsonian Institution, 1979.

———. "Sandia Pueblo, New Mexico: A Linguistic and Ethnolinguistic Investigation." PhD diss., Southern Methodist University, 1970.

Brayer, Herbert O. *Pueblo Indian Land Grants of the "Rio Abajo," New Mexico.* Albuquerque: University of New Mexico Press, 1939.

Brescia, Michael. "Historical Assessment of Ohkay Owingeh's Water Rights in the Santa Cruz Valley Prior to 1924." Unpublished manuscript, 2009.

Brooks, James F. *Captives and Cousins: Slavery, Kinship, and Community in the Southwest Borderlands.* Chapel Hill: University of North Carolina Press for the Omohundro Institute of Early American History and Culture, 2002.

Brown, Donald Nelson. "Picuris Pueblo." In vol. 9 of the *Handbook of North American Indians: Southwest*, edited by Alfonso Ortiz, 268–77. Washington, D.C.: Smithsonian Institution, 1979.

———. "Structural Change at Picuris Pueblo, New Mexico." PhD diss., University of Arizona, 1973.

Brown, Stephen R. *1494: How a Family Feud in Medieval Spain Divided the World in Half.* New York: St. Martin's Press, 2011.

Burke, Joseph C. "The Cherokee Cases: A Study in Law, Politics and Morality." *Stanford Law Review* 21, no. 3 (1969): 500–531.

Burt, Larry. *Tribalism in Crisis: Federal Indian Policy, 1953–1961.* Albuquerque: University of New Mexico Press, 1982.

Calvin, Ross. *Lieutenant Emory Reports.* Albuquerque: University of New Mexico Press, 1968.

Canes of Power. DVD, Silver Bullet Productions, 2012.

Carrillo, Charles M. "Oral History-Ethnohistory of the Abiquiú Reservoir Area." In *History and Ethnohistory along the Rio Chama*, 109–69. Albuquerque, NM: U.S. Army Corps of Engineers, 1992.

C. de Baca, Vincent Zachary. "Death Becomes the Patriarch: Luis María Cabeza de Baca, 1754–1827." Paper presented at the annual conference of the Historical Society of New Mexico, Santa Fe, May 2012.

Chardon, Roland. "The Elusive Spanish League: A Problem of Measurement in Sixteenth-Century New Spain." *Hispanic American Historical Review* 60, no. 2 (1980): 294–302.

Chávez, Angélico. *Archives of the Archdiocese of Santa Fe, 1678–1900.* Washington, D.C.: Academy of American Franciscan History.

———. *Chávez: A Distinctive Clan of New Mexico.* Santa Fe, NM: William Gannon, 1989.

———. *Origins of New Mexico Families: A Genealogy of the Spanish Colonial Period.* Rev. ed. Santa Fe: Museum of New Mexico Press, 1992.

———. "Valle de Cochiti." *New Mexico Magazine* 51, (Jan.–Feb. 1973): 8–12.

Clifford, Frank. "Albert Fall: New Mexico's Dark Knight." *El Palacio* 117, no. 1 (2012): 52–59.

Collins, Dabney Otis. "Battle for Blue Lake: The Taos Indians Finally Regain Their Sacred Land." *American West* 8, no. 3 (1971): 32–37.

Crane, Leo. *Desert Drums: The Pueblo Indians of New Mexico, 1540–1928*. Boston: Little Brown, 1928.
Cunningham, Charles H. *The Audiencia in the Spanish Colonies*. Berkeley: University of California Press, 1919.
Cutter, Charles R. *The Legal Culture of Northern New Spain, 1700–1810*. Albuquerque: University of New Mexico Press, 1995.
———. *The Protector de Indios in Colonial New Mexico*. Albuquerque: University of New Mexico Press, 1986.
———. "The 'Spurious' Seventeenth-Century Pueblo Grants of New Mexico: A Closer Look." Unpublished manuscript, 1987.
Davis, W. W. H. *El Gringo*. New York: Harper and Bros., 1857.
del Río, Ignacio. *Guía del Archivo Franciscano de la Biblioteca Nacional de México*. Washington, D.C.: Instituto de Investigaciones Bibliográficas, Universidad Nacional Autónoma de México and Academy of American Franciscan History, 1975.
del Rosal, Francisco. *Diccionario etimológico: Alfabeto primero de origen y etimología de todos los vocablos originales de la lengua castellana*. Facs. ed. Madrid: Consejo Superior de Investigaciones Ciéntificas, 1992.
de Tocqueville, Alexis. *Democracy in America*. New York: Knopf, 1945.
"Disposiciones sobre fundo legal y ejidos de los pueblos." *Guía práctica de derecho: Legislación, derecho y jurisprudencia*, 1 Sept. 1892, 389–95.
Doolittle, William E. *Pre-Hispanic Occupancy in the Valley of Sonora, Mexico: Archaeological Confirmation of Early Spanish Reports*. Tucson: University of Arizona Press, 1988.
Dory-Garduño, James. "The 1766 Ojo del Espíritu Santo Grant: Authenticating a New Mexico Land Grant." *Colonial Latin American Historical Review* 16, no. 2 (2007): 157–96.
Dozier, Edward P. *Hano: A Tewa Indian Community in Arizona*. New York: Holt, Rinehart and Winston, 1966.
Duarte, Carlos F. "El mobiliario de la época republicana en Venezuela." *Armitano arte* 1 (Dec. 1982): 11–42.
Dublan, Manuel, and José María Lozano. *Legislación mexicana*. 54 vols. Mexico City: Imprenta del Comercio a cargo de Dublan y Lozano, 1876–1904.
Dunbar, John B. "Massacre of the Villasur Expedition by the Pawnees on the Platte in 1720." In vol. 11 of *Kansas Historical Collections*, 397–423. Topeka: Kansas State Printing Office, 1909–1910.
Dunham, Harold. "Historical Study of Land Use Eastward of the Taos Indians' Pueblo Land Grant." In *Pueblo Indians*, edited by David Agee Horr, 313–44. New York: Garland, 1974.
———. "Spanish and Mexican Land Policies and Grants in the Taos Pueblo Region." In *Pueblo Indians*, edited by David Agee Horr, 151–313. New York: Garland, 1974.
Ebright, Malcolm. *Advocates for the Oppressed: Hispanos, Indians, Genízaros, and Their Land in New Mexico*. Albuquerque: University of New Mexico Press, 2014.

———. "Advocates for the Oppressed: Indians, Genízaros, and Their Spanish Advocates in New Mexico, 1700–1786." *New Mexico Historical Review* 71, no. 4 (1996): 305–39.

———. "Breaking New Ground: A Reappraisal of Governors Vélez Cachupín and Mendinueta and Their Land Grant Policies." *Colonial Latin American Historical Review* 5, no. 2 (1996): 195–233.

———. Final application for state register status for the Guadalupita-Coyote Historic District to the New Mexico State Register of Cultural Properties. Property No. 1968, listed 14 Oct. 2011. nmhistoricpreservation.org/assets/files/register-nominations/Guadalupita-Coyote%20Historic%20District_FINAL%20 Nomination_9-9-11.pdf. Accessed 28 Mar. 2013.

———. "Frontier Land Litigation in Colonial New Mexico: A Determinant of Spanish Custom and Law." *Western Legal History* 8 (1995): 199–226.

———. *Land Grants and Lawsuits in Northern New Mexico*. Albuquerque: University of New Mexico Press, 1994.

———. "Sharing the Shortages: Water Litigation and Regulation in Hispanic New Mexico." *New Mexico Historical Review* 76, no. 1 (2001): 3–45.

———. *The Tierra Amarilla Grant: A History of Chicanery*. Santa Fe, NM: Center for Land Grant Studies, 1980.

Ebright, Malcolm, and Rick Hendricks. "Pueblo League and Pueblo Indian Land in New Mexico, 1692–1846." In vol. 4 of *Ysleta del Sur Pueblo Archives*, 91–193. El Paso, TX: Sundance Press, 2001.

———. *The Witches of Abiquiu: The Governor, the Priest, the Genízaro Indians, and the Devil*. Albuquerque: University of New Mexico Press, 2006.

Elliott, Michael L. "Mission and Mesa: Some Thoughts on the Archaeology of Pueblo Revolt Era Sites in the Jemez Region, New Mexico." In *Archaeologies of the Pueblo Revolt: Identity, Meaning, and Renewal in the Pueblo World*, edited by Robert W. Prucell, 45–60. Albuquerque: University of New Mexico Press, 2002.

Ellis, Florence Hawley. "Anthropological Data Pertaining to the Taos Land Claim." In *Pueblo Indians*, edited by David Agee Horr, 29–150. New York: Garland, 1974.

———. "Anthropological Evidence Supporting the Land Claim of the Pueblos of Zia, Santa Ana, and Jemez." Unpublished manuscript, 1956, document P-483, Laboratory of Anthropology, Santa Fe, NM.

Enote, Jim. Introduction to *Mapping Our Places: Voices From the Indigenous Community Mapping Initiative*, edited by Clay Scott, Alvin Warren, Jim Enote, and Indigenous Communities Mapping Initiative, 12–13. Berkeley, CA: Mapping Initiative, 2005.

Espinosa, J. Manuel. *The First Expedition of Vargas into New Mexico*. Albuquerque: University of New Mexico Press, 1940.

———. "Governor Vargas in Colorado." *New Mexico Historical Review* 11, no. 2 (1936): 179–87.

———. *The Pueblo Indian Revolt of 1696 and the Franciscan Missions of New Mexico*. Norman: University of Oklahoma Press, 1988.

Ferguson, T. J., and E. Richard Hart. *A Zuni Atlas*. Norman: University of Oklahoma Press, 1985.
Fernández, Domingo, Antonio B. Vigil, and Donacio Vigil. *Vigil Index, Spanish Archives and Mexican Archives of New Mexico, 1681 to 1846*. Edited by Julián Josué Vigil. Springer, NM: Editorial Telaraña, 1984.
Folsom, Franklin. *Indian Uprising on the Rio Grande: The Pueblo Revolt of 1680*. Albuquerque: University of New Mexico Press, 1973.
Forbes, Jack D. *Apache, Navajo, and Spaniard*. Norman: University of Oklahoma Press, 1960.
Ford, Richard I., Albert H. Schroeder, and Steward L. Peckham. 1972. "Three Perspectives on Puebloan History." In *New Perspectives on the Pueblos*, edited by Alfonso Ortiz, 19–39. Albuquerque: University of New Mexico Press, 1972.
Forrest, Suzanne. *The Preservation of the Village: New Mexico's Hispanics and the New Deal*. Albuquerque: University of New Mexico Press, 1989.
Frank, Ross. *From Settler to Citizen: Economic Development and the Creation of Vecino Society, 1750-1820*. Berkeley: University of California Press, 2000.
Galván Rivera, Mariano. *Ordenanzas de tierras y aguas*. 1868. Facs. of the 5th ed. Mexico City: Registro Agrario Nacional and Centro de Investigaciones y Estudios Superiores en Antropología Social, 1998.
Gibson, Charles. *The Aztecs Under Spanish Rule: A History of the Indians of the Valley of Mexico, 1519-1810*. Stanford, CA: Stanford University Press, 1964.
González de Villarroel, Diego. *Examen y práctica de escribanos*. Madrid: n.p., 1631.
Gordon-McCutchan, R. C. *The Taos Indians and the Battle for Blue Lake*. Albuquerque: University of New Mexico Press, 1995.
Gortner, Willis A. "Evidence for a Prehistoric Petroglyph Trail Map in the Sierra Nevada." *North American Archaeologist* 9, no. 2 (1988): 147–54.
Graybill, Andrew. "'Strong on the Merits and Powerfully Symbolic': The Return of Blue Lake to Taos Pueblo." *New Mexico Historical Review* 76, no. 2 (2001): 125–60.
Greenleaf, Richard E. "Land and Water in Mexico and New Mexico, 1700–1821." *New Mexico Historical Review* 47, no. 2 (1972): 85–112.
Grimes, John S. *A Treatise on the Law of Surveying and Boundaries*. 4th ed. Indianapolis, IN: Bobbs-Merrill Company, 1976.
Gulliford, Andrew. *Sacred Objects, Sacred Places: Preserving Tribal Traditions*. Boulder: University Press of Colorado, 2000.
Gutiérrez, Ramón A. *When Jesus Came the Corn Mothers Went Away: Marriage, Sexuality, and Power in New Mexico, 1500-1846*. Stanford, CA: Stanford University Press, 1991.
Hackett, Charles W., ed. *Historical Documents Relating to New Mexico, Nueva Vizcaya, and Approaches Thereto to 1773*. 3 vols. Washington, D.C.: Carnegie Institution, 1923–1937.
Hackett, Charles W., ed., and Charmion Clair Shelby, trans. *Revolt of the Pueblo Indians of New Mexico and Otermín's Attempted Reconquest, 1680-1682*. 2 vols. Albuquerque: University of New Mexico Press, 1942.

Hall, G. Emlen. *Four Leagues of Pecos: A Legal History of the Pecos Grant, 1800–1933*. Albuquerque: University of New Mexico Press, 1984.

———. "Giant Before the Surveyor-General: The Land Career of Donaciano Vigil." In *Spanish and Mexican Land Grants in New Mexico and Colorado*, edited by John Van Ness and Christine M. Van Ness, 64–73. Manhattan, KA: Sunflower University Press, 1980.

———. "Juan Estevan Pino, 'Se Los Coma': New Mexico Land Speculation in the 1820s." *New Mexico Historical Review* 57, no. 1 (1982): 27–42.

———. "The Pueblo Grant Labyrinth." In *Land, Water, and Culture: New Perspectives on Hispanic Land Grants*, edited by Charles Briggs and John Van Ness, 67–138. Albuquerque: University of New Mexico Press, 1987.

Hall, G. Emlen, and David J. Weber. "Mexican Liberals and the Pueblo Indians, 1821–1829." *New Mexico Historical Review* 59, no. 1 (1984): 5–32.

Hall, Kermit. *The Oxford Companion to the Supreme Court of the United States*. New York: Oxford University Press, 1992.

Hammond, George, and Agapito Rey, eds. *Don Juan de Oñate: Colonizer of New Mexico, 1595–1628*. 2 vols. Albuquerque: University of New Mexico Press, 1953.

———, eds. *The Rediscovery of New Mexico, 1580–1594*. Albuquerque: University of New Mexico Press, 1966.

Hanke, Lewis. *The Spanish Struggle for Justice in the Conquest of America*. Boston: Little, Brown and Company, 1965.

Haring, C. H. *The Spanish Empire in America*. New York: Harcourt Brace Jovanovich, 1975.

Harrington, John Peabody. *The Ethnogeography of the Tewa Indians*. Washington, D.C.: GPO, 1916.

Hart, E. Richard. *Zuni and the Courts: A Struggle for Sovereign Land Rights*. Lawrence: University Press of Kansas, 1995.

Hendricks, Rick. "David J. Miller." newmexicohistory.org/people/david-j-miller. Accessed 1 Dec. 2011.

———. "David V. Whiting." newmexicohistory.org/people/david-v-whiting. Accessed 21 Dec. 2011.

———. *New Mexico in 1801: The Priest's Report*. Los Ranchos, NM: Rio Grande Books, 2008.

Hendricks, Rick, and John P. Wilson, eds. *The Navajos in 1705: Roque Madrid's Campaign Journal*. Albuquerque: University of New Mexico Press, 1996.

Herzog, Tamar. "La política espacial y las tácticas de conquista: Las 'Ordenanzas de descubrimiento, nueva población y pacificación de las Indias' y su legado (siglos xvi–xvii)." In *Felipe II y el oficio de rey: La fragua de un imperio*, edited by José Román Gutiérrez, Enrique Martínez Ruiz, and Jaime González Rodríguez, 293–303. Madrid: Sociedad Estatal para la Conmemoración de los Centenarios de Felipe II y Carlos V, 2001.

Hibben, Frank C., and W. S. Stallings. *Excavation of the Riana Ruin and Chama Valley Survey*. Albuquerque: University of New Mexico Press, 1937.

Hill, W. W., and Charles H. Lange. *An Ethnogeography of Santa Clara Pueblo, New Mexico.* Albuquerque: University of New Mexico Press, 1982.

"History of The Pueblo of Jemez." www.jemezpueblo.com/content.asp? CustComKey =364865 &Category Key=364886&pn=Page&DomName=jemezpueblo.com. Accessed 1 Dec. 2011.

Hoberman, Louisa Schell. Conclusion to *Cities and Society in Colonial Latin America,* edited by Louisa Schell Hoberman and Susan Migden Socolow, 313–31. Albuquerque: University of New Mexico Press, 1986.

Hodge, Frederick Webb. *Handbook of American Indians North of Mexico.* 2 vols. Totowa, NJ: Rowman and Littlefield, 1975.

Hordes, Stanley M. "History of the Boundaries of the Pueblo of Sandia, 1748–1860." Prepared for U.S. Forest Service Southwest Region, Albuquerque, NM, 1 Mar. 1996.

Horr, David Agee, ed. *Pueblo Indians.* 5 vols. New York: Garland, 1974.

Icaza Dufour, Francisco de. *La abogacía en el reino de la Nueva España, 1521–1821.* Mexico City: Miguel Ángel Porrúa, 1998.

Jeançon, J. A. *Excavations in the Chama Valley, New Mexico.* Smithsonian Institution Bureau of American Ethnology Bulletin 81. Washington, D.C.: GPO, 1923.

Jefferson, James, Robert Delaney, and Gregory Thompson. *The Southern Utes: A Tribal History.* Ignacio, CO: Southern Ute Tribe, 1972.

Jenkins, Myra Ellen. "The Baltasar Baca Grant: History of an Encroachment." Pt. 1. *El Palacio* 68, no. 2 (1961): 47–64.

———. "The Baltasar Baca Grant: History of an Encroachment." Pt. 2. *El Palacio* 68, no. 3 (1961): 87–105

———. "History and Administration of the Tigua Indians of Ysleta del Sur during the Spanish Colonial Period." In vol. 3 of *Ysleta del Sur Pueblo Archives,* 101–38. El Paso, TX: Sundance Press, 2000.

———. "The Pueblo of Sandia and Its Lands." Unpublished report in author's possession, 1986.

———. "Some Eighteenth-Century New Mexico Women of Property." In *Hispanic Arts and Ethnohistory in the Southwest: New Papers Inspired by the Work of E. Boyd,* ed. Marta Weigle with Claudia Larcombe and Samuel Larcombe, 335–45. Santa Fe, NM: Ancient City Press, 1983.

———. "Spanish Land Grants in the Tewa Area." *New Mexico Historical Review* 47, no. 2 (1972): 113–34.

Jenkins, Myra Ellen, and Albert Schroeder. *A Brief History of New Mexico.* Albuquerque: University of New Mexico Press, 1974.

Jones, Oakah L., Jr. *Pueblo Warriors and Spanish Conquest.* Norman: University of Oklahoma Press, 1966.

Julyan, Robert. *The Place Names of New Mexico.* Albuquerque: University of New Mexico Press, 1996.

Keene, Milford T. "A Report of the Sandia Pueblo East Boundary on Sandia Mountain." 15 Oct. 1985.

———. "Report on the Boundaries of the Santa Cruz Tract." Southern Pueblos Agency, Bureau of Indian Affairs, 26 Feb. 1981.

Kelley, Henry W. "Franciscan Missions of New Mexico, 1740–1760." *New Mexico Historical Review* 16, no. 2 (1941): 41–69.

Kelly, Lawrence C. *The Assault on Assimilation: John Collier and the Origins of Indian Policy Reform*. Albuquerque: University of New Mexico Press, 1983.

———. "History of the Pueblo Lands Board, 1922–1933." Unpublished manuscript in author's possession, 1980.

———. "The Pueblo Lands Act and the Problem of Overlapping Pueblo and Non-Indian Grants." Unpublished manuscript in author's possession, 1987.

———. "Section 17 of the Pueblo Lands Act: A Study of Legislative History and Administrative Practice." Unpublished manuscript in author's possession, 1984.

Kessell, John L. *Kiva, Cross, and Crown: The Pecos Indians and New Mexico 1640–1840*. Washington, D.C.: National Park Service, 1979.

———. *Pueblos, Spaniards, and the Kingdom of New Mexico*. Norman: University of Oklahoma Press, 2008.

———, ed. *Remote Beyond Compare: Letters of don Diego de Vargas to His Family from New Spain and New Mexico, 1675–1706*. Albuquerque: University of New Mexico Press, 1989.

Kessell, John L., and Rick Hendricks, eds. *By Force of Arms: The Journals of don Diego de Vargas, New Mexico, 1691–1693*. Albuquerque: University of New Mexico Press, 1992.

Kessell, John L., Rick Hendricks, and Meredith D. Dodge, eds. *Blood on the Boulders: The Journals of don Diego de Vargas, New Mexico, 1694–1697*. 2 vols. Albuquerque: University of New Mexico Press, 1998.

———, eds. *To the Royal Crown Restored: The Journals of don Diego de Vargas, New Mexico, 1692–1694*. Albuquerque: University of New Mexico Press, 1995.

Kessell, John L., Rick Hendricks, Meredith D. Dodge, and Larry D. Miller, eds., *A Settling of Accounts: The Journals of don Diego de Vargas, New Mexico, 1700–1704*. Albuquerque: University of New Mexico Press, 2002.

———, eds. *That Disturbances Cease: The Journals of don Diego de Vargas, New Mexico, 1697–1700*. Albuquerque: University of New Mexico Press, 2000.

Knaut, Andrew. *The Pueblo Revolt of 1680: Conquest and Resistance in Seventeenth-Century New Mexico*. Norman: University of Oklahoma Press, 1995.

La Farge, Oliver. "Indians on the New Frontier." *Indian Affairs* 41 (1966): 1–2.

Lamar, Howard. *The Far Southwest, 1846–1912*. Rev. ed. Albuquerque: University of New Mexico Press, 2000.

Lange, Charles H. *Cochiti: A New Mexico Pueblo, Past and Present*. Albuquerque: University of New Mexico Press, 1959.

Las Casas, Bartolomé de. *In Defense of the Indians*. Translated by Stafford Poole. Dekalb: University of Northern Illinois Press, 1992.

———. *Tears of the Indians*. Williamstown, MA: John Lilburne, 1970.

Las siete partidas del rey don Alfonso El Sabio: Cotejadas con varios códices antiguos por la Real Academia de la Historia. Facs. rpt. Madrid: Edición Atlas, 1972.

LeCompte, Janet. "The Independent Women of Hispanic New Mexico, 1821–1846." *Western Historical Quarterly* 12, no. 1 (1981): 17–35.

Levine, Frances. *Our Prayers Are in This Place: Pecos Pueblo Identity over the Centuries*. Albuquerque: University of New Mexico Press, 1999.

Liebmann, Matthew. *Revolt: An Archaeological History of Pueblo Resistance and Revitalization in 17th Century New Mexico*. Tucson: University of Arizona Press, 2012.

Liebmann, Matthew, and Robert Preucel. "The Archaeology of the Pueblo Revolt and the Formation of the Modern Pueblo World." *Kiva: The Journal of Southwestern Anthropology and History* 73, no. 2 (2006): 195–217.

Lockhart, James. "Encomienda and Hacienda: The Evolution of the Great Estate in the Spanish Indies." *Hispanic American Historical Review* 49, no. 3 (1969): 411–29.

Long, Anton V. "Senator Bursum and the Pueblo Indian Lands Act of 1924." Master's thesis, University of New Mexico, 1949.

Manje, Juan Mateo. "Diary of an Expedition." In *Kino and Manje, Explorers of Sonora and Arizona: Their Vision of the Future*, edited by Ernst J. Burrus, 284–99. St. Louis, MO: St. Louis University Press, 1971.

Mathews-Benham, Sandra K. "The Cruzate Grants of 1689 and Modern Pueblo Land Claims." In *Sunshine and Shadows in New Mexico's Past: The Spanish Colonial and Mexican Periods, 1540–1848*, edited by Richard Melzer, 60–78. Los Ranchos, NM: Rio Grande Books, 2010.

Mathews-Lamb, Sandra K. "'Designing and Mischievous Individuals': The Cruzate Grants and the Office of the Surveyor General." *New Mexico Historical Review* 71, no. 4 (1996): 341–59.

———. "The 'Nineteenth-Century' Cruzate Grants: Pueblos, Peddlers, and the Great Confidence Scam." PhD diss., University of New Mexico, 1998.

McKnight, Joseph W. "Texas Community Property Law: Conservative Attitudes, Reluctant Change." *Law and Contemporary Problems* 56, no. 2 (1993): 71–98.

Merlan, Thomas. Report in support of final brief of San Felipe Pueblo, Apr. 2003. Unpublished manuscript in author's possession.

Meyer, Michael C., and Susan M. Deeds, "Land, Water, and Equity in Spanish Colonial and Mexican Law: Historical Evidence for the Court in the Case of the State of New Mexico vs. R. Lee Aamodt, et al." Unpublished report on file in *New Mexico v. Aamodt*, No. 6639 (D.N.M., 1979).

Miller, Michael. "The Papers of Francis C. Wilson: Santa Fe Attorney and Oil Industry Pioneer, 1876–1952." *Greater Llano Estacado Southwest Heritage* 12, no. 2 (1983): 2–8, 23–24.

Minge, Ward Alan. *Acoma: Pueblo in the Sky*. Albuquerque: University of New Mexico Press, 1991.

———. "The Pueblo of Santa Ana's Ranchito Purchases." Manuscript in author's possession, Oct. 1983.

Montgomery, C. M. "Corn Shrine of the Tanos: Galisteo Basin, New Mexico." *Desert* 27, no. 12 (1964): 26–28.

Mora, José María Luis. *México y sus revoluciones*. Mexico City: Porrúa, 1965.

Morgan, William A. "'And on the East . . .': The Sandia Eastern Boundary Issue and Land Policies of Three Nations." Unpublished report in author's possession, 1988.

Nabokov, Peter. *Where Lightning Strikes: The Lives of American Indian Sacred Places*. New York: Viking, 2006.

Naranjo, Tessie. "Thoughts on Migration by Santa Clara Pueblo." *Journal of Anthropological Archaeology* 14, no. 2 (1995): 247–50.

Newman, Roger K. *The Yale Biographical Dictionary of American Law*. New Haven, CT: Yale University Press, 2009.

Newton, Nell J., Robert Anderson, et al., eds. *Cohen's Handbook of Federal Indian Law*. Newark, NJ: Matthew Bender, 2012.

Norris, Jim. "Franciscans Eclipsed: Church and State in Spanish New Mexico, 1750–1780." *New Mexico Historical Review* 76, no. 2 (2001): 161–74.

Olson, Jerry, ed. "GLO Surveyor Personal Notes." olsonengr.com/download/glo surveyorsnotes.pdf. Accessed 19 Dec. 2011.

Ortiz, Alfonso. "Ritual Drama and the Pueblo World View." In *New Perspectives on the Pueblos*, edited by Alfonso Ortiz, 135–61. Albuquerque: University of New Mexico Press, 1972.

———. *The Tewa World: Space, Time, Being and Becoming in a Pueblo Society*. Chicago: University of Chicago Press, 1969.

Parry, J. H., *The Audiencia of New Galicia in the Sixteenth Century*. Cambridge: Cambridge University Press, 1948.

Pecos, Regis. "The History of Cochiti Lake from the Pueblo Perspective." *Natural Resources Journal* 47, no. 3 (2007): 639–42.

Perdue, Theda, and Michael D. Green. *The Cherokee Nation and the Trail of Tears*. New York: Penguin, 2008.

Perez, Nicolas, Jr. "Locating the Ysleta Grant: Affidavit and Exhibits." In vol. 3 of *Ysleta del Sur Pueblo Archives*, 337–68. El Paso, TX: Sundance Press, 2000.

Philp, Kenneth R. *John Collier's Crusade for Indian Reform*. Tucson: University of Arizona Press, 1973.

Pinel, Sandra Lee. "Stopping the Flood of Damages from Cochiti Dam." *Cultural Survival Quarterly* 12, no. 2 (1988): 25–28.

Prechtel, Martín. *The Toe Bone and the Tooth*. London: Harper Collins, 2003.

Preucel, Robert, and Matthew Liebmann, eds. *Archaeologies of the Pueblo Revolt: Identity, Meaning, and Renewal in the Pueblo World*. Albuquerque: University of New Mexico Press, 2007.

Prucha, Francis Paul. *The Great Father: The United States Government and the American Indians*. Lincoln: University of Nebraska Press, 1984.

Recopilación de leyes de los reinos de las Indias. 4 vols. 1681. Facs. ed. Foreword by Ramón Menéndez y Pidal. Madrid: Cultura Hispánica, 1973.

Riley, Carroll L. *The Kachina and the Cross: Indians and Spaniards in the Early Southwest.* Salt Lake City: University of Utah Press, 1999.

Rixon, Theodore F. *Report on and Examination of the Taos Forest Reserve, Territory of New Mexico.* Washington, D.C.: U.S. Geological Survey, 1905.

Roeder, Fred. "John W. Garretson." *American Surveyor.* amerisurv.com/content/view/6009/1361. Accessed 4 Apr. 2009.

Rosen, Deborah A. "Acoma v. Laguna and the Transition from Spanish Colonial Law to American Civil Procedure in New Mexico." *Law and History Review* 19, no. 3 (2001): 513–46. http://www.historycooperative.org/journals/lhr/19.3/rosen.html. Accessed 17 June 2011.

Rothman, Hal K. *Bandelier National Monument: An Administrative History.* Professional Paper No. 14. Santa Fe, NM: Southwest Cultural Resources Center, 1988.

———. *On Rims and Ridges: The Los Alamos Area Since 1880.* Lincoln: University of Nebraska Press, 1992.

Salazar, Richard J. *The Felipe Tafoya Grant: A Grazing Grant in West Central New Mexico.* Center for Land Grant Studies Research Paper No. 28. Guadalupita, NM: Center for Land Grant Studies, 1994.

Sando, Joe S. "Jemez Pueblo." In vol. 9 of the *Handbook of North American Indians: Southwest,* edited by Alfonso Ortiz, 418–29. Washington, D.C.: Smithsonian Institute, 1979.

———. *Nee Hemish: A History of Jemez Pueblo.* Albuquerque: University of New Mexico Press, 1982.

———. *The Pueblo Indians.* San Francisco: Indian Historian Press, 1976.

———. *Pueblo Nations: Eight Centuries of Pueblo Indian History.* Santa Fe, NM: Clear Light Publishing, 1992.

———. "The Pueblo Revolt." In vol. 9 of the *Handbook of North American Indians: Southwest,* edited by Alfonso Ortiz, 194–97. Washington, D.C.: Smithsonian Institution, 1979.

Scholes, France V. "Church and State in New Mexico." *New Mexico Historical Review* 11, no. 4 (1936): 297–349.

———. "Civil Government and Society in New Mexico in the Seventeenth Century." *New Mexico Historical Review* 10, no. 2 (1935): 71–111.

———. *Troublous Times in New Mexico, 1659–1670.* New York: AMS Press, 1977.

Schroeder, Albert H. *A Brief History of Picuris Pueblo: A Tiwa Indian Group in North Central New Mexico.* Adams State College Series in Anthropology 2. Alamosa, CO: Adams State College, 1974.

———. "Pecos Pueblo." In vol. 9 of the *Handbook of North American Indians: Southwest,* edited by Alfonso Ortiz, 430–37. Washington, D.C.: Smithsonian Institute, 1979.

———. "Pueblos Abandoned in Historic Times." In vol. 9 of the *Handbook of North American Indians: Southwest,* edited by Alfonso Ortiz, 236–54. Washington, D.C.: Smithsonian Institution, 1979.

Schroeder, Albert H., and Daniel S. Matson. *Colony on the Move: Gaspar Castaño de Sosa's Journal.* Santa Fe, NM: School of American Research Press, 1965.

Seed, Patricia. *Ceremonies of Possession in Europe's Conquest of the New World, 1492–1640*. Cambridge: Cambridge University Press, 1995.

———. "Taking Possession and Reading Texts: Establishing the Authority of Overseas Empires." In *Early Images of the Americas: Transfer and Invention*, edited by Jerry M. Williams and Robert E. Lewis, 111–47. Tucson: University of Arizona Press, 1993.

Sherry, Ashley. "I Interact Therefore I Am: La Donna Harris and the Return of Taos Blue Lake." newmexicohistory.org/people/i-interact-therefore-i-am-ladonna-harris-and-the-return-of-taos-blue-lake. Accessed 15 May 2012.

Sides, Hampton. *Blood and Thunder: An Epic of the American West*. New York: Doubleday, 2006.

Simmons, Marc. *Albuquerque: A Narrative History*. Albuquerque: University of New Mexico Press, 1982.

———, ed. and trans. *Father Juan Agustín Morfi's Account of Disorders in New Mexico, 1778*. Santa Fe: Historical Society of New Mexico, 1977.

———. "The Mysterious A Tribe of the Southern Plains." In *The Changing Ways of Southwestern Indians: A Historic Perspective*, edited by Albert Schroeder, 73–89. Glorieta, NM: Rio Grande Press, 1973.

———. *Spanish Government in New Mexico*. Albuquerque: University of New Mexico Press, 1968.

Smith, Daniel Blake. *An American Betrayal: Cherokee Patriots and the Trail of Tears*. New York: Henry Holt, 2011.

Snow, David. "A Note on Encomienda Economics in Seventeenth-Century New Mexico." In *Hispanic Arts and Ethnohistory in the Southwest*, edited by Marta Weigle with Sarah Larcombe and Claudia Larcombe, 347–57. Santa Fe, NM: Ancient City Press, 1983.

Stavig, Ward. "Ambiguous Visions: Nature, Law, and Culture in Indigenous-Spanish Land Relations in Colonial Peru." *Hispanic American Historical Review* 80, no. 1 (2000): 77–111.

Stevens, John. *A New Spanish and English Dictionary*. London: Printed for George Sawbridge at the Three Flower-de-Luces in Little Britain, 1706.

Stoller, Marianne L. "Grants of Desperation, Lands of Speculation: Mexican Period Land Grants in Colorado." In *Spanish and Mexican Land Grants in New Mexico and Colorado*, edited by John R. and Christine M. Van Ness, 22–39. Manhattan, KS: Sunflower University Press, 1980.

Swentzell, Rina. "An Architectural History of Santa Clara Pueblo." Master's thesis, University of New Mexico, 1976.

———. "Conflicting Landscape Values: The Santa Clara Pueblo Day School." In *Canyon Gardens: The Ancient Pueblo Landscapes of the American Southwest*, edited by V. B. Price and Baker Morrow, 125–32. Albuquerque: University of New Mexico Press, 2006.

Taos Pueblo Council. *The Blue Lake Area . . . An Appeal from Taos Pueblo*. N.p., n.p., [1969].

Taylor, Morris F. "Campaigns Against the Jicarilla Apache, 1854." *New Mexico Historical Review* 44, no. 4 (1969): 274–78.

Taylor, William B. "Colonial Land and Water Rights of New Mexico Indian Pueblos." Report on file in *New Mexico v. Aamodt*, No. 6639 (D.N.M., 1979).

———. *Landlord and Peasant in Colonial Oaxaca*. Stanford, CA: Stanford University Press, 1991.

Terrell, John Upton. *Pueblos, Gods and Spaniards*. New York: Doubleday, 1973.

Thomas, Alfred B. *After Coronado: Spanish Exploration Northeast of New Mexico, 1696-1727*. Norman: University of Oklahoma Press, 1935.

———. "Documents Bearing Upon the Northern Frontier of New Mexico, 1818–1819." *New Mexico Historical Review* 4, no. 2 (1929): 146–64.

———. *The Plains Indians and New Mexico, 1751-1778*. Albuquerque: University of New Mexico Press, 1940.

Tigges, Linda. "The Pastures of the Royal Horse Herd of the Santa Fe Presidio, 1692–1740." In *All Trails Lead to Santa Fe: An Anthology Commemorating the 400th Anniversary of the Founding of Santa Fe*, 237–66. Santa Fe, NM: Sunstone Press: 2010.

Todorov, Tzvetan. *The Conquest of America: The Question of the Other*. Norman: University of Oklahoma Press, 1999.

Tórrez, Robert. "The Taos Tax Revolt of 1816." *Ayer y Hoy in Taos* 27 (Spring 1999): 3–6.

———. "The Vara: Weights and Measurements in Colonial New Mexico." *Tradición revista* 9 (Spring 2004): 38–43.

Twitchell, Ralph Emerson. *Leading Facts of New Mexican History*. 2 vols. Cedar Rapids, IA: Torch Press, 1912.

———. *Old Santa Fe: The Story of New Mexico's Ancient Capital*. Chicago: Rio Grande Press, 1925.

———. *The Spanish Archives of New Mexico: Compiled and Chronologically Arranged with Historical, Genealogical, Geographical, and Other Annotations, by Authority of the State of New Mexico*. 2 vol. Glendale, CA.: Arthur H. Clark, 1914.

Tyler, Daniel. "Ejido Lands in New Mexico." In *Spanish and Mexican Land Grants and the Law*, edited by Malcolm Ebright, 24–35. Manhattan, KA: Sunflower Press, 1989.

———. "Land and Water Tenure in New Mexico: 1821–1846." Unpublished report on file in *New Mexico v. Aamodt*, No. 6639 (D.N.M., 1979).

U.S. Bureau of Indian Affairs. *1979 Land Status Report: Eight Northern Pueblos, Taos*. Albuquerque, NM: Bureau of Indian Affairs, 1979.

———. *Authorization of Appropriations to Pay in Part the Liability of the United States to Certain Pueblos: Hearings on HR 9071 before the House Committee on Indian Affairs, 72nd Congress, 1st session, February 17 and February 19, 1932*. Washington, D.C.: GPO, 1932.

———. *Report on the Pueblo of Santa Ana: House Report 70, 40th Congress, 2nd Session, July 1, 1868*. Washington, D.C.: GPO, 1868.

U.S. Indian Claims Commission. *Final Report*. Washington, D.C.: GPO, 1979.

U.S. Senate. *Cochiti Pueblo-Corps of Engineers Dam Project: Hearing before the Select Committee on Indian Affairs, 100th Congress, 2nd Session, March 15, 1985*. Washington, D.C.: GPO, 1985.

———. *Hearings on S. 3855 and S. 4223 before the Subcommittee of the Senate Committee on Public Lands and Surveys, 67th Congress, 1st Session, January 15–31, 1923*. Washington, D.C.: GPO, 1923.

———. *Joint Hearing before the Senate Committee on Energy and Natural Resources and the Committee on Indian Affairs on Senate Bill 2016, 107th Congress, 2nd Session, October 8, 2002*. Washington, D.C.: GPO, 2002.

———. *Senate Report 105-506, To Settle the Land Claims of the Pueblo of Santo Domingo, 106th Congress, 2nd Session, October 18, 2000 [to accompany S.2917]*.

———. *Senate Report 109-252, To Resolve Certain Native American Claims in New Mexico, and for Other Purposes, 109th Congress, 2nd Session, May 3, 2006 [to accompany S. 1773]*.

———. *Survey of Conditions of the Indians throughout the United States: Hearings before a subcommittee of the Committee on Indian Affairs, 71st Congress, 2nd Session, January 21, 1932, February 4, 1932*. Washington, D.C.: GPO, 1932.

———. *Taos Indians Blue Lake: Hearings before the Subcommittee on Indian Affairs of the Committee on Interior and Insular Affairs, 90th Congress, 2nd session, on H.R. 3306, an Act to Amend Section 4 of the Act of May 31, 1933 (48 Stat. 108), September 19–20, 1968*. Washington, D.C.: GPO, 1968.

———. *Taos Indians Blue Lake: Hearings before the Subcommittee on Indian Affairs of the Committee on Interior and Insular Affairs, 91st Congress, 2nd session, on S. 750 and H.R. 471, Bills to Amend Section 4 of the Act of May 31, 1933 (48 Stat.108), to Add Certain Lands to the Wheeler Peak Wilderness, Carson National Forest, N. Mex., and for other Purposes, July 9–10 1970*. Washington, D.C.: GPO, 1970.

Verdejo Gonzales, Francisco. *Arte de medir tierras, y aforar los líquidos y sólidos*. Madrid: Imprenta de Sancha, 1796.

Vigil, Julián Josué. *Picuris, N.M. Marriages, 1726–1775*. Guadalupita, NM: Center for Land Grant Studies, 1984.

Vitoria, Francisco de. *De Indis et de iure belli relectiones*. Lyon: Jacques Boyer, 1557.

Vlasich, James A. *Pueblo Indian Agriculture*. Albuquerque: University of New Mexico Press, 2005.

Wagner, Henry. *The Life and Writings of Bartolomé de las Casas*. Albuquerque: University of New Mexico Press, 1967.

Walker, Deward. "American Indian Sacred Geography." *Indian Affairs: Special Supplement-American Indian Religious Freedom* 116 (Summer 1988): iii–vii.

Warren, Alvin H. "Defining a Homeland: A History of 26,228.17 Acres of Land in Northern New Mexico." Honors Thesis, Dartmouth College, 1991.

———. "Sustaining the Revolution: Adaptations and Transformations in New Mexico State-Tribal Relations." In *White Shell Water Place: An Anthology of Native American Reflections on the 400th Anniversary of the Founding of Santa Fe, New Mexico*, edited by F. Richard Sanchez with Stephen Wall and Ann Filemyr, 155–66. Santa Fe, NM: Sunstone Press, 2010.

Warren, Charles. *The Supreme Court in United States History*. 2 vols. Knoxville, IL: Beard Books, 1999.

Waters, Frank. *The Man Who Killed the Deer*. New York: Washington Square Press, 1942.

Weber, David. *The Spanish Frontier in North America*. New Haven, CT: Yale University Press.

Westphall, Victor. *Mercedes Reales: Hispanic Land Grants of the Upper Rio Grande Region*. Albuquerque: University of New Mexico Press, 1983.

Whatley, John T. "The Saga of Taos Blue Lake." *Indian Historian* 2, no. 1 (1969): 22–28.

White, Koch, Kelley, McCarthy, and the New Mexico State Planning Office. *Land Title Study*. Santa Fe, NM: State Planning Office, 1971.

White, Leslie A. "The Pueblo of Santa Ana, New Mexico." Pt. 2. *American Anthropologist* 44, no. 4 (1942): 1–360.

Whitely, Peter M. "Reconnoitering 'Pueblo' Ethnicity: The 1852 Tesuque Delegation to Washington." *Journal of the Southwest* 45, no. 3 (2003): 437–518.

Williston, S. W., and H. T. Martin. "Some Pueblo Ruins in Scott County Kansas." In vol. 6 of *Kansas Historical Collections*, 124–30. Topeka: Kansas State Printing Office, 1900.

Wolf, Tom. "The Los Utes Case: Forestry Seeks Its Soul." *American Forests* 96, nos. 11–12 (1990): 28–32, 66–68.

Zubrow, Ezra B. W. *Population, Contact, and Climate in New Mexican Pueblos*. Tucson: University of Arizona Press, 1974.

Newspaper Articles

Baca, Kim. "More Than 70 Years After Exhumation Pecos Pueblo Ancestors Are Reburied." *Santa Fe New Mexican*, 23 May 1999.

Coleman, Michael. "Leased Town Didn't Meet Expectations for Pueblo." *Albuquerque Journal*, 29 June 1998.

Ebright, Malcolm. "What History Has to Say: Who Owns Sandia Peak Becomes Perfectly Clear When One Takes a Historical Look, a New Mexico Lawyer Says." *Albuquerque Tribune*, 13 Oct. 1998.

Graves, Howard. "Taos Leader, 90, to Take Plea to Capital." *Albuquerque Journal*, 14 June 1970.

Griffith, Winthrop. "The Taos Indians Have a Small Generation Gap." *New York Times Magazine*, 21 Feb. 1971, 25–27.

"The Indians Need Blue Lake." *New York Times*, 17 Jul. 1968.

Jadrnak, Jackie. "Feds Seek Dismissal of Land Suit." *Albuquerque Journal North*, 19 Feb. 2013.

Lezon, Dale. "Commission Questions Pueblo Land Acquisitions." *Albuquerque Journal*, 31 Jul. 1999.
Linthicum, Leslie. "The Long Way Home to Jemez: Ceremonial Objects End Journey to Pueblo Tonight." *Albuquerque Journal*, 30 Oct. 1993.
Nauman, Talli. "Jemez Pueblo Regains Land Church Leased." *Albuquerque Journal North*, 10 Nov. 1984.
———. "U.S. Sues to Settle Santo Domingo Land Claim." *Albuquerque Journal*, 10 Mar. 1989.
Neary, Ben. "Picuris Reclaims Clay Site." *Santa Fe New Mexican*, 17 May 2005.
"The Question Settled." *Santa Fe New Mexican*, 24 Oct. 1913.
Romancito, Rick. "Fighters for Blue Lake Return." *Taos News*, 26 Aug. 1993.
"Sandia Plan Gets Rocky Reception." *Santa Fe New Mexican*, 6 Apr. 2000.
Schiller, Mark. "Picuris Pueblo Files Claim to Aboriginal Lands." *La Jicarita News*, 9 Mar. 2004.
Simmons, Marc. "Pablo Abeita, A Leader; Isleta Pueblo's 'Grand Old Man' Led a Colorful Life." *Santa Fe Reporter*, 5 Jul. 2000.
———. "A Primer on Rope-Making." *Santa Fe Reporter*, 13–19 Dec. 1995.
———. "The Saving of Blue Lake." *Santa Fe Reporter*, 22–28 Aug. 1990.
Walker, Hollis. "Eight-Year Effort Pays Off for All." *Santa Fe New Mexican*, 23 May 1999.
"Wilson Replies to A. B. Renehan Interview." *Santa Fe New Mexican*, 22 Oct. 1913.
Whiteley, Peter M. "Law, Fact Legitimize Claim Up to Crest." *Albuquerque Journal*, 28 Aug. 1998.

INDEX

Abeita, Pablo, 273, 410n22
Aberle, Sophie, 200, 298
Abiquiu, 23, 109, 185, 330, 370n98
Abréu, Santiago, 43–45
Acoma Pueblo, 96, 219, 381n1, 391n42, 391n45; Cruzate grant to, 205, 208, 214–15, 218, 222, 228–29, 233, 244, 392n63; as encomienda, 3–4; lands of, 288, 327, 335; litigation by for documents and land, 230–32
Act to Regulate Trade and Intercourse with the Indian Tribes, 240, 243, 249, 251, 260–62, 276, 278
Aguilar, Juan de, 34–35
Aguilar, Rafael, 42
Alameda, 70–71, 81–82, 193
Alameda Pueblo, 92, 125
Alarid, José Rafael, 36
Allande, Pedro María de, 153; and Cochiti dispute with Cabeza de Baca, 172–73, 175–77
American Indian Defense Association, 275, 279, 297, 411n32
Anderson, Clinton P., 166, 293, 300–301, 304, 306–12, 314–16
Angostura, 51, 55, 58, 63, 71, 81, 331, 355n23, 364n152; dispute over by Santa Ana Pueblo and San Felipe Pueblo at, 69–70, 72, 74–75, 82; Indian lands at, 16, 68; land grant, 67–68; removal of Hispanos from lands, 76–79, 83
Anza, Juan Bautista de, 24, 45, 193; and enforcement of Cañada de Santa Clara grant, 161; and measurement of Santa Clara Pueblo league 25–27, 151
Apaches, 58–59, 90–91, 95, 107, 113, 175, 210, 365n7; Picuris Indians living among, 96, 98; raids by, 5, 132, 206–7; raids on Picuris Pueblo by, 101, 106, 110; relationship of with Genízaros, 109; role of in Pueblo Revolt, 92–93; Spanish military campaigns against, 101–2, 106
Arce, José María de, 71–72, 359n77, 359n91, 360n92
Archibeque, Juan Domingo, 76, 80
Archuleta, Diego, 138–39
Archuleta, Juan, 159–60
Arellano, Cristóbal, 18, 329
Argüello, José Miguel, 117
Ariluead, Vicente, 230–31
Armenta, Antonio, 193, 331
Armijo, Manuel, 131, 197, 221, 223, 225, 231–32, 374n26, 388n5, 397n129
Arvide, Martín de, 91, 111, 189–90
Atkinson, Henry M., 162, 208, 215, 226, 408n118
Atwood, Stella, 271–73
Audiencia of Guadalajara, 67, 73, 332, 360n101; and Cochiti Pueblo lawsuit against Cabeza de Baca, 171, 175, 177–78; and Santa Ana Pueblo and San Felipe Pueblo boundary dispute, 72, 74–77, 79, 81, 83, 85; and Taos Pueblo land dispute, 32
Audiencia of Mexico City, 124, 177, 360n101

Baca, Antonio, 56–59, 170, 332
Baca, Bartolomé, 79, 362n123; redistribution of Indian lands under, 37–39
Baca, Cristóbal, 51, 56; San Felipe Pueblo purchase of lands from, 60, 67, 71, 78
Baca, Diego, 194–95

441

Baca, Josefa, 55, 67–68, 70, 354n22, 409n130
Baca, Juana, 16, 20, 54, 343n23
Baca, Manuel, 19, 52, 60, 170, 329, 353n10, 409n130; dispute by, with Durán y Chaves over land boundaries, 53–54; Santa Ana Pueblo purchase of land from, 51, 55–56, 67
Baca, Vicente, 45–46
Baca Location No. 1, 164, 167, 408n125
Bandelier, Adolph F., 197, 210, 215–17, 391n46
Barker, Elliot, 295
Barreiro, Antonio, 218, 220, 394n75
Benedict, Kirby, 230–32, 249, 397n134
Berle, Adolf A., 275–77, 411n32
Bernal, Paul J., 294, 300, 311–12, 315, 317
Blue Lake, 9, 146, 294; efforts for return to Taos Pueblo, 300, 302–19, 324, 417n25; as sacred shrine of Taos Pueblo, 293, 295, 305, 308, 311; Taos Pueblo usage permit for, 298, 301
Bonavía y Zapata, Bernardo, 21, 152, 172–73, 331
Borah, William, 270, 272–73
Bowannie, John, 183, 384n49
Bracho, Rafael, 172–73, 177, 331
Bratton, Sam, 285–87
Brown, Henry Billings, 196, 386n39
Bureau of Indian Affairs, 149, 166, 182, 248–49, 269, 271, 280, 298, 301, 311, 372n137; administration of San Isidro grant by, 199–200; and Cochiti Dam and town, 183–84, 186; and encroaching grants on Ojo del Espíritu Santo, 195; management of Santa Clara Reservation by, 164–65
Burke, Charles, 269, 271, 273, 280, 295–96
Bursum, Holm O., 268–73, 275, 290, 324, 414n61
Bursum Bill (1922), 198, 268–74, 290, 324
Bustamante, Felipe, 109–11
Bustamante, Juan Domingo de, 20–21, 103–4, 155, 158–59
Bustamante y Tagle, Bernardo, 127, 131, 134–36

Caballero, Antonio, 28, 347n87
Cabeza de Baca, Luis María, 73, 164, 186, 194, 360n92, 408n125; land dispute with Cochiti by, 170–78
Caja del Río land grant, 179–81, 185–86
Calhoun, James S., 207, 388n5, 400n24, 400n26, 400n29; and protection of Pueblo Indians, 242–44
Campo Redondo, José, 26–27
Cañada de Cochití grant, 170, 174, 186, 347n87, 408n124
Cañada de Juan Tabovo, 128, 136
Cañada de Santa Clara Grant, 8, 160–61, 164–65, 223, 263–64; confirmation of by United States, 162–63
Canjuebe, Roque, 151–53, 330–31
Cañón de Picurís. See Vadito
Cargo, David, 308, 310, 312, 318
Carson National Forest, 121, 294–96, 302–4
Catití, Alonso (Santo Domingo Indian), 92, 94
Catron, Thomas B., 201, 216, 251–53; claim in Ojo del Espíritu Santo grant by, 195–96
Chacón, José Albino, 83, 323, 364n154
Chamisal, 115, 120
Chimayo, 102, 225
Ciénega Pueblo, 5, 15, 21, 36, 329
Cieneguilla, 67, 113, 358n69
Cieneguilla Pueblo, 5, 36, 76, 96, 113, 219, 408n124
Claramonte, fray Andrés, 108; as priest at Picuris Pueblo, 111–12
Clark, John A., 84, 221, 246, 248, 402n55
Clements, Reuben E., 137, 146, 214, 283, 376n53, 376n58; Sandia Pueblo grant survey by, 138–40
Cochiti Dam, 182–84, 186
Cochiti Lake, Town of, 182, 184, 186
Cochiti Pueblo, 8, 16, 19, 28, 69, 138, 177, 180, 200, 211, 219, 327, 329, 332, 360n92, 384n49, 360n92; adjudication of Cruzate grant to, 178–79, 205, 208, 211, 218–19, 233, 244, 263–64, 283, 335, 390n35, 391n37, 408n124; and building of Cochiti Dam

INDEX

and town, 182–85; *Cochiti v. Cabeza de Baca*, 176; Hispano encroachment on, 170, 180; history of, 169; and La Majada grant, 181; litigation by in land disputes, 20–21, 28, 73, 170–78, 186, 249–50, 343n23; revolt by, 96; study of land dealings of, 185, 384n55; use of land-title system by, 322; and reburial of Pecos Indians, 203
Cochrane, Walter, 279, 289
Codallos y Rabal, Joaquín, 330; and land grants, 67, 109–11, 151, 180; and peace with Comanche and Ute Indians, 23; and resettlement of Sandia Pueblo, 127–29; to Sandia Pueblo, 208; and Sandia Pueblo grant, 134, 223, 226
Collier, John, 324, 410n12, 412n50, 413n53, 413n57, 413n59; and actions of Pueblo Lands Board; 277–82, 284–87; background of, 270; land-reform program by, 199–201; and Pueblo Lands Act, 271–76, 290; and return of Blue Lake to Taos Pueblo, 294, 297–99, 302–3, 308, 318
Comanches, 23, 31, 107, 113, 139, 203, 206, 313, 369n91; alliance with Ute Indians by, 107; attacks on Pueblo Indians by, 90, 108–10, 132, 134, 340n7; attacks on Jicarilla Apaches by, 107; relationship of with Picuris Indians, 90; Spanish campaigns against, 102, 106.
Commissioner of Indian Affairs, 120, 165, 195, 242, 295; John Collier as, 199, 287, 297–98
Contereras, Quiteria, 56, 65–66, 358n66, 364n155, 409n130
Córdoba, Lázaro de, 103–4
Cortes of Cadiz, 30, 34, 36, 131, 174, 237, 398n1; and privatizing of Indians lands, 28–29, 32–33, 37, 40, 323, 332
Cota, José, 42–43, 197
Court of Private Land Claims, 23, 164, 248; adjudication of Pueblo land grants by, 68, 264; and Cañada de Santa Clara grant, 8, 55, 157, 163, 165; confirmation of land grants by, 8, 84, 167, 179, 323, 347n87, 354n16, 372n123, 403n63; creation of, 263; and Laguna Pueblo Cruzate grant, 215, 217, 220, 228, 264, 388n2, 401n44; and La Majada grant by, 180–81; and Ojo del Espíritu Santo grant by, 191, 193–96, 202
Crane, Leo, 198, 259, 407n111
Cruzate grants, 263, 324, 335, 347n87, 387n1, 389n22, 391n45, 392n62, 393n66, 395n89, 397n129, 401n44; for abandoned pueblos, 224; for Acoma, 214–15, 231; analysis of handwriting of, 218–19; authenticity of, 205–6, 215–16, 220–23, 228, 232; as basis for land-grant confirmations, 8, 210, 248; for Cochiti, 178–79, 181; confirmation of by U.S. Congress, 244; content of, 210–11, 214–15, 229; description of documents of, 208–9; documents of held by de la O, 232; filing of, 118–19; for Jemez and Pecos, 191, 224; for Laguna pueblo, 216–18, 228, 264; photos of documents of, 212–13; for Picuris Pueblo, 120; purpose of creation of, 233–34; for San Cristóbal Pueblo, 224–25; for Sandia Pueblo, 227, 246; for Zuni Pueblo, 226
Cruzat y Góngora, Gervasio, 106, 113, 330, 368n76; land-grant petitions to, 21–22, 125; nullifying of Santa Ana land purchase, 54–55, 60; and Tafoya grant near Santa Clara Pueblo, 155–56
Cuartelejo Apaches, 102, 367n44; Picuris and Taos relationship with, 91, 107, 112; Picuris Indians living with, 98–113, 150
Cuervo y Valdés, Francisco, 19, 99–100, 367n48
Curtis, Charles, 268, 275

Davis, James P., 304, 308
de la Concha, Fernando, 161–62
de la O, Gregorio, 231–32
de la O, Victor, 215, 230–32, 246
de la Peña, José Mariano, 75–78, 80–81
de la Vega y Coca, José, 103–6
Del Real Alencaster, Joaquín, 129, 323

Department of Agriculture, U.S., 141, 165, 201; and Blue Lake, 294, 296, 299–302, 306, 308, 311, 313, 315, 317
Department of Interior, U.S., 201, 206, 241, 244, 264, 286, 289, 391n45, 406n99; and Blue Lake, 294–95, 301–2, 306, 308–9, 311–12, 315, 317; and Sandia Pueblo boundary dispute, 141–42, 145
Department of Justice, U.S., 145, 284, 286, 289
Domínguez, Francisco Atanasio, 108, 111–12, 132, 331, 355n30
Domínguez de Mendoza, Juan, 124, 219
Domínguez de Mendoza, Tomé, 124
Durango, Mexico, 73–74, 130, 132, 152–53, 177, 322, 364n151, 369n76; Cochiti lawsuit heard in, 171, 173, 178; commanding general in, 129, 171, 177
Durán y Chaves, Fernando, 16, 53–54, 92, 353n10, 354n13, 354n16

Earle, Henry, 195–96
Eastern Association on American Affairs, 274, 278
Eaton, Ethan, 225, 395n100
Elena Gallegos land grant, 144
"El Jaca" (Taos Indian), 92, 94
Elkins, Stephen B., 249, 251–52
Ellis, Florence Hawley, 304, 353n4, 417n25
Ellison, Samuel, 194
El Paso del Norte, 14–15, 33, 95, 131, 209–10, 229, 389n24; Hispanos retreat to during Pueblo Revolt, 22, 54, 93, 125
El Picurí. See Tupatú, Luis ("El Picurí")
El Ranchito. See Ranchiit'u
Ely, Northcutt, 286–87
Embudo de Picurís, 96, 103–4, 106, 112, 370n98
Embudo land grant, 103–6, 112
encomienda, 3–6, 12, 124, 340n17, 341n22
Ezeiza, fray Juan Antonio de, 107, 369n79

Fall, Albert B., 268–72, 279, 410n12
Fernández, Bartolomé, 28, 144, 176, 179–81, 185, 192–93, 331, 383–84n40

Fernández, Carlos, 24–27, 105, 330–31
Fernández, Domingo, 37–38, 43–44, 76, 225, 333, 349n125, 362n123
Fernández de la Pedrera, Juan, 179–80, 383n40
Flores Mogollón, Juan Ignacio, 101, 104
Franciscans, 4, 94–95, 113, 124–25, 127, 134; archives of in Mexico City of, 128, 135–36, 216; and jurisdictional conflict with Bishop of Durango, 369n76; missions among Jemez, 189–90; at Picuris Pueblo, 91, 112; and resettlement of Sandia Pueblo, 4, 22, 127, 132, 134–35
Fraser, George A. H., 279–80, 282, 288–90

Gallegos, Juan Jose, 67–68
García, Alonso, 52, 76, 93, 124
García, José, 76, 80
García, Rafael, 44–45, 191
García de Noriega, Juan Esteban, 22, 159
Garretson, John W., 370n99; survey of Pueblo grants by, 119, 137–40, 155, 179, 191
General Land Office, 137–38, 140, 164, 179, 207, 214–16, 224, 244, 277, 402n55; Cruzate grant documents filed with, 214–15, 226, 248
Genízaro Indians, 23, 109, 125, 330, 370n92
Gildersleeve, Charles, 195
Gómez Robledo, Franciso, 3–4
González, Prudencia, 159, 161
González, Juan Bautista, 76–79, 81, 116, 362n129
González, Miguel, 43–44, 372n125
González Bas, Juan, 54, 354n22, 409n130
Greeley, Arthur W., 305–6
Greene, Harold, 144–47
Greene Kilberg, Bobbie, 313–14
Greiner, John, 83–84, 118
Griffin, Robert, 316–17
Griffin-Harris amendment, 316–17
Guadalajara, Mexico, 73, 176–78, 186, 322, 360n101
Gutiérrez, Felipe, 58, 61
Gutiérrez, Francisco, 76–77

Gutiérrez, Juan José (governor of Santa Clara Pueblo), 165
Gutiérrez, Juan José, 21, 45, 173–74
Gutiérrez, María Victoria, 80–81
Gutiérrez, Pedro Miguel, 80, 363n142

Hagerman, Herbert, 278–81, 283–87, 289, 413n54, 413n57, 413n59
Haley, James, 308–9, 311–12, 316
Hall, Wendell, 214, 283
Hanna, Richard H., 259, 267–69, 279–80, 284–86, 289–90, 407n111, 415n70
Hardin, Clifford M., 311, 313
Harris, Fred, 293, 313–18
Harris, LaDonna, 313
Hernández, Juan José, 127, 134
Herrera, Antonio de, 371n119
Hewett, Edgar Lee, 164, 367n44
Hickle, Walter, 311–12
Hopi Indians, 8, 22, 353n4; encomienda tribute collected from, 3–4, 6; Pueblo Indians with, 125, 150, 190, 225, 330; at Sandia Pueblo, 132, 134
Hordes, Stanley M., 137, 146, 221, 376n50
House Indian Affairs Committee, 273, 287
Howard, George Hill, 163–64, 195–96, 217, 264–65
Hurtado, Andrés, 53–54

Ickes, Harold, 201
Indian Affairs, Commissioner of, 120, 195, 199, 287, 413n53
Indian agents, 113–14, 154, 162, 164, 207, 242, 251, 253. *See also* Commissioner of Indian Affairs
Indian Claims Commission, 248, 399n12, 403n63; act establishing, 182, 214, 300; and Cochiti Pueblo petition to, 179, 181–82, 185–86; and Ojo del Espíritu Santo grant, 202; and Santa Clara lands, 165–67; and Taos Pueblo claim for Blue Lake, 300–301, 303–5, 315, 416–17n25
Indian Service, Office of, 195, 253–54, 258–59, 264, 408n125

Inouye, Daniel, 145–46
Isleta Pueblo, 22, 104, 125, 127, 261, 262, 273; kachina dances of, 124; lands of, 4, 245, 247, 327, 335, 397n128, 408n124

Jackson, Henry, 314, 316–17
Jemez, 62, 70–71, 74, 81, 83
Jemez Pueblo, 95, 127, 190, 199–200, 242, 330; and boundaries of San Isidro grant, 199–200; consolidation of with Pecos Pueblo, 198; Cruzate land grant and other land grants to, 205, 208, 211, 229–30, 244, 263–64, 335, 356n36, 408n124; encroachment on lands of, 193; history of, 189; land-boundary disputes of, 46, 51, 193, 199–200, 364n153; lands of, 199, 288, 290, 327, 331; measurement of Pueblo league of, 44–45, 173, 191; and Ojo del Espíritu Santo grant, 8, 191–96, 200–202; Pecos Indians at, 197–98, 224; repatriation of human remains and ceremonial objects to, 202–3, 387n60; role of in Pueblo Revolt, 92–93, 96, 211; San Diego de la Congregación, 189–90; San Diego del Monte, 189–90; San Diego de los Jémez, 189; San Juan de los Jémez, 189–90
Jemez River, 50, 54, 64, 86, 189, 190, 209, 246, 288; Santa Ana purchase of farmlands along, 51–52, 55–56
Jenkins, Myra Ellen, 304, 315, 393n67, 417n25
Jennings, Charles, 278–79, 281, 285
Jicarilla Apaches, 101, 107, 189, 203; attacks by, 114, 340n7; Picuris and Taos relationship with, 107, 112–13; pottery making by, 113–14
Jironza Pétriz de Cruzate, Domingo, 209–10, 387n1, 389n24, 390n27; background of, 209; Cruzate documents of, 211, 214, 218, 220, 228, 244; land grants by, 205, 208, 213–14, 217–218, 223, 227, 229; reconquest of New Mexico attempt by, 209–10; signature of, 219. *See also* Cruzate Grants
Johnson, Justice, 251–52
Johnson v. M'Intosh, 238–40, 247

Jones, Andrieus, 273, 275
Joseph, Antonio, 251–53
Joy, Francis C., 163, 259, 267, 270, 274, 277
Julian, George W., 162–63, 199

Kearny, Stephen Watts, 134, 223, 238, 388n5, 398n2
Kelley, Dean, 307–8
Kennedy, Robert F., 293, 305
Keown, Allan, 218–19, 393n66
Keres Indians, 15, 95, 169, 193, 209, 219, 329, 353n4, 381n1; history of, 50; role of in Pueblo Revolt, 92–94, 210. *See also* Santa Ana Pueblo
Kiowa Indians, 109, 203, 367n44
Koslowski, Martin, 251–52

Ladrón de Guevara, Pedro, 218–19
La Farge, Oliver, 294, 299, 301–3, 308, 318
Laguna Pueblo, 211, 219, 230, 381n1, 391n42, 391n45; Cruzate grant to, 208, 214–18, 220, 223, 228, 231–32, 260, 264, 323, 388n2, 391n45, 401n44; disputes with Acoma by, 214; lands of, 327, 335, 408n124; purchase of lands by, 263, 392n62
La Majada land grant, 179–81, 185–86, 283
Landa, Francisco Antonio de, 172–73
Las Casas, Bartolomé de, 12, 237, 341n6, 343n25
Las Lemitas, 78–79, 331
Las Trampas (settlement), 108–9
Las Trampas land grant, 106, 109
Las Vegas, 40, 164
Laughlin, N. B., 179
La Ventana, 191–92, 201
Lenroot, Irvine, 270, 273–75
Le Sage, Robert, 306, 308
Leshy, John, 145–46
Lobato, Miguel Antonio, 45, 247, 333, 397n128
Locker, Corinne, 303, 306–7
López del Castillo, María, 54, 129
López de Mendizábel, Bernardo, 91, 124
Los Trigos, 34, 175
Lovato, Miguel Antonio, 137–38, 376n50

Lucero, Antonio Benito, 117, 186, 250, 347n87
Lucero, Marcos, 23–28, 82–83, 150
Lucero, Miguel, 60, 364n153
Luhan, Mabel Dodge, 270–72, 287
Lujan, Joseph, 141–42
Luján, Juana, 23–25, 330
Lujan, Manuel, 312, 318

Mairo, Eusebio, 69, 359n81
Manrique, José, 34, 70–72, 171, 323, 331, 359n77
Marín del Valle, Francisco Antonio, 24, 158–60, 162, 391n42
Márquez, Juan, 56–57, 103–4
Marshall, John, 238–39, 241, 247
Martín, Antonio, 102, 109–11
Martín, Cristóbal, 54, 60–61, 63, 67, 71, 354n22
Martín, Francisco, 103, 104, 106
Martín, Jacinto, 109–10
Martín, Juan Antonio, 116–17
Martín, Juan Francisco, 109–11
Martín, Pedro, 31–32
Martín, Sebastián, 31; land grant of, 102–3, 106
Martínez, Cristóbal. *See* Martín, Cristóbal
Martínez, Salvador, 59, 128, 129
Martinez, Seferino, 294, 299–303, 309, 311
Martinez, William, 314, 316
Martínez de Lejanza, Mariano, 46, 333
Martínez Gallego, Cristóbal. *See* Martín, Cristóbal
Martínez Gallegos, Mariano, 62–63, 65
Matos, José, 152–53
Mayers, Abraham G., 154, 229–30
Maygua, Andrés, 82, 364n152
Máynez, Alberto, 28, 73, 152, 171, 176, 323, 332, 361n105; and encroachment of Hispanos on Pueblo land, 29–32; and land grants, 34, 45, 76, 208, 331
McElroy, Stephen, 199–200
McGovern, George, 309, 313–14, 316–17
Melgares, Facundo, 32, 36, 113, 129, 225, 332, 364n152, 398n1; and Santa Ana and San Felipe boundary dispute, 75, 78, 82, 85

INDEX
447

Menchero, fray Juan Miguel, 8, 127, 132, 330, 394n85; description of Picuris Pueblo by, 107–8; and Sandia land grant, 22, 134–35

Mendinueta, Pedro Fermín de, 39, 108, 263, 331, 354n16, 369n91, 403n63; land grant to San Felipe Pueblo and Santo Domingo Pueblo by, 28, 76, 174–76

Mendiola Velarde, Mariano, 73–75, 176–78

Mendoza, Gaspar Domingo, 158, 180, 391n42

Mestas, Antonio, 23–24

Mestas, Joaquín, 158–59

Metcalf, Lee, 305, 309, 315–17

Mexican Republic, 2, 32, 36–37, 42, 92, 123, 182, 220–21, 230–31, 238, 323, 402n62; land grants by, 8, 224, 233, 243, 244, 269, 282, 324; privatizing of pueblo lands by, 28, 33, 39–40, 46; protection of Indians under, 237; Pueblo Indians as citizens of, 38, 237, 241, 249

Miera y Pacheco, Anacleto, 129–30

Miera y Pacheco, Bernardo, 56–57, 62, 64, 66, 129, 355n30

Miller, David J., 207, 215–16

Miller, Samuel, 252–53

Miranda, Feliciana, 58–60, 356n36

Miranda, Javier de, 58, 60–61, 356n36

Mizquía, Lázaro de, 15–16, 329

Montaño, José de Jesús, 62–63, 65

Montoya, Andrés, 67, 170, 358n69

Montoya, Antonio, 19–20, 80, 329

Montoya, Cristóbal, 56–57

Montoya, Diego, 16, 54, 343n23

Montoya, Nerio Antonio, 56–57, 64, 69, 72, 174, 193, 359n77

Montoya, Pablo, 69, 75–76, 79–81

Montoya, Salvador, 44–45, 80, 173

Moqui Indians. *See* Hopi Indians

Moquino, José María, 131

Mora, Alejandro, 57–60, 63–64, 356n36, 409n130

Nambe Pueblo, 4, 38, 245, 280–82, 285, 327, 335, 378n1

Naranjo, José, 100, 150

Narbona, Antonio, 39, 41–42, 130–31, 323

National Congress of American Indians, 310, 312

National Council of Churches, 307–8

National Park Service, 165, 185, 384n55

Navajo Indians, 102, 107, 190, 191, 194, 203, 279, 284, 299, 340n7, 373n137

Navarro García, Luis, 144

Neblett, Colin, 280–81, 284, 290

New Mexico Association on Indian Affairs, 274–75

New Mexico Commission on Indian Affairs, 138, 310

New Mexico Council of Churches, 304, 308

Oñate, Juan de, 1, 3, 33, 63, 89, 91, 113, 123, 149, 339n1, 348n108

Ortiz, Antonio, 171, 349n117

Ortiz, Antonio José, 21, 171, 174, 176

Ortiz, Francisco, 151, 330

Ortiz, Matías, 34, 38–39

Ortiz, Nicolás, 110, 180

Otermín, Antonio de, 22, 92–93, 124–25, 170, 209, 227, 389n22

Padilla, Diego, 34, 37

Páez Hurtado, Juan, 17–18, 21–22, 101–2, 156, 329–30, 344n33

Paisano, Stewart, 146–47

Pajarito Plateau, 155, 164, 167, 169, 390n35

Pawnee Indians, 109, 359n91

Payne, John B., 267, 269

Payupki Pueblo, 125

Pecos, Regis, 182–83

Pecos Pueblo, 36, 90, 92, 95, 101, 107, 333, 414n65; attempt by to regain lands of, 197–98; Cruzate grant to 198, 208, 211, 224, 244, 335, 395n89; as an encomienda, 3–4; encroachment on lands of, 29, 33–37, 41, 251, 333; measurement of Pueblo league at, 175, 341n12, 349n117; move to Jemez Pueblo by, 196–98, 224; recognition of lands of, 37–43, 47; during reconquest, 96, 211; redistribution of

lands of, 36–40, 42–43; repatriation of human remains to, 203
Peláez, Jacinto, 180–81
Pelham, William, 341n1, 388n13, 389n15, 395n100; confirmation of Pueblo Indian land grants by, 84, 134, 137–38, 140, 154–55, 179, 244–47, 264, 266, 391n45, 402n55; confirmation of Spanish and Mexican land grants by, 3, 225; Cruzate-grant documents delivered to, 208, 214–15, 220, 222, 224, 226, 228, 389n20, 397n128, 401n44; search for Pueblo grant documents by, 229–30, 232; as surveyor general of New Mexico, 206–7, 244
Peña, José Mariano de la, 171–72
Peñasco, 118, 120, 288. *See also* Santa Bárbara (settlement)
Perea, Baltasar, 82, 85, 364n152
Pereyro, fray José Benito, 30–32
Phillips, Orie, 280–81, 285, 412n41
Picuris Pueblo, 89–90, 94–96, 108, 111, 119, 121, 269n79, 365n7, 365n14, 373n137; abandonment of, 99–100, 120–21; Comanche raids on, 108–9, 11; Cruzate land grants of, 119–20, 205, 208, 211, 244, 327, 335, 372n17; encroachment on lands of, 43, 102–6, 109–11, 116–18; flight of to Cuartelejo Apaches, 97, 99–100, 150; forced labor of, 91–92; Pueblo league of, 118, 370n99; relationship of with Apaches, 114–16, 120, 284, 288; return of land to, 43–44, 319; role of in Pueblo Revolt, 92–94
Pinchot, Gifford, 294, 300, 306
Pinillas, Ángel, 153, 172
Pino, José, 70–72, 359n77
Pino, Juan Esteban, 42–43, 69, 75–76, 80–81, 197
Pino, Pedro Bautista, 80–81, 173–75
Plan de Iguala, 237, 241, 404n72
Pojoaque Pueblo, 137, 245–46, 327, 335, 373n137, 378n1
Polvadera, 143, 231, 247, 397n128
Poole, Rufus, 303, 308

Pope, John H., 256–57
Porter, Eliot, 308
Proctor, George, 302–3
Protector of Indians, 19, 105, 173, 237, 322, 343n25, 363n146, 398n1; Alfonso Rael de Aguilar, 16–17, 18, 20, 329, 358n70; Felipe Sandoval, 30, 34, 69–71, 73, 171, 331; Ignacio María Sánchez Vergara, 73–75, 81–82, 186, 363n146; José Joaquín Reyes (in Durango), 171, 172, 173, 178, 186; Mariano Mendiola Velarde (in Guadalajara), 176, 178; Vicente Villanueva, 173–76, 186
Proudfit, James K., 194–95, 215, 220, 264
Pueblo Indian Agency, 162–63
Pueblo Lands Board, 165–66, 276, 278; Congressional review of actions of, 284–86; hearings and rulings on claims by, 119–20, 198, 226, 279–84, 290, 348n102, 393n66, 414n65; impact of decisions by, 267, 288, 324; procedures of, 277–78; and return of Blue Lake to Taos Pueblo, 295–96, 298
Pueblo league, 7, 25, 347n87; as basis for Pueblo Indians landholdings, 8, 11, 19–21, 35, 45–46, 103, 248, 323; of Cochiti Pueblo, 28, 170, 172–73, 180; encroachment on, 16–20, 29–32, 41, 43, 50–51, 79–80, 83, 102–6, 109–11, 114, 116–18, 171, 176, 193, 251, 253, 263–64, 333, 348n102, 362n123; of Jemez Pueblo, 44–45, 173, 191; measuring of, 10, 23, 25, 118–19, 175, 190–91, 331, 333, 341n12, 358n70; origins and definition of, 6–7, 12, 46, 343n23; of Pecos Pueblo, 29, 37–38, 41, 197, 333; of Picuris Pueblo, 118, 370n99; privatization of, 36, 38–40; of Sandia Pueblo, 123, 127–28; of San Felipe Pueblo, 16–18, 21–28, 35, 137, 329–31, 346n78; of San Ildefonso Pueblo, 14, 21–22, 26–28, 35, 137, 329–31, 346n78; of Santa Ana Pueblo, 86, 246; of Santa Clara Pueblo, 150, 155; of Santo Domingo, 8, 21, 45–46, 171–74, 333; of Taos Pueblo, 30–32, 294,

348n102; use of in New Mexico, 28, 176, 237, 321, 341n2
Pueblo Revolt, 1, 12, 18, 20, 22, 50, 54, 69, 108, 124, 149, 209, 219, 224, 232, 321, 348n108, 389n22; described, 93; as mentioned in Zuni Cruzate document, 226; role of Pueblo Indians in, 92, 99, 111, 150, 169, 190, 224, 227
Puyé Cliffs, 164–65
Puyé Pueblo, 149, 155

Quintana, José, 69
Quitoyo, Bartolomé, 156

Radcliffe, Mark, 186
Rael de Aguilar, Alfonso, 16–17, 129, 329, 343n23, 358n70; measurement of Pueblo leagues by, 20, 22, 170; as Protector of Indians, 17–18, 27, 176
Rael de Aguilar, Eusebio, 129–31
Rael de Aguilar, Julián, 129
Rainer, John, 294, 310, 312
Ranchiit'u, 50, 55, 64, 83–84, 86, 264, 327, 408n124; Santa Ana Pueblo purchase of lands of, 51, 58, 61, 64, 79
Rancho de Peña Blanca, 172, 176–78
Rancho de Sile, 21, 171
Rancho Viejo land tract, 58
Recopilación, 16, 23, 25, 346n79, 367n48; citation of in land disputes, 27, 73, 152, 160, 172–73, 176–78, 330; protection for Indian lands in, 12, 17, 74, 104–5, 237
Renehan, A. B., 256, 259, 269–70, 273
Reneros Posada, Pedro, 125, 209, 227
requerimiento, 2–3, 6, 340n11
Reyes, José Joaquín, 171–73, 178, 186
Reynolds, Matthew Givens, 196, 216, 263–65
Rhoads, Charles, 120, 286, 413n54
Riaño Tagle, José, 21–22, 330, 345n52, 346n70, 346n78
Ribera, Miguel, 37, 333
Río de Las Trampas, 102–3
Río de Picurís, 44, 114, 117. *See also* Rio Pueblo

Río de Picurís grant, 105, 114–17, 372n123
Río de Santa Ana. *See* Jemez River
Rio Pueblo, 107, 114, 120, 293, 296. *See also* Río de Picurís
Rio Puerco, 58, 61, 192, 247, 354n16, 356n36, 397n128
Robledo, Francisco Gómez, I, 124
Robledo, Francisco Gómez, II, 124
Rodríguez, Mariano, 43–44, 116, 333
Rodríguez Cubero, Pedro, 6, 16, 180, 216, 219; granting of land grants by, 16
Romero, Baltasar, 54–55, 60–61, 330, 368n76
Romero, Domingo, 170, 186
Romero, José, 31–32, 197
Romero, Juan de Jesús, 294, 296, 300, 314–17
Romero, Miguel, 170, 186
Romero, Pedro, 60–61, 356n36
Romero, Querino, 294, 309, 314–15, 317
Roosevelt, Franklin D., 287, 410n22, 411n32, 413n53
Roosevelt, Theodore, 164, 264, 294, 408n125
Roybal, Ignacio, 17–18, 384n40

Salas, José Benito, 117–18
San Agustín de la Isleta Pueblo. *See* Isleta Pueblo
Sanches, Ramón, 230
Sánchez, José de Jesús, 45–46
Sánchez, Pedro, 23–25
Sánchez de Tagle, Isidro, 134–35
Sánchez Vergara, Ignacio María, 330–31, 362n123, 363n146, 364n152, 374n26; altering of Sandia Pueblo grant documents by, 129–31, 133, 135–36, 333; and Cochiti land dispute with Cabeza de Baca, 173–74; *Sánchez Vergara vs. Sandia,* 333: and Santa Ana–San Felipe boundary dispute, 73–78, 332; schemes of to get Cochiti and Santo Domingo lands, 81, 83, 85, 175–76, 178, 186, 361n105
San Cristóbal grant, 181, 225, 395n100
San Cristóbal Pueblo, 95, 208, 211, 224–25, 227, 349n125, 408n124

Sandia Mountain, 63–64, 84, 123–24, 132, 138, 142, 354n22, 355n22, 376n50; as boundary for Sandia land grant, 22, 128, 139–44

Sandia Pueblo, 3–4, 59, 95, 124–25, 132, 134, 151, 170, 381n1; Cruzate grant to, 123, 128, 133–37, 139–40, 227–29, 208, 226, 230, 244, 246, 248, 335; destruction and resettlement of, 22, 124–25, 127; history of, 12, 123–24, 131, 330, 335, 401n45; land disputes of, 129–31, 141–45, 374n26; land grant to, 22, 127–28, 139; lands of 8, 11, 223, 327, 332; map of land grant of, 126; and T'uf Shur Bien Preservation Trust Area, 146–47

Sandoval, Felipe, 30, 34, 69–71, 73, 171, 175, 256, 259, 331

San Felipe Pueblo, 70, 95, 290, 329, 353n10; Cruzate land grant to, 205, 208, 211, 214, 216, 223, 229, 233, 244, 263–64, 395n87; and land dispute with Santa Ana Pueblo, 55, 63, 67–72, 74–76, 80, 82–83, 359n81, 364n152; land purchases by, 59–62, 64, 67; lands of, 28, 49, 81, 174, 327, 329, 331–32, 335, 362n123, 362n129; privatization of lands of, 38–39; and Pueblo Lands Board, 281; Pueblo league of, 16–17, 22; as Spanish allies during reconquest, 96, 210; schemes to take land from, 175–76

San Ildefonso Pueblo, 91, 166, 180, 330, 378n1, 384n40; encroachment of Hispano land grants on, 17; land dispute with Santa Clara by, 150–51; land grants of, 4, 245–46; lands of, 319, 327, 335; litigation of land disputes by, 23–28, 35, 330–31, 346n78; measurement of Pueblo league of, 14, 21–22, 26–28, 35, 137, 329–31, 346n78; and Roybal grant, 17–18

San Isidro grant, 191, 193, 195, 199–200

San José de la Laguna Pueblo. *See* Laguna Pueblo

San José de los Jémez, 189–90

San Juan (settlement), 91–93, 95

San Juan de los Caballeros, 32–33, 39

San Juan Pueblo, 4, 102, 120, 149, 225, 331–32, 348n108, 378n1, 412n50, 413n57; Cruzate grant to, 205, 211, 219, 228–29, 244, 288, 327, 335, 391n37

San Lázaro Pueblo, 92, 227

San Lorenzo Pueblo (El Paso area), 33

San Marcos Pueblo, 4, 93, 170, 408n124

San Miguel del Bado (town), 37, 41

Santa Ana Pueblo, 53, 61, 73–74, 81, 86, 95, 330, 353n4, 381n1; confirmation of land grants to, 245–46, 248; encroachment on lands of, 50–51, 79–80, 83, 193, 263–64; land dispute with San Felipe by, 67–72, 74–75, 77–78, 81, 359n77, 359n81, 361n152, 364n153; land purchases by, 7, 53–57, 59–61, 64–66, 86, 354n22, 368n76; lands of, 288, 290, 323, 327, 331, 335, 362n129, 363n142, 402n55, 402n57, 409n130; litigation of land disputes of, 76, 79, 82, 264n155, 282; loss of lands of, 83–84, 86, 288, 361n105; map of lands of, 53; and Ojo del Espíritu Santo grant, 191–96, 202; *Santa Ana v. San Felipe,* 331; as Spanish ally, 96, 170, 210; Tamaya, 50–51, 58, 64, 74, 84, 86, 246, 353n4, 356n36; use of land-title system by, 49–50, 83, 322

Santa Bárbara (settlement), 106, 108–10, 115, 117–19, 370n99. *See also* Peñasco

Santa Clara Canyon, 157, 163–65, 167, 408n125

Santa Clara Creek, 155, 158, 160–61, 163, 167

Santa Clara Pueblo, 98, 99, 149–51, 155–56, 160, 256, 322, 329–31, 378n2; and Cañada de Santa Clara grant, 160–63; confirmation of land grants to, 154–55, 245, 263–64, 323; land disputes of, 21–22, 25, 150–53, 155–59; land grants to, 4, 8, 223, 246; lands of, 1, 154, 288, 327; map of, 57; measurement of Pueblo league of, 14, 26–28, 35, 137, 331, 346n70, 346n78; reservation for, 164–65, 408n125

Santa Cruz, 16, 97, 109, 161

Santa Cruz spring, 180, 185–86

Santo Domingo Pueblo, 3, 46, 92, 95, 132, 169–70, 219, 230, 264, 272, 329, 344n43,

INDEX

381n1, 407n111; Cruzate land grant to, 205, 208–9, 212–14, 218–19, 221, 223, 230, 233, 244, 263–64, 347n87, 389n15; encroachment on lands of, 16, 19–20, 171, 176; lands of, 20, 28, 73, 76, 319, 327, 331–32, 335, 362n123, 408n124, 414n64; privatization of lands of, 38–39; and Pueblo Lands Board, 282–83; Pueblo league of, 8, 21, 45–46, 171–74, 333; schemes to take land from, 175–76
Sarracino, Francisco, 44, 46, 80, 221, 232
Sawyer, Daniel, 103, 199–200
Schaab, William, 303, 308, 311
Second Mesa (Hopi), 125
Senate Indian Affairs Committee, 268, 284, 286, 298
Senate Interior Committee, 309, 316
Senate Public Lands Committee, 270, 273
Senate Subcommittee on Indian Affairs, 285, 305, 309–10, 316
Slough, John P., 249–50, 252, 403nn67–68
Snyder, Homer, 269, 273
Socorro, 76, 222, 229–31, 247, 268, 397n128
Surveyor General of New Mexico, 135, 137, 215–16, 277, 347n87; confirmation of land grants by, 44, 51, 68, 84, 103, 116, 134–38, 162, 178, 191, 194, 197, 230, 246, 248, 262–63, 403n64; creation and duties of, 8, 244; and Cruzate grants, 119, 211, 215, 218, 220–22, 224, 226, 228–29, 231, 264, 323, 347n87, 388n2, 391n37, 392n63

Tafoya, Antonio, 155–56, 158–59, 161–62
Tafoya, Cristóbal, 155, 159
Tafoya, Felipe, 193, 345n62; as defender of Indian property, 23–25, 27, 105, 176, 191
Tafoya, Juan, 155–56, 158, 161–62
Tafoya, Juan Miguel, 117, 371n119
Tafoya, Pedro, 134–35
Tamaya. *See* Santa Ana Pueblo
Taos (settlement), 44, 89, 106–7, 118, 270–72, 287–88, 302, 348n102; ayuntamiento of, 44, 115, 117; land dispute of with Taos Pueblo, 30–31, 303

Taos Pueblo, 3–4, 9, 31, 90, 95–96, 98–99, 101, 104, 107–8, 112–13, 146, 254, 271, 295, 315; Blue Lake as shrine to, 293, 295, 307–8; confirmation of grant of, 208, 244, 248, 335; encroachment on lands of, 29–31, 102, 253, 348n102; efforts by to regain Blue Lake, 294–96, 298–306, 308–19, 324, 417n25; lands of, 288, 327; litigation of land disputes by, 32, 251, 281, 284; Pueblo league of, 152, 401n45; relationship of with Forest Service, 294, 296–97, 302; return of Blue Lake to, 299, 308, 417n25; Tarr Opinion, 141–42, 144–45, 377n61
Tenorio land tract, 31, 294
Tenth Circuit Court of Appeals, 120, 260, 281, 290, 414n61, 415n70
Tesuque Pueblo, 3, 95–96, 207, 244, 267, 378n1; lands of, 137, 245–46, 327, 335; Pueblo Lands Board hearings for, 279–80, 285
Thomas, Benjamin, 162, 367n44
Tipton, Will, 216, 263–64, 393n64; background, 215; and Cruzate documents, 8, 217–19
Toledo, George (governor of Jemez Pueblo), 200
Tosa, Paul (governor of Jemez Pueblo), 203
Toya, Juan Antonio (governor of Pecos Pueblo), 197
Treaty of Guadalupe Hidalgo, 8, 182, 238, 241–42, 244, 248–51, 269, 398n2, 402n62, 403n63
Tupatú, Antonio, 95–98
Tupatú, Lorenzo, 94, 96–99, 97–98, 366n19; as ally of Spaniards, 95, 100–101
Tupatú, Luis ("El Picurí"), 92, 94–95, 97–98, 366n19
Twitchell, Ralph Emerson, 257, 269–71, 273, 279, 347n87, 409n8

Udall, Stewart, 293, 305, 308–9, 311–12
Ulibarrí, Juan de: expedition of to retrieve Picuris Indians, 99–100, 113

United States v. Antonio Joseph, 252–55, 258–61, 274, 291, 324
United States v. Lucero, 249, 251–52, 254, 291
United States v. Sandoval (1913), 121, 257, 259–61, 263, 267, 274, 324
United States v. Thompson, 218, 221, 393n66
U.S. Congress, 183, 206, 216, 221, 241, 299n12, 372n123; confirmation of Pueblo Indian grants by, 119, 137, 144–45, 158, 162, 179, 181–82, 191, 194–95, 197, 205, 208, 214–15, 218, 220, 224, 226, 245–48, 263–64, 377n60, 388n2, 390n34, 392n62, 393n66, 397n128, 401n44; and legal status of Pueblo Indians, 250, 253, 257–62; legislation regarding Pueblo lands, 84, 146–47, 166–67, 186, 254, 282, 289–90, 295, 311, 317, 319, 347n88
U.S. Forest Service, 141, 166, 185, 294–95, 306, 308, 316; and dispute over Sandia Pueblo boundaries, 123, 141, 145–47; relationship with Taos Pueblo over Blue Lake, 296–99, 301–07, 310–12; and timber industry, 308

Vadito, 44, 116–17, 120, 288
Valles Caldera, 155, 167
Van Devanter, Willis, 257–58, 260, 406n99
Varela, Manuel, 251, 252
Varela Jaramillo, Cristóbal, 16–17, 358n70
Varela Jaramillo, Juan, 16–17, 358n70
Vargas, Diego de, 6, 12, 180, 219, 223, 329; campaigns against Indians by, 94–95, 97–98, 190; death of, 354n13; encomienda of, 341n27; and land grants, 14–17, 51, 53–54, 102, 180, 354n16, 358n70; reconquest of New Mexico by, 6, 49–50, 54, 96, 125, 170, 210, 225
Vélez Cachupín, Tomás, 45, 60, 108, 111, 170, 369n76, 370n98; and Cañada de Santa Clara grant, 159–65; land grants by, 8, 23, 70, 103, 109, 151, 330, 356n36, 386n38, 403n63; and land sales to Santa Ana Pueblo, 58–59, 62, 64; and Ojo del Espíritu Santo grant, 191–92, 196; ruling on Santa Ana Pueblo–Baca litigation, 56–57; and San Ildefonso Pueblo lawsuit, 24–25, 27
Vélez de Escalante, fray Silvestre, 216, 219, 355n30; *Extracto de noticias* by, 216, 219
Vigil, Carlos (governor of Teseque Pueblo), 245–46
Vigil, Donaciano, 83–85, 221–23, 225, 229–30, 232–33, 245, 388n5, 397n129, 402n57
Villanueva, Vicente, 34–35, 173–76, 186, 349n117
Vitoria, Francisco de, 238, 240

Walker, Roberts, 278–79, 412n38
Ward, John, 198, 249
Warner, Louis H., 281, 285, 412n38
Waters, Frank, 294, 299
Watts, John S., 215, 220, 230, 249–50, 252, 264
Whiting, David V., 220, 229, 244, 388n5, 390n33; background of, 206–7; translation of grant documents by, 107, 136–37, 140, 143
Wilson, Francis C., 181, 256–57, 259, 272–76, 285, 406n96, 407n111
Work, Hubert, 278, 280, 283, 296

Zamora, Francisco de, 90, 113, 365n7
Zia Pueblo, 49, 95, 125, 381n1, 390n27; Cruzate grant to, 205, 208–9, 244, 263–64, 389n20; lands of, 288, 290, 327, 335, 408n124; and Ojo del Espíritu Santo grant, 8, 191–92, 193–96, 200–2, 356n36; role of in Pueblo Revolt and reconquest, 96, 190, 209–11, 227
Zuni Pueblo, 2, 4, 5, 108, 340n8; Cruzate grant to, 8, 205, 211, 226, 327, 335, 388n2, 401n44

www.ingramcontent.com/pod-product-compliance
Lightning Source LLC
Chambersburg PA
CBHW030515230426
43665CB00010B/620